Microsoft®
Commerce
Solutions

Micro Modeling Associates, Inc.

PUBLISHED BY
Microsoft Press
A Division of Microsoft Corporation
One Microsoft Way
Redmond, Washington 98052-6399

Library of Congress Cataloging-in-Publication Data
Microsoft Commerce Solutions / Micro Modeling Associates,
   Inc.
      p. cm.
   ISBN 0-7356-0579-3
   1. Internet programming.   2. Web site development.   3. Retail
trade--Computer networks.   I. Micro Modeling Associates.
QA76.625.O24   1999
658'.054678--dc21   99-10307
                                           CIP

Printed and bound in the United States of America.

1 2 3 4 5 6 7 8 9   WCWC   4 3 2 1 0 9

Distributed in Canada by Penguin Books Canada Limited.

A CIP catalogue record for this book is available from the British Library.

Microsoft Press books are available through booksellers and distributors worldwide. For further information about international editions, contact your local Microsoft Corporation office or contact Microsoft Press International directly at fax (425) 936-7329. Visit our Web site at mspress.microsoft.com.

Macintosh is a registered trademark of Apple Computer, Inc. used under license. ActiveX, BackOffice, FrontPage, JScript, Microsoft, the Microsoft Internet Explorer logo, Microsoft Press, MSDN, NetShow, Outlook, Visual Basic, Visual C++, Visual InterDev, Visual J++, Visual Studio, Windows, and Windows NT are either registered trademarks or trademarks of Microsoft Corporation in the United States and/or other countries. Other product and company names mentioned herein may be the trademarks of their respective owners.

The example companies, organizations, products, people, and events depicted herein are fictitious. No association with any real company, organization, product, person, or event is intended or should be inferred.

Technical Editor: Richard Collins
Manuscript Editor: Anne Owen
Graphic Artist and Desktop Publisher: Lulu Shellhase
Proofreader: Mildred Rosenzweig
Indexer: Robert Saigh
Project Manager: Brian Miller

For Microsoft Press:
Acquisitions Editor: Juliana Aldous
Project Editor: Thom Votteler

Contents

About This Book

Welcome to *Microsoft Commerce Solutions*. This book will help you make sense of the technology surrounding the design, development, and deployment of commerce related Web sites. It is intended for technical managers of Web development efforts, business managers who want some insight into the technology, and developers who need to understand the big picture. This book does not cover the business and marketing strategy side of e-commerce. While this side of the equation is of equal importance to the technology side (and typically must be addressed before embarking on a development effort), there are only so many pages in a book, and we could not have done the topic justice without another volume.

The technology presented is the Microsoft platform and tools—Windows NT, Internet Information Server, Site Server, Internet Explorer, Active Serve Pages, and COM, as well as open Internet standards such as HTML, CSS, DHTML, and XML. Web development is notorious for involving scores of tools and technologies, and this book will help you understand how they fit together and how to design complete solutions using them. The level of detail is generally at the architecture/design level, with frequent dives into detail for newer technologies as well as advice on avoiding common pitfalls and getting your site designed right the first time.

BOOK ORGANIZATION

Each section of this book covers a general category of technology typically worked on by staff with the same skill sets. Feel free to read the book cover-to-cover, or to skip around to topics that interest you. In any event, we recommend that everyone read chapters 1 and 2 before the rest of the book. These chapters present the big picture issues of commerce on the Web, and provide an overview of all the major technologies covered in the book. Reading this introductory material will give you context for delving into specific chapters. The sections are organized as follows:

- **I: Getting Started** presents the case for commerce over the Web, the aspects of the Web medium that make it unique, and an overview of the technologies available to build commerce applications.

- **II: Infrastructure and Security** discusses the hardware, connectivity, and security issues you must address to provide a solid platform for commerce application development. It also covers issues related to secure payment over the Web.

- **III: The Site Server Commerce Platform** covers the basic services available in Microsoft Site Server to run and administer a Web site, and the specific commerce functionality provided by Site Server Commerce Edition.

- **IV: Server-Side Components** explains the role of Active Server Pages (ASP) as a "glue" technology for integrating components and ActiveX Data Objects (ADO) as a universal technology for accessing relational and other types of data stores. It then proceeds to detail all aspects of writing custom business logic to run on the server side of a Web application.

- **V: Web User Interfaces** provides a guide to building compelling user interfaces using the standard tools of the Web: HTML, DHTML, Cascading Style Sheets (CSS), client-side scripting, and client-side components. It also describes the role of XML as a method of exchanging data between the server and browser, how to use Microsoft Office as an alternative user interface, how to integrate collaboration into commerce workflows, and how to add dynamic video and audio content to provide a more compelling user experience.

COMPANION CD

Included with the book is a companion CD. This CD contains the sample code and files referenced in each chapter. It is organized by chapter number (one directory for each chapter), and each chapter will tell you where to look for sample files on the CD. Please note that most, but not every, chapter has sample code.

COMPANION WEB SITE

In order to make it possible for you to view some of the more complex demos without setting them up yourself, a companion Web site has been created. This site has running versions of relevant demos which illustrate key concepts in the book. The site can be found at *http://www.micromodeling.com/commercebook.* I hope you find the book informative, enlightening, and enjoyable to read.

Steve Harshbarger
harshbargers@micromodeling.com

Acknowledgments

Electronic commerce (e-commerce) became a reality in 1998. Between November 26 and December 27, 1998, America Online (AOL) had 1.25 million members who became first-time Web shoppers. AOL claims that when surveyed 98 percent of their shoppers said they "would be motivated" to make an online purchase in the next six months. E-commerce will be a necessity in 1999 and beyond for companies with goods and services to sell.

Micro Modeling would like to express heartfelt thanks to the folks at Microsoft Press who gave us the opportunity to write about such a timely and important topic. Thanks to Casey Doyle and David Clark who helped get us started, and to Juliana Aldous and Thom Votteler who helped us finish. Thanks also to the technical editing team at Syngress Media—Richard Collins, Brian Miller, Anne Owen, Lulu Shellhase, Mildred Rosenzweig, and Robert Saigh—who helped us get it right.

Much of this book was written on personal time. As project manager and internal editor, I would like to thank Steve Harshbarger, technical manager, and the incredibly talented author team for their professionalism and hard work (and for abiding by the "no whining" rule). Thanks also to Ken Heft, Brad Patch, Mary McCann, Joseph Campise, Deborah Kunesh and the other Micro Modelers, spouses, significant others, and friends who edited, commented on, and helped make this book a better product.

Lenore Michaels
michaelsl@micromodeling.com

Part I

Getting Started

Chapter 1

Commerce and the Web

by Andy Maretz

It's hard to forget the hysteria that surrounded the rise of the Web in the early 1990s. Generally unknown to mainstream business people and even many computer professionals as late as 1993, the Web became overwhelmingly familiar to these groups, along with virtually all others, by about the first half of 1995. Around this time, business cards, stationery, and advertisements started mentioning, or even primarily featuring, *Uniform Resource Locators*, or *URLs*. By 1996, it became pretty normal to recite a URL in everyday conversation, and people quickly figured out that you could even omit the http:// part of a URL, and everyone still knew what you were talking about. Time went on, and the Web continued to permeate daily life. Entire businesses sprang up to exploit it, and a general flood of activity developed around it.

It's now the early part of 1999 as we write this book, and the flood of activity just continues to intensify. The Web is entrenched in our culture and our economy, and legitimately credited with transforming both. It's a publishing medium, an entertainment form, a social device, a commerce instrument, and so many other things. And it's still surrounded by the same hysteria as when it first surfaced from obscurity just five years ago.

Most crazes don't last this long. Those that do usually owe their above-average shelf life to some actual substance beneath the veneer, and the Web seems to fit pretty well into this category. The Internet data network brought the possibility of cheap, easy connectivity to essentially every desktop in the world, and with the easy-to-use Web user interface, technical laymen became able and willing to use this connectivity. These innovations have had profound implications for those engaging in commerce. But although a few Web commerce success stories have made news over the last few years, the Web remains much more a story of untapped potential. Most attempts to use the Internet for profit have failed, and most businesses haven't even given the Internet a try so far. One big reason is a lack of understanding of how to approach the Web from a business and marketing standpoint. In fact, getting the business strategy down should be the first step for any company. That topic, however, is very deep and not the subject of this book. This book addresses the other big reason for this slow progress in tapping the potential of the Web: the technical difficulty of implementing effective Web commerce solutions. We hope this book makes it easier.

This book is about building commerce-enabled software for use over the public Internet or a private intranet. It discusses both the special nature of commerce-enabled applications, as well as the special nature of the Web as an application platform. It then describes the key technologies and techniques necessary to build Web commerce solutions. Whether you're specifically trying to do business on the Internet, or just interested in getting a better understanding of the practical issues behind Web commerce, this book should help.

The book is organized into the following major sections:

- **I: Getting Started** presents the case for commerce over the Web, the aspects of the Web medium that make it unique, and an overview of the technologies available to build commerce applications.

- **II: Infrastructure and Security** discusses the hardware, connectivity, and security issues you must address to provide a solid platform for commerce application development. It also covers issues related to secure payment over the Web.

- **III: The Site Server Commerce Platform** covers the basic services available in Microsoft Site Server to run and administer a Web site, and the specific commerce functionality provided by Site Server Commerce Edition.

- **IV: Server-Side Components** explains the role of Active Server Pages (ASP) as a "glue" technology for integrating components and ActiveX Data Objects (ADO) as a universal technology for accessing relational and other types of data stores. It then proceeds to detail all aspects of writing custom business logic to run on the server side of a Web application.

■ **V: Web User Interfaces** provides a guide to building compelling user interfaces using the standard tools of the Web: HTML, DHTML, Cascading Style Sheets (CSS), client-side scripting, and client-side components. It also describes the role of XML as a method of exchanging data between the server and browser, how to use Microsoft Office as an alternative user interface, how to integrate collaboration into commerce workflows, and how to add dynamic video and audio content to provide a more compelling user experience

This chapter, along with the more hands-on Chapter 2, provide the overview materials that make up Part I.

COMMERCE: ELECTRONIC AND OTHERWISE

Before getting into the technology issues surrounding Web commerce, it's necessary to talk a bit about commerce itself, with special consideration of how the Web changes the topic.

Commerce

Commerce refers to all the activities surrounding the purchase or sale of goods or services. It involves a wide range of activities starting long before an actual transaction is ever contemplated, and lasting until long after the transaction has been executed. These activities fall roughly into the following categories:

■ **Marketing.** Activities associated with reaching out to customers and potential customers to provide information about your company, brand, and product/service. This also includes market research activities to improve your understanding of existing and potential customers, with an eye toward refining product (or service) features, pricing, or message.

■ **Sales.** Activities specifically associated with an actual sales transaction, including the transaction itself.

■ **Payment.** Activities associated with the buyer meeting his or her obligations under the terms of the sale—the actual "transaction" at the heart of e-commerce. The ability to *securely* accept payment over the Web is fairly new; its acceptance has been key to the growth of e-commerce.

- **Fulfillment.** Activities associated with the seller meeting its obligations under the terms of the sale or, put more simply, the delivery of goods and services to the buyer. There are many hidden costs in fulfillment—particularly customer service, communications, warehousing, shipping, insurance, and storage.

- **Customer service.** Follow-up activities after fulfillment for problems and questions, as well as pre-sales support, general inquiries, and so on.

Note that it doesn't matter whether we're talking about traditional brick and mortar commerce or the Web variety: business is business, so the preceding list still applies. It's just that business activities are done a little differently on the Web, due to the special nature of the Web as a setting for commerce. Most of the remainder of this chapter talks about the special nature of the Web, along with an overview of the technologies created for this environment. At the end of the chapter, we'll revisit the statement that commerce activities are done a little differently on the Web.

Web Commerce

What's so special about the Web? It's not just that it's an electronic medium. Companies have used private networks for years to exchange order and invoice information, but without nearly the fanfare of the Web. What's really so special about the Web is that it's available everywhere and there are so many companies and people using it, with more and more jumping on every day.

Private networks are expensive and difficult to set up, so they're really only appropriate for trade partners anticipating a fairly significant, ongoing volume with each other. A Web connection, by contrast, is often already set up before anyone even contemplates doing commerce over the connection. This radically changes the economics of electronic commerce, because low-volume trade partners (such as one-time or emergency suppliers, merely *prospective* customers, or ordinary retail customers) are now prime candidates to participate. In other words, if there's no need to justify the setup costs of connectivity, then the "marketplace" consists of everyone, rather than the precious few. Small businesses and individual consumers, previously all but ineligible for e-commerce, are now right in the middle of it.

But universal reach has a downside, too. Appealing to a mass audience is a big, creative challenge, and doing so in a secure, dynamic way is a big, technical challenge. To put it another way: Writing great software is hard under the best of circumstances, and the Web is among the worst of circumstances. The data transfer rates are typically slow, which severely undermines the ability to create a great user experience. Security is vitally important on a public network, but also difficult to achieve. Development tools are immature and rapidly changing. Multiple, incompatible payment standards exist. The list of difficulties goes on and on— not enough to dissuade most people from attempting Web commerce, just enough to make life difficult for those who do. And it is why we are writing this book: to provide some guidance for those who want to try.

The Technical Challenge of the Web

Table 1-1 summarizes the main challenges in building great Web commerce solutions.

Table 1-1
CHALLENGES TO BUILDING GREAT WEB COMMERCE SOLUTIONS

Challenge	Explanation
The Basics	The Web was designed as a publishing medium for generally static documents but has been twisted into being a client/server application platform. Writing a relatively simple Web application is significantly harder than writing a comparable, non-Web application (in Visual Basic or Visual C++, for example). This is true even without developing any commerce-specific features. The most basic challenge of the Web, therefore, is simply writing a functional client/server application that physically spans the Internet or an intranet.
Special Effects	The boundary between entertainment and business on the Web is unclear, often very deliberately so. The effectiveness of a Web commerce application often hinges on how visually appealing or dynamic the application is. Another important challenge of Web commerce is therefore creating an exceptionally strong user interface, often under exceptionally difficult circumstances (slow modems, poor UI tools, incompatible browsers, and so on).
Scalability	The Web is a great reminder of the familiar saying: Be careful what you wish for; you just might get it. Sellers generally like the idea of getting lots of customers. But a Web commerce application, down deep, is just a computer program, and most computer programs can't handle hundreds or thousands of concurrent users as easily as they can handle one user. Most computer

(continued)

Table 1-1 *(continued)*

Challenge	Explanation
	programs can't handle hundreds or thousands of concurrent users at all. Effective Web commerce therefore depends heavily on features of scalability.
Security	The Web is as accessible for acts of malice as for acts of commerce, not to mention acts of well-intentioned thick-headedness. Another important aspect of building a Web commerce solution is therefore securing the application and its data against both deliberate and accidental harm.
Commerce "Extras"	At a high level, the elements of commerce—sales, marketing, and so on, as listed earlier in the chapter—are constant across all businesses. Microsoft and other software vendors are increasingly providing modular Web-based solutions to common components of business processes. An important skill as a creator of Web commerce solutions is to become acquainted with this pre-built infrastructure and learn how to use it effectively to build a robust and profitable business on the Web.

The remainder of this chapter provides an overview of building client/server commerce applications for the Web. As such, it describes the tools and techniques available for responding to the challenges listed in this table.

TECHNICAL OVERVIEW OF WEB COMMERCE

In its simplest form, the Web exists to facilitate reading ordinary documents that are physically located on other people's computers. This is certainly what the Web was first designed for, though it has grown into much more than that. To set the stage for looking at how full-blown, client/server, commerce-enabled applications are deployed over the Internet, we should first review the basic mechanics of the Web.

The Basics: Static Web Content

The Internet is a big data network with decent (but not great) reliability and generally mediocre data transfer speeds. It is, in any case, widely available and accessible, the implications of which were touched on previously. Computers attached to the Internet communicate with each other through a variety of applications and communications protocols. Two applications of special interest here are Web servers and Web browsers, which communicate with each other through *HyperText Transfer Protocol (HTTP)*.

The primary purpose of a Web browser is to display files for reading. An important aspect of the Web browser's functionality is that it downloads these files on an "as-needed" basis from other computers; that is, the browser is constantly contacting Web servers, sending requests (typically filenames), and processing responses (typically file contents) throughout a given user's session. The purpose of the Web server, on the other hand, is to listen for, and fulfill, these requests from Web browsers. The format of most of the files requested and downloaded over the Web is *HyperText Markup Language*, or *HTML*, which is how the HyperText Transfer Protocol, or HTTP, gets its name. The mechanics of the Web, in simple form, are illustrated in Figure 1-1. Although things will get a bit more complicated than this momentarily, it's worth noting that a person can spend all day "surfing" the Web and never go much beyond what's shown in this figure.

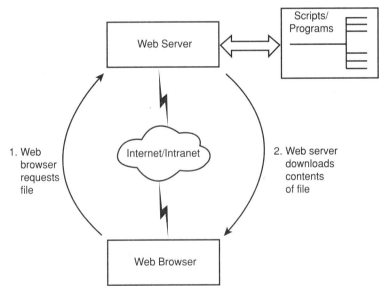

Figure 1-1. *Core Web application architecture, static content only.*

As Figure 1-1 shows, a Web browser sends the server a request—typically a simple URL. The Web server takes this simple URL and uses it to locate a particular file that the server sends back to the browser.

Dynamic Web Content

The preceding description is concerned solely with "static Web content," a phrase that denotes all the millions of files in the world that are sitting on Web servers waiting to be downloaded as is. There are some excellent Web sites consisting of nothing more than static content, but browsing such sites is not quite the same type of computing experience as using a "real" application (like Microsoft Excel, Microsoft Word, Visio, and so on). What's missing is a rich set of user input facilities and the associated richness of output. On the Web, the foundation of these application-like qualities is provided by two important features: HTML forms and server-side program execution. HTML forms facilitate user input, and server-side program execution facilitates dynamically generated output.

HTML forms are simply graphical user interfaces that Web browsers render and process, based on specifications contained in Web pages. Forms themselves are not dynamic, but their ability to call and pass parameters to automated scripts or programs on the server makes them an integral part of the solution. An HTML form can occupy the entirety of a Web page, or can show up as user input elements sprinkled throughout a Web page that otherwise contains ordinary text and graphics. In case you have any doubt as to what an HTML form is, look at Figure 1-2; you'll see that HTML forms are very familiar to you.

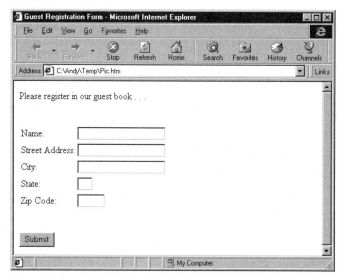

Figure 1-2. *A simple HTML form.*

Server-side program execution is a slight variation on the file-request/file-download paradigm described in the previous section. When Web browsers

request content from a Web server, they can send a program name (and optionally some program parameters) in place of a filename. In this case, the Web
server executes the program, and then downloads the *output of* the program
in place of where it normally downloads the *contents of* a requested, ordinary
file. This mechanism, which is illustrated in Figure 1-3, goes by a few different
names, depending on the specific details of a given Web server's architecture.
For most non-Microsoft Web servers, the mechanism is called *Common Gateway Interface*, or *CGI*. On a Microsoft Web server, dynamic content sometimes
comes from *Internet Server Application Programming Interface DLLs (ISAPI
DLLs)* but more commonly comes from *Active Server Pages (ASP)*. ASP is covered heavily throughout the remainder of this book.

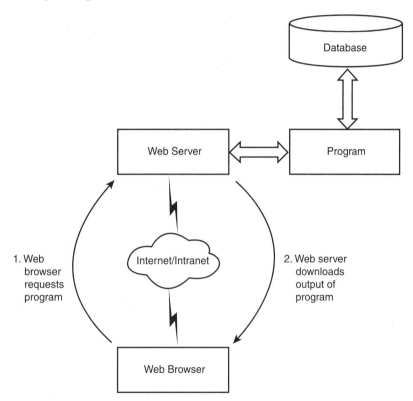

Figure 1-3. *Core Web application architecture, with dynamic content.*

As shown, in response to user input, a Web browser sends a request to
the server. The request contains two parts: the name of the program and its parameters or input. The server routes the parameters to the indicated program,
and then takes the results from the program and sends it back to the requestor.

HTML forms and server-side program execution are closely related topics, because they provide the richness of input and output that are missing from ordinary, static Web pages. The interplay between these two bits of functionality works as follows:

- When the user clicks the Submit button[1] on an HTML form, the Web browser extracts a program name from the form specification and appends the parameters to it—the specific values that were either entered manually by the user or came from hidden fields in the form.

- The Web browser then transmits this request (program name plus parameters) to the Web server in place of where it normally transmits a filename.

- The Web server then executes this program with these parameters as arguments or input and downloads the output for the Web browser to display. The specific form or content of this output is thus constructed "on-the-fly," based on whatever the user entered prior to clicking the submit button.

By tying an HTML form with a program that transforms the form's data values into some logically resulting output, a Web designer can create an application that flows sensibly from one screen to the next, soliciting user input, performing database queries and updates, displaying graphics or text, and so on—just like a conventional application. This is the basic mechanism that all Web applications employ, from the very simple to the very complex, though there are many technologies that enhance this mechanism, either by adding functionality, easing the programming challenge, or both.

The Microsoft Distributed Internet Applications Architecture (DNA)

In the Microsoft world, the set of technologies used for building N-tier[2] applications, including Web-based applications, is collectively labeled the *Distributed interNet Applications Architecture*, or *DNA*. Table 1-2 is an abridged list of the technologies under the DNA umbrella[3].

Table 1-2

TECHNOLOGIES UNDER THE DNA UMBRELLA

Technology	*Description*
Internet Information Server (IIS)	Microsoft's Web server.
HTML	The core language of Web browsers—whether Microsoft's or anyone else's.
Active Server Pages (ASP)	A scripting environment that facilitates server-side program execution under the control of IIS.
Client-Side Scripting and Dynamic HTML	Some features that extend ordinary HTML to facilitate client-side processing of user input, or general client-side program execution.
Microsoft Transaction Server (MTS)	A technology that eases the development and administration of scalable, secure N-tier applications.
Component Object Model (COM)	An interface standard, together with a set of operating system services, that facilitates interoperability between software components.
Microsoft Message Queue Server (MSMQ)	A technology that facilitates interoperability in some ways not offered directly by COM—specifically asynchronous communications between systems that might not have a reliable real-time connection.
ActiveX Data Objects (ADO)	A generic data access layer that permits DNA applications to be indifferent as to which vendor's database they're using.

A COMMENT ON VENDOR BIAS

Much of the discussion of *server-side* technology in this book is very Microsoft specific. In contrast, most of the discussion of *browser-side* technology is vendor neutral, or at least pretty much neutral between the two dominant browsers. Why the different treatment of servers vs. browsers? Because it turns out that there's a lot more vendor-specific functionality to benefit from on the server—starting with IIS, but also including a large number of other technologies described in this chapter and throughout the remainder of the book. Browsers have a lot of important functionality, but this functionality is largely consistent across vendors (although you will need to develop a thorough understanding of the differences in order to write applications that work well on all browsers). In any case, you can choose your server platform, but your users will choose your browser platform for you. So if you're going to exploit vendor-specific features, the server is both the more compelling place to do so and the easier place to get away with it.

Simple Web applications under DNA

The core architecture for Web applications under Microsoft's DNA is shown in Figure 1-4. It consists of:

- HTML hosted by a Web browser
- One or more Active Server Pages under the control of IIS
- Miscellaneous business logic packaged as COM objects
- One special set of COM objects, ADO, providing data storage services

Note the similarity to the architecture shown previously (refer to Figure 1-3) describing dynamically created Web content in a *vendor neutral* way. As indicated in that discussion, ASP is Microsoft's version of server-side program execution, and ASP is also the centerpiece of a Web DNA application.

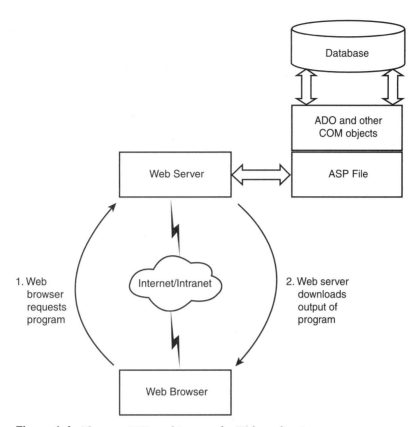

Figure 1-4. *The core DNA architecture for Web applications.*

As shown in Figure 1-4, in response to user input, a Web browser sends a request to the server for a URL ending in .asp. IIS retrieves the ASP file. For portions of the file designated as script code, IIS hosts execution of the script fragments and downloads any output the script code generates. For the other portions (which are typically ordinary HTML), IIS simply downloads the file content as is.

Active Server Pages

ASP is a scripting environment hosted by IIS. The set of ASP pages that make up a particular Web site, along with all the software objects the ASP pages invoke, together constitute the *server* half of a Web client/server application under DNA. The HTML (and other) output of these same ASP pages then becomes the *client* half of the client/server application, with a little help from a Web browser. Again, this is just server-side program execution, though ASP adds several notable twists to the concept.

Unlike traditional CGI applications, which were free-standing programs connected to the Web server through only a few invocation parameters and environment variables, ASP scripts are very tightly integrated with the Web server, IIS—even sharing the IIS process space, if you choose to configure it that way. This tight integration shows up in a lot of different ways, probably the most important being a handful of built-in objects that provide convenient programmatic access from ASP code to the IIS host environment. These objects expose to the ASP programmer:

- Readable fields corresponding to each part of the incoming HTTP request

- Writable fields corresponding to each part of the outgoing HTTP response

- Several mechanisms for storing state information throughout a user's application session, or even across all users of the application

- Access to the resource pooling and transactioning features of Microsoft Transaction Server (MTS)

- Access to a few miscellaneous utility functions

This functionality represents an enormous improvement over the bare-bones facilities of traditional CGI.

Another important feature of ASP is the ability to mix plain HTML and script code in a single file—a hybrid approach between static content and dynamically created content. ASP files contain both types of content, with the dynamic portions identified by appearing between special ASP markers: <% at the beginning of a script segment and %> at the end of a script segment. The processing of an ASP file is as you'd expect. Text outside the ASP markers is downloaded as is, whereas text inside the ASP markers is executed as a script, and the output of the script code is downloaded. The nice part about this is that many Web pages are neither totally dynamic nor totally static; they're a mixture of both types of content. Accordingly, ASP lets Web developers create Web pages with some *portions* that are static, and others that are dynamic.

The Component Object Model (COM)

ASP alone is pretty good, but the real power of ASP comes from using existing software components—including components purchased commercially, components bundled with the Windows operating system, or components that you or others write in almost any programming language. The way ASP gets at all this code is through COM, a technology of enormous importance to ASP specifically, but more generally a technology that represents the basic glue that holds the entire DNA framework together.

COM is an industry standard that facilitates interoperability of software components. Originally devised by Microsoft, but now administered and maintained by an independent organization, COM specifies all the details necessary for software components to communicate with each other under a diverse and otherwise extremely difficult set of circumstances. On the Microsoft platform, if you want to get two pieces of code to interact with each other, it's very often through COM. And if the two pieces of code are written in different languages, or by different organizations, or if they run on different machines, you'll almost certainly want to use COM to achieve interoperability.

COM can be discussed, praised, critiqued, and debated endlessly on a purely technical level. At a very practical level, however, the really significant thing about COM is its prevalence: It's totally established as the interoperability standard on the Windows platform, and it's widely adopted on many non-Windows platforms as well.

The power of ASP rests in large part on the fact that ASP is a COM client. That is, ASP script code can instantiate and use COM objects. Using ASP to automate COM objects is not *required* because ASP code can do all server-side processing by itself. Much more often, however, Web developers use the ASP code as a high-level control mechanism, invoking the services of COM objects to do all the heavy processing. One big reason for this, as stated earlier, is that COM objects can be purchased off the shelf, or very often just already exist in the Web developer's own code libraries.

And even for code that doesn't already exist, a Web development team gets several more big benefits from implementing functionality as COM components rather than directly in ASP script code. First, they can code in their favorite (or the most appropriate) language for a given task, rather than directly in ASP script. For example, some processes must be written in a compiled language like C++ in order to perform well. Second, by ensuring that the bulk of their business logic is housed in COM objects, a development team can reuse this code in any other COM client, which means almost any other Windows application. A third benefit is that a COM component can be moved very easily to some machine other than the actual Web server. This provides performance and scalablity by distributing the server processing across machines.

One set of COM objects that's especially useful to a Web application under DNA is *ActiveX Data Objects*, or *ADO*, which is concerned with vendor-neutral access to databases.

ActiveX Data Objects (ADO)

Several years ago, Microsoft created a standard called *Open Database Connectivity*, or *ODBC*, with which applications could write code that was independent of the particular brand of database to be used by the application at runtime. In other words, applications could perform all database operations using ODBC calls, and then the user of the application could configure their system in such a way that the ODBC calls were translated into whatever vendor-specific calls matched the particular database product in use in their environment.

ODBC caught on quite well and is still a dominant standard for vendor-neutral database access. Virtually all database vendors provide ODBC drivers for their products, so that writing applications to the ODBC specification is still a great hedge for an organization to make against its own future database decisions.

Unfortunately, the ODBC interface is not a COM interface, and as mentioned earlier, the Microsoft world has become a world of COM objects and COM clients. In addition, people have recognized a need to create uniform access mechanisms for many data sources other than relational databases, such as in-memory object hierarchies or real-time network data feeds. ODBC can be stretched to handle these types of tasks, but an enhanced, COM-based interface can handle them better.

Therefore, Microsoft created two mechanisms that provide vendor-neutral data source connectivity, in a more flexible way than ODBC and in the form of COM objects. The first mechanism, called OLE DB, is the more "hard core" of the two, in the sense that it's harder to use, more powerful, more sophisticated, and so on. The second mechanism, ADO, is essentially a programmer-friendly layer on top of OLE DB. ADO can be used with any OLE DB provider, and Microsoft supplies an OLE DB provider for ODBC, which, as mentioned earlier, covers virtually every database on the market. The result is that ADO, though fairly new as a standard, has become widely adopted very quickly by leveraging the existing installed base of ODBC drivers in the world.

ADO is a good, simple interface for data operations. It can be used from any COM client, the particularly relevant such client to this discussion being ASP. And because most applications of any reasonable size create and use some sort of persistent data, it turns out that most DNA Web applications use ADO.

Better Web applications under DNA

The technologies discussed up until now provide a good framework for building client/server applications for deployment over the Web. But high-end Web applications, of the sort that a serious commercial venture can be formed around, really need some other features. This section covers some of the notable ones.

User Interface enhancements

People's attention spans are at their very shortest when they're surfing the Web. The browser paradigm of being one click away from the next page is powerful and probably a big part of the Web's success, but it works against you if your page is the one being clicked away from, rather than the one being clicked to. People expect a responsive, visually appealing, well laid-out user interface, and the fact that achieving such a user experience is difficult in a Web application (which it is) is immaterial because, of course, others are doing it. Several technologies exist to help.

The first such technology, *Cascading Style Sheets (CSS)*, is a set of formatting directives and syntax additions that extend HTML. HTML and CSS together represent a significantly more powerful formatting toolset than HTML alone. CSS gets its name from the fact that multiple styles can be applied to a given element in a Web page; the CSS standard contains cascading—that is, precedence—rules specifying which of the multiple styles should be applied. CSS permits Web developers to define named sets of formatting directives for subsequent use, to define global styles for use throughout one or several pages, and to define families of styles that differ only by some subset of the family's formatting elements. CSS also allows much greater control over the layout of elements on a page, including positioning on the Z axis (that is, specifying which element appears in front of others when elements overlap).

Client-side scripting is another important technology for enhancing the user interface of a Web application. Whereas CSS is generally concerned with enhancing static content on Web pages, client-side scripting is concerned with giving dynamic qualities to a user interface, *without* server-side processing. There are two main reasons why this is important. First, certain types of processing, such as sanity checking a user input value as the user tabs from field to field, must be done almost instantaneously to avoid annoying the user to death. Server-side processing won't suffice in this situation, because it relies on a network round trip and a browser screen refresh in order to show any effect—a sequence of processes far too slow for anyone to tolerate on every tab from field to field. The other main reason client-side processing is preferable to server-side processing in many situations is simply for load distribution reasons: The more you can offload error checking, input processing (for example, converting various hand-entered dates to some uniform format), or even simple calculations or animation effects to the browser machine, the more compute resources will be left on the server machine to handle its own load. All that being said, it should be noted that client-side scripting is not appropriate for all types of processing. This includes any proprietary calculations (because client-side script can be read in source code form by your users), any highly compute-intensive tasks (because client-side script is interpreted and therefore much slower than compiled, server-side COM code), and also any database-intensive operations (because the server machine presumably has much faster access to your database than any machine that a browser is running on).

Although many different types of processing are possible with client-side scripting, one deserves special mention. *Dynamic HTML*, or *DHTML*, is a technology that, in a sense, combines HTML, CSS, and client-side scripting. Under DHTML, the elements of the browser's state (including the currently displayed page) are exposed for manipulation by client-side script. This includes both content and formatting directives. Changes made to content or formatting via DHTML are reflected in the browser display without any need for a request to the Web server and without even any need for reloading the currently displayed page.

The final two user interface enhancements we'll mention here are ActiveX controls and Java applets. Controls and applets are compact pieces of code that are designed to be downloaded along with the HTML of an ordinary Web page, but then executed on the client machine. This is very different from how HTML is processed. HTML really just *guides* the browser as to how it should alter its display area. Controls and applets are much more "autonomous" in that they (typically) lay claim to an area of the browser's display, and then proceed to perform sometimes elaborate processing with often limited interaction with the host browser. The difference between controls and applets is simply the language they're written in, as well as how they're physically packaged for distribution. Controls are compiled COM objects that execute on the browser's computer's CPU, whereas applets are Java classes that execute in the browser's *Java Virtual Machine (JVM)*. Controls and applets are valuable user interface elements because, even with all the user interface technologies discussed earlier, there are still many user interface features and effects that are possible only with full access to the Win32 API (for controls) or the Java language (for applets)[4]. Controls and applets can therefore round out the toolset for a Web application that seeks to have an exceptionally strong user interface.

Scalability, transactioning, and security features

If you're fortunate enough to attract multiple concurrent users to your Web site, you immediately become vulnerable to performance degradations that will make those users vow never to come back. And even if the performance of the system holds up okay, the possibility of *any* concurrent access (just two users can be enough) exposes your data to the risk of corruption. Finally, once you take care of performance and concurrency issues, you still need to worry about who is authorized to access which parts of your application and data. *Microsoft Transaction Server*, or *MTS*, is a powerful technology available to help with these problems, as well as provide a robust infrastructure for transaction processing on or off the Web.

MTS works as a silent "middle man" between COM clients and COM servers. In the case of a DNA Web application, MTS sits between ASP script code and whatever COM servers that script code uses. If a COM server is registered to run under MTS (either an installation program or a system administrator can so register it), then MTS keeps track of all running instances of the COM server system wide and permits subsequent requests for the COM server to reuse an existing instance where appropriate. If developers of COM objects take a few simple steps to make COM objects "MTS-friendly," then it turns out that MTS can allow this sort of reuse very easily. It also turns out that such reuse can have a massive, beneficial effect on the scalability of an application.

Another service that MTS provides is transaction support. When multiple applications, or multiple instances of the same application, attempt to modify a particular piece of data concurrently, the data can become corrupted if the concurrent accesses are not synchronized. A transaction, in the context of database systems, is simply a set of operations that an application developer identifies as being logically atomic—that is, the operations in the transaction must either all succeed or all fail. Most database products provide transactioning features, but achieving transactional integrity can be difficult if the atomic operation set spans multiple databases or multiple computers. MTS facilitates transactioning in these situations and also provides some programming conveniences that make transactioning much easier to implement in any situation.

The final MTS service alluded to at the start of this section is security. As the intermediary between the ASP script code and the various COM servers that together constitute the server half of an application, MTS is in a good position to allow or disallow object instantiation or object method invocation. MTS has a concept called a "role," which is a category of users defined by the application developer. For example, a bank application might have roles for "Customer," "Teller," "Bank Officer," and so on, such that different COM operations would be allowed or disallowed for the different categories of users. Once the system is ready to be deployed, the actual users and groups in the machine's normal NT security can be assigned to the different roles to control what these actual users can do. To enforce security, MTS facilitates two different approaches, known as *declarative security* and *programmatic security*. In declarative security, the permissions are declared by the application's administrator through the MTS administration utility; the code inside the COM objects doesn't explicitly participate in security operations. In programmatic security, the code itself performs security checks by utilizing an internal COM interface implemented by the MTS runtime.

Chapter 11, on transaction processing and scalability, fills in the details. For the current discussion of DNA Web applications, it's sufficient to note that MTS is a technology that addresses scalability, transactioning, and security in a particularly effective way, and these three issues are almost by definition going to be relevant to any serious Web commerce application, so MTS is likely to play a role in such an application. MTS also comes for free as part of the NT Server operating system and like ASP itself, is very tightly integrated with IIS (there's a built-in ASP object whose sole purpose is to provide MTS functionality to ASP code). The case for using MTS is therefore extremely compelling.

Commerce-specific features

At a high level, all commerce—whether electronic or conventional—is basically the same. A commercial enterprise can be anything from an ordinary plumbing supply store to a tax preparation Web site. In some form or other, commerce always includes marketing, sales, payment, fulfillment, and support; and, there is a lot of similarity of tasks within these overall activities. For this reason, several technologies have been created that attempt to provide broadly applicable commerce infrastructure. One such technology, Microsoft Site Server Commerce Edition (SSCE), is a Microsoft product that integrates particularly well with the DNA framework.

SSCE is actually a superset of the more generic Microsoft Site Server (SS), a product designed to help Web application developers accelerate development of certain types of Web applications. SSCE extends the functionality of SS by providing a large set of generic COM objects for handling the different tasks in the overall commerce process. SSCE uses the term *pipeline* to refer to this overall process and builds its functionality around the pipeline concept: There are several pipeline component objects (one for each step in the commerce process), a pipeline object (the container for all the pipeline components), and an order form object (the place where state information is stored between steps in the pipeline).

The individual tasks represented by pipeline components are things like tax calculation, credit card processing, inventory control, and so on. SSCE provides simple implementations of these specific tasks and roughly 50 others, and also provides two different implementations of the pipeline object itself, one that supports MTS transactions, and the other that runs under MTS but without transactioning. Depending on the complexity of the Web application you're building, the Microsoft-supplied pipeline components may be sufficient for many or even most of your needs. It's fine if they're not, though; they're just COM objects, and the interface they implement is documented and available for you to implement in COM objects of your own. In this way, you can enhance the pipeline framework with business rules as complex as they need to be for your application. Chapter 6, "Site Server Commerce Services," provides details on customizing the pipeline framework, as well as information on a few pieces of SSCE functionality separate from the pipeline framework.

Before concluding this section on commerce-specific technologies, it's worth mentioning one technology that's not commerce-specific strictly speaking but is important nonetheless, and offers powerful capabilities to commerce applications. This technology, *Extensible Markup Language (XML)*, is an open standard for passing structured data between Web servers and Web browsers. Like HTML, XML is a text-based markup language—that is, a human-readable format that interleaves data with descriptive information about the data. But whereas HTML is concerned with the formatting characteristics of the embedded data, XML is concerned with the structural characteristics of the embedded data, as well as the relationship between different pieces of data. If you want to download some text, and specify certain portions of it as being bold font or left justified, then HTML is designed for the task. If you want to download a detailed catalog of product information, with prices, descriptions, and inter-product relationships (such as the dependency of a certain disk drive on a certain disk controller card), then XML is designed for the task.

XML permits Web applications to convey rich detail about the structure of data being downloaded. At the browser end of the connection, the XML data is automatically parsed and built up into an in-memory tree structure that client-side script code can easily examine and manipulate. This makes it reasonable to pass significant quantities of structured data back and forth between server and browser, with many implications for commerce applications. Product catalogs, order forms, customer records, inventory information, and so on, which were previously really only practical as server-side data structures, can now be downloaded for client-side processing where appropriate. This takes the arguments given previously for client-side processing (UI responsiveness and distribution of processing load) and extends their applicability into much more substantive commerce-related tasks. Chapter 16, "Information Exchange with XML," covers this topic.

WEB COMMERCE: REVISITED

Many pages ago, we observed that electronic and traditional commerce are basically the same at a high level, except that some of the specific activities change a bit for the electronic form. It's time to elaborate on that now. This section provides brief comments on how the general activities of commerce are, or should be, different on the Web.

Marketing

Marketing is all about knowing your customers. The Web, for its part, can help you do that. When a person visits your Web site, you can track and record everything they click, everything they examine, everything they type, and, most importantly, every transaction they make. You can then use this information to send targeted mailings, prompt human phone calls, or modify the behavior of the Web application on a customer-by-customer basis. This type of one-on-one marketing and site personalization makes for a richer and more satisfying customer experience.

One obvious example of modifying an application's behavior for a particular customer is simply storing mailing address and payment information so that this customer needs to enter the information only once. A more interesting example is actually modifying the product catalog and site naviga-tion pattern to reflect the customer's previously exhibited preferences and habits.

In the traditional (non-electronic) setting, truly personalized treatment exists but is rare. Most people really appreciate it, though, and will go out of their way to patronize businesses that know their favorite sandwich toppings, know their shirt size, or know which musician's new releases they'd like ad-vance warning about. Most people will pay a little extra for this sort of buying experience and will similarly hesitate to jump to a competitor.

A person's surfing and transaction history represent extremely valuable marketing information. Beyond this, most people will happily provide additional information not implied by their surfing or transaction history if they know it will make your Web site behave better for them. You can use this information by defining site behavior in terms of what you know about the current visitor. And at the aggregate level (that is, considering shopping and purchasing pat-terns exhibited by all your customers as a group), you can use this information to continually evolve your product offerings, your pricing, your promotion strat-egy, and your distribution channels, based on what you know to have been appealing or successful with existing customers. You can also use this informa-tion *proactively*, to provide your customers with complimentary products and services based on their purchasing patterns. For example, Amazon.com provides individualized suggested reading lists based on past book purchases.

Sales

Sales refers to the steps leading up to the actual commercial transaction, along with the transaction itself. Probably the biggest difference between a traditional sales transaction and an electronic one is the lack of human contact, which implies some things about "closing" and also implies some things about the anxiety surrounding the transaction moment.

Anyone who has done some selling knows there's a huge difference between getting someone very interested in a product or service and getting them actually to purchase it. In a traditional setting, closing the deal often de-pends heavily on the interpersonal qualities of the salesperson, on the ability of that person to convey the excitement, value, or necessity of the product. On the Web, that excitement has to come from a tremendously strong user interface, coupled with insightful bits of personalized *software* behavior as described in the previous section on marketing.

And just as a traditional buying experience might be appealing for its human touch, the Web buying experience can be appealing for its convenience. At any point in a Web application, a person might decide to execute the trans-action. The application should make it convenient for them to do so.

Payment

Payment is probably the greatest focus of anxiety in the Web buying experience. Although people seem to be slowly coming to grips with the idea that the Web is a safe place to exchange payment information, there's still a lot of apprehension around it. When credit cards first came out, there was a long ritual performed to indicate the importance and seriousness of the "credit card enabled transaction." Now people swipe their own credit cards, and it is no big deal. Now there is a new mystique about the "Web-enabled transaction," so we begin again. You should do everything you can to make it ordinary, normal, simple, and safe.

A lot of the anxiety arises from the perceived complexity of security measures designed to safeguard payment data being transmitted over a public network. The disorderly growth of payment methods and security measures has prompted vendors and standards-setting bodies to create stable protocols and products to shield electronic merchants from complexity. It is exactly this shielding from complexity that this book is all about — using Microsoft's components and tools, you can make your client's visit to your commerce Web site a pleasant and enjoyable process.

See the section on payment in Chapter 4, "Security Planning and Implementation," for the details on the topics mentioned in the previous paragraphs, along with many other topics.

Fulfillment

Fulfillment is concerned with providing the goods or services to the customer. In the case of tangible goods, fulfillment might be the phase of commerce that differs least between the traditional and the Web settings, in the sense that both types of merchants frequently just hand off fulfillment responsibility to an outside firm. In this case, a seller could use the Web to transmit instructions automatically to the shipping firm to fulfill orders. Amazon.com, for example, does not stock all the books it sells. Many orders are fulfilled directly by the publisher based on instructions sent to them from Amazon when a customer makes an order. This business-to-business electronic communication is growing rapidly under the paradigm of electronic data interchange (EDI), which is itself changing because of the growing ability to transmit EDI standard documents from business to business over Web transport protocols. Fulfillment depends, fundamentally, on secure EDI. It also depends on the traditional ability to ship and track goods and services.

For purely electronic products or information-based services the Web setting offers a distinct advantage. For example, purchased software can be downloaded directly from the Web. Similarly, online services, such as tax preparation or electronic news and analysis, meet their basic fulfillment obligation directly through the Web.

Customer Service

Like marketing, customer service is a great candidate for "mass-personalization." Just as you can use your knowledge of a customer's past habits, preferences, and transactions to do a better job selling them more things, you can use that same knowledge to do a better job making their ownership experience better for the things you've already sold them.

As in the sale itself, the personal touch is as yet lacking in electronic service but can be nicely compensated for with convenience. If the service portions of a Web site are nicely laid out, rich in information, and easy to use, a lot of people would probably view that as a nice step up from the crap shoot that most human-powered service offerings seem to be. For example, a Web service center can be open around the clock. Personal e-mails addressing customer service needs or suggestions can be much better than holding for hours on a toll-free line. In the future, as high bandwidth becomes commonplace, customer support staff will likely talk directly to the client using Internet phone and video. In short, the Web will get more and more personal over time.

Maybe the most important observation about service in any setting, whether traditional or electronic, is that it is an integral part of the marketing and selling process. The information picked up from processing customer problems is valuable marketing data, and if the service experience is great, that turns into a powerful sales pitch for this same customer, or his or her friends. Great Web commerce applications have great service components, with great user interfaces and great personalization features. Most importantly, these components are tightly integrated with all other parts of the Web site.

COMPLEMENTS TO COMMERCE

Although this book is primarily about deploying commerce sites that directly transact business, some of the technology can be applied in complementary ways that provide substantial business value. Businesses make money not only by increasing sales, but also by lowering costs of operations and being more capable in what they do. Therefore, we will take an occasional opportunity to show commerce-related scenarios such as streaming multimedia within an organization via NetShow, using Microsoft Office to collaborate on marketing documents, and implementing customer support workflow with Microsoft Exchange.

SUMMARY

The Web presents tremendous opportunities and challenges, both of which are accentuated by the primitive nature of life on the Web. The technologies available have been weak up until very recently, remain unfamiliar to many and are rapidly evolving. Succeeding in such an environment offers extra-big rewards to those who can select and apply these new technologies.

The Microsoft Distributed Internet Applications Architecture (DNA), along with the many complementary technologies discussed in this chapter and the remainder of the book, represent a breadth and quality of tool set that finally make large-scale commercial Web development a reasonable undertaking. All built up from, and around, the basic request and response paradigm of HTTP, these tools cover everything from user interfaces to data storage, as well as all the business logic in between.

This chapter, hopefully, has helped illustrate the big picture of these technologies. The next chapter provides some hands-on exercises to reinforce concepts discussed here. After that, the topics of this chapter, along with many others, are covered in much greater detail in the remaining chapters of the book.

---

[1] We're speaking a bit loosely here of a "Submit" button in the sense that the control on an HTML form which triggers a new request to a Web server does not need to be a button, nor does it need to be labeled with the actual text, "Submit."

[2] The term "N-tier" refers to a generic architectural framework for building client/server applications in a flexible, scalable way. The N tiers which give the framework its name are the user interface, the database, and one or several business logic layers in between. Chapter 2 provides an example of a simple N-tier application, and the remainder of the book provides details on filling in the various tiers as they manifest themselves in a Web application.

[3] See *http://www.microsoft.com/dna/tech.asp* for the full list of technologies.

[4] Strictly speaking, ActiveX controls actually don't have full access to the Win32 API, and Java applets don't have full access to the Java language. Both controls and applets are prevented from doing a few isolated operations in their respective environments, mainly for security reasons. But the accessible portions of their respective environments are still far more feature rich than any other Web UI technology.

Chapter 2

The Core Technologies in Action

by Andy Maretz

The list of technologies in a modern, full-featured Web application can be daunting: There's a huge number of them, they're changing extremely rapidly, and many of the really important ones are new or even unreleased. Chapter 1 provided an architectural overview of these technologies, which is probably the best starting point. But there's still nothing quite like seeing them in action.

This chapter illustrates the steps necessary to build a simple Web application. We start by reviewing the steps necessary to build an ordinary Microsoft Visual Basic application—no Web, no network, just a normal Windows executable. Then, we show how to use DCOM to split this application across two computers, with the user interface on one machine, and the business services and database on a different machine. Finally, we show how to use a Web server and Web browser to operate this same application across an intranet or the Internet.

NOTE ON HARDWARE AND SOFTWARE REQUIRED

The hardest part about building everything in this chapter probably is gaining access to the hardware and software used in the examples. Ideally, you'll have two computers. The first is a Microsoft Windows NT 4 Workstation with Microsoft VB 6, IE 5, and Microsoft Access 2000. The second machine is an NT 4 Server with Microsoft IIS 4 and VB 6 (you can actually get away with just having the VB runtime, but it's probably easiest just to install the full VB development environment). If you have only a Windows NT Server, that's fine; you can do everything on that one machine. If there's a Windows NT Server available on your network but you don't have administrative rights to it, you can make it through the following examples by submitting a very small number of simple requests to your local system administrator. These are clearly marked in the text.

You'll see that things get relatively easy once the initial, non-networked VB application is done. That's because it's implemented as a three-tier architecture. Two tiers, a Data tier and a Business Services tier, will be totally reused, without change, for the DCOM and Web versions that follow. Of course, this is exactly the sort of flexibility that motivates people to use the N-tier approach in the first place, so it's encouraging to see the architectural payoff in these simple examples.

If you tried to implement an N-tier system even as recently as two or three years ago, you know that this sort of payoff hasn't always been so easy to come by. For all its architectural appeal, the N-tier approach has really been held back by the sheer difficulty of implementing it. But the current set of development tools and middleware have finally given developers sufficient power to tackle N-tier projects without too much pain. Recent releases of Microsoft Visual Basic, Microsoft Visual C++, and Microsoft Visual J++ have made it easy to create and use COM objects. In addition, Active Server Pages and Microsoft Transaction Server have drastically eased the deployment and management of N-tier systems. You'll use a lot of these technologies in the exercises in this chapter.

Of course, a Web application implemented in the space of one chapter lacks a lot of features found in a real application. Therefore, the chapter concludes by listing a few of the notable deficiencies of the application, along with references to later parts of the book that explain how to fix them.

APPLICATION PREVIEW

Before getting started, take a quick look at what you're about to build. The application is a very simple automated teller machine. It doesn't dispense cash, it doesn't accept deposits, and, in fact, it doesn't do anything at all except process transfers of funds from a savings account to a checking account. It's basically a utility for people who write bad checks.

In its VB incarnation, whether operating locally on one computer or operating in a distributed fashion using DCOM, the user interface looks like Figure 2-1. In its Web incarnation, it looks like Figure 2-2. In either case, the use of the application is very simple. You fill in a username, a transfer amount, and then click the Execute button. If your username is valid and if you have enough funds in your savings account to cover the transaction, the transfer succeeds; otherwise, the transaction fails.

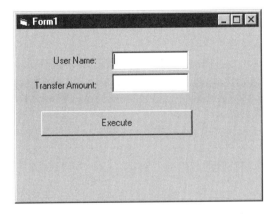

Figure 2-1. *User view as a Visual Basic application.*

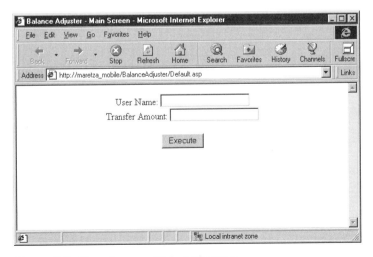

Figure 2-2. *User view as a Web application.*

BUILDING THE SHARED COMPONENTS

Again, the ultimate goal of this chapter is to compare a conventional VB application, a distributed VB application, and a Web application side by side. As noted earlier, however, these aren't three different applications. They're three different ways of facilitating user interaction with a single, shared infrastructure, consisting in this case of a COM object (the Business Services tier) and a simple relational database (the Data tier). Figure 2-3 shows this graphically. In this first section, you'll build this common infrastructure.

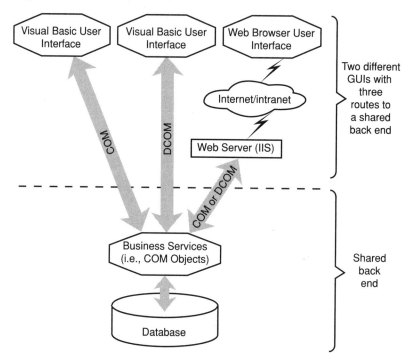

Figure 2-3. *Architecture of the sample applications. The Data and Business Services tiers of the three-tier architecture are shared.*

The Data Tier

To get things going, start up Microsoft Access, and follow these steps to create a simple database with one table:

1. Either select Blank Database from Access's initial greeting screen or, if you're already in Access, select New Database from the File menu,

and choose Blank Database from the gallery of templates. In either case, you'll end up at the file save dialog shown in Figure 2-4.

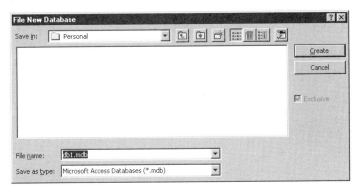

Figure 2-4. *Creating a new Access database.*

2. Save the database file under the name BankDatabase.mdb. This will put you into the datasheet view of a new table.

3. In the View menu, select Design View.

4. Now add the following three fields to the table:

Field Name	*Data Type*
UserName	Text
SavingsBalance	Currency
CheckingBalance	Currency

5. Highlight the entire UserName row by clicking on the small gray box immediately to the left of the text, UserName. With this row highlighted, select the Primary Key command from the Edit menu. A picture of a key should appear at the left of this row. At this point, the screen should appear as shown in Figure 2-5.

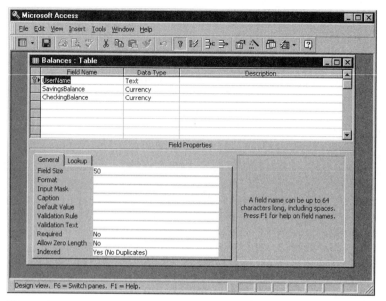

Figure 2-5. *Creating a simple table and setting its primary key.*

6. Save the table under the name Balances by selecting File Save. Then close the table by selecting File Close.

7. Finally, add some sample data to the database. Double-click the table in the main Access explorer window to open it for editing, tab from field to field and row to row, and type two or three rows of sample data. Use whatever usernames and balances you'd like, but remember at least one of the usernames so you can test the application later.

8. When you're done adding sample data, choose File Close to close the table, followed by File Exit to leave Access altogether.

You now have a functional database, but it's useful to associate the database with an ODBC data source. There are many reasons why this is so; the immediate benefit is that the ODBC link makes it more convenient to use the database from VB code, which you'll be doing momentarily. Follow these steps to create an ODBC data source for your database:

1. From the Windows Start menu, select Settings Control Panel.

2. Double-click the ODBC applet in the control panel.

3. Click the Add button to create a new data source, and then select Microsoft Access Driver (*.mdb) from the list of choices. Click Finish.

4. Fill in SampleBankData as the data source name.

5. Click the Select button to select the database and navigate your way to the BankDatabase.mdb file you created earlier. Once you locate this file, highlight it and click OK to select it.

6. Click OK two more times to close the ODBC applet, and close the control panel now as well.

You now have a functional database in a convenient form. That's one tier down and two to go. The next task is to create the middle tier, which, in this case, is a single business object that encapsulates and operates on the data.

The Business Services Tier

Chapter 1 discussed the COM architecture at some length and described the important role that COM objects, also known as COM servers, play in both traditional and Web applications on the Windows platform. In this section, you'll use Visual Basic to create a COM object.

Start up Visual Basic and select ActiveX DLL from the New Project dialog box. This brings you into VB and creates a class module, which is a set of code and data that will be bundled together to become a COM server. In general, a COM server has data members (also known as "properties") and code procedures (also known as "methods" or "events," depending on whether the COM client is calling the COM server or vice versa). In the case of the object you're creating here, there will be no properties, no events, and only one method. Follow these steps to create the method:

1. From the Tools menu, select the Add Procedure command.

2. Fill in Transfer as the name of the procedure.

3. Click the Function option button.

4. Click OK.

You should now be in the VB code editor with the following code showing:

```
Public Function Transfer()
End Function
```

Now replace this code with the following (and don't despair at the amount of code you need to type; this is the entire Business Services tier, and you'll be using it exactly as is for all three applications):

```
'/ Return:
'/  0 for OK
'/  1 for unknown UserName
'/  2 for insufficient funds
'/  3 for miscellaneous other error

Public Function Transfer(vUserName As Variant, vTransferAmount As
Variant, _
  vSavingsBalance As Variant, vCheckingBalance As Variant) As
Variant

  '/ Declare local variables
  Dim cyTransferAmount As Currency
  Dim strQueryString As String
  Dim rsBankData As ADODB.Recordset
  Dim objContext As ObjectContext

  '/ Set up to handle errors
  On Error GoTo ErrorHandler

  '/ Initialize context object for MTS
  Set objContext = GetObjectContext()
  Set rsBankData = CreateObject("ADODB.Recordset")

  '/ Construct query string and open recordset
  strQueryString = "Select * from Balances " & _
    " where (UserName = '" & vUserName & "')"
  rsBankData.LockType = adLockOptimistic
  rsBankData.Open strQueryString, "DSN=SampleBankData"

  '/ Process Transfer request
  If rsBankData.EOF Then
    '/ UserName not found in database
    Transfer = 1
  Else
    cyTransferAmount = CCur(vTransferAmount)
    vSavingsBalance = rsBankData("SavingsBalance")
    vCheckingBalance = rsBankData("CheckingBalance")
    If vSavingsBalance >= cyTransferAmount Then
      '/ UserName found and sufficient funds available
      Transfer = 0
      vSavingsBalance = vSavingsBalance - cyTransferAmount
      vCheckingBalance = vCheckingBalance + cyTransferAmount
      rsBankData.Update "SavingsBalance", vSavingsBalance
      rsBankData.Update "CheckingBalance", vCheckingBalance
    Else
      '/ UserName found, but insufficient funds available
```

```
Transfer = 2
    End If
  End If

  '/ Close recordset and release object
  rsBankData.Close
  Set rsBankData = Nothing

  '/ Finish transaction successfully
  If Not objContext Is Nothing Then
    objContext.SetComplete
  End If

Exit Function

ErrorHandler:
  ' Abort transaction
  If Not objContext Is Nothing Then
    objContext.Abort
  End If

  Transfer = 3

End Function
```

This code implements the transfer of funds from savings to checking. Although the database, which you created previously, stores all the relevant data for this application, it's incomplete without some well-defined rules for how this data should be accessed, how it can be legitimately changed, what should be done in the event of errors, and so on. That's what the Transfer method is all about. It implements the business rules associated with the handling of this data.

The Transfer method accepts four arguments:

■ **Username.** The user name, as entered on the first screen of either the VB or Web application

■ **TransferAmount.** The transfer amount, as entered on the first screen of either the VB or Web application

■ **SavingsBalance.** An output parameter used to store the ending balance in the savings account

■ **CheckingBalance.** An output parameter used to store the ending balance in the checking account

It then returns a code indicating if the transfer was successful.

The first few lines of the method declare variables to be used in the remainder of the method. After that, an MTS context handle is obtained (see the sidebar on MTS). Next, an ADO recordset object[1] is created and initialized with a query that's constructed at runtime. If the recordset contains any records (in which case the EOF, or end-of-file, property is initially False), the requested username was found in the database. This just establishes that the customer exists, so the next step is to check that there are sufficient funds in savings to cover the transfer. If there are, the Transfer method changes the balances for both accounts appropriately. Eventually, the method returns a 0, 1, 2, or 3 to indicate what happened; the comment at the start of the code sample indicates the meaning of these return values.

THE MTS CONTEXT HANDLE

So what's this MTS context handle that's obtained at the start of the code? MTS, as described in Chapter 1, is a middleware technology that performs a variety of services on behalf of COM servers and COM clients. The service that helped give MTS its name is transactioning support, which refers to the set of protocols and technologies that ensure data integrity under concurrent database access conditions. Later in this chapter, you'll install this COM server under the control of MTS; the MTS context handle shown in the code sample earlier is the means by which this COM server will communicate with the MTS runtime. Specifically, objContext.SetComplete tells MTS that everything executed successfully, and objContext.Abort tells MTS that there was a problem. MTS uses this information, in turn, to commit or roll back a database transaction it sets up and manages automatically for you.

In the absence of transactioning, concurrent attempts to transfer funds within the same user's account could result in a corrupted database or other incorrect behavior. This is because there's a window of vulnerability between these two lines in the TransferAgent object's Transfer method:

```
rsBankData.Update "SavingsBalance", vSavingsBalance
rsBankData.Update "CheckingBalance", vCheckingBalance
```

In other words, if two different transfers were being attempted simultaneously on the same user account, and the second transfer happened to execute just as the first was paused between these two lines (such as from an operating system timeslice), the semantics of the transfers would be incorrect, and the database would be left in a corrupt state. By running this COM server under the control of MTS and coding the COM server to utilize MTS's transactioning support, you ensure that the transfer operation is either done correctly or not done at all. This type of transactional integrity is critical for any application, especially one that transfers funds from one bank account to another. You'll activate this feature later in the chapter when you install the COM server under MTS.

Creating the DLL

That's *almost* all there is to be done for this COM server. All that remains is to save it in such a way as to make it accessible to other applications (such as the VB application and Web application you'll be writing momentarily). Follow these steps:

1. Click the project name (Project1) in the project explorer, go to the properties sheet, and change the name from Project1 to TransferDLL.

2. Click the class module name (Class1) in the project explorer, go to the properties sheet, and change the name from *Class1* to TransferAgent.

3. Now save the project, using whatever names you like for the class file and project file.

4. Finally, select the Make TransferDLL.dll command from the File menu and choose a location to put the DLL file. You can put the DLL file wherever you like, but remember where you put it, since you'll need to find it in a few minutes.

That's it for the shared infrastructure. Here's a quick review of what happened here:

■ **The Data.** You created a database and made it accessible via an ODBC data source.

■ **The Business Rules.** You created a COM server with code implementing connectivity to the database.

■   **Installing Components.** Finally, you packaged the COM server as a dynamic link library (DLL) and advertised it in the Windows Registry (though you may not have realized you were doing the latter part).

In the next section, you'll create the first user interface, so you'll finally get to see something working.

BUILDING A TRADITIONAL WINDOWS APPLICATION

Start up Visual Basic if you're not already in it and select Standard EXE from the New Project dialog box. You can also get the New Project dialog box by selecting New Project from the File menu. Once you've selected Standard EXE, your screen should look something like Figure 2-6.

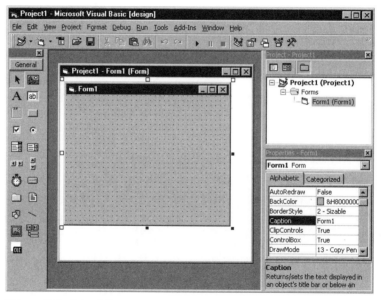

Figure 2-6. *Initial VB environment.*

Now create a simple user interface, similar to the form shown in Figure 2-7.

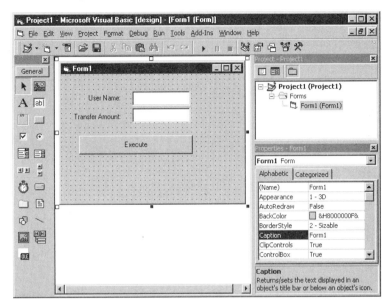

Figure 2-7. *VB user interface being built.*

Start by creating the User Name: and Transfer Amount: fields as follows:

1. Click on the Label tool in the tool palette on the left side of the workspace and use the mouse to drag a rectangle on the form big enough to hold the User Name: text.

2. Go to the property sheet at the bottom-right of the VB workspace and change the Caption property to User Name:.

3. Click on the TextBox tool in the tool palette and place the input box for the username next to the User Name: label on the form.

4. Go to the property sheet at the bottom-right of the screen and change the Name property from Text1 to txtUserName.

5. While still in the property sheet, delete the value from the Text property.

6. Repeat Steps 1 through 5 for the Transfer Amount: label and input box, using the name txtBalanceAmount in this case for the input box.

Now create the Execute button by following these steps:

1. Click the CommandButton tool on the tool palette and place a button at the appropriate place on the form (refer to Figure 2-7).

2. In the property sheet, change the button's Name property to cmdExecute and change its Caption property to Execute.

3. Double-click the button itself on the form to bring up the associated code window and fill in the command handler procedure as follows:

```
Private Sub cmdExecute_Click()

    Dim vResult As Variant
    Dim vSavingsBalance As Variant
    Dim vCheckingBalance As Variant
    Dim vUserName As Variant
    Dim vTransferAmount As Variant
    Dim vBalanceString As Variant
    Dim vTransferAgent As Variant


    '/ Create TransferAgent COM server
    Set vTransferAgent = CreateObject("TransferDLL.TransferAgent")
    vUserName = txtUserName.Text
    vTransferAmount = txtTransferAmount.Text
    '/ Call the Transfer method of the TransferAgent COM server
    vResult = vTransferAgent.Transfer(vUserName, _
      vTransferAmount, vSavingsBalance, vCheckingBalance)

    '/ Check the return code and report on the results
    If vResult = 0 Then
      vBalanceString = _
        Format(vSavingsBalance, "Currency") & _
        "/" & _
        Format(vCheckingBalance, "Currency")
      MsgBox "Succeeded, new balances (savings/checking): " _
        & vBalanceString
    ElseIf vResult = 1 Then
      MsgBox "Transfer failed: user name unknown"
    ElseIf vResult = 2 Then
      vBalanceString = Format(vSavingsBalance, "Currency")
      MsgBox "Transfer failed: insufficient funds (only " _
        & vBalanceString & " available)"
          Else
            MsgBox "Transfer failed: unknown error"
    End If


    '/ Set vTransferAgent to the special value 'Nothing' to
    '/ signal to VB to release its handle on the COM server
    Set vTransferAgent = Nothing

End Sub
```

4. Now close this code window and save your project under whatever name you like. You'll actually be prompted to save two files: one for the project as a whole and another for the form. Any names you want to use are fine here.

Running the Application

The VB application is now ready to run. Select Run Start to try it out, and you should be able to change some balance values in your database, as long as you can come up with a valid username and transfer amount.

Before moving on, take a quick look at what's going on behind the scenes. You've implemented, in very simple form, a three-tier application. Although you implemented the application from back to front, the sequence of processing actually goes from front to back, as follows:

1. The user starts up a Visual Basic form.

2. When the user clicks the Execute button, this invokes the click event handler (known by the name cmdExecute_Click) associated with the button.

3. This event handler gathers together the username and transfer amount from the input screen.

4. Next, the event handler calls the Transfer DLL:

    ```
    CreateObject("TransferDLL.TransferAgent")
    ```

5. The CreateObject call goes to the Windows Registry and looks up the key TransferDLL.TransferAgent to find the location of the COM object that goes by this name.

6. In this case, the location is a DLL on the local filesystem, so this DLL gets loaded into the VB address space, and the cmdExecute_Click procedure uses the Transfer method that the COM object implements.

7. The Transfer method, in turn, uses COM to create an ADO recordset object for use on an Access database. The Transfer method also enforces the business semantics of a monetary transfer, specifically by making sure the person doing the transfer has a valid account with sufficient funds.

8. When the transfer is done, the ADO recordset object is closed and released, and the Transfer method returns a result code back to cmdExecute_Click.

9. Finally, cmdExecute_Click examines the return code from the Transfer method and uses the results to put an appropriate message on the screen.

The next section brings a network into the picture, and the section after that gets to the long-awaited Web application.

DISTRIBUTING OVER THE INTERNET USING DCOM

A COM client needn't know or care where its server is located. When a COM client (such as the VB user interface you wrote earlier) needs to use a COM server (such as the TransferDLL.TransferAgent object you also wrote earlier), it simply calls CreateObject to create the server, and then accesses the methods, properties, and events of the server. If the server happens to be in a different Windows process, or even a process that executes on an entirely different machine, the COM infrastructure of the Windows operating system steps in to handle the inter-process or inter-machine communication, but the COM client remains unaware of the fact that such intervention is taking place behind the scenes. This feature of COM is called *location independence* and is discussed in detail in Chapter 9 of this book. For our immediate purposes, location independence means that the Windows application you wrote earlier, in which a COM server DLL was loaded in-process, should work exactly "as-is" if you decide to move the COM server to a different computer. And this, in fact, is the case, except that there are a few complications to take care of first.

The first is that you need to install the COM server physically on a different computer. The second is that you need to update the registry on the client computer so that it knows what machine the server is installed on. The third complication is that the COM server you wrote is a dynamic link library, or DLL, which is a code form incapable of executing except in the process space of a normal program (typically an EXE). The problem is that the DLL is now on a different computer from the EXE in which it previously executed, which eliminates this EXE as a candidate to play host to this DLL. The server thus needs some other EXE to play host to it on the remote computer, and you need to arrange for this to happen.

None of these complications is insurmountable, but they're each a little bit of a hassle to deal with. It turns out that Microsoft Transaction Server, or MTS, takes care of all three of these complications for you, along with performing a large variety of other services, such as the transactioning support discussed earlier in this chapter. MTS is not required in order to achieve DCOM connectivity, but it's a fairly harmless bit of overkill that makes DCOM connectivity easier to accomplish. We, therefore, will use MTS in the steps that follow to help with DCOM setup. A significant·side benefit of this is that by installing the TransferAgent under MTS, the transactioning operations of the server's Transfer method (the objContext.SetComplete and objContext.Abort calls in the code sample starting on page 36) will now have the protective effect they were put in for.

> **NOTE**   You will need administrator rights on the NT Server for most of the following steps.

Follow these steps to split the balance transfer application across two computers:

1. Locate the directory on the local computer where you saved the VB project file and class file (a .vbp file and a .cls file) for the TransferDLL, and copy these files to your Microsoft NT server machine.

2. Open the project file on the server machine, select the Make TransferDLL.dll command from the File menu, and then exit VB.

3. Start up the Microsoft Transaction Server Explorer on the NT Server machine and navigate your way down the tree control to a folder called Packages Installed under the My Computer icon.

4. Right-click on Packages Installed and select New Package from the pop-up menu.

5. Click the Create an Empty Package button.

6. Name the package *Bank Utilities*, and then click the Next button.

7. Leave the next screen as is and click Finish to leave the Package Creation Wizard.

8. Now navigate down to the components folder under the Bank Utilities package you just created.

9. Right-click the components folder and select New Component from the pop-up menu.

10. Click the button labeled Import components that are already registered.

11. Scroll down and select TransferDLL.TransferAgent from the list.

12. Once the component is into MTS, locate it in the MTS Explorer, right-click the component, and select Properties from the pop-up menu.

13. On the Transaction tab, select Requires a transaction.

The COM server is now registered on the server machine, and MTS is all set to play host to the DLL. There are just two things that remain to be done: configuring the client registry and configuring an ODBC data source on the server. Follow these steps to use a convenient mechanism that MTS provides to ease the task of registering COM servers on client machines:

1. Go again to the MTS Explorer and find the Bank Utilities package under Packages Installed.

2. Right-click Bank Utilities and select the Export command from the pop-up menu. This brings up a dialog that prompts you for a file name to create.

3. Click the Browse button here to get a Save As dialog box and save the export package under whatever name you'd like.

4. Now click the Export button to save the package file.

5. When you go into the Windows Explorer to look at the package file you just created, you'll see that the MTS Explorer also created a subdirectory there called "clients" and placed in that directory a file with an .exe ending.

6. If you copy that .exe file over to the client computer and simply execute it by double-clicking it, your client application will now know where to locate this COM server.

You can actually run the application right now, and the basic DCOM connectivity between client and server should be all set up and working. The only problem is that when you execute the Transfer method of the TransferDLL.TransferAgent COM server, it will trigger an error on the server machine, since the Transfer code expects to use an ODBC data source (called SampleBankData) which is not yet created. You did create this data source on the client machine, which was necessary to run the application as a fully local client-server pair. You just need to set up a data source with this same name on the new server machine if you want to run as a distributed client-server pair. To do this, first copy the Microsoft Access database file (a file with an .mdb extension) over to the server machine. Then follow the same steps you performed on page 34 above to create a User ODBC data source, but this time perform these steps on the System DSN tab in the ODBC Administrator control panel applet.

The application should work now. If you invoke the application on the client machine, you may notice a longer-than-usual delay while it performs the transfer operation. That's because it's doing a lot more than it used to do, albeit in a way that's invisible to you, except for the extra delay. But it should eventually come back with the "Transfer succeeded…" message.

To review what's going on, here's the same recap of the "behind-the-scenes" processing that was shown on page 43, but this time with modifications (shown highlighted in gray) to describe the changes associated with the move from a local COM server to a distributed COM server:

1. The user starts up a Visual Basic form.

2. When the user clicks the Execute button, this invokes the "click event handler" (known by the name cmdExecute_Click) associated with the button.

3. This event handler gathers together the username and transfer amount from the input screen.

4. Next, the event handler calls the Transfer DLL:

    ```
    CreateObject("TransferDLL.TransferAgent")
    ```

5. The CreateObject call goes to the Windows Registry and looks up the key "TransferDLL.TransferAgent" to find the location of the COM object that goes by this name.

6. In this case, the location is a remote machine, so the local machine contacts the remote machine in order to start up the COM server.

7. When the remote machine goes to start up TransferDLL.TransferAgent, however, it sees that this particular COM server is designated to be hosted by MTS. The server machine, therefore, tells MTS to start up TransferDLL.TransferAgent, which it does.

8. Once this is done, the COM infrastructure on the remote machine returns control to the COM infrastructure on the local machine, which in turn returns control to the cmdExecute_Click procedure. The cmdExecute_Click procedure now has a valid object reference in hand through which it can invoke server methods.

9. As before, the cmdExecute_Click procedure calls the Transfer method of this COM server. In the non-networked case, the communication between cmdExecute_Click and the COM server is fairly simple. This is not so in the networked case, however, where the communication of method name, method arguments, and method return value all must occur across a network. The nice part of this complexity, at least, is that COM handles all of it for you automatically.

10. The Transfer method, in turn, uses COM to create an ADO recordset object for use on an Access database. The Transfer method also enforces the business semantics of a monetary transfer, specifically by making sure the person doing the transfer has a valid account with sufficient funds.

11. When the transfer is done, the ADO recordset object is closed and released, and the Transfer method returns a result code back to cmdExecute_Click.

12. Finally, cmdExecute_Click examines the return code from the Transfer method and uses the results to put an appropriate message up on the screen.

The next section provides instructions on building another distributed version of the balance transfer application, but this time the underlying communications mechanism is HTTP (that is, a Web server and a Web browser) instead of DCOM.

BUILDING A WEB APPLICATION

Take another look at Figure 2-3. You'll notice that the connection between the shared infrastructure and the Web user interface (UI) is a lot more complicated than the connection between the infrastructure and the VB UI. The VB version of the UI is a simple Windows application that calls directly into the TransferDLL.TransferAgent object when the user clicks the Execute button. The Web version of the UI, on the other hand, is the combined effect of several different pieces of software. At a very high level, the Web application is simply a pair of Web pages: one that greets the user and accepts input of a username and a transfer amount, and another that announces the results of the transfer operation. The trick to making these two Web pages function as a unified application is the hand-off of information from the form on the first Web page to the code that creates the second Web page. This is one of the basic services provided by the Active Server Pages (ASP) framework that operates under Internet Information Server (IIS).

Probably the easiest way to understand the behavior of the Web application is just to go ahead and build it. There are some extremely feature-rich tools out in the world for creating Web pages, including some that are covered later in this book. The Web application under consideration here, however, is so simple that an ordinary text editor, such as Notepad, will work just fine. So open up Notepad and enter the following text:

```
<HTML>
<HEAD>
<TITLE>
Balance Adjuster - Main Screen
</TITLE>
</HEAD>
<BODY>
<CENTER>

<FORM name="frmMain" action="Results.asp" method="POST">
User Name: <input type=text name="UserName" size=20>
<BR>
Transfer Amount: <input type=text name="TransferAmount" size=20>
|<BR><BR>
<input type="submit" value="Execute">

</CENTER>
</BODY>
</HTML>
```

This is ordinary HTML that describes an input form containing:

1.   A text input field called UserName

2.   A text input field called TransferAmount

3.   A command button called Execute

Save this file under the name Default.htm in a directory visible to your Web server. When a Web browser downloads this file for display, it renders an input form on the screen, as shown in Figure 2-2.

> **NOTE**   If you don't have administrative access to your NT Server computer, you'll need an administrator to create a directory for you and also to grant you write permission to that directory.

Take a closer look at the HTML that describes the form in Default.htm. Of special interest is the <FORM> tag itself, which specifies that the "action" associated with the form is something called Results.asp. This is simply the name of a different Web page—the second of the two Web pages that make up the Web UI of this application. The effect of this is that when the user clicks the Execute button, the browser knows to bundle up the data from the form (just two items: a UserName and a TransferAmount) and to request a page called Results.asp from the Web server, passing to it these two data items.

Now create Results.asp in Notepad with the following contents and save it in the same directory as Default.htm (which you created earlier):

```
<HTML>

<HTML>
<HEAD>
<TITLE>
Balance Adjuster - Results Screen
</TITLE>
</HEAD>

<BODY>

<CENTER>
<%
Function Format(vNumber, vStyle)
      Format = "$" & vNumber
End Function
%>

<%
Dim vResult
Dim vSavingsBalance
Dim vCheckingBalance
Dim vUserName
Dim vTransferAmount
Dim vBalanceString
Dim vTransferAgent

Set vTransferAgent = CreateObject("TransferDLL.TransferAgent")
vUserName = Request.Form("UserName")
vTransferAmount = Request.Form("TransferAmount")
vResult = vTransferAgent.Transfer(vUserName, _
  vTransferAmount, vSavingsBalance, vCheckingBalance)

If vResult = 0 Then
  vBalanceString = _
    Format(vSavingsBalance, "Currency") & _
    "/" & _
    Format(vCheckingBalance, "Currency")
  Response.Write "Succeeded, new balances (savings/checking): " _
    & vBalanceString
ElseIf vResult = 1 Then
  Response.Write "Transfer failed: user name unknown"
ElseIf vResult = 2 Then
  vBalanceString = Format(vSavingsBalance, "Currency")
  Response.Write "Transfer failed: insufficient funds (only " &
vBalanceString & " available)"
Else
```

```
Response.Write "Transfer failed: unknown error"
End If

Set vTransferAgent = Nothing
%>
</CENTER>
</BODY>
</HTML>
```

This is the bulk of the Web UI. Recall that this page is requested in response to the user clicking the Execute button on the Default.htm screen. When the Web server sees that a requested page has the .asp extension, as this one does, it scans the file for VB Script (everything between matching <% and %> markers) before downloading it to the Web browser.

In the case of this page, there are two different blocks of VB Script code. The first one defines a function called Format, which will be used during execution of the second block of VB Script. Now look at the second block of code; we'll return to the Format function in a moment.

First, this code declares some variables. Next, it calls CreateObject("TransferDLL.TransferAgent") to create the TransferDLL.TransferAgent COM object, the exact same object created long ago as part of the VB application. Then this ASP code extracts the UserName and TransferAmount values from the requesting form, and passes these values to the Transfer method of the COM object.

As a quick aside, the syntax shown, in which the requesting form's data is accessible via Request.Form(...) is one of the standard, core features of Active Server Pages. ASP automatically creates an object called Request and arranges for that object to be visible to your VB Script code. The VB Script code then simply calls the Form method of the Request object. This Form method, in turn, knows where to find the user-entered data that the Web browser transmitted along with the request for the currently executing ASP page.

At this point, the remaining processing is simply concerned with examining the return value from the Transfer method. Recall that Transfer returns 0 on success, 1 on failure due to an unknown user, 2 on failure due to insufficient balances, and 3 on miscellaneous other errors. The processing of these result codes in the VB Script is pretty easy to follow. There are just two additional things to point out, however.

First, output is generated by calling the Write method of the Response object. Like the Request object, the Response object is one of the built-in objects in ASP, and the Write method is one of the key features of the Response object. You'll notice that there's ordinary HTML laced throughout this ASP file. The way output gets downloaded to the Web browser is that the Web server simply downloads text as it proceeds from top to bottom through the ASP file.

For everything outside the <% … %> markers, the Web server copies text exactly as is. For everything *inside* the <%…%> markers, the Web server does *not* copy the text to the Web browser. Instead, it processes the code and generates downloaded output only when instructed to do so by the code, such as in a Response.Write statement.

The second thing to point out is the Format function, which we briefly mentioned earlier. If you look back for a moment at the cmdExecute_Click procedure you wrote in Visual Basic previously, you'll see that it bears an extremely strong resemblance to the VB Script code in Results.asp. This was almost inevitable, in the sense that cmdExecute_Click and Results.asp are doing exactly the same thing, using the same underlying business object. It was, however, deliberate that these two procedures look exactly alike. As I assembled the examples in this chapter, I used cmdExecute_Click as the starting point for Results.asp because, in addition to saving me some keystrokes, it also underscores the similarity between the non-Web and Web implementations of the application. The problem with the Format function, however, is that it's built into VB, but not into VB Script. Therefore, to follow through on keeping cmdExecute_Click and Results.asp as similar to each other as possible, I just included a home-made definition of the Format function at the top of Results.asp. This has the nice side effect of illustrating how to define a function in ASP, but be warned that this implementation of Format is embarrassingly incomplete compared with the real Format function from VB.

Running the Application

At this point, you should be able to run the application. Start up a Web browser and enter the URL for the Default.htm file you created earlier. As long as you can remember a valid username and transfer amount, you should be able to transfer some imaginary funds through the Web application you just built.

CONCLUSION: BUILDING A BETTER APP

The Automated Teller you just built suffers from a lot of problems, ranging from pure cosmetics to serious security holes. The remaining sections provide brief explanations of these problems, and then refer you to chapters that address relevant topics more thoroughly.

Security

The application in this chapter is so small that it's hard to believe there's even room for gaping security holes, but they're there. A real application would, at the very least:

- Ask for a password in addition to a username

- Encrypt the username, password, and transfer amount before transmitting them over the public Internet

- Encrypt the calculation results before transmitting them back to the browser

A *thoroughly secured*, real-world application would very likely do much more than this.

Chapter 4 provides a detailed overview of security in the context of Web applications. The more specific topic of electronic payments (such as the processing of credit card numbers) is obviously of great importance to E-Commerce applications; this topic is also covered in Chapter 4. You'll also find discussions of security in a few other places in the book, including the following:

- Chapter 3, which discusses the infrastructure of e-commerce applications, including several security-related components

- Chapter 5, which discusses security in the context of the Microsoft Site Server product

- Chapter 11, which discusses Microsoft Transaction Server, a product with significant features that assist in the administration of Web application security

Client-Side Processing

Apart from the complete lack of graphics, colors, and so many other visual appeals, probably the most notable UI deficiency of the Web application in this chapter is the lack of client-side processing. If someone leaves an input field blank, or if they type a value that's clearly invalid as a monetary value into the

TransferAmount field, this application has no ability to catch the error until the form contents have been transmitted to the server, possibly over a slow Internet link. Although server-side processing is appropriate for substantive business rules (such as implementing the semantics of a funds transfer), client-side processing is good for providing very quick feedback to the user. This certainly includes catching simple errors (like forgetting to fill in a required value) but also includes cleaning up or "cooking" manual input (such as by changing the text "23.1" into the text "$23.10" automatically as the user tabs out of the field). Chapter 14 provides a detailed discussion of client-side scripting, along with a few related topics pertaining to processing on the client-side of the Web connection.

Scalability

One of the "good-news/bad-news" stories of developing applications for the Web is that it's amazingly easy to reach customers, suppliers, and business partners, but applications fortunate enough to do so often die under the load of their own popularity. The Web forces application developers to face the topic of scalability in a serious way. Several technologies and design techniques exist to help developers create scalable applications. The most important technology supporting scalability on the Microsoft platform is Microsoft Transaction Server (MTS), which you used earlier as a quick aid in implementing DCOM connectivity and transaction support.

MTS supports scalability through a variety of services, most notably resource pooling, in which key system resources (such as COM objects, database connections, and threads) are shared among MTS clients, often yielding huge efficiency gains. By installing TransferDLL.TransferAgent in MTS on the Web server, rather than hosting it in a less intelligent EXE, you (perhaps unknowingly) made your application much more scalable than it would otherwise have been. The problem is that some objects are "MTS friendly," and others are not, in the sense that a COM object must adhere to a few important rules in order to enjoy the benefits of scalability offered by MTS hosting.

It's very likely that you would violate one or more of these rules if you simply started enhancing TransferDLL.TransferAgent without first learning about what makes a COM object "MTS friendly." These are relatively simple rules to follow as a developer of COM servers, but failure to follow them can have devastating performance effects. You can read about these rules, along with a number of other MTS features, in Chapter 11, which is devoted to MTS.

Server-Side State Management

Also in the category of potential problems, in the simple examples of this chapter, is the lack of state management on the Web server. In all likelihood, any attempt to make this application more "real" would force you to look for ways to build up state information cumulatively over the course of a user's session. This might be in the form of a "shopping cart" (that is, a running list of transactions the user may, or may not, eventually execute), a set of session specific preferences, or any number of other types of session-global information.HTTP, the protocol of the Web, is stateless, which means that a Web application needs to craft some mechanism above and beyond HTTP in order to track the actions of a user from page to page. In a normal, non-Web application, this state is typically maintained in global variables of some sort. In a Web application, session-global state has typically been implemented in the past through a mechanism called *cookies*, which are local data files for recording state information. These local files are maintained by the Web browser but used by the Web server.

The Active Server Platform, which is the runtime environment that supports Active Server Pages, offers some state management services that are almost always needed by a Web application of any reasonable size. These are, in fact, implemented internally on the same cookie mechanism that has been used for state management prior to ASP, but the state management programming model of ASP is much more convenient and powerful than raw cookie-based state management. ASP provides a mechanism for application-global state (global variables visible across all users of a particular Web application), as well as session-global state (global variables visible across all pages hit by a particular user). These services, along with a variety of other ASP features not covered in the examples of this chapter, are covered in Chapter 7.

Non-VB Development

It's very likely that a development team would want to work in some language other than Visual Basic or Microsoft Visual Basic Scripting. This could be due to performance issues, developer skill sets, management views about future industry direction, or any number of other reasons. This chapter used VB and VBScript for illustration reasons, but COM is very much a language-neutral protocol. This means that the TransferAgent DLL could have been written in any of a large number of languages (including C++, Java, or even COBOL). Similarly, all the client code (the VB user interface and the Active Server Pages) could have been written in different languages. Chapter 12 discusses language-specific issues of implementing COM servers, focusing on C++, Java, and Visual Basic. Chapter 7 discusses all aspects of Active Server Pages, one of which is that ASP supports JavaScript in addition to VB Script.

SUMMARY

The purpose of this chapter is to make Web application development seem a little less daunting and a little more comprehensible to newcomers by walking through some simple examples. Apart from this, there's one key lesson worth taking away from the chapter: Web application development can be approached in a way that is fundamentally the same as conventional application development, with only minor techniques and technologies that you need to learn to accommodate the slight platform differences.

At a high level, most Windows applications developed in the future will look a lot like the simple balance transfer utility demonstrated earlier. They will involve some user interface technology selected from a large and growing list of COM clients, with COM servers implementing the core application functionality, and databases to store information between sessions. The complete reusability of TransferDLL.TransferAgent illustrated the significant overlap between Web and non-Web development. The nearly identical implementation of cmdExecute_Click and Results.asp was another illustration of this. The remainder of this book goes into all the details of a lot of new technologies, but the big picture stays surprisingly constant. Hopefully, this statement has been made more understandable and more believable by the exercises of this chapter. Hopefully, as well, the details that follow are a bit easier to absorb with the benefit of these same exercises.

---

[1]   ADO is explained briefly in Chapter 1, and in more detail in Chapter 8.

Part II

Infrastructure and Security

Chapter 3

Establishing an E-Commerce Infrastructure

by Steve Waldon

This chapter, and Chapter 4, will help you understand the infrastructure necessary to run an electronic commerce Web site—from both an architectural and operational perspective. There are large variations in the level of service and commitment needed to support e-commerce on the Web, and there is no magic blueprint that can guarantee good results for your particular situation. For example, a simple Web site can run virtually unattended for less than $100 a month and can be developed for well under $50,000. Larger sites might require dozens of full-time staff to update, cost several million dollars to create, with annual operating budgets in the millions. Given this variability, the task of determining what type of infrastructure is right for your business might seem daunting to you. The topics covered in this chapter, as well as those in Chapter 4, have been carefully chosen to help you understand how to navigate the e-commerce landscape and plan intelligently to make the right decisions in the early stage of your venture.

This chapter, designed to help you in your role as architect or e-commerce manager, assumes your Internet venture is mission-critical to the operation of your business. For example, you need to think about possible service outages and dealing with large numbers of users accessing your site. You need to plan for disasters such as flooding of your Web server hosting facility. You need to worry about criminals, vandals, and competitors tampering with or stealing equipment and information. You need to understand what types of resources are required to run and maintain your operation, and, if pressed for capital or time, you might need to know what options exist for outsourcing. Finally, because you are reading a book about e-commerce, you are probably interested in selling goods and services using the Internet, which should make you very curious about convenient and secure Internet mechanisms for billing and re-ceiving payment.

The remainder of this chapter is organized around four major topics that shed light on these concerns:

- Reliability and Scalability

- Performance

- Operational Issues

- Outsourcing Options

Two additional topics, security and electronic payment, are complex enough to warrant the attention of dedicated chapters. You will find more in-depth discussions of these topics in Chapter 4.

RELIABILITY, SCALABILITY, AND CAPACITY PLANNING

Assuming you have an effective business plan, a well-designed user interface, quality products, and a commitment to your customers, how do you assure that the Web site you build will provide reliable service and grow with you as your business expands? On the surface, reliability and scalability might seem like separate issues. However, deeper examination reveals that they are very closely related. Consider the example of an Internet stock brokerage site choking under the high-trading volumes encountered during a market collapse. Angered cus-tomers will take little comfort in the explanation that you have a very reliable system when it takes two hours to process their trades during busy times. In addition to the perception that a slow and unresponsive system is not reliable, there are additional architectural couplings between reliability and scalability.

As you will see shortly, a number of the same techniques used to make a system reliable also make it scale well under heavy load.

Reliability, scalability, and capacity planning are rich and complex subjects, and a thorough discussion of them could easily fill an entire book. The purpose of this chapter is to introduce you to some of the issues to consider when starting out and to give you a sampling of the things that are possible.

Understanding Reliability Requirements

Depending on the specifics of your e-commerce initiative, you might have varying requirements for how long a service outage you can tolerate from your Web site. For some businesses, their Web site is the sole mechanism of contact with customers. If your site falls into this category, any break in service might translate to heavy losses in terms of lost revenue from lost sales and the risk of losing customers to competitors. On the Web, going to the store next door is a simple matter of a click of a button. Any break in service can translate into dissatisfied customers and lost sales. This is a function of the immediate situation where customers cannot access your site to buy what they need, and your long-term commitment to the customer and to customer service. One company with loyal customers will weather a storm, while another company that does not communicate with its customers will not survive.

In other cases, your Web-based services might be crucial to the operation of someone else's business. This dependency also means that service outages in your operation could jeopardize their operations, causing them financial harm and placing you at risk from a liability standpoint. If your business falls in this category, you need even greater certainty that your site will stay up and running. You also should start thinking about acquiring service guarantees and insurance policies from your infrastructure suppliers.

Finally, there are sites where service interruptions put people's lives in jeopardy as in the case of patient record retrieval from an Internet-based record keeping facility used by a hospital's emergency room. Clearly, reliability of these systems is of the highest concern, and reliability guarantees need to be on the same order as those mandated for systems such as air traffic control and medical equipment.

Estimating reliability

There are many ways of estimating the reliability of a Web site. The Mean Time Between Failure (MTBF) is a standard term applied to the average time that a given system will run before a catastrophic failure occurs. The general mechanisms for calculating MTBF are based on underlying physical models that govern system behavior and are beyond the scope of this book. However, most infrastructure components have previously determined MTBFs; ask your vendor for them if they are not readily available. MTBF will provide a general indication of the reliability of any single component of your system.

Uptime is another measure that is more typically used in service industries such as telecommunications. Uptime numbers are typically given in percentages, such as 99.9 percent uptime. This is the amount of time you can expect a system to be available during a given time period. For an e-commerce infrastructure, this is typically a more meaningful number than MTBF. You can calculate the uptime for a given component of your system if you know the MTBF and length of time it takes to replace or repair it once it breaks down.

Once you have an understanding of the reliability of the components of your system, you can begin to evaluate the weaknesses in the system as a whole. If there are any single points of failure in your system, the reliability of the entire system can be compromised. The goal for producing a highly reliable system is to design it so that it does not have any single points of failure. You can design your system to be more reliable by building parallel processes for every critical component that might fail. Your "contingency plans" lay out what you will do if your primary server breaks down or is hacked, if your telecommunications becomes unavailable, if key staff are lost, and so forth.

Think about the probability that both of your ISPs will fail within a given time period or the probability that a network connection will fail in San Francisco while simultaneously two servers in New York come down. Because these probabilities are low, it's probably best to leave the calculations alone and spend your time documenting and rehearsing procedures for what are some of the more likely disaster scenarios. You can find more information on this topic in the section on disaster recovery at the end of the chapter.

Capacity Planning and Scalability Requirements

Determining the performance demands that can be placed on your e-commerce infrastructure is a difficult task. Predicting in advance the average load and the variability you want to handle might involve lots of guesswork. To better understand how to characterize your requirements, you should partition your needs into two categories: *reserve capacity* and *long-term capacity*.

- Reserve capacity is the immediately available capacity that allows your system to scale up instantaneously and is what you must invest in to handle short-term usage increases.

- Long-term capacity is the maximum future load your infrastructure can handle when it is maximally configured. Ideally, this capacity can be added incrementally by adding hardware and network bandwidth as demand warrants.

Reserve capacity for peak demand

Understanding the characteristics of short-term usage increases is a difficult task, and it might take you a few months of operation to understand exactly how much reserve capacity you actually need. There are a number of techniques you can use to predict the load your site may need to handle; however, this is not an exact science.

You might want to determine whether you are going to attempt to handle an extreme load or take the view that when the store is full, customers will just have to wait. Some heavily trafficked Web services such as weather and online trading have shown that it is possible to see daily surges in the order of 50 to 300 percent. Handling a 300 percent increase in short-term demand can be an expensive proposition. However, if you believe that service outages pose a liability risk, or you cannot afford to turn away customers, you will need to put in place the facilities to manage peak demand.

Long-term increase in demand

Long-term increases in average demand are much different than short-term usage spikes in the sense that you usually have more time to react to them, assuming that you have invested in an infrastructure that is scalable. Investing in an infrastructure that can scale as your demand increases will let you add capacity without throwing away old equipment, software, management structure, backup facilities, and other infrastructure components. This usually means spending more money up front on a well-designed system. Cutting corners in the beginning can result in the need to start from scratch when you realize that your original system has run out of gas.

Before you invest in infrastructure, analyze the number of customers you expect your site to receive and how this number will grow over time. Many successful Internet ventures significantly underestimated demand and had to scramble to ensure that they could continue to provide a reasonable level of service. Do your market research; know your clients and their needs. Build into your plans ways to monitor the growth and patterns of demand on your site.

Redundancy

Redundancy is the name of the game when designing an infrastructure that keeps running in the event of equipment failure. It is also a very useful mechanism for providing reserve capacity to handle short-term increases in load. There are three primary areas to focus on when thinking about e-commerce infrastructure redundancy: computer hardware, telecommunications services/Internet connectivity, and software. Infrastructure redundancy should also include personnel. The people who run and maintain the system are as critical as the systems themselves. When something breaks, you need the right people.

Computer hardware

There are two basic approaches you can take to making computing hardware more reliable and scalable. You can focus on a single computer and make it as reliable and scalable as possible, or you can utilize a number of computers in a cluster as a single unified system. The individual computers in the cluster might not be very reliable by themselves, but as a group they exhibit a high degree of fault-tolerance, and the failure of one or two computers will be compensated for by the remaining working systems. In addition, multiple copies of the same software application running on different machines enable many requests to be processed in parallel, increasing performance.

Increasing single host reliability

Making a single host computer more reliable involves replicating the major computing subsystems. This is usually accomplished by including two or more redundant copies of each of the CPUs, power supply, and disks/storage devices.

Even though it is possible to make a single computing host reliable and scalable, there are two disadvantages to this approach. The first is cost. As you increase reliability and performance, your system costs begin to increase exponentially; systems with 128 or more processors and hundreds of gigabytes of RAM also come with multimillion-dollar price tags. The second reason is that no matter how many extra CPUs your Web server has, it will not be able to recover from the gasoline tanker that just exploded and leveled the building where your Web server was located. Looking at this from another perspective reveals that even though redundancy has been used at the component level to increase reliability, on the macro or system level there is still a single point of failure.

Server clustering

Server clusters, redundant aggregations of independent computers, are one of the most common ways to increase Web site reliability and provide a cost-effective mechanism for scaling. Figure 3-1 shows a sample network architecture for a server cluster.

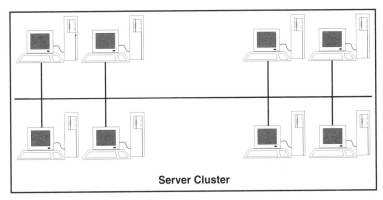

Figure 3-1. *A redundant set of computer servers attached to a high-speed network.*

Scalability is achieved because each computer handles a portion of the service load. Adding more computers increases capacity. If one or more of the systems fails, the load is redistributed among the other servers. This also makes the cluster very reliable.

Computers providing identical services are clustered together to create a pool of redundant devices. Should any single system fail or should several systems fail at the same time, the remaining systems will take over until the broken ones can be repaired. Adding geographically separated clusters enhances this configuration. The geographic separation of the units provides insulation from local catastrophic events such as fire or flooding.

Telecommunication services

Along with your computing infrastructure, your telecommunications infrastructure is probably your biggest concern for reliability and scalability. It is usually the area that is most likely to have single points of failure. As with a number of other topics in this chapter, the design of reliable and scalable telecommunications networks is a deep subject discussed only briefly in this section.

Network reliability

The reliability of your own local area networks is a key issue. It is on the LAN where your servers reside, and unless the local network is working, connectivity to the outside world won't even be possible. The good news is that this part of the problem is under your own control. That is not the case for the next issue.

Telecom reliability

Unfortunately, one of the important issues you will face when designing your telecom infrastructure is that, for the most part, it is not something you have complete control of. Fortunately, the majority of the problems that occur are specific to a very small section of the public infrastructure, mainly the section that connects you to your ISP. This is true because the Internet is by definition a very redundant network. Therefore, if you have enough redundant connections to the Internet, a failure in one segment will not necessarily cause a service outage. To better understand telecom issues, it is best to first understand how information flows from your Web site to a customer's Web browser.

As you can see in Figure 3-2, the connection between the Web server and the ISP represents a single point of failure. If it is damaged, the Web site will be out of service. There is a fairly simple solution to this problem, though: Simply increase the number of connections to the ISP. To improve reliability, however, you will need to request that the physical cable routes be different for each connection. This might be rather costly and might not even be possible. A more realistic solution is to increase the number of ISPs you use. Try to arrange for service from organizations in different geographic locations because telecom infrastructures are susceptible to natural localized disasters. This might not be easy either, because many ISPs tend to cluster in small areas so that they are close to major network access points reducing telecom costs for the ISPs themselves.

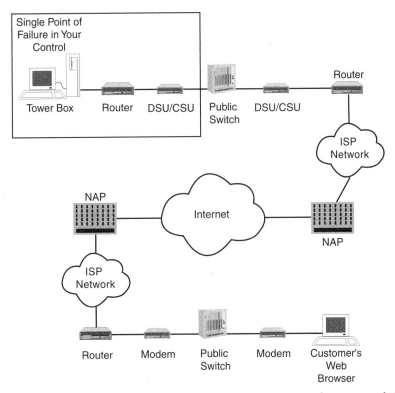

Figure 3-2. *A representative network architecture covering the entire path from a Web server to the Web browser client.*

Scalability

Like server clustering, increasing telecom service redundancy also increases capacity. Many small network connections can be used to transfer as much information as a single high-speed network. Pricing of telecom services is very region-specific, so you need to examine the solution that gives you the best capacity and reliability for your area.

Software Architecture

Creating reliable and scalable hardware and network architectures is the easy part of your job. The more difficult task is implementing software that takes advantage of the redundancies in your base infrastructure. Redundancies created by reliable and scalable computer hardware and network architectures can be utilized in many different ways. Some of these are reliable, and some of these are scalable, but accomplishing both takes a little skill. For example, you can create a very reliable but poorly scalable software architecture built on top of a small two-server cluster.

In this two-server cluster example, each server runs a duplicate copy of a Web server, and each maintains a duplicate copy of the content. Only one of the servers is used at any given time. The backup server monitors the running server, and if a failure occurs, the backup server reassigns its IP address to that of the running server and assumes the responsibilities of main system. Adding a third backup server can further increase reliability. Backup systems that can instantaneously take over in the event of a failure are often called *hot-spares*. This architecture can be implemented using Microsoft's cluster technology and applications software such as Microsoft SQL server. Unfortunately, this system does not scale any better than a single server because there is only one system functioning at any given time. Essentially, the backup servers remain idle except when a failure occurs. It is useful, however, for applications that are difficult to decompose or replicate into independent redundant services.

For an example of a system that is scalable but not reliable, consider another two-server cluster. This system uses virtually the same software configuration as the previous one. This time, however, client requests are equally divided between the servers, distributing the load. The system is scalable because you can add more servers as you add more clients. This system is not very reliable, though, because an outage of a single server leaves a number of users without service. You could even measure the potential economic impact of this event. If you define "client request service reliability" as a percentage of client requests that are served within a given period of time, and then you can show that the two-server clusters with assigned client requests can go from 100 percent to 50 percent reliability if one server goes down. The economic impact of these missed client requests can tell you what you should be willing to spend to increase reliability. What is needed is a way for the clients to be reassigned transparently to a working server. Ideally, client requests should be assigned to the server with highest available capacity.

As you can see, just because the underlying hardware and network architectures are scalable and reliable, it does not mean that the system as a whole exhibits the same properties. The key to creating a successful system architecture is to address reliability and scalability at the computer hardware, network, *and* software levels. To ensure that the software architecture has these properties, you must replicate software components as well as intelligently distribute service requests (also called *load balancing*).

Replicating system components

To take advantage of redundant hardware, it is necessary to replicate independent software components onto separate servers. This results in increased capacity to process requests for a given piece of functionality so that the maximum number of requests now equals the total number of requests that each server can handle multiplied by the number of servers.

In some cases, this replication may be a fairly easy task. For example, a Web site that contains only static HTML content can easily be duplicated onto multiple machines. Any Web server can service requests for any page. In other instances, replication might not be possible because there is some underlying physical device or data source that cannot be replicated. This is often the case for legacy databases. Although database replication technology exists and can solve the problem for new systems, there are a significant number of legacy data stores that would be impractical to convert to replication-based database architectures. This usually requires moving to the latest version of a database vendor's software and might not be feasible. Therefore, many legacy databases are often constrained to running on a single server. In this case, the best mechanisms for reliability and scalability are to use a combination of a fault-tolerant, high-performance server and a hot-spare.

Load balancing

One of the most critical components of a scalable and reliable architecture is the mechanism used to distribute requests for services. In more formal software engineering terminology, this is often referred to as a *load balancing mecha-*

nism. There are many schemas that can be employed to route service requests. You can get fairly creative in the way you perform this task, taking into account such things as the current load of the server resource pool and the shortest logical path from client to server. You can also use more simplistic mechanisms such as round-robin scheduling that just cycle through servers in a sequential manner. You will find discussions of specific implementations of these load balancing mechanisms in the examples that follow.

Web site software architecture examples

Following are two examples of scalable and reliable software architectures that can be used as a basis for electronic commerce. The first solution is a low-cost option that is commonly utilized to increase the reliability, scalability, and capacity of a legacy Web site. The reason for examining this solution is because of its popularity and to expose some of its limitations. The second solution provides an example of state-of-the-art high-end technology that could be used for a very high-traffic site.

Example 1

The first approach (shown in Figure 3-3) utilizes a round-robin Domain Name Service (DNS) to balance the load on a Web server cluster. This approach is fairly popular because it provides a way for existing sites to scale fairly easily and economically. Each Web server uses Active Server Pages to generate dynamic pages and talk to a single database (this is a very typical architecture for a first-generation e-commerce Web site). The database represents a single point of failure, so it has been placed on a high-performance, fault-tolerant server with additional backup from a hot-spare. There are two main problems that will limit the scalability and reliability of this site. The first is the use of the round-robin DNS as a mechanism for load balancing Web servers. The second is the monolithic structure of the Web server software architecture. Even with these limitations, however, this architecture is much better than that of a single Web server connected to a single ISP over a single telecom line.

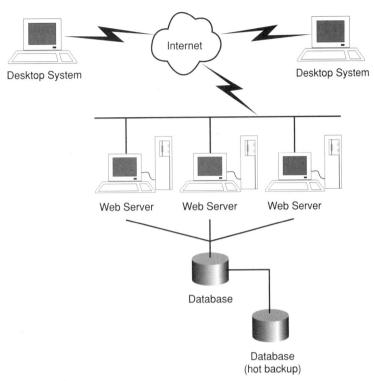

Figure 3-3. *A round-robin Domain Name Service balancing the load on a Web server cluster.*

To elaborate a little more on the problems associated with round-robin DNS, it is first necessary to discuss a few of the details of how DNS and the round-robin feature function. DNS is a mechanism used to resolve a given host name into an IP address such as when you ask your Web browser to find a resource located at a give URL. For example, say you are trying to access *http://www.aWebsite.com*. The first thing your browser does is contact a local DNS server to ask it if it knows the IP address for the server named *www.aWebsite.com*. If the local DNS server does not have this information, it forwards the request on to another DNS server to see if it has the information. This forwarding of requests continues until the request reaches the DNS responsible for the server *www.aWebsite.com*. When this DNS receives the request, it resolves the name by returning the appropriate IP address and sends this response back through the chain of original DNS-forwarded requests. Eventually, the results are returned to your Web browser, and the IP address is used to make a request to the Web server for the default home page.

The preceding process works very similar with a round-robin DNS except that when the DNS responsible for *www.aWebsite.com* is asked for the IP address, it returns a different value each time it is asked by cycling through a list of IP address for all the Web servers in the cluster. In this way, you have an equal probability of receiving an IP address for any of the servers in the cluster, and your browser's request has an equal probability of being assigned to any of the servers in the cluster. Theoretically, this should distribute the load equally among all the servers. In addition, this architecture also affords some help with reliability. If one of the servers fails, the System Administrator can remove the IP address of the failed server from the DNS and consequently redistribute the load over the remaining servers.

Unfortunately, there are two problems with this approach. The first problem is that during the process of forwarding your DNS request, some of the intermediate DNSs might store the name address pair so that the next time it is requested, they can respond immediately. This speeds the address translation problem but also disrupts the round-robin scheme, foiling its fault-tolerant characteristics. To combat this problem, you can control the length of time a hostname address pair stays cached on a DNS, and you can, in fact, even set this value to zero. Unfortunately, this also increases the time it takes to make a request to your site because the name translation step must propagate all the way back to your DNS for every page request. The second problem is that round-robin load balancing does not take into account the current load of the servers in the cluster. Because not all Web server requests require equal processing, there is a chance that a request will be forwarded to a server that is busy processing a dynamic page request instead of one that is sitting idle.

Example 2

The second example uses sophisticated technologies to create a set of Web server clusters geographically and logically dispersed across the country. The system uses Cisco's Distributed Director to route requests to the logically nearest Web server cluster. Distributed Director utilizes a special protocol and a series of agents—the Distributed Request Protocol (DRP) agent—to measure the response between various points on the Internet and the two Web server clusters. This enables routing of client requests to the logically closest cluster. Within each cluster, requests are routed to specific Web servers based on server loading using Cisco's Local Director. In addition, each server cluster utilizes a DCOM-based architecture for distributing processing of dynamic page generation across multiple servers (the component servers). Finally, database replication is used to maintain consistent customer and product information across all server clusters and to improve performance of database queries.

In this architecture, there are no single points of failure. The most critical components from a reliability standpoint are the Distributed Director, Local Director, and databases. As you can see from the diagram in Figure 3-4, each one of these components has at least one redundancy, and, therefore, the entire system exhibits high reliability. More details on this architecture can be found on Cisco's Web site at *http://www.cisco.com*.

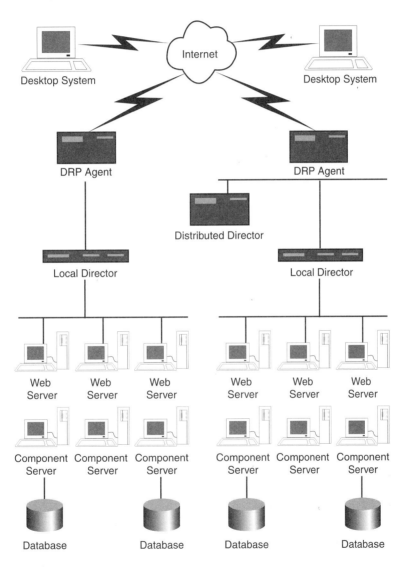

Figure 3-4. *A very sophisticated Web site infrastructure using a hardware load balancer that distributes requests based on server utilization.*

Although your needs will probably fall somewhere between these two architectures, you can still pick and choose aspects of each to create your desired level of performance, reliability, and scalability.

Optimizing Performance of Your Web Site

Up to this point, there has been very little discussion of the performance of individual components and services used to build your e-commerce infrastructure. The architecture discussions presented so far have attractive properties that make it easy to increase performance and reliability by adding network connections and hardware. These methods, however, are a brute force way of scaling the performance of your Web site and can be a very expensive way to proceed. Making efficient use of your current infrastructure ensures that you are not wasting your hardware and network investments. However, the gains afforded by increased efficiency do not come for free either. You can just as easily go overboard and create very complicated software that ekes every last ounce of performance out of your hardware. Heavily optimized software can be costly to build, and you have to trade off the cost of software development with returns in performance. Keeping this in mind, the material that follows will provide information on the low-hanging software optimization fruit that can help you save precious CPU cycles, memory, and network bandwidth.

Web Server Optimization

There are three main issues to consider when performance optimizing your Web server:

- The amount of server memory and network bandwidth your content is using

- The number of connections required to transfer the content

- The amount of CPU used to create and distribute each page

In general, delivering a large piece of content in one request is much more efficient than many small pieces delivered over multiple connections because of the significant overhead required to establish and set up a connection (remember the previous DNS example). HTTP is especially susceptible to this problem because as a connectionless protocol, the connection setup overhead is incurred on every request. Early Java applets suffered a very heavy penalty during download because each class needed to be transferred in a separate HTTP request. The later introduction of CAB and JAR archives fixed this problem by bundling all classes together in a single file and transferring them in a single request.

So you do not have to learn from scratch all the hard lessons of those who have toiled before, here are some rules of thumb that have been utilized by some of the more highly stressed sites on the Internet:

- **Do not use frames.** Frames increase the number of page downloads which, in turn, increases the number of connections that need to be made.

- **Use images sparingly.** This has a two-pronged benefit. It reduces the demand on both network bandwidth and server memory. It also reduces the number of connections that need to be made because each image gets transferred as a separate file.

- **Use server-side scripting as sparingly as possible.** The less VB script or ASP code the better. Move all your logic into separate objects and only use ASP as a mechanism to instantiate the objects and pass them data.

- **Consider an architecture that allows the functionality of your site to be reduced during times of heavy load.** For example, some weather sites only allow the access of critical information during periods where severe weather is threatening people's lives.

- **Take advantage of the bandwidth limiting capabilities of your software such as those that come with Microsoft's IIS4.0.** This feature enables you to "throttle" the amount of bandwidth utilized by any given client. Your site might benefit from this approach if you believe a number of users are accessing your site over very high-speed lines, thereby placing a larger-than-average burden on your site.

Decomposing Functionality into Components

Because an e-commerce Web site is unlikely to be built with static HTML pages, a large portion of the performance bottlenecks will come from the dynamic generation of Web pages and associated database queries. You need to be smart about how you perform these dynamic page computations. One of the best mechanisms for dealing with this problem is to decompose your page generation system into independent components. Microsoft's ASP and COM technologies are ideal foundations for component-based Web sites. The details of building components using Microsoft's COM technology are covered in more detail in Chapter 10. An introduction to COM is also given in Chapter 9. This section will briefly cover some of the higher-level architectural concerns of a component-based Web architecture. There are two issues to deal with when deciding how to decompose the system. The first is the size of a single standalone unit of functionality—or how small a component should be. The second is the creation of stateless components. The stateless property of a component addresses its independence and efficiency.

Level of decomposition

The benefit of decomposing your software into components is that they can "fit" and perform well on smaller, cheaper servers. Under this method, the power of the hardware needed to suitably process requests for a given component is reduced. Your infrastructure then scales more cost effectively because you can add smaller and cheaper computers to your server cluster. If your functionality is all bundled up in a single monolithic structure, the only choice for scaling is to purchase faster computing hardware, which is typically more expensive than equivalent performance obtained through a number of lower-priced units.

There is a point, though, where the communication overhead between components on different machines begins to remove the advantages gained by dedicating the component to a separate server. Improving the network bandwidth between computers in the cluster is a solution to this problem. A lot of effort is currently being applied to developing technologies such as HIPPI, Fiber-Channel, and Gigabit Ethernet. These technologies show great promise in helping solve network bottlenecks in server clusters. The price of these technologies has yet to reach commodity levels, so the need to use them might eliminate some of the cost advantages of using a server cluster.

Stateless servers

Through trial and error, it has been established that when it comes to transaction processing systems, it is best to eliminate the coupling of state between individual service requests. This is a fancy way of saying that each request should be self-contained and should not depend on information from previous requests. The reasoning behind this is the difficulty in knowing how long to save the state-related information. Precious memory will be used up storing information for future requests, robbing currently executing transactions of vital resources. In addition, it is difficult to remove state information that is no longer needed. The process of reclaiming resources can itself waste valuable CPU cycles and memory.

OPERATIONAL ISSUES AND STAFFING

In this section, you will find a collection of topics that deal with the everyday operation of your infrastructure, such as site monitoring, disaster recovery, implementation, and the staffing required to deal with these topics.

Monitoring

One problem you will face is determining the current state of your infrastructure. There are a number of mechanisms and services you can utilize to monitor the health of your system, and it is extremely advisable that you invest in some of them. There are many ways to implement this functionality, but, in general, it means that you must build into each component and service from the beginning the ability to send or respond to some signal that shows its current state. An industry-standard technology called Web Based Enterprise Management (WBEM) deals with this issue directly. See *http://microsoft.com/management/wbem/default.htm* for more information.

Disaster Recovery

Once catastrophe strikes and you need to recover from an earthquake that just wiped out your Santa Clara facility, it is way too late to start figuring out how to recover. Whole industries have developed to provide services that can help keep a business operational in the event of a catastrophe. One of the most important assets you will have in a crisis situation is a detailed disaster recovery plan. This plan must be rehearsed and periodically reviewed. A good plan should include:

- A detailed list of all equipment and software needed to bring a site back online. If you have a fire, you will need new licenses. If you change hardware, you will need the original software.

- A current list of vendors that stock all the equipment needed to get back online and that can get it to you fast

- A contingent site (hosting facility) for locating your new infrastructure

- A thorough plan for assembling all equipment and loading all software from backups

- Complete documentation of how to bring the system back online

- Procedures for saving copies of the system and data, along with how these will be kept off-site and restored in the event of disaster

- Plans for how to recover from loss of client transaction information

- Strategies to deal with hacked systems that compromise client information

- Software licenses and points of contact with hardware and software vendors

- Contract information for all the equipment

Testing and Deployment

Designing proper processes to ensure that new content and other updates don't break your working site is essential. Figure 3-5 shows an architecture that will make the process easy to accomplish. Note that production systems are separated from the test and deployment server. The function of the test and deployment infrastructure is to stage content so it can be tested before it is rolled out to your live site. New components from your software engineers and new HTML pages from your graphic designers are first placed on the test and deployment server, and then thoroughly tested and debugged. When the new content is deemed ready, it is pushed from the deployment server to the production machines when system load is at a minimum. Microsoft's Site Server deployment capabilities provide a convenient mechanism to help automate this phase of this process. You will notice that in Figure 3-4 the test and deployment portion of the architectures is a scaled-down version of the production infrastructure. In some cases, this will not be adequate for testing purposes, and it might be necessary to create a test "sand-box" that duplicates the entire production environment.

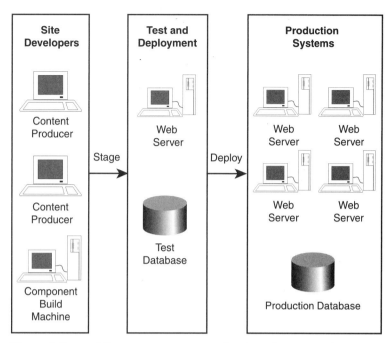

Figure 3-5. *Workflow processes associated with updating a Web site.*

Staffing

Determining the human resources required to operate your infrastructure is also an important consideration. The following list identifies the roles required to run a moderate-to-large-size venture. If you are running a small operation, a single individual can perform a number of these roles. In addition, you will see that there are also a number of third-party resources you can use to outsource a number of the roles. As an example of combining multiple roles in a single individual, the Web site technical operations functions could be staffed by using a single person who maintains and services the entire Web site. This person would perform all functions from DBA to hardware technician and would leave only the monitoring functions unfulfilled. Because hiring and maintaining a 24 x 7 monitoring staff is a costly and difficult task, the monitoring functions would be best served by outsourcing.

Development

■ **Project manager.** Has the ultimate responsibility of making sure that the development of your Web site happens according to your expectations.

- **System architect.** Provides the technical vision for the Web site. This person is responsible for making sure that the site will function as planned and includes responsibility for meeting performance and reliability expectations.

- **Creative lead/Information architect.** Provides the artistic and aesthetic vision for the Web site. This person is responsible for the look and feel as well as the overall site usability.

- **Security architect.** This person ensures that the system architecture will be adequate from a security perspective. It is still common for this role to be embodied by the system architect.

- **Database developer.** Provides the design and implementation of most functionality specific to the database. This includes designing the schema and writing stored procedures. This person will work closely with the Web site operation's DBA when the site is rolled out to performance-tune the application.

- **Component developer.** Implements middle-tier components for business logic.

- **UI developer.** Is responsible for the implementation of the user interface. This person works closely with the graphic artists and the HCI engineers to deliver a well-designed UI.

- **Graphic artists.** Are responsible for creating the multimedia objects that provide a good portion of the Web site's look and feel.

- **Human computer interface (HCI) engineer.** Performs usability testing and workflow analysis to aid in the design of the user interface.

Testing

- **Testing lead.** Heads up the test team and coordinates the activities of all the people on the test team. This person is ultimately responsible for the quality of the site's content and software.

- **Component testers.** Because it is usually necessary to test a Web site in a short period of time (so that content does not become stale), it is necessary to subdivide the task of testing a Web site. Each component tester is assigned a specific area or areas to test.

Web site technical operations

- **Webmaster.** The webmaster and associated technical staff have the ultimate responsibility of keeping your technical infrastructure running on a daily basis. The webmaster is essentially the head of technical operations.

- **Computer hardware and network technicians.** These technicians are responsible for keeping the computer servers, disk arrays, routers, switches, and so on in healthy working order. They are also responsible for being on call to fix any problems in the event of failures outside of normal business hours.

- **Backup operators.** These people are responsible for performing backups of all software. This job usually involves loading and maintaining a tape archive as well as ensuring that all media is properly deposited in a secure offsite location.

- **Database administrators.** These people will make sure that your databases are working properly and that they have adequate space as they grow.

- **Uptime monitors.** You will need someone to sit in front of the dashboard you created to monitor the pulse of your infrastructure. This person is very similar to the plant monitors that watch the control board at a manufacturing facility.

- **Security monitors.** These folks are responsible for monitoring all relevant items related to security of the information systems.

Marketing

- **Content producers and editors.** These people are responsible for the creation of new content that will attract new visitors to a site. Examples of these people would be news editors at a financial site or the generators of product reviews at a consumer products site.

- **Direct eMarketers.** These people are responsible for analyzing the buying patterns and usage patterns of site visitors, and developing rules for automated cross-selling and marketing campaigns. They will interact directly with your e-commerce infrastructure or through your technical staff to mine customer data and create business rules.

Again, do not be dismayed by the complexity of the organization that is needed to run an effective commerce operation. You can always consider outsourcing some of your site's operations. Outsourcing options are discussed in the next section.

OUTSOURCING

There are two areas of site creation and operation that are strong candidates for outsourcing: the creation and evolution of your site and the technical operations. The decision to outsource the creation of your site will depend on your desire and ability to manage and recruit a software development organization. It will not be dealt with here. This section provides information on choosing a Web site hosting company and services for monitoring your infrastructure.

Outsourcing Web Site Technical Operations

One of the most important decisions you must make when assembling your e-commerce infrastructure is finding a home for your Web site and a staff to operate it. You may have faced a similar decision if you work in the IT department of a large corporation and have had to decide where to locate your corporate data center. Internal hosting is still the choice for those corporations that have existing and appropriate facilities. However, as you have seen in the earlier part of this chapter, the complexity and the amount of capital required to build and to maintain a mission-critical infrastructure can be overwhelming. This is especially true for new Internet-only businesses that are starting from scratch. In fact, more and more high-profile Web sites are externally hosted; FrontierGlobal hosts Yahoo, and Exodus hosts Lycos.

The Web hosting market has matured significantly over the past several years, and you will find a wide range of service offerings. In most cases, these services can be broken into four categories:

- Shared Hosting Services

- Dedicated Services

- Co-Location Services

- Specialty Services

At the low end, a shared hosting service provides a home for your Web site that is shared with other sites. This service limits your access for tasks such as debugging and deployment. It also exposes you to performance and reliability risks if other sites suddenly rise in popularity or perform actions that cause your server to fail. At the high end, co-location and specialty services provide almost unlimited flexibility (for a price, of course).

Shared services

If you select a shared hosting service, your Web site will share space on a server with other applications. Because of the limitations imposed by this approach, it is not recommended for anything but a very small-scale venture with few security or performance requirements.

Dedicated services

The next step up in service from a shared server is a dedicated server. For many hosting companies, this still means that you will be limited to using software preloaded by the hosting company. However, you have much better access to it than with a shared site, and you get the added benefit of not sharing server CPU cycles with anybody else's Web application. Other benefits of this service are that all hardware and network connections are taken care of by the hosting company, 24 x 7 monitoring of all equipment is typically available, as well as service level guarantees regarding uptime.

Co-location and other specialty services

If your needs cannot be met by the services just discussed, a co-location service in conjunction with some high-end specialty services will probably do the trick. A co-location service lets you locate your own equipment in a secured area of a third-party Web hosting facility. This differs from the previous service because you are free to choose the specific hardware and software you need. Essentially, you are renting space to house your own equipment. The down side is that you will probably have to contract a separate service organization to maintain it for you. However, you still benefit from immediate access to a very fast network backbone with multiple redundant connections to the Internet.

In addition to the ability to quickly increase your network bandwidth, high-end hosting services have started to offer a number of specialty services that make it difficult to find an excuse to do it yourself. As an example of the kinds of services you can use, consider the following list of services provided by Exodus *http://www.exodus.com*, one of many premium hosting companies.

Power services

- 1.6 megawatts (MW) premise power
- Customer-dedicated power backed up by Uninterruptible Power Supply (UPS)
- High-capacity diesel generator

- Customer-dedicated circuit breaker protection
- Scalable customer power

Fire protection

- State-of-the-art, gas-based fire protection system
- Separate fire zones below the floor and above the ceiling
- Specialized heat/smoke sensors
- Automatic local fire department notification
- Physical plant
- Raised floor
- HVAC
- Separate cooling zones
- Seismically braced racks

Server hosting facilities

- Secured scalable areas, cabinets, full open racks, and shared open racks
- Call Management and Incident-Tracking System:
- Advanced Call Distribution system (ACD)
- 24x7 notification and monitoring

Facility security system

- Motion sensors
- Secured access
- Video camera surveillance
- Security breach alarm
- 24x7 automatic police department notification

Personal security system

- 24x7 card key customer access to Internet Data Centers
- 24x7 monitoring by on-site personnel

Evaluating an outsourcing vendor

In addition to the major issues outlined earlier in the chapter—reliability, scalability, performance, and an assortment of operational issues—there are three other issues that are of concern when considering the possibility of outsourcing Web hosting services. These are access, security, and disaster protection.

Clearly, there are organizations whose overriding security concerns would never allow external hosting to be an option. One might question the rationale for using the Internet for delivering information in this case, but that is a different story. Should you choose to outsource, then access, then both physical access and virtual access, can be major issues when considering a hosting service. If you are planning to use one of the commodity services listed later in the chapter, virtual access is probably all that is allowed. In addition, there may be restrictions in the types of physical access, even for high-end services. This can be problematic, especially if your business is not geographically close to the hosting location. If any equipment needs servicing, you might be at the mercy of your hosting organizations, so it's important that responsibilities of the different parties be well understood. For example, if you have equipment that needs to be serviced by parties other than your hosting company, it is important that they are provided with necessary access and that it is clear which pieces of equipment they are responsible for.

As you can see by some of the specialty services provided by Internet hosting companies, you can find a fairly high level of service with regards to physical security. Some of the things you should consider when evaluating your security needs are:

- Are all employees bonded?

- How is physical access to the premises and specifically access to your equipment handled?

- Does the company offer an insurance policy?

- What kind of surveillance does the company use?

- What is the response time for additional security personnel or police?

Finally, even if you are planning to take advantage of a hosting service that can provide geographically dispersed and redundant hosting locations, it still makes sense to consider the following disaster planning concerns.

- Are adequate precautions being taken for weather-related issues? Is the hosting service located in a flood plane or earthquake zone?

- What happens in the event of a power outage?

■ Are there any issues related to electric use? Has the ISP contracted a reduced rate of electricity based on participation in a rotating outage program during peak demand? Has the ISP completed its Year 2000 preparations and verified the Y2K status of all vendors and service providers? An ISP that doesn't have a clear plan can be in for trouble.

Monitoring Alternatives

There are two types of external monitoring services that are worthwhile to consider when deciding how to keep watch over your Web site. These are performance monitoring and security monitoring.

Services such as those offered by Keynote (*http://www.keynote.com*) provide an alternative to maintaining an in-house monitoring staff. In addition to monitoring the performance of your site, they also can perform the following services:

■ Web site management to compare your site's performance to that of key competitors and to internal performance objectives

■ Customer-service personnel to respond accurately to user complaints about perceived poor performance on the Internet site from specific geographic locations

■ Operations personnel to diagnose performance problems at various points on the Internet, instead of limited to their own Web server and connections

■ Network engineers to improve your Web server, client, or network infrastructure based on accurate and comparative measurement data

As you can probably imagine, duplicating this level of service using your own resources would be a large undertaking, so it is certainly worth considering leaving at least a portion of this task to others.

Security monitoring services

Security monitoring services have been around for a much longer period of time than Internet performance monitoring services. There is a growing number of companies that offer some form of continuous equipment monitoring. These organizations employ individuals who monitor your system around the clock and respond immediately to suspicious behavior. In addition to the monitoring services offered, a number of organizations also provide periodic intrusion assessments and audits. When you use one of these services, you sanction the provider to attempt to break into your system to provide you with important advice on where your security infrastructure is weak and needs improvement.

SUMMARY

As you have probably gathered by now, there is a lot to think about when you decide to set up an e-commerce infrastructure. Hopefully, you have found the information in this chapter helpful in understanding the types of issues you will need to deal with when embarking on your venture. As discussed in the chapter introduction, there are two more topics you might want more information on: security and electronic payment/billing. The next chapter provides you with more details on these topics.

Chapter 4

Security Planning and Implementation

by Steve Waldon

When you think about e-commerce security, what comes to mind is all the media hype on the dangers of using your credit card to purchase goods over the Internet. Although this is an important issue, it is also just the tip of the iceberg. While you will certainly find a discussion of electronic payment here, the purpose of this chapter is to provide a general overview of security-related technology. Beyond the world of digital certificates, SSL, and firewalls, it also includes information on how to assess your security needs.

As you might expect, a thorough discussion of these topics could fill several books. While most of the material presented here will be introductory in nature, it should still give you a good feel for the basic elements to be considered when setting up an electronic defense.

IN CASE YOU ARE NOT CONCERNED

So you have read this far and now you're thinking, "Do I really need to read this chapter?" Before you make that decision, consider the following: In a September 1998 *CNet* article, it was revealed that of 1,600 corporations surveyed in 50 countries, 79 percent had experienced some form of security breach. The more telling statistic, however, is that 69 percent of all e-commerce Web sites have experienced some form of security breach. Considering the scope of this problem, sticking your head in the sand when it comes to security is probably the wrong approach.

A METHOD FOR THE MADNESS

Bruce Schneier, president of Counterpane (*www.counterpane.com*), along with several colleagues at the National Security Agency (NSA, *www.nsa.gov*) and Defense Advanced Research Projects Agency (DARPA, *www.darpa.mil*), have published a framework and methodology for thinking about and designing secure systems: "Toward a Secure System Engineering Methodology;" C. Salter, O. Saydjari, B. Schneier, and J. Wallner; New Security Paradigms Workshop, September 1998. This section is based primarily on this methodology. If you would like the specific details, check out the white paper found on the Counterpane Web site.

The methodology provides a systematic approach for determining and countering the vulnerable portions of your system. The first step is to understand your adversaries and what they have to gain by attacking your infrastructure. Based on this information, they can determine the major weaknesses of your system. Once you have determined what your risks are, you can begin to design and implement countermeasures to reduce them.

Understanding Your Adversaries

You may already have an idea of who is a potential threat to your organization. The better you understand the nature of these people, the better you will be able to understand your security needs. Schneier recommends that you classify your adversaries according to four attributes: resources, access, risk tolerance, and objectives. Understanding an attacker's objectives will also give you some insight into the other three attributes. For the purposes of Internet commerce, it is helpful to partition malicious individuals into two groups based on their objectives: those seeking material gain, and those seeking to commit vandalism or acts of vengeance.

The first group consists of all those individuals whose primary motive is to steal your information or disrupt your services in hope of gaining some material reward. The term "reward" is used here in a generic sense, and is not limited to purely financial gain. For example, stealing and releasing financial information could be used to damage a political campaign. Typically, the level of material reward they are seeking determines the amount of risk and resources that these individuals will exert. Therefore, an understanding of the types of information that your organization has, and its external material value, will provide significant insight into an adversary's behavior.

The second type of adversary is one whose primary objective is non-material gain. This includes hackers who want to break in for the fun of it, and disgruntled former employees who want to disrupt your operation. This class of attackers may not necessarily try to steal information but will meet their objectives by simply corrupting or shutting down your system. Because their motives are less tangible and their behavior sometimes irrational, they are also a more difficult group to deal with.

The External Value of Your Information Assets

Identifying sensitive information and understanding its external value will be helpful in understanding the motivation of your adversaries who want to steal it. In the world of e-commerce, there are typically three areas of specific concern: customer information, internal corporate information, and vendor information. For each one of these categories, there is usually a specific subset of information that must be protected.

Customer information

Although theft of customer personal information (name, address, phone number, and so on) may be cause for dismay, it does not usually lead to significant physical or financial harm (...a few extra junk e-mails, perhaps). Bulk theft of personal information may be of value when sold as a targeted mailing list, but this information is often already available from many organizations. A highly publicized release of personal information could create a substantial amount of bad will for your company. At best, such an incident will probably reduce your customers' trust in you, resulting in a temporary loss of business. The external value of customer information is, therefore, primarily useful to someone whose objective is harm to your business. This would make it a significant target for vandals and disgruntled employees.

For other types of personal information such as medical and certain types of financial records, the scenario is quite different. This information can be very sensitive and possibly be used for blackmail or fraud. Owning this type of information puts you on the radar screen for a host of very sophisticated criminals, from terrorists to organized crime. It also increases the level of harm that could occur from public release of the information, thereby increasing its attractiveness to vandals, hackers, and disgruntled employees.

Internal corporate information

The problems that can occur if sensitive corporate information is stolen by competitors need very little elaboration. Determining if you need to worry about your competitors actually taking the risk to do this is another story. (You should consult professional advice on the particulars of your industry for more on this topic.) Whether competitive espionage is a genuine threat or not, you still need to worry about vandals and disgruntled employees. Also, do not forget that your e-commerce infrastructure may contain key aspects of your competitive advantage. It most certainly will contain your pricing strategy. Hiding your pricing strategy in a retail site is not practical. However, for private Extranet-based sales channels, you may have negotiated special pricing agreements that need to be kept confidential from both competitors and other customers.

Supplier and vendor information

During the course of doing business, it is quite normal to have acquired sensitive information from and about your vendors. This may include future product roadmaps, strategic marketing agreements, and so on. It is also standard practice for this information to be shared under a non-disclosure agreement. Letting this information slip into the hands of your vendors' competitors could result in a liability suit. This gives the information some external value if it is used to damage your organization through time- and resource-consuming litigation. Although this is a possible scenario, it is more likely that the information would be stolen by your vendor's competitors.

System Vulnerabilities and Countermeasures

After understanding your attacker, the next order of business is for you to understand the vulnerabilities of your infrastructure. In general, when you begin analyzing your system for potential weaknesses, you need to consider not only the system software and hardware, but also all of the associated policies, procedures, and personnel required to run them. For critical system components, you need to understand vulnerabilities through the complete lifecycle of creation. This means analyzing the security-related aspects of the system components during design, construction, deployment, operation, and disposal.

Elaborating on the security issues related to each one of these lifecycle phases as well as security concerns related to process and personnel are beyond the scope of this chapter. However, to provide context for the technology-related material in the later sections, a discussion of some common operational vulnerabilities is provided next.

Categorizing operational vulnerabilities

Although the bag of tricks that hackers use is continually growing, it is helpful to classify them into three very general categories of attack. The first category contains attacks whose purpose is to gain access to secured areas. This type of attack, if successful, is usually potent because information inside the secured area is usually not very strongly guarded. A physical analogy of this would be gaining access to a secure file room. Once access to the room has been obtained, it is easy to get information. The second category of attacks is that of intercepting information as it is transmitted from one place to another. Expanding the last example, rather than breaking into the filing room to steal information, you could listen to a phone conversation of someone reading information in the files to someone at another location. A third category is used to classify all attacks that render the secure system unusable (sometimes referred to as "denial of service" attacks). Although media attention on denial of service attacks has focused on cases where vandalism had been the prime motive, it can also be used as part of a strategy to steal information. Users may be forced to utilize stopgap measures in order to keep business running. Because time is usually critical in getting things running again, there is a good chance that security will not be the first priority. As a result, would-be attackers may have a better opportunity to infiltrate the temporary system.

Breaking into a secured area

While time and energy are devoted to setting up a secure electronic perimeter, inside that perimeter, more attention is paid to convenience of access than security. This means, for instance, that once you have gained access to a given computer, it is usually possible to read the files on that computer regardless of who you are. This is not universally true, as password files are usually encrypted, but in the majority of cases, access to a computer usually means access to the files that are on it. The same holds true for entire networks of computers. For example, it is commonplace for a single ID and password combination to provide access to almost every computer on an organization's entire network.

Designing counter-measures for this broad class of attacks is a very rich subject. The section on firewalls will give you a brief introduction to the topic.

Message and communication channel compromise

With the rise in popularity of the Internet, there has also been an increase in opportunities to listen in on private conversations. This is not a new threat, but one that has significantly increased in likelihood. Prior to the Internet, most information was exchanged via the public telephone system. In general, this system is not secure either but more difficult to gain access to. (This too is changing, and anyone who uses the phone system to transfer sensitive information should use protective measures as well.)

The technology used to help counterattacks that try to compromise communication channels generally falls under the domain of cryptography. A brief introduction to the relevant technologies is given later in the chapter.

Denial of service

There are many ways to stop an e-commerce infrastructure from functioning, and it is not necessary to enumerate the more sinister ones. Unfortunately, there is usually not much you can do to prevent some of these things from occurring, especially those in the domain of natural disasters. The best you can do is to develop a good disaster recovery plan. There are, however, a number of common electronic denial of service attacks that are starting to be addressed by the makers of firewalls and operating systems.

CREATING A SECURE PERIMETER: THE FIREWALL

The technologies and techniques described in this section provide a means to create a firewall, a virtual security fence around your organization. Unfortunately, organizations that use these techniques often reduce the amount of energy applied toward protecting information behind the firewall. While this strategy makes life easier for operations inside the perimeter, it can have bad consequences once someone manages to break through. Later in this chapter, you will see how cryptography can be used to protect sensitive information enroute over the public networks. In some cases, it may make sense to use cryptographic techniques to protect sensitive information inside the organization as well. You might, for instance, consider encrypting sensitive files stored on desktop computers. Should someone manage to break in or steal them, the information would be useless unless the thieves had access to the cryptographic keys. More about this later, but first let's look at creating a solid fence.

Technology for Securing the Perimeter

Before delving into a description of the different architectures you can use to build an electronic shield around your organization, you need a little information on the tools and building blocks used to assemble such a shield. There are two basic technologies that are appropriate here. The first one, usually referred to as a filtering device, controls the flow of traffic in and out of your internal network. (The term "firewall" can also be used to describe some of these devices, but in this chapter the term firewall is used to describe the entire infrastructure used to secure the perimeter.) The second technology is automated intrusion detection, software guardians who watch for suspicious activity on specific computers and send off an alarm alerting appropriate personnel when such activity occurs.

Filtering the good from the bad: The e-membrane

An electronic filtering device is akin to an electronic membrane—letting some packets in, while stopping others from entering. It can also do the reverse; that is, limit access by internal users and systems to the outside world. Devices and software that perform this function come in all shapes and sizes. They include screening routers, firewalls (for example, Checkpoint's Firewall-1, Gauntlet's Raptor), Virtual Private Network (VPN) software, and so on. In general, all these systems serve the same function. They use a set of rules to examine packets that are flowing across the perimeter. Based on these rules, the packets can be dropped, modified, or allowed to pass unaltered. The amount of intelligence used in analyzing the flow of information is what distinguishes the different systems.

Packet-filters utilize information contained in the packet header such as destination and origination addresses. Some of the smarter packet-filters use state information gathered from previous packets to increase the ability to detect potential problems. A further level of intelligence in filtering technology uses application proxies to analyze information at the level of specific application protocols. This means that multiple packets are examined in the context of a specific application-layer protocol. It provides a means of detecting certain classes of attacks that "tunnel" rogue information streams through firewall openings configured specifically for certain services. For example, an http application proxy will detect any sequence of packets that does not specifically conform to the http protocol. This makes it difficult to try to sneak an unauthorized data transmission through a hole that is supposed to be used to communicate with a Web server on the internal network.

Both packet-filters and application proxies can be utilized to provide a service known as network address translation (NAT). This is a process whereby the filtering device translates the IP address of internal computers to a different external address. From a security perspective this hides the address of internal computers from the outside world. Knowledge of internal IP addresses is a common requirement for many types of attacks that attempt to gain access through the firewall.

Although application-level proxies and, to a lesser degree, packet-filters both provide significant protection from would-be intruders, a third level of sophistication can be provided by virtual private networking (VPN) technology. This type of device has been gaining popularity over the last several years. It uses cryptographic techniques (like those discussed later in the chapter) to encrypt packets and provide the ability to identify the sender of each packet using much more specific information than that available to application proxies and packet-filters.

Firewall Architectures

There are many different architectures that can be used to create a secure electronic fence around your corporate network. In this section, you will find information on two popular firewalls. Each one allows information to flow in both directions across the perimeter. The first architecture, the single-stage firewall, is sometimes referred to as a dual-home host. The second architecture, the dual-stage firewall is sometimes referred to as Demilitarized Zone (DMZ) architecture. You should be aware that there does not seem to be a strict use of terminology in this area, so the names associated with the following architectures are not universal.

Single-stage firewall

Figure 4-1 shows a single-stage firewall architecture. This system utilizes either a packet-filtering or application proxy filter on a single host.

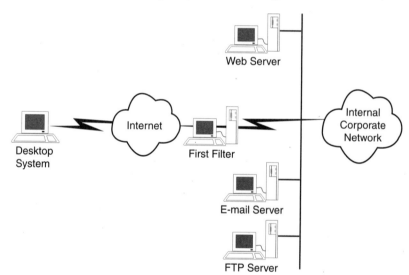

Figure 4-1. *A single-stage firewall.*

The firewall in Figure 4-1 utilizes a single filtering device on a dual-home host. The filtering device has been set up to allow network traffic to flow into three specific servers behind the firewall (Web, E-mail, and FTP). It also allows all internal systems behind the firewall to access resources on the Internet.

The host maintains a connection to the Internet on one side and a connection to the internal network on the other. Rules are set up in the filtering device to restrict access to only those internal systems that require it. In Figure 4-1 this is a Web server, FTP server, and E-mail server. Users inside the firewall are allowed to access resources on the Internet. However, the addresses on all machines on the internal network are hidden from the outside using NAT. The limitation of this architecture is that should someone compromise any single internal server (for example, the Web server), they would have full access to the internal network. The firewall in this case only provides a single line of defense.

Dual-stage firewall

Figure 4-2 shows a more enhanced firewall architecture.

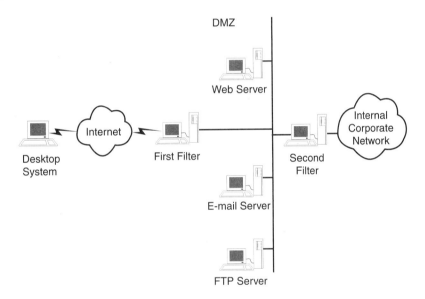

Figure 4-2. *A two-stage firewall.*

The firewall in Figure 4-2 utilizes two filtering devices to create a safe zone, which some people refer to as a "demilitarized zone" DMZ. The first filtering device allows network traffic to flow only to those computers in the safe zone. The second device allows network traffic to flow into the internal network only if it originates from a computer in the safe-zone.

This architecture creates a buffer that shields the internal network. If someone compromises one of the machines in the safe-zone, they are severely limited to what they can do because they need to traverse another firewall to get to internal machines. A would-be attacker would have to load special software onto one of the machines in the DMZ, and then utilize one of the open ports in the second firewall to get in. This is an order of magnitude more complicated than penetrating a single-stage firewall.

Monitoring

The subject of monitoring was briefly discussed in the last section; however, the details of what needs monitoring have not yet been discussed. It is important to point out that all filtering devices, all machines in the safe-zone, as well as all machines directly accessible behind the single-stage firewall, should be continuously monitored and logged for security purposes. These systems are exposed to the outside world and, as such, are strong candidates for attack. These are also good machines to think about running intrusion detection software on.

AUTHENTICATION AND ACCESS CONTROL

Although firewalls provide means to monitor network traffic that crosses the perimeter, they do not (except in the case of VPNs) provide a way to determine who the sender of a packet is and what they should be allowed to see. This is normally the job of applications that sit on the internal network or in the safe-zone. For example, a firewall will monitor network traffic accessing a Web server and can be configured to limit only legitimate http commands to reach the server. However, the Web server is still responsible for determining who is at the other end of a request and what Web pages they should be able to see. In the security world, two well-defined terms have been applied to this process. Authentication is the process that decides if a person is who they say they are, and access control is the process of deciding what someone is allowed to do and see.

Authentication

There are many schemes that people have created to identify someone electronically. You may already be familiar with a number of them—username and password, fingerprint recognition, challenge response cards, and so on. In order to organize the discussion, authentication technologies can be broke into three categories: single-factor, two-factor, and biometric schemes.

Single-factor authentication

As the name implies, single-factor authentication schemes rely on ownership or knowledge of a single entity. This entity is something that only a given individual knows or owns. For example, the username and password scheme is a single-factor scheme. Your password is a single item (known only to you) that is secret in the process. Your username is usually not secret since it is widely distributed throughout an organization. For purposes of e-mail, this username may even be distributed publicly. An ATM card that does not require a PIN number would be another example of a single-factor authentication scheme In this case, the possession of the card is the only factor needed to prove your identity.

In general, single-factor schemes are difficult to make secure. For example, the typical username and password scheme suffers from a number of pitfalls. The biggest problem with this scheme is that passwords that are easy to remember are generally easy to guess. When using the username and password authentication mechanism, it is essential to have strict policies for what are acceptable passwords. As a safety check, you can obtain software (such as Crack) that tries all the passwords that are easy to guess. Users whose passwords fail this test should be asked to change them immediately.

Two-factor authentication

Two-factor authentication schemes get their name from the notion that you need to have ownership of two entities to authenticate. Something you know and something you physically possess. An example of this is the SecurID system from Security Dynamics. It utilizes a credit-card size card that uses a special algorithm and synchronized clock to generate a temporary password. The ATM utilizes another two-factor scheme. For this one, you need to have in your possession both the card and knowledge of the PIN. Two-factor authentication is generally thought to be much better than single-factor since you are required to possess two unique objects or characteristics when you are authenticated. Guessing passwords or PIN numbers is just not enough to get through. In the latter half of this chapter, two-factor authentication based on modern cryptography will be discussed.

Biometric authentication

Although two-factor authentication is generally much better than single-factor methods, it still suffers from the problem of inconvenience for users. You need to remember passwords and you need to keep track of the "something you possess." The solution that is starting to gain some media attention (if the latest showing at Comdex was any indication) is biometrics. These devices measure a unique aspect of the human body and compare it to some previously measured value. If there is a match, then you are who you say you are. Some of the devices—retina and iris scanners, voice and face recognition, palm scanners, and so on—are straight out of your favorite sci-fi movies. Cost, accuracy, and user acceptance are still basic problems prohibiting widespread use. The technology is starting to mature, however, and this may be the preferred mode of access in three to five years. Another interesting problem with it is the ability to recognize when the measurement of a particular aspect of the body is still attached to the body it is suppose to be identifying. For example, early fingerprint scanners did not require that the finger used in the device be attached to the owner's hand. A morbid thought, but something you might want to consider when contemplating deployment.

Access Control

Once you have figured out who someone is, your next challenge is to determine what they are allowed to do and see. Your infrastructure may contain a very large number of possible resources that need to be protected such as printing services, access to files, database entries, Web pages, and so on. The general technique is to label each resource with a set of permissions that are required for access. There are a number of ways of doing this. The NT operating system uses an access control list (ACL). The access control list specifies who is able to access the resource and specifically what they are allowed to do with it. It determines if someone is allowed to read and modify a file or just read it. In systems with very large numbers of users, it is not practical to label each resource with privileges for each specific user. For some installations, this list could require millions of entries and would be impossible to maintain as new users were added to the system and old ones removed. To get around this problem, the concept of role-based security was created. Using this approach, a user is assigned a role or a set of roles. Each ACL in the system then contains only a list of roles and the privileges that are granted to each role.

CRYPTOGRAPHIC BUILDING BLOCKS

This section contains a description of some of the more popular mechanisms for encrypting information. In the next section, you will find discussions of how these techniques are applied to some popular secure Internet protocols. The cryptographic systems discussed here rely heavily on the concept of an electronic key. A key is essentially a number (usually a very large number) that is used in combination with a special algorithm for scrambling or encrypting data into an unreadable form. These cryptographic algorithms have special properties that make it extremely difficult to unencrypt the coded information, requiring more computing power than is economically feasible to possess. As you learn more about electronic commerce, you will often encounter terms and phrases closely related to this basic key; for instance, "digital signature," "Digital ID from a trusted source," "public and private keys." In the next sections, we will give you a basic explanation of these. The thing that you will be using most and that is fundamental to the whole area of secure commerce is the "Digital ID."

Public- and Private-Key Algorithms

For the purposes of this discussion, you need to be aware of two types of algorithms for encrypting information. The first class is the symmetric algorithm. Symmetric algorithms use a single key (or pair of keys where one is derivable from the other) for encryption and decryption. Symmetric key algorithms were pretty much the entire game in town until the mid-1970s. This is when two researchers, Whitfield Diffie and Martin Hellman, invented the concept of public-key cryptography (actually a third researcher, Ralph Merkle, discovered this concurrently). A public-key algorithm is one where different keys are used to encrypt and decrypt the data. The two keys are completely distinct and one cannot be derived from the other. In 1978, a trio of researchers, Ron Rivest, Adi Shamir, and Leonard Adleman, introduced the first usable public-key algorithm called RSA. They later become a company by the same name.

Symmetric and public-key technologies, along with another concept called digital signatures, form the basis for emerging standard secure protocols in use today on the Internet. Let's look at a few more details on these technologies.

Digital Signatures

A concept that you will see used repeatedly in cryptographic protocols is a digital signature. Although the actual algorithms are somewhat complex, the concept is quite simple and elegant. In order to understand it, you will need to first understand a concept known as a one-way hash. A one-way hash is an algorithm that creates a unique number (a hash) for each unique message. In addition, the hash cannot be used to recover the original message. If the document or message is altered, the value of its one-way hash will be different. Add in the concept of public-key cryptography for encrypting the hash and you now have a way of transmitting an electronic message that is tamper-proof. In general, the scheme looks something like this:

- First, agree on a one-way hash algorithm to use with the person you want to send the message to.

- Compute the one-hash of the document.

- Encrypt the hash value using your private-key to produce a digital signature.

- Send the document, the digital signature, and your public-key to the receiving person.

- The receiving person first computes the one-way hash of the received document.

- Then, using the sender's public-key, the receiver decrypts the digital signature the computed one-way hash.

- If these values match, the document has arrived safely intact.

Since only the sender of the document possesses the private-key that matches the public-key, it would be impossible to intercept the document, alter it and compute a new one-way hash. Alterations to the message would be detected because the one-way hash of the received document would not match the original. Unfortunately, this scheme is flawed since a mischievous person could intercept the public-key and replace it with an imposter. This would allow them to alter the message, recompute the hash, and re-encrypt it. What is needed is a way to ensure that the public-key comes from the person who sent the original message. One mechanism for doing this, Digital Certificates, will be discussed later in this chapter.

SECURE INFORMATION EXCHANGE ON THE INTERNET

In this section, you will see how the basic building blocks of cryptography, introduced in the last section, are used to create useful and practical protocols for exchanging information. The protocols and infrastructure described here provide solutions to some of the common security problems associated with sending sensitive information from one party to the another over an insecure channel (such as the Internet). These problems include:

- **Protection from message tampering.** This property means that it is very difficult to intercept a message and change it or create an alternate message.

- **Hiding sensitive information from view.** This is typically the most commonly associated property. It means that if a message is intercepted, it will be very difficult to determine what it says.

- **Protection from impersonation of either sender or receiver.** A common trick is to mislead one of the parties into believing you are someone else and therefore tricking them into sending you sensitive information. This is essentially a problem of authentication. All the protocols listed later provide for enhanced mechanisms for authenticating both senders and receivers.

Digital Certificates and Certificate Authorities

Before proceeding to the discussion of the protocols, there is a piece of infrastructure that needs some more elaboration. This infrastructure has evolved around a set of standards for using public-key cryptography and digital signatures to create what is known as a digital certificate. As discussed previously, the concept of a digital certificate solves the problem of how to safely distribute public-keys. A digital certificate is an electronic packet of information that binds together a public-key and a set of information that can be used to identify the owner of the private-key/public-key pair. If you remember from the last section, the problem with distributing a public-key is that you can never be certain it has not been intercepted and a rogue substitute inserted in its place. The digital certificate solves this problem by introducing a third party that is trusted by both sender and receiver to certify that the public-key and associated identifying information have not been tampered with. This third party is known as a certificate authority (CA). You probably have heard of some of popular CA's, for example, Verisign and GTE. These folks are essentially in the trust business (if you look at the amount of venture capital that has been thrown at this industry, you will see that trust is a valuable thing).

The basic operation of a CA is pretty simple (in reality, things can get pretty complicated but the details are not necessary here): The steps involved in obtaining a digital certificate are as follows:

- The user decides they need to obtain a certificate and requests their application, such as a Web browser or e-mail client to begin the process. The first thing that happens is usually the generation of a public-key/private-key pair.

- Once the keys have been generated, the application requests the user to supply the necessary information (such as name, address, e-mail address, and so on) required for the certificate.

- The private-key/public-key pair generated in the first step along with the identifying information collected in the previous step is then bundled up and sent to a CA for certification.

- The certificate authority processes the request by performing whatever due diligence is necessary to be certain that the request is legitimate and that all information in the certificate is correct. This may be as simple as sending an e-mail message to an appropriate address and having the user respond thus verifying the legitimacy of the user's e-mail address (this is essentially what happens for class 1 user certificates). The process can be much more involved for higher-level certificates. For instance, a business applying for a certificate to identify itself on a Web server may need to pass a stringent investigation into its legitimacy.

■ Once the CA is satisfied that everything is okay, it computes a one-way hash of the message containing the user's identifying information and public-key and signs the hash with the CA's heavily guarded private-key (for a public CA like Verisign, this key is generally protected by military-grade controls). This digital signature securely binds the public-key and the identifying information.

■ The CA finishes the preparation of the certificate, attaching the digital signature along with the identifying information for the CA.

■ The certificate is then sent back to the requesting party. Since the certificate is generally useful only to the person who owns the private-key that matches the embedded public-key, the process of sending the certificate back to the user is generally a low-risk procedure.

■ To prove the authenticity of a certificate, you need to have copy of the CA's public-key. This is a special certificate that you trust to be authentic. Essentially all trust flows from this entity. You use the CA's public-key to verify the authenticity of any certificate that it certifies.

You can now use this certificate in place of a raw public-key to create a robust mechanism for sending tamper-proof electronic documents. Instead of sending the raw public-key along with the document and digital signature, you can send your digital certificate. In addition, the receiving person needs to obtain the CA's certificate. This is usually fairly transparent to the receiver if they are using a popular Web browser or e-mail client since the big CA's have pre-arranged agreements with Internet application developers to embed their certificates in the released versions of the applications. When a certificate is received, the public-key in the CA's certificate is used to first determine if the sender's certificate has been tampered with. If it has not, then the receiver uses the public-key in the sender's certificate to check the authenticity of the message. Again, this whole process assumes that you trust the CA to do its job.

Digital certificate standards

To enable the interoperability of certificates generated from different CA's, standards for the structure and information of different types of certificates have been created. You may have heard the term X.509. This term refers to ANSI standard for the format of a digital certificate, and it is quickly becoming the leading standard for all certificates. There are different grades or classes of certificates. Each class contains a different level of information and is meant for use in different situations. To get more information on the types of digital certificates, visit Verisign's Web site at *http://www.verisign.com*.

Generic Secure Protocols

There are numerous protocols that have been created to transfer information securely over insecure channels. In the following sections, you will find a description of two of the more popular ones that are gaining wide acceptance for use on the Internet. As with most Internet technologies, the reason for their acceptance lies in the fact that they are published standards with support from a number of vendors. The interoperability between different vendors is generally quite good and is key to the proliferation of the standard. The protocols listed here can also be thought of as generic protocols since they are rather low level and are not domain specific.

Secure sockets layer (SSL)

SSL is quickly becoming one of the most widely used protocols on the Internet when secure exchange of information is required. SSL is a lower-level protocol because it works directly on top of TCP/IP and is implemented in such a way that it is very transparent to any information that rides at a higher level. This makes it very easy to add security support to protocols used for Web communication (for example, HTTP). In general, SSL functions by using public-keys to facilitate the exchange of private-keys. After the handshake, all information is exchanged using the private-key algorithm. This improves efficiency and solves the problem of private-key distribution.

There are a number of ciphers (algorithms) that can be used for the public-key, message digest, and symmetric key portions of the protocol. This set of algorithms is often referred to as the cipher suite. Because SSL implements a wide range of cipher suites, the exact details of how the protocol functions depend on which suite is used. Even though this level of detail is beyond the scope of this chapter, the following explanation will give you a sense of the basic workings of SSL.

The overall SSL protocol is divided into two subprotocols, the record protocol and the handshake protocol. As mentioned previously, the handshake protocol is what governs the exchange of private-keys. The record protocol is what governs how encrypted packets are formatted. The most interesting portion of the protocol is the handshake. It takes place as follows:

- The client sends the server its SSL version, cipher settings and a randomly generated message.

- The server responds with the same, plus the server's certificate.

- If required, the server requests the client's certificate.

- The client authenticates the server and creates the pre-master secret for the session, encrypts it with the server's public-key, and sends it to the server.

- If client authentication is requested, then the client signs another piece of data with its private key and sends it along with its certificate.

- The server authenticates the client, if needed, then decrypts the pre-master key with its private-key.

- Both client and server user the pre-master key to generate a master key, which is then used to generate session keys.

- Session keys are used for the symmetric encryption algorithm.

- Client and server exchange messages telling each other they are going start encrypting messages with session keys.

- The handshake is complete.

During both the server and client authentication steps, the respective certificates are checked for validity using an algorithm similar to the one described in the previous section on Digital Certificates. In addition, each party can check if the certificate is still valid (for example, not out of date). During client authentication, it is also possible to perform access control. This means that certain fields in the client's certificate can be used to determine if the user should be allowed access to resources and if so how this should be restricted. At present, Microsoft's IIS Web server allows certificates to be mapped to NT accounts. If the certificate is determined to be authentic and valid, a search is performed to see which account it maps to. If a match is found, then the user is given all the privileges associated with the account.

S/MIME and secure e-mail

Secure/Multipurpose Internet Mail Extensions (S/MIME) is emerging as the protocol of choice for asynchronous messaging over the Internet. Essentially, this covers everything from standard e-mail to automated EDI applications. S/MIME is supported by the two largest vendors of e-mail client software, Microsoft and Netscape, and is starting to gain wider acceptance. In its initially released version (version 2), it suffered from a limitation that 40-bit RC2 (RC2 is a symmetric cipher created by RSA) was the only mandated encryption algorithm. Other symmetric algorithms (DES and triple-DES) could be used, but support for them was not guaranteed. Since the security of 40-bit algorithms is not very strong, many people criticized the standard. Version 2.0 will remove this limitation and will make it easier to utilize a wider variety of cipher suites.

S/MIME in itself is not a protocol, but rather, a specification of the format and related issues needed to encrypt MIME objects. In this sense, S/MIME is independent of the actual protocol used to transfer the data. In this section, the transport is assumed to be the simple mail transfer protocol (SMTP). The combination of the two creates a way to send secure e-mail messages across the Internet. In order to support the greatest flexibility, the S/MIME standard is structured is such a way that an encrypted or signed MIME attachment is just another MIME type. In general, this means that it is possible to encrypt or sign only the portions of a complex message that require it.

To see how S/MIME can be used to send secure e-mail, you can break it down into three parts. The first part involves retrieving and validating all the public-keys (certificates) for all desired recipients of a given message. The next part involves constructing the secure message and sending it. The final part involves receiving the message and decrypting it. The latter two steps are discussed first.

The details of constructing a S/MIME message involve a standard known as PKCS#7. This is standard procedure and format for creating cryptographic messages developed by RSA labs (*http://www.rsa.com*). The details of creating a PKCS#7 vary according to the specific cipher suite used. Since S/MIME allows for a message to be either encrypted (enveloped) and signed, just enveloped, or just signed, there are further permutations on the how things are performed. This is very similar to SSL. There are additional details required for formatting the PKCS#7 message as a MIME message, but they are not particularly relevant to the security discussion. The following process is taken from the PKCS#7 specification (available at ftp://ftp.rsa.com/pub/pkcs/ascii/pkcs-7.asc).

- A content-encryption key for a particular content-encryption algorithm is generated at random. In version 2.0 of S/MIME, the only required support was RC2. But DES and Triple-DES could be optionally supported.

- For each recipient, the content-encryption key is encrypted with the recipient's public-key.

- For each recipient, the encrypted content-encryption key and other recipient-specific information are collected into a RecipientInfo field.

- For each signer, a message digest is computed on the content with a signer-specific message-digest algorithm. (If two signers employ the same message-digest algorithm, then the message digest needs to be computed for only one of them.)

- For each signer, the message digest and associated information are encrypted with the signer's private-key, and the result is encrypted with the content-encryption key.

- For each signer, the doubly encrypted message digest and other signer-specific information are collected into a SignerInfo field.

- The content is encrypted with the content-encryption key (the symmetric key).

- The message-digest algorithms for all the signers, the SignerInfo values for all the signers, and the RecipientInfo values for all the recipients are collected together with the encrypted content into a SignedAndEnvelopedData field.

As with SSL, this process utilizes the benefits of public-key cryptography with the processing efficiencies of private-key algorithms. The most problematic portion of this process is the need to posses all the public-keys of all the recipients of a given message. Currently, the only way for this to take place is for the users to send their certificates to the party they want to receive mail from. There are several proposals for better ways to do this using directory services, but none of these have yet to catch on.

Payment Systems and Protocols

While the protocols described in the previous section can be used for transmitting any kind of information, they do not contain any inherent support for e-commerce-related payment activities. This means, for example, that even though you can use SSL to collect payment information (including credit-card numbers), there is no direct support for verifying if the number is stolen or a person's credit limit has been reached. If S/MIME and SSL are your only tools, then you will need to build a significant amount of functionality from scratch. There are a number of schemes that are currently vying for attention in the space of Internet payment. Peter Wayner's book, *Digital Cash*, provides an interesting overview of the wide variety of options that are currently being tested. Since the vast majority of systems are currently in experimentation or early trial phases, the material in this section will be limited to discussions on protocols and systems that focus on credit card based mechanisms.

There are several vendors that provide services to solve the Internet Payment problem. CyberCash, Verifone, IBM, and GlobalSet are all big players in this space. At present, there are variations in each vendor's solution. This is beginning to change, however, with the maturing of the SET (secure electronic transaction) standard. In general, there are three sets of services and software that are needed to create a payment solution: one for the consumer, one for the merchant, and one for the merchant's credit-card processing institution.

The customer

For the customer to make secure electronic payments, some software, usually called a "wallet," needs to be installed on the user's computer. The "needs to be installed" portion of the statement can be a bit of an issue, so wallet makers are looking to make deals with browser vendors to distribute their wallets as part of the browser. A wallet serves as the consumer's interface to the payment infrastructure. It holds certificates, private-keys, payment information, and customer demographics, and is responsible for sending this information to the merchant's system and to the financial institution.

The merchant

For the merchant, the payment infrastructure provides point of sale (POS) functionality similar to that used by brick-and-mortar retailers. Having POS functionality in your e-commerce infrastructure will allow you to:

- Perform credit-card authorizations in real time.

- Verify addresses to see if the billing address presented at purchase time matches that listed by the card issuer.

- Signal the credit-card processor to transfer funds to your account after goods have been shipped.

Credit institutions

Finally, for the organization that processes credit-card transactions, a gateway is needed from the Internet to the processor's private network. This gateway allows requests for authorization, capture, and voided transactions from the merchant's server to be processed by the same infrastructure that handles brick-and-mortar merchant requests.

The details of how these elements interact are dependent on the particular vendor's solution. The SET standard (described at *http://www.SETCO.org*) formalizes how each of the components interact so any wallet will interact with any merchant server and any merchant server will interact with any processor gateway. In order to get a feel for how the different elements of the payment infrastructure interact to process payment information, take a look at the following process:

- The customer first browses a catalog on a commerce Web site and selects the set of products they wish to purchase (call this the shopping basket).

- The information in the shopping basket is sent to the commerce Web server that then forwards it to the merchant's payment server.

- The merchant's payment server computes the cost of the goods and formats an order for the goods.

- The order is sent from the payment server back to the customer's computer and displayed in the wallet. Before the wallet and the merchant's payment server establish a connection, they use a handshake (similar to the one in SSL) to establish authenticity of both parties. After this step, all sensitive information is encrypted.

- The wallet then prompts the user to select the appropriate credit card.

- The customer selects the desired card and authorizes the transaction to purchase the goods. At this point, the wallet signs the order with a digital signature to provide strong confirmation that the user has requested the transaction.

- The signed transaction (including order and payment information) is then returned to the merchant's payment server. In some systems (and by design, in all SET systems), the merchant does not receive the customer's credit card number. This information remains encrypted and is sent on for processing to the payment gateway. This is expected to cut down on fraudulent merchants that set up Web sites for the sole purpose of collecting credit card numbers.

- Finally, once the transaction is processed by the payment server (in this sequence, it would normally be the approval of an authorization request), confirmation is sent back to the merchant and back to the consumer.

For the non-SET compliant systems that are in use today (such as older versions of CyberCash), the public-key-based authentication steps do not explicitly utilize standard certificates and certificate authority infrastructures. This will change if the SET standard takes hold. The need to obtain a certificate in order to use your credit card for Internet purchases is one of the main features of SET. The due diligence required to obtain this digital ID should significantly increase the difficulty in defrauding the system. However, as you will see later, it is also one of the stumbling blocks that may prevent a massive role-out of the technology.

PKI Management

Now that you have had a taste of the things that are possible using basic cryptographic building blocks, it is time to take a look at some of the practical issues of utilizing this technology. As you might have noticed while reading the previous section, the problem of distributing and managing a large volume of private-keys and public certificates was glossed over. Unfortunately, this problem has been one of the major stumbling blocks for widespread utilization of the strong form of client authentication provided by SSL and other public-key based protocols.

The infrastructure needed to run a CA is substantial and can be very expensive to maintain. Since the security of a CA's private-key underlies the security of the certificates it issues, it is necessary to provide the strongest guarantees that this key will not be compromised. In addition, you will see shortly that "out-of-the-box" application software on the client does not support the secure storage of private-keys. Aside from the technical complexities of maintaining a PKI, there are a host of operational and legal issues that are still being ironed out. For instance, the legal framework for digital signing of documents and transaction has not been fully established.

Portability and security of certificates and private-keys

As hinted to in the last section, significant ease-of-use and security problems exist with end-user applications distributed by most Internet application vendors. The problems with ease of use are two-fold. The first basic problem is that the private-key is locked to the computer that the application software has been installed on. This means, for example, that you would need a different certificate and private-key to access your health records from your office computer than from your home computer. The use of two certificates creates a major administrative burden for you as well as for the information service provider. The second ease-of-user issue is one of general knowledge of PKI. If you have ever walked through the process of obtaining a certificate and installing it in a browser, you will probably remember that you were confronted by a number of unfamiliar terms and difficult questions. The knowledge of PKI has not reached the general Internet-aware user, and as a result, the possibility for error and misuse is still very high. Much work is needed by application vendors in order to streamline the process and make it more understandable.

Another problem with PKI is the basic assumption of the previously described protocols (SSL and S/MIME). They assume that the person who currently posses the private-key is its rightful owner. Since this is one of the most basic assumptions of the entire infrastructure, it would seem essential for any PKI to protect private-keys from theft. Unfortunately, this has been a very poorly implemented feature on both Netscape and Microsoft browsers. Netscape Navigator uses software encryption to store the private-key on the user's computer, and Microsoft Internet Explorer 4, by default, uses no protection at all. Even though Netscape uses encryption, the scheme is so weak that it can be easily penetrated using simple desktop computing hardware.

As an example of the problems this can cause, imagine an online banking application that authenticates users based on certificates. Losing the laptop computer that contains your private-key would be almost equivalent to losing a cash card with your PIN written on it. Fortunately, you cannot dispense cash through a computer (yet, anyway), so the best someone could to do is to transfer money to another account and make a quick withdrawal. The possibility for vandalism, however, is much greater.

There are alternatives to using the built-in functionality that ships with the brand name Web browsers. Smart cards initially showed a great deal of promise for solving this problem. These devices utilize a credit card size computer to store a user's private-key and have been shown to provide very strong protection from attack. However, they require a specialized card reader to be installed on the host computer in order to be used. Some manufacturers are starting to offer this as an option at the time of purchase but widespread usage still faces an uphill battle since the installed base is so large. It is difficult to imagine that people will be willing to purchase and install the device just so they can shop over the Internet. There is some possibility that certain Internet services might distribute the smart-card devices as a part of a specialized service offering (for example, online banking), but the cost and logistics would seem to be overburdening.

There is a second alternative that is worth mentioning. This involves increasing the security of the private-key storage on the client machine. This is the approach of a small company known as Arcot Systems. The solution they have created involves a secure wallet that has a number of the properties of a smart card with the added ease of portability of software-only module. If you would like more details, check out *http://www.arcot.com*.

How Secure Is This Stuff?

A natural question to ask at this point is: How secure is all the stuff? Unfortunately, this is a very difficult question to answer. Most of the public knowledge of how to subvert or crack modern protocols with large keys (such as those described earlier) suggests that it is a very challenging task and that you would need to spend a lot of money to do it. One of the problems with this assumption is that for most of the recent past, the majority of cryptographic research has been performed in a classified setting. It is generally known ("rumored" is probably the correct term) that the NSA has much more cryptographic knowledge then exists in the public domain. Given some of the events of the past 20 years (for example, the knowledge of DES before it was released publicly), it would seem that a good gauge of an algorithms effectiveness is the degree to which the NSA complains of its use in the civilian sector. The theory is that given the NSA's mission, they will be real nervous about algorithm's and techniques that they cannot crack. Therefore, if the NSA has a fairly laissez-faire attitude to a specific technology (like algorithms with 40-bit keys), then we can assume that they (and probably others) have mechanisms to subvert it. Their initially strong resistance to allow 56-bit or greater algorithms to be exported is probably a sign that they provided fairly strong protection. Since these restrictions are starting to be lifted, it is either a sign that the business community now has a stronger voice in Congress than the NSA, or that the NSA has had sufficient time to build up techniques and defenses against the protocols.

PUTTING IT ALL TOGETHER

To give you some idea of how the technology in this section can be used in a commercial setting, an example will be given utilizing the high-performance e-commerce architectures described in Chapter 3. There are three basic areas that you need to think about when using the architecture in Figure 3-4 on page 73 for this type of secure e-commerce site. They are:

- Secure communication between users (customers) of the service and the commerce site during transfer of order, personal, and payment information

- Secure transmission of the information (such as orders to a fulfillment house) between the site and suppliers

- Protection of sensitive information contained in company databases as well as general protection of non-public infrastructure such as the distributed object servers

If you look back at Figure 3-4, you will notice that security was basically ignored when discussing the features of this architecture. Using the material presented in this chapter, you can begin to see how some of the desired improvements might be carried out. However, before making any modifications, its worthwhile to note that the existing system already had a small degree of security built in. The local director hardware used mainly for load-balancing purposes also functions essentially as a packet-filter. It provides NAT services and therefore can hide the true IP addresses of all machines behind it. As described in the previous sections, this feature hides internal machines from external view. This would be essential for databases and internal distributed object servers. Figure 4-3 shows the architecture of Figure 3-4 reincarnated, with the security improvements listed earlier.

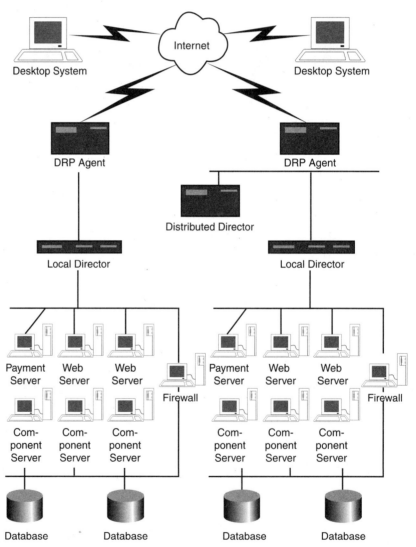

Figure 4-3. *This network diagram shows a security-enhanced version of the architecture originally presented in Figure 3-4.*

You will notice that there have been several significant improvements and modifications. A set of special Web servers has been added for order-taking purposes. The reason for the use of separate servers for this purpose is several-fold. First, SSL is not a stateless protocol (you need to have the same private-key on either side of a connection for each http request). In its current implementation by all vendors, there is no mechanism to share the private-keys for the symmetric algorithms. This means that you either need to make the secure portion of your order process a single step (something that may be very difficult) or you need to return to the same Web server for each step in the process. The second reason is that as site volume increases, it may be necessary to take advantage of cryptographic accelerators to improve the performance of cryptographic calculations. In general, you probably do not want to put this hardware (for cost reasons) on all the servers in your cluster.

While the payment servers add the needed security for collecting sensitive information during order processing, a filtering device has been added between the Web servers and the rest of the infrastructure. This filtering device, in combination with the Local Director, creates a two-stage firewall. The firewall is configured to only let packets flow in from those machines in the DMZ, that is, the Web servers. This wall will protect sensitive information in the databases should someone compromise any of the Web servers.

Finally, after orders are processed, information needs to be sent to the place of fulfillment. Since this information contains sensitive customer information, sending it in the clear is not acceptable. In the past, if this function was handled electronically, the information was usually sent over a private value added network (VAN). This requires setting up a private leased line to the network or directly to the supplier (a costly endeavor). To eliminate this expense, S/MIME over SMTP is used to transfer orders. This is accomplished by adding a mail server to the DMZ and configuring the firewall to allow SMTP traffic to flow out. The mail server can also be used to send order confirmation to customers.

Defining a Security Policy

Although the technology side of the security infrastructure is important, you will see that taking a few steps back and understanding process and policy can make an even bigger impact. Imagine how foolish it would be to install the best lock you could find on your front door then to leave the key hanging around the doorknob. The information technology analog of this is precisely what happens in many organizations and even to those organizations that you are trusting with some of your most sensitive personal information. Next time you are in a hospital, look around at the computer terminals. You are very likely to find username and passwords posted right on the front of the screen. The security of any system whose users freely give out passwords is significantly compromised, and all the technology in the world will not help make it more secure. Nothing can take the place of clear policies and well-educated and trained employees. To this end, there are many issues that need to be considered when constructing a policy, and you may want to enlist the help of a professional when implementing one for your organization. Just to give you a taste of what is needed, the rest of this section gives a few examples of the issues that need to be dealt with.

Let's start with some of the basics. You need to decide what the policy is for creating and sharing passwords. For example, you need to decide what the policy will be for letting a user of the system "logon" for someone else. This is especially sensitive for employees with root access or Administrator privilege. If your answer is never, then you need to make sure all employees follow that rule. As an aside, this seems like the right answer, but consider scenarios where this may cause some hardship, for example, what happens when you need a vendor to install or service software? What are the procedures for doing this? Do you leave them alone on your network, or does someone have to watch over their shoulder while they work? If you are planning to set up access to your system from outside your facility (a safe bet if you have outsourced the hosting of your site), how will these users log on, and what access rights will they have? Another issue that needs to be dealt with is the policy for leaving sensitive information on external computers. Consider the fact that the default setting for your Web browser is to cache pages on your local hard drive. Now imagine what would happen if that computer was stolen by a malicious individual (or left a trade show and picked up by one of your competitors). All the cached information could be easily recovered by just using the Web browser on the machine and setting it to work offline. You might want to consider restricting access to the corporate information from only approved equipment and using appropriate authentication and access control measures for all portable computers.

As you may begin to realize, creating a security policy is not a trivial exercise and is not something you should do without the help of someone with a lot of experience. The main goal in creating the policy is to address the issues that will have potential to cause the greatest harm to your organization. In addition, this needs to be done in such a way that it does not overly burden the users of the system. The more burdensome a policy is, the less likely it is going to be followed.

Defining a Privacy and Confidentiality Policy

Even though the media has been hyping the message about the general public's resistance to sending credit card numbers over the Internet, you might want to consider a related problem as possibly even a greater barrier to e-commerce in the near future. Although credit card numbers are definitely a concern, consumers are starting to be more fearful of what happens to all the rest of the information that is collected during the order-completion process. In some ways, your credit card number is the least problematic portion of this information. Consider the type of information that you need to complete an online mortgage application. Allowing this type of information to pass into the wrong hands has strong implications for those that collect it. If the fears of consumers are not calmed, you may suffer lost business.

Issues of privacy and confidentiality as they relate to Internet e-commerce are starting to become the focus of government regulation. Several bills are pending in the U.S. Congress and Europe has already enacted legislation. Given the rise in public awareness and possibility of government regulation, you probably need to think about creating a privacy and confidentiality policy. This policy formally states what you will do with the information that you collect. You should view such a policy as a competitive advantage.

In order to give your policy the muscle that it needs to convince people that their private information is safe with your business, you will also need to have an independent auditor routinely validate your compliance with the policy.

The Need for an Independent Auditor

If you managed to read this far, congratulations! You are well on your way to understanding the security and technology issues that need to be considered when running an e-commerce business. If you skipped down to this section, that's fine too because this is probably the most important part of this chapter.

Regardless of what technical infrastructure you have constructed and what policies you have created, the best thing you can do to ensure the safety of your information is to hire an outside firm to perform regular audits. This will ensure everything is functioning as you think it should. You may need to enlist more than one firm to provide full coverage. For example, a security firm may be very good at auditing your security policy and determining if your infrastructure has holes in it. They may not, however, be the right folks to audit your privacy and confidentiality practices.

SUMMARY

The material in this chapter gave you a brief introduction to the world of computer information security. Firewall technology was discussed and shown to be useful in creating an electronic fence around your private corporate network. In addition, a few basic cryptographic concepts were introduced. These concepts gave you the basic building blocks of some of the more common protocols used on the Internet. In addition to technology, the need for sound policy and methodology was stressed throughout the chapter. As part of the policy discussions, it was recommended that you seek the services of an outside auditor to ensure your technical infrastructure is sound and you are following proper policy.

Part III

The Site Server Commerce Platform

Chapter 5

Core Site Server Services

by *Andy Hoskinson*

At first glance, the task of developing extensible, scalable, and secure Web commerce solutions with the least possible resource expenditure and technical risk might seem to be a daunting one, indeed. The Web commerce developer must ensure the successful, rapid completion of many difficult and critical tasks: redundancy, fault tolerance, load balancing, high availability, risk analysis, bastioning, access control, user authentication, encryption, object-oriented design, personalization, and so on. Failure to attend to these details can cause many bad things to happen, including loss of revenue, loss of job, and potential legal liability. To even the most hardened IT veteran, this can seem a bit overwhelming at times.

The good news is this: For the most part, you do not need to "reinvent the wheel." Most software vendors sell server products that provide "out-of-the-box" functionality for a majority of the aforementioned tasks. Moreover, these vendors also provide APIs (application programming interfaces) that serve as programming "hooks" into their basic services. These hooks allow application developers to extend and customize the functionality of these core services to fit their own unique requirements.

Microsoft is certainly no exception. With its BackOffice family of server products, its Visual Studio family of development products, and its COM architecture, Microsoft provides Web commerce developers with a rich foundation of core functionality on which to build sophisticated, scalable, secure, and extensible solutions. The next two chapters will start the process of "drilling down" into some of these products by covering the Microsoft Site Server family of products, which includes two discrete products: Site Server Core, and Site Server Commerce Edition. Site Server Commerce Edition is covered in the next chapter; this chapter will cover Site Server Core.

WHAT IS SITE SERVER 3.0?

Microsoft Site Server 3.0 extends the Microsoft Active Server platform by providing a substantial collection of services, components, APIs, and applications that automate the advanced management and targeted delivery of information. Site Server is not a stand-alone product; its services run on top of Windows NT Server 4.0 and Internet Information Server 4.0. Site Server adds value to any NT- and IIS-based Web site by giving the site builder sophisticated and cost-effective Internet, extranet, and intranet solutions "out of the box." Moreover, Site Server 3.0 ships with a SDK (Software Development Kit), and virtually every Site Server service provides a COM object model to allow the site builder to extend the functionality of the underlying services, and build rich custom solutions in a relatively short period of time. Site Server's functionality is broken down into several distinct areas. These areas include Publishing, Search, Personalization and Membership, Push, Knowledge Manager, and Analysis.

Publishing

Site Server Publishing provides the Web developer with core services and components that allow easy implementation of end-to-end, Web-based document publishing systems. Components and services include the Microsoft File Upload ActiveX control (for client applications), the Microsoft Posting Acceptor ISAPI extension (for RFC 1867 HTTP Post file uploads), and the Site Server Content Deployment Service, which automates the process of replicating content, IIS metabase settings, and even COM components between servers.

WHAT IS ISAPI?

ISAPI is the Microsoft *Internet Server Application Programming Interface*. It is the API that developers use to extend the functionality of IIS. With ISAPI, you can write two types of components: an extension or a filter. An ISAPI extension is invoked by URL. For example, let's say you write an extension called MyCustomFunctionality.dll. To implement this, you would put it in an executable IIS virtual directory, and the end user would run the application by opening its URL, just like he would with a CGI program:

```
http://www.mydomain.com/scripts/MyCustomFunctionality.dll
```

The advantage you gain by using an ISAPI extension is that it runs (by default) in the process space of IIS, rather than spawning a new process, like a CGI program would do.

An ISAPI filter, on the other hand, loads with IIS, continuously monitors inbound HTTP requests, and responds accordingly to events for which it is registered to handle. For example, you could write a custom authentication filter that authenticated remote users against a SQL Server user database.

Search

Site Server Search provides a service that indexes the contents and meta-data (properties) of documents into catalogs. It also provides a COM object model that application developers can use to search these catalogs.

If you are familiar with Index Server, another Microsoft BackOffice product, you are probably thinking, "Hey, isn't that what Index Server does?" The short answer is yes. In fact, Site Server Search uses some of the underlying functionality of Index Server to do its catalog builds. The one thing you get with Site Server Search that you don't get with Index Server is the ability to perform a remote catalog build (a "crawl") and to propagate the completed catalog to another server. This gives you the ability to set up both a dedicated catalog build server and a dedicated search server for your entire Web farm. This obviously helps out your performance and scalability.

Personalization and membership

Site Server Personalization and Membership (P&M) allows you to manage user communities of virtually any size. P&M has services and components that run the entire gamut of user management and personalization issues.

The user data access and storage piece is handled by the Site Server LDAP (Lightweight Directory Access Protocol) service, which handles the interface between client applications and the membership directory. The membership directory stores user attributes, such as name, address, password, and preferences, and uses SQL Server or Microsoft Access as its backend data storage mechanism. The authentication piece is handled by the Site Server Authentication Service, which works in conjunction with a custom ISAPI authentication filter to authenticate remote Web visitors against a Site server membership directory.

The personalization piece includes Active User Object (AUO), a COM object that retrieves the current logged on user's attributes, and facilitates the process of delivering personalized content to the user based on his or her preferences. It also includes Direct Mail, which uses a variety of different services to send out personalized content to distribution lists via SMTP mail. These lists can be either static or dynamic. An example of a static list would be a list of users who want to be kept informed of a new product launch in a particular product category. An example of a dynamic list would be a list that is developed by querying Site Server Analysis for users who expressed an implicit interest in a particular area by visiting certain pages.

LDAP, ADSI, AND OTHER ACRONYMS

The Lightweight Directory Access Protocol (LDAP) is an industry-standard application layer protocol that abstracts the process of implementing a directory service on a TCP/IP network. Simply put, LDAP gives Internet developers a common standard with which they can implement and manage user communities. LDAP is a subset of the X.500 Directory Access Protocol (DAP), and is defined by RFC 2251.

LDAP provides a portable C API for writing client applications that must interact with a LDAP service. There is only one problem, though; as you can well imagine, this API is fairly difficult for the typical Visual Basic developer to master and use.

Fortunately, Microsoft has a solution: Active Directory Service Interfaces (ADSI). ADSI is a collection of COM interfaces that provide a layer of abstraction between client applications and underlying directory services. ADSI itself does not provide any concrete functionality. Functionality comes from ADSI providers which handle the low-level details of interacting with a particular directory service, and return objects that implement the appropriate ADS interface to client applications. This gives application developers the ability to access a wide variety of directory services, including LDAP, from a single code base. ADSI is the preferred method of accessing data in a Site Server membership directory. Later in this chapter, we'll look at a VB 6 example of how to do this.

Push

Site Server Push automates the process of targeted information delivery to users. Push is based on Microsoft's Active Channel Technology, which was first introduced about a year and a half ago with Internet Explorer 4 (see sidebar). Site Server Push has two main components: Active Channel Server, and Active Channel Multicaster. Active Channel Server is a NT service that builds and manages Channel Definition Format (CDF) files that are based on user preferences. Users can then subscribe to these channels, and have targeted information pushed to them whenever content is updated. The Active Channel Multicaster is an NT service that simultaneously delivers content to multiple users through a process called multicasting. Multicasting allows a server to send the same piece of data to multiple clients at the same time, much the same way that a television broadcast is sent to multiple TV sets simultaneously.

AN OVERVIEW OF MICROSOFT ACTIVE CHANNEL TECHNOLOGY

Microsoft Active Channels and desktop items provide an easy authoring mechanism for Web developers to create subscription content for their Microsoft Internet Explorer users without having to do a lot of programming. With this authoring technology, Web developers can create "push" channels that provide their visitors with the following functionality:

■   Automatic notification of Web site content changes through a notification channel, which notifies users of new or updated channel content on a scheduled basis.

(continued)

An Overview of Microsoft Active Channel Technology *(continued)*

■ Automatic download of Web site content for off-line viewing through an immersion channel. When users subscribe to the channel, its content is downloaded for off-line viewing. That way, they can view the channel's content at their leisure, even when they are not connected to the Internet.

■ The ability to track and view breaking information (such as stock quotes, sports scores, and breaking news) on the desktop through an Active Desktop Item. In addition to automatically updating content on a regular basis, Active Desktop Items allow users to view updated information on their desktop without having to open up their browser.

This technology, while frequently described as a "content push" technology, is actually implemented through "scheduled pull" operations by Microsoft Internet Explorer. Therefore, all of the "leg work" is done on the client. When a user subscribes to a channel, Internet Explorer will download the Channel Definition Format (CDF) file that defines the channel, and will present the user with a Subscription wizard. CDF is an XML-based mark-up language used to define channel content. With the Subscription wizard, the user can choose many different subscription options, including the update schedule, e-mail notification of updated content, and downloading for off-line use. Once the subscription process is complete, Internet Explorer will check the content identified by the channel for changes based on the interval specified in the schedule. The end user is notified of any new or updated content by a red gleam on the channel bar icon, and by e-mail, if the user selected that option on the Subscription wizard.

An Active Desktop Item is a component (such as an HTML page or an image) displayed directly on the desktop. Like Active Channels, Active Desktop Items are delivered via CDF files. By residing directly on the desktop, Active Desktop Items are a useful way to put and keep information on a user's "radar screen."

Microsoft Internet Explorer Active Channels and Active Desktop Items allow you to provide your Web site visitors with an easy, unobtrusive way of checking your Web site for content changes. There are many different ways to exploit Microsoft Active Channel technology to deliver content to your users in an interesting, innovative manner. Some examples include:

- Authoring an immersion channel for your intranet site to allow your mobile laptop users to view important content while off-line

- Creating an Active Desktop Item search form to give your users one-click access to your site's search engine

- Creating a personalized channel or Active Desktop Item for your e-commerce site that notifies customers of new products in which they are interested

- Designing an Active Desktop news ticker that keeps your readers notified of breaking news, such as stock price updates

Knowledge manager

Knowledge Manager is a customizable ASP application that "brings together" all of the aforementioned services into a robust intranet knowledge management application. With Knowledge Manager, users can stay up to date on the information in which they are most interested. Knowledge Manager uses Site Server Search for document indexing and searching; P&M for user management, authentication, and site vocabulary; Site Server Publishing for document submission and content replication; and Site Server Push for targeted information delivery via Active Channels.

Analysis

Analysis provides tools that allow you to perform both content and usage analysis. These tools include the Content Analyzer, Custom Import tool, Report Writer, and the Usage Import tool.

The Content Analyzer tool allows you to analyze the structure and integrity of your site. In addition to providing a graphical view of your Web site structure and over 20 different content reports, it will also perform such critical yet time-consuming tasks as checking for broken links.

With the Usage Import tool, you can import your Web server's log files, and then use Report Writer to generate a wide variety of usage analysis reports for your Web site. These reports can be created quickly from a template, or can be built from scratch, if the need arises. These reports will tell you a lot about how people are using your site: what pages they are visiting, what browser/ OS combinations they are using, how they are stepping through your site, how they are finding your site (search engines, referring pages, etc.), where they are originating from, how long they are staying at your site, and other useful information.

With the Custom Import tool, you can import data from other sources to integrate this data with the log file data you imported using Usage Import. For example, you can use the Usage Import tool to import data from your Site Server Commerce Edition Ad Server database to integrate this data into your log file analysis reports. See the next chapter for more information on Ad Server.

Site Server for the Web Commerce Developer

As we have seen from the previous section, many of Site Server's features are targeted toward knowledge management. In other words, Site Server is typically used to power corporate intranet-based document management systems, where a premium is placed on automating and managing the publishing, indexing, searching, and targeted delivery of corporate knowledge assets. Nevertheless, Site Server can provide the Web commerce site builder with a timely and cost-effective way of solving some of the thornier problems with deploying a secure, scalable, and usable e-commerce site. These include:

- Using Site Server Content Deployment to replicate Web content, IIS metabases, and even COM objects across your entire Web farm

- Using Site Server Search to provide a powerful and scalable way of allowing users to find the information they are looking for quickly

- Using the Site Server Authentication Service, ADSI, and the Membership Directory to manage large membership communities and implement access control and user authentication

- Using Site Server Personalization and Membership (P&M) and the Active User Object (AUO) to provide customers with a personalized shopping experience that provides them with the information in which they are most interested

To illustrate this, the remainder of this chapter will walk you through specific examples of how you can use the underlying services of Site Server 3.0 to enhance your e-commerce site. These scenarios include:

- Using Site Server Publishing to replicate your site content and IIS metabase across a Web farm

- Using Site Server Search to create a Web site search engine

- Using P&M for user authentication and personalization.

USING SITE SERVER PUBLISHING ACROSS A WEB FARM

One of the keys to running a successful Web commerce site is to achieve scalability. In other words, your Web site must be able to handle constantly increasing numbers of transactions without going down or requiring major changes to your application logic. How does one achieve this? Frequently, Web developers of high-volume sites will use a "Web farm" to achieve scalability.

A Web farm is a cluster of Web servers that provide identical and redundant content and services. Web farms provide fault tolerance, high availability, and reliability by eliminating the Web server as a single point of failure. In a typical Web farm configuration, a "local director" product (such as the Cisco LocalDirector) balances load among two or more identically configured Web servers. LocalDirector is an embedded OS product that can intelligently balance load between multiple Web servers.

LocalDirector's HTTP daemon responds to requests for the Web site's URL, and passes the request off to the Web server that is most capable of handling the load at that particular time. LocalDirector brings servers in and out of service automatically, based on hardware or daemon availability. LocalDirector ensures that a given client is handed off to the same Web server each time, which allows ASP developers to use the ASP Session object within their applications, if desired. Figure 5-1 shows this configuration.

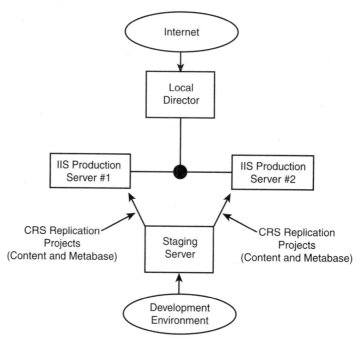

Figure 5-1. *Site Server Content Deployment Architecture overview.*

In addition to providing redundancy, this configuration also provides scalability, in that the developer can accommodate traffic increase by simply putting more servers on line. The key to this strategy, though, is finding an automated way to ensure that each server's content and configuration is kept identical. Site Server Publishing provides the tools to accomplish this.

The Scenario

You can use Site Server Publishing to automate the deployment of content, IIS metabases, and components. This section will describe how to create both a content deployment and a metabase deployment project to replicate information from a staging server to multiple production servers. Before diving into the details, let's quickly review the scenario (shown in Figure 5-1):

1. You have a small Web farm of two production servers and one staging server, with Cisco LocalDirector answering HTTP requests from the Internet and handing the requests off to one of the two

production servers. Even though you only have two production servers right now, you plan on growing your Web farm as your traffic increases.

2. Once content is developed, tested, and released in your development environment, it gets pushed to the staging server. From there, you need a reliable way to replicate your content to all of the production servers. Bottom line: the content and metabase settings of your staging server and production servers need to be exactly the same at all times.

Creating a Content Deployment Project

Site Server provides three tools for creating content deployment projects. The first one is the Site Server MMC (Microsoft Management Console) snap-in, shown in Figure 5-2. You can access this by clicking on Start, Programs, Site Server, Administration, and Site Server Service Admin (MMC). The second tool is the browser-based admin tool, which you can access by pointing your browser to *http://your_server_name/siteserver/admin*. The third way is through code, via the Content Replication Service (CRS) object model. This object model allows you to create and manipulate content deployment projects from any COM client. It also provides an IReplicationEventSink interface to allow you to write your own "Event Sink" components. An Event Sink component allows you to implement custom handling of CRS events.

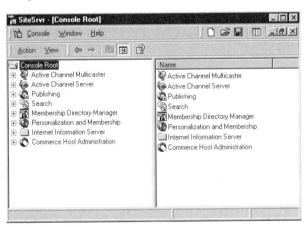

Figure 5-2. *The Site Server MMC snap-in.*

For our content deployment project, we will use the MMC snap-in. To get started, expand the Publishing node and the node corresponding to your staging server. This will display three nodes called Event Reports, Projects, and Routes. Right-click on the Projects node. On the resulting pop-up menu, click on New, then click on Project With A Wizard. This will start the New Project Wizard. Click the Next button to advance to the next frame (see Figure 5-3). Type in a name for your project, and click Next.

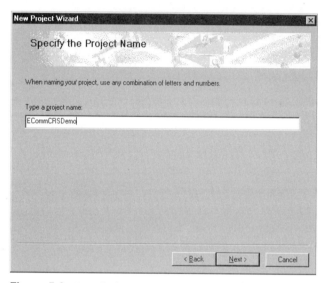

Figure 5-3. *Specify the project name.*

In this frame, you will select the content deployment project type. This frame is shown in Figure 5-4. There are four choices. If you want to push local content from your server to a remote server, select the first choice. If you want to deploy a COM component packaged in a cabinet (.cab) file, select the second choice. If you want to create a "content retrieve" project that crawls a Web or FTP server, select the third or fourth choice, respectively. For our example, we will select the first choice.

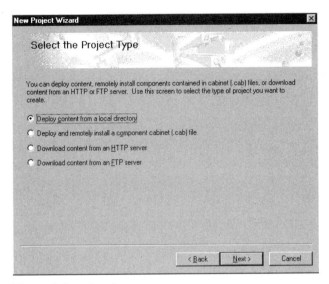

Figure 5-4. *Select the project type.*

In the next frame, type (or select, using the Browse button) the path of the local directory that contains the content that you want to deploy to remote server(s). This frame is shown in Figure 5-5. In our case, we'll type in the root directory of our Web site.

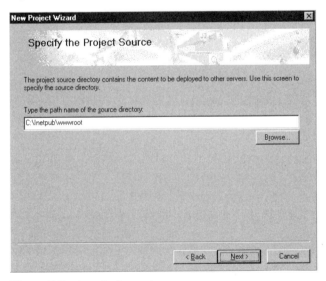

Figure 5-5. *Specify the project source.*

The next step is to specify the project destinations, shown in Figure 5-6. With this dialog, you will add the production servers to which you want to replicate the content identified in the previous step. To add a server, click the Add button, and type in the server name and destination directory to which to replicate your staging server's content. Once you are done, click the Next button.

The next dialog allows you to instruct Site Server to create and configure an IIS virtual directory on the destination servers that correspond to the replicated content, if needed. For this example, we will skip this step, because, as you will see later, we will create a metabase replication project to replicate the metabase from the staging server to the production servers.

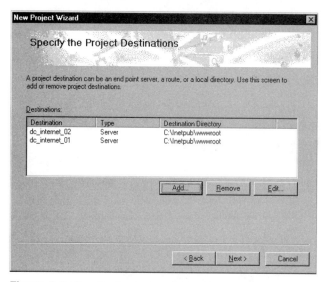

Figure 5-6. *Specify the project destinations.*

The next frame of the wizard allows you to create the project schedule. This frame is shown in Figure 5-7. A content deployment project can be scheduled one of three ways: either on demand, which requires you to manually start the deployment; on a particular time schedule; or automatically as content changes. For our scenario, we want new and changed content to be automatically deployed to the production servers when posted to the staging server, so we'll check the Deploy Content Automatically As Content Changes box, and click the Next button. As the Create Project Schedule Dialog indicates, we must manually start the project once the wizard is finished to enable automatic replication.

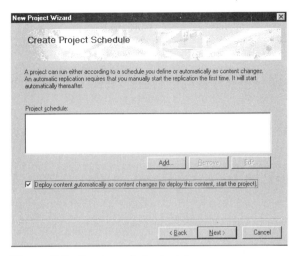

Figure 5-7. *Create project schedule.*

If we wanted to put the deployment on a particular time schedule, we could accomplish this by clicking the Add button, and specifying the schedule using the New Schedule dialog, shown in Figure 5-8.

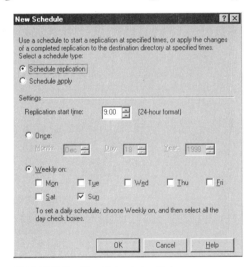

Figure 5-8. *New Schedule dialog.*

The final frame of the New Project Wizard will give us a summary of the content deployment project we are about to create. To close out the wizard and create the project, click on the Finish button. At that time, Site Server will create the project with the indicated settings on both the staging server and the production servers. If you selected automatic replication, your project will initially be created in an idle state. To enable automatic replication, you must start the project. To do this using the Site Server MMC snap-in, perform the following steps:

1. Expand the Publishing Node.

2. Expand the node for your staging server.

3. Double-click the Projects node. In the listview object on the right side of the MMC, right-click on your project.

4. In the pop-up menu, select Start.

Once you have created your content deployment project using the wizard, you can modify its attributes at any time by editing the project's property sheet. To access the property sheet, simply right-click on the project and select Properties from the pop-up menu. This will invoke the property sheet. The property sheet allows you to edit the following attributes:

■   Project directory and destinations.

■   Include and exclude filtering. With this feature, you can instruct Site Server to include or exclude certain file types when replicating content. For example, you might add an exclude filter of *.DLL to prevent the replication of any DLLs.

■   E-mail notification: This allows you to instruct Site Server to send e-mail alerts to notify you of deployment success or failure.

- Scripts: This allows you to instruct Site Server to run a particular script before or after any content is sent or received. This is useful if you have any pre- or post-processing requirements for your replicated content. For example, you could replicate your content in a Zip file to save bandwidth, and then have a script on the destination server unzip it.

- Security: This allows you to specify any security information, such as NT accounts that have Administrator or Operator access to the project, an NT account that the project uses to access resources across the domain, and ACL replication options.

- Schedule: This allows you to add, edit, or delete deployment schedules.

- Other attributes, such as remote IIS virtual root creation and configuration, and advanced file matching options.

> **NOTE** You can create a content deployment project without using the wizard. We will illustrate this when we go through the metabase deployment project example. One thing to remember though: If you create a content deployment project without using the New Project Wizard, you must remember to create a project of the same name on the destination servers to receive the replicated content.

Creating a Metabase Deployment Project

Now that we have set up a deployment project to replicate our content from the staging server to the production servers, the next step is to create a project to replicate our IIS metabase settings. This will allow us to make our metabase changes on the staging server only, and replicate them to all of the production servers, either as a scheduled task, or manually with just a few mouse clicks.

WHAT IS THE IIS METABASE?

The Internet Information Server (IIS) metabase is a registry-like data store that is used to store configuration information used by the various services that ship with IIS. These services include the WWW service, the File Transfer Protocol (FTP) service, the Simple Mail Transfer Protocol (SMTP) service, and the Network News Transfer Protocol (NNTP) service.

Like the Windows registry, the IIS metabase uses a tree hierarchy to store configuration data. This tree hierarchy uses a classic container-object taxonomy, with the Computer node as the root object. The Computer node contains a node for each of the various services, which contain nodes for each of the service instances, and so on. The IIS metabase supports property inheritance, which allows you to set properties on upper-level nodes and propagate these changes down the entire depth of the taxonomy. This allows you to make global data changes quickly and easily.

There are several tools available to edit the IIS metabase. The most obvious one is the "Internet Service Manager" MMC snap-in. Another option is the Web-based Internet Service Manager application that ships with IIS. Yet another popular tool is MetaEdit, which ships with the IIS Resource Kit. MetaEdit exposes the IIS metabase taxonomy using the familiar RegEdit interface. You can also manipulate the IIS metabase through code by using the IIS Admin objects. These objects provide an ADSI implementation for the IIS metabase, thereby allowing you to write COM clients that manipulate the IIS metabase using the ADSI object model.

To get started, open up your Site Server MMC snap-in and expand the Publishing node and the node corresponding to your staging server. Right-click on the Projects node. On the resulting pop-up menu, click on New, then click on Project. This will invoke the New Project dialog, shown in Figure 5-9. Type in a project name, select Content Deploy Project as the project type, and click OK. This will automatically open the project's property sheet, shown in Figure 5-10.

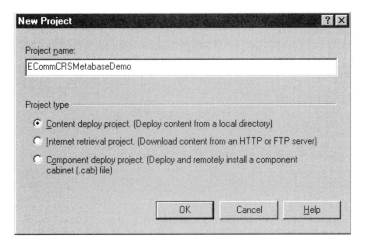

Figure 5-9. *Creating a new metabase replication project.*

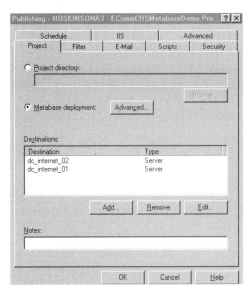

Figure 5-10. *The Metabase deployment project property sheet.*

On the Project tab of the property sheet, select the Metabase Deployment radio button, and click the Advanced button. This will invoke the IIS Metabase Deployment dialog, shown in Figure 5-11.

In the IIS Metabase Deployment dialog, select the Web site for which you want to replicate metabase settings, and click OK. Then, returning to the project property sheet, add your destination servers. Fill out the rest of the property sheet appropriately, and click OK when you are done. At this time, Site Server will create the project on the staging server.

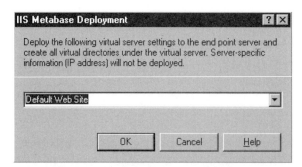

Figure 5-11. *Selecting an IIS virtual root for metabase deployment.*

To complete the task, you must now create a metabase deployment project of the same name on each of the destination servers. The destination servers' projects will be identical to the staging server's project, with one exception. Since the destination servers' projects exist merely to receive incoming metabase data, their destination list will be empty. Once you have done that, you can start the project to force a manual metabase deployment, or schedule a deployment for a specific time. There is one scheduling limitation, though; you cannot schedule a metabase replication to occur automatically as content changes, like you can with a content deployment project. This option is disabled for metabase deployments.

USING SITE SERVER SEARCH TO CREATE A WEB SITE SEARCH ENGINE

Every good Web site needs a search engine to allow visitors to quickly find the information in which they are most interested. This section will show you how to accomplish this quickly and easily using Site Server Search.

The Scenario

To illustrate this, let's say you run a Web storefront that sells outdoor adventure gear. You want to provide your customers with the ability to conduct focused searches of your Web site to virtually any degree of sophistication; anything from simple keyword searches to complex Boolean expressions. You also want to reserve the option to isolate the catalog build and search servers from your production Web servers, if needed, to improve performance and facilitate scalability. Your Web site is a combination of static documents and dynamic, database-driven ASP scripts.

To meet these requirements, we will walk through the following tasks:

1. Building a search catalog to index your Web storefront's content

2. Writing an ASP script that uses the MSSearch.Query object to search your catalog

Building a Search Catalog

We will use the New Catalog Definition Wizard to build our search catalog. To access this wizard, open the Site Server MMC snap-in, expand the Search node, expand your server's node, and right-click on the Catalog Build Server node. From the pop-up menu, select New Catalog Definition With A Wizard. This will invoke the opening frame of the wizard. To get started, click the Next button.

The next frame in the wizard is entitled Name the Catalog. This frame is shown in Figure 5-12. Type in a descriptive catalog name, and click Next.

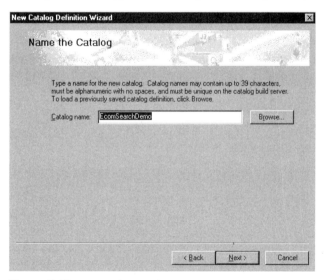

Figure 5-12. *Name the Catalog.*

The next step is to specify the crawl type, shown in Figure 5-13. There are three types of crawls you can do: a Web link crawl, which builds the catalog by following links from a top-level document and indexing all pages encountered; a File crawl, which indexes all files and subdirectories in a given directory; and an Exchange crawl, which indexes all MAPI objects in a given exchange server public folder. Select Web link crawl, and click Next.

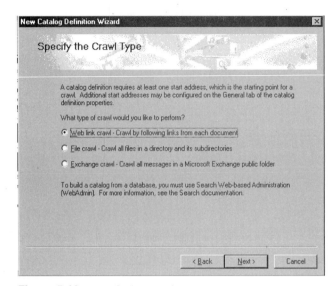

Figure 5-13. *Specify the crawl type.*

Next, you will configure a start address. This is shown in Figure 5-14. A start address is the URL of the top-level document of the site you want to index. Site Server will index this document first, follow all of the hyperlinks on that document, and index those documents as well. You can also use this frame to limit the depth to which Site Server will crawl the site. For example, as Figure 5-14 shows, you can tell Site Server not to follow any external links by checking the Site Hops check box, and specifying 0 as the number of site hops to make.

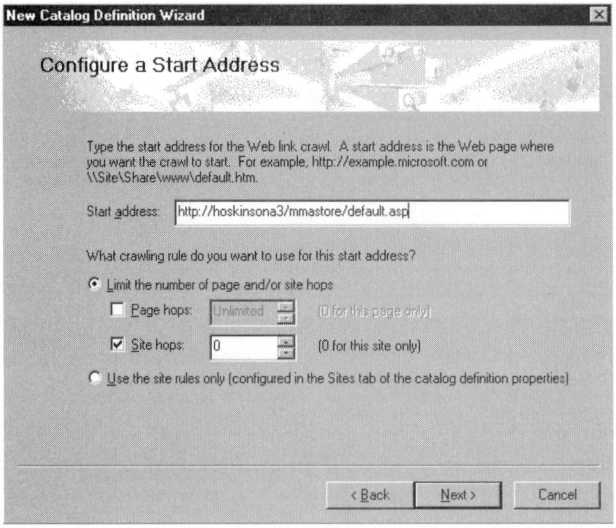

Figure 5-14. *Configure a start address.*

The next step is to select the search servers to which you want to propagate the completed catalog. This step is shown in Figure 5-15. One of the advantages of Site Server Search is that it allows you to isolate both the catalog build and the search process to separate, dedicated servers, if desired. That way, the WWW service on your production Web servers is not competing with Site Server Search for server resources.

Figure 5-15. *Select search hosts.*

The next frame, shown in Figure 5-16, allows you to complete the catalog creation process. To do this, simply click the Finish button. If you want, you can start the build process immediately by checking the check box labeled Start Build Now.

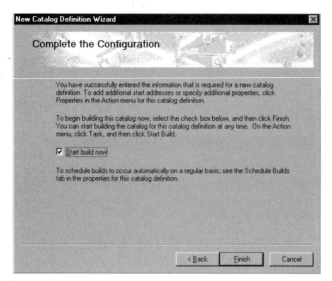

Figure 5-16. *Build the catalog.*

Once you have built your catalog, you can modify your catalog definition by editing the property sheet shown in Figure 5-17. For example, you can use the property sheet to schedule incremental or full catalog builds to keep the content in your search catalog up to date. You can access the property sheet by right-clicking on your newly created catalog build definition, and selecting Properties from the pop-up menu. For our example, we will go to the URLs tab, and ensure that the Follow URLs Containing Question Marks check box is checked, since our site uses a lot of ASP scripts with query strings that perform database queries. One thing to remember: If you modify your catalog definition, it is a good idea to rebuild your catalog. You can do this at any time by right-clicking on your catalog build project, selecting All Tasks from the pop-up menu, and then selecting Start Build.

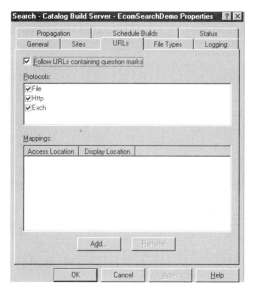

Figure 5-17. *The Catalog Build Project property sheet.*

Writing an ASP Search Script

Once you have defined, built, and propagated your Site Server search catalog, you can write ASP scripts to allow your end users to search the catalog. Site Server Search provides a COM object called MSSearch.Query that allows you to put together fairly sophisticated search engines rather quickly. Putting together an ASP search script for your search catalog is a simple four-step process:

Step 1: Create an instance of MSSearch.Query:

```
set objConn = Server.CreateObject("MSSearch.Query")
```

Step 2: Set some properties of your MSSearch.Query instance. These properties define the search string, which catalog to search, how to sort the search results, which document properties to return, and a limit on the number of records to return:

```
objConn.Query = strFilter
objConn.SortBy = "rank[d]"
objConn.MaxRecords = 300
objConn.Catalog = "EcomSearchDemo"
objConn.Columns = "DocTitle, DocAddress, " &_
                  "FileSize, FileWrite, rank"
```

Step 3: Execute the search. This will return an ADODB.Recordset object:

```
Set objRS = objConn.CreateRecordSet("sequential")
```

> NOTE   For more information on ActiveX Data Objects (ADO) in general
> and the ADODB.Recordset object in particular, please see Chapter 8. For
> more information on ASP scripting, see Chapter 7. For more information
> on HTML, see Chapter 13.

Step 4: Display the returned recordset as an HTML table.

The following code listing gives you a complete example of how to create a Site Server Search ASP script. This script is also located on the companion CD-ROM, in the SSSearch.asp file. Figure 5-18 on page 150 shows how this script looks when executed in a Web browser.

```
Code Listing for SSSearch.asp

<%
'***********************************
'This ASP script executes a search
'against a Site Server Search catalog
'***********************************
Option Explicit

On error resume next

'Boolean flag that indicates whether
'or not to execute the search
Dim boolCanRun

'The Site Server Search Query object
Dim objConn

'The returned recordset object
Dim objRS

'The search string
Dim strFilter

'A counter object
Dim intRecordCount

'Initially set the flag to true
boolCanRun = true
```

```
'Get the search string from the ASP request object
strFilter = Request("filter")

'If the search string is null or zero length, don't
'execute the search; display the search form only.

if IsNull(strFilter) or strFilter = "" then

    boolCanRun = false

end if

%>
<html>

<head>
<meta http-equiv="Content-Type"
content="text/html; charset=iso-8859-1">
<title>Site Server Search Sample</title>
</head>

<body bgcolor="#FFFFFF">

<p align="center"><font color="#000080" size="5" face="Arial">
<strong>Site Server Search Sample</strong></font></p>

<p><font face="Arial">This script is an example of how to use
the <i>MsSearch.Query</i> object in an ASP script to search data
in a Site Server Search catalog.</font></p>

<p><font face="Arial">Using the form below, enter a query.
This query can include boolean operators (such as AND, OR, and
NOT):</font></p>

<form action="SSSearch.asp" method="POST">
    <p><font color="#000080" face="Arial">
    <strong>Query:</strong></font>
    <font face="Arial">
    <input type="text" size="30" name="filter"
value="<%=server.HTMLEncode(strFilter)%>">
    <input type="submit" value="Submit"></font></p>
</form>

<%
'Now search the catalog, if appropriate
if boolCanRun then
```

(continued)

147

Code Listing for SSSearch.asp *(continued)*

```
    set objConn = Server.CreateObject("MSSearch.Query")

    objConn.Query = strFilter
    objConn.SortBy = "rank[d]"
    objConn.MaxRecords = 300
    objConn.Catalog = "EcomSearchDemo"
    objConn.Columns =    "DocTitle, DocAddress, " &_
                         "FileSize, FileWrite, rank"

    Set objRS = objConn.CreateRecordSet("sequential")

    'As long as no errors occur...
    if err.number = 0 then

        'Set our counter to zero
        intRecordCount = 0
%>

<p><font face="Arial" size="4">Search Results for query
'<%=strFilter%>':</font></p>

<table border="1" cellspacing="0">
    <tr>
        <td bgcolor="#C0C0C0"><font face="Arial">Title</font></td>
        <td bgcolor="#C0C0C0"><font face="Arial">URL</font></td>
        <td bgcolor="#C0C0C0"><font face="Arial">Size</font></td>
        <td bgcolor="#C0C0C0">
            <font face="Arial">Last Modified</font>
        </td>
        <td bgcolor="#C0C0C0"><font face="Arial">Rank</font></td>
    </tr>

<%
    'Loop through the recordset until there are no more records...
    Do while not objRS.EOF

        'For each record, insert the value of each field into
        'the appropriate HTML table cell
%>
    <tr>
        <td><font face="Arial">
            <%=objRS("DocTitle")%> </font>
        </td>
        <td><font face="Arial">
            <a href="<%=objRS("DocAddress")%>">
              <%=objRS("DocAddress")%>
            </a> 
```

```
                        </font>
            </td>
            <td><font face="Arial">
                <%=objRS("filesize")%> bytes </font>
            </td>
            <td><font face="Arial">
                <%=objRS("filewrite")%> </font>
            </td>
            <td><font face="Arial">
                <%=objRS("rank")%> </font>
            </td>
        </tr>
<%

        'Move the pointer to the next record
        objRS.MoveNext

        'Increment our counter by one
        intRecordCount = intRecordCount + 1


    loop
%>
</table>
<%

    'If our counter is still zero at this point,
    'then there were no records in our recordset.
    'Therefore, we need to display the appropriate message
    'to the user.

    if intRecordCount = 0 then
%>
<p><font face="Arial">
Your search did not return any products. Please try again.
</font></p>
<%else%>
<p><font face="Arial"><b>Record Count:</b>
<%=intRecordCount%>
</font></p>
<%end if

    'If there was an error...
    else%>
 <p><font face="Arial"><strong>Your search returned the following
error:</strong></p>
 <p><strong>Number:</strong>   <%=err.number%></p>
 <p><STRONG>Description:</STRONG>   <%=err.description%></p>
```

(continued)

(continued)

```
<p>Please try again.</font></p>
<%
end if

set objRS = nothing
set objConn = nothing

end if
%>

</body>
</html>
```

Figure 5-18. *The completed search engine.*

USING P&M FOR USER AUTHENTICATION AND PERSONALIZATION

Site Server P&M gives developers a great toolset for managing large communities of users and building personalization into Web commerce solutions. As Figure 5-19 shows, P&M gives you the ability to:

■   Implement a variety of different authentication scenarios with the membership authentication service, including HTTP basic authentication, HTML Forms authentication, and automatic cookie authentication.

■   Store a variety of different user attributes and preferences in a LDAP-compliant membership directory that can be accessed and manipulated by any COM client using the ADSI object model.

■   Create personalized content based on a user's preferences quickly and easily using the Active User Object (AUO).

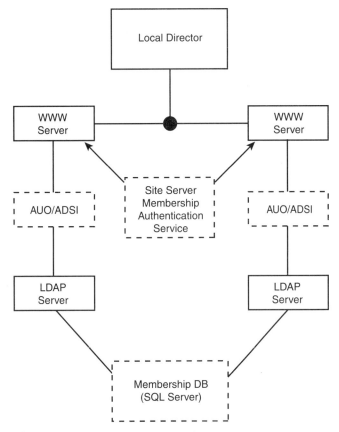

Figure 5-19. *Site Server's P&M architecture.*

To illustrate these capabilities, this section will walk you through the creation of a simple P&M framework for a hypothetical customer extranet. Building this framework will involve the following tasks:

1. Creating a new membership server instance

2. Binding this membership server instance to a Web site

3. Writing a user registration ASP application

4. Creating a personalized product page using AUO

The Scenario

You're a wholesaler. Your organization sells bulk quantities of outdoor adventure equipment to retailers, who then turn around and sell the merchandise to consumers. To automate the supply chain, you want to set up a private extranet for your customers, the retailers.

This extranet will provide a secure way for your customers' purchasing agents to find out about available product inventory, and to order bulk quantities of merchandise online. It will also offer personalization; purchasing agents will be able to specify a product category in which they are interested, and the extranet's home page will be personalized to display available products in that category.

Creating a New Membership Server Instance

The first task is to create a new membership server instance. You can accomplish this using the New Membership Server Wizard. To start the wizard, open your Site Server MMC snap-in, expand the Personalization and Membership node, right-click on your server's name, select New from the pop-up menu, and then select Membership Server Instance. This will invoke the wizard's welcome frame. Click the Next button to continue with the wizard.

The first step is to select your configuration mode. This step is shown in Figure 5-20. Since we are building our membership server from scratch, select Complete Configuration, and click Next.

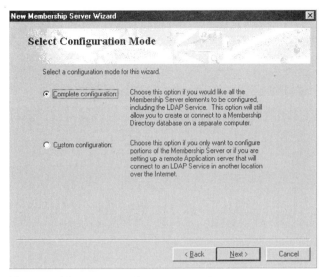

Figure 5-20. *Select Configuration Mode.*

The next step is to select the membership directory to connect to. This is shown in Figure 5-21. Once again, since we are building our membership server from scratch, we will select Create a New Membership Directory.

Figure 5-21. *Select the Membership Directory.*

The next step is to select an authentication mode. This is shown in Figure 5-22. There are two choices: to use membership authentication, or Windows NT authentication. Since we are going to use this membership server instance with our fictional customer extranet, we will use membership authentication.

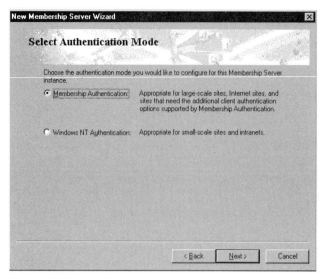

Figure 5-22. *Select Authentication Mode.*

The next step is to name the membership directory and specify a password for the Administrator account. This is shown in Figure 5-23. We will name our membership directory EcomPMDemo.

> **WARNING!**   The Administrator account in a membership server instance is, by default, a SUPERBROKER account. This basically means that anybody logged onto the membership server as the Administrator can do anything they want. Consequently, you should take care to ensure that the Administrator password is as "crackproof" as possible (that is, use a mixture of uppercase and lowercase letters and numbers, as well as other common safeguards), and you should write it down and store it in a secure place, such as a safe. Please see the Site Server documentation for more guidance.

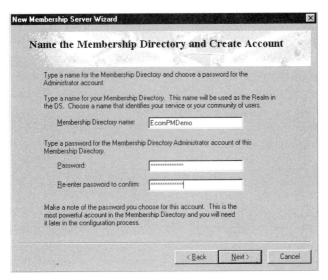

Figure 5-23. *Name the membership Directory and Create Account.*

The next step is to select the database type. This is shown in Figure 5-24. There are two choices: Microsoft Access, or SQL Server. For large-scale production sites, you should definitely use SQL Server, because Access does not scale well to high-volume sites. For small-scale sites, such as workgroup or departmental intranets, development servers, or demo servers, you can get away with using Microsoft Access. For the purposes of this demo, we will use Microsoft Access.

NOTE   When in doubt, use SQL Server as your Membership Directory backend database.

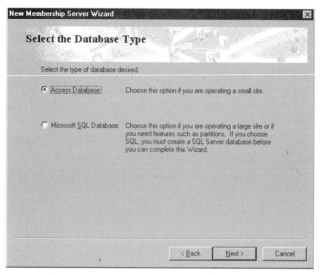

Figure 5-24. *Select the database type.*

The next step is to create the new database. This is shown in Figure 5-25. If you selected Microsoft Access as your membership directory backend, this portion of the wizard will allow you to identify the location and the name of the MS Access database that will host your membership directory. The wizard, of course, will generate the actual MDB file and database schema.

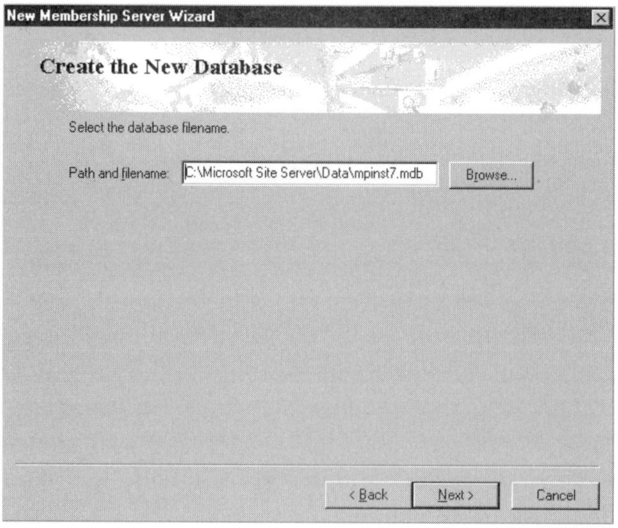

Figure 5-25. *Create the new database.*

The next step is to create the local LDAP service. This is shown in Figure 5-26. This frame allows you to select the IP address and port for the LDAP service instance that will be bound to your membership server instance. The IP address defaults to All Unassigned, and the port number defaults to the next available IP port, but advanced users can modify this to meet their specific needs.

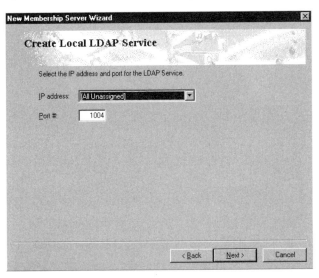

Figure 5-26. *Create local LDAP service.*

The last step is to configure the message builder service. This is shown in Figure 5-27. As we mentioned before, the message builder service gives you the ability to create targeted mailings based on users' preferences, both stated (for example, preferences indicated on a user registration form) and implied (for example, preferences gleaned from Web site usage analysis). The only thing the message builder service needs to know is to what SMTP service to connect for sending outbound mail.

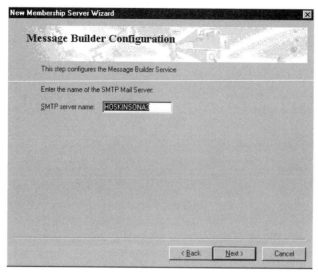

Figure 5-27. *Message builder configuration.*

WARNING!   A newly created membership server instance allows unrestricted, anonymous access. This allows you to use P&M prior to deciding on how secure your implementation needs to be, and also helps prevent accidental lock-outs. Nevertheless, for most production environments, you will need to tighten up the security of your membership server instance considerably. Please consult the "Securing a Membership Directory" topic in your Site Server online help for detailed information on how to do this.

Binding Your Membership Server to a Web Site

Once you have created your membership server instance, you must bind it to an IIS virtual root (Web site) to use it. To do this, perform the following steps:

1.   In the Site Server Admin MMC snap-in, open up the Internet Information Server node.

2.   Open up the node for your server.

3.   Right-click on the Web site to which you want to bind your membership server instance.

4.   From the pop-up menu, select All Tasks, and then select Membership Server Mapping. This will invoke the membership server mapping dialog.

5.   Select the membership server to which you want to bind this Web site, and click OK.

Once you are done, take a look at the property sheet for your Web site. You will notice a new property page called Membership Authentication. This is shown in Figure 5-28. For our fictional customer extranet demo, we will use HTML Forms Authentication, and we will also disallow anonymous access. To implement this, clear the Allow Anonymous check box, select HTML Forms Authentication, and click OK.

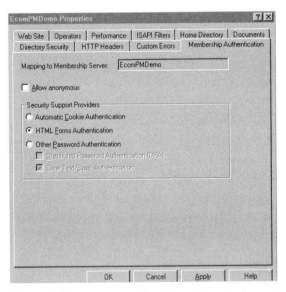

Figure 5-28. *Setting membership authentication properties for your Web site.*

Creating a User Registration Application Using ADSI

Now that you have created your membership server instance, bound it to your Web site, and configured your Web site to use HTML Forms authentication, you must create a way to register users for new accounts. To demonstrate this, we will create a Web-based user registration application. This application will consist of the following components:

1. An HTML form that collects the appropriate user information and posts it to an ASP script

2. A COM DLL, written in Visual Basic 6, that actually writes the new account to the membership directory

3. An ASP script that creates the aforementioned COM object and passes it the new user account information, encapsulated in the ASP Request object

Writing the HTML form

The first step is to write the HTML form that is used to collect account registration information from the end user. This form is shown in Figure 5-30 on page 168, and is also located on the companion CD-ROM in a file named UserReg.htm. This form can be created using any HTML editor, including FrontPage. This form will collect the following information:

■ The new account's userid, password, and the retyped password for confirmation

■ Personal information, such as name, street address, and e-mail address

■ A "preferred product category" for personalization (more on this later)

When the Submit button is clicked, the browser will post this information to an ASP script named register_user.asp. We'll take a look at how to write this script a little later. In the meantime, this is what the code looks like for the HTML form:

UserReg.htm Code Listing

```
<html>

<head>
<meta http-equiv="Content-Type"
content="text/html; charset=iso-8859-1">
<meta name="GENERATOR" content="Microsoft FrontPage Express 2.0">
<title>User Registration Form</title>
</head>

<body bgcolor="#FFFFFF">

<h1 align="center" style="BACKGROUND-COLOR: white">
<font color="#000080" size="6" face="Arial">User Registration
Form</font></h1>

<form action="register_user.asp" method="POST">
    <p style="BACKGROUND-COLOR: white"
    title="User Registration Form"><font face="Arial">Please fill
    this form out completely</font></p>
    <table border="0" cellspacing="1">
        <tr>
            <td valign="top"><table border="0" cellspacing="1">
```

```
<tr>
    <td><p align="left"><font face="Arial">
    UserID:  
    </font></p>
    </td>
    <td><font face="Arial"><input type="text"
    size="20" name="userid"></font></td>
</tr>
<tr>
    <td><p align="left"><font face="Arial">
        Password: 
    </font></p>
    </td>
    <td><font face="Arial"><input type="password"
    size="20" name="password"></font></td>
</tr>
<tr>
    <td><p align="left"><font face="Arial">Confirm
    Password:  </font></p>
    </td>
    <td><font face="Arial"><input type="password"
    size="20" name="confirmpassword"></font></td>
</tr>
<tr>
    <td><p align="left"><font face="Arial">
        Street: 
    </font></p>
    </td>
    <td><font face="Arial"><input type="text"
    size="20" name="street"></font></td>
</tr>
<tr>
    <td><p align="left"><font face="Arial">
        City: 
    </font></p>
    </td>
    <td><font face="Arial"><input type="text"
    size="20" name="city"></font></td>
</tr>
</table>
</td>
<td valign="top"><table border="0" cellspacing="1">
    <tr>
        <td><font face="Arial">First name: 
            </font></td>
        <td><font face="Arial"><input type="text"
```

(continued)

UserReg.htm Code Listing *(continued)*

```
                        size="20" name="firstname"></font></td>
            </tr>
            <tr>
                <td><font face="Arial">Last Name: 
                </font></td>
                <td><font face="Arial"><input type="text"
                size="20" name="lastname"></font></td>
            </tr>
            <tr>
                <td><font face="Arial">Email: 
                    </font></td>
                <td><font face="Arial"><input type="text"
                size="20" name="email"></font></td>
            </tr>
            <tr>
                <td><font face="Arial">State: 
                </font></td>
                <td><font face="Arial"><input type="text"
                size="3" name="state"></font></td>
            </tr>
            <tr>
                <td><font face="Arial">Zip: 
                </font></td>
                <td><font face="Arial"><input type="text"
                size="11" name="zip"></font></td>
            </tr>
        </table>
        </td>
    </tr>
</table>
<p><font face="Arial">Please select the product category in
which you are most interested:<br>
<select name="interests" size="1">
    <option selected>Backpack </option>
    <option>Parka </option>
    <option>Tent </option>
    <option>Carabiner </option>
    <option>SleepingBag </option>
    <option>Harness </option>
    <option>Supplies </option>
    <option>Boot </option>
    <option>Crampon </option>
</select></font></p>
    <p><input type="submit" value="Submit"> </p>
</form>
</body>
</html>
```

Writing the VB component

The second step is to write the COM object that will take the user's input and create a user object in the membership directory that encapsulates this input. The VB component uses ADSI to create the account. The entire project is located on the book CD-ROM. Creating the component is a relatively simple process:

1. Create an ActiveX DLL project.

2. Add an early binding reference to the ADSI and ASP type libraries (See Figure 5-29).

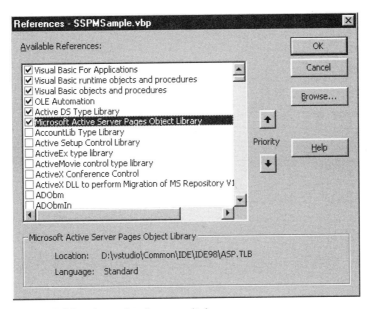

Figure 5-29. *The VB6 References dialog.*

3. Add constants for your membership directory's URL moniker, and the account you will use to log on your membership directory's LDAP service.

    NOTE The account you use to create your users' accounts must have sufficient access permissions to write a user object to your directory's *ou=members* container. Please see the Site Server documentation for more information.

4. Create a public method that actually creates the account. For this example, we'll call this method *CreateNewUser*. This method reads the new account information from the ASP Request object (which is passed to the method from the calling ASP script), and uses the ADSI

object model to connect to your LDAP server and add the account. The most important thing to remember when writing this method is that the element names in the Forms collection of the ASP Request object must match their counterparts in the HTML form.

To give you an example that illustrates this, let's take the user's first name. As you will recall from the previous section, the HTML form's input object into which the user types his first name looks like this:

```
<input type="text" size="20" name="firstname">
```

The line of code in the VB component that sets the first name looks like this:

```
objUser.Put "givenName",CStr(Trim(objRequest("firstname")))
```

Notice how they both use "firstname" as the identifying key.

Here's the complete code listing for our VB user registration component:

MembershipManager.cls Code Listing

```
''*******************************************
'  LDAP business object
'  Written by Andy Hoskinson
'*******************************************
Option Explicit

'The path to our Site Server Membership Directory
Private Const LDAP_PATH = "LDAP://hoskinsona3:1004/" &_
                          "ou=Members,o=EcomPMDemo"

'Logon credentials for our membership directory
Private Const ADMIN_USER = "cn=UserRegAccount,ou=Members, " &_
                           "o=EcomPMDemo"
Private Const ADMIN_PASSWORD = "password"


Public Sub CreateNewUser(ByVal objRequest As Request)

    On Error GoTo errorhandler

    'An object reference that points to our LDAP Namespace
    Dim objNamespace As ActiveDs.IADsOpenDSObject

    'An object reference that points to our membership directory
    Dim objDirectory As ActiveDs.IADsContainer

    'An object reference that points to a user in the directory
```

```
Dim objUser As ActiveDs.IADs

Dim strCurrUser As String

'Site Server's GUID generator
Dim objGuidGen

'The user's GUID
Dim strGUIDVal As String

'Get the UserID from the ASP Request object
strCurrUser = Trim(CStr(objRequest("userid")))

'Before adding the user, verify that the passwords match...
If PasswordsMatch(CStr(objRequest("password")), _
        CStr(objRequest("confirmpassword"))) Then

    'Hook into LDAP first
    Set objNamespace = GetObject("LDAP:")

    'Log onto our membership server instance
    Set objDirectory = objNamespace.OpenDSObject(LDAP_PATH,_
                    ADMIN_USER, ADMIN_PASSWORD, 0)

    'Create our new user
    Set objUser = objDirectory.Create("member",_
                "cn=" & strCurrUser)

    'Generate a unique GUID for the user
    Set objGuidGen = CreateObject("Membership.GuidGen.1")
    strGUIDVal = objGuidGen.GenerateGuid
    objUser.Put "GUID", CStr(strGUIDVal)
    Set objGuidGen = Nothing

    'Set the user's properties
    objUser.Put "userPassword",_
                CStr(Trim(objRequest("password")))
    objUser.Put "mail", CStr(Trim(objRequest("email")))
    objUser.Put "givenName",_
                CStr(Trim(objRequest("firstname")))
    objUser.Put "sn", CStr(Trim(objRequest("lastname")))
    objUser.Put "street", CStr(Trim(objRequest("street")))
    objUser.Put "l", CStr(Trim(objRequest("city")))
    objUser.Put "st", CStr(Trim(objRequest("state")))
    objUser.Put "postalCode", CStr(Trim(objRequest("zip")))
    objUser.Put "topicInterests",_
```

(continued)

MembershipManager.cls Code Listing *(continued)*

```
                CStr(Trim(objRequest("interests")))

        'Set the account status to active (1)
        objUser.accountstatus = 1

        'Commit the changes
        objUser.SetInfo

        'Release our objects
        Set objUser = Nothing
        Set objDirectory = Nothing
        Set objNamespace = Nothing

    Else

        'If the passwords didn't match, raise an error back
        'to the client

        App.LogEvent "SSPMSample logged the following error: " &_
                "The two passwords sent to the " &_
                "CreateNewUser method do not match. " &_
                "These passwords were submitted by " &_
                strCurrUser & "."
        Err.Raise 9999 + vbObjectError, "SSPMSample",_
                "The two passwords " &_
                "sent to the CreateNewUser method " &_
                "do not match."
        Exit Sub

    End If

Exit Sub
Errorhandler:

    'If a runtime error occurs, log it and raise it back to
    'the client

    App.LogEvent "SSPMSample logged the following error in " &_
                "the CreateNewUser method: " & Err.Number &_
                ", " & Err.Description & ". This error " &_
                "was caused by " & strCurrUser & "."
    Err.Raise Err.Number, "SSPMSample", Err.Description

End Sub

Private Function PasswordsMatch(strPassword As String,_
                strConfirmPassword As String) As Boolean
```

```
        'This function checks the two passwords to ensure
    'that they match

    Dim intComparevalue As Integer

    intComparevalue = StrComp(strPassword,_
                    strConfirmPassword, vbBinaryCompare)

    If intComparevalue = 0 Then

        PasswordsMatch = True

    Else

        PasswordsMatch = False

    End If

End Function
```

Writing the ASP script

Finally, we need to write an ASP script that "glues" together our HTML form
(shown in Figure 5-30 on the next page) and our VB component. This ASP script,
which is our HTML form's action handler, creates an instance of our VB component, and calls the CreateNewUser method, passing a copy of the ASP Request object to it. If the account creation succeeds, it let's the user know. If it
fails, it informs the user of whatever error occurred. Our ASP script, entitled
register_user.asp, is located on the book CD-ROM. This is what the code looks like:

Register_user.asp Code Listing

```
<%
option explicit
on error resume next
%>
<HTML>
<HEAD>
<TITLE>
Registration Status
</TITLE>
</HEAD>
<BODY bgcolor="#FFFFFF">

<%dim objMemMgr
```

(continued)

Register_user.asp Code Listing *(continued)*

```
set objMemMgr =
Server.CreateObject("SSPMSample.MembershipManager")

objMemMgr.CreateNewUser Request
if err.number = 0 then
%>
<font face="Arial">
<p>
Your registration was successful!
</p>
</font>
<%else%>
<font face="Arial">
<p>
Your registration failed with the following error:
<BR>
Number:   <%=err.number%>
<br>
Description:   <%=err.description%>
</p>
</font>

<%end if%>
</body>
</html>
<%set objMemMgr = nothing%>
```

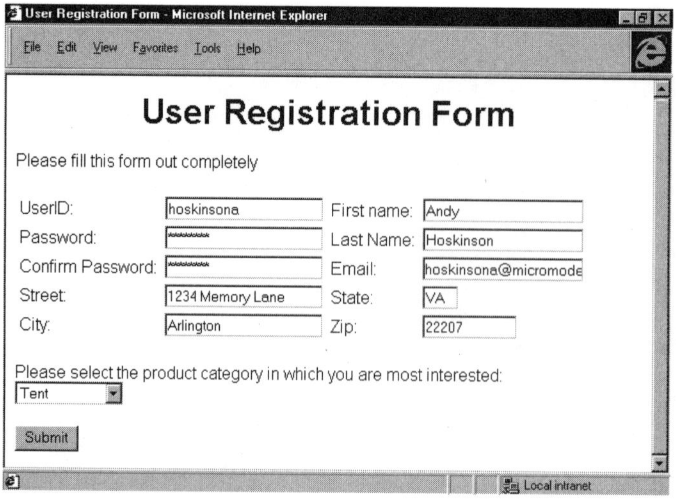

Figure 5-30. *The completed user registration application.*

We now have a browser-based application that we can use to create new user accounts for our customer extranet. Of course, we can also use the Site Server Membership Directory Manager to add, edit, delete, or administer user accounts. To access this, open up the Site Server Admin MMC snap-in, and right-click the Membership Directory Manager node. You will see the Membership Directory Manager Properties dialog, shown in Figure 5-31. Make sure that the entries for host name and port are correct, and click OK.

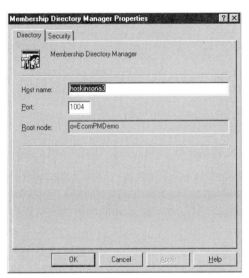

Figure 5-31. *Connecting to your Membership Directory using Membership Directory Manager.*

Open up the container marked ou=members, and double-click on one of the users. This will open up the User Properties dialog, shown in Figure 5-32. From this dialog, you can edit the user's attributes, consistent (of course) with your account's permissions.

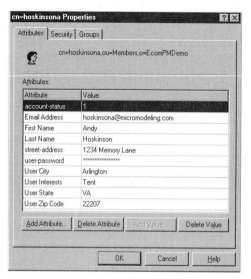

Figure 5-32. *Editing a user using Membership Directory Manager.*

Implementing Personalization Using AUO

Thus far, in building our customer extranet, we have created a membership server, bound it to a Web site, implemented HTML Forms authentication, and built a user registration application. Now, we will finish up by designing a personalized products page for our users. We will accomplish this using the AUO, or Active User Object.

Before diving into the AUO code, let's review how HTML Forms authentication works. When an anonymous user first accesses a Web site that is secured with HTML Forms Authentication, an authentication ISAPI filter redirects the user to an HTML login form. This form is shown in Figure 5-33. The user supplies his credentials, and clicks the Login button. A backend ASP script authenticates the user against the membership directory. If authentication succeeds, the user is redirected to the originally requested page. If authentication fails, the user is redirected back to the Login page.

> **NOTE**   The Login form in Figure 5-33 is the default form that ships with Site Server 3.0. Web developers can certainly modify this form, if desired, to fit their site's "look and feel."

Figure 5-33. *Logging on a Web site using HTML Forms Authentication.*

Once authentication succeeds, the Membership.verifusr.1 object writes a FormsAuth cookie to the client. This is a RAM-based cookie that contains the user's hashed credentials. Subsequent requests to the Web site within a certain timeout period are automatically authenticated using the credentials contained in the FormsAuth cookie. The cookie expires when the browser session is ended or is idle for a length of time exceeding the timeout period. By default, the timeout period is 10 minutes, although administrators can change this using the Site Server MMC snap-in.

> **NOTE** For an additional layer of security, Webmasters should consider using SSL (Secure Socket Layer) encryption on top of HTML Forms Authentication. This will greatly reduce the risk of a third party using a protocol analyzer to "sniff" userids and passwords sent in the clear. It will also greatly reduce the risk of a "replay" attack using the FormsAuth cookie. Please see the Site Server documentation for more information.

Once a user is logged on, you can use AUO to obtain all of the information stored about that user in the membership directory. In fact, it takes literally only one line of ASP code to do this:

```
set objUser = server.createobject("Membership.UserObjects")
```

With this line of code, you now have a pointer to the ADSI user object representing the logged-on user. If you want to greet the user by name, you can do it with this single line of code:

```
Hello, <%= objUser.givenName %>!
```

It gets better, though. Remember how, when we were writing the user registration application, we decided to store a product category preference for each user? With AUO, we can query a products database for all products that match this preference by constructing a SQL statement that looks like this:

```
strSQL = "select * from Products where ProductType like '" &_
         objUser.topicInterests & "' Order By ProductName"
```

We can then execute this query using ADO, and display the "preferred products" to the user, as shown in Figure 5-34 on page 176.

Here's the code listing for our personalized product page:

Code Listing for default.asp—Our Personalized Home Page

```
<%
Option Explicit

'The ADO connection object
Dim objConn

'The ADO recordset object
Dim objRS

'The SQL statement
Dim strSQL

'A counter object
Dim intRecordCount

'The current user
Dim objUser

'Instantiate AUO
set objUser = server.createobject("Membership.UserObjects")
%>
<html>
<head>
```

```
<Title>
<%= objUser.givenName & " " & objUser.sn %>'s Custom Product Page
</title>
</head>
<body bgcolor="#ffffff">
<font face="Arial">
<h1 align="center"><font color="#000080">
<%= objUser.givenName & " " & objUser.sn %>'s Custom Product Page
</font></h1>
<h3>
Hello, <%= objUser.givenName %>!
</h3>
<p>
Thanks for coming back!  How are things in
<%= objUser.l %>, <%= objUser.st %> this fine day?
</p>


<p>
Here are some products we know you'll be interested in:
</p>
<%
'Create the ADO connection object
set objConn = Server.createObject("ADODB.Connection")

'Open the Adventure Works database
objConn.Open "DSN=AdvWorks"

'Create our SQL statement based on the value of the current user's
preferences
strSQL = "select * from Products where ProductType like '" &_
        objUser.topicInterests & "' Order By ProductName"

'Execute the search. This will return an ADO recordset
set objRS = objConn.Execute(strSQL)

'Set our counter to zero
intRecordCount = 0
%>
<table border="1" cellspacing="0">
    <tr>
        <td bgcolor="#C0C0C0"><font face="Arial">Name</font></td>
        <td bgcolor="#C0C0C0"><font face="Arial">Type</font></td>
        <td bgcolor="#C0C0C0">
            <font face="Arial">Description</font>
        </td>
        <td bgcolor="#C0C0C0">
```

(continued)

Code Listing for default.asp, Our Personalized Home Page *(continued)*

```
                <font face="Arial">Available Sizes</font>
        </td>
        <td bgcolor="#C0C0C0"><font face="Arial">Price</font></td>
    </tr>
<%
    'Loop through the recordset until there are no more records...
    Do while not objRS.EOF

        'For each record, insert the value of each field into
        'the appropriate HTML table cell
%>
    <tr>
        <td>
            <font face="Arial">
                <%=objRS("ProductName")%> 
            </font>
        </td>
        <td>
            <font face="Arial">
                <%=objRS("ProductType")%> 
            </font>
        </td>
        <td>
            <font face="Arial">
                <%=objRS("ProductDescription")%> 
            </font>
        </td>
        <td>
            <font face="Arial">
                <%=objRS("ProductSize")%> 
            </font>
        </td>
        <td>
            <font face="Arial">
                <%=FormatCurrency(objRS("UnitPrice"))%> 
            </font>
        </td>
    </tr>
<%
        'Move the pointer to the next record
        objRS.MoveNext

        'Increment our counter by one
        intRecordCount = intRecordCount + 1

    loop
```

```
%>
</table>
<%
    'If our counter is still zero at this point, then
    'there were no records in our recordset. Therefore, we
    'need to display the appropriate message to the user.

    if intRecordCount = 0 then
%>
<p><font face="Arial">
Your search did not return any products. Please try again.
</font></p>
<%
    end if

'Clean up our ADO objects by closing down all
'connections and releasing the objects

objRS.close
objConn.close

set objRS = nothing
set objConn = nothing

'Clean up our user object
set objUser = nothing
%>
</font>
</body>
</html>
```

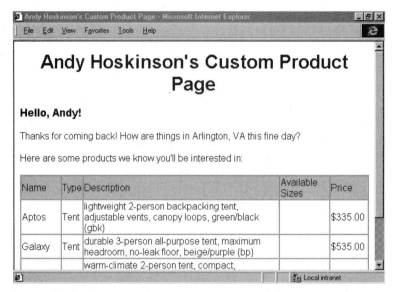

Figure 5-34. *The personalized home page.*

SUMMARY

In this chapter, we discussed a few ideas about how you can use the core services of Microsoft Site Server 3.0 to facilitate the process of building feature-rich, scalable, user-friendly Web commerce solutions in a relatively short period of time. There are many other ways to use Site Server's core services to enhance your Web site; one chapter is insufficient to cover them all! The best thing to do is to get your hands on the product, and start using it. In the next chapter, we will discuss ways you can use the commerce-specific functionality that is available with Site Server Commerce Edition to rapidly build sophisticated, scalable, and extensible business-to-consumer and business-to-business e-commerce solutions.

Chapter 6

Site Server Commerce Services

by Andy Hoskinson

It's Monday morning, and you're reading the business section of the local newspaper before going to work. As CIO of a retail operation, you want to stay on top of business trends that might impact your company and market. You know you are going to have a bad day when you read an article entitled "Is Your Company Falling Behind in the Race to Stake an E-Commerce Homestead on the Web?" You know your boss, the CEO, is probably reading this article, too, and there's going to be trouble when you get to work. Sure, you have a Web site, but it's just "brochureware"; while it provides a useful presence for your company on the Web, it doesn't generate any revenue. Your boss has been on you for the past few months about getting this fixed, but you haven't made any tangible progress, aside from conducting research on the barrage of products out there.

Sure enough, when you get to work, your assistant tells you that the boss needs to see you "yesterday." You trudge over to his office, and he is waiting for you with the newspaper in hand, pointing at the article. "I pay you big bucks to keep us ahead of the IT power curve. I want to sell products over the Web ASAP, and I want it done right. Get this fixed!"

As you go back to your office, you review the options. You know it is not as simple as that. This requirement has a lot of "implied" tasks and unstated requirements. You know you can buy an off-the-shelf third-party e-commerce application, but what happens when you need to customize it? What happens when you need to make radical changes to the look and feel of the site? What happens when you need to add components to the site to implement your company's proprietary business logic? Will it scale to your site's inevitable exponential grow in traffic? Will it integrate with your suppliers' and business partners' systems?

What you really need is a product that will get your site up and running quickly, while at the same time allowing an almost infinite level of customization. It should provide authoring wizards that will quickly create fully functional Web storefronts that are based on Web commerce best practices. At the same time, you should have complete control over the end product and should be able to make whatever changes you need to make. It should provide an application development framework and APIs that allow your in-house developers (or third-party ISVs) to create reusable custom components that plug into your commerce application with little effort. It should be based on open architecture and should interact well in a heterogeneous environment.

If this describes your situation, you should take a look at Microsoft Site Server 3.0 Commerce Edition. This product builds on the Microsoft Active Server platform by providing an extensive collection of COM objects, services, and Win32- and browser-based authoring tools that allow you to create sophisticated Web-based business-to-consumer and business-to-business e-commerce solutions. With Site Server Commerce Edition, you can create fully functional Web storefronts quickly and easily, and customize and extend the look, feel, and functionality of the resulting e-commerce site to meet your specific needs.

WHAT IS SITE SERVER COMMERCE EDITION?

Site Server Commerce Edition creates Web storefronts that are three-tier ASP applications hosted on a server running Microsoft Windows NT Server and Microsoft Internet Information Server (and optionally, Microsoft Transaction Server). These ASP applications are written using VBScript, JScript, or any other scripting language that has an interpreter written to the Microsoft Active Scripting

Interface standard. They use all of the usual COM objects that ASP developers find useful, such as the intrinsic ASP objects (Application, Session, Response, Request, and Server) and ActiveX Data Objects (ADO) for OLE DB data access. What makes them unique is that they also use a collection of over 50 custom COM objects that ship with Site Server Commerce Edition. These COM objects each encapsulates a particular commerce-related business rule, such as credit card validation, price adjusting, inventory control, and purchase order generation. Therein lies the heart of Site Server Commerce Edition's utility. Figure 6-1 shows the typical architecture of a Site Server Commerce Edition application.

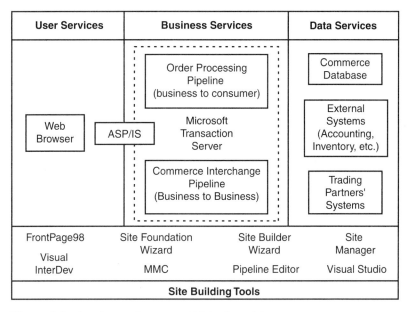

Figure 6-1. *Site Server Commerce Edition's architecture.*

Site Server Commerce Edition's Pipeline Framework

What makes these COM objects unique is the fact that they plug into a common framework called a *pipeline*. Site Server Commerce Edition's pipeline framework gives the e-commerce site builder an extensible, scalable architecture and API for creating highly specialized e-commerce applications of virtually any degree of complexity.

What is a pipeline?

In the commerce world, a *pipeline* is a generic term that describes a business process model composed of a list of tasks that are performed in a particular sequence to facilitate the orderly transfer of goods and services in exchange for money. Simply put, a pipeline is a channel that gets a product from the manufacturer to the consumer. To put this in perspective, let's say that you are going to the grocery store. There are certain tasks you and the merchant will perform to get you the groceries you want and to get the merchant the money he wants. For example:

1. You browse around the store, looking at product information such as cost, ingredients, and brand name to determine the best deal.

2. When you find a product you want, you put it in your shopping cart.

3. If you decide that you don't want a particular product after all, you take it out of your shopping cart and put it back on the shelf.

4. When you have everything you need, you go to the checkout counter.

5. The cashier rings up your order and calculates your total cost.

6. You swipe your credit card through the credit card machine.

7. If your credit card account has enough available credit, funds are committed, your bill is paid, you get a receipt, and you leave the store with your goods.

Site Server Commerce Edition automates the pipeline process by defining two generic COM object interfaces: IPipeline to represent the pipeline (the collection of tasks) and IPipelineComponent to represent the pipeline components (the tasks themselves).

NOTE   For more information on Microsoft's COM (Component Object Model) architecture, please take a look at Chapter 9.

Pipeline objects

A Site Server Commerce pipeline is a COM object that implements the IPipeline COM interface. A pipeline wraps a collection of components that each implements the IPipelineComponent COM interface. These COM objects are known simply as *pipeline components*. Site Server 3.0 Commerce Edition provides three generic types of pipeline classes:

■ *MtsTxPipeline,* which holds an (MTS) Microsoft Transaction Server transaction across all of its components. You should use this pipeline object when you need to maintain transactional integrity across components and retain the ability to commit or abort an entire pipeline as a single unit. See Chapter 11 for more information on MTS.

■ *MtsPipeline*, which is registered under MTS but does not support transactions. You should use this pipeline object if maintaining transactional integrity across components is not important.

■ *OrderPipeline*, an older object that ships with version 3.0 to provide backward compatibility with Site Server 2.0 commerce sites.

> NOTE The (MSDTC) Microsoft Distributed Transaction Coordinator service must be running in order to use the MtsTxPipeline object. If you are having problems creating and executing a MtsTxPipeline pipeline, this is one of the first things you should check.

Pipeline components

Pipelines execute their pipeline components in sequence. Each pipeline component encapsulates code that enforces a particular business rule on a business object. Site Server Commerce Edition typically uses two types of business objects in a pipeline: the Commerce.OrderForm object (also known as the OrderForm object) for business-to-consumer transactions and the Commerce.Dictionary object (also known as the Transport Dictionary) for business-to-business transactions. These objects are used to maintain state throughout the execution of the pipeline.

An OrderForm object is, as the name implies, an object that stores information relevant to a particular customer's order. For example, the OrderForm object stores a customer's shipping address, credit card information, a list of the products he or she wishes to purchase, among other information.

The Transport Dictionary stores a collection of key-value pairs that associate transactional meta-data (such as the transaction ID and whether or not a receipt is requested) with a business data object, such as the OrderForm object mentioned earlier.

Functional types of pipelines

Site Server Commerce Edition defines two different *functional* types of pipelines: the Order Processing Pipeline (OPP) for business-to-consumer transactions and the Commerce Interchange Pipeline (CIP) for business-to-business transactions.

The Order Processing Pipeline

The Order Processing Pipeline encapsulates logic that implements business-to-consumer transactions. The most common scenario for an OPP is a Web storefront, where individual customers shop for retail goods using secure, online credit card processing. As Figure 6-2 shows, a Web storefront's OPP is divided into three separate stages:

- The *product pipeline*, which executes components that compute price and discount information on individual products

- The *plan pipeline*, which executes components that present the shopper with an order total, including all discounts, taxes, and shipping and handling charges

- The *purchase pipeline*, which executes components that perform credit card validation and fund commitment, write the order to the store's database, and generate a receipt for the customer

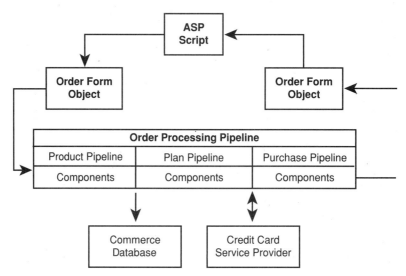

Figure 6-2. *The Order Processing Pipeline.*

The Commerce Interchange Pipeline

The Commerce Interchange Pipeline encapsulates logic that implements business-to-business transactions. There are many different scenarios under which two or more trading partners can conduct business, and the CIP architecture reflects this; Microsoft designed the CIP to be data and transport independent, to allow it to be used in virtually any supply chain automation scenario (more on this later). Some examples include:

- An online bookseller using an (EDI VAN) Electronic Data Interchange Value-Added Network to exchange purchase orders, invoices, and other EDI business documents with its suppliers (see EDI sidebar on page 191)

- An online retailer using SMTP e-mail with S/MIME encryption to exchange XML-formatted business documents with its suppliers over the Internet

- A large, worldwide franchiser using (DCOM) Distributed Component Object Model to exchange persisted COM business objects with its franchisees via a (PPTP) point-to-point tunneling protocol virtual private network (VPN)

But how, one might reasonably ask, does it work if it is not tied to a particular data format or transport protocol? The beauty of the CIP is that it automates a process and a framework, into which you can plug components that implement specific functionality, such as enforcing a proprietary business rule or integrating with an external system. Many of the components you would need are already provided to you as a part of Site Server Commerce Edition. Others can be purchased from third-party vendors. If all else fails, you can develop your own custom CIP component by implementing IPipelineComponent.

The CIP is divided into two distinct pipelines: the Transmit pipeline and the Receive pipeline. The Transmit pipeline, as Figure 6-3 shows, models the following process:

- **Mapping.** Takes information from a business data object (such as an OrderForm object) and maps it to virtually any type of business document format, such as an EDI 850 PO (purchase order) or an XML document. Site Server Commerce Edition ships with a MakePO component that allows you to generate text-based purchase orders in any format from a VBScript template.

- **Header data generation.** Appends transaction meta-data, such as a transaction ID, the transaction's date and time, a return receipt request, and sender and receiver addresses, to the aforementioned document.

- **Digital signing.** Signs the business document with a digital certificate to allow your trading partner to authenticate that it came from you.

- **Encryption.** Encrypts the document to prevent third-party interlopers from snooping into your business.

- **Transport.** Sends the document to your trading partner. Again, this process is protocol independent. Site Server Commerce Edition ships with SendHTTP, SendSMTP, and SendDCOM components, but nothing precludes you from writing your own CIP transport component to support your own unique needs. For example, if you needed to support Microsoft Message Queue transport, you could write your own custom SendMSMQ component. Moreover, many EDI VAN service providers are providing their customers with custom CIP transport components to integrate with proprietary networks.

■   **Audit**. A general-purpose stage that covers the need to ensure transactional reliability. This can be anything from e-mail notification to responsible parties, to updating an accounting system to "close the loop" on the transaction.

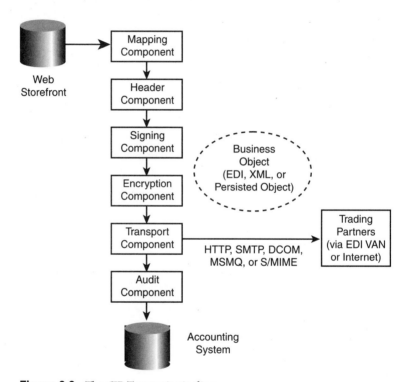

Figure 6-3. *The CIP Transmit pipeline.*

The CIP Receive pipeline, in essence, models the reverse of the Transmit pipeline. The Receive pipeline takes the inbound document, decrypts it, checks the digital signature for authenticity, parses it, and then updates the appropriate databases with the enclosed data. Figure 6-4 shows the flow of a typical CIP Receive pipeline.

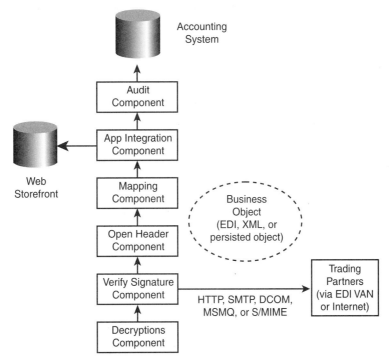

Figure 6-4. *The CIP Receive pipeline.*

Pipeline files

Information about a pipeline (both OPP and CIP) is stored in a pipeline file. A pipeline file is a binary file (normally with a .pcf extension) that provides persistent storage for pipeline meta-data. This meta-data includes the names of the components that are part of the pipeline, the order in which they should be executed, and state information that the pipeline components use when executing. This information is set using the pipeline editor, a tool that is available as both a Win32- and browser-based application. Figure 6-5 shows the Win32 pipeline editor. The pipeline object uses information stored in the pipeline file to determine how to execute it.

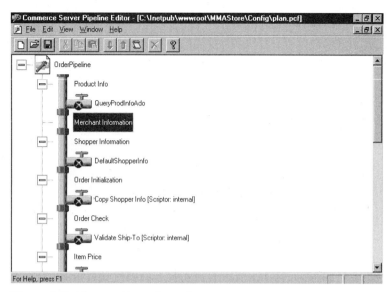

Figure 6-5. *The Win32 pipeline editor.*

Putting it all together

To give you a more concrete example of how the process works, let's follow a shopper around a virtual store. As the shopper goes through the site and selects items for purchase, the ASP script fills out the OrderForm object. When the shopper wants to "check out," the ASP script creates the pipeline object and passes it the OrderForm object. The pipeline object gives the OrderForm object to the first pipeline component in the pipeline by calling that component's Execute method. The Execute method is defined by the IPipelineComponent interface, and any COM object implementing IPipelineComponent must define an Execute method with the signature required by IPipelineComponent (more on this later).

Once the first pipeline component receives the OrderForm object, it evaluates its contents based on a certain set of business rules and modifies the values accordingly. Take, for example, a hypothetical "Discounter" component. The Discounter component's business rules might be to give a shopper a 5 percent discount if the total bill exceeds $100. When the Discounter component receives the OrderForm object from the pipeline, it will look at the total price. If it exceeds $100, the component will apply the discount. If not, it will do nothing.

When the pipeline component is done executing, it will return a status code to the pipeline object to indicate success or varying degrees of failure. The pipeline object uses this information to either continue executing the pipeline, or aborting and rolling back the pipeline and returning an error to the calling ASP scripting environment. If transactional integrity is required, the MtsTxPipeline object can use the underlying services of Microsoft Transaction Server to commit or abort an entire pipeline as a single transaction.

WHAT IS EDI?

Several places in this chapter refer to EDI. What is EDI, anyway? *EDI*, or *Electronic Data Interchange*, is an interoperability standard that allows businesses with different underlying systems to conduct seamless electronic transactions, such as purchase orders, invoices, inventory data, and shipping notices, in a reliable manner. The most popular EDI standard in place today (at least in North America) is the X12 ANSI standard.

Trading partners usually exchange EDI documents via a private network called an *EDI VAN (Value-Added Network)*. In addition to providing bandwidth, EDI VAN providers will normally provide some type of mapping software that "maps" relational DBMS data to the various EDI "flat-file" document formats, as well as guarantee timely delivery of EDI documents to the right trading partner (that's the "value-added" part of it). EDI VAN subscription fees that cover leased lines, dedicated connections, delivery services, and EDI mapping software are usually pretty steep, which is driving an industry trend toward less expensive alternatives, such as EDI over the Internet. Popular with smaller businesses that cannot afford expensive EDI VAN services, EDI over the Internet uses common TCP/IP application layer protocols such as HTTP and SMTP, and the Internet backbone to deliver documents, with various encryption technologies such as SSL, PPTP, PGP, and S/MIME to ensure data security, and digital signing to ensure sender authentication.

To put this in perspective, let's look at a hypothetical supply chain scenario involving an online bookseller and various publishing houses. The bookseller makes sales online but does not have any inventory. As each sale is made, the bookseller will send a purchase order via an EDI VAN to the appropriate publisher, who will then fulfill the order by shipping the book. Here's how the process works:

Step 1. After receiving an order from a shopper, the bookseller generates an EDI 850 purchase order addressed to the appropriate publisher. The bookseller submits it via FTP to the appropriate host on the EDI VAN. The EDI VAN service provider ensures that purchase order gets delivered to the publisher.

(continued)

What Is EDI? *(continued)*

Step 2. Upon receipt of the 850 PO, the publisher sends an 855 PO ACK (Purchase Order Acknowledgment) back to confirm receipt of the PO and provide shipping status information. If the product is back ordered, the 855 will indicate this.

Step 3. The publisher ships the book to the customer and sends an 856 ASN (Advanced Shipping Notice) to the bookseller. The 856 ASN includes shipping information, such as the delivery company's tracking number.

Step 4. The publisher will then bill the bookseller by sending an 810 Invoice document to the bookseller.

Step 5. From time to time, publishers will send 832 price updates to the bookseller, to inform them of price changes in their titles.

Step 6. Also, from time to time, publishers will send 846 inventory documents to update the bookseller with their on-hand merchandise balances. This will reduce the number of incidents where the bookseller executes sales against a zero-balance inventory.

Site Building Tools for Non-Programmers

If this sounds like a programmer's paradise, it is. The COM-based pipeline framework allows a degree of customization and extensibility that is limited only by the skills of your programming staff. Moreover, it opens up a whole new market for third-party off-the-shelf components, which make it easy to assemble sophisticated custom solutions in a short period of time. Site Server Commerce Edition is not a "for programmers only" product, though; it makes the chore of building, maintaining, and administering an e-commerce site easy for non-programmers as well. It integrates various tools to make the Web storefront building process relatively painless for programmers and non-programmers alike. These tools include:

- Core Site Server 3.0 features (for example, Personalization/ Membership, Push, Search, and Analysis).

- A Microsoft Management Console (MMC) snap-in.

- A collection of Win32- and browser-based wizards that generate ASP scripts, SQL Server database schemas, and even pipeline files. It is important to note that you always have the option of modifying, customizing, and extending the output from any of these wizards.

■ Other development tools, such as Microsoft FrontPage 98 and Microsoft Visual InterDev.

BUILDING YOUR FIRST WEB STOREFRONT

To illustrate the ease with which you can use Site Server Commerce Edition to create, customize, extend, and deploy a fully functional Web-based e-commerce application, let's spend the rest of this chapter going through the development of a sample Web storefront. This Web storefront, which lets customers purchase retail items via secure credit card transactions, will illustrate the following concepts:

■ Creating a commerce site's database using Microsoft SQL Server Enterprise Manager

■ Creating and configuring an IIS virtual root to host the site using the Site Foundation Wizard

■ Adding content and functionality to the site using the Site Builder Wizard

■ Administering the site using the Site Manager application

■ Adding cross promotions and price promotions to the storefront

■ Customizing the site by modifying wizard-generated ASP scripts

■ Extending the functionality of the site by creating custom pipeline components

■ Creating and implementing advertising campaigns using Ad Server

For this sample Web storefront, use the product data found in the Adventure Works Microsoft Access database that ships with IIS.

Software and Hardware Requirements

Before proceeding with the construction of the site, make sure that you have all of the software and hardware needed to run Site Server Commerce Edition. Required software is:

- Windows NT Server 4.0 with Service Pack 3 (or higher)

- Microsoft Internet Explorer 4.01 or higher

- Windows NT Server Option Pack, which includes IIS 4 and Microsoft Transaction Server

- Microsoft SQL Server 6.5 with Service Pack 4 (or higher)

- Microsoft Site Server 3.0

> NOTE   Your Windows NT Server should be set up as either a PDC (primary domain controller) or a standalone server. Installing Site Server 3.0 Commerce Edition on a backup domain (BDC) controller is unsupported.

Hardware requirements depend largely on your scalability requirements. If you are selling to millions of customers, you will need a lot more horsepower than if you are selling to only a couple of hundred. At a minimum, you will need a server with these specs:

- Either a Pentium 100 or higher (Pentium 166 recommended), or a DEC Alpha processor

- At least 64 MB of RAM (128 MB recommended)

- At least 1 GB of available hard disk space (2 GB recommended)

- A VGA or Super VGA monitor that is Windows NT server compatible, set to 1024 by 768 resolution (many of the browser-based wizards and admin tools don't look good at a lower resolution)

> NOTE   You should periodically check Microsoft's Site Server Commerce Edition update page (*http://www.microsoft.com/siteserver/commerce/Update/*). This page contains free service pack downloads, implementation tips, sample code, and links to frequently asked questions (FAQs) and Knowledge Base articles. This information will help you stay on top of software updates and bug fixes.

Step 1: Create Your Commerce Site's Database Using SQL Server Enterprise Manager

The first thing to do is to create an empty SQL Server 7 database to store all of the data used by the Web storefront, including product data, order data, customer data, and promotions data. You don't have to worry about creating any tables or other objects for this database; the Site Builder Wizard will generate a schema for you (more on this later). To create a database, perform the following steps:

1. Open the SQL Server Enterprise Manager by selecting Start, Programs, Microsoft SQL Server 7.0, and Enterprise Manager. This will open the Microsoft Management Console (MMC) and load the SQL Server 7.0 snap-in.

2. In the TreeView pane on the left side, find and expand your server. Locate the Databases folder and right-click on it.

3. Select New Database. This will open the Database Properties dialog box (shown in Figure 6-6).

4. Type in a name for your database and click OK. For this sample Web storefront, choose MMAStore as the name of the database.

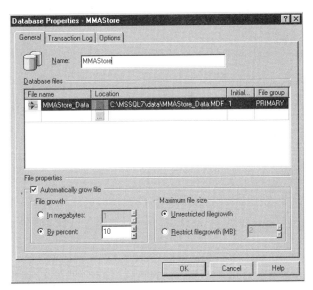

Figure 6-6. *The SQL Server 7 Database Properties dialog box.*

After you create the database, you will need to set up a System data source name (DSN) for it. To do this, open Control Panel, start the ODBC32 applet, click the System DSN tab, and then click the Add button. This will start the Create New Data Source Wizard, which will create a System DSN. Create a System DSN called MMAStore.

Step 2: Create and Configure an IIS Virtual Root to Host Your Site Using the Site Foundation Wizard

Once you have created a SQL Server database and System DSN for the Web storefront, the next step is to create and configure an IIS 4 virtual root to host the commerce site. To facilitate this process, Site Server Commerce Edition provides a browser-based tool called the Site Foundation Wizard. To start this wizard, point your Web browser to *http://your_server_name/siteserver/admin/commerce/* and click the *Server Administration* link in the frame on the left side. This will start the server administration tool, shown in Figure 6-7.

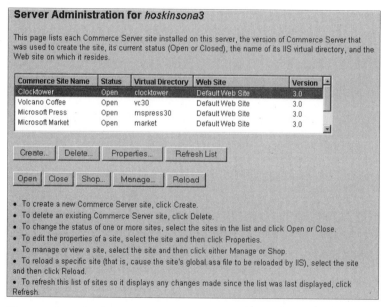

Figure 6-7. *The browser-based Commerce Server Administration tool.*

Clicking the Create button will load a frame that will ask you to select a currently installed Web site to host your new Web storefront. This frame is shown in Figure 6-8. Select the appropriate Web site and click the Next button (for this example, select the Default Web Site).

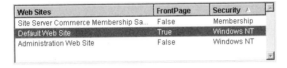

This page lists the Web sites available on this server. Sites listed as TRUE in the FrontPage column can be edited using Microsoft FrontPage and Microsoft Visual InterDev. The Security column indicates the type of security model in use on each Web site. Sites listed as Windows NT use Windows Access Control Lists (ACLs) to restrict access. Sites listed as Membership are mapped to a Membership server and use Membership security.

Select the Web site on which you want to create the new foundation and then click Next.

Web Sites	FrontPage	Security
Site Server Commerce Membership Sa...	False	Membership
Default Web Site	True	Windows NT
Administration Web Site	False	Windows NT

Figure 6-8. *The Site Foundation Wizard.*

The next frame asks you to select both a short and a long name for your storefront. The short name is used to name directories and database tables, and therefore must be unique. As you can see in Figure 6-9, existing sites are contained in a list box, so you can check which names are taken. The long name exists for display purposes and should be sufficiently descriptive to reflect the nature of the storefront.

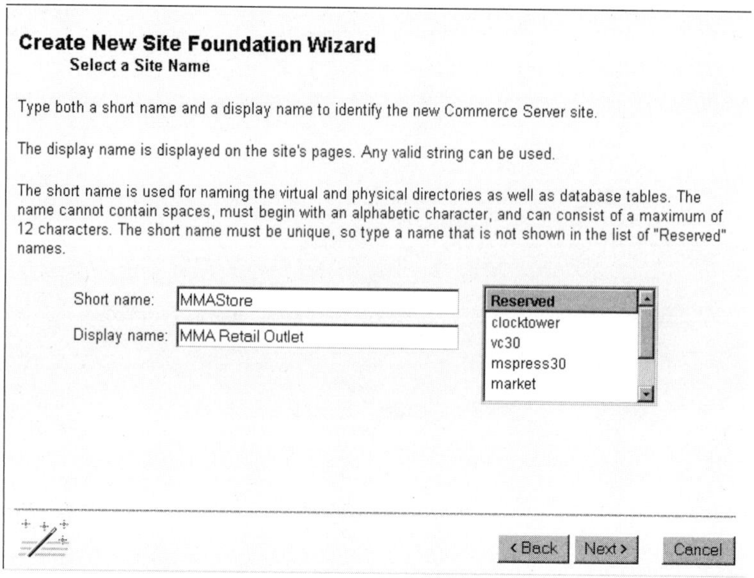

Create New Site Foundation Wizard
Select a Site Name

Type both a short name and a display name to identify the new Commerce Server site.

The display name is displayed on the site's pages. Any valid string can be used.

The short name is used for naming the virtual and physical directories as well as database tables. The name cannot contain spaces, must begin with an alphabetic character, and can consist of a maximum of 12 characters. The short name must be unique, so type a name that is not shown in the list of "Reserved" names.

Short name: MMAStore

Display name: MMA Retail Outlet

Reserved
clocktower
vc30
mspress30
market

< Back   Next >   Cancel

Figure 6-9. *Selecting a site name for your Web storefront.*

Type in a physical path on the server for the storefront's files. As Figure 6-10 shows, the default physical directory is *c:\inetpub\wwwroot\your_store_ name*, unless you specify a different directory. This physical directory will be mapped to the IIS virtual directory for the site.

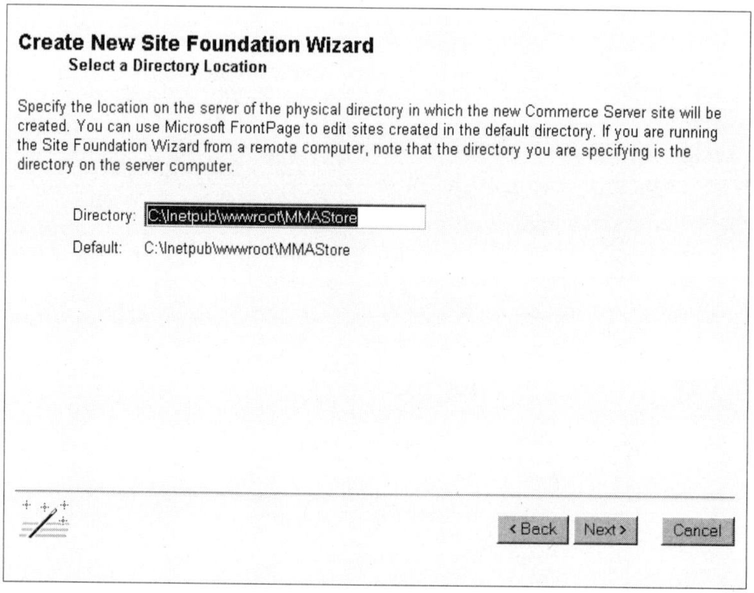

Create New Site Foundation Wizard
Select a Directory Location

Specify the location on the server of the physical directory in which the new Commerce Server site will be created. You can use Microsoft FrontPage to edit sites created in the default directory. If you are running the Site Foundation Wizard from a remote computer, note that the directory you are specifying is the directory on the server computer.

Directory: C:\Inetpub\wwwroot\MMAStore

Default: C:\Inetpub\wwwroot\MMAStore

< Back   Next >   Cancel

Figure 6-10. *Selecting a directory location for your Web storefront.*

The next frame (shown in Figure 6-11) asks you to select a System DSN (data source name) from the list of available DSNs. This DSN will be used as the default data source for the Web storefront. You also need to specify a valid SQL Server user account to log on to this database. In our case, we will use the database and System DSN we created earlier for our sample site.

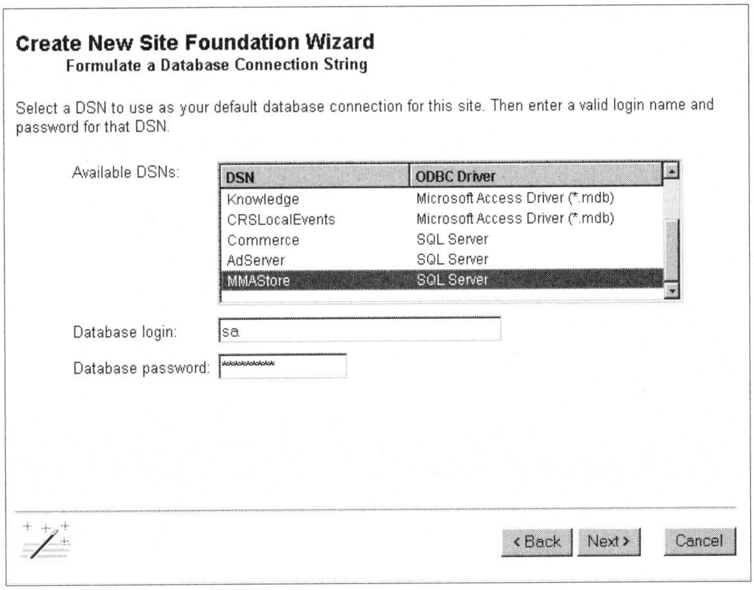

Create New Site Foundation Wizard
Formulate a Database Connection String

Select a DSN to use as your default database connection for this site. Then enter a valid login name and password for that DSN.

Available DSNs:

DSN	ODBC Driver
Knowledge	Microsoft Access Driver (*.mdb)
CRSLocalEvents	Microsoft Access Driver (*.mdb)
Commerce	SQL Server
AdServer	SQL Server
MMAStore	SQL Server

Database login: sa
Database password: **********

< Back | Next > | Cancel

Figure 6-11. *Selecting a DSN for your Web storefront.*

NOTE For demo purposes, we are using the SQL Server SA account. However, for a production site, you probably want to use another account for database login rather than your SA account. This will greatly enhance your site's security posture.

The next step is to identify who will administer this particular site. You do this by identifying a Windows NT user account in the next two frames of the wizard. This is shown in Figure 6-12. The Site Foundation Wizard will give the selected account the appropriate permissions to modify the site's content, run the Store Manager application, and perform other administrative tasks. It will accomplish this by creating a NTFS local group called Commerce_ YourSiteName_1 (Commerce_MMAStore_1 in the case of this example), adding the selected account to this group, and modifying the Windows NT Access Control Lists (ACLs)to give this group full control over the site's directory.

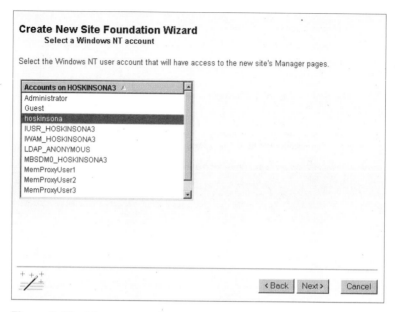

Figure 6-12. *Selecting an administrator for your Web storefront.*

Once you are done, click the Finish button. The Site Foundation Wizard will create and configure the IIS virtual root, and then bring up a page with a hyperlink to the custom Site Manager application. From there, you can run the Site Builder Wizard, which lets you add content and additional functionality. This page is shown in Figure 6-13.

If you want to make any changes to the configuration of your storefront, you can do so by using any number of NT tools and MMC snap-ins. For example, you can implement Secure Sockets Layer (SSL) on your site using the IIS and Site Server MMC snap-ins. If you want to change which users can manage the site, you can open your server's User Manager for Domains application and add and remove users appropriately from the Commerce_YourSiteName_1 local group.

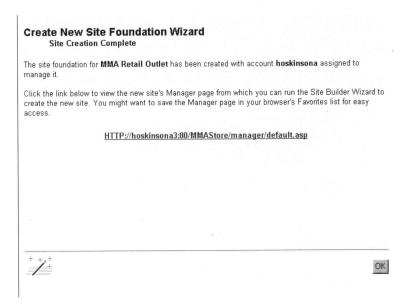

Figure 6-13. *Generating the site foundation.*

Step 3: Add Content and Functionality to Your Site Using the Site Builder Wizard

The Site Builder Wizard adds content and functionality to an existing site. Specifically, it creates the following items:

- ASP scripts for both your storefront and manager applications

- Order Processing Pipeline files, including the Plan pipeline, the Product pipeline, and the Purchase pipeline

- A SQL script to build the schema for your site's database

One important note about the Site Builder Wizard: generally, you will want to run this only once. As you can see in the warning in Figure 6-14, after you start making custom changes to ASP scripts or .pfc (pipeline) files, you don't want to run the Site Builder Wizard again on this particular site. If you do, you will overwrite any changes you have made.

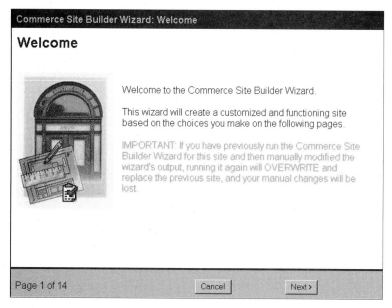

Figure 6-14. *The Site Builder Wizard.*

The first step is to determine whether you want to create a custom site from scratch or to use a copy of an existing site. Site Server Commerce Edition ships with several different sample sites, which can be reused and customized for your own purposes. For the purpose of this demo, select *Create a Custom Site*, as shown in Figure 6-15.

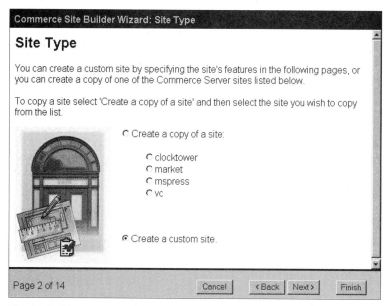

Figure 6-15. *The Site Builder Wizard Site Type frame.*

USING THE SAMPLE SITES THAT COME WITH SITE SERVER COMMERCE EDITION

Take note: copying an existing site is a great option if you want to create a specialized e-commerce site that maps to the functionality offered by one of the four sample sites that ship with Site Server Commerce Edition. Here's a brief description of the four sites:

- **Clocktower:** This fictional clock shop is a simple example of a business-to-consumer retail Web storefront.

- **Microsoft Market** corporate purchasing site: This sample site is a scaled-down version of the corporate purchasing intranet that Microsoft actually uses to allow their employees to submit purchase orders for office supplies to various vendors and suppliers, with management review and approval where appropriate. This is an excellent example of a business-to-business e-commerce site that uses the CIP.

- **Microsoft Press**, an online bookstore. This sample site is a good demonstration of how a Site Server Commerce Edition storefront can integrate the core Site Server Analysis feature (see Chapter 5 for more information on Site Server Analysis).

- **Volcano Coffee**, a fictional business-to-consumer Web storefront that sells gourmet coffee and accessories. This is the most feature-rich of the business-to-consumer sample sites and serves as an excellent example of the use of promotions, shopper management and registration, and Microsoft Wallet integration.

Type in contact information for your site. This information will be displayed on the site's About page, shown in Figure 6-16.

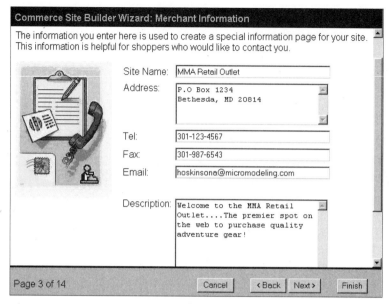

Figure 6-16. *The Site Builder Wizard Merchant Information frame.*

Next, you'll want to define style attributes for your site using the Site Style form displayed in Figure 6-17. You can specify whether you want a vertical or horizontal navigation bar, as well as font, background color, and button style. If you check the Use Logo check box, the Site Builder Wizard will put a place-holder logo on the site, which you can replace later with your own branded logo. Of course, any of these appearance attributes can be changed later by modifying the wizard-generated ASP scripts.

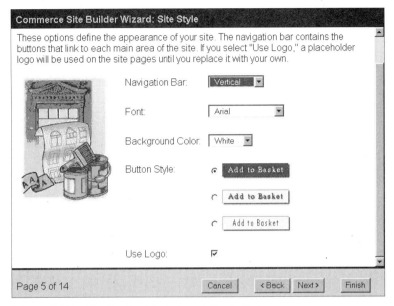

Figure 6-17. *The Site Builder Wizard Site Style frame.*

The next frame allows you to stipulate if you want to build support for promotions into your Web storefront. Once you build in support for this, you can create promotions through Site Server's administration tools after the site is in production. More on this later in the chapter. As you can see in Figure 6-18, there are two types of promotions:

- **Price Promotions** allow you to tie a discount for a particular product to the purchase of a certain quantity of another product. An example of a price promotion is "Buy two copies of product A, get one copy of product B at 50% off."

- **Cross promotions** create a relationship between multiple products. This facilitates "cross-selling" by allowing you to enumerate related products for any given product. For example, if a customer is browsing the product data for product X, he would be presented with a list of other related products he might be interested in, the intent being that this will increase the odds of the shopper purchasing additional products.

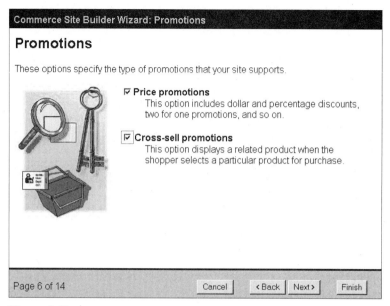

Figure 6-18. *The Site Builder Wizard Promotions frame.*

The next frame prompts you to select options for shopper registration, department type, and product searching. This frame is shown in Figure 6-19. For registration, you can select None, On Entry, or When Ordering.

- If you select None, the wizard will not build shopper registration capabilities into the site.

- If you select On Entry, first-time users will be required to register upon entry and return visitors to log on upon entering the site.

- If you select When Ordering, the site will prompt shoppers to register or log on the first time during any given session that they try to add a product to their shopping basket.

For this sample application, select When Ordering.

Department type allows you to define a hierarchy structure for your products. There are two choices: Simple and Variable Depth. Simple creates a taxonomy that is one level deep; there is one tier of departments, and each department can contain products but cannot contain other departments. Variable Depth creates a multi-tiered taxonomy, where a department can contain both products and other departments. For this sample site, select Simple.

The third configurable option on this frame is Product Searching. It is highly recommend that you enable this; product searching capabilities are (or at least should be) a standard feature in any Web storefront.

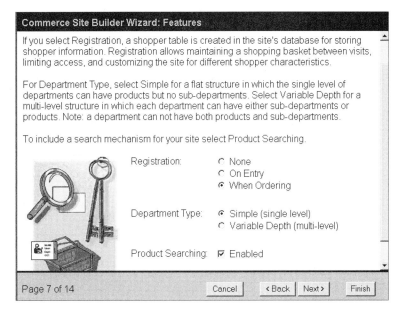

Figure 6-19. *Registration, Department Type, and Product Searching options.*

The next step requires that you identify what type of attributes (meta-data) your products will have. As shown in Figure 6-20, you can select either Static or Dynamic Attributes. Static is appropriate if your Web storefront will sell only products that are of the same class. Dynamic is appropriate if you will sell a lot of different products with many different characteristics.

For example, suppose that your Web storefront is an electronic software download service. In this case, you could make the argument for using static product attributes, because all of your products will be of the same class (for example, software products) and will have the same attributes (for example, filename, description, format, size, type, vendor, and so on).

On the other hand, if you are running a retail operation that sells everything from shoes to toys to appliances, you will want to select Dynamic Attributes, because there is no way to adequately abstract such a diverse set of product classes to one set of fixed meta-data.

When in doubt, always select Dynamic Attributes. Select it now for this sample application.

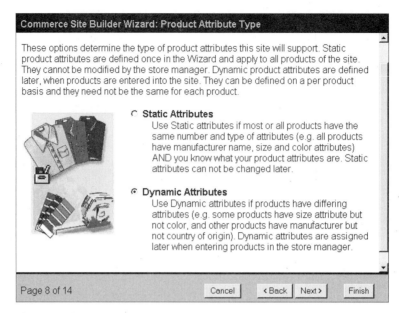

Figure 6-20. *Product Attribute types.*

Assuming you chose Dynamic Attributes in the previous frame, the Site Builder Wizard will ask you to select the maximum number of multi-valued attributes per product. As Figure 6-21 shows, a site using Dynamic Attributes can have an unlimited number of single valued attributes per product. However, you can only have a maximum of five multi-valued attributes per product. What's the difference? A single valued attribute has only one value. An example would be "manufacturer." A product has only one manufacturer (for example, the XYZ Widget Company). A multi-valued attribute has many values. An example would be "size," which would have numerous values, such as small, medium, large, and extra large.

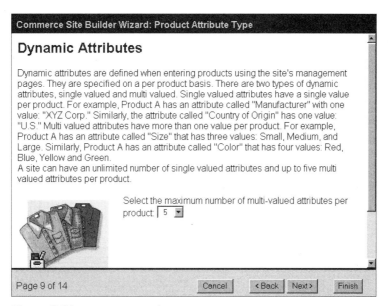

Figure 6-21. *Dynamic Attributes.*

The next step is to define Shipping and Handling rules. For shipping, you can enable up to three different scenarios, as Figure 6-22 shows. For example, you can specify an overnight delivery cost of $10 and a second day delivery cost of $8. You can also enable handing charges and assign a dollar value cost.

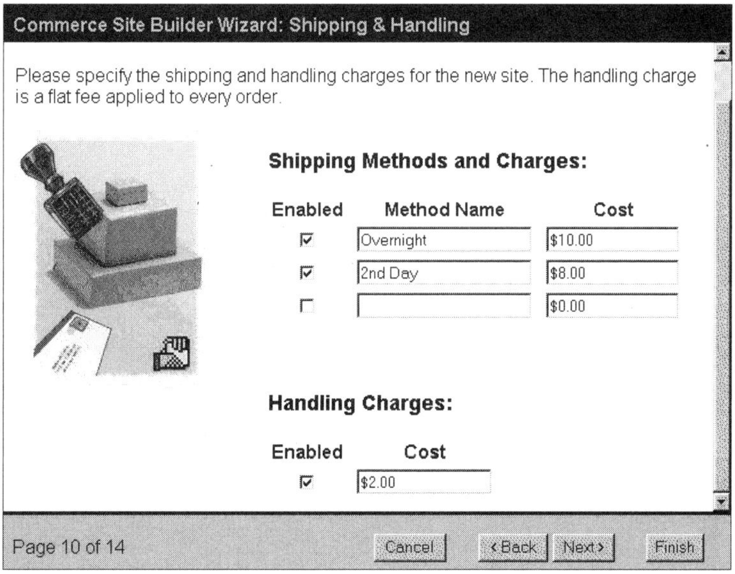

Figure 6-22. *Shipping and handling business rules.*

The next frame allows you to designate tax rates for residents of various states. Create a business rule that will add a 5 percent sales tax to any shopper with a Maryland address. (As the note on Figure 6-23 points out, you should consult a qualified tax professional to ensure that your site is in compliance with the appropriate tax laws.)

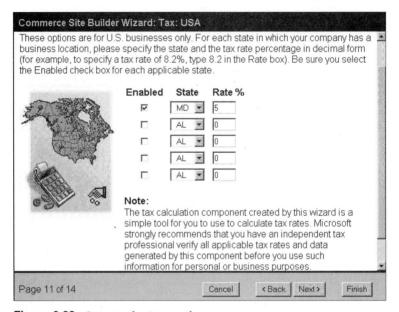

Figure 6-23. *State tax business rules.*

The next frame allows you to select which major credit cards you will accept. As Figure 6-24 shows, the wizard will support Visa, MasterCard, American Express, and Discover. Your selection will depend largely on which credit cards are supported by your credit card service provider. For the purposes of demonstration, select all four.

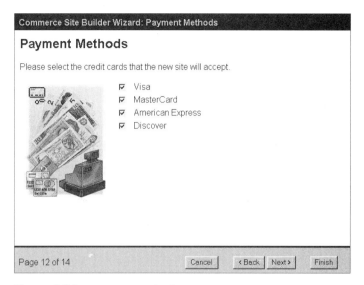

Figure 6-24. *Payment methods.*

The "order history" frame asks you whether you want to retain past order data for your customers. You should retain this information for several reasons. First, as Figure 6-25 explains, this will enable your customers to view their order history at any time. Second, it provides historical data that you can use to personalize the shopping experience and maximize "cross-sell" and "up-sell" opportunities. For example, by retaining and querying customers' order history, you can recommend products to customer's based on their previous shopping history.

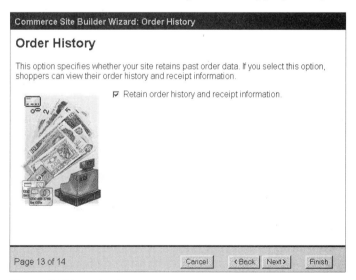

Figure 6-25. *Order history.*

The final frame of the Site Builder Wizard is a summary page that lists the tasks that will be performed by the wizard. As you can see from Figure 6-26, the wizard will generate ASP scripts for both the store and the manager site, pipeline files for the store's Order Processing Pipeline (OPP), and SQL scripts to create a schema and sample data for your storefront's SQL Server database. You can control the output of the wizard by selecting or deselecting any of the listed options. For this site, select the first six options to generate the site's logic, but leave the seventh unchecked so we can populate the site's database with sample data from Microsoft's Adventure Works MS Access database.

Once you are done selecting your options, click the Finish button. The wizard will now generate the site.

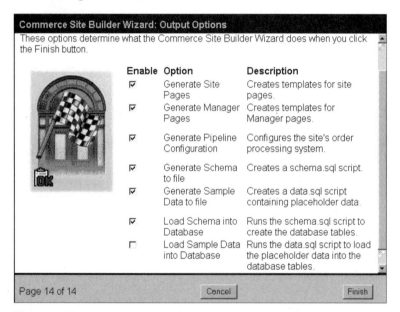

Figure 6-26. *Output options.*

You're done! You now have a simple, functional Web storefront. To view it, point your browser to the following URL: *http://your_machine_name/your_store_name.*

Touring Your Completed Site

Figure 6-27 shows what our MMA Retail Outlet storefront looks like. There are a few things to note. First, the SQL Server database tables created by the Site Builder Wizard have been populated with sample product data obtained from the Adventure Works database. Chapter 8 will discuss tools and techniques for doing this. Second, the logo being used on the site was modified. If you recall, frame 5 of the Site Builder Wizard gave you the opportunity to check the Use Logo option for your site. If you checked that, the wizard created a placeholder image at *http://your_machine_name/your_store_name/Assets/images/Logo.gif.* To replace this image with your own logo, simply name your logo logo.gif and overwrite the existing file.

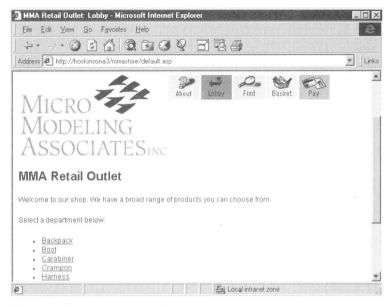

Figure 6-27. *Web Storefront home page.*

Shopper registration

If you selected When Ordering as the registration option for your shoppers in frame 7 of the Site Builder Wizard, your new site will redirect shoppers to register or log on the first time they try to add a product to their shopping basket in any given browser session. The registration script, shown in Figure 6-28, gives two options: log on using an existing account or create a new account.

Figure 6-28. *Shopper Lookup page.*

SSL: Making the site secure

One thing you might have noticed about the URL of this page is that the protocol is https instead of http. This is because we are using Secure Sockets Layer (SSL) to encrypt the packets that are passed between the client (the Web browser) and the server. This is a critical step for any e-commerce site. Packets sent via "plain vanilla" HTTP are sent in the "clear"; anybody with a protocol analyzer can "sniff" the packets and get sensitive information, such as passwords and credit card numbers. Failure to use SSL encryption on your e-commerce site will cause many bad things to happen, including (but not limited to) a lack of customers (because people will be too afraid to shop at your site), and liability problems (that is, you might get sued because a hacker sniffed your customers' credit card numbers).

Fortunately, the site generated by the Site Builder Wizard provides support for SSL. However, actually implementing it is not automatic. There are a couple of things to do:

■ Implement SSL on the IIS virtual root hosting your Web storefront. Obtain a server certificate from a valid CA (Certificate Authority, such as Verisign), using Key Manager to create a SSL key pair to bind to this certificate and the Internet Service Manager MMC snap-in to implement SSL on that virtual root. For more information on how to do this, please see Chapter 4.

■ Enable HTTPS on your storefront: Start the Site Server Admin MMC snap-in, Open the Commerce Host Administration node, expand the node representing your server, and right-click on your site. Select Properties from the pop-up menu and check the Enable HTTPS check box, shown in Figure 6-29.

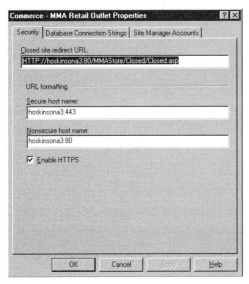

Figure 6-29. *The Commerce Host Administration property page for your Web storefront.*

Microsoft Wallet

When a new shopper registers with your site, he will be directed to a page that requests his e-mail address, physical address, and a password. This page is shown in Figure 6-30. If the shopper is using Internet Explorer or Netscape Navigator, he will have the opportunity to use Microsoft Wallet to provide this information.

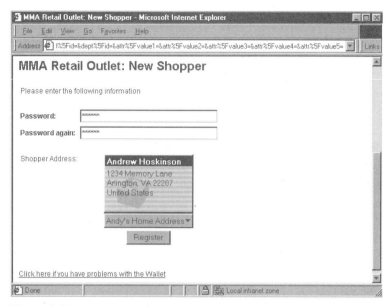

Figure 6-30. *The New Shopper Registration page.*

Site Server Commerce Edition provides built-in support for Microsoft Wallet. Microsoft Wallet is a component that is implemented as both an ActiveX control and a Netscape plug-in. To implement Wallet support, your Site Builder Wizard-generated Web storefront contains ASP code that determines what browser the shopper is using. If the shopper is using Internet Explorer 3 or 4, your Web storefront will stream the necessary <OBJECT> tag markup to the browser to implement the ActiveX version of Wallet. If the shopper is using Netscape Navigator version 3 or 4, your Web storefront will stream the necessary <EMBED> tag markup to the browser to implement the Netscape plug-in version of Wallet. If the shopper is using some other browser type, the Web storefront will stream a regular HTML form to the browser to collect the shopper's address information.

Microsoft Wallet contains two objects: an Address Selector and a Payment Selector. Microsoft Wallet allows users to store sensitive information, such as their home address and credit card numbers, on their local hard disk in a secure manner. Wallet ensures security by storing this information in an encrypted, password-protected file on the local file system. Users can store multiple addresses and credit card numbers in this file. This offers a great convenience to end users; when shopping at sites that provide support for Microsoft Wallet, users do not have to keep retyping the same repetitive address and credit card information into HTML forms. The downside of Microsoft Wallet is that it takes a long time to download when a shopper initially installs it on his machine, especially the Netscape plug-in version, which does not use Authenticode technology for seamless installation within the browser environment. This might be a "point of friction" for an impatient shopper, especially if he is shopping your site via a dial-up analog modem connection. Moreover, many shoppers will visit your site using their computers at work, school, or some other public location, and they will be leery about allowing their sensitive information to be stored on the local hard disk, even if it is encrypted and password-protected.

NOTE When using Microsoft Wallet on an e-commerce site, you must *always* give your shoppers the option to provide registration information via a regular HTML form. Relying solely on Microsoft Wallet to collect shopper information will most likely result in lost sales for your Web storefront.

When a user registers, he will first create a password for his account. Next, using Microsoft Wallet, he will select an existing address to be used as the default shipping address for this storefront.

If he prefers, the user can create a new address within Wallet by filling out the dialog box shown in Figure 6-31.

Figure 6-31. *Microsoft Wallet's Add a New Address dialog box.*

After providing all the necessary information, the user clicks the Register button, and an account will be created. On subsequent visits to the site, the user will log on using this account.

As mentioned earlier, if the shopper is using a browser that is not ActiveX or Netscape plug-in-capable, the site will serve a regular HTML form that will allow the user to register and create an account. For the shopper's convenience, this information is stored in the storefront's SQL Server database in the yourstorename_shopper table (mmastore_shopper for our sample storefront).

In subsequent visits to the site, the shopper will not have to retype this information, although he can certainly modify it if required.

NOTE The Site Builder Wizard-generated site uses the Microsoft Browser Capabilities component (MSWC.BrowserType). This component uses information stored in the browscap.ini file to determine what content types a given browser can handle. For maximum accuracy in browser detection, you should download the most current version of the *browscap.ini* file from *http://backoffice.microsoft.com/downtrial/moreinfo/bcf.asp*.

Shopping basket

Once the shopper has created an account with your store, he can add products to his shopping basket by clicking the Add to Basket button located on the product page, which is shown in Figure 6-32. Once this is done, the site will take the shopper to his shopping basket.

Figure 6-32. *The Web storefront's product page.*

The shopping basket is shown in Figure 6-33. Here, the shopper can perform a variety of tasks, including removing individual items, changing purchase quantities, and deleting all items from the shopping basket. The shopper can also "check out" by clicking the Purchase button.

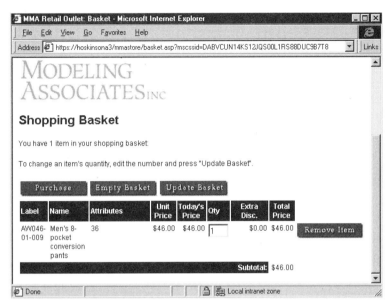

Figure 6-33. *The Shopping Basket.*

Shipping

Once the shopper clicks the Purchase button, the Shipping page appears, shown in Figure 6-34. There, the shopper can select which shipping method to use (for example, overnight, second day, and so on), which you built into the site on frame 10 of the Site Builder Wizard. If the shopper is using Internet Explorer or Netscape Navigator, he will have the opportunity to use the Microsoft Wallet Address Selector control to select the shipping address. If he is using a browser that does not support ActiveX controls or Netscape plug-ins, he will get a standard HTML form.

Figure 6-34. *The Shipping page, showing integration with the Microsoft Wallet Address Selector control.*

Payment

When the shopper clicks the Total button, he is taken to the Payment page, shown in Figure 6-35. There, he will have an opportunity to review a payment summary and select a credit card to pay for the transaction by using the Microsoft Wallet Payment Selector control. This process is shown in Figure 6-36.

Figure 6-35. *The Payment page, showing integration with the Microsoft Wallet Payment Selector control.*

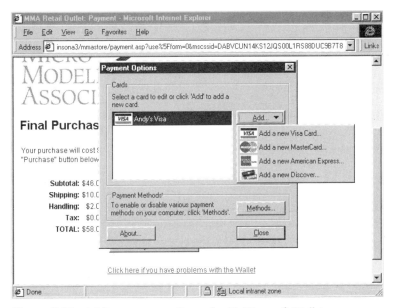

Figure 6-36. *Adding a new credit card with Microsoft Wallet.*

Purchase

When the shopper is ready to check out, he clicks the Purchase button. As Figure 6-37 shows, Wallet will prompt him for the password to access his credit card information.

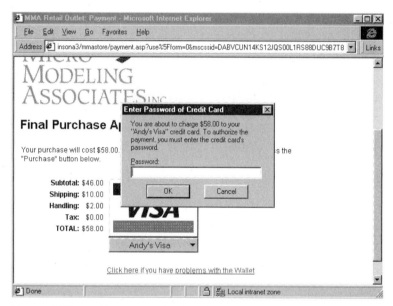

Figure 6-37. *Wallet prompts the user for a password before posting credit card information.*

Confirmation

Once he provides the correct password and is authenticated, the transaction will be posted to an ASP script on your site, which creates and executes the site's Purchase pipeline. Upon successful execution of the pipeline, the storefront will serve the user a purchase confirmation page, complete with an order number. This page is shown in Figure 6-38.

NOTE   The default purchase pipeline created by the Site Builder Wizard contains the ValidateCCNumber component, which performs a checksum test on the credit card number to ensure that its format is correct. It does not actually reserve or commit any funds against a particular account. To do that, you must contract with a credit card service provider, such as CyberCash or ICVerify. There are several credit card service providers that will provide their clients with a custom component that will plug into a Site Server Commerce Edition purchase pipeline. Visit *http://www.microsoft.com/ siteserver/commerce/partners/partners.asp* for more information.

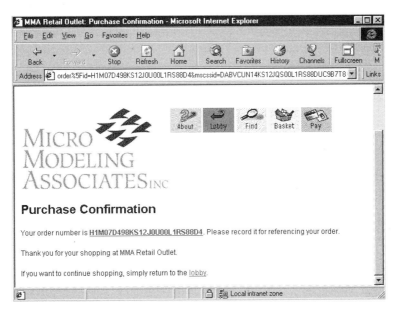

Figure 6-38. *The Purchase Confirmation page.*

ADMINISTERING YOUR SITE USING THE SITE MANAGER

In addition to creating the Web storefront, the Site Builder Wizard will also create a Site Manager application. You (and any other authorized NT account) can use this browser-based ASP application to administer the store. Access the Site Manager application by pointing your browser to *http://your_machine_name/ your_store_name/manager*. There, you will see the Site Manager application's home page, which is shown in Figure 6-39.

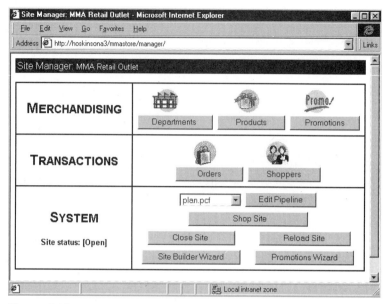

Figure 6-39. *The Site Manager application.*

Overview

The Site Manager application lets you perform the following administrative chores:

- Add, edit, or delete products and departments.

- Assign products to departments.

- Query shopper and order data.

- Delete shoppers.

- Edit pipeline files.

- Close the store. Closing the store will redirect all incoming site visitors to a page that informs them that the Web storefront is temporarily unavailable.

- Reload the site. Reloading the site calls the Reload method of the Commerce.AdminSite object, which executes the ASP Application and Session object OnStart event handlers in the site's global.asa file, thereby refreshing data that has application and session scope.

- Rerun the Site Builder Wizard. Please note that this is not recommended after you have made custom changes to the site's ASP scripts or pipeline files, because the Site Builder Wizard will overwrite your changes.

- Implement promotion support.

Promotions

In frame 6 of the Site Builder Wizard, we enabled promotion support for the Web storefront by checking the two boxes for price and cross promotions. Now let's use the Site Manager to implement specific promotions.

To get started, go to the Site Manager's home page and click the Promotions button. This loads the Promotion Manager page, shown in Figure 6-40.

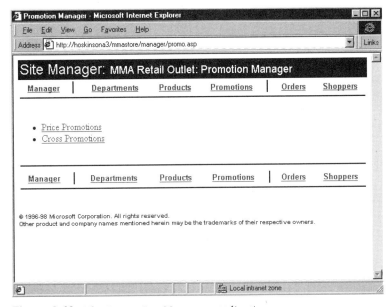

Figure 6-40. *The Promotion Manager application.*

Price promotions

First, add a price promotion. Figure 6-41 shows the Price Promotions page. For this demonstration, choose Buy X Get Y At Z% Off from the choice list and click the Add button.

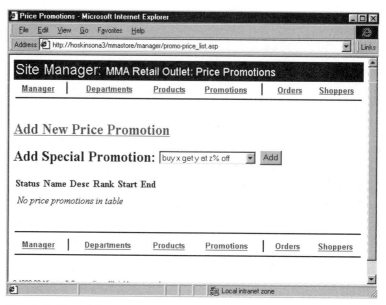

Figure 6-41. *Adding a new price promotion.*

This brings up the price promotion form, shown in Figure 6-42. Fill out this form by typing in a name for your promotion and specifying the Buy and Get quantities and products. Give shoppers one Black Diamond Quicksilver II carabiner for free if they purchased two Edgehugger crampons. (For those of you who are not familiar with mountaineering equipment, a *carabiner* is a hook-like device that is used to snap ropes and harnesses together, and a *crampon* is a type of footgear used for traction during ice climbing.) The other options on the form, such as Status, Rank, Start date, and End date, will be filled out with default values, although you can certainly modify them if desired. Once you have completely filled out the form, click the Add Price Promotion button.

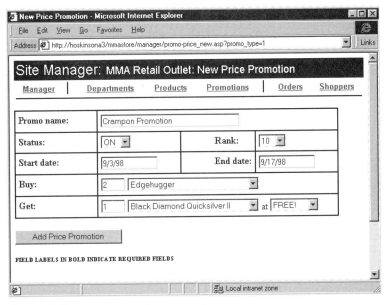

Figure 6-42. *Price promotion properties.*

Now go back to your shopping site and log in as a shopper. Add two Edgehuggers and one Black Diamond Quicksilver II to your shopping basket. As you can see in Figure 6-43, a discount of the entire sales price of the Black Diamond Quicksilver II is applied to your total.

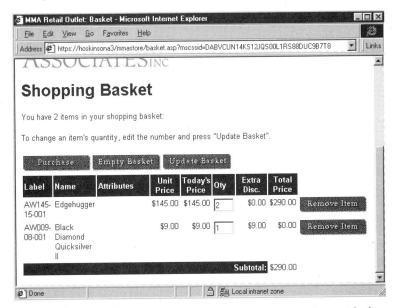

Figure 6-43. *The Shopping Basket, showing a price promotion applied.*

Cross promotions

To add a cross promotion, go back to the Promotion Manager home page and click the *Cross promotions* hyperlink. This will bring you to the New Cross Promotion page. Select the two products for which you want to establish a relationship. As Figure 6-44 shows, establish a relationship between the Gold-Series Locking D carabiner and the Black Diamond Quicksilver II. Click the Add Cross Promotion button.

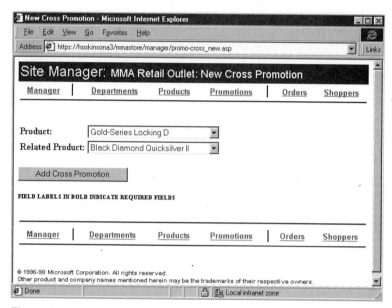

Figure 6-44. *Creating a new cross promotion.*

Now go back to the shopping site and look at the Gold-Series Locking D product record. As Figure 6-45 shows, a See Also list now appears at the bottom of the page, with a hyperlink to the Black Diamond Quicksilver II.

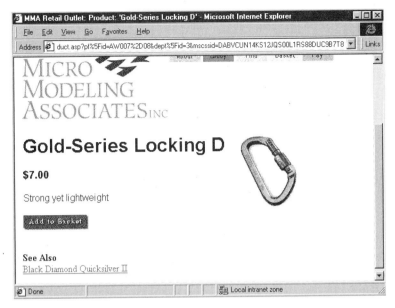

Figure 6-45. *The Product page showing a related product.*

To make this a more effective cross-sell tool, change See Also to something more descriptive. To do this, locate the *product.asp* file located in the root of your shopping site and open it using Visual InterDev. Go to the 220th line of code in this file (or thereabouts) and locate this code fragment:

Code fragment from product.asp (before)

```
REM display up to 5 related products:
    if Not rsRelated.EOF then
            %>      <BR>     <B>See Also</B>
```

Change *See Also* to *Here are some other products you might be interested in...Check them out!*

Now go back to your browser and refresh the page. Your shoppers will now see a much more effective "cross-sell" message, shown in Figure 6-46. Please refer to *product.asp* on the sample CD for a complete listing of this example.

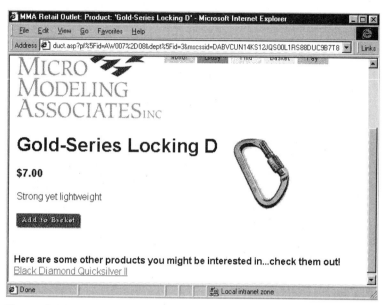

Figure 6-46. *The Product page after the change to product.asp.*

ENHANCING YOUR SITE

The Site Builder Wizard creates basic Web storefronts rather quickly. Most people, though, will want to make custom changes to the basic site created by the wizard. For example, you might want to change the site's look and feel to reflect your company's branding. You might want to implement a custom business rule in your Order Processing pipeline. You also might want to use an existing product database, rather than migrating your data to the wizard-generated database schema. Fortunately, you have complete control over the output of the Site Builder Wizard and can make whatever custom changes you deem appropriate.

Customizing the Wizard-Generated ASP Scripts

As you have already seen with the product.asp example earlier, it is relatively easy to modify wizard-generated ASP scripts to change the appearance of your site. You can also modify ASP to change the functionality of your site. For example, the site's search engine, which is contained in the find.asp script, implements a search of the name field in your database's product table. This is useful, but what might be even more useful would be to modify the SQL statement for this search to perform an inclusive search by both product name and description.

To implement this, open *find.asp* (located in the root directory of your Web storefront site) using Visual InterDev. Go to line 58 (or thereabouts) and modify the SQL statement located there to include a search of the description field. Please refer to *find.asp* on the sample CD for a complete listing of this example:

Old SQL Statement

```
CmdTemp.CommandText = "SELECT p.pf_id, p.name, p.list_price,
dp.dept_id FROM mmastore_product p, mmastore_dept_prod dp WHERE p.name
LIKE '%" & safeFindSpec & "%' and p.pf_id = dp.pf_id ORDER BY name"
```

New SQL Statement

```
cmdTemp.CommandText = "SELECT p.pf_id, p.name, p.list_price,
dp.dept_id FROM mmastore_product p, mmastore_dept_prod dp WHERE
(p.name LIKE '%" & safeFindSpec & "%' or p.description LIKE '%" &
safeFindSpec & "%') and p.pf_id = dp.pf_id ORDER BY name"
```

This is just one example of how you can customize the appearance and functionality of your Web storefront by modifying the wizard-generated ASP scripts. The possibilities are virtually endless. There are two things to keep in mind, though: before modifying the ASP script, you should examine the existing code very thoroughly so your changes don't inadvertently "break" your site. Also, you should keep in mind that once you start modifying code, you should not run the Site Builder Wizard against your site again. Doing so will result in your custom modifications being overwritten. For more information on the powerful things you can do with ASP, please take a look at Chapter 7.

SEPARATING DESIGN FROM CONTENT IN YOUR WEB STOREFRONT

As mentioned earlier, one of the advantages of using the Site Builder Wizard is that it creates a fully functional site quickly and easily. But, as you will soon learn when you start digging into the ASP code, it could be a difficult and time-consuming process to put your company's "look and feel" onto the wizard-generated site. Why is this? Because the Site Builder Wizard-generated ASP scripts contain a great deal of application logic mixed in with the HTML elements that implement the site's design. Even with the business logic and design separation achieved by using pipelines, there is still a lot of logic implemented in ASP script. For example, our sample application's wizard-generated ASP scripts contains 13 different

(continued)

Separating Design from Content in Your Web Storefront *(continued)*

references to the ADODB.Connection and ADODB.Recordset objects, which are used to conduct database queries and transactions (see Chapter 9 for more information on ADO). The *find.asp* script is a perfect example of this.

For long-term maintainability, you should separate the site's hardcore logic from its design. Here are a few techniques that will help you do this:

■ Once you have run the Site Builder Wizard, port the application logic contained in ASP scripts to middle tier "business objects" where possible. A "business object" is an in-process COM component that encapsulates an organization's business rules. Business objects can be written in any language that supports the creation of in-process COM servers, such as Visual Basic, Visual C++, or Visual J++. See Chapter 7 for more information on creating business objects.

■ Use the ASP scripts as your design templates. Ideally, the only programmatic functions your ASP scripts will perform is to create, execute, and release your business objects. See Chapter 7 for more information.

■ Use new Microsoft technologies such as Visual Basic 6 Webclasses and the Visual J++ 6 wfc.html classes to merge dynamically generated content with HTML templates at runtime. This will greatly facilitate the ability to make rapid changes to your site's look and feel without needing to change the underlying logic of your Web storefront.

Writing Custom Pipeline Components

Another advantage of Site Server Commerce Edition is that it provides a framework for running third-party components that implement custom business logic. This pipeline framework makes it easy for you to extend the functionality of your e-commerce site with third-party components, written by you or purchased from a third party ISV. This makes it easy for your Web storefront to integrate existing systems. For example, a vendor that makes an accounting system might provide a pipeline component that integrates Site Server Commerce Edition-based Web storefronts with that system. An EDI VAN provider can develop an EDI mapping component. A shipping service might create a tracking component.

If all else fails and you must implement an unusual or proprietary piece of business logic, you always have the option of writing your own pipeline component. How, then, do you write your own pipeline component? There are basically two ways. The first way is to create an in-process COM server that implements the IPipelineComponent interface. The second way is to write your custom object using an Active Scripting language, such as VBScript or JScript, and execute it using the pipeline Scriptor component.

COM servers

If performance and scalability are your biggest criteria, you should write a COM pipeline component. You can write a COM pipeline object in any language or development environment that supports the creation of in-process COM servers. For the best performance, though, using the Visual C++ ATL (Active Template Library) is recommended. In fact, the Site Server SDK (which ships with Site Server) provides a Pipeline Component Wizard add-in that allows you to turn a standard ATL/COM project into a pipeline component.

> NOTE You can write pipeline components using Visual Basic. However, due to threading limitations, you should include pipeline components written in Visual Basic in pipelines that are created and executed on a per-ASP script basis only. You should *not* include a Visual Basic-written pipeline component in a Commerce Server 3.0 pipeline object (MtsPipeline or MtsTxPipeline) that is stored in the ASP Application or Session object.

By definition, a pipeline component must implement the PipelineComponent interface. This interface defines two methods, the most important of which is the Execute method. The pipeline object fires the Execute method and passes four parameters to it:

- An IDispatch pointer to the OrderForm object.

- An IDispatch pointer to the pipeline's Context object.

- A long "flag" value, which is currently not used (but is reserved for future use).

- A long pointer to an error level code. This value will be set by the component's Execute implementation and will be used by the calling pipeline object to indicate success (or varying degrees of failure). The pipeline object then uses this information to determine whether to abort the pipeline or continue executing it.

In Visual C++, the Execute method returns a HRESULT. In Visual Basic and Java, the signature is slightly different; the Execute method will take three parameters (the OrderForm, the Context, and the flag) and return the error level code.

In addition to IPipelineComponent, there are other COM interfaces available for custom components to implement. These interfaces allow components to implement persistent storage of state data, provide implementation information, and provide a UI to facilitate configuration. These interfaces include:

- **IpipelineComponentAdmin.** To expose a dictionary of custom properties.

- **IspecifyPropertyPages.** To provide a property page for editing the component's custom properties using the pipeline editor.

- **IpersistStreamInit.** To provide a means of persistent storage of custom properties.

- **IpipelineComponentDescription.** To enumerate which elements it reads or writes in the OrderForm and pipeline context objects. This assists site builders in identifying which data elements are analyzed and changed by a given pipeline component.

For more information on creating custom pipeline components, please consult the Site Server SDK.

The Scriptor Component

But what if your scalability and performance requirements are not too steep, and you want to implement a custom business rule into your OPP (Order Processing Pipeline) without going to all the trouble of creating an in-process COM server? If this is your situation, you can write a custom pipeline script and implement it in your pipeline using the Scriptor Component. This is a pipeline component that executes a script written in an Active Scripting language, such as VBScript or JScript. This is the easiest way of extending your Web storefront with custom functionality.

Writing your script

Going back to the MMA Retail Outlet sample site, suppose we wanted to extend our purchase pipeline by adding code that automatically e-mailed a purchase order to our shipping department for fulfillment, as well as a courtesy e-mail to the shopper after he has purchased from your site. We can do this easily with a little VBScript code and the Win32 Pipeline Editor. When writing your VBScript code, it is important to remember that Scriptor Component scripts have a certain signature. This signature looks like this:

Scriptor Component VBScript Code Signature

```
function MSCSExecute(config, orderform, context, flags)
'*****************************************************************
'*    This function is called by the pipeline object,
'*    which passes the following objects:
'*
'*        config:  a dictionary containing custom parameters
'*        orderform:  the order form object
'*        context:  a dictionary containing references to
'*                  objects and data that the site stores in
'*                  the ASP intrinsic Application object
'*        flags:  This parameter is reserved for future use
'*
'*        Returns:  an error level; 1 = success, 2 = failure
'*****************************************************************
end function

sub MSCSOpen(config)
'Initialization code goes here
end sub
·sub MSCSClose(
·'Clean up code goes her

end sub
```

As you can see, a Scriptor Component script defines three methods: MSCSExecute, MSCSOpen, and MSCSClose. The first one, MSCSExecute, is the most important and bears a strong resemblance to the Execute method of the IPipelineComponent interface discussed earlier. MSCSExecute is called by the Scriptor Component, which passes four parameters received from the pipeline object:

- **Config.** This is a dictionary object that contains an arbitrary list of key-value pairs that constitute, in essence, custom properties for the script. This list is created by typing a semicolon delimited list of key-value pairs (for example, prop1=value1;prop2=value2) in the Scriptor Component's property page (more on that later). You refer to it in code by calling config.keyname, where keyname is the name of your custom property.

- **Orderform.** This is the pipeline's OrderForm object.

- **Context.** This is a Dictionary object that contains pointers to the various objects that make up the pipeline's execution context.

- **Flags.** This parameter is currently not used but is reserved for future use.

MSCSExecute should return a value of *1* or *2* to inform the calling pipeline of the status of its execution. A return value of 1 indicates success to the calling pipeline, and *2* indicates failure.

The second method is MSCSOpen. This is called when the host Scriptor Component is first created and should contain any initialization or start-up code required. MSCSOpen receives the aforementioned config object from the calling pipeline. MSCSClose is called when the host Scriptor Component is destroyed. It should contain any necessary clean-up code.

Let's put all of this together to write a script that will e-mail an abbreviated purchase order to our shipping department once a shopper executes a purchase, and then send a courtesy e-mail to the shopper. This script will be appended to the tail end of our purchase pipeline. Let's review the requirements and design specifications of this script:

- The config object will contain three custom properties: StoreEmail (the e-mail address of your Web storefront's point of contact), ShippingEmail (the e-mail address of your shipping department), and CustTable (the data table to query for the shopper's e-mail address).

- Using information from the OrderForm object, the MSCSExecute method will construct an e-mail purchase order and send it to config.ShippingEmail using Collaboration Data Objects (CDO). (See Chapter 18 for more information on CDO.) Moreover, it will run a Select query against config.CustTable to get the shopper's e-mail address (using orderform.shopper_ID in the Where clause) and send the shopper a courtesy message via CDO.

- The MSCSExecute function will return *1* if it succeeds. It will include error handling and will return *2* if an error occurs.

- We will save this script using the filename *FulfillOrder.vbs*. This file is also located in its entirety on the sample CD:

FulfillOrder.vbs Code Listing

```
'****************************************
'  FulfillOrder Pipeline Script
'  Written by Andy Hoskinson
'  August 10, 1998
'  Micro Modeling Associates, Inc.
'  This script emails an abbreviated
'  PO to a shipping dept. from a Site
'  Server Commerce Edition Order
'  Processing Pipeline
'  It also emails an order
'  acknowledgement to the customer.
'****************************************
function MSCSExecute(config, orderform, context, flags)
'*********************************************************************
'     This function is called by the Purchase pipeline,
'     which passes the following objects:
'          config:     a dictionary containing custom parameters
'                      (config.custTable, config.ShippingEmail,
'                      and config.StoreEmail)
'          orderform:  the order form object
'          context:    a dictionary containing references to
'                      objects and data that the site stores in
'                      the Application object
'          flags:      Reserved. This parameter should be zero
'*********************************************************************
Dim intResult 'the function's return value (1=good, 2=bad)
'Send the PO to the Shipping department
intResult = NotifyShipping(config, orderform)
'If this succeeds, send a courtesy email to the shopper
if intResult = 1 then
    intResult = NotifyCustomer(config, orderform, context)
end if
MSCSExecute = intResult
End function


Function NotifyShipping(config, orderform)
'*********************************************
'  This function emails an abbreviated
'  PO to a shipping dept. It returns
'  an error code (1=success, 2=failure)
'*********************************************
on error resume next
Dim strSubject 'The email's subject
Dim strMessage 'The mail message
Dim intResult 'the function's return value (1=good, 2=bad)
```

(continued)

FulfillOrder.vbs Code Listing *(continued)*

```vbs
'Construct the email message using
'information from the orderform object
strSubject = "New Order: " & orderform.order_id
strMessage = "A new order has been received " &_
             "and validated. " &_
             " Please fulfill this order. Here " &_
             "are the details:" &_
             vbcrlf & vbcrlf & "Customer " &_
             "Name: " & orderform.ship_to_name &_
             vbcrlf & "Order ID: " &_
             orderform.order_id &_
             vbcrlf & "Total Sale: $" &_
             CCur(orderform.[_total_total]/100) &_
             vbcrlf &_
             "Please go to the following URL for " &_
             "more information:" & vbcrlf & vbcrlf &_
             "http://hoskinsona3/mmastore/manager/" &_
             "order_view.asp?order_id=" &_
             orderform.order_id & vbcrlf
' Send email message...we get the email addresses
' from the config object...
' We will send it high priority (2)
intResult=SendMail(config.StoreEmail,_
      config.ShippingEmail,strSubject,strMessage, 2)
'return Result
NotifyShipping = intResult
End function
·Function NotifyCustomer(config, orderform, context
·'********************************************
·' This function sends a courtesy emai
·' via CDO to the customer with inf
·' about the order. It returns an error cod
·' (1=success, 2=failure
·'********************************************
·on error resume nex

·Dim strSubject 'The email's subjec
·Dim strMessage 'The mail messag
·Dim objConn 'the ADODB connectio
·Dim objRS   'the ADODB recordse
·Dim strSQL 'the SQL statemen
·Dim strRecipien
·Dim intResult 'the function's return value (1=good, 2=bad

intResult = 1'Create a SQL statement that will get the
```

```
'email address in the table name
'passed via the config object using
'the shopper_ID passed via the
'orderform object as a filter.
strSQL = "select email from " & config.custTable &_
        " where shopper_id = '" & orderform.shopper_ID & "'"
set objConn = CreateObject("ADODB.Connection")
'If this succeeds...
if err.number = 0 then
    'We get the site's connection string
    'from the context object
    objConn.open context.DefaultConnectionString
    'If this succeeds...
    if err.number = 0 then
        'Execute the query
        set objRS = objConn.execute(strSQL)
        'If this succeeds...
        if err.number = 0 then
            do while not objRS.EOF
                strRecipient = trim(objRS("email"))
                objRS.MoveNext
            loop
            'Clean up our ADO objects
            objRS.close
            objConn.close
            set objRS = nothing
            set objConn = nothing
            'Construct the email message using
            'information from the orderform object
            strSubject = "Your Order Number " & orderform.order_id
            strMessage = "Dear " & orderform.ship_to_name &_
                    "," & vbcrlf & vbcrlf &_
                    "Your order has been received and" &_
                    " validated. " &_
                    " Thank you " &_
                    "for shopping at the " &_
                    context.sitename &_
                    "! You should be receiving your" &_
                    " product " &_
                    "soon.  If you " &_
                    "have any questions or comments, " &_
                    "please " &_
                    "feel free to " &_
                    "contact our toll free customer " &_
                    "support line at " &_
                    "1-800-xxx-xxxx.  Please use this " &_
```

(continued)

FulfillOrder.vbs Code Listing *(continued)*

```
                              "information when " &_
                              "referring to your order:" &_
                         vbcrlf & vbcrlf &_
                         "Order ID: " & orderform.order_id &_
                         vbcrlf &_
                         "Total Sale: $" &_
                         CCur(orderform.[_total_total]/100) &_
                       vbcrlf &_
                       "Please go to the following URL " &_
                       "for more " &_
                       "information:" &_
                        vbcrlf & vbcrlf &_
                       "http://hoskinsona3/mmastore/" &_
                       "receipt.asp?order_id=" &_
                        orderform.order_id & "&mscssid=" &_
                        orderform.shopper_ID & vbcrlf
                ' Send email message...we get the email addresses
                ' from the config object
                ' and from the database query we did earlier...
                ' We will send it normal priority (1)
                intResult=SendMail(config.StoreEmail,_
                        strRecipient,strSubject,strMessage, 1)
            else
                intResult=2  'the shopper email lookup query failed
            end if
        else
            intResult=2   'Unable to connection to our DB
        end if
    else
        intResult=2   'Unable to instantiate ADO
    end if    'return Result
    NotifyCustomer = intResult
    end function


    sub MSCSOpen(config)
    'Initialization code goes here
        'Not used in this script...no startup code
    end sub


    sub MSCSClose()
    'Clean up code goes here
        'Not used in this script...no cleanup code
    end sub


    function SendMail(strFrom, strTo, strSubject, strBody,
    intImportance)
```

```
'*************************************'
This is a helper function that' sends an email via CDO and
returns' an error code
'*************************************
on error resume next
Dim objMail 'The CDO instance

' Instantiate CDO
Set objMail = CreateObject("CDONTS.NewMail")
'If this raises an error, return 2 and exit
if err.number <> 0 then
    SendMail = 2
exit function
end if
objMail.From=strFrom
objMail.To=strTo
objMail.Subject=strSubject
objMail.Body=strBody
objMail.importance=intImportance
objMail.MailFormat=0
objMail.Send
'If this raises an error, return 2 and exit
if err.number <> 0 then
    SendMail = 2
Exit function
end if
'Release the object
Set objMail = nothing
SendMail = 1
end function
```

NOTE For the CDONTS.NewMail object to work properly, you must ensure that your IIS 4 SMTP Service is running and that it is configured properly. Please see your IIS documentation for more information.

Adding your script to the purchase pipeline

Once you have written your script, you need to add it to your Purchase pipeline using the pipeline editor. You can use either the Win32-based pipeline editor or the browser-based pipeline editor that is accessible via your Site Manager application. Let's walk through adding your script to the pipeline using the Win32 pipeline editor:

1. To start the pipeline editor, click Start, Programs, Microsoft Site Server, Commerce, and Pipeline Editor.

2. Open your Purchase pipeline by clicking File, Open, and browsing for your site's *purchase.pcf* file. This file should be located at *c:\Inetpub\wwwroot\your_store_name\Config\purchase.pcf* (unless you installed it to a different location when you ran the Site Builder Wizard).

3. Select the last component in the pipeline (it should be the SaveReceipt component). Right-click this component. From the resulting pop-up menu, select Insert Component, and then select After. This will invoke the Choose a Component dialog box, shown in Figure 6-47.

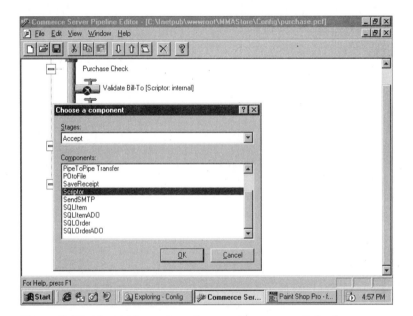

Figure 6-47. *The Pipeline editor Choose a Component dialog box.*

4. Select Scriptor and click OK. The Scriptor Component should now be the last component in the pipeline.

5. Double-click the Scriptor Component. This will invoke the Component Properties property page shown in Figure 6-48.

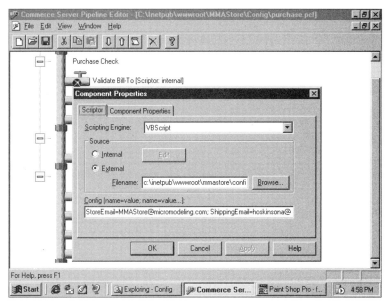

Figure 6-48. *The Scriptor Component's Component Properties dialog box.*

6. Ensure that VBScript is selected as the scripting engine.

7. Under Source, check the External radio button. Click the Browse button and locate your *FulfillOrder.vbs* file using the Open dialog box.

8. In the Config text box, type in your semicolon-delimited list of custom properties. It should look like this: StoreEmail=my_store_email@ myhost.com;ShippingEmail=my_shipping_dept@myhost.com; CustTable=MySiteName_shopper

9. Click the Component Properties tab. Type *FulfillOrder.vbs* in the Label field. Click the OK button.

10. Now, when a shopper purchases an item or items from your site and the purchase pipeline is executed, the FulfillOrder script will send an e-mail message to your shipping department for fulfillment. An example of this message is shown in Figure 6-49.

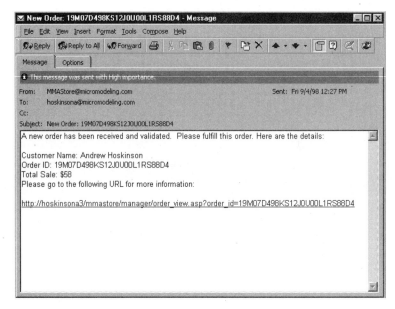

Figure 6-49. *The PO generated by the FulfillOrder pipeline script.*

Clicking the hyperlink will bring up the order view page from the Site Manager application, shown in Figure 6-50. This will provide the shipping department with all the information required to fulfill the order.

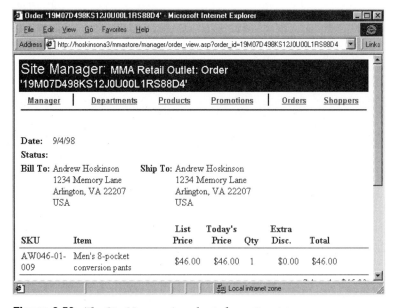

Figure 6-50. *The Site Manager's order information page.*

Also, our FulfillOrder script will send the courtesy e-mail message shown in Figure 6-51 to the shopper following a successful purchase transaction.

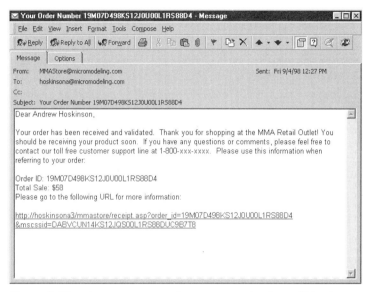

Figure 6-51. *The courtesy e-mail message sent by the FulfillOrder script to the shopper.*

When the customer clicks the URL in the mail message, he can view his receipt online. Figure 6-52 shows an example of what this receipt looks like.

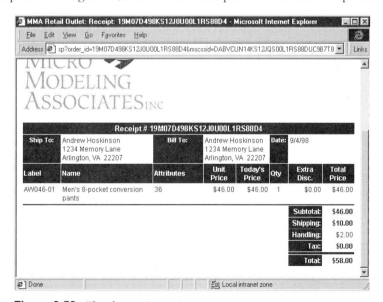

Figure 6-52. *The shopper's receipt.*

BUSINESS-TO-BUSINESS E-COMMERCE PLANNING CONSIDERATIONS

The Web storefront we built is a fairly typical example of a business-to-consumer e-commerce implementation. To be complete, though, we need to build in some backend business-to-business functionality. For example, we need to have a way to automate the submission of purchase orders to the suppliers and wholesalers who would actually ship the product to the customer. Suppliers need a robust, automated way to send us invoices to bill us for the products they shipped. We both need an automated way of receiving shipping notices, product inventory reports, price reports, and other business documents.

In our MMA Retail Outlet sample site, we implemented a simple business-to-business transaction with the FulfillOrder.vbs Scriptor Component sample. As you might recall, one of the tasks performed by this script is to send out an abbreviated purchase order to the shipping department for fulfillment.

This works fine for small Web storefronts that do not move a great deal of inventory. However, for high-volume production sites, you would probably want something a little more robust. Fortunately, the Site Server Commerce Edition CIP (Commerce Interchange Pipeline) framework provides you with all the tools necessary to implement virtually any business-to-business e-commerce scenario.

As mentioned earlier, the CIP automates a process and a framework, and is therefore data and transport independent. This is ideal because business-to-business e-commerce scenarios are situation dependent. There are many different ways to implement business-to-business e-commerce, and implementation strategies vary from organization to organization depending on scalability and security requirements, existing architecture, and trading partner requirements. Regardless of implementation, the desired end results are:

■ The efficient, secure transmission of business documents.

■ Seamless integration with existing systems.

A Web retailer needs to coordinate with suppliers and trading partners to determine the most efficient way of doing this. There are three broad areas that the Web retailer and his trading partners should plan for:

■ **Data format standards** What data format will be used to exchange data between trading partners?

■ **Data transport** How will data actually be moved to trading partners' computers and back?

■ **Security** How will data be protected to ensure that proprietary and sensitive information does not fall prey to prying eyes?

Data Format Standards

The first thing you should coordinate with your trading partners is what data format standard you should use to exchange data. The options are virtually endless; there are no hard and fast rules, and the standard that you and your trading partners should choose is the one that integrates best with the existing systems of all involved parties. There are, however, some common business document data formatting options available that facilitate the exchange of structured data in a heterogeneous environment. These options include EDI and XML.

EDI

Electronic Document Interchange (EDI) has been around for a while (see sidebar) and has a large installed user base. If you are getting into the online retail business, chances are good that many of the suppliers and wholesalers you will deal with already have the infrastructure in place to support EDI. Moreover, virtually all the major e-commerce software vendors provide "out of the box" support for EDI. This allows you to integrate easily with an organization that is using a different application or architecture for its e-commerce platform.

Site Server Commerce Edition supports EDI in several different ways. The CIP MakePO component is written generically enough to allow you to generate EDI documents. You can accomplish this by writing a VBScript template that merges your Commerce.OrderForm object's data elements with the X12 ANSI standard EDI markup. In fact, the Microsoft Market sample site has an excellent example of using the MakePO component to generate an EDI 850 PO (purchase order) document. This example is located at *c:\Microsoft Site Server\SiteServer\Commerce\SDK\Commerce\Samples\PO850Template.txt* on your server. Moreover, there are several third-party ISVs that sell EDI mapping pipeline components that snap right into the CIP.

XML

XML, or *eXtensible Markup Language*, is a Web-friendly markup language that provides a platform-independent way of marking up structured data sets. Chapter 16 has a more thorough description of XML; for now, suffice it to say that in Web terms, XML does for relational databases what HTML did for documents. XML has many of the same advantages that EDI has: it is ASCII text-based and has multi-vendor support; all of the major players either support it now or have pledged to support XML in their products, and XML parser APIs are available for many different programming languages and object request broker technologies. XML has one key advantage over EDI: it offers a much greater degree of business document customization and flexibility. Site Server Commerce Edition ships with two components, MapToXML and MapFromXML, that allow you to send and receive your business documents as XML documents.

Data Transport Options

The next thing you should plan for is how you will physically transport your business documents to your trading partners. When planning for transport, you should plan for what network(s) and protocols you will use to exchange data with your trading partners.

Network

There are several networking options available. The first one is simply to use the Internet. This is the least expensive option but is also the least secure. As new encryption and authentication technologies emerge, though, security becomes less of a concern. An example of this is using an Internet-based VPN (virtual private network) that uses PPTP (point-to-point tunneling protocol) to encrypt data as it moves over the Internet backbone to your trading partners. Another option is to communicate with your trading partners via a private WAN, such as an EDI VAN. This is the most secure option, but it is also the most expensive.

Protocols

There are also several protocol options available. The first option (and perhaps the most common) is to use TCP/IP application layer protocols, such as HTTP, SMTP, and FTP. Site Server Commerce Edition ships with several pipeline components that provide this functionality "out of the box," including a SendSMTP component and a SendHTTP component. FTP is not currently supported out of the box (which is unfortunate, because FTP is the typical protocol used to exchange documents on many EDI VANs), but writing an FTP pipeline component would be a relatively simple exercise for an experienced COM programmer on your staff.

If your trading partners are using DCOM-based solutions, you should also consider using DCOM or Microsoft Message Queue (MSMQ) as your transport. Site Server Commerce Edition ships with a SendDCOM component to facilitate this. If you plan on using MSMQ, Site Server Commerce Edition does not ship with a Send MSMQ component at this time (although Microsoft plans on doing so in a future release). Nevertheless, it would be pretty easy to write your own, or simply to write a Scriptor Component pipeline script that sends your business document via MSMQ. See Chapter 11 for more information on MSMQ.

Security

The third factor you should plan for is security, especially if you plan on conducting business-to-business commerce over the Internet. At a minimum, you should encrypt your business documents to prevent compromise of sensitive data. You should also sign your documents with a digital certificate so your trading partners can verify that the documents actually did come from you when they receive them. Site Server Commerce Edition includes the EncodeSMIME, DecodeSMIME, DigitalSig, and VerifyDigitalSig components to allow you to do this from a CIP.

ADDING ADVERTISING CAMPAIGNS USING AD SERVER

Once you have created and deployed your Web storefront, chances are that it will generate a significant amount of traffic. Once this starts to happen, it opens up another new source of revenue for your site: online advertising. Fortunately, Site Server Commerce Edition includes Ad Server, which makes it easy to integrate online ad campaigns with your e-commerce site.

What Is Ad Server?

Ad Server has three distinct pieces to it. The first piece is a COM Component called Commerce.AdServer. The second piece is a SQL Server database that is used to provide persistent storage for ad campaign data. This database is created during a normal installation of Site Server Commerce Edition. The third piece is the Ad Manager, a browser-based front end to the Ad Server database. Ad Manager lets you create and modify your online ad campaigns. This architecture is shown in Figure 6-53. Together, these tools let you:

- Create targeted ad campaigns for your Web sites
- Schedule ad campaigns by either ad requests (impressions) or clicks
- Support a variety of different ad types, including images, plain text, HTML, Buy Now, and NetShow
- Integrate ad campaigns into existing ASP scripts with only a few lines of code
- Provide your sponsors (advertisers) with detailed impressions and click-through reports to show them the effectiveness of their ad campaign

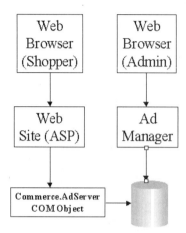

Figure 6-53. *Ad Server Architecture.*

To give you an idea of how easy it is to support online advertising using Ad Server, let's go through an example of how to create a simple ad campaign and integrate it into an existing site. For this demo, we will continue to use our MMA Retail Outlet sample site. Our sponsor is a fictional company called Adventure Works Outdoor Sports Company. They will provide four 468 x 60 .gif ad banners, which they want rotated randomly throughout the site. They want to pay you for a certain amount of clicks, which will be different for each ad banner.

Adding a Customer to Ad Server

The first step is to open Ad Manager by pointing your browser to *http://your_machine_name/admanager/default.asp*. Click the *Customers* hyperlink, and then click the Add New Customer button. This will load the New Customer page. This page contains a form to capture basic contact information about the sponsor, shown in Figure 6-54. Fill out the form, and then click the Add Customer button.

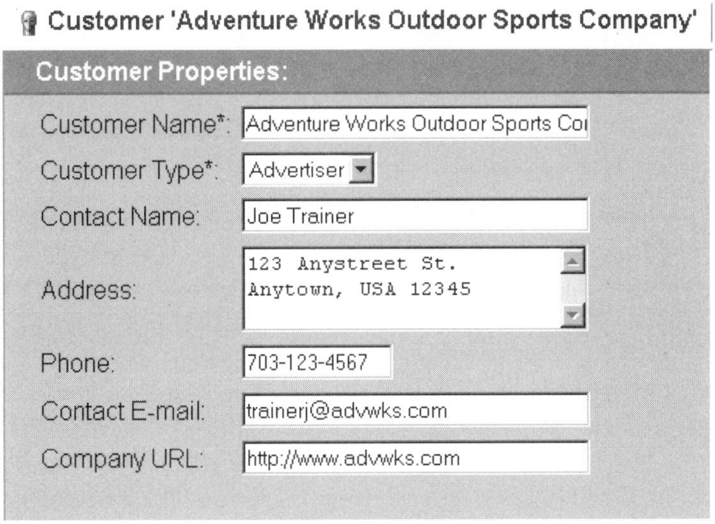

Figure 6-54. *The Ad Server Customer property page.*

Creating an Ad Campaign

Once you have added a customer, the next step is to add a new campaign. A *campaign* is a set of ad banners associated with one customer and scheduled for delivery over a specific period of time. To add a new campaign for the customer you just created, go to the Ad Manager home page, click the *Customers* hyperlink (the hyperlink for the customer you just created), and then click the Add New Campaign button. You will see a form that looks something like the one shown in Figure 6-55.

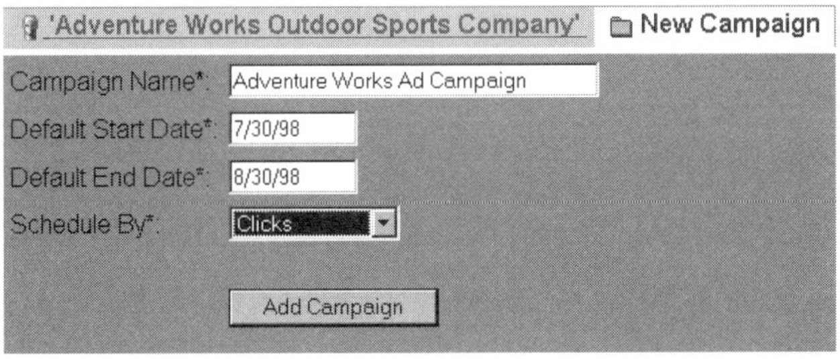

Figure 6-55. *The Add Campaign property page.*

Type a descriptive name for the campaign. Specify the period of time for the campaign by modifying the Default Start Date and the Default End Date. Select your Schedule By parameter from the choice list. This last parameter allows you to make one of two choices:

- *Ad Requests* are used to allow your sponsors to schedule a certain number of impressions. An *Ad Request* occurs when the server delivers the ad banner to a Web browser. For example, if a sponsor buys 100 ad requests for a particular ad banner, Ad Server will serve only that particular ad banner 100 times.

- *Clicks* are used to allow your sponsors to schedule a certain number of clicks. A click occurs when a user actually clicks on a particular ad banner. For example, if a sponsor buys 100 clicks for a particular ad banner, Ad Server will serve that particular ad banner until it reaches a click count of 100.

Once you have filled out this form, click the Add Campaign button.

NOTE   All ads in a given campaign must be scheduled the same way: either by ad request or clicks. If your sponsor wants to buy ad space by clicks for some banners and requests for others, you must segregate those banners into two different campaigns.

Adding Campaign Items

Once you have created a campaign, you can add campaign items to it. A campaign item is basically an ad banner. The Ad Manager has an Add New Campaign item form that allows you to stipulate the ad banner, schedule, ad request or click limit, exposure limit, hyperlink URL, and alternate text to display in lieu of the image (in case a visitor has image loading turned off on his browser). Figure 6-56 shows this form.

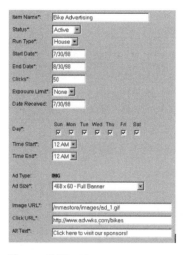

Figure 6-56. *The Campaign Item property page.*

Modifying Your Storefront's ASP to Implement the Ad Campaign

Once you have added all the ad banners to be displayed as part of your sponsor's campaign, you must add some code to your existing ASP to implement ad delivery. Doing this is an easy four-step process:

1. Copy two files to the root of your Web site.

2. Modify your Web site's global.asa file.

3. Add a few lines of code to the pages on which you want to display the ads.

4. Reload your ASP Application object.

Copy two files to the root of your web site

There are two ASP scripts that you must copy to the root of your Web site to implement Ad Server support. These files are amrefresh.asp and adredir.asp, and they are located in the root directory of the *http://your_machine_name/ AdSamples* application.

Amrefresh.asp is used by the Ad Manager's synchronize.asp script to allow you to perform a manual refresh of your Ad Server instance. When you "refresh" your Ad Server instance, you are instructing your instance of Commerce.AdServer to hit the database and update its state with any changes or new data.

Adredir.asp is used to redirect users who click a given ad banner to the advertiser's URL. For example, if an advertiser wanted his ad banner to link to *http://www.mycompany.com/myproduct*, the ad banner's hyperlink constructed by the AdServer object would actually be *http://my_machine_name/my_store/ adredir.asp?ciid=1&url=http://www.mycompany.com/myproduct*. Why do it this way? Because this is how the Ad Server counts clicks on a given ad banner. Prior to redirecting the user to the new URL, adredir.asp calls the RecordEvent method of your Ad Server instance, which logs the event to the IIS log and updates the count in memory.

Modify your web site's global.asa file

The next step is to add some code to the Application_OnStart event handler of your site's *global.asa file*. This code will create an Ad Server instance for your Web site, configure it, and store it in your site's Application object. Please refer to *global.asa* on the sample CD for a complete listing of the following example:

Global.asa Code Fragment: Implementing Ad Server's Application Scope

```
'Create the AdServer object
Set  Ad = Server.CreateObject("Commerce.AdServer")

'Set the connection string to your Ad Server database
Ad.ConnectionString = "DSN=adserver;UID=sa;PWD=;"
•'Set AdServer propertie

•'This is the HTML displayed if AdServer cannot fin
•'an appropriate ad to displa
•Ad.DefaultAd = "<br>

•'This is the refresh interval in seconds.  Refres
•'interval means the amount of time AdServer wait
•'before going back to the database for an updat
•Ad.RefreshInterval = 90

•'This is the number of seconds that AdServer wait
•'between attempts to reconnect with the database i
•'the connection fail
•Ad.RetryInterval = 6

•'The URL of the redirecting ASP file, which logs th
•'click and redirects the user to the advertiser's pag
•Ad.RedirectURL = "/mmastore/adredir.asp

•'If this is set to true, then AdServer will retur
•'an error if it cannot find a suitable ad to display
•'If false, then it will display the default a
•Ad.DesignMode = Fals

•'This is used to distinguish separate instances of th
•'AdServer in the NT Event lo
•Ad.Application = "/MMAStore

•'This assigns your AdServer instance to your ASP app'
•'Application objec

Set Application("Ad")  = Ad
```

Add a few lines of code to the pages on which you want to display the ads. Once you have updated your site's global.asa file, the next step is to add the following lines of code to ASP scripts in which you want to display ads:

```
<% Set Ad = Application("Ad") %>
<%=Ad.GetAd(Response)%>
```

This will display random ad banners (consistent, of course, with the schedule you set for your ad banners) from your ad campaign at the spot on the page where these two lines of code were added.

Two lines of code were added to the i_header.asp file and located in the root directory of the sample MMA Retail Outlet. *I_header.asp* is a header file that is included in every page to ensure a standard look and feel to the site as a whole. By adding these lines of code to this one file, every page on the site will display a random ad banner. Please refer to *i_header.asp* on the sample CD for a complete listing of this example.

I_header.asp Code Fragment: Implementing Rotating Ads (lines 6-15)

```
<TABLE BORDER="0">
<% '****** Added to implement Ad server support   %>
<tr>
<p align="center">
<% Set Ad = Application("Ad") %>
<%=Ad.GetAd(Response)%>
</p>
<br>
</tr>
<% '******* End Ad server support ****** %>
<TR ALIGN="LEFT">
```

Reload your ASP application object

Before ad banners are displayed, the application object must be refreshed by reexecuting the Application_OnStart event handler for the site to ensure that the Ad Server instance is created in the first place. The easiest way to do this is to go to the Site Manager application for the Web storefront and click the Reload Site button. Once you have done that, go back to the shopping site, refresh any page, and you'll see one of your ad banners displayed at the top. Take a look at Figure 6-57, and you'll see what we mean.

Figure 6-57. *The Web storefront after Ad Server support has been implemented.*

Reporting Data to Your Advertisers

One of the things your sponsor will certainly require is a periodic report on how frequently his ads are being displayed and also (perhaps more importantly) how frequently people are actually clicking on those ads to go to his Web site. Fortunately, the Ad Manager application already provides this report. Figure 6-58 shows an example of what this report looks like. To view it, go to the Ad Manager home page, click Customers, click your customer's name, and then click Performance.

Performance Summary							
Customer/Campaign	From	To	Scheduled	Ad Requests	Clicks	Click Rate	Performance
Adventure Works Outdoor Sports Company							
Adventure Works Ad Campaign	7/30/98	8/30/99	320	1286	8	0.62%	Clicks
Training Ad Banner	7/30/98	8/30/99	100 (H)	330	1	0.30%	
Bike Advertising	7/30/98	8/30/99	50 (H)	315	3	0.95%	
Footgear Advertising	7/30/98	8/30/99	80 (H)	342	2	0.58%	
ClockTower Advertising	7/30/98	8/30/99	90 (H)	299	2	0.67%	

Figure 6-58. *The ad campaign performance summary report.*

Targeting Your Ad Campaign

With Ad Server, you also have the ability to create *targeted ads*. A targeted ad is an ad that is displayed only to those shoppers who are likely to have some interest in the product or service being advertised. Ad Server implements targeted ad creation by matching "tags" stored with the ad campaign item in the Ad Server database with tags that are passed to the GetAd method of your site's Ad Server instance at runtime. A *tag* is simply a keyword. You can create tags for your ad campaign items using the Ad Manager application. There are three types of tags you can store with an ad campaign item:

- **Target tags.** A target tag will increase an ad's selection weight when the target tag matches a tag passed to the GetAd method.

- **Required tags.** A required tag will cause the ad to be selected only if the target tag matches a tag passed to the GetAd method.

- **Exclude tags.** An exclude tag will prevent an ad from being selected if the exclude tag matches a tag passed to the GetAd method.

How, then, do you determine at runtime what tags to pass to your Ad Server instance's GetAd method? There are a couple of different techniques you can use:

- On your shopper registration page, you can add some logic that allows shoppers to select preferences from a list. As a shopper moves through your site, you can get these preferences from the database and feed them to the GetAd method's optional TagList argument.

- You can also base the TagList argument on the currently displayed content. For example, if the shopper is looking at backpacks, you can code your ASP to pass "backpack" as a tag to the GetAd method. That way, your Ad Server instance will serve up an ad banner that relates to backpacks, assuming you added a target or required tag called "backpack" to some of your ad campaign items.

To give you a specific example of how to do this, start your Ad Manager application, click the customer hyperlink, select any customer, select one of that customer's campaigns, and then select a campaign item. On the right side of the page where it says "Campaign Item Targets," type *Backpack* in the text box, and then click the Add New Target button. Next, open your i_header.asp script and replace your existing Ad Server implementation code with this code fragment:

```
<% '****** Added to implement Ad server support ****** %>
<tr>
<p align="center">
<%
Set Ad = Application("Ad")
'This variable will hold the current script we are running on
Dim strScriptName

'Get the current script from the Request object
strScriptName = Request.ServerVariables("SCRIPT_NAME")

'Since I_header.asp is an included file, we need to first
'find out what page we are on. If we are on the department
'script or the product script, we will assign the value of
'the dept_name variable to an array, and pass that array to
'the Taglist argument of our Ad Server instance's GetAd method.
'(dept_name is read from the DB on those 2 pages). When we are
'on the backpack department page or one of the backpack product
'pages, dept_name will be equal to "backpack."  Otherwise,
'we'll simply call Ad.GetAd(Response), just like before.
if (instr(strScriptName,"dept.asp") > 0) or _
(instr(strScriptName,"product.asp") > 0) then
    dim strTaglist(1)
    strTaglist(1) = dept_name
%>
<%=Ad.GetAd(Response, strTaglist)%>
<%else%>
<%=Ad.GetAd(Response)%>
<%end if%>
</p>
<br>
</tr>
<% '******* End Ad Server support ****** %>
```

Next, shop your site. You will notice that, for most pages, Ad Server is serving up random ad banners. However, if you go to the Backpack department page or the product page for any of the individual backpack products, the only ad banner you will get is the banner to which you added the "Backpack" tag.

For more information on Ad Server tagging, consult the Site Server SDK.

SUMMARY

Site Server 3.0 Commerce Edition builds on the Microsoft Active Server platform by providing an extensive collection of COM objects, services, and Win32 and browser-based authoring tools for creating sophisticated Web-based business-to-consumer and business-to-business e-commerce solutions. With Site Server Commerce Edition, you can create fully-functional Web storefronts quickly and easily, while at the same time retaining the ability to fully customize and extend the look, feel, and functionality of your e-commerce site.

Of course, most sophisticated production e-commerce sites will, at one point or another, involve writing custom COM objects from scratch. This is the topic of the next chapter. Happy coding!

Part IV

Server Side
Components

Chapter 7

Active Server Pages

by Steve Gilmore

Microsoft developed *Active Server Pages (ASP)* as a server-side scripting architecture for building dynamic Web applications. With ASP, you can combine client-side HTML, scripting, and ActiveX controls with server-side scripting and COM/DCOM components to create dynamic content and sophisticated Web-based applications. ASP is included with Internet Information Server (IIS) on Windows NT Server, Peer Web Services on Windows NT Workstation, and Personal Web Server (PWS) on Windows 9X and Macintosh platforms.

ASP applications can be powerful and complex yet easy to create and extend. ASP enables component-based Web development in any language, including Visual Basic, C++, and J++. This allows developers to leverage their existing skillsets to build browser-independent Web applications with tools and languages they already know. ASP allows you to separate the programming and logic from the design and content of a Web page.

BENEFITS OF USING ASP

With so many server-side development technologies available today, why would you want to use ASP? ASP is an ideal environment for building Web-based Commerce solutions. The following list highlights some of the benefits you can realize by building and deploying your Web solutions using ASP:

- **Browser-neutral.** All application logic can be executed on the server, with complete control over what is sent to the browser.

- **No new languages to learn.** ASP pages can be written in languages such as VBScript, JScript, and Perl. This allows both Web page designers and application programmers to leverage their existing skillsets.

- **No complicated development tools to learn.** Although powerful development tools exist, ASP pages can be created using your favorite HTML editor.

- **Component-based.** Like other Windows application environments, ASP pages can use COM or DCOM objects for maximum reuse. You can use the components that are included with ASP, third-party components, or your own components.

- **Transactional.** ASP pages and their objects can run within a transaction, allowing object-level rollback and commit functionality for increased system integrity.

- **Robust debugging.** The Script Debugger supports interactive debugging of both client- and server-side scripts.

- **Secure.** Unlike client-side scripting and components, ASP pages reside and run only on the server. Users cannot view the ASP pages in their browsers; they can only view the HTML output from those pages.

- **Stable.** Each ASP application can be isolated in its own memory space separate from the Web server. If one Web application fails, the other applications and the Web server will continue running.

CREATING ASP PAGES

ASP pages can be created in any scripting language that complies with the ActiveX Scripting standard. VBScript and JScript scripting engines ship with ASP, but compliant third-party scripting engines for languages such as Perl and REXX are also available.

An ASP page is simply a file with an .asp file extension that contains any combination of text, HTML, XML, client-side script, and server-side script. When a browser requests an .asp file, IIS passes the request to the ASP engine (ASP.DLL). The ASP engine parses the file line by line, executes any server-side script logic, and sends any output to the browser. Because ASP scripts run on the Web server and return only the script's output to the browser, ASP script logic cannot be viewed from the browser.

It's easy to create an .asp file; just change the file extension of any HTML page to .asp. If you then request the .asp file, you'll see the original HTML page in the browser (the .asp file or its directory will need Script or Execute permission enabled). Though the resulting Web page looks the same, the .asp file was processed by the ASP engine *before* its output was returned to the browser.

> **NOTE** Only pages that contain server-side script should have .asp file extensions. The ASP engine represents additional server processing that isn't necessary for static HTML Web pages.

Development Tools

Although you can use any text editor to create .asp files, using a tool designed to support ASP development, such as Microsoft FrontPage or Visual InterDev, will yield the best results. FrontPage allows you to add ASP logic to Web pages using the Insert Script command. Visual InterDev is designed specifically for ASP-based Web site development and provides a sophisticated environment for creating, debugging, and deploying advanced Web applications. Visual InterDev is shown in Figure 7-1.

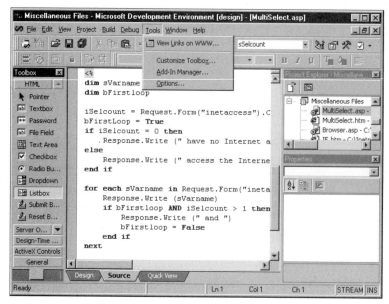

Figure 7-1. *Microsoft Visual InterDev.*

GENERATING WEB PAGES DYNAMICALLY WITH ASP

Server-side script can be added to an ASP page by placing any valid scripting command between the <% and %> delimiters. For example, the following ASP page uses the VBScript Date function to display the Web server's current date:

```
<HTML>
<BODY>
The current date on the Web server is <%= Date %>.
</BODY>
</HTML>
```

The equal sign (=) within the delimiters is one way to direct ASP to return the results of the Date function to the Web browser. The ASP engine processes the page, calls the Date function, and replaces <%= Date %> with the current date before returning the page to the browser. Each time the ASP page is requested, it dynamically calls the Date function and builds the Web page returned to the browser.

NOTE   The examples in this chapter assume you have a working knowledge of HTML. For more information on HTML, see Chapter 13 in this book.

You can mix server-side script and HTML in an ASP page as needed. For example, a page using server-side VBScript that determines whether today is a workday or not looks like this:

```
<HTML>
<BODY>
<% If Weekday(Date)< 2 or Weekday(Date) > 6 Then %>
It's the Weekend!
<% Else %>
It's a workday.
<% End If %>
</BODY>
</HTML>
```

If today happens to be Tuesday (that is, weekday 3), then ASP processes the page and sends only the following HTML back to the Web browser:

```
<HTML>
<BODY>
It's a workday.
</BODY>
</HTML>
```

Setting the Default Scripting Language

Microsoft Visual Basic Scripting Edition (VBScript) is the default scripting language for ASP pages. VBScript is a subset of Visual Basic providing fewer features such as no support for variable data types. To learn more about VBScript, see the Microsoft Scripting site at *msdn.microsoft.com/scripting*.

The default can be changed at three levels if you want to use a different language: Web server, ASP application, or ASP page. You define an ASP application by designating a starting directory in Internet Service Manager. All files and folders under that directory are considered part of the application until another application's starting directory is reached. IIS can host multiple applications. To change the default language for the entire Web server or an ASP application, change the Web server or application's Default ASP Language property in Internet Service Manager.

To override the default language for a single ASP page, place the following directive at the top of the ASP page before any server-side script:

```
<%@ LANGUAGE=ScriptingLanguage %>
```

The @ sign is used to indicate an ASP processing directive that sends information to IIS about how to process an .asp file. In this case, IIS is being explicitly told what language the ASP page's script is written in.

Multiple scripting languages can be used on an ASP page by using the HTML <SCRIPT> tag and its LANGUAGE and RUNAT attributes. The syntax looks like this:

```
<SCRIPT LANGUAGE=ScriptingLanguage RUNAT=Server>
    script goes here
</SCRIPT>
```

Although you can use multiple server-side scripting languages in a page, it is preferable to use a single language for all script in a page and the entire application if possible. The use of multiple languages requires the ASP engine to load multiple scripting engines and perform more work as it determines which piece of script should be sent to which scripting engine. While this performance hit might not be noticeable on low-volume Web sites, it will reduce the responsiveness and scalability of the application. In addition, your staff and support costs could increase due to the burden of maintaining code in different languages.

ADDING COMMENTS TO ASP PAGES

To add comments to your server-side scripts, use an apostrophe for VBScript and two slashes for JScript. A comment in each language looks like this:

```
'This is a VBScript comment.
//This is a JScript comment.
```

Unlike HTML comments, server-side script comments are not sent to the browser. However, they do need to be parsed by the ASP engine. Therefore, the more comments you add, the longer the ASP page will take to process. Although the additional time is usually insignificant, it can reduce the scalability of high-volume sites. So plan your comments wisely.

THE SERVER-SIDE #INCLUDE DIRECTIVE

Server-Side Includes (SSI) provide a way to insert the content of a file into your ASP pages. A good way to reduce maintenance and increase code reuse is by creating a file of common script, style sheets, or HTML, and then including the file in multiple ASP pages. Multiple files can be included in an ASP page, allowing a modular development approach. Include files typically have an .inc extension, but this is not required, so you can give them any unique extension that helps you identify them as include files.

To include a file into an ASP page, place the #INCLUDE directive and either the VIRTUAL or FILE keyword inside HTML comment tags. Including a file with the FILE keyword indicates the file is located in a path relative to the ASP page, and it looks like this:

```
<!--#include file="common/copyright.inc"-->
```

NOTE If you want to include a file from a parent directory, make sure you have Enable Parent Paths selected in Internet Service Manager.

Internet Service Manager

The Internet Service Manager (shown in Figure 7-2) is a Microsoft Management Console (MMC) snap-in used to configure settings for IIS and the ASP environment. Use it to start and stop, configure, and tune your Web server. Right click on the Web server or a Web site you want to configure, and then select Properties to access the settings as shown in Figure 7-3.

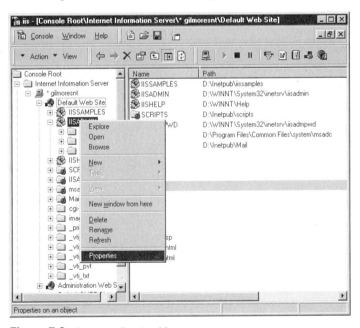

Figure 7-2. *Internet Service Manager.*

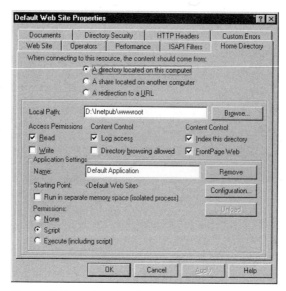

Figure 7-3. *Web Site Properties page.*

Including a file with the VIRTUAL keyword indicates the file is located in a path beginning with a virtual directory, and it looks like this:

```
<!--#include virtual="/corp_images/header_logo.inc"-->
```

Although the include file concept sounds simple, there's more to it than it may seem. Understanding the following include file characteristics will save you some time:

- When you include a file in an ASP page, the ASP engine locates the file and adds it to the ASP page before the page is processed. This means you cannot use script to build the name of an include file.

- Include files can be added to ASP pages or other include files. The same include file can also be added to another file more than once. However, if you create two include files that include each other or an include file that includes itself, you will get an error message.

- You cannot use an opening script delimiter (<%) in an ASP file, and its closing delimiter (%>) in an included file, and vise versa. Both tags must be either inside or outside of the include file.

- ASP detects changes to include files that are contained under an application's root or home directory and will reflect those

266

changes the next time the include file is requested. However, the application needs to be restarted using the Internet Service Manager before changes to referenced include files residing outside the application are reflected.

A common use for include files is to contain page footer information such as a disclaimer or copyright text. For example, a copyright include file containing a copyright symbol and a date could look like this:

```
<i>&copy; Copyright 1999</i>
```

An ASP page could then add the include file to the bottom of any page. An example of this can be found on the companion CD in the \Chapter 7\ directory and looks like this:

```
<%@ Language=VBScript %>
<HTML>
<HEAD>
<TITLE>Include file example</TITLE>
</HEAD>
<BODY>
<h3>Server Side Includes (SSI) example</h3>
The copyright text below is from a separate include file.
<p> <!--#INCLUDE FILE="copyright.inc"--> </p>
</BODY>
</HTML>
```

What ASP returns to the browser looks like this and is shown in Figure 7-4:

```
<HTML>
<HEAD>
<TITLE>Include file example</TITLE>
</HEAD>
<BODY>
<h3>Server Side Includes (SSI) example</h3>
The copyright text below is from a separate include file.
<p> <i>&copy; Copyright 1999</i>
 </p>
</BODY>
</HTML>
```

Figure 7-4. *SSI output.*

Though the previous example is simple, you can see how much maintenance could be eliminated by placing common elements in include files. If fifty of your application's Web pages have a standard menu and that menu changes, just modify the include file containing the menu to update each of the fifty pages the next time a browser requests it.

INTRINSIC ASP OBJECTS

ASP provides built-in objects that make it easy for Web pages to receive and respond to browser requests as well as manage application-level and user-level information. Because these objects are intrinsic to the ASP environment, you do not need to create an instance of a built-in object before you use it in your scripts. Here are the objects automatically available to ASP scripts:

- **Application.** Used to share information among all users of the Web application. The Application object is a good place to store anything common to the application such as database connection strings, frequently used lookup lists, and environment information.

- **Session.** Used to maintain user information across multiple Web page requests. The information is kept for the duration of a user's session (which can be configured with the Session object's TIMEOUT property), and is therefore a good place to store data specific to the user.

- **Request.** Used to access information passed from the browser when requesting a Web page. This includes HTML form fields, client certificate information, and cookies.

- **Response.** Used to send information back to the browser. This includes dynamic Web pages and cookies as well as instructions that redirect the browser to another URL.

- **Server.** Primarily used to instantiate objects in your ASP scripts using its CreateObject method. This will be discussed in detail later in this chapter.

- **ObjectContext.** Used to commit or abort transactions managed by Microsoft Transaction Server (MTS).

Accessing Objects with Script

Interacting with objects from script is identical to working with objects from languages like VB and C++. Let's quickly review how to reference an object's properties and methods from VBScript.

Setting and getting properties

To set the value of an object's property, place the object and its property to the left of the equal sign and the value the property on the right, like this:

```
<% Object.Property = Value %>
```

To get a value contained in an object's property, do the opposite, like this:

```
<% Value = Object.Property %>
```

Value can be a variable, the results of a function or method call, or the property of another object. This line of code moves the value of a property of one object to the property of another object:

```
<% Object1.Property = Object2.Property %>
```

Calling methods

Object method calls can be written two ways:

```
Object.Method [Param1, Param ...]
```

Or

```
Call Object.Method([Param1, Param ...])
```

Parameters are optional. However, if the Call keyword is used, the parameters must be included in parentheses. If the Call keyword is used and the method has no parameters, empty parentheses are required. Method return values can be captured in variables using syntax similar to that of setting properties earlier, like this:

```
MethodResults = Object.Method([Param1, Param ...])
```

The following script example updates a user-defined Application object variable called "hits." Notice the Application object's Lock and Unlock methods are used. This prevents contention if two users try to access an Application-level variable at the same time.

```
<%
Application.Lock
Application("hits") = Application("hits") + 1
Application.Unlock
%>
Total page hits:<%=Application("hits")%>
```

The next example, found on the companion CD in the \Chapter 7\ directory, uses the Request object to detect whether the browser is Internet Explorer or not. If the browser is IE (as shown in Figure 7-5), the Response object's Redirect method is called, returning a different page to the browser. If the browser is not IE, the HTML in this page is returned to the browser.

```
<%@ Language=VBScript%>
<%
if inStr(Request.ServerVariables("HTTP_USER_AGENT"),"MSIE") then
      Response.Redirect ("ie.htm")
else
%>
<HTML>
<HEAD>
</HEAD>
<BODY>
This page is displayed for Non-Internet Explorer browsers.
</BODY>
</HTML>
<%end if%>
```

Figure 7-5. *Detecting browser type.*

The following example, found in the \Chapter 7\ directory of the companion CD, retrieves all the values from the Request object's ServerVariables collection and displays them in an HTML table. Notice how the server-side script and the HTML are combined to build each row of the table inside the VBScript For loop:

```
<%@ LANGUAGE = VBScript %>
<HTML>
<HEAD>
<TITLE>Server Variables Example</TITLE>
</HEAD>
<BODY>
<H3>Server Variables Example</H3>
<TABLE BORDER=1>
<TR><TH>Variable Name</TH><TH>Value</TH></TR>
<%
      dim varname
      for each varname in Request.ServerVariables
             Response.Write ("<TR><TD>" & varname & "<
TD><TD>" & Request.ServerVariables(varname)& "</TD><
TR>")
      next

%>
</TABLE>
</BODY>
</HTML>
```

In addition, the Response.Write method is used to return content to the browser. This method has the same behavior as using its shortcut, the equal sign (=), shown earlier. Figure 7-6 shows what this page looks like in a browser.

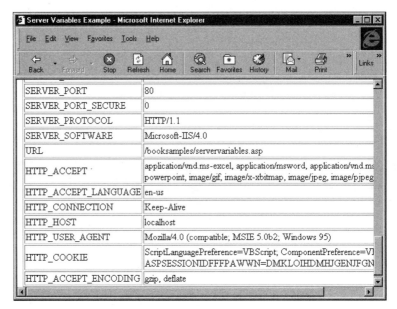

Figure 7-6. *Request.ServerVariables.*

Example: Collecting user input

It is common to require information from your customers to complete orders and transactions. ASP makes collecting user input easy by providing the Request object's Form collection. If the browser submits a form to your Web server, ASP automatically parses the HTML form element names and values and then puts them in the Form collection.

> **NOTE** If data is sent to the Web server by appending it to the URL or by submitting the form using the Get method, ASP will put the data in the Request object's QueryString collection instead of the Form collection.

The following HTML page, from the \Chapter 7\ directory of the companion CD and shown in Figure 7-7, allows the user to make multiple selections for the same input element. When the Submit button is clicked, the browser posts the form information to the *multiselect.asp* page:

```
<HTML>
<HEAD>
<TITLE>Multi-select Form Example</TITLE>
</HEAD>
<BODY>
<FORM ACTION="MultiSelect.asp" METHOD="post">
<TABLE BORDER=0>
<TR>
<TD ALIGN=right VALIGN=top>
Business:
</TD>
<TD>
<SELECT MULTIPLE NAME="business" SIZE=5>

<OPTION VALUE=1>Banking</OPTION>
<OPTION VALUE=2>Finance</OPTION>
<OPTION VALUE=3>Government</OPTION>
<OPTION VALUE=4>Medical</OPTION>
<OPTION VALUE=5>Education</OPTION>
<OPTION VALUE=6>Computer Related</OPTION>
<OPTION VALUE=7>Other</OPTION>
</SELECT>
</TD>
</TR>
<TR>
<TD ALIGN=right VALIGN=top>
Where do you access<BR> the Internet from:
</TD>
<TD>
<INPUT TYPE="checkbox" NAME="inetaccess" VALUE="at home">At home
<INPUT TYPE="checkbox" NAME="inetaccess" VALUE="at work">At work
</TD>
</TR>
<TR><TD COLSPAN=2 ALIGN=middle><INPUT TYPE=submit value="Submit
Query"></TD></TR>
</TABLE>
</FORM>
<DIV></DIV>
</BODY>
</HTML>
```

Figure 7-7. *Multiselect.htm.*

The *multiselect.asp* page uses the Form collection's Count property and a For loop to retrieve and display the multiple values selected as shown in Figure 7-8:

```
<%@ LANGUAGE = VBScript %>
<HTML>
<HEAD>
<TITLE>Multi-select Example</TITLE>
</HEAD>
<BODY>
<H3>Multi-select Example</H3>
You selected
<%
dim iSelcount
iSelcount = request.form("business").count
select case iSelcount
      case 0
            response.write (" no businesses")
      case 1
            response.write (" 1 business")
      case else
            response.write (" multiple businesses")
end select
%>
<P>You
<%
dim sVarname
```

```
dim bFirstloop
iSelcount = Request.Form("inetaccess").Count
bFirstLoop = True
if iSelcount = 0 then
        Response.Write (" have no Internet access")
else
        Response.Write (" access the Internet ")

end if
for each sVarname in Request.Form("inetaccess")
        Response.Write (sVarname)
        if bFirstloop AND iSelcount > 1 then
                Response.Write (" and ")
                bFirstloop = False
        end if
next
%>
</P>
</BODY>
</HTML>
```

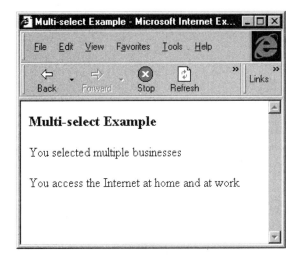

Figure 7-8. *Multiselect.asp.*

Using Components in Active Server Pages

Although components have been discussed in previous chapters, here's a quick review. A *component* is a unit of compiled or scripted code that encapsulates a set of business functionality. For example, a query component might retrieve a customer's order history from a database based on the user account parameter passed to it.

Components allow developers to provide the same sophisticated business logic in Web sites as in applications written in languages like Visual Basic or Visual C++. Because the code is encapsulated, components provide consistent, reusable functionality that is easy to maintain and share. A component can be modified or enhanced without affecting the rest of the application.

Several components come with ASP. You can also use components from third-party developers or write your own components in any programming language that supports the Component Object Model (COM), such as Visual Basic, C++, or J++.

> **NOTE**   Components run on the Web server; therefore, they should not have any graphical user interface elements (including error message boxes) because no one will be able to interact with them or respond to them.

Creating an Instance of a Component's Object

A component exposes one or more objects through its interface: the component's properties, methods, and events. To use a component's object, create an instance of the object and assign it to a variable with the ASP Server.CreateObject method. For example, the ASP Ad Rotator component randomly rotates through a series of graphical advertisements. The Ad Rotator component provides one object, the Ad Rotator object, whose registered name (PROGID) is "MSWC.AdRotator." To create an instance of the Ad Rotator object, use the following statement:

```
<% Set AdRotObj = Server.CreateObject("MSWC.AdRotator") %>
```

COMPONENTS INCLUDED
WITH ACTIVE SERVER PAGES

The easiest way to start developing Web applications using components is to use the server components included with ASP. Table 7-1 lists the available components.

Table 7-1
ASP SERVER COMPONENTS

Component	PROGID	Description
Ad Rotator	MSWC.AdRotator	Automatically rotates ad banners displayed on a page according to a configurable schedule
Browser Capabilities	MSWC.BrowserType	Determines the features available in each browser that accesses your Web site
Content Linking	MSWC.NextLink	Creates a table of contents of Web page links like pages in a book
Content Rotator	MSWC.ContentRotator	Like the Ad Rotator except it's for HTML content strings (not ad banners)
Counters	MSWC.Counters	Creates and manages any number of individual counters
File Access	Scripting.FileSystem Object	Provides access to flat file input and output
MyInfo	MSWC.Myinfo	Tracks personal information, such as display choices
Page Counter	MSWC.PageCounter	Classic Web page counter that records page hits
Permission Checker	MSWC.Permission Checker	Uses IIS authentication to determine whether a user has permissions to access a file
Tools	MSWC.Tools	Provides common utilities (like generating random numbers and checking for the existence of a file)

One of the most useful of these objects is the File Access object. With it, you can handle most file system functions such as reading, writing, or getting file size and date. Files are often good alternatives to databases when the information they contain is small and simple, such as application initialization files (.ini files).

To demonstrate, the following example collects order information from a customer, writes it to a file, and then displays the contents of the order file in the browser. The order entry form (shown in Figure 7-9) can be found in the \Chapter 7\ directory of the companion CD, and its source code looks like this:

```
<HTML>
<HEAD>
<TITLE>Order Form</TITLE>
</HEAD>
<BODY BGCOLOR="#ffffff" TEXT="#000077" LINK="#ff0000">
<DIV ALIGN=center>
<FORM ACTION="orderform.asp" METHOD="post">

<TABLE BORDER=0>
<TR><TH colspan=2>Order Information</TH></TR>
<TR>
<TD>
Product:
</TD>
<TD>
<SELECT NAME="product" SIZE=1>
<OPTION VALUE=1 selected>Product A</OPTION>
<OPTION VALUE=2>Product B</OPTION>
<OPTION VALUE=3>Product C</OPTION>
<OPTION VALUE=4>Product D</OPTION>
<OPTION VALUE=5>Product E</OPTION>
<OPTION VALUE=6>Product F</OPTION>
</SELECT>
</TD>
</TR>

<TR>
<TD>
Color:
</TD>
<TD>
<SELECT NAME="color" SIZE=1>
<OPTION VALUE=1 selected>Red</OPTION>
<OPTION VALUE=2>Green</OPTION>
<OPTION VALUE=3>Blue</OPTION>
<OPTION VALUE=4>Black</OPTION>
<OPTION VALUE=5>White</OPTION>
```

```
</SELECT>
</TD>
</TR>

<TR>
<TD>
Size:
</TD>
<TD>
<SELECT NAME="size" SIZE=1>
<OPTION VALUE=1 selected>S</OPTION>
<OPTION VALUE=2>M</OPTION>
<OPTION VALUE=3>L</OPTION>
<OPTION VALUE=4>XL</OPTION>
    </SELECT>
</TD>
</TR>

<TR>
<TD>
Quantity:
</TD>
<TD>
<SELECT NAME="quantity" SIZE=1>
<OPTION VALUE=1 selected>1</OPTION>
<OPTION VALUE=2>2</OPTION>
<OPTION VALUE=3>3</OPTION>
<OPTION VALUE=4>4</OPTION>
<OPTION VALUE=5>5</OPTION>
</SELECT>
</TD>
</TR>

<TR><TH colspan=2>Shipping Information</TH></TR>
<TR>
<TD>
Name:
</TD>
<TD>
<INPUT NAME="name" LENGTH  = 30 SIZE=30>
</TD>
</TR>

<TR>
<TD>
```

(continued)

(continued)

```
Account Number:
</TD>
<TD>
<INPUT TYPE=password NAME="account" LENGTH = 30 SIZE=30>
</TD>
</TR>


<TR>
<TD>
E-mail Address:
</TD>
<TD>
<INPUT NAME="email" LENGTH = 30 SIZE=30>
</TD>
</TR>

<TR>
<TD>
Address:
</TD>
<TD>
<INPUT NAME="street" LENGTH  = 30 TYP = TEXT SIZE=30>

</TD>
</TR>


<TR>
<TD>
City:
</TD>
<TD>
<INPUT NAME="city" LENGTH = 30 SIZE=30>
</TD>
</TR>

<TR>
<TD>
State:
</TD>
<TD>
<INPUT NAME="state" LENGTH = 2 SIZE=2>
</TD>
</TR>
```

```
<TR>
<TD>
Zip Code:
</TD>
<TD>
<INPUT NAME="zip" LENGTH = 10 SIZE=10>
</TD>
</TR>
<TR>
<TD COLSPAN=2 ALIGN=middle>
<INPUT TYPE=submit value="Submit Query">
</TD>
</TR>
</TABLE>
</FORM>
</DIV>
</BODY>
</HTML>
```

Figure 7-9. *Orderform.htm.*

The *orderform.asp* page, from the \Chapter 7\ directory of the companion CD, uses the Session object's SessionID property to create a unique order file name. The File Access object is used to first read and then write the order file back to the browser (as show in Figure 7-10):

```
<% @Language=VBScript%>
<HTML>
<HEAD>
<TITLE>Chapter 7 Example - Order Form.</TITLE>
</HEAD>
<BODY>
<H3>Order Results</H3>

<%
'set file path and name using the Server and Session objects
DefaultDir = Server.MapPath("\")
sFileName = session.SessionID & ".txt"

'open file
Set fs = Server.CreateObject("Scripting.FileSystemObject")
Set sFile = fs.CreateTextFile(DefaultDir & "\" & sFileName)

'write all form field values to the file
FOR EACH elementname IN Request.form
sFile.WriteLine (elementname & ":" & Request.Form(elementname))
NEXT

'close file
sFile.Close
%>

The order file <%=DefaultDir & "\" & sFileName%> was just created.
<P>Here is the contents of the order file:</P>

<%
Set sFile = fs.OpenTextFile(DefaultDir & "\" & sFileName)
DO WHILE NOT sFile.AtEndOfStream
      Response.Write (sFile.ReadLine & "<BR>")
LOOP
%>
</BODY>
</HTML>
```

Figure 7-10. *Orderform.asp.*

DATABASE ACCESS WITH ACTIVE DATA OBJECTS

Although knowing how to use text files as shown in the example in the preceding section is an important skill to have, the preferred approach to storing and securing order information is via a relational database. This can be accomplished by using *ActiveX Data Objects (ADO)*, a technology that provides connectivity to any ODBC or OLE DB data source. Using ADO, databases can be accessed from ASP scripts and common languages such as Visual Basic and C++. This allows you to integrate your Web Commerce applications with legacy accounting and fulfillment systems so that changes in an inventory or pricing database will be reflected in the Web application immediately without changing code. For more on accessing data sources from ASP, see Chapter 8.

CREATING ASP APPLICATIONS

Now that you know many of the details of ASP, we'll take a brief look at some of the issues relating to ASP applications as a whole. These include the Global.asa file, object scope, session management, and the implications of using Web farms.

Global.asa

The *Global.asa* file is an optional file in which you can specify application and session start and end event scripts. An application starts when the first user visits an ASP application and ends when the last user leaves. A session is started when each user first visits an ASP application and ends, by default, after 20 minutes of inactivity. Only one Global.asa file is allowed per application, and it is used to perform processing when these application and session events occur. Reading configuration information or creating objects and variables used globally by the application might be typical tasks.

Global.asa can also contain other script routines, but these routines are accessible only from within the Global.asa. They cannot be referenced from other ASP pages in the application. To use this file, it must be named Global.asa and must be placed in the root directory of the application. The following four event routines can be included in any combination and in any order in *Global.asa:*

GLOBAL.ASA EVENT ROUTINES

Event Routine	*Description*
Application_OnStart	Occurs when the first user accesses the Web application. Useful for setting up application-level information like common lookup lists and application settings.
Application_OnEnd	Occurs after the last user's session is terminated (see Session_OnEnd for a definition of how the end of a session is determined). Useful for updating and closing global resources.
Session_OnStart	Occurs when each user first accesses the Web site. Useful for validating login information and retrieving personalization information.
Session_OnEnd	Occurs when each user's session times out. The default timeout is 20 minutes after the user's last request. The session can be terminated explicitly in script using the Session.Abort method. Doing so also causes the Session_OnEnd event to occur.

These event routines are enclosed in <SCRIPT></SCRIPT> tags as described earlier in this chapter, like this:

```
<SCRIPT LANGUAGE=ScriptingLanguage RUNAT=Server>
  script goes here
</SCRIPT>
```

You only need to include script tags and code for the events you want to use. For example, if you did not need the Session_OnEnd event, you could leave it out. The structure of the Global.asa would then looks like this:

```
<SCRIPT LANGUAGE=VBScript RUNAT=Server>
Sub Application_OnStart
'application startup code goes here
End Sub
</SCRIPT>

<SCRIPT LANGUAGE=VBScript RUNAT=Server>

Sub Application_OnEnd
'application shutdown code goes here
End Sub
</SCRIPT>
<SCRIPT LANGUAGE=VBScript RUNAT=Server>
Sub Session_OnStart
' session startup code goes here
End Sub
</SCRIPT>
```

When you make a change to Global.asa, IIS finishes processing all current requests in its queue and then restarts the Web application and reflects the changes made to Global.asa. Though this process does not take much time, additional requests cannot be processed while the Web application is being restarted.

NOTE Changing a file that Global.asa refers to does not cause IIS to recompile Global.asa. IIS only watches for changes to Global.asa itself.

Setting Object Scope

The scope of an object determines which scripts can use the object. An object that you create on an ASP page by using Server.CreateObject exists for the life of that page (until the page is finished processing).

An object that has session scope is created for each new session in the Web application and destroyed when the session ends. A Session Scope object can be referenced from multiple scripts, but it affects only one user session. To give an object session scope, store the object in the intrinsic ASP Session object, like this:

```
<% Set Session("AdRotObj") = Server.CreateObject("MSWC.AdRotator")
%>
```

To use the object, set a local variable to point to the session variable, and then work with the local variables properties and methods, like this:

```
<%
Set AdRotObj = Session("AdRotObj")
Response.write  AdRotObj.GetAdvertisement("myAddData.txt")
%>
```

An object with application scope is a single instance of an object that is available to all users of the Web application. Objects such as counters are good candidates for application scope.

Give objects session or application scope only when needed. Because these objects linger until the session or application has finished running, they consume resources, such as memory or database connections, that might be better used in other ways. In addition, the threading model of a component affects the performance of objects you create from it, especially objects with session or application scope. (For more information on threading models and object scope, please refer to Chapter 11.)

Application- and session-level variables can be effective for sharing resources, but you should avoid creating application- and session-level objects when possible. For example, you should not give an ADO Connection object session or application scope because the connection it creates remains open for an extended amount of time and because your script can no longer use ODBC connection pooling.

Storing shared parameters for that Connection object (such as the data source information) in the session or application name space and accessing them from a page-level Connection object is a more efficient use of resources.

ASP and Session Management

One of the benefits of ASP is that it has powerful session management built right in. The Session object will maintain the information stored for the user's session in memory on the server. The user is provided with a unique session ID (via an HTTP cookie) that ASP uses to match user requests with the information specific to that user's session. Each subsequent request by the browser to the server includes the cookie. When ASP receives a browser request, it uses the cookie to retrieve and restore the session information. This allows session information to span multiple Web page requests. If users have cookies disabled in their browser, ASP's built-in session management cannot be used.

Web Farms and ASP Session State

Web farms are a technique for scaling a Web site with hardware. Typically, a Web farm consists of multiple Web servers running identical copies of the same Web site. As requests come in to the farm, each request is distributed among the Web servers in the farm. When more capacity is needed, more hardware is added. While this technique works great for Web sites that don't track session information, it poses a problem for ASP applications because the ASP session object is specific to a Web server, and a single user can be rerouted to a different server each time a request is made. If it is anticipated that multiple Web servers will be used or required for a single application, use the Session object carefully. Here are some alternatives to using the Session object for Web applications that reside on multiple machines:

- **Develop stateless applications where session information is not collected and managed.** While this is an option, it is rarely practical in an electronic Commerce environment.

- **Pass state information from page to page using the HTML form's Get or Post mechanisms.**

- **Manage state information with client-side cookies.** This option requires browsers to have cookies enabled, which is not guaranteed.

- **Use session aware load balancing.** This technique assigns each user to one machine for the duration of a session. While it allows developers to continue to use the ASP Session object (provided all URLs within the application are relative), it isn't true load balancing and doesn't provide failover support.

- **Centralize session state.** True server-side session state can be achieved by centralizing session state on a dedicated server that is accessible to the Web servers in the farm. To accomplish this, the Personalization component of Microsoft Site Server can be used. It provides a persisted User Property database that is appropriate for storing temporary session information. Unlike the ASP Session object, state information can be persisted between sessions. The User Property database also features replication and hot backups. A disadvantage is that session information is written to disk and could potentially reside on a remote computer. Therefore, this option is slower than using the ASP Session object.

WRITING TRANSACTIONAL ACTIVE SERVER PAGES

It is often important to ensure that several tasks complete successfully as a unit or transaction. Customer account activity is a good example of this. When transferring money from a customer (or business partner) account to your account, a debit from one account and a credit to another must occur for the transaction. In this case, a transfer must be completed successfully. A transaction is a server operation that includes one or more individual tasks that succeed or fail as a whole. You can create ASP scripts that run within a transaction so that if any piece of the script fails, the entire transaction is rolled back.

ASP transactions are made possible by Microsoft Transaction Server (MTS), which includes an object model and run time environment for deploying and managing distributed applications. Unlike transactional support in databases, MTS can manage updates to heterogeneous, distributed data sources within a transaction. This functionality is integrated into both IIS and Personal Web Server.

MTS transactions apply only to database access; MTS cannot roll back changes to the file system. MTS works with any database that supports the XA protocol from the X/Open consortium, including SQL Server.

The @TRANSACTION Directive

When you declare a page transactional, any script commands and objects used on the page are considered part of the transaction. To declare a page transactional, add the @TRANSACTION directive to the top of the page:

```
<%@ TRANSACTION=value %>
```

Value can be one of the following:

@TRANSACTION DIRECTIVE VALUES

Value	Description
Requires_New	Always starts a new transaction.
Required	Starts a new transaction unless called from another transactional page, in which case it would be included in the first transaction.
Supported	Does not start a transaction. Can be included in a transaction if called from a transactional page.
Not_Supported	Does not start or become included in a transaction.

The @TRANSACTION directive must be the very first line on the page and must be included in each transactional ASP page. A transaction ends when its ASP page finishes processing. When a transactional ASP page completes, all objects included in the transaction are released. Therefore, you should not include application- and session-level objects in transactions.

MTS automatically commits or aborts any changes made to resources that support transactions based on their success status. You can also explicitly commit or abort a transaction by calling ObjectContext.SetComplete or ObjectContext.SetAbort, respectively.

> **NOTE** The transaction is also aborted if the page times out before the transaction is completed.

To determine whether a transaction has succeeded or failed, you write event routines that will be automatically called by MTS. To do this, add the OnTransactionCommit and OnTransactionAbort event routines to the transactional ASP page, like this:

```
<%
Sub OnTransactionCommit()
  'Called by MTS when transaction succeeds.
end sub

Sub OnTransactionAbort()
  'Called by MTS when transaction fails.
End sub
%>
```

The following transactional page, from the \Chapter 7\ directory of the companion CD, includes the OnTransactionCommit and OnTransactionAbort event routines:

```
<%@ TRANSACTION=Required LANGUAGE="VBScript" %>
<HTML>
<HEAD>
<TITLE>Transactional example</TITLE>
</HEAD>
<BODY>
<h3>Transactional example</h3>
<% 'ObjectContext.SetAbort%>

</BODY>
</HTML>
<%
Sub OnTransactionAbort()
```

(continued)

(continued)

```
    Response.Write "The Transaction Aborted."
end sub
Sub OnTransactionCommit()
    Response.Write "The Transaction Committed."
end sub
%>
```

Notice in the body of the page that the ObjectContext.SetAbort method is commented out. When this page runs, MTS considers the transaction a success and calls the OnTransactionCommit event routine as shown in Figure 7-11. If the comment is removed from in front of the ObjectContext.SetAbort method, MTS calls the OnTransactionAbort event routine and the resulting HTML looks like Figure 7-12.

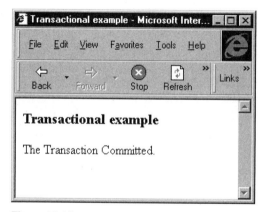

Figure 7-11. *Transactional ASP—Committed.*

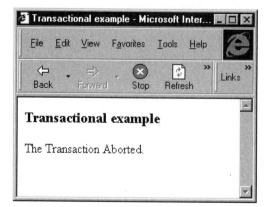

Figure 7-12. *Transactional ASP—Aborted.*

Components must be registered in MTS and must be configured to require a transaction before they can be used in a transaction. Use MTS Explorer to do this. You must set the transaction attribute of each component to either Requires a Transaction or Requires a New Transaction. For more on MTS, see Chapter 11.

DEBUGGING YOUR ASP APPLICATIONS

ASP scripts can be difficult to design, build, and debug because they usually contain several languages, client- and server-side elements, as well as user interface and business logic—all in one file. To tackle this complexity, you can use the Microsoft Visual InterDev debugger, shown in Figure 7-13. Similar to the Visual Basic debugger, the Visual InterDev debugger allows you to step through code, set break points, check variable values, and view the call stack. It also allows you to debug script running on a remote server. If you haven't used a debugger like this before, the online documentation will get you up to speed quickly.

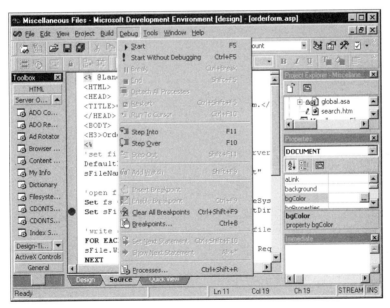

Figure 7-13. *The Visual InterDev debugger.*

Knowing how server-side scripts are processed will help you develop and debug your ASP pages. When an ASP is requested, the ASP engine processes the entire page serially, from top to bottom. Server script outside of functions and subroutines is executed immediately. Script within functions and subroutines is executed only when called.

Before you can debug ASP scripts, you must enable the debugger. To configure Visual InterDev to automatically enable script debugging in ASP pages, install Visual InterDev and follow these steps:

1. Right-click the project and select Properties.

2. Select the Launch tab.

3. Under Server script, check Automatically Enable ASP Server-Side Debugging On Launch. This instructs Visual InterDev to modify the Server debugging settings prior to launching the debugger and to restore the settings to their previous values when the debugging session ends.

Debugging *Global.asa*

Unlike ASP pages, the *Global.asa* file is event driven. Therefore, you must embed calls to the debugger in the Global.asa event routines, and then restart the application.

To call the debugger, set a breakpoint in script, restart the Web application, and then request any ASP page that is part of the application. This causes the Global.asa file to execute the Application_OnStart and Session_OnStart event routines. Adding the Session.abandon method to an ASP page and then executing it causes the Global.asa file to execute the Session_OnEnd event routine. If this is the only active session, the Application_OnEnd event routine will also be called.

As mentioned earlier, making a change to the Global.asa file will also cause it to be restarted, executing its event routines as described earlier.

SECURING YOUR ASP APPLICATIONS

An important part of any application accessible to the public is security. Because of its multitiered nature, security can be employed at many levels throughout the Web application: NT file system (NTFS), IIS, MTS, databases, ASP scripts, authentication, client certificates, and Secure Sockets Layer (SSL). An ASP application security scheme typically involves several of these.

■ Use NTFS to secure your ASP application's files and directories by applying various levels of file and directory access permissions assigned to a user or user group.

■ Use IIS to configure Web permissions. Unlike NTFS permissions, Web server permissions apply to all users. Read, Script, and Execute permissions can be applied to directories and files.

■ Use MTS to control access to components or groups of components. By assigning permissions to component "packages," access to application resources can be granted or denied by user or group.

■ Use native database security features to control access to tables, views, and stored procedures.

■ Use ASP to insulate the users from the underlying system below. For example, the users of your site should never have database information such as database name, table names, or database account and password.

■ Use authentication if your Web application requires the user to have a valid Windows NT account. This is typically used for sites with sensitive information and a small finite number of users. Enabling "Basic authentication" will prompt the user for a name and password. Enabling "Windows NT Challenge/Response authentication" will prompt the user and encrypt a name and password for additional security. Note that this option works only with Internet Explorer browsers.

NOTE If Anonymous access is enabled on the Web server, the user will not be authenticated.

■ Use client certificates to verify the identity of a user. Users apply for and install these certificates on their browsers. If you configure your IIS server to Accept or Require client certificates, the user's Web browser will automatically send the certificate to the Web server for verification. While client certificates don't really apply to commercial sites, they are particularly important in business-to-business Commerce applications where you need to verify your trading partner's identity.

■ Use the Secure Sockets Layer (SSL) protocol to encrypt communication with browsers. SSL prevents the interception of sensitive data (such as credit card information) exchanged between the user and a Web application.

ACTIVE SERVER PAGE BEST PRACTICES

Multitier Web applications pose a different set of challenges for developers than desktop and client/server applications. Every aspect of the environment needs to be considered—from graphics to the operating system. Understanding where the common Web bottlenecks occur is also critical. The two primary concerns are to keep data access and network traffic to an absolute minimum. These issues can be minimized with techniques such as performing form validation in client-side script and storing common data, such as list box entries, in the Application object instead of repeatedly issuing the same database query. However, there is more to creating a well-oiled Web site than just addressing the bottlenecks. Use the following best practices when tuning and configuring your Web site to ensure that you consider the whole system, not just ASP.

Windows NT Server 4.0 Tuning

Windows NT Server should be tuned to dedicate as many resources as possible, including CPU cycles, memory, hardware, and network bandwidth to the Web server. When configuring a Windows NT Server as a dedicated Web server, everything non-essential to the Web environment should be removed or turned off.

■ Install service packs and hotfixes when they become available, particularly when related to security fixes. All service packs, fixes, and patches are available on the Microsoft Web site.

■ Dedicate hardware to the Web server and do not share it with other applications.

■ Turn off or disable unnecessary and non-IIS related NT services. The services required by IIS can be found in the Microsoft Knowledgebase article Q164885.

> **NOTE** Many NT Server services are interdependent so use caution when disabling them.

■ Remove unnecessary software (including development tools and server extensions) from the production Web server.

■ Rename the default IIS account for anonymous logins. This account is automatically created when IIS is installed. Because the account includes the computer's name, renaming it improves security.

■ Install the minimum network protocols required to run Web applications (preferably only TCP/IP). Remove other installed protocols if they're unnecessary.

- Set the NT Server service to Networked Applications to allow NT to focus more on network I/O than disk I/O. This setting can be changed by right-clicking Network Neighborhood, selecting Properties, selecting the Services tab, and then double-clicking the Server service.

- Maximize the Network Interface Card (NIC) Receive Buffers setting. Increasing this value lets the Web server accommodate more simultaneous requests.

- Set the Foreground Application Boost to *None* for Web servers. This will dedicate more system resources to the Web server. This setting can be changed by double-clicking System in the Control Panel and then selecting the Performance tab.

Internet Information Server 4.0 Tuning

Tune Internet Information Server to use the available NT Server resources as efficiently as possible for serving Web applications and to secure the environment from malicious or accidental harm.

- Increase the IIS metabase setting AspMemFreeFactor. AspMemFreeFactor specifies the ratio (as a percentage) of free memory to used memory within IIS. When the ratio exceeds the value of this setting, IIS gives memory back to NT Server's virtual memory pool. The default value is 50, which means when free memory exceeds 50 percent of used memory, IIS returns memory to the virtual memory pool. For NT Servers dedicated to serving ASP pages, this value should be substantially increased so that IIS has the memory it needs on hand rather than going to the pool to find more before continuing. Setting this value in the range of 500 percent will improve performance.

- If pages are static and don't contain server-side logic, give them an .htm file extension instead of .asp. This reduces the load on the ASP parser and improves scalability.

- For security reasons, always place .htm files in a different directory than .asp files. Make sure the .htm files directory has only read access and the .asp files directory has read access disabled.

- Create subdirectories instead of virtual directories when possible. Virtual directories take longer to resolve.

■ Avoid creating virtual directories that map to other machines because accessing such directories will be slower. The remote machine or network could also be down.

■ Enable buffering. Buffering can improve performance. Buffering also allows developers more programmatic control over if and when the browser receives output. To enable buffering for an ASP application, click the Enable Buffering property in Internet Service Manager. To enable buffering for an ASP page, set the Response.Buffer property to True. Be aware, though, that buffering consumes resources, particularly if large pages are being sent to the browser.

■ Adjust the Maximum Daily Connections setting on the Performance tab. The default value is Less Than 100,000. Optimize this setting by changing the value to just more than the anticipated maximum daily connections. This will free server resources. However, a value too low or too high will consume resources.

■ Set Cache ISAPI Applications to True. This configuration will improve performance.

■ HTTP Keep-Alives is enabled by default. This feature keeps a TCP/IP connection alive between client requests. Server resources should be freed by disabling this, but connections will be slower. How the Web server responds to Keep-Alives can be tested using the Web Capacity Analysis Tool. WCAT is a free download on the Microsoft Workshop site (*www.microsoft.com/workshop*).

■ Set Enable Parent Paths to False. While this does not adversely affect performance, it does present a potential security risk. A value of True allows clients to navigate to directories on the disk drive hierarchy that are above the Web site's root directory.

■ Set the Default Language to the language most commonly used. It is more efficient to set this value to the language most commonly used throughout an application than it is to place a directive at the top of each ASP page in the application. This value can be set at the application level allowing different groups using the same Web server to build ASP applications in the language of their choice.

■ Set Script File Cache to Cache All ASPs. In general, caching ASP scripts will improve performance.

- Run ASP applications in a separate process only when the application is unstable or when it coexists with mission-critical ASP applications on the same Web server. Though this option provides protection for the Web server and other Web applications from failure, it does consume additional memory and CPU cycles, resulting in reduced application performance. This setting is typically used for new production applications until they prove themselves stable.

- Only enable logging periodically when specific analysis is needed. Logging is often useful during development and for production Internet applications. The value of logging is considerably reduced for production intranet applications because the continuous collecting of data on internal activity is usually unnecessary. Logging reduces application performance because the Web server needs to manage logging in the background, and disk I/O is taking place. However, the decision to enable logging is usually driven more by business need or policy than by pure performance considerations.

- Set the ASP Script Timeout setting as low as possible. The default is 90 seconds. When the value is reached, the script will be terminated. While this value might need to be raised for long running scripts, it should be kept as low as possible. This helps reduce the amount of time each script is consuming resources and will terminate malfunctioning scripts faster.

ASP Application Tuning

Tune ASP applications to consume as few system resources as possible. Applying the following resource-reducing techniques will result in better performance and improved scalability.

Active Data Objects (ADO) and database connectivity

- All object variables, especially ADO objects like Recordsets and Connections, should explicitly be set to NULL (in JavaScript) or NOTHING (in VBScript) immediately after they are no longer needed. For example, just issuing a Connection.Close method won't release the memory and reference to the Connection object.

- Access the database as little as possible. Even though database connection pooling has improved data access performance, focus your design on reducing trips to the database. Consider techniques such as issuing one query to retrieve common data, such as list box entries, and then storing the results in Application object variables instead of repeatedly issuing the same database query.

- Use connection pooling. Opening and closing database connections is very expensive and time consuming. Connection pooling is configured by setting the CPTimeout registry entry.

- Consider de-normalizing the database. The performance of Web applications can be improved by reducing the number of joins in SQL statements.

- Encapsulate data access in components rather than script. Some advantages of using components over script to access data are that they are easier to share and reuse, they are more secure, and they provide better performance, increased scalability, and more sophisticated error handling.

- If using ADO directly from an ASP script, use constants instead of the large (10 K) ADO constant files adojavas.inc and adovbs.inc. Take only the constants needed from those files and put them in their own .inc file, or add them directly to the ASP file. A typical page uses only two or three of the constants in these include files. The potential disadvantage is that it is possible that the constant values could change in future releases of the product, so the custom .inc file would need to be updated as part of the upgrade.

- Use the ADO Recordset object's Open method instead of the ADO Connection or Command object's Execute method for returning data when possible. It offers the most optimization control via the CursorType, LockType, and Options parameters of its Open method and its CursorLocation property. When using the ADO Recordset object's Open method, explicitly set these parameters because the default settings can vary based on the data source and ODBC driver's capabilities. Another advantage of using the ADO Recordset object over the ADO Connection or Command object is that an ADO Connection object does not need to be created to use the Recordset object, thereby reducing resource consumption and simplifying code.

■ Reference Recordset object fields by name rather than index when possible. For example, use rs.fields("city_name") instead of rs.fields(2). Index references pose potential maintenance problems if table or query columns are added, dropped, or reordered. Names are also easier to read than indexes.

ASP scripting

■ Mix scripting languages in a single ASP file as little as possible. This will improve performance.

■ Reference the intrinsic Server object only once if possible. The Server object gets and returns all the HTTP properties when any one of its properties is referenced, which degrades performance.

■ Use as few Response.Write calls as possible by concatenating multiple lines of HTML into one string, and then sending that string. All object calls take time and should be minimized for scalability. Because Response.Write is used frequently in ASP pages, it is a good candidate to be tuned.

■ Create all objects immediately before they are needed and destroy them immediately after they are no longer needed. This ensures each object's lifespan is as short as possible.

■ Explicitly set all object variables to NULL (in JavaScript) immediately after they are no longer needed. In VBScript, set object variables to NOTHING instead of NULL. This ensures the object is destroyed and resources are released.

■ Minimize dependencies on networked resources. This includes data sources, file shares, and DCOM components. The network is the major bottleneck in distributed applications and should be avoided as much as possible.

■ Use fewer <%...%> pairs by creating distinct blocks of HTML and script and by using string concatenation. This will improve performance because the less the ASP engine has to switch back and forth between languages in a page, the faster it executes the page.

■ Put <% and %> on the same line of code if possible. Because the ASP engine has to read and interpret every character in an ASP page, carriage returns and line feeds reduce performance particularly on high-volume sites.

■ Because ASP files are interpreted, the ASP parser reads every character in the file, including carriage returns and comments. With this in mind, consider these two techniques:

❑ Remove as many blank lines from ASP files as possible (the tradeoff for doing so is reduced readability).

❑ Remove comments from production code. Code-level documentation is critical. However, when it's thorough and extensive, it can slow ASP script execution. Be conscious of this and create clear, concise comments. Moving code comments to a separate file or files is another possible solution.

■ Build a separate error handling ASP file and call it when needed. This not only makes your applications more modular, it also improves performance because the ASP engine doesn't need to load and parse extra error handling code on every page.

■ Use relative URLs instead of absolute URLs when possible. This makes the ASP application more portable.

■ Use Server.MapPath instead of a literal for specifying Web server paths. This increases application portability.

■ Use the Application and Session objects to store commonly referenced information. Database access can be greatly reduced by storing a query's results in one of these objects rather than repeatedly executing the same query.

■ If it is anticipated that multiple Web servers will be used or required for a single application, design the use of the Session object carefully. Because the Session object is specific to a Web server, other options must be considered in a Web farm environment. The following list outlines possible alternatives to using the Session object for applications that reside on multiple machines:

❑ Develop stateless applications. While this is an option, it is rarely practical in an intranet environment.

❑ Pass state information from page to page using the HTML form's Get or Post mechanisms.

❑ Manage state with client-side cookies. This option requires the browsers to have cookies enabled, which is not guaranteed.

❑ Use session aware load balancing. This technique assigns each user to one machine for the duration of a session. While it allows developers to continue to use the ASP Session object (provided all URLs within the application are relative), it isn't true load balancing and doesn't provide failover support.

❑ Centralize Session State. True server-side session state can be achieved by centralizing session state on a dedicated server that is accessible to the Web servers in the farm. To accomplish this, the Personalization component of Microsoft Site Server can be used. It provides a persistent User Property database that is appropriate for storing temporary session information. Unlike the ASP Session object, state information can be persisted between sessions. The User Property database also features replication and hot backups. A disadvantage is that session information is written to disk and could potentially reside on a remote computer. Therefore, this option is slower than using the ASP Session object.

Before implementing any of these options, be sure the ASP application requires multiple servers. A single Web server on fault-tolerant hardware is sufficient for some cases.

■ Use include files for modularity and reuse. However, excessive use of include files will reduce performance. This is because the ASP parsing engine needs to perform additional work to locate each include file, read it from disk, and add it to the script before code interpretation can begin.

■ Business logic should be contained in components. Components offer better performance, better error handling, and more sharing and reuse capability than ASP and include files do.

■ Avoid using a file data source name (DSN) configuration. Its use is encouraged in the Visual InterDev tool, but it is twice as slow, on average, as system DSN. In addition, it's less secure because the database name, username, and password are all in one text-based file on the Web server.

■ Consider moving as much data and logic to the browser as possible via technologies like DHTML and XML. This not only improves the user's experience by presenting a more robust user interface, but it also reduces demand on the Web server.

■ Use Visual InterDev and IIS to debug applications rather than adding debug code to script files. If runtime-logging logic is needed, it should be encapsulated in a logging component and called with a parameter to toggle logging off and on.

■ Keep ASP files as small as possible.

■ Disable session state on any page that doesn't use it:

```
(<%@EnableSessionState=False%>)
```

■ Object variables should be early bound to their type libraries by declaring them using the Server.CreateObject() method. If the object's type library isn't specified, performance diminishes because the system has to determine at runtime what type of object the variable references and then retrieve the appropriate type library before continuing. For example, the first object declaration here will yield better performance than the second:

```
Set rs = Server.CreateObject("ADODB.Recordset")
Dim rs
```

MTS and Component Development

The following are tips for building components that run under the control of Microsoft Transaction Server. Chapter 10 provides a much more detailed view of the issues surrounding this topic.

- Build stateless components if possible. This means that data should be passed as method parameters instead of as properties to reduce object life span and network trips.

- Components should not generate events or utilize callback techniques. These features increase the life span of a component and reduce its scalability.

- Pass arguments by value when possible because passing by reference causes an additional trip across the network.

- Avoid passing objects (including Recordsets) to and from components. Objects should be passed by reference.

Processes and Standards

Your development team should agree on, and then follow, a structured set of processes and standards. The following list presents the major issues to consider in this area:

- Define a standard Web application directory structure and apply it to all Web applications. This adds consistency, making maintenance and support easier. A typical structure might look like the following:

```
Web Site Root/
        Asp/
        Controls/
        Classes/
        Docs/
        HTML/
        Images/
        Includes/
```

NOTE   Do not place the Docs directory in a production structure or anywhere accessible by users.

- Define database standards (including table and column naming conventions) and the locking order for the tables in the database. The locking order standard will help avoid potential locking problems and contentions.

■   Define code standards for every language used by the development community. Microsoft supplies suggested standards as part of the documentation of most languages. These standards make an excellent baseline.

■   Build and manage a component and object repository. Reusing common components and business logic is key to lowering development expense and providing consistent application behavior.

■   Conduct architecture, design, and code reviews. This is especially important for the first applications developed using new technologies, and it aids in getting everyone up to speed on the technology.

■   Create an internal user group. This is particularly valuable when your organization is going through a technical transition period. Developers will benefit from training sessions, vendor presentations, knowledge transfer, and peer support.

■   Select product and tool champions from within the development community. Both management and staff will benefit from having access to the company expert on a product or tool. Champions should be selected for technologies such as Visual InterDev, DHTML, XML, MTS, or Exchange.

Development and Management Tools

The following tools can be invaluable in helping you design your application, measure performance, control your source code, and get detailed questions answered during the development process.

■   *Web* **Capacity Analysis Tool.** This tool simulates Web site workloads under various conditions. Results can be used to identify bottlenecks and tune Web applications. WCAT is a free download available on the Microsoft Workshop site (*www.microsoft.com/ workshop*).

■   **InetMonitor 3.0.** InetMonitor is for capacity planning and load monitoring for Web applications. InetMonitor replaces InetLoad and InetMon and is a free download available from Microsoft (*www.microsoft.com/msdownload*).

- **Visual Studio Tools**

  - ❑ **Visual Source Safe.** This source code control application tightly integrates with most other Visual Studio tools. Visual Source Safe offers many features, including team development support, branching and merging of code, and release marking.

  - ❑ **MS Component Manager and MS Repository.** The Component Manager and Repository provide a common place to store and manage objects and information about how those objects relate to each other.

  - ❑ **Visual Studio Analyzer.** The Visual Studio Analyzer allows you to debug and analyze distributed and multitier applications. This tool can provide a high-level view of all components and their relationships in an application and identify individual problem components.

  - ❑ **Visual Modeler.** A subset of Rational's Rose modeling tool, Visual Modeler is a graphical object-oriented modeling tool that integrates with Visual Studio. Visual Modeler offers features like model building, code generation, and reverse engineering.

- **The Microsoft Sitebuilder Web site** (www.microsoft.com/sitebuilder). The Workshop area, in particular, is an excellent resource for information on everything Microsoft offers for building Web sites. It includes articles, downloads, samples, documentation, and training.

- **The Visual Studio Web site** (www.microsoft.com/vstudio). Covers all the tools included in the Visual Studio suite. It includes articles, downloads, samples, documentation, and multimedia training demos.

- **The Microsoft Development Network (MSDN) subscription includes CDs of all Microsoft operating systems, development tools, products, and documentation.** This is an excellent way for developers to test, evaluate, and gain exposure to the latest Microsoft tools and technologies. For more information, go to *msdn.microsoft.com/ developer/join/subscriptions.htm*.

SUMMARY

You have seen how easy it is to create dynamic Web applications using only ASP. ASP is a platform for creating and managing dynamic Web-based Commerce applications. Sophisticated development tools, session management, easy integration with components and backend systems, and support for all browsers are features of this technology.

However, the biggest strength of ASP is its tight integration with other Windows technologies. Integrating ASP with products such as Site Server, SQL Server, and Microsoft Exchange makes for a complete Commerce solution. ASP is the ideal framework for accessing legacy systems, integrating with the corporate infrastructure, hosting today's Commerce initiatives, and providing a foundation for future applications.

Chapter 8

Data Access Technologies

by Andy Hoskinson and Paul Drumgoole

In the "old days," developing a data access application for your enterprise was a no-brainer. First, you developed a relational data model to host your data—identifying entities, attributes, and relationships that described data storage in terms that were important for your organization. Next, you developed a physical data model using a relational database management system (DBMS). Entities became tables, attributes became fields, and relationships became table joins. After that, you populated your database with data. Finally, you wrote a client application that used the proprietary API exposed by the underlying DBMS to add, edit, delete, and search data stored therein. If your organization used several different DBMSs to store data, your application developers needed to know the various APIs to write applications that could mine that data.

THE PROBLEM

Realizing that this diverse set of APIs and consequential program development and support costs was a problem, Microsoft developed the Open Database Connectivity (ODBC) API. ODBC gave relational database developers a common API for writing applications to access any relational DBMS for which an ODBC driver had been written. This was a definite improvement in that database developers had to learn only one API. Nonetheless, many programmers found ODBC to be a difficult API to learn and use.

Microsoft responded to this with two products: Data Access Objects (DAO) and Remote Data Objects (RDO). DAO provided developers with an object-based interface to the Jet database engine (the underlying engine of Microsoft Access), offering easy access to a wide variety of desktop database products. For enterprise database developers, Microsoft released RDO, which was a thin COM object model that wrapped the ODBC API. RDO greatly simplified database development, particularly for Visual Basic programmers. Client/server relational database applications quickly became the standard for enterprise data access.

The only problem was that the tight structure of a relational DBMS did not always fit how the typical user likes to work. The average user likes to produce data in the form of documents. For example, if you told a user to capture topics discussed in a staff meeting, that user would typically create a document using a word processing application, such as Microsoft Word. This creates an obvious problem: If you want that data to be available to your enterprise using your client/server relational DBMS application, you must parse the contents of that document, fit the document's data to your relational data model, and add it to your database. In addition to being a time-consuming and redundant process, this is frequently like trying to fit the proverbial "square peg into a round hole."

Nevertheless, this relational data access technology model persisted for a few years. What changed everything was the explosion in popularity of the Web, which caused two things to happen:

- The entire Internet was now exposed as a data source that was easily accessible to most computer users. From an enterprise computing standpoint, the Internet became a *de facto* "official" source of data for many organizations.

- The document-centric nature of HTTP (and, therefore, the Web) shifted the architectural "balance of power" from relational DBMS to document repository-based systems. To be sure, there continues to be a need for relational DBMS, but the Web has caused people to expect the same ease of access to data in document repositories that they have traditionally had with data stored in relational DBMS.

Today, enterprise data access application developers are expected to build applications that provide their organizations with integrated access to data from a wide variety of data sources. Users expect to be able to access and search:

- Different relational DBMSs from different vendors, such as Oracle and Microsoft SQL Server

- Meta-data and contents of documents in various different formats

- Messaging system data stores (such as Exchange Server public folders)

- Data from a wide variety of different directory services

This point is especially true in the world of Web commerce. Let's say, for example, that you run a Web storefront, selling retail goods on the Internet. Your product database uses Microsoft SQL Server. Your accounting system uses Oracle. You store your customer data in a Site Server 3.0 LDAP membership directory. Your EDI system stores commerce documents from trading partners in an LDAP directory service from yet another vendor. Your Web site's static documents are "harvested" by Index Server. Then you are faced with the task of writing a Web commerce application that accesses and integrates those different data stores as efficiently and seamlessly as possible.

The key challenge is this: How do you write such an application in a timely and cost-effective manner, without having to learn and use a bunch of different APIs?

THE SOLUTION: UNIVERSAL DATA ACCESS

Microsoft's solution to this problem is a strategy called Universal Data Access (UDA). Simply put, the goal of the UDA initiative is to give developers a common interface for writing high-performance, easy-to-maintain applications that access a variety of different data sources, both relational and non-relational. This interface is called OLE DB.

What Is OLE DB?

OLE DB is an interface specification that provides a layer of abstraction between a data provider (such as a relational DBMS) and a data consumer (such as a business object or a client application). OLE DB interfaces describe what certain objects should look like when passed from the provider to the consumer. Because OLE DB interfaces are abstract, they do not provide any inherent functionality. The functionality is implemented by the underlying OLE DB providers.

An OLE DB provider is a component that creates a data source-specific implementation of the OLE DB interfaces. In other words, the provider component talks to the underlying data source, gets data from it, and then returns that data to the consumer in a manner that adheres to the OLE DB specification.

Therein lies the advantage of OLE DB: The data consumer does not need to know anything about the underlying data provider. All it needs to know the details of the underlying data provider, only how to use the objects that implement the OLE DB interfaces. As long as the underlying data source has an OLE DB provider, the consumer will be able to access its data.

What Is ADO?

To simplify writing OLE DB clients, Microsoft created ActiveX Data Objects, or ADO. ADO is a COM wrapper for the OLE DB interfaces. ADO allows developers to access, through OLE DB providers, a wide variety of different data sources using a common, easy-to-use object model.

With ADO, developers do not need to know about the internal workings of any given data source. As long as they know how to use the ADO object model, they can write applications that can access virtually any data source, as long as an OLE DB provider has been written for that data source.

Conversely, data source developers do not have to worry about developing a proprietary API to allow application developers to write client applications for their data source. All they have to do is write an OLE DB provider for their data source, and their data source is automatically exposed to the legions of application developers who know ADO. Figure 8-1 shows this architecture. It's a win-win situation.

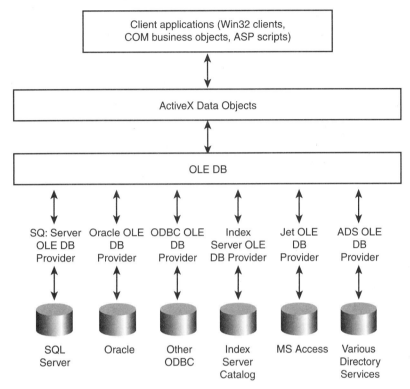

Figure 8-1. *Microsoft's Universal Data Access architecture.*

To date, Microsoft (and other third-party vendors) have written OLE DB providers for a wide variety of different data sources, including ODBC data sources, SQL Server, Oracle, Jet databases (such as Microsoft Access), Index Server catalogs, and ADS (Active Directory Service). Moreover, numerous directory services for which Active Directory Service Interfaces (ADSI) providers have been written (such as LDAP, NT, and NDS) are accessible via the ADS OLE DB provider. Finally, developers can write their own OLE DB providers using the Microsoft Data Access SDK. For up-to-date information, you can always refer to *http://www.microsoft.com/data/*.

To put this in perspective, the rest of the chapter will show you how to develop Web-based and N-tier universal data access applications using ADO and OLE DB. Specifically, it covers the following topics:

■   Writing ASP scripts that use, via ADO, the various OLE DB providers that ship with Microsoft Data Access Components (MDAC) 2.0

- Writing an N-tier Web-based application with a middle-tier COM object that uses ADO to query an OLE DB data source, and then returns results to an ASP script for presentation to the user

- A discussion about what other third-party OLE DB providers are available to allow heterogeneous data access using ADO and how to find them

- How to write a simple OLE DB provider for your own proprietary data source

WRITING DATA ACCESS APPLICATIONS WITH ADO

Now that we've covered the history and overall architecture of data access technologies on the Microsoft platform, we'll take a specific look at how to write data access applications using ADO.

MDAC 2.0

Before you can write ADO applications, you must first install MDAC (Microsoft Data Access Components) on your computer. Because MDAC is shipped with a variety of different Microsoft products (such as Microsoft Internet Information Server 4.0 and Microsoft Visual Studio 98), there is a good chance that it's already installed on your machine. If not, you can download it free of charge from Microsoft's Universal Data Access Web site at *http://www.microsoft.com/data*. The most current version of MDAC is 2.0.

MDAC comes in several different flavors. The first one is the Microsoft Data Access Components 2.0 Redistribution Minimal Setup, which includes only the core components: ADO, OLE DB, RDS (Remote Data Service components, which allow you to interact with an OLE DB data source over HTTP), and the core ODBC drivers.

The second MDAC flavor is Microsoft Data Access Components 2.0 Redistribution Typical Setup, which includes the core components discussed earlier, as well as some additional OLE DB providers and ODBC drivers for various different database products.

The third flavor is the Microsoft Data Access Components 2.0 Typical Redistribution Plus ActiveX Data Objects for Multidimensional Data (ADO MD) Setup. This includes all of the previously mentioned components, plus the ADO MD components, which can be used to query OLE DB data sources that provide N-dimensional data.

Last, but not least, is the Microsoft Data Access SDK 2.0. In addition to the aforementioned components, this download, which weighs in at a whopping 37.8 megabytes, includes comprehensive API and object model documentation, development tools, and code samples for building everything from a simple client to a complete OLE DB provider.

The ADO Object Model

Once you have MDAC 2.0 installed, you are ready to start writing data access applications using ADO. ADO provides a robust, easy-to-use object model that encapsulates a vast majority of the functionality provided by OLE DB. For those developers who have used RDO and DAO before, ADO will look very familiar and should be easy to pick up. Here's a quick review of the ADO object model (see Figure 8-2):

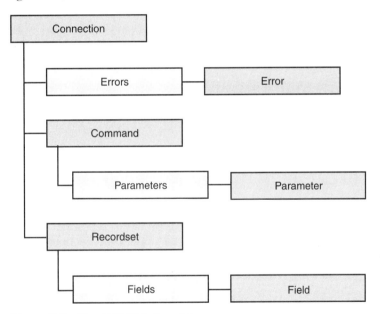

Figure 8-2. *The ADO Object model.*

■   **The Connection object.** Encapsulates the functionality needed to establish, persist, and close a connection with a remote OLE DB data source. A Connection object contains a collection of Error objects (discussed later), into which provider-specific error conditions are placed as they occur. This allows the developer to query the Connection object for error conditions that might have occurred during operations on that particular Connection object.

■   **The Command object.** Encapsulates a command (such as a query) that will be sent to and executed on the remote data source. This command is generally a Structured Query Language (SQL) statement but can also be a provider-specific command, such as a SQL Server stored procedure. A Command object contains a collection of Parameter objects (discussed next), which are used to pass one or more parameters to the Command object.

■   **The Parameter object.** Encapsulates a parameter of a Command object. This includes a parameter passed to a stored procedure or parameter query, or any other type of provider-supported command that accepts parameters.

■   **The Recordset object.** Encapsulates the entire set of records returned from the execution of a command (for example, a SQL Select statement). In an ADO recordset, data is arrayed in a tabular fashion, in rows and columns. Recordsets also contain a variety of methods that allow manipulation and navigation of the data by the client application. Each recordset contains a collection of Field objects, which contain the column names and data.

■   **The Field object.** Encapsulates a column of a Recordset object.

■   **The Error object.** Encapsulates an error condition on a Connection object.

■   **The Property object.** Encapsulates a custom OLE DB provider-specific attribute of an ADO Connection, Command, Recordset, or Field object. The attributes represented by Property objects are normally unique to a particular provider. Property objects are stored in a Properties collection in each of the aforementioned objects (see Figure 8-3).

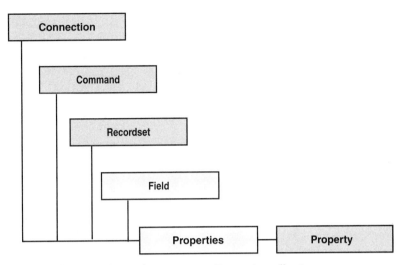

Figure 8-3. *ADO objects that contain a Properties collection.*

For additional information on the ADO object model, a great reference source is the Microsoft Data Access SDK, which you can download from Microsoft's Universal Data Access Web site at *http://www.microsoft.com/data.*

Using the Various OLE DB Providers

The MDAC 2.0 ships with several different OLE DB providers including ODBC, Jet, SQL Server, Oracle, Index Server, and ADS. Additionally, there are numerous other providers available for third-party data sources. This section will show you the basics of writing ADO applications that target each of the providers that ship with MDAC 2.0, and will culminate with a discussion on what other OLE DB providers are available.

The ODBC OLE DB provider

With the ODBC OLE DB provider, you can use ADO to access data from any data source with an ODBC driver. This includes Microsoft Access, SQL Server, Oracle, and numerous other popular DBMS. The ODBC OLE DB provider is the default provider for ADO; if you do not explicitly specify another provider, ADO will automatically use the ODBC provider.

To illustrate how to use the ODBC OLE DB provider in an ADO application, let's create two versions of a simple product search ASP script. You will find both versions of the script on the book CD-ROM:

■ The first version, SimpleADO.asp, will demonstrate how to access an ODBC data source using ADO from an ASP script.

■   The second version, SimpleADO2.asp, will demonstrate a three-tier version of the product search ASP script. In this example, the ADO logic is moved from the ASP script into a middle tier in-process COM object written using VB 6. The COM object will, in turn, be called by an ASP script to present the data to the user.

For both examples, we will use the Adventure Works Microsoft Access database that ships as a sample with both IIS and MDAC. After installing those products, there should be a system DSN set up for this database. To verify this, perform the following steps:

1.   Click on Start, and then Settings, and then Control Panel.

2.   Double-click on the ODBC 32 applet icon.

3.   Click on the System DSN tab. Verify that there is a System DSN called AdvWorks, as shown in Figure 8-4.

4.   If not, find Advworks.mdb on your hard disk (it should be located at c:\Program Files\Common Files\System\msadc\Samples\adv-works.mdb if you installed MDAC 2.0 to the default location specified by the setup program), and create a System DSN called AdvWorks using the ODBC 32 Control Panel applet's Create New Data Source Wizard.

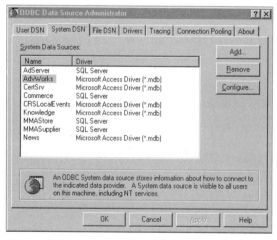

Figure 8-4. *The ODBC Data Source Administrator, showing the System DSN tab.*

Accessing ODBC data from an ASP script

First, you should model how your product search page will look to the user. You can do this using virtually any HTML editor, including Microsoft Visual InterDev or Microsoft FrontPage. For that matter, you could use Notepad if you wanted to and code the HTML markup by hand. The only things you need to remember are to save the file with an .asp extension and to make sure that your server-side script is properly delimited. For more information on ASP scripting, please refer to Chapter 7. For more information on HTML, please refer to Chapter 13.

For my sample product search script, I created a script that initially presents the user with a form that contains a text input box and a Submit button (see Figure 8-5). The user enters his or her search string in the text box and clicks the Submit button. The server reexecutes the script, this time passing the search string in as a parameter using the ASP Request object. The script then executes the ADO code to perform the search and returns results to the user as an HTML table. Here's how to put together the ADO code:

Step 1. Create the ADO Connection object, using the following line of code:

```
set objConn = Server.CreateObject("ADODB.Connection")
```

Step 2. Open a connection to your ODBC System DSN. Once the Connection object is created, open a specific ODBC DSN using the Open method of the ADODB.Connection class. In this case, I'm using the AdvWorks DSN, which represents our Adventure Works MS Access database. Please note that I did not specify a provider because I want to use the ODBC OLE DB provider, which is the default provider used by ADO if none is specified:

```
objConn.Open "DSN=AdvWorks"
```

If I had wanted to explicitly specify the ODBC OLE DB provider, then this line of code would look like this:

```
objConn.Open "Provider=MSDASQL;DSN=AdvWorks"
```

Here is yet another way that I could have written this line of code:

```
objConn.Open "DSN=AdvWorks;UID=admin;PWD=;"
```

Notice that this Connection string includes a UserID and password. The Adventure Works database we use in our example has not been secured using the MS Access Security Wizard, so we are not required to supply login credentials with the Connection string. However, if you are using the ODBC OLE DB provider with an enterprise DBMS such as SQL Server, you will most likely be required to connect using a valid account.

There is yet a fourth way to write this line of code:

```
objConn.Open "Driver={Microsoft Access Driver (*.mdb)};" &_
             "DBQ=advworks.mdb;" &_
             "DefaultDir=c:\Program Files\Common " &_
             "Files\System\msadc\Samples;" &_
             "Uid=Admin;Pwd=;"
```

You will notice that, in this example, I do not use a System DSN. Instead, I instruct the Open method to use the MS Access ODBC driver and tell it where on the hard drive to find the specific Access database.

What are the advantages of doing it this way, as opposed to using a System DSN? Let's say that your Web site resides on a Windows NT Server run by a Web hosting service, and you need to query an Access database from an ASP script. There are two courses of action you can pursue to accomplish this objective:

1. E-mail the Web hosting service's tech support department requesting that they set up a System DSN for you. You might get it sometime next week.

2. Use the Connection string listed earlier, and you're done today.

Step 3. Formulate the SQL statement for your search. The SQL statement, represented by the variable strSQL, will retrieve all records from the Products data table that contain the search string (represented by the variable strFilter) in the ProductName field or the ProductDescription field. Moreover, the resulting recordset will be sorted by ProductName, in ascending order. The value of strFilter is passed to our ASP script using the ASP Request object. For more information on the ASP Request object, please see Chapter 7.

```
strSQL = "select * from Products where ProductName like '%%" &_
         strFilter & "%%' OR ProductDescription like '%%" &_
         strFilter & "%%' Order By ProductName"
```

Step 4. Execute the search by passing the SQL statement to the OLE DB data source and get the results back as an ADODB.Recordset object. There are a couple of different ways to do this. The way we do it in this sample is to call the Execute method of our ADODB.Connection instance, passing our SQL statement as an argument. We will cover other ways later in the chapter.

```
set objRS = objConn.Execute(strSQL)
```

Step 5. Loop through the recordset. As you loop through each record, read the field values for that record into the HTTP response stream. For brevity, I have omitted the HTML markup used to format the results as a table. While looping through the recordset, we'll keep track of how many records we have by using a counter variable (intRecordCount). If intRecordCount is still zero by the time we have reached the end of the recordset, that means our search returned no results, and we'll tell the user that:

```
<%
'Set our counter to zero
intRecordCount = 0

'Loop through the recordset until there are no more records...
Do while not objRS.EOF

'For each record, insert the value of each field into the
'appropriate HTML table cell
%>
    (Some HTML Here)
    <%=objRS("ProductName")%> 
    (Some HTML Here)
    <%=objRS("ProductType")%> 
    (Some HTML Here)
    <%=objRS("ProductDescription")%> 
    (Some HTML Here)
    <%=objRS("ProductSize")%> 
    (Some HTML Here)
    <%=FormatCurrency(objRS("UnitPrice"))%> 
    (Some HTML Here)
<%

    'Move the pointer to the next record
    objRS.MoveNext

    'Increment our counter by one
    intRecordCount = intRecordCount + 1

loop

'If our counter is still zero at this point, then there were
'no records in our recordset.  Therefore, we need to display
'the appropriate message to the user.

 if intRecordCount = 0 then
%>
<p>
    <font face="Arial">
        Your search did not return any products.  Please try
again.
    </font>
</p>
<%end if%>
```

Step 6. Finally, we need to "clean up" by closing our connection(s) and releasing our objects:

```
<%
'Clean up our ADO objects by closing down all connections and
'releasing the objects

    objRS.close
    objConn.close

    set objRS = nothing
    set objConn = nothing

end if
%>
```

Here's the complete SimpleADO.asp code listing (shown in Figure 8-5 on page 325):

Code Listing Sample ADO

```
<%
Option Explicit

'Boolean flag that indicates whether
'or not to execute a database query
Dim boolCanRun

'The ADO connection object
Dim objConn

'The ADO recordset object
Dim objRS

'The SQL statement
Dim strSQL

'The search string
Dim strFilter

'A counter variable
Dim intRecordCount

'Initially set the flag to true
boolCanRun = true

'Get the search string from the ASP request object
strFilter = Request("filter")
'If the search string is null or zero length, don't
```

```
'execute any ADO operations; display the search form
'only.
if IsNull(strFilter) or strFilter = "" then

boolCanRun = false

end if
%>
<html>

<head>
    <meta http-equiv="Content-Type"
    content="text/html; charset=iso-8859-1">
    <title>Simple ADO Sample</title>
</head>

<body bgcolor="#FFFFFF">

<p align="center">
    <font color="#000080" size="5" face="Arial"><strong>Simple
ADO Sample</strong></font>
</p>

<p><font face="Arial">This script is an example of how to use
ActiveX Data Objects (ADO) in an ASP script to search data in an
OLE DB data source. In this case, the OLE DB data source is an
Access database (the sample &quot;Adventure Works&quot; database
that ships with IIS and MDAC). This database is set up as a
System DSN called &quot;AdvWorks&quot; using the ODBC32 Control
Panel applet.</font></p>

<p><font face="Arial">Using the form below, enter a search
string. This search string will be used to search the ProductName
and ProductDescription fields in the Products table of the
Adventure Works database:</font></p>

<p><font face="Arial"></font> </p>

<form action="SimpleADO.asp" method="POST">
    <p>
    <font color="#000080" face="Arial"><strong>Search String:</
strong></font>
    <input type="text" size="20" name="filter"
            value="<%=strFilter%>">
    <input type="submit" value="Submit">
  </p>
</form>
```

(continued)

Code Listing Sample ADO *(continued)*

```
<p><font face="Arial"></font> </p>
<%
'Now search the database, if appropriate
if boolCanRun then

'Create the ADO connection object
set objConn = Server.createObject("ADODB.Connection")

'Open the Adventure Works database
objConn.Open "DSN=AdvWorks"

'Create our SQL statement based on the value of
'the search string
strSQL = "select * from Products where ProductName like '%%" &_
         strFilter & "%%' OR ProductDescription like '%%" &_
         strFilter & "%%' Order By ProductName"

'Execute the search.  This will return an ADO recordset
set objRS = objConn.Execute(strSQL)

'Set our counter to zero
intRecordCount = 0
%>

<p>
    <font face="Arial" size="4">Search Results for search string
    '<%=strFilter%>':</font>
</p>

<table border="1" cellspacing="0">
<tr>
    <td bgcolor="#C0C0C0">
        <font face="Arial">Name</font>
    </td>
    <td bgcolor="#C0C0C0">
        <font face="Arial">Type</font>
    </td>
    <td bgcolor="#C0C0C0">
        <font face="Arial">Description</font>
    </td>
    <td bgcolor="#C0C0C0">
        <font face="Arial">Available Sizes</font>
    </td>
    <td bgcolor="#C0C0C0">
        <font face="Arial">Price</font>
    </td>
</tr>
</table>
```

```
<%
'Loop through the recordset until there are no more records...
Do while not objRS.EOF

'For each record, insert the value of each field into the
'appropriate HTML table cell
%>
<tr>
    <td>
       <font face="Arial">
           <%=objRS("ProductName")%> 
       </font>
   </td>
   <td>
       <font face="Arial">
           <%=objRS("ProductType")%> 
       </font>
   </td>
<td>
    <font face="Arial">
        <%=objRS("ProductDescription")%> 
    </font>
</td>
<td>
    <font face="Arial">
        <%=objRS("ProductSize")%> 
    </font>
</td>
<td>
    <font face="Arial">
        <%=FormatCurrency(objRS("UnitPrice"))%> 
    </font>
</td>
</td>
</tr>
<%

   'Move the pointer to the next record
   objRS.MoveNext

   'Increment our counter by one
   intRecordCount = intRecordCount + 1

loop
%>
</table>
<%
```

(continued)

Code Listing Sample ADO *(continued)*

```
'If our counter is still zero at this point, then there were
'no records in our recordset.  Therefore, we need to display
'the appropriate message to the user.

  if intRecordCount = 0 then
%>
<p>
    <font face="Arial">
        Your search did not return any products.  Please try
again.
    </font>
</p>
<%
  end if

'Clean up our ADO objects by closing down all connections and
'releasing the objects

  objRS.close
  objConn.close

  set objRS = nothing
  set objConn = nothing

end if
%>
</body>
</html>
```

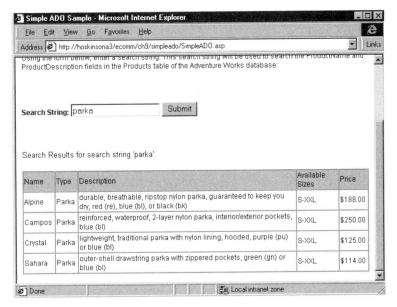

Figure 8-5. *SimpleADO.asp's output.*

Accessing ODBC Data from a COM object

SimpleADO.asp is a good example of using ADO within an ASP script, useful if your Web site is hosted by a third-party hosting service and it is not convenient or possible for you to install COM objects on the server. There are problems with using this approach, though. As we have seen in earlier chapters, when you put a lot of logic in an ASP script, it is virtually impossible to reuse this code in another application. It is also difficult to separate design from content and functionality. Application performance suffers because interpreted script runs slower than compiled components. Application maintainability and developer productivity suffers.

A better way of writing ASP data access applications is to move your ADO logic out of the ASP script and into a middle-tier business object. A business object is a COM DLL that encapsulates a particular business rule. This is the subject of our next example.

In this example, we will rewrite our Adventure Works product database search application as a three-tier application. We will separate our user presentation (in the form of HTML) from our data access logic (in the form of ADO code) by writing a COM object in Visual Basic to access our data source via ADO. We will use the ASP script to create and execute our COM object, and then stream the results to the user as HTML.

Writing the business object

The first step is to write the COM object. For this example, we will use Visual Basic 6, although you can use any language or development system that can create in-process COM servers, including Visual C++ and Visual J++. To do this, perform the following steps:

Step 1. Create a new Visual Basic 6 ActiveX DLL project called SimpleADO. The entire project is contained on the book CD-ROM.

Step 2. Click on Project in the menu bar, and then Properties to bring up the Project properties dialog box (see Figure 8-6). Make sure that the General tab is selected. Check the Unattended Execution block and make sure that Apartment Threaded is selected as the threading model.

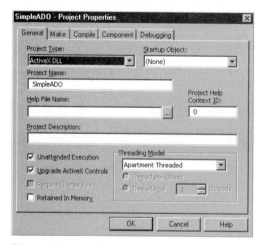

Figure 8-6. *SimpleADO Project Properties dialog box.*

Step 3. Click on Project in the menu bar, and then References to bring up the References dialog box. Check the box for Microsoft ActiveX Data Objects 2.0 library and click OK. This will allow us to use "early binding" with our ADO objects (see Figure 8-7).

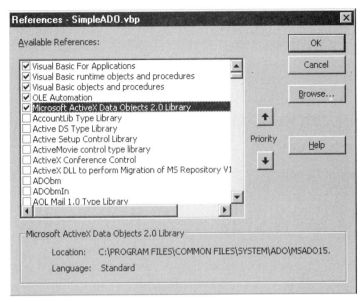

Figure 8-7. *SimpleADO References dialog box.*

Step 4. Create the component's object model. For our SimpleADO component, create three classes: Product, which encapsulates each product record; Products, a collection class that holds all the Product objects returned by our search; and the ProductSearch class, which encapsulates a particular search.

Step 5. Next, add an Execute method to the ProductSearch class. As the name implies, the Execute method executes the actual search. It takes a search string as an argument and returns a Products object that holds all the products returned by the search. Here's the code for the Execute method of the ProductSearch class:

```
Public Function Execute
(strFilter As Variant) As Products
On Error GoTo errorhandler

'Create an instance of our Products collection
Dim objProducts As New Products

'An individual product reference
Dim objProduct As Product

'Create an instance of the ADO Connection class
Dim objConn As New ADODB.Connection

'The ADO recordset
```

(continued)

327

(continued)

```
Dim objRS As ADODB.Recordset

'The SQL statement
Dim strSQL As String

'Open the Adventure Works database
objConn.Open "DSN=AdvWorks"

'Create our SQL statement based on the value of the
'search string passed to the Execute method

strSQL = "select * from Products where ProductName " &_
         "like '%%" & strFilter & "%%' OR " &_
         "ProductDescription like '%%" &_
         strFilter & "%%' Order By ProductName"

'Execute the search.  This will return an ADO recordset
Set objRS = objConn.Execute(strSQL)

'Loop through the recordset until there are no more records...
Do While Not objRS.EOF

'For each record, add a new Product object to our Products
'collection
Set objProduct = objProducts.Add(objRS("ProductName"),_
                ObjRS("ProductDescription"),_
                ObjRS("ProductType"),_
                ObjRS("ProductSize"),_
                ObjRS("UnitPrice"))

'Go to the next record
objRS.MoveNext

Loop

'Clean up our database connections and ADO objects
objRS.Close
objConn.Close
Set objRS = Nothing
Set objConn = Nothing

'Return our Products collection to the calling application
Set Execute = objProducts

Exit Function
```

```
errorhandler:

'If an error occurs, log it to the NT Event log and inform
'the calling application

App.LogEvent "The SimpleADO COM Object raised the following " &_
             "error in it's ProductSearch class and Execute " &_
             "method: " & Err.Number & ", " &_
              Err.Description

Err.Raise Err.Number, "SimpleADO Component", Err.Description

End Function
```

Step 6. Compile the project, and build the DLL.

Writing the ASP script

Once you have written the COM business object, you can reuse it in a variety of different applications. In this example, we will modify our SimpleADO.asp script to use the COM object, rather than using ADO directly. We will do this by performing the following steps:

Step 1. Create and execute the object:

```
set objProductSearch = Server.CreateObject("SimpleADO.ProductSearch")

set objProducts = objProductSearch.Execute(strFilter)
```

Step 2. If the object returns search results, build an HTML table to display those results; otherwise, tell the user that their search did not return any results. This is what the code looks like to accomplish this. For the sake of brevity, the HTML markup used to construct the table has been omitted:

```
<%if objProducts.Count > 0 then%>

(HTML Table markup here)

<%For each objProduct in objProducts%>

    (HTML Table markup here)
    <%=objProduct.ProductName%>
    (HTML Table markup here)
    <%=objProduct.ProductType%>
    (HTML Table markup here)
    <%=objProduct.ProductDescription%>
    (HTML Table markup here)
    <%=objProduct.ProductSize%>(HTML Table markup here)
```

(continued)

(continued)

```
        <%=FormatCurrency(objProduct.UnitPrice)%>
        (HTML Table markup here)

    <%Next%>

    (More HTML markup here)

    <%else%>

    (Inform the user that the search did not return any results)

    <%end if%>
```

Step 3. Release the objects:

```
set objProduct = nothing

set objProducts = nothing

set objProductSearch = nothing
```

You can find the complete code listing for this modified product search ASP script in the SimpleADO2.asp file on the book CD-ROM.

The Jet OLE DB provider

The Microsoft Jet OLE DB provider allows you to access Microsoft Jet databases, including Microsoft Access, via ADO. Additionally, it is a good data access option for accessing a variety of other popular desktop database products, as Jet provides native access to Paradox, dBase, and other database file formats.

For the most part, switching from the OBDC OLE DB provider to the Jet provider is a simple matter of modifying only one line of your ADO code. To demonstrate, let's modify the original Adventure Works product search ASP script (SimpleADO.asp) to use the Jet OLE DB provider instead of the ODBC OLE DB provider. This sample is located in its entirety on the book CD-ROM in a file called AccessADO.asp.

The Adventure Works database is a Microsoft Access database, which uses the Jet database engine. Therefore, you need to make only one change to the existing script to use the Jet OLE DB provider. Instead of using DSN=AdvWorks as the connection string when calling the Open method of the ADODB.Connection object, use a connection string that identifies Jet as the OLE DB provider, the path to our MDB file, and the userid and password (which will generally be admin with a zero-length string password, unless you have secured your Access database). The call to the Open method of the ADODB.Connection object looks like this:

```
objConn.Open "PROVIDER=Microsoft.Jet.OLEDB.3.51;" &_
             "DATA SOURCE=c:\Program Files\Common Files\"&_
             "System\msadc\Samples\advworks.mdb;" &_
             "User id=admin;password=;"
```

The SQL Server OLE DB provider

The SQL Server OLE DB provider allows your ADO applications to access SQL Server databases without having to go through ODBC. Moreover, the SQL Server OLE DB provider offers a greater variety of connection parameters. It also allows greater syntactic flexibility in the commands you send to the backend data source; in addition to ODBC and ANSI standard SQL, the SQL Server OLE DB provider will also accept Transact-SQL statements.

To use the SQL Server OLE DB provider, specify SQLOLEDB as the provider in the Connection string. For example:

```
Set objSQLSession = Server.CreateObject("ADODB.Connection")

objSQLSession.Open "PROVIDER=SQLOLEDB;DATA SOURCE=DBServerName;" &_
                   "DATABASE=DBName;USER ID=DBUserName;" &_
                   "PASSWORD=myPassword;"
```

In this example, DBServerName is the NetBIOS name of your database server, DBName is the name of the database you want to open, and DBUserName and myPassword are the credentials you want to present to the database server.

The Oracle OLE DB provider

The Oracle OLE DB provider allows your ADO applications to access Oracle databases without having to go through ODBC. To use the Oracle OLE DB provider, you should specify MSDAORA as the provider in the Connection string. For example:

```
Set objOracleSession = Server.CreateObject("ADODB.Connection")
objOracleSession.Open "PROVIDER=MSDAORA;" & _
             "DATA SOURCE=MyOracleServer;" & _
             "USER ID=myUserName;PASSWORD=myPassword;"
```

In this example, MyOracleServer is the hostname of your database server, and myUserName and myPassword are the credentials you want to present to the database server.

The Index Server OLE DB provider

The four OLE DB providers examined earlier were similar in that they each provided data access to relational data sources. But what if you need to search documents as well as relational DBMSs, and you prefer to use ADO for coding consistency? Fortunately, MDAC 2.0 provides a solution: the OLE DB provider for Index Server.

What is Index Server?

Microsoft Index Server 2.0 is a BackOffice product that allows you to integrate document searching functionality into your IIS Web sites. With Index Server, you can create (rather quickly and easily) tools that will search many different types of documents on your intranet or public Web site. These document types include HTML files as well as files created by the various Microsoft Office applications. Index Server can also index Network News Transfer Protocol (NNTP) stores. Index Server includes an API that allows you to create custom filters to index other file types.

In addition to a file's content, Index Server will also index its "meta-data." Meta-data are properties that describe the document's attributes (such as the title, author, and so on). For Microsoft Office documents, meta-data is stored as OLE Structured Storage document properties, and for HTML documents, as META tags. This allows you to create search scripts that will conduct both content searches and meta-data (document property) searches.

Index Server performs "near real-time" indexing of documents. In a nutshell, Index Server continuously monitors the file system for changes, and indexes documents when changes occur. When a file is created, changed, or deleted on an IIS virtual root for which indexing has been enabled, the NT file system informs Index Server, which then opens it at the earliest possible moment using the appropriate filter (depending on the file type). It then extracts both the content and the meta-data of the document, and stores it in a catalog. Index Server's indexing thread is a minimum priority thread, so it will generally take a few seconds or more to index a file, depending on the size of the file(s) being indexed and other activities on the server at that particular time.

An Index Server catalog is a collection of rather large files with cryptic file names stored in a directory called Catalog.wci. The exact location of this catalog depends on how you installed and configured Index Server but is usually located in the c:\inetpub directory by default. Once Index Server has populated its catalog with data, you can search the data securely using a variety of different techniques. Index Server ensures security by returning only those documents for which the calling client's security context (that is, the NT user account under which it is running) has "read" access.

The easiest and perhaps the most common way to create an Index Server search engine for your site is to write an IDQ script and companion HTX template. IDQ scripts are simple Index Server queries. They are ASCII text files that are saved with an .idq file extension and are executed by an ISAPI filter called idq.dll. When an IDQ script is executed, Index Server retrieves the search results and merges them with the .HTX template, which is then streamed back to the browser. IDQ scripts are easy to create, and the Index Server documentation provides numerous examples that site builders can customize for their own use.

One of the disadvantages of IDQ scripts and HTX templates is that they are rather primitive in the amount of logic you can code into them. Consequently, Microsoft provides a COM object (ixsso.Query) that you can use to conduct Index Server searches within the context of an ASP script (or, for that matter, any other COM client). This COM object allows you to write infinitely more sophisticated Index Server search scripts, while retaining the familiar IDQ query syntax.

There is a third way to write Index Server search tools: ADO. Because MDAC ships with an OLE DB provider for Index Server, you can use the familiar ADO object model to write tools that allow your visitors to conduct document searches on your Web site.

Why would I want to use ADO to search an Index Server catalog?

There are several reasons why you would want to use ADO to conduct Index Server searches. First, you (or others on your staff) probably already know ADO pretty well. Even if you don't, by learning ADO, you can leverage this knowledge and apply it to write data access tools for a wide variety of data sources. Second, the Index Server OLE DB provider uses SQL for its command syntax, as opposed to the proprietary query language used by conventional Index Server search mechanisms. Finally (and perhaps most importantly), using ADO will allow you to achieve the tightest degree of integration between your Index Server searches and searches against other OLE DB data sources. Using ADO and the Index Server OLE DB provider to search an Index Server catalog gets you search results in the form of an ADODB.Recordset object. You can then pass this recordset to any component that has been written to manipulate and consume ADODB.Recordset objects.

Writing an ASP script to search an Index Server catalog

To illustrate how to use ADO to search an Index Server catalog, let's write an Index Server document search ASP script. This script is located in its entirety in the IndexADO.asp file on the companion CD-ROM:

Step 1. Create your ADODB.Connection object and tell it to use the Index Server OLE DB provider:

```
set objConn = Server.CreateObject("ADODB.Connection")
objConn.Open "provider=msidxs;"
```

Step 2. Formulate your query string as a SQL SELECT statement. There are a couple of things to keep in mind here. First, your field names will map to the various document properties stored by Index Server. These document properties are listed, in great detail, in your Index Server documentation at *http://*

your_server_name/iishelp/ix/htm/ixseovr.htm. Here are the ones used in IndexADO.asp:

- **DocTitle.** This is the document title. For HTML documents, this will return the text between the <TITLE>...</TITLE> tag pair. For Microsoft Office documents, this will return the OLE DocTitle property.

- **Vpath.** This is the file's virtual URL.

- **Size.** This is the file's size, in bytes.

- **Write.** This is the file's last modified date.

- **Rank.** This is the "relevance" rank of the file. When Index Server executes a search, it scores each file based on how many times the search terms showed up in the file's contents.

Second, your "table" name will use the Index Server provider-specific Scope() function. Using the Scope() function without any parameter will tell Index Server to search the entire scope of the catalog, starting from the Web site's root directory and working all the way down. Of course, you can restrict that by passing the appropriate virtual path into the Scope() function. Third, your WHERE clause will generally include the Contains() function, to which a Boolean search expression is passed to limit the search results returned:

```
strSQL = "Select DocTitle, path, rank, size, Vpath, write " &_
         "FROM scope() WHERE CONTAINS(' " & strFilter & " ') " &_
         "> 0 ORDER BY rank desc"
```

Step 3. Create your ADODB.Command object. Associate the Command object with the Connection object created in Step 1 and assign it the SQL statement created in Step 2:

```
Set objCommand = Server.CreateObject("ADODB.Command")
set objCommand.ActiveConnection = objConn
objCommand.CommandText = strSQL
```

Step 4. Create the recordset object to hold the search results, ensuring that no more than 300 records are returned. Otherwise, a user might try to run a query that could return too many records, and this might bring your server to its knees:

```
set objRS = Server.CreateObject("ADODB.Recordset")
objRS.MaxRecords = 300
```

Step 5. Execute your search by calling the Open method of the ADODB.Recordset object and passing the ADODB.Command object to it as a parameter:

```
objRS.open objCommand
```

Step 6. Loop through the recordset. As you loop through each record, read the field values for that record into the HTTP Response stream. For brevity, the HTML markup for the table that displays the search results has been omitted:

```
<%
'Set our counter to zero
intRecordCount = 0
%>
(HTML Table Markup here)
<%
'Loop through the recordset until there are no more records...
Do while not objRS.EOF

    'For each record, insert the value of each field into the
    'appropriate HTML table cell
%>
    (HTML Table Markup here)
    <%=objRS("DocTitle")%>
    (HTML Table Markup here)
    <%=objRS("Vpath")%>
    (HTML Table Markup here)
    <%=objRS("size")%>
    (HTML Table Markup here)
    <%=objRS("write")%>
    (HTML Table Markup here)
    <%=objRS("rank")%>
    (HTML Table Markup here)
<%
    'Move the pointer to the next record
    objRS.MoveNext

    'Increment our counter by one
    intRecordCount = intRecordCount + 1

loop
%>
```

Step 7. If the recordset contained zero records, inform the user of this:

```
<%if intRecordCount = 0 then%>
<p><font face="Arial">Your search did not return any products.
Please try again.</font></p>
<%end if%>
```

Step 8. Finally, "clean up" by closing your connection(s) and releasing your objects:

```
<%
objRS.close
objConn.close

set objRS = nothing
set objCommand = nothing
set objConn = nothing
%>
```

Once you upload this script to your IIS Web server and run it from your browser, you will get output that looks similar to Figure 8-8.

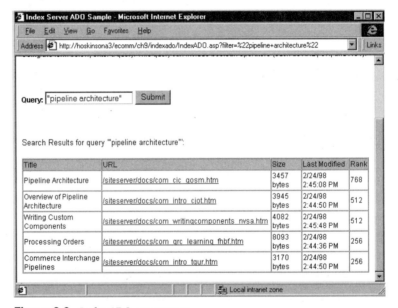

Figure 8-8. *IndexADO.asp output.*

The ADS OLE DB provider

The OLE DB provider for ADS (Active Directory Service) opens up a whole new world of data sources to ADO programming. With this provider, virtually any directory service for which an ADSI provider has been written can be accessed by ADO clients. This section will show you how.

What is an Active Directory Service?

An *active directory service* is any directory service for which an ADSI provider has been written. What, then, is *ADSI?* ADSI, or Active Directory Service Interfaces, is a collection of COM interfaces that provide an abstract description of what objects from a generic directory service (see sidebar) should look like. As such, ADSI provides a layer of abstraction between client applications and underlying directory services.

WHAT IS A DIRECTORY SERVICE?

A *directory service* stores data using a hierarchical tree structure. At its most basic level, a directory service is a taxonomy of containers and objects, with a root container that hosts objects and other containers. The subordinate containers can, of course, host more objects and containers, and so on. The "data" stored in a directory service is actually the persisted state of instances of given classes. The directory service also stores the schema, or public members, of these classes, thereby allowing client applications to determine, at runtime, the attributes (properties) of a given object.

Traditionally, directory services are used to store user, group, organization, and service information, thereby allowing organizations to locate resources dynamically, in much the same manner that you would get somebody's telephone number by looking them up in the phone directory. Nevertheless, directory services are certainly not limited to these uses; any taxonomy that uses the container/object tree hierarchy paradigm can, with the right provider, be mapped to a directory service. An example of this includes the IIS 4.0 metabase.

Like OLE DB, ADSI itself does not provide any concrete functionality. Functionality comes from ADSI providers that handle the low-level details of interacting with a particular directory service, and return objects that implement the appropriate ADS interface to client applications. This gives application developers the ability to access a wide variety of directory services from a single code base. For example, using ADSI, you could write one application that you could then use to access multiple directory services, such as NT, Novell Directory Service (NDS), Lightweight Directory Access Protocol (LDAP), or any other directory service for which an ADSI provider has been written.

For simple enumeration through an Active Directory data store, you can use the ADSI object model to open an ADS container and access the objects therein. You do this by passing the URL moniker of the underlying provider to the VBScript GetObject function. GetObject will instantiate the underlying provider, which will grab the object from the underlying directory service and return a reference to the IADs interface implementation of the underlying object. From there, you can enumerate through the objects that live in the container you just opened using the For Each…Next VBScript loop.

For example, let's say we had a Site Server 3.0 Membership Directory and we wanted to write an ASP script that lists the name, e-mail address, and street address of the users in that directory. A Site Server Membership Directory is an LDAP-compliant directory service used to store, among other things, user data, such as a user's e-mail address, street address, preferences, and so on. Such an ASP script might look something like this:

```
<%
Option Explicit

'An object reference that points to our membership directory
Dim objDirectory

'An object reference that points to a user in the directory
Dim objUser

'Our directory's URL moniker
Dim strDirURL
%>
<html>

<head>
<meta http-equiv="Content-Type"
content="text/html; charset=iso-8859-1">
<title>Simple ADSI Sample</title>
</head>

<body bgcolor="#FFFFFF">

<p align="center"><font color="#000080" size="5" face="Arial">
<strong>Simple ADSI Sample</strong></font></p>

<p><font face="Arial">This script is an example of how to use
the ADSI object model to enumerate through a Site Server 3.0
LDAP-compliant membership directory.</font></p>
<%
'Open up the directory

strDirURL = "LDAP://hoskinsona3:1002/
```

```
ou=MMA,ou=Members,o=Microsoft"
set objDirectory = GetObject(strDirURL)
%>
<table border="1" cellspacing="0">
    <tr>
        <td bgcolor="#C0C0C0">
            <font face="Arial">Name</font>
        </td>
        <td bgcolor="#C0C0C0">
            <font face="Arial">Email</font>
        </td>
        <td bgcolor="#C0C0C0">
            <font face="Arial">Street Address</font>
        </td>
        <td bgcolor="#C0C0C0">
            <font face="Arial">City, State</font>
        </td>
        <td bgcolor="#C0C0C0">
            <font face="Arial">Zip</font>
        </td>
    </tr>

<%
'Loop through the directory until there are no more users...
For each objUser in objDirectory
%>
    <tr>
        <td>
            <font face="Arial">
                <%=objUser.givenName & " " & objUser.sn%> 
            </font>
        </td>
        <td>
          <font face="Arial">
            <a href="mailto:<%=objUser.mail%>">
                <%=objUser.mail%>
            </a> 
          </font>
        </td>
        <td>
            <font face="Arial">
                <%=objUser.street%> 
            </font>
        </td>
    </td>
    <td>
```

(continued)

(continued)

```
        <font face="Arial">
            <%=objUser.l & ", " & objuser.st%> 
        </font>
    </td>
    <td>
        <font face="Arial">
            <%=objUser.postalCode%> 
        </font>
    </td>
</tr>
<%next%>
</table>
<%
'Release our objects
set objUser = nothing
set objDirectory = nothing
%>
</body>
</html>
```

The output of this script is shown in Figure 8-9. The script itself (SimpleADSI.asp) is on the book CD-ROM.

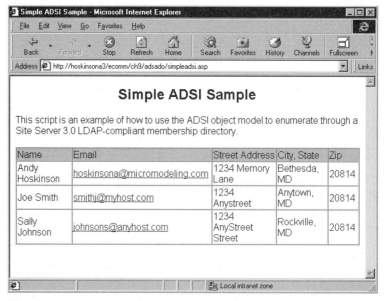

Figure 8-9. *SimpleADSI.asp output.*

NOTE Please refer to the ADSI 2.0 SDK for more information about the ADSI object model. You can download this SDK from *http://www.microsoft.com/adsi*. For more information on Site Server Membership, please see Chapter 5.

But what if you want to search for only a few users who meet certain criteria? Well, you could enumerate through the entire directory using ADSI to find the users you are looking for. This works fine if you have only a few users in your directory. But if you are running a popular Web storefront, you might find that your user directory is filled with tens of thousands of users. When that happens, looping through the entire directory to find a couple of users doesn't make much sense. In that case, you want to use ADO and the ADS OLE DB provider to conduct narrow focused searches on a large ADS data store.

Writing an ASP script to search a Site Server Membership Directory
As an example, let's walk through how to write an ASP customer search script. This script will allow you to search for customers who live in a particular U.S. state. It will use ADO and the ADS OLE DB provider to search the contents of an LDAP-compliant Site Server 3.0 Membership Directory. This script (ADSADO.asp) is located in its entirety on the book CD-ROM:

Step 1. Create your ADODB.Connection object and tell it to use the ADS OLE DB provider by setting the Provider property of the ADODB.Connection object. For the ADS provider, the Open method can just take a zero-length string, because the connection information is included in the query string in Step 2:

```
set objConn = Server.CreateObject("ADODB.Connection")
objConn.Provider = "ADsDSOObject"
objConn.Open ""
```

Step 2. Formulate your query string. When using the ADS OLE DB provider, your query string will be formatted a little differently than it is with the other providers covered so far, which all use SQL. The format for an ADS query string is <BaseDN>;(Filter);PropertyList;Scope, where:

■ *BaseDN* = The distinguished name of the ADS container to search

■ *Filter* = The search filter, given in the form of (propertyname= propertyvalue)

■ *PropertyList* = A comma-delimited list of ADS object properties to return as fields in the *ADODB.Recordset* object

■ *Scope* = The scope of the search; either base (the BaseDN container only), OneLevel (one level down from the BaseDN container), or SubTree (the BaseDN container and all its children)

This is what the query string will look like:

```
strSearch = "<LDAP://hoskinsona3:1002/ou=MMA,ou=Members,o=Microsoft>;"
&_
            "(st=" & strFilter & ");adspath;subtree"
```

Step 3. Execute your search:

```
set objRS = objConn.Execute(strSearch)
```

Step 4. Loop through the recordset, creating a user object for each record from the value of the ADSPath field. The ADSPath points to the "distinguished name" of the object that encapsulates membership data for a particular customer. From the ADSPath, you can instantiate an ADSI object using the GetObject() function. The ADSPath returned in each record of the ADODB.Recordset object will look something like this:

```
LDAP://hoskinsona3:1002/cn=Hoskinsona,ou=MMA,ou=Members,o=Microsoft
```

Where "cn=Hoskinsona" is the "common name" for the particular customer (see sidebar).

Step 5. Once you instantiate the ADSI object that encapsulates a record, you can put its attributes into the Response stream by reading the object's properties. Once again, for the sake of brevity, the HTML markup has been omitted from this code sample:

```
<%intRecordCount = 0%>
(HTML Markup here)
<%
Do while not objRS.EOF

    set objUser = GetObject(objRS("adspath"))
%>
    (HTML Markup here)
    <%=objUser.givenName & " " & objUser.sn%>
    (HTML Markup here)
    <%=objUser.mail%>
    (HTML Markup here)
    <%=objUser.street%>
    (HTML Markup here)
    <%=objUser.l & ", " & objuser.st%>
    (HTML Markup here)
    <%=objUser.postalCode%>
    (HTML Markup here)
```

```
<%
    objRS.MoveNext

    intRecordCount = intRecordCount + 1

loop
%>
```

MORE ON THE OBJUSER OBJECT

The objUser object returned by ADSADO.asp is an instance of the standard Site Server Membership Directory's Member class. This class is used to encapsulate user data in a Site Server Membership Directory. To code this object, you need to be aware of its schema. This class contains a large list of allowable properties, also known as attributes. The sample ASP scripts use the following properties:

- *cn*: The member's common name

- *c*: The member's country

- *mail*: The member's e-mail address

- *givenName*: The member's first name

- *sn*: The member's last name

- *street*: the member's street address

- *l*: The member's city

- *st*: The member's state

- *postalCode*: The member's zip code

Step 6. If the recordset contained zero records, inform the user of this:

```
<%if intRecordCount = 0 then%>
    (Inform the user that his search returned zero records)
<%end if%>
```

Step 7. Finally, "clean up" by closing your connection(s) and releasing your objects:

```
objRS.close
objConn.close
set objRS = nothing
set objConn = nothing
```

This script's output is shown in Figure 8-10.

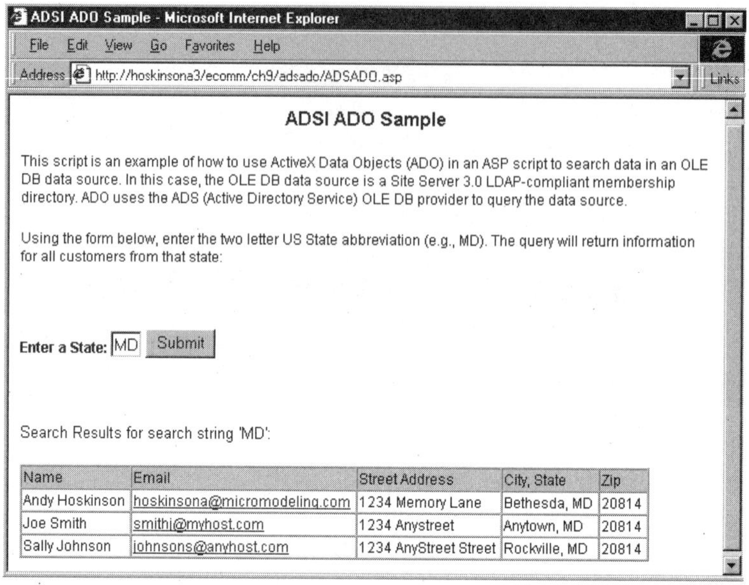

Figure 8-10. *ADSADO.asp's output.*

Other OLE DB providers

As we mentioned earlier, one of the advantages of Universal Data Access is that it provides developers with a common API (ADO) to access a virtually limitless number of data sources. This is because any data product vendor can write an OLE DB provider to expose its product to access from ADO client applications.

In addition to the core OLE DB providers that ship with MDAC, there are OLE DB providers available for many other database products on the market. Microsoft maintains a fairly comprehensive and up-to-date list of these providers at *http://www.microsoft.com/data/oledb/products/product.htm*. Some of the more interesting ones include:

■ Microsoft SNA Server, a BackOffice product used to integrate NT domains with mainframe-based networks, ships with two OLE DB providers that allow developers to access mainframe data using ADO. The OLEDB/DDM provider for IBM's Distributed Data Management (DDM) architecture allows you to access data stored in VSAM and

AS/400 file systems with ADO. The Component Object Model Transaction Integrator (COMTI), formerly code-named "Cedar," allows you to access data and post transactions against the IBM Customer Information Control System (CICS) and Information Management System (IMS) environments.

■ ObjectStore Active Toolkit, from Object Design, Inc. (*http://www.odi.com*), includes an OLE DB provider that allows ADO to access the popular ObjectStore object database system.

Of course, you always have the option of writing your own OLE DB provider if you need to access data from a proprietary or obscure data source using ADO. This is the topic of the next section.

CREATING AN OLE DB PROVIDER

The previous sections of this chapter discuss accessing your data using ADO. When writing ADO code, you do not need to concern yourself with how the actual data is retrieved. You probably want to know whether or not your data is stored in a relational database, but for the most part, you can remain ignorant of the intricacies of the data storage and retrieval mechanism. You have data, and you want to write the most efficient code to retrieve it.

This section focuses on the other end of the picture: retrieving the data and making it accessible to ADO. Simply put, ADO sits on top of OLE DB. All the data that ADO uses comes from OLE DB providers. Many data stores have an OLE DB provider written specifically for them that knows the ins and outs of the actual data. Certain data sources do not have a native OLE DB provider written for them yet; in that case, they can use the OLE DB provider for ODBC. So, if the data source in question has an ODBC driver, it is accessible through OLE DB and ADO. If you like using ADO, you can thank the kind and generous souls (mainly from Microsoft) who have gone out and written OLE DB providers.

Why Would I Want to Create My Own OLE DB Provider?

Suppose you have data that you want to make available to ADO. In other words, you want to read, update, insert, and delete this data using ADO. Maybe your company has a proprietary data source that does not have an OLE DB provider written for it, so all data from this source is retrieved via a proprietary interface. In the future, your company might move this data to SQL Server, at which point all code written in the proprietary interface has to be scrapped. Even if your data will not be moved to another data source, it is still advantageous for all your programmers to code to one interface. It is hard enough to get new developers up to speed in Visual Basic (VB), Visual C++, and/or Visual J++. On top of that, they must learn ADO for dealing with your company's mainstream data. Then you give them the additional requirement that they must learn your proprietary interface. By the time they are up to speed, they might be ready to move on to another job.

The idea behind Universal Data Access (UDA) is to give developers one interface to access all data. In a perfect world, C++ gurus will have written OLE DB providers for every possible data source, including that cryptic flat file that the company accountant uses to store important financial information, and all you need to worry about is creating your ADO Command objects and opening your recordsets. However, because that is not the case, you have a few decisions to make if you want to use ADO for all your data access:

■ Put all future data in data stores that have OLE DB providers and port all existing data to stores that have OLE DB providers.

■ Give up on UDA—who needs another acronym, anyway.

■ Code your own OLE DB provider(s) for data stores you use that do not have OLE DB providers available.

If you fall into either of the first two categories, you have permission to skip this section completely. If you're still with me, get ready to roll up your sleeves and get your hands dirty.

The OLE DB Simple Provider Toolkit

The bad news is a complete OLE DB provider can be written only in C++. Doing so is beyond the scope of this book, but you can get started by downloading the Microsoft Data Access Software Development Kit (SDK) 2.0 from *http://www.microsoft.com/data/mdac2.htm*.

The good news is you can write what is called an OLE DB Simple Provider (OSP) using VB, Visual J++, or Visual C++. To do this, you will still need to download the Microsoft Data Access Software Development Kit (SDK) 2.0 from *http://www.microsoft.com/data/mdac2.htm*. A simple provider does not support many of the advanced capabilities of OLE DB. The capabilities of OLE DB are exposed via COM interfaces, and OSPs only support a subset of the complete OLE DB interfaces. There is no way around these limitations; you cannot add additional code to the OSP in order to support additional OLE DB interfaces. Therefore, before you jump up and begin to write your first OSP, make sure that it can do the things you need it to do.

One important limitation of OSPs is that you cannot use OLE DB commands. In ADO terms, this means that you will not be able to use the Command object with your OSP; you must open Recordsets directly off of the Connection object. OSPs are good if most of your data can be accessed by opening single tables. I use the word "table" in a generic sense: A table can be a flat file or anything else you want it to be. You cannot easily perform complex joins across tables within your OSP. You could open a number of ADO Recordsets using your OSP, one for each table, and then perform the join using logic coded in a Visual Basic object, but this can get messy. If you find yourself writing your own query processor that sits on top of your OSP, then at this point it is probably better to write your own OLE DB provider in C++. Consult the OSP documentation for further details concerning the limitations surrounding the OSP toolkit.

A sample OSP project is included in each of the three languages. These projects can be found in C:\MSDASDK\Samples\OSP (assuming you accepted the default installation path). The documentation for the OSP Simple Provider Toolkit can be found at *http://www.microsoft.com/data/reference/oledb2.htm*. [Expand the OLE DB Simple Provider (OSP) Toolkit leaf in the tree on the left.]

An OLE DB simple provider example

A sample OSP written in VB 6.0 is included on the CD with this book in the Ch06\OLEDBProvider\VB directory. When you open this sample in the VB development environment and select Project/References from the toolbar, you might notice that the reference to Microsoft OLE DB Simple Provider 1.5 Library (C:\Windows\System\simpdata.tlb) is missing, and VB is looking in a different directory. If that is the case, click the Browse button in the References dialog, navigate to C:\Windows\System, and select simpdata.tlb.

Notice in the General tab of the Project Properties dialog box that the Threading Model is set to Apartment Threaded and that the "Unattended Execution" check box is checked. If you are planning on using your OSP from Active Server Pages (ASP) running under Internet Information Server (IIS), these settings must be as described earlier. While we're at it, go to the Compile tab and notice that the DLL Base Address has been changed from its default setting of &H11000000 to &H15360000. It is important that each component that is running in a given process space have a different DLL BaseAddress. Doing so can really help your component's memory usage. Search for Setting Base Addresses in Visual Basic Books Online.

Concurrency is an important issue to consider for your OSP. Can multiple people update the data simultaneously? If the answer is yes, your OSP must take action to ensure that errors do not occur from multiple people accessing the data at the same time. In addition, you might want to write code to ensure that one person's changes do not overwrite another person's. My example takes care of the first case, but it does not inform someone if they try to update data that someone else has just changed. Because this sample is meant to run under IIS and IIS has multiple threads (remember, the sample OSP can run in multiple threads under IIS's process space because the component is apartment threaded and has unattended execution), it is possible that one thread will try to update the file while another thread is already reading it. Because we are always opening the file for exclusive access, the second open call will generate a runtime error. To solve this problem, each thread in my sample application opens a *mutex* before trying to read and write to the file. A mutex is an object that is used to ensure exclusive access to a shared resource in a multithreaded environment. When two or more threads need exclusive access to a shared resource (such as a file), the programmer can synchronize this access by requiring each thread to defer execution of code that acts on the shared resource until it has ownership of the mutex. Getting back to our example, if another thread tries to open the mutex while it is locked, that thread will sleep until the first thread is done using it. Any further threads that try to open the mutex will queue up and wait in line. When the original thread is done, it will release the mutex, and the next thread in line will get access. If this still sounds a little funny, looking at the sample code on the CD should help.

With the overview out of the way, let's dig into the details. As an example, lets say a company wants to make its product list available to customers. Typically, there are a number of ways to create this products page, including (but not limited to):

- Use ASPs to access product data stored in SQL Server and dynamically build the products page.

- Use the SQL Server Web Assistant to automatically generate a static Web page based on data stored in a SQL table.

- Store all the product information in an HTML page.

Although storing the product list in a database seems like the obvious solution, perhaps the company is not ready to make the investment in SQL Server and wants to start small. One solution is to build an OSP that interfaces with HTML tables to read, insert, update, and delete data from the product page. Once you complete development of the OSP, it will be a simple task to build ASP pages that use the OSP to modify the product table.

"Why would I create an OSP instead of writing a VB component that performs file I/O on the products page?" you ask. That is a good question. You might be able to get the I/O solution up and running faster, but you gain some rather nice advantages with the OSP:

- If you later move the products listing out of the HTML page and into a SQL Server database, the ASP pages that access the data will be very easy to change. The code that loops through and works with recordsets can remain largely unchanged. You will just need to add Command objects to call SQL Server stored procedures. If you have used the file I/O approach, the changes to your code could be very significant. Depending on how widespread use of your file I/O component is, there might be many thousands of lines of code that require changing all over your enterprise.

■ Your data will play nice with other ADO data. If you create an OSP to access your data, you will be able to open updateable recordsets on that data. These recordsets can be passed around in code just like a recordset containing SQL Server data. This flexibility could become very important as you find yourself dealing with many different types of data. There is one common way to access it, and you can write generic, reusable routines to work with this data.

■ You get some powerful ADO functionality at a cheap price. For example, you can write ADO code to filter your recordsets and find individual records. Internet Explorer HTML controls will be able to bind to your data, providing easy browsing and updating ability.

■ You get support from plug-and-play service providers, including query processors and cursor engines. These additional components can be added to the OLE DB environment, providing features that the OLE DB provider itself does not make available.

The OSP documentation (*http://www.microsoft.com/data/reference/oledb2.htm*) does a nice job of giving you all the nitty gritty details. Here is a simple overview of how to implement your OSP. If you want to know the "why" behind all of this, consult the help file.

To code your own OSP, you need an ActiveX DLL. This DLL will contain at least two classes. The first class (named MyDataSource in the sample, but you can name it anything you want) is used just to get a foot in the door, so to speak. This class must be MultiUse, and you must implement two trivial methods (msDataSourceObject and addDataSourceListener). The implementation of those methods in the sample should give you a useful template to work from. The second class (MyOSPObject) must implement the OLEDBSimpleProvider interface. This interface contains 14 methods, shown in Table 8-1.

Table 8-1

OLEDBSIMPLEPROVIDER METHODS

GetRowCount	Retrieve the number of rows in the recordset.
GetColumnCount	Retrieve the number of columns in the recordset.
GetRWStatus	Retrieve the read-write status of a field.
GetVariant	Get the value of a field.
SetVariant	Set the value of a field.
InsertRows	Insert one or more rows into the recordset.
DeleteRows	Delete one or more rows from the recordset.
Find	Find a value in the recordset.
GetLocale	You can return an empty string for this method.
IsAsync	Return true if your OSP works asynchronously; false otherwise. The sample is not asynchronous.
GetEstimatedRows	If your OSP is not asynchronous, return the total number of rows in the recordset. If your OSP is asynchronous, return the estimated number of rows in the recordset.
StopTransfer	If your OSP is not asynchronous, this method can be ignored; otherwise, you should stop retrieving rows.
AddOLEDBSimpleProviderListener	Just return a reference to the OLEDBSimpleProviderListener.
RemoveOLEDBSimple ProviderListener	You don't need to implement this for an OSP. Just include a comment in the method implementation.

The msDataSourceObject method of MyDataSource is your OSP's entry point into the world of OLE DB. It receives a single parameter: DataMember$. This is your Connection string, so to speak. Based on its format, you decide which OSP object to instantiate. In this example, the DataMember$ parameter is just the path to the HTML file whose table we are editing.

```
Public Function msDataSourceObject(DataMember$) As
OLEDBSimpleProvider
    Dim oMyOSP As MyOSPObject

    If DataMember$ = "" Then
        Err.Raise E_FAIL
    End If

    Set oMyOSP = New MyOSPObject
    With oMyOSP
        .FilePath = DataMember$
        .LoadData
    End With

    Set msDataSourceObject = oMyOSP
    Set oMyOSP = Nothing
End Function
```

Notice that the DataMember$ parameter is used to set the FilePath property of my OSP object. The LoadData method is then called and reads in the first HTML table it encounters in the file represented by the FilePath property. The OSP object exposes this table as an OLE DB rowset. The LoadData method is responsible for taking the data in its raw format and translating it into a form that allows you to easily expose it through the methods on the MyOspObject object. In this case, the HTML table is stored in a VB collection.

The 14 methods on the OSP object are called to read and update the data. When the Class Terminate event is fired (MyOspObject is terminated because the ADO recordset has been closed), the private SaveData method is called. This method is responsible for taking the VB collection and writing it out as the newly updated HTML table.

Registering MyOSP.dll

You need to complete three steps to register MyOsp.dll:

1. Register msdaosp.dll. This file is automatically registered when you install the OLE DB SDK, and it should reside in the C:\Program Files\Common Files\System\ole db directory. If it is registered else-where, you will need to change the path referenced in the MyOsp.reg file, discussed later.

2. Register the OSP. Double-click on MyOsp.reg to merge the contents of this file with your registry.

3. Copy MyOSP.dll to your hard drive and register it. You can register it by selecting Run from the Start menu and typing

```
regsvr32 <path to MyOsp.dll>\MyOsp.dll
```

That's it. You're now ready to use the OSP.

The OSP in action

Three ASP pages and an HTML page are included on the CD (look in the ASP directory) along with the VB project code. The HTML page is Products.htm. It contains the name, description, price, and a picture of all the products currently available from Awesome Computers. The three ASP pages manage adding, de-leting, and editing the products page, using the OSP we created. When you copy the files to your hard drive, make sure that you remove the read-only attribute from Products.htm. If Products.htm is read-only, the OSP will not function correctly.

Move these four files and the images subdirectory to a directory under IIS. First, view Products.htm to get a feel for the data you'll be editing (see Figure 8-11). There are currently six products offered by Awesome Computers. (You can tell I haven't purchased computer equipment in a while based on my prices.)

Next, go to EditProd.asp (see Figure 8-12). From here, you can click on links to edit, delete, and add new products. Editing and adding is done on Edit.asp. By clicking on the link for one of the items, you are brought to the edit page. You can change data and press Save or Cancel. Also on the EditProd.asp page is a link to the FilterPr.asp page, which allows you to filter your view of the products page. I can say that I only want to see all products whose price is less than or equal to $99.99. Figure 8-13 shows the updated Products.htm page after all my editing is complete.

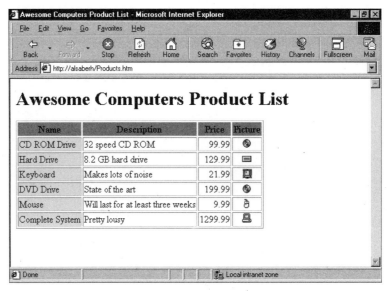

Figure 8-11. *The original Products.htm page.*

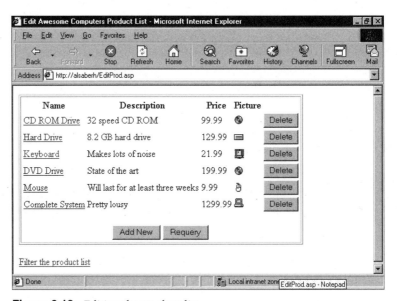

Figure 8-12. *Editing the product list.*

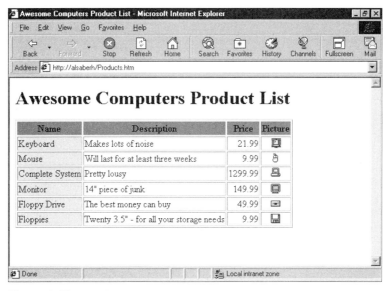

Figure 8-13. *The final Products.htm page.*

Limitations of this example

The sample MyOSP.dll is not perfect. It is designed only to read and update the first HTML table it encounters in a given file. To keep the code simple, there is a minimum of error handling. It is also not too forgiving if your HTML syntax is incorrect. It does not handle nested tables: One of your table cells cannot contain another HTML table as its contents. It assumes that the first column of the table is your key: You should not have duplicate values in the first column, or problems will arise. This should not be a problem for Products.htm because the first column is the name.

One more annoying shortcoming is that it will not allow the use of spaces in column names. The OSP assumes the first row of your table will have <TH> tags. It takes each of those <TH> tags and stores them as column names. If those column names have spaces in them, the Find and Filter commands on the recordset will not work. One workaround (which is left to the reader to code) is to remove the spaces before storing the column names and putting them back in when saving the data.

MyOsp.dll handles two data types: string and numeric. The numeric data type is stored as a double in VB. The OSP determines the data type of a cell by trying to convert it to a double. If that fails, it assumes it is a string. You could easily add support for dates and other data types by adding code to the GetTable function of MyOsp.cls, part of which is shown here:

```
On Error Resume Next
' Try to convert the cell value to a double.
avColumns(ospColValue, lColIndex) = CDbl(sCol)
If Err <> 0 Then
' The data is not numeric; store it as a string.
   Err.Clear
   avColumns(ospColValue, lColIndex) = sCol
End If
On Error GoTo LoadDataErr
```

So while MyOsp.dll is far from perfect, it is still useful for updating simple HTML tables. Feel free to build on it and make it more robust. One nice addition would be automatically sorting the rows based on the values of the first column before saving the data. You will notice that Products.htm does not display the products in any particular order. Because the rows are stored in a collection, doing a quick sort on the data and rearranging the rows in the collection is not too tough. Think of this as your extra-credit assignment.

Registering your OSP

If you recall in the "Registering MyOSP.dll" section earlier, you had to double-click on MyOsp.reg, a registry file created based on a template provided by the SDK. You will need to create a similar file for your OSP. Take the sample registration file included with the SDK (C:\MSDASDK\Samples\OSP\registerprovider.reg) and substitute your own values. C:\MSDASDK\Samples\OSP\registerprovider.txt as well as the Help file contain detailed instructions on how to do this.

When you compile your ActiveX DLL, VB creates a Globally Unique Identifier (GUID) for each public class in your project. However, you will need another GUID to register your DLL as an OSP. The Help file suggests you use a GUID creation tool, but in case you do not have one available, here is a little workaround:

1. Create a new ActiveX DLL in VB and change the project name to GUIDTest.

2. Compile the DLL.

3. Select Run from the Start menu, type in **regedit**, and press Enter.

4. Select Find from the Edit menu, type **GUIDTest.Class1** in the Find dialog (shown below in Figure 8-14) box. Make sure the Keys check box is checked, and press Enter.

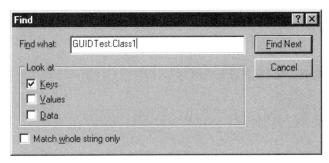

Figure 8-14. *The Regedit Find dialog.*

5. When regedit finds the GUIDTest.Class1 entry, expand the tree, and you will find your GUID as shown in Figure 8-15.

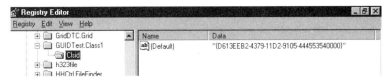

Figure 8-15. *Finding your GUID.*

6. Copy this to the clipboard or write it down; you will need it for your registration file.

7. To clean up your registry when you are done, type **regsvr32 –u <*full path to your dll*>\GUIDTest.dll**.

OLE DB is a very powerful technology. When it comes to UDA, most developers will concern themselves with writing good ADO code. However, some of us might need to get a little deeper into the UDA universe. For the rocket scientists among us, you can go out and write a complete OLE DB provider in Visual C++. Sometimes, that is the only thing that can be done. As mentioned earlier, the OSP has some serious limitations. However, there are times when the OSP offers a very nice solution. If you have simple data (a flat file that can be mapped into arrays or collections), an OSP just might be the answer to your Data Access quandary.

SUMMARY

Today, end users expect Data Access applications to provide seamless access to a wide variety of different data sources. At the same time, software developers need to be able to crank out applications in a timely, efficient, and robust manner. Meeting both goals requires a common, easy-to-use API with which developers can access myriad different data storage products. Microsoft's Universal Data Access architecture, with its underlying OLE DB and ADO technologies, provides this and gives developers a framework with which they can rapidly develop high-performance Data Access applications for the enterprise.

Chapter 9

COM Primer

by Frank J. Campise

This book spends a great deal of time talking about developing Web-based commerce solutions. It covers topics ranging from building HTML front-ends to using MTS for transactions and scaling. But at the heart of almost every chapter implicitly lies this concept known as *Component Object Model* or *COM*. COM is used throughout the book as a mechanism for automating one application or extending the functionality of another. COM is everywhere! If you have ever embedded a Microsoft Excel spreadsheet into a Microsoft Word document, used a ActiveX control from a Web page or a Microsoft Visual Basic application, or retrieved data from a database using ADO, then you have used COM. This is due to the fact that COM is Microsoft's foundation for component-based software solutions.

According to the latest statistics compiled by Microsoft and the Giga International Group, COM is currently being used in over 150 million systems worldwide. The market for third-party COM-based components is estimated at around $670 million in 1998 and growing toward $3 billion in the year 2001. COM is here to stay! If you are an architect or developer on the Windows platform, there is virtually no way to avoid it. COM is currently being used in almost every Microsoft product as well as by many third-party vendors. Along with the recent emergence of some complementary enterprise technologies such as Microsoft Transaction Server (MTS) and Microsoft Message Queue (MSMQ), COM promises to be the preferred way to build solutions for years to come.

NOTE Many Microsoft products such as Word, Excel, and Outlook use COM in the form of an *object model*. An object model is basically a set of COM components that work together to programmatically provide the same functionality as can be obtained from the application's user interface (this is sometimes referred to as *Automation*).

It's also important to understand the COM is not inherently tied to the Windows platform. The original implementation of COM was created by Microsoft to run on the Windows and Windows NT platforms, but Microsoft has also released it for the Macintosh, Sun Solaris, as well as some limited support on the Windows CE platform. Microsoft is leaving the task of supporting COM on other operating systems up to third-party vendors. For example, as of the time of this writing, Digital Equipment Corporation is currently working on a version for their DIGITAL UNIX platform as well as the OpenVMS platform.

With that said, it is imperative that you have a good conceptual understanding of COM if you want to continue to be successful at implementing solutions—large or small—on the Windows platform. That is where this chapter comes in. It is geared toward the individual who would like to get an architectural overview of COM without drudging through every grueling detail about this technology.

UNDERSTANDING COM

Historically, most developers' first encounter with COM was involved in working with compound documents and the OLE technologies that allowed a Microsoft Excel spreadsheet to be linked or embedded into a Microsoft Word document. These battles left many developers disenchanted with building components and overcome with the impression that there was some "black magic" involved. Most of the confusion, however, was due to the fact that developers were trying to implement COM components without a basic understanding of COM. This was partially due to the fact that in OLE's first incarnation, COM didn't exist as a formal specification and was not officially invented until the second release of OLE. The other half of the problem was the lack of good documentation surrounding the "COM architecture," which refers to operating system features or programming environment features that implement the COM specification. This problem is slowly dissolving as more and more books (as well as this chapter) enter the market with an emphasis entirely on COM.

Microsoft has primarily used COM technology to solve many specific problems such as compound documents, user interface controls, and application automation, but it is important to realize that COM is a generic foundation for building component-based software. COM, or Component Object Model, defines a standard way for a developer to package functionality into reusable software modules or components. Like any standard, COM comes with its very own specification. This specification is a document that was created by Microsoft and defines everything about COM—from the high-level motivations behind its creation to the nitty gritty details for programming with it. The complete COM specification can be downloaded from the Microsoft's Web site (*http://www.microsoft.com/com*).

Figure 9-1 shows the COM foundation and many of those technologies that Microsoft has built on top of this foundation. It would be impossible to cover every one of these technologies in just one chapter; therefore, this chapter will concentrate on the COM foundation in the context of building custom business components. It will help you gain an understanding of COM by looking at it from a couple of different angles:

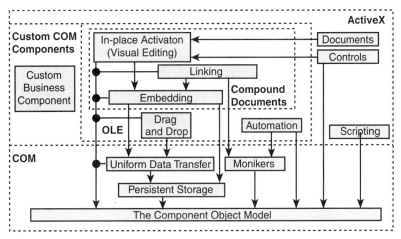

Figure 9-1. *COM as the foundation for component-based software.*

■ **Why Components?** You might want to know the reasons behind component technology and why it fits so well in building software.

■ **Fundamental Building Blocks.** You need to understand the fundamental concepts and entities used in building COM-based component solutions.

■ **COM vs. Object-Orientation.** There has been much debate over whether or not COM is an object-oriented technology. This section will attempt to clarify the issues as well as describe why traditional object-oriented languages have fallen short of creating universally accepted software components.

■ **COM Architecture.**–You need to understand the runtime aspects of COM, including the facilities and structures that are in place for building and using COM components.

WHY COMPONENTS?

Building a product out of components is definitely not a new idea. In the mid-1800s, the parts for a gun were standardized so that blacksmiths could build parts without having to specially create them for each individual gun. During the Industrial Revolution, the assembly line was created as a way to quickly and efficiently build products out of parts (that is, components). For the past few decades, computer hardware designers have built their products from existing integrated circuit (IC) components. But what do all of these scenarios have in common? Well, by using components to build their products, these businesses were able to achieve some competitive advantages, such as shorter times to market, higher quality, and even lower production costs.

What Is a Component?

At a minimum, you can think of a *component* as a self-contained unit that performs a specific set of functions and has well-defined interfaces. To give a concrete analogy, let's take a look at the engine in an automobile (see Figure 9-2). An automobile is simply a collection of components (that is, parts) that are put together to provide some overall functionality (that is, moving people from one place to another), and an engine is just one of those components. An engine performs a specific function; it is responsible for providing the power needed to move the automobile. An engine can also be thought of as self-contained; how it is internally built to provide the power is of no concern to any of the other parts of the car. The engine itself can even be made up of other components, each performing its own function to collectively provide the power. The engine must also provide a well-defined interface; whether you are adding a six-cylinder engine or a four-cylinder engine, there must be a common mechanism that the rest of the car can use to harness the power provided by the engine. For example, a variety of engines from different manufacturers, in a range of power and torque characteristics, built of a variety of materials, and using various internal technologies and fuels can be used in the same automobile—if the "engine" has standard mounting bolts, size, and connections to the automobile.

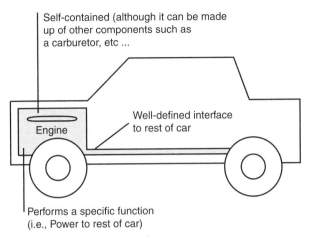

Self-contained (although it can be made up of other components such as a carburetor, etc ...

Engine

Well-defined interface to rest of car

Performs a specific function (i.e., Power to rest of car)

Figure 9-2. *The engine as a component to a car.*

Component Benefits

As mentioned at the beginning of this section, there are a number of benefits that come from using components to develop your product. Following is a list and description of some of these benefits and competitive advantages.

- **Manageability.** Breaking down a product into a collection of components allows a designer to break down a complex monolithic problem into a collection of smaller, more manageable problems.

- **Economies of Scale.** Components are self-contained units and therefore can theoretically be implemented independently of one another, assuming that all aspects of the interfaces between components have been well defined. Multiple developers can work in parallel to implement individual components.

- **Solve the Problem Once; Reuse Many Times.** Another benefit of building and using components is that you have to solve an individual problem only once. For the managers out there, this translates into having to incur the time and cost associated with building the component only once. You can then reuse this component over and over again by applying it to similar projects.

- **Explicit Dependencies.** Well-defined interfaces define explicit dependencies between components. Because a component hides the implementation details about how it accomplishes a task and exposes only a well-defined interface, any errors in the implementation details are self contained. Therefore, errors can be fixed in isolation, and only the behavior of the interface for the given component needs to be retested.

- **Domain Expertise.** Components allow companies to concentrate on their individual domain expertise. A company can buy additional components as needed when they do not have the individual expertise in-house or the cost of building the component themselves is prohibitive. For example, Microsoft Transaction Server (MTS) is a framework that allows a company to build a scalable distributed application. MTS deals with all of the issues related to scalability and transactions, so companies using MTS need to worry only about implementing the business logic components for their specific applications.

- **Shorter Development Cycles.** Theoretically, with a large number of prefabricated components in the marketplace, a company has to write only the "glue" or logic to put these components together to form an application. Today, however, components fall somewhere in the middle ground between completely writing an application from scratch and just writing some "glue."

The Software Industry

When thinking about components and the advantages they offer, it seems to make sense that the software industry could benefit from using components. You would not be alone with this thought; the idea of component software has been around for about 30 years. So why isn't it a reality? Well, one of the main obstacles in the software industry was that the mechanisms were not present to facilitate component-based software. Sure, there have been a number of technologies that have started us on the road to component-based software, such as code libraries and object-oriented programming, but they all have fallen short of being a universal solution. A "universal" software component not only has to take on the three characteristics mentioned earlier (self-contained, perform specific function, well-defined interface) but also needs to posses the following attributes in order to be accepted and used by a large number of developers:

- **Binary Standard.** Software components need to be used at the binary level. A third-party component vendor should not have to release their proprietary source code for other companies to use their products.

- **Language Independent.** There are numerous languages in the marketplace for developing software, and a software component should be capable of being used and created by a vast number of these languages.

- **Location Transparency.** One of the goals of a true component-based solution is to allow the client program to interact with a component the same way regardless of where the component is located. This should hold true whether the component is on the same machine or it is located 1,000 miles away on some other machine on a network.

- **Versioning.** A software component should not break existing software when a new version of the component is released.

FUNDAMENTAL BUILDING BLOCKS

Despite the fact that there are a lot of details surrounding COM, you will find out that COM really boils down to some simple but very powerful concepts. A COM component can be broken down into two fundamental building blocks: *interface* and *implementation*.

The Interface

The interface is everything! It is the standard mechanism in COM by which software modules can communicate with one another. As defined by the COM Specification:

> An interface is a strongly typed contract between software components to provide a relatively small but useful set of semantically related operations. An interface is an articulation of an expected behavior and expected responsibilities, and the semantic relation of interfaces gives programmers and designers a concrete entity to use when referring to the contract.

To better understand this definition, let's take a deeper look at how the COM interface is involved in building and using components. When thinking about communication between software modules, you can conclude that there are usually two parties involved: a software module that provides some functionality (that is, component) and a software module that wants to use the functionality (that is, client). Technically, these two software modules are bound by whatever protocol is used for exchanging the functionality (that is, function call, RPC, windows messages, and so on). However, from a functional point of view, there really is no need for these two parties to be intimately coupled with one another. They should simply connect and exchange the given functionality at the appropriate time. That is where the interface comes in (see Figure 9-3). It acts as a mediator between the two parties so that they can exchange the functionality without even being aware of who is on the other side, requesting or providing the functionality, respectively. This ability to connect two software modules at runtime versus compile time is known as *late binding*.

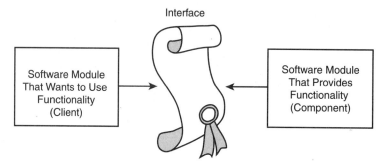

Figure 9-3. *The interface as a software contract between software modules.*

Now, think about how much trouble you have getting two software modules to communicate together when they are being developed by two different individuals within the same organization. Throw in late binding, and you can imagine a scenario where these two software modules can be developed by two different people working for different companies in different parts of the world. Also, imagine that any number of client applications might want to use the functionality that this interface provides, and any number of components might want to provide the implementation for this functionality. For example, assume that someone has created a spell-checking interface. There might be several applications that want to use spell checking, such as a word processing application, a spreadsheet application, or maybe an e-mail program. There might also be a number of third-party vendors who have implemented spell checkers (see Figure 9-4). With that potential de-coupling, you can see why it is imperative to have a well-defined interface or "contract" between the parties involved. The next few sections explore in greater detail the contractual obligations that come along with COM interfaces.

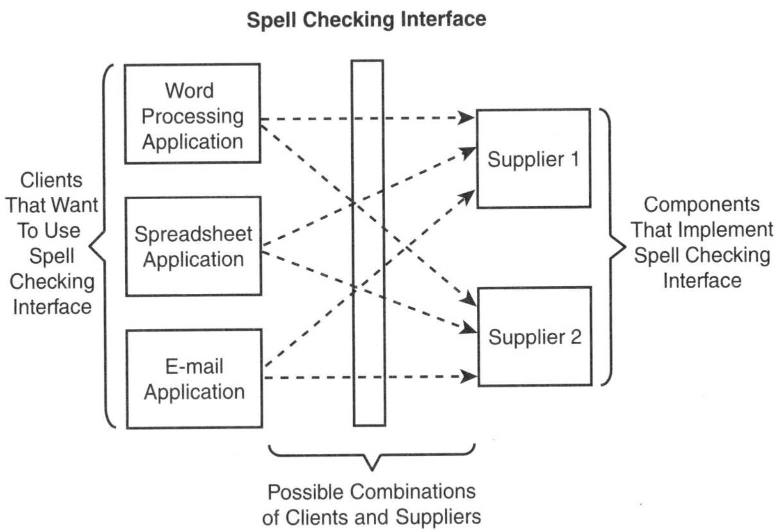

Spell Checking Interface

Figure 9-4. *The interface as the constant between an unknown group of clients and suppliers.*

Formal side of the contract

When most developers think of interfaces, they are generally referring to the formal aspect of the contract. An interface is formally defined as a collection of *methods* (that is, callable functions). These methods define the programmatic syntax or protocol for executing the desired behavior. The interface lets a component know how to expose the functionality it is implementing and lets the application using the component know how to tap into the desired functionality.

> NOTE Some languages like Visual Basic lead you to believe that an interface can contain both properties and methods. However, this is merely a programming convenience. Under the covers, an interface's property is just two method calls: one that returns a value and one that sets a value.

Although not a specific requirement of COM, most interfaces today are described using the Interface Description Language or IDL. COM's version of IDL is largely borrowed from the IDL used in the Open Software Foundation's Distributed Computing Environment (OSF DCE). IDL provides a mechanism that is a language-independent way of describing the functions and the parameters that make up an interface.

Let's take a look at a department store's point of sale system as an example. A department store typically allows its customers to pay for merchandise using credit cards. Assume that a bank or clearing house provides the store with a component that allows the store to debit or credit an individual's account for a given merchandise transaction. This component might expose an individual's account through an interface. As defined in IDL, it might look something like this:

```
[
object,
uuid(62839981-32E8-11d2-A5F6-F0CD600000000),
pointer_default(unique)
]
interface IBankAccount : IUnknown
{
        HRESULT Debit(  IRetailStore* pStore,
                        BSTR UPCCode,
                        CURRENCY amount,
                        long* pTransNumber);
        HRESULT Credit( IRetailStore* pStore,
                        long OriginalTransNumber,
                        CURRENCY amount,
                        long* pTransNumber );
}
```

This bank account interface has two functions: Debit and Credit. The Debit function accepts three inputs—a pointer to the department store's component (via an interface) so that the bank can retrieve additional information about the store (for example, store number, and so on), the universal product code (UPC) for the product or service being purchased, and the amount of the purchase. It returns a transaction number through the pTransNumber parameter. The Credit function accepts a pointer to the store component handling the return, the original transaction number (from the customer's receipt), and the amount to credit for the return. It returns a new transaction number also through the pTransNumber parameter. You should notice that both functions have a return value known as an HRESULT. An HRESULT is a 32-bit status code that contains information on success or failure of the function call as well as the general nature of any errors that occurred. Following is some sample code written in C++ that shows how this interface can be used by the department store's system to debit an individual's account.

NOTE   Some languages like Visual Basic hide the HRESULT values from the programmer and simply throw an exception if an ewCor is incurred.

```
    . . .

long transNumber;
IBankAccount* pBankAccount;
//logic to retrieve Bank Account interface for the given
//customer's account  - omitted for clarity
    . . .

//Attempt to debit individual's account
    HRESULT hr = pBankAccount->Debit( pDepartmentStore,
                              "781673312167",
                              34.95,&transNumber);

    if ( SUCCEEDED (hr) )
        //logic to handle successful transaction
    else
        //logic to handle an error condition

    . . .
```

NOTE   For more detailed information about IDL, refer to the COM specification at *http://www.microsoft.com/com.*

Informal side of the contract

An interface is more than just the operations that are defined for it. One of the least emphasized aspects of an interface is the informal side of the contract. This includes many of the functional and non-functional requirements associated with an interface. These requirements are generally taken into account during the process of creating a new interface. Unfortunately, the COM specification does not provide any formal mechanism for recording these requirements. Many times some or all of these requirements will go undocumented. However, most of the standard Microsoft-defined interfaces cover some of these requirements in their online help.

Following is a list of some of these informal requirements that you might expect to see associated with a COM interface:

■   **Intended Purpose.**–For you to use or implement an interface, you must be aware of what the intended purpose is for the interface and what its expected behaviors are. The department store is aware that the bank account interface lets them accept credit cards as payment for merchandise or services. The store also expects the bank to pay them for any charges made through the interface with an understanding that the bank will now be responsible for collecting the payment from the individual account holder.

■   **Pre- and Post-Conditions.** When using an interface, the client application might need to be aware of any pre- or post-conditions that are required when calling the operations on a interface. There might also be some predefined sequence in which the operations should be called.

■   **Valid Inputs and Outputs.** To successfully interact with an interface, you must be aware of the valid values that can be passed into the inputs for an operation and the valid outputs that can be returned. This might include boundary conditions related to input values (that is 0 >= credit limit <= 20,000) or the enumeration of all types of supported error conditions that can result by calling an operation.

■   **Performance Requirements.**–When a client application uses an interface, the client might have some timing requirements for any component that intends to implement the interface. The department store's point of sale application might depend on the fact that the component that implements the bank account interface will return a result within a predetermined number of seconds. This constraint might be due to the fact that a customer is willing to wait only so long for credit approval.

■   **Resource Consumption Requirements.** A client application might need to run in an environment that has limited resources such as physical memory. This application will function properly only if the components that it uses also are constrained by the same physical memory requirements. Likewise, a component might need a certain amount of minimum memory to accomplish its tasks.

Strongly typed

As defined earlier, interfaces are contracts between software components. For this to work, however, both parties involved in the contract must agree on the contract. To agree, they must both be sure they are looking at the same contract. The COM specification deals with this problem by requiring every interface to have its own unique identifier, sometimes referred to as an IID or Interface ID. An IID is derived from a globally unique identifier or GUID (discussed later in the chapter); a GUID is virtually guaranteed to be unique across time and space. As can be seen from the earlier IDL snippet, the IID for the bank account interface is defined by the hexadecimal number contained within the *uuid* tag (that is 62839981-32E8-11d2-A5F6-F0CD600000000). The IID for an interface helps avoid any chance of collisions and guarantees that both parties are agreeing to the same contract.

As a side note, each interface is also given a human readable name. This name is usually prefixed with the letter *I* (short for *Interface*) and used as a convenience to the developer. For example, the bank account interface discussed earlier has the human readable name of IBankAccount. However, unlike their corresponding IIDs, these human readable names are not guaranteed to be unique.

Immutable

In an effort to further de-couple any dependencies between a client and a component, the COM specification states that once an interface is published, it should not be changed. This again goes back to the fact that an interface is a contract. If one side was able to change the contract without the other side knowing, it would effectively break the contract; both sides would have different ideas about what the contract was about and what it supported. This one-sided change could cause the two software modules to either crash or produce some erroneous results when being run together. Obvious inconsistencies can occur when changes have been made to the formal side of the contract, such as adding or removing methods, or parameters to methods. However, the impact of changes to the informal side of the contract is less obvious but still can break the contract. Once again, let's look at the department store and bank. Assume now that the bank came out with a second release of the credit card component that used more advanced encryption algorithms to send information back and forth, but as a result, the debit operation took twice as long. This could break the contract without physically breaking the client application. Customers might find it unacceptable to wait twice as long to check out at the store; as a result, the customer decides to shop elsewhere. Although this scenario is a little exaggerated, it attempts to show the importance of all aspects of an immutable contract.

It is also important to note that COM does not provide any physical checks to make sure that both sides have complied with the immutability of an interface. Therefore, it is up to the designers to make sure that they do not change an interface definition once it has been made public. The act of going public can simply be defined as releasing the interface to customers outside your control. This could mean that your product was released to the general public through some distribution channel, or you simply e-mailed the interface to a different department within your organization. The main consequence of disobeying this rule is that you are likely to have one less customer if your interface changes cause the customer's product to crash.

Versioning

There might be one question left on your mind in regards to immutable interfaces: How does a developer deal with a second release of an interface? The answer is simple. The developer simply creates a new interface with its own unique identifier (IID). This interface might include any or all of the functions from the first interface, and it might include adjustments made to parameter lists for a given function as well as any new functions that need to be added. Older client applications that have not changed can use the old interface, while newer client applications can take advantage of the new interface (see Figure 9-5). In its human readable form, the next release of an interface is generally post-fixed with its version number. For example, if one was to come out with a second release of the bank account interface, it might have the name IBankAccount2.

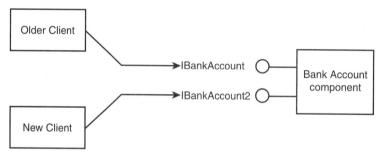

Figure 9-5. *Two clients using different versions of a component.*

The Implementation

The interface defines the terms of the contract or "what" should happen between two software modules. As you might know, this contract is meaningless unless someone actually fulfills or implements the terms of the contract. That is where the COM component comes into play. The COM component provides an implementation to determine "how" a contract will be fulfilled.

A COM component is in many ways very similar to the notion of an object in the object-oriented community. A COM component (for convenience, the word *component* is used to refer to the definition of component class as well as the instantiation of the component), like an object, can define a set of data that is private to that particular component and encapsulates the state of the component. The methods of a component are defined by the methods of the interfaces that it implements. In that sense, you can think of a COM component as a specific implementation for a set of interfaces. It implements the logic and stores the data necessary to provide the functionality promised by the interfaces.

DIAGRAMMING COMPONENTS

In object-oriented analysis and design, developers often attempt to model a system by using standard diagrams to show the relationships and interactions that occur between objects in the system. The COM specification defines a standard way to extend these diagrams to add COM components. As you can see in Figure 9-6, when diagrammed, a COM component generally appears as a rectangle, and the interfaces that it implements appear as "lollipops" or "plug-in jacks." Generally, the IUnknown interface is separated from the rest of the interfaces and appears on the top of the rectangle as it is the only required interface. Other supported interfaces are usually extended out of the left side of the component. Finally, the relationship between a client application and an interface on a component is generally represented by an arrow that indicates that the client application uses this interface.

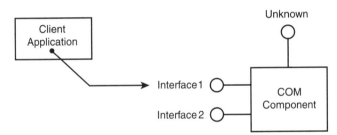

Figure 9-6. *Basic notation for a COM component and the interfaces it implements.*

Uniquely identified

Like its interface, a COM component also needs to be uniquely distinguished in time and space. A client application might need to differentiate between different implementations for a set of interfaces. Each COM component is also assigned a globally unique identifier (GUID), which in this case is sometimes referred to as a Class Identifier or CLSID.

Relationship to interfaces

A COM component has a one-to-many relationship with interfaces. It has to implement at least one interface but can implement many interfaces. Also, by definition, a COM interface is an atomic unit. Therefore, to implement a particular interface, a COM component has to provide code for every function declared in that interface (albeit the function does not have to do anything).

> **NOTE**   For the C++ programmer, think of an interface as an abstract base class in C++ that contains nothing but pure virtual functions. For a C++ class to inherit from that abstract class, it must implement every function in that class.

The only interface that every COM component has to implement is the IUnknown interface. This is also the base interface on which every other interface must be derived. It contains three methods: AddRef, Release, and QueryInterface. These three methods exist to support two primitive functional requirements of COM. The AddRef and Release methods are around for managing a component's lifetime, which we will talk about in our discussion of the COM Architecture. The QueryInterface method is the mechanism that allows a client application to navigate to other interfaces that a component supports.

Relationship to client applications

A client application never has direct access to a COM component. A client application can talk to a COM component only through the interfaces it supports. To be more specific, a client application only gets a pointer to an interface, and then through that pointer, it can call the functions on that interface. However, as mentioned earlier, a COM component can implement multiple interfaces in which the client application might be interested in using. Unlike traditional object-oriented languages where all inherited classes and methods are grouped together under the child object, each COM interface remains separate in a component and must be accessed independently of one another. This separation helps maintain the de-coupling between a client application and the components that it uses. But the question still remains regarding how a client application can get to other interfaces on the same component. Remember that every interface must be derived from the IUnknown interface, which means every interface contains a QueryInterface method. If a client application has an interface pointer to one of the interfaces that the component supports, the client can then call through the QueryInterface method using an IID to receive additional interfaces. Therefore, at any given point in time, a client application might have multiple interfaces to a single component (see Figure 9-7).

> **NOTE**   For the Visual Basic Programmer, the IUnknown interface to a COM component is not directly accessible. It is, however, called indirectly every time you assign a COM component to a new variable of a different type.

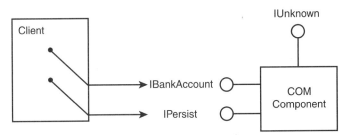

Figure 9-7. *A Client application accessing a component through two different interfaces.*

DESIGNING INTERFACES AND COMPONENTS

Interfaces are everything! This is an important statement to reiterate, because the design of your interfaces for your given project could mean the difference between success and failure. A set of well-designed interfaces can create a successful set of flexible and reusable components that can be used on many projects to come. Poorly designed interfaces might create a set of highly coupled components that are destined to the same maintenance nightmares we have seen with past programming models. Although one could fill an entire book on designing good COM interfaces and components, here are a few quick tips for creating reusable interfaces:

■ **Whenever possible, use a standard set of interfaces.–** Before creating your own custom interface to solve a problem, look at the standard interfaces, including those published by Microsoft to support ActiveX and OLE (for example, IStream defined for reading and writing data from a stream).

■ **An interface should be a small set of functionally related methods.** If you have to create custom interface, it should have one purpose, and all the methods on that interface should help you accomplish that purpose. A well-designed interface is generally thought of as having less than 10 methods. One of the biggest problems developers have when creating their own interfaces is that they tend to create

(continued)

(continued)

> one interface per component. This leads to an interface that does a little of everything and probably will never fit the need of another project. A COM component can support multiple interfaces for a purpose. If your component needs to do multiple tasks, it should support multiple interfaces.

COM VS. OBJECT-ORIENTATION

One of the most common scenarios for a group of developers standing around the water cooler is to argue about the virtues of their favorite technologies. With the advent of COM, one of the most common debates is to determine whether or not COM can truly be classified as an object-oriented technology. This is not a question that one can try to answer without spurring an onslaught of religious battles. So in an effort to avoid spoiling hours of fun around the water cooler, we can simply sidestep the issue and call COM a component-based technology that just happens to have many object-oriented features.

You have already discovered that a COM component is in many ways very similar to an object in the object-oriented world in the fact that it can contain a set of data as well as the methods (as defined by the interface) to act on the data. But COM also supports the three main features of object-oriented technology: encapsulation, polymorphism, and inheritance. These terms are described later. Many of the definitions come from *Understanding ActiveX and OLE*, a book by David Chappell.

Encapsulation

Encapsulation means that an object's internal data (its state) is not directly accessible to the user of the object. This is sometimes referred to as *data hiding*. A user of the object can only access or manipulate the object's state from the object's methods (or operations). Encapsulation allows a developer to build an object that can perform a given set of functionality without exposing the mechanics of how it performs the functionality to the rest of the program. For example, the credit card component in our department store analogy provides the ability to credit and debit an individual's account. The credit card component might communicate with the bank by using telephony and its data structures; it might use secured sockets; or it might even use Distributed COM. The point is that it does not matter how this communication is implemented to the rest of the point of sale application; the application only cares about the functionality provided by the credit card component's interface or methods. Therefore, a developer can change how the communication works and its underlying data structures without affecting the rest of the application.

As you might have already derived for yourself, COM, through its basic definition of separating the interface from the component (that is, the implementation), supports the notion of data encapsulation. A client program can access a component only though the component's interfaces. Therefore, the client has no way of getting at the internal data contained within the given component.

Polymorphism

Polymorphism simply means that a program can deal with different objects as if they were the same while allowing the objects to behave differently. Again, let's go back to the department store analogy. The store currently allows customers to buy merchandise using cash or a credit card. However, many customers would like to go to the store and buy merchandise using their checking account without the hassle of writing and getting approval for their personal check. (Likewise, many customers would like to go to an ATM and get cash using their line of credit.) Through the use of polymorphism, this is possible. Many banks now issue debit cards that have the charge card logo on them. These cards are not credit cards, but the logo indicates that they adhere to the charge card interface for crediting and debiting an account. This allows a debit card to be used seamlessly by a store as if it were a credit card, while still behaving like a debit card. Stores can handle both kinds of transactions the same way, while remaining unaware of the differences that don't concern them. The two types of cards behave according to their intended purpose. The charge card will debit the line of credit; which basically means increasing the amount of money that has been loaned to the user, while the debit card will decrease the amount of money in the user's checking account.

Every COM interface is polymorphic. This again can be attributed to the separation of interface and component. A client application always writes code to interact with the COM interface and the contract it provides. The exact behavior of the interface, however, depends on the specific COM component that is used with the client (see Figure 9-8).

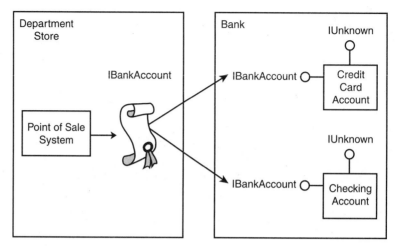

Figure 9-8. *Department store's point of sale system using both credit cards and debit cards as if they were the same.*

Inheritance

Inheritance is the ability for an object to include some or all of the existing features of another object. There are really two types of inheritance: *interface inheritance* and *implementation inheritance*. COM supports only interface inheritance. This partial support for inheritance is often the spark that ignites the COM and object-orientation debates.

Interface inheritance

Interface inheritance means that an object can only take on the definition of features from another object but remains responsible for implementing the code behind the features. Again, the debit card was able to fool the store's system by inheriting or taking on the features of the credit card interface, while how it actually implemented those features varied greatly from that of the charge card.

COM supports the notion of interface inheritance. In fact, it is a requirement in COM. For COM to work correctly, every interface must be either directly derived from the IUnknown interface or an interface that is a descendant of IUnknown.

Implementation inheritance

Implementation inheritance, on the other hand, has basically meant that an object not only takes on the definitions of the features from another object but also the code or implementation behind those features.

COM does not allow for implementation inheritance. Implementation inheritance follows what is known as *white-box* reuse, or put simply, the fact that both components' implementations are tightly coupled and dependent on one another. The designers of COM felt that implementation inheritance could cause serious dependency problems in an architecture that promotes loosely coupled, evolving, decentralized objects. However, the ability to reuse code that is already contained within a component was still a very important issue that needed to be addressed. So the designers of COM provided two alternatives for reusing a component: *containment* and *aggregation*. Both of these mechanisms follow *black-box* reuse, or the fact that both components know nothing about the implementation details of each other but simply depend on a well-defined interface. The following paragraphs provide a quick overview of containment and aggregation. However, you should refer to the COM specification or one of the COM books suggested at the end of this chapter for a more detailed discussion of these topics.

Containment is a concept that is simply centered around the fact that a COM component can itself be a client and instantiate other COM components from within its implementation and make calls into them. As shown in Figure 9-9, when a client application makes a call into a component's (outer component) methods, the component might make calls into another component (inner component) in the process of fulfilling the client's request. The client will not even be aware that its component is using another component to complete its tasks. This form of reuse simply takes advantage of the mechanisms that were already in place within the COM architecture. The outer component is simply a "client" of the inner component and, therefore, is isolated from the exact implementation of the inner component just like any client-component relationship in COM.

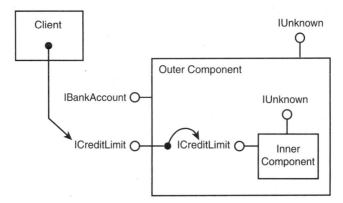

Figure 9-9. *COM containment.*

Aggregation is very similar to containment, except for the fact that a component exposes another component's interface directly to the client as if it were its own. As can be seen in Figure 9-10, the client application believes that it has an interface from the outer component, while the actual implementation is provided by the inner component. If the outer component does not need to make any pre- or post-processing of the method calls on the exposed inner component's interface, aggregation saves the additional overhead of having the outer component forward all calls to the inner component.

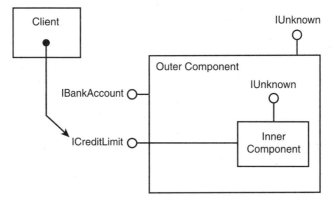

Figure 9-10. *COM aggregation.*

Object-Oriented Shortcomings

In our earlier discussion, we talked about the fact that there were a number of technologies that started the software industry on the road to components. The object-oriented programming paradigm has been the most prominent and comes the closest toward realizing the promised benefits. This paradigm meets the minimum requirements of being a component (self-contained, perform specific function, well-defined interface) but falls short of creating universally accepted components.

Language dependence

Traditional object-oriented programming is language specific. Although most object-oriented languages follow the same basic concepts, each language uses its own constructs to define an object, its data, and the operations that act on that data. Therefore, one cannot create an object in Java that can be used directly by Smalltalk or C++. This presents a very large problem for the software industry because there is no way in this world you will be able to get all developers to agree on one language to develop with.

No binary standard

Even if you look past the language-specific problem, you run into an even larger problem: There is no standard binary format for object-oriented components. Let's say that you decide C++ should be the standard language for developing components. The problem lies in the fact that each compiler company is free to generate certain language features in their own proprietary ways. Don Box's book *Essential COM* goes into great detail and gives some good examples, such as name mangling and exception handling. It is highly likely that a component compiled using Company A's compiler will not work correctly with a client program compiled using Company B's compiler and vice versa. This means that there is really no way for a company to sell its components to the rest of the industry in a binary format.

Location dependency and lack of versioning

Object-oriented languages by themselves provide no means for executing their objects in different locations or dealing with different versions of an object. Traditionally, all objects are compiled into one large executable and run in the same process space. For a developer to run an object on a separate machine transparently or handle different versions of an object concurrently, a developer would have to come up with some proprietary scheme to accomplish this. Each object developer might then provide a different mechanism and incur the extra cost of implementing their proprietary solution.

COM ARCHITECTURE

Now that you know the basic constructs for COM and how COM compares to object-oriented technologies, let's move away from the theoretical and see how COM puts these pieces together to form a flexible and robust runtime architecture. Our discussion of the COM runtime architecture will center mostly around the ability to create and use COM components directly from within a client application. In the book *Understanding ActiveX and OLE*, David Chappell presents a diagram that pretty much sums up the COM runtime architecture into one picture. As you can see in Figure 9-11, this overall process can be broken down into a sequence of eight general interactions:

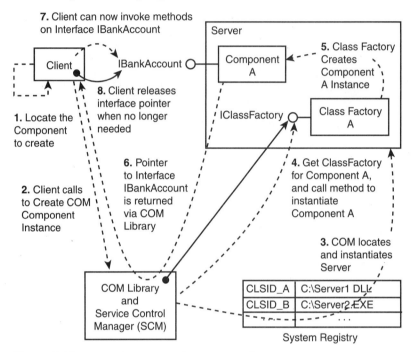

Figure 9-11. *General overview of creating and using a COM component.*

1. Client needs to locate the exact component to use for the type of functionality needed.

2. Client will ask the COM architecture to create an instance of the component as well as the interface to retrieve.

3. The COM architecture locates the server, and instantiates it if it is not already loaded and running.

4. The COM architecture retrieves the class factory for the component, and then calls into it to create an instance of the component.

5. The class factory in turn creates an instance of the component.

6. The interface for the component is then returned back through the COM architecture to the client application.

7. The client application can now invoke methods on that interface or call QueryInterface to retrieve additional interfaces for the component.

8. When the client no longer needs the interface, it releases it, and the component is destroyed (assuming that no other clients are using it).

These interactions, and the overall picture they present, are meant to set the context for the rest of the discussion to follow. The following sections will go into greater detail about some of the more important aspects of the COM runtime architecture and explain some of the preceding steps.

Binary Standard / Language Independence

The first thing to note about building and using COM components is that COM itself is not a computer language but rather defines a binary specification for components. Therefore, COM components can be built or used by any language that supports its binary format. This feature of COM overcomes one of the shortcomings that was pointed out related to the object-oriented programming model. A developer can build a COM component in Java that can interoperate directly with an application written in C++. By being language independent, COM allows a developer to choose his or her favorite language to build and use components. It also allows a company to leverage in-house programming skills while taking advantage of the many features components have to offer. It is important to note, however, that some languages are easier than others to implement and use COM components. For more details about these language differences, you should read Chapter 12.

For a language to support COM's binary standard, it has to support the binary format specified for COM interfaces. As the mediator between client applications and COM components, the interface has to remain consistent no matter what language is being used for the client or component, respectively. Figure 9-12 shows an example of the binary format implemented for an interface associated with a component. As you can see in the diagram, the department store application holds an interface pointer to the IBankAccount interface, while in reality, it actually holds a pointer to a table of function pointers. This table is called a vtable or virtual function table. Likewise, the bank application holds the interface pointer to the ICreditLimit interface which, in turn, follows the same format. When a method is actually called on the interface, the pointers are traversed, and the corresponding method is called from the vtable. If you are a C++ programmer, this structure might look very familiar because the COM interface was modeled directly from the class layouts created by the C++ compiler. It is one of the reasons C++ maps so nicely to COM.

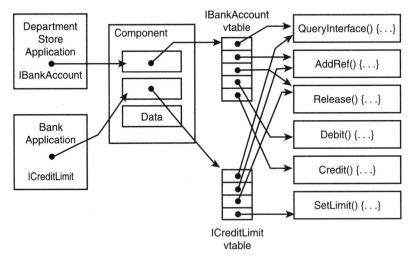

Figure 9-12. *What an interface looks like in a component.*

Following is a partial list indicating some of the languages that can be used to implement or automate COM-based components:

- **Languages for building components:** C, C++, Visual Basic, Java, PowerBuilder, and Delphi

- **Languages for automating components:** C, C++, Visual Basic, Visual FoxPro, Java, PowerBuilder, Delphi, VBScript, and JScript

COM, AUTOMATION, AND VISUAL BASIC

For the Visual Basic programmer reading this chapter, you might be pondering the fact that you have used automation from within Visual Basic and that you did not have to know anything about interfaces and components. You are right. The Visual Basic environment hides many of the details about COM from the application programmer. However, every new release of the Visual Basic language seems to be exposing more and more of the details and power associated with COM programming.

Late binding

In the early days of Visual Basic and automation, the only way to use a COM component was to declare a variable as type "Object" and then call the CreateObject (or FindObject) function to instantiate a new instance of the COM component. You could then make method calls on the object but could not find out if the object supported the given method until runtime. This form of programming became known as Automation programming. Under the covers, COM and all of its concepts still existed, but the Visual Basic environment was not capable of dynamically walking the vtables associated with COM interfaces. So, in an effort to make COM work with Visual Basic, Microsoft created an interface known as IDispatch.

The IDispatch interface is just a normal interface that exposes a set of methods; these methods allow a client application to execute the functionality of a component by passing in a string naming the function as well as a collection of parameters. This interface created a mechanism to dynamically execute functionality without having to walk the vtable of an interface. Visual Basic basically hard-coded the vtable for the IDispatch interface and, therefore, was the only interface through which a Visual Basic application could talk to a COM component.

Behind the scenes, every time a COM component was created and used by Visual Basic, the following events took place: Visual Basic called the CoCreateInstance API (for CreateObject) to instantiate the component and return an IDispatch pointer for the component; for each method call associated with the component, Visual Basic would call the GetIDsOfNames function of IDispatch to retrieve a dispatch identifier or DISPID based on the string name for the functionality, pack all of the parameters into a data structure, call the Invoke method of IDispatch by passing in the DISPID and the data structure, and, finally, unpack any data returned from the function. This is referred to as late binding.

(continued)

(continued)

This solved the problem of getting COM components to talk with Visual Basic applications, but a couple of problems remained:

- A component had to expose all of its functionality through one interface in order to be used by Visual Basic.

- A component developer now had to specially code for Visual Basic, while other languages supported COM natively.

- Every method call initiated from Visual Basic required two roundtrips: one call to get the dispatch identifier for a function and another call to actually make the function call.

- For the component developer, the IDispatch interface was a cumbersome interface to implement. The IDispatch interface required a model where parameters needed to be packed by the sender and then unpacked by the component. This was significantly more difficult than a simple function call.

ID binding

Microsoft soon realized that although that version of automation programming worked, it had significant performance penalties compared to calling a COM interface's function directly. To improve on the performance problems, the Visual Basic environment added support for Type Libraries (which are discussed in the COM architecture section). This allowed the Visual Basic environment to look up the DISPIDs for a method prior to execution, and thus simply call the Invoke method with the appropriate DISPID at runtime. This solution became known as *ID binding*. This new way of using components solved the roundtrip problem associated with late binding but still did not address the other issues related to IDispatch programming.

Vtable binding

With the release of Visual Basic 5.0, the Visual Basic environment was able to get another step closer to calling COM natively. Along with the support for Type Libraries, the Visual Basic environment now allowed a developer to create a variable of the component type and then call "new" to instantiate a new instance of the component. This variable actually holds an interface pointer to the default interface for the component. Now, every method call from that variable actually walks the vtable and truly is a simple function call. It is also important to note that a Visual Basic application can use other interfaces on the component by simply declaring a variable of the interface type and then assigning the component to that variable (under the covers, Visual Basic will perform a QueryInterface for the desired interface).

Packaging Components

In spite of the fact that COM components can be written in any number of languages, they all need to conform to a standard physical format in order to be distributed and used by other programs. COM components are physically packaged into *servers*. A server can be created as either a Win32 dynamic linked library (.dll) or as an executable (.exe). A server has a one-to-many relationship with COM components and can contain one or several different types of COM components.

The server will look like an ordinary executable or dynamic linked library, and can be compiled to statically or dynamically link with other supporting DLLs. It can make system calls or even communicate with some other device via sockets or named pipes. The fact is that a server has the full set of capabilities that any standard Windows executable or DLL has. The only difference is that a COM server has to support some extra functionality in order to work properly with the COM architecture. A COM server has to support these standard tasks:

- It needs to provide the ability to register and un-register the components it contains with the system.

- It needs to provide the capability to create new instances of the components it contains.

- It needs to indicate to the system when it is no longer needed (that is, none of its components are currently being used). However, this functionality is only needed by the DLL version of a COM server so that the system can unload the DLL from a given process's address space when it is no longer being used. An executable server can simply stop running when it is no longer needed.

How this functionality is accomplished varies depending on whether or not the server is an executable or a DLL. The DLL version of the server exposes this functionality by exporting and implementing a set of predefined function calls, such as DLLRegisterServer, DLLUnregisterServer, DLLGetClassObject, and

DLLCanUnloadNow. The executable version of the server uses some command line arguments as well as some COM facilities to accomplish these tasks.

Class factory

A *class factory* is a special instance of a COM component that is required by the COM architecture (otherwise, it is just another COM component). The COM architecture relies on the fact that there is one class factory for each type of component in a server. A class factory's only job in life is to create instances of the type of component it represents. When you ask the operating system to create an instance of the component, it will ask your server for the corresponding class factory. It will then invoke a method on the class factory to create an instance of the desired component.

At first glance, the class factory might seem unnecessary. You might be asking yourself, "Why doesn't the COM architecture just create the component instance directly?" Well, this is one of those cases where the COM architects designed for performance. If you look back at Figure 9-11, you will see that to create a single instance of the component, the COM architecture has to go through the COM library, which in turn goes through the Windows system registry, which will load the server and then go through the class factory to create the component. Although these steps run fairly quickly, they could become a performance bottleneck if your application wanted to create a large number of the same type of component (that is, go through each one of those steps for each instantiation of the component). The COM architecture allows you to bypass this unnecessary redundancy and inefficiency by allowing the client application to directly request the interface to a component's class factory from the COM library using the CoGetClassObject; then the client application can invoke the creation method on the class factory as many times as it likes (at the minimal cost of a single function call). Note that all of the steps required for COM library to locate the right server and load it still need to occur, but they only happen on the initial request for the class factory.

Type library

A server can also optionally contain what is known as a *type library*. A type library is a standardized binary mechanism for retrieving meta-data about COM components and interfaces. A type library can include things such as the definitions of all the components contained in the server, definitions of the interfaces that a component supports, descriptions of the properties and methods for each interface, as well as links to help files. A type library is generally used by a development tool to aid in the process of using components. Although it's usually included as part of the server package, a type library can also exist outside a server as a separate binary file (.olb or .tlb).

Finding a Component

One of the features of COM is that it supports a plug-and-play architecture. This allows a client program to dynamically load a component at runtime instead of having to statically link with it at compile time. This adds a very powerful dimension to COM. This section will present some of the various ways a client application can go about finding the right component to use for the task at hand.

> **NOTE** Although not a specific requirement of COM, the Windows system registry is used as the data store for the various meta-data used to locate and use COM components on the Windows platform. Other future implementations of COM on different platforms might use some other data store. Currently, COM uses the HKEY_CLASSES_ROOT section of the registry to store some of the following information that is needed by the COM library and other facilities:

- ProgIds for a component
- A components class identifier (CLSID)
- The name, location, and type of server for a component
- The location of a component's type library
- Interface identifiers (IID)
- Component categories

GUIDs

The first way for a client application to locate a component is to simply ask for it directly (that is, by its CLSID). Remember, both interfaces and components are given identifiers (IID and CLSID, respectively) to be able to uniquely identify them. Both of these identifiers are defined as Globally Unique Identifiers, also known as GUIDs (pronounced as either *goo-ids* or *gwids*). A GUID is a 128-bit integer that is virtually guaranteed to be unique in the world across space and time, because the generation of a GUID is based on an algorithm that takes into account various factors, such as the current timestamp, the address of your network card if you have one, and some other factors (for more information, refer to the COM specification). The GUID is based on Universally Unique IDs (UUIDs) which are defined in the Distributed Computing Environment's Remote Procedure Call (DCE RPC) specification. When displayed in textual form, a GUID is generally represented as a set of hexadecimal numbers:

```
BCEAC531-2C9A-11d2-A5EC-C22E9C000000
```

ProgIDs

To account for the fact that some scripting languages such as VBScript cannot deal with CLSIDs directly, the COM architecture supports programmatic identifiers. The programmatic identifier, or ProgId, is a human readable string that can be used to look up a specific component. A ProgId takes on the format:

```
Vendor.Component.Version
```

However, one should note that the vendor portion of this format is usually filled in with a product name instead of the vendor name. For example, to locate the document object in Microsoft Word, you would form a ProgID that looks like this:

```
Word.Document.6
```

The one caveat to using a ProgId instead of the CLSID is that a ProgID is not guaranteed to be unique and might potentially cause name collisions.

Component categories

Sometimes you might want to give the user of an application a chance to specify which component to use. For example, you might let the user choose which spell checker to use for their application. One of the problems with this scenario is that the chosen component might be expected to support a number of interfaces. It would not be very efficient for your application to instantiate every COM component in your system to find the ones that support all the required interfaces. Therefore, COM provides a concept known as *component categories*. A component category provides a generic mechanism that allows developers to group together collections of components with the same type of functionality. An application can then query the facility for a list of components that are contained within a given category.

Monikers

A user might also want to reconnect to the same exact instance of a component that they had been using earlier. This is where the *moniker* comes in. A moniker is simply a COM component that implements the IMoniker interface and is used as a way to identify a particular instance of a component. The moniker component wraps the necessary data needed to instantiate a particular component and return it to the state it was in when the moniker was created. Monikers can come in all shapes and sizes; there are file monikers that point to a particular file in the file system; there are item monikers that point to data within a document; there are URL monikers that wrap a Web address; there are even composite monikers that are made up of other monikers. For example, a client application might want to use the moniker in Figure 9-13 to load the given Microsoft Excel spreadsheet and get an interface pointer to an instance of its range component.

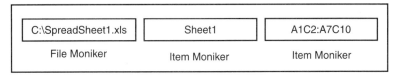

Composite Moniker

Figure 9-13. *Composite moniker.*

The COM Library

Another very powerful feature in COM is that it abstracts a component's identity (that is, CLSID) from its physical packaging (executable file type and location). This allows an application's logical design to be de-coupled from the actual physical deployment layout. After initially deploying the application, a developer might decide to repackage the components of an application differently for performance reasons or might decide that a given component should be run on a separate machine for load-balancing. In any case, these deployment issues should not affect the client application or its code. However, to pull this off, the COM architecture needs to take control of the instantiation process of a component. The COM library was created to handle this task as well as some other services, such as some memory management functions and functions for exposing a server's components.

Component creation and location transparency

The COM library provides a set of APIs, such as CoCreateInstance, CoCreateInstanceEx, CoGetClassObject, and so on, that allow a client application to create a component by simply specifying its class identifier or CLSID. The COM library internally uses the Service Control Manager (SCM) to associate a CLSID with the server that implements the component, as well as the location of the server executable file. The COM library will then use the SCM to create the component for the client application.

A client application can use a component the same way regardless of whether the component is being run in the same process as the client application or is being run on a separate machine located somewhere else on a network. To the client application, both types of components can be used by simply invoking the methods on a component's interface (that is, a function call). This location transparency truly simplifies the design of a client application and moves much of the burden of this transparency to the COM architecture. The COM architecture allows a COM component to be instantiated in three different ways (see Figure 9-14).

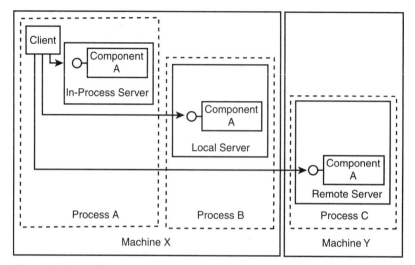

Figure 9-14. *Different ways of running a COM server.*

- **In-Process.** A component can be created in an in-process server, which means that the component will run in the same address space as the client process. The main advantage to using in-process components is performance. When a component is run in-process, you will not incur the overhead of the context switching that happens every time you switch back and forth between processes. It is also important to note that only DLL versions of servers can run in-process.

- **Local.—**A component can be created in a local server, which means that the component will run in its own address space (or as its own process). This can be significantly slower than the in-process component because for every method called, the system must perform a context-switch as well as copy any data passed via the parameters. Note that both DLL and EXE types of servers can be run as local servers. (The DLL version of a server can run in a surrogate process. The default process provided by the system is dllhost.exe.)

- **Remote.** Finally, a component can be created in a remote server, which means that the component will run as a separate process on a separate machine that is connected via a network. The ability to run a component remotely only became available with the advent of DCOM (Distributed COM). As you might imagine, a remote server has the worst performance of them all but offers an architecture that promotes scalability.

For in-process servers, the COM architecture simply loads the server into the process space of the client application. Because they share the same memory address space, invoking a method is truly a simple function call. However, when a component is loaded as a local or remote server, the COM architecture has to do some extra work to make the client feel like it is making a simple function call (see Figure 9-15). The COM architecture has to create two entities behind the scenes to allow this transparency to occur. It creates a proxy component in the address space of the client that looks like the real component from the outside, but inside does nothing more than forward method requests via a remote procedure call. It also creates a stub component in the process space of the real component to receive the remote procedure calls and pass them on to the real component. This extra work by the COM architecture lets both the client application developer as well as the component developer avoid dealing with any of the remoting issues related to out-of-process components.

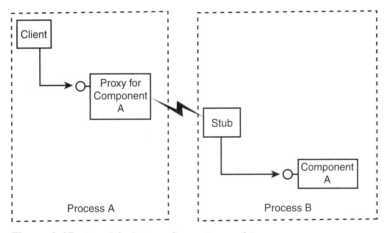

Figure 9-15. *Simplified view of remoting architecture.*

Using a Component

Finally, once a client application creates a component and gets handed back the interface pointer to it, the client can now start using the functionality provided by the component. This generally includes invoking the function calls of an interface. However, there are a few more issues related to using components.

Managing a component's lifetime

An instance of a component is only around as long as it needs to be. In the COM architecture, a component instance is obligated to delete itself from memory when it is no longer needed. COM uses a mechanism that is known as *reference counting*. Reference counting simply refers to the fact that a component is responsible for keeping track of the number of clients currently using it. When this number reaches zero, the component will delete itself. How can this be done? Remember that a client can only access a component through its interfaces and that every interface must be derived from the IUnknown interface. Also, remember that the IUnknown interface has two methods, AddRef and Release, that were created for memory management. Well, the AddRef method is used to increment the reference count, and the Release method is used to decrement the reference count. These two methods, along with the COM specification, detail the rules that a client and component must follow when passing around the interface pointers, managing a component's lifetime.

Threading models

No matter how many benefits a new technology has to offer, sooner or later performance becomes an issue. As we have already mentioned, the COM architecture allows a client program to run a component in-process, which is effectively the same as a local function call. This can solve the performance problem for the traditional application where one task happens at a time. But today, as more and more applications are being created to take advantage of the Win32 architecture, there is a demand for applications that can perform multiple tasks simultaneously. This is known as *multithreading*, where a process can have multiple threads of execution. Multithreaded programming adds a level of complexity to the traditional single-threaded programming model. Programmers who want to take advantage of multiple threads of executions have to add extra code to make sure that the various threads do not attempt to do things such as access a variable concurrently.

In an effort to keep a component as simple as possible while keeping performance in mind, the COM architecture provides two threading models for programming COM components:

- **STA (Single-Threaded Apartment).** A single-threaded apartment is a logical grouping of components that allows only one thread to be executed at a time. Any component created in an STA does not have to worry about synchronization issues, because all requests are serialized in a message queue and then executed by the thread that created the component on behalf of the other threads. COM allows there to be any number of STA groupings within a given process.

- **MTA (Multithreaded Apartment).** A multithreaded apartment is a logical grouping of components that allows multiple threads to execute at one time on a single component. Components created in an MTA need to worry about synchronization but can benefit from the performance improvements. COM allows there to be only one MTA grouping for a given process.

Security

How do you allow certain users access to a component while denying access to other users? Security is a topic that is becoming more and more important as systems are becoming more distributed and being exposed to larger numbers of users. COM bases most of its security model on the RPC security model on which it sits. At a high level, COM provides three categories for securing your COM component: authentication security, activation security, and token management. Many of these security attributes can be configured through registry settings without modifying the actual code. You can also specifically add code to your component to deal with security.

- **Authentication.** Mechanisms that deal with verifying that the message sent over the network is authentic and that the user who sent the message was indeed who he or she claims to be

- **Activation Security.**–Mechanisms that determine who is permitted to launch or connect to your components

- **Token Management.**–Mechanisms that dictate what user security credentials are used when launching or using the component

SUMMARY

This chapter has provided an architectural overview of COM. Although it has not given you enough information to go off and start coding, it has hopefully given you a better understanding of COM from both a conceptual point of view as well as its runtime architecture. COM promises to become one of the universally accepted ways to build components. It meets the three minimum requirements (self-contained, perform specific function, well-defined interface) as well as the four additional requirements defined earlier: binary standard, language independent, location transparency, and versioning support.

For More Information

If you are interested in more detailed information about COM or component-based development, you might want to refer to *http://www.microsoft.com/com/default.asp* and also explore some of the following books:

- *Understanding ActiveX and OLE* by David Chappell (Microsoft Press, 1997)

- *Essential COM* by Don Box (Addison-Wesley, 1998)

- *Inside COM* by Dale Rogerson (Microsoft Press, 1997)

- *Component Software: Beyond Object-Oriented Programming* by Clemens Szyperski (Addison-Wesley, 1998)

Chapter 10

Building Custom Commerce Components

by Biff Gaut

This chapter will provide some very useful tips for designing COM objects providing Web services. But, in order to successfully augment your Active Server Pages with COM, it is important to follow seven very basic rules. If you do, then you will avoid the most common mistakes encountered when programming on a grander scale. First you will hear about two fictional Web sites that make some fundamental mistakes in their development and get a taste of the dangers that lie in wait for careless COM developers. After hearing their plight, you will find seven simple rules that would have helped them and definitely will help you.

Active Server Pages (ASP) is definitely the way to begin programming a Web application. It lets you create dynamic content on a Web server in a very straightforward way. Why, then, is it only the start? Why shouldn't all Web content be developed with ASP? If you've read Chapter 7, you know that ASP is easy to write and provides decent performance. Before you start doing the final design of your new site, however, let's look at two examples where you might need to start thinking about the next step.

REUSE, REUSE, REUSE

The Web site at *www.webofdeceit.com* is home to a brand new Internet startup company peddling mystery novels over the Web. (Don't bother looking. I'm making this up.) They've assembled a vast database of mystery trivia in a comprehensive database with access by an ASP application. Now your aunt can go to the Web and find out that Jimmy Soames was killed by a pathological unicycle rider in *A Spoke Too Soon*. This application then allows, even encourages, a user to jump directly to the storefront page to place an order for the book. Fortunately, it seems that *www.webofdeceit.com* strikes a nerve, and everyone who ever read a mystery decides to go out and try the database and buy a book. Overwhelmed by their good fortune, the owners decide to open up a storefront to start selling books over the counter as well as over the Web. A customer can come into the store and ask who was the serial killer of street performers in *A Mime Is a Terrible Thing to Waste*. The clerks figure that because the machine with the search application is connected to their workstations by a Local Area Network, they should be able to get a little better performance and a little more functionality than someone coming over the Web. Oops. All the logic is in ASP pages. ASP pages can operate only under the auspices of the Internet Information Server (IIS), so the clerks have to log on to the Web site like everybody else. A better design would locate the logic where the ASP pages can still use it, but other applications can use it as well without having to go through IIS. This is the first big argument for COM. Consider that this site will also rely heavily on Site Server Commerce services (see Chapter 6) with all of its COM object needs, and you should be just about convinced that writing COM objects is in your future. Just in case you're still skeptical, here's one more example.

DEVELOPING ON A GRAND SCALE

A home improvement company offers a Web site with the capability to enter the dimensions of your kitchen, along with options as to your decorating desires (cabinet style and location, appliances, and so on) to produce a three-dimensional rendering of what your new kitchen will look like. Unfortunately, these extremely complex calculations take a long time to run, especially written in interpreted ASP. Though the site designers are not worried about making the would-be redecorator wait several seconds to see the results, they are concerned that a couple of users browsing for a new kitchen could slow their server to the point where a potential customer can't log on to the site to get the phone number of the firm. Their need is to write the rendering code in a faster language and run it on a different machine. Both these goals can be met by COM as well. COM will allow functionality to be written and shared in any language and, through distributed COM, allow the processing load to be shared across many machines.

The point of these two examples (and many other situations that aren't listed here) is that ASP can take you only so far. If you are creating a large-scale Web site, you will soon find yourself at a point where you can't add any more processors to your Web server, and your calculations are taking too long to run in ASP. Make no mistake, ASP is instrumental to the development of any Web site, large or small. The best way to use ASP, however, is as a scripting language to control your COM components. Avoid the situation described in these examples by planning for them up front and putting your code in reusable COM objects. Other benefits you'll see from using COM objects to implement your business rules are:

- The object-oriented nature of COM will allow more compartmentalized development. This will enable more developers to work together and reduce the likelihood of dreaded spaghetti code.

- COM objects allow you to take advantage of the scaling and transaction features of Microsoft Transaction Server, described in Chapter 11.

COM SERVERS FOR THE WEB

Hopefully, by this time you're convinced that it's important to move functionality into COM components to make your Web site run. But what type of functionality is appropriate to implement with a COM component? Just about anything. If you have been programming in a Microsoft desktop environment, you have probably already used many COM components, maybe without even knowing it. A number of places where you might have used a COM object are:

- ActiveX Controls in Microsoft Visual Basic. ActiveX Controls are simply COM objects that expose a set of interfaces defined for ActiveX Controls[1].

- Programming Microsoft Office, either from outside using Visual Basic or from within using VBA. The object hierarchies exposed by the Office Applications are really a set of COM objects.

■   Writing a Visual Basic class. A Visual Basic class, in reality, is a COM object.

Making your own COM objects is a relatively simple and straightforward process. Microsoft has supplied wizards in all of their major languages to simplify COM programming. Chapter 12 demonstrates the basics of creating a COM object in Visual Basic, Microsoft Visual C++, and Microsoft Visual J++.

Although almost any piece of code can be implemented as a COM object and any COM object can be run on a server, the demands on a server-side component require special consideration. For instance, although Microsoft Excel exposes almost all of its functionality through a hierarchy of COM interfaces, several features discussed later in this chapter make it a poor choice for most server-side functions.

SEVEN RULES OF COM DEVELOPMENT

If you follow a few rules when you develop your COM components, your site will be faster, easier to support, and less likely to crash. Learning these rules in advance can save you hours of heartbreak and lost sleep in the last few weeks before delivery.

Rule #1: Server-Side COM Objects Have No User Interface

The first rule when designing a COM object to run on the server is that the object is not allowed to have *any* user interface. Think about this for a minute. These objects will be running on the server where they will be created and manipulated by IIS. IIS runs as an NT Service, so it, along with the objects it instantiates, has no access to the desktop. If an object attempts to display a dialog box asking for additional user input or displaying information, it will fail. If the UI requires input before processing can continue, the http request will freeze. Although the client side will eventually time out, the request will remain frozen on the server side. Because IIS has the capacity to service a limited number of http requests simultaneously, every time one request gets halted, the overall response of your site will worsen. Freeze enough sessions, and IIS will halt altogether. Sooner or later, this process will end with you or the System Administrator getting awakened in the middle of the night to go down to the office to restart IIS so your site can resume business.

Because we already determined that all user interface functionality should be handled by the browser using ASP-generated HTML and DHTML, this rule might seem to be redundant. But obeying this rule might not be as straightforward as you first think. Your object must have *no* user interface, not even something stuck in by the compiler itself. For instance, in VB any uncaught error will throw a dialog box up on the screen (see Figure 10-1). Even though you did not put a dialog box in your code, the IIS session is frozen. Similar things can happen in VC as well. When implementing your object, you have to be sure that you have planned for these contingencies. In Visual Basic, go to the Project Properties dialog box and check the Unattended Execution box (see Figure 10-2), and write error handling code in every routine to catch exceptions. In Visual C++, make sure that you catch all exceptions by setting up a try/catch block at the beginning and end of each interface method.

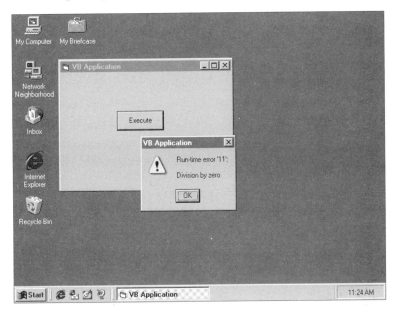

Figure 10-1. *Did you see this one coming? An error that is bothersome in Visual Basic is disastrous on a Web site.*

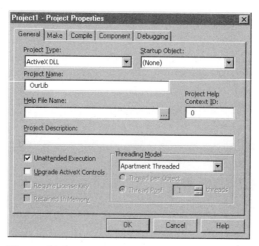

Figure 10-2. *The Unattended Execution feature will prevent unwanted user interface.*

The other place to watch out for unexpected UI is inside existing, or legacy, code. One common use of COM is to wrap legacy code in COM objects to provide its functionality to a whole new set of clients and thereby extend its life. Make sure you scour that old code well for any hint of a user interface before you put it on your server or some long-forgotten dialog box in a low-level function will slow your site to a crawl. So, although this seems like a straightforward rule, it's important not to overlook anything, or you'll inconvenience your customers and annoy your coworkers.

Rule #2: Report User Errors to the User and System Errors to the System

Two things can go wrong while a user is using your Web site. First, the user might enter bad information. If this happens, your COM objects should catch the error and, in conjunction with the ASP code, inform the user of the mistake in as helpful a manner as possible. These are normal errors, and programming for them on the Web is very similar to programming for them on the desktop.

The other type of error is a system error. This might include things like a database crash or a disk full error. Although these are errors, they must be handled quite differently from user error. How many times have you been using a Web site and instead of a.page you were expecting, you got a message like the one in Figure 10-3?

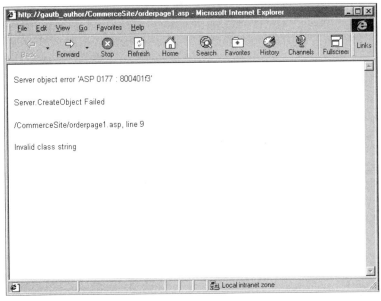

Figure 10-3. *Reporting a system error to the user.*

This is a situation where you, as a developer, must be intelligent in your error handling and, when the site has problems, inform the user in a clear and non-threatening way. If a site was down, wouldn't you rather see a message more like the one in Figure 10-4?

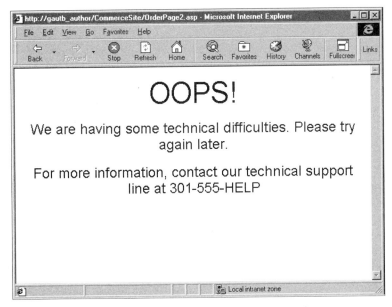

Figure 10-4. *Hiding system error information from the client.*

Unfortunately, if your code encounters a system error and you shield the user from the details, your job is only half done. You must record the error somewhere and notify someone that the error has occurred. Appropriate places to log errors include the NT Event Log (pictured in Figure 10-5), a SQL Server database, or a simple disk file. In Visual Basic, putting an entry in the event log is as easy as calling the *LogEvent* method on the *App* object. To notify the System Administrator, your options are limited only to how creative you are and how much time you have. One relatively simple option is to use MAPI (another COM interface!) to create an e-mail message to the System Administrator detailing the problem. This message can then be sent to multiple locations, including mail addresses acting as a front for a pager.

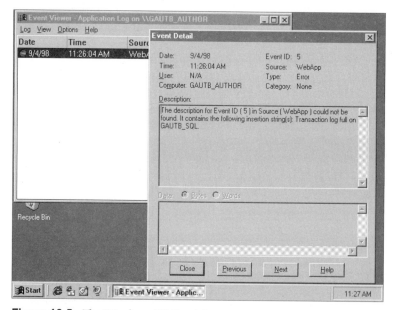

Figure 10-5. *The Windows NT Event Log.*

Rule #3: If At All Possible, Server Objects Must Be in Process

COM objects can be implemented in two ways: In Process and Local. In Process objects are implemented in a dynamic link library (DLL) and run in the same process space as the client program. In this way, they essentially become a part of the client program when loaded (see Figure 10-6). Local objects are implemented as executable programs that run in their own process space. When they are created, the object's executable program is loaded and runs alongside the client program (see Figure 10-7). Although this doesn't seem to be a significant difference, the difference in performance between the two implementations can be substantial.

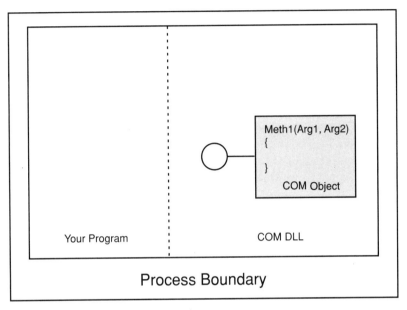

Figure 10-6. *An In Process COM object.*

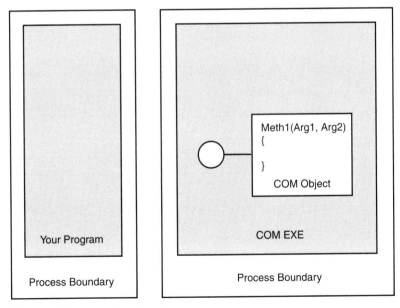

Figure 10-7. *A Local COM object.*

Figure 10-8 shows a client calling a method on an In Process object. When the method is called, the arguments are packaged up into an area of memory called the stack. The In Process object can access them directly. Compare this with Figure 10-9, which shows a client calling a method on a Local object. When the method is called, the arguments are again packaged up into the stack, but because the object is in a different process that has its own stack, it cannot access the stack that contains the arguments. COM steps in to help at this point. COM automatically takes the arguments, converts them to a buffer of raw binary information, and transfers them over to the process containing the COM object and reassembles them in the stack for the COM object to access. Once the method is complete, the return values are treated the same way to get back to the client. This system of automatically moving arguments and return values from one process to another is called *marshalling*, and although it happens automatically, it can be very expensive from a performance perspective.

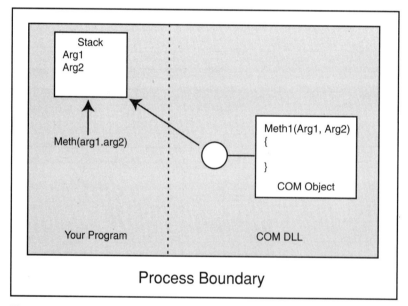

Figure 10-8. *Sharing arguments with an In Process server object.*

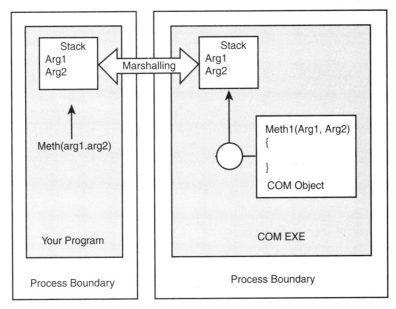

Figure 10-9. *Sharing arguments in a Local server object.*

Just how expensive is marshalling? I have run tests that do nothing but execute extensive COM calls and have found that the Local versions of objects have performed up to 5,000 times slower than the In Process test. These tests, however, didn't do anything other than make calls to empty methods. In a real-world application, the code implemented within a method would take much longer to execute than the duration of the marshalling, thereby lessening marshalling's influence on the overall performance of the object.

Rule #4: Server-Side Objects Must Be As Small As Possible

This rule applies to almost all programming situations, but it is brought up here to highlight some special aspects of server programming that make it all the more important. Let's say you have a very sophisticated financial model implemented in an Excel worksheet that you want to make available to your users over the Web. Because Excel is an automation server, it is possible, in fact, it is pretty simple for you to write ASP code that instantiates Excel, loads the worksheet, runs the spreadsheet model, and returns the result. Let's look at two situations that suggest that this is not such a good idea.

The first user of the day logs onto your site and runs the financial model. In response to that request, you are going to load Excel and load a spreadsheet. Do that once by hand on your computer and see how long it takes. Considering that a responsive Web site generates its pages in well under a second on the server side, imagine how responsive your site is going to seem to your user. One of the reasons these objects must be very small is so that load time is very short.

Later in the day, as more users arrive at the office, they all start logging on and requesting models. Even if you have set up your system so that one instance of Excel can service many requests, you're still creating a new workbook object for each user. If you have hundreds of users logged on at the same time, you're going to have a lot of memory on your server taken up by Excel. Remember that any object you use could conceivably get instantiated hundreds of times—another good reason to keep them small.

Don't let this section make you think that there is no place on a Web server for Excel—quite the contrary. Excel is a wonderful tool for Web applications; it just needs to be used correctly. We'll take a look at an application that uses Excel appropriately in Chapter 17.

Rule #5: Handle Errors According to COM Conventions

A key aspect of developing in any type of environment is error handling. Whether the error is system generated or based on invalid user input, a development team must decide how they are going to notify each other of errors and then stick to that standard (hopefully!) across the entire project. Developers working on a COM object or a hierarchy of COM objects is no different. There are many ways to get error information from a COM object back to your clients. For instance, you can set up a system of return values or use an attribute of each object that defines error status. One key point that slips by many new COM developers is that COM has already defined a standard method to notify clients of errors. It is in your best interest to learn and implement COM's standard for two reasons:

- In the general sense, because COM is set up as an industry standard for component software, clients that have no advance knowledge of your component will be able to read your errors without changing their code.

- From a more pragmatic point of view, Visual Basic, Visual C++, and Visual J++ automatically support the standard COM error system when writing both clients and components, making it very easy to implement the COM standard. ASP also looks for the COM error standard.

So, besides being the proverbial "right thing to do," using the COM error mechanism is easier than defining your own. Let's talk about how it works, first from a detailed point of view, and then from a more practical point of view.

COM errors

Although the Microsoft Visual Studio languages all have features that make using the COM error mechanism relatively simple, it is best that you have a reasonable understanding about what is going on under the hood as well. This will make things much clearer when you start developing your objects in multiple languages.

In COM, an error is associated with a concept called a "logical thread." A logical thread is a series of nested method calls, similar to a call stack in a single language. The difference between a logical thread and an operating system thread (to be discussed shortly) is that a logical thread may actually span more than one operating system thread.

When an error occurs in a COM method, an object following the COM standard will handle the error by creating an object that supports the IErrorInfo interface. An object that implements the IErrorInfo interface is referred to as an ErrorInfo object. This interface provides a large amount of information about the error, including:

■   The interface where the error occurred

■   The text name of the class where the error occurred

■   A textual description of the error

■   The filename of the Windows help file with the full documentation
    of the error

■   A help context into the Windows help file

The object might either implement its own ErrorInfo object, or it might use a default implementation exposed by the COM libraries. Needless to say, the default implementation is a lot more popular. Once this object has been created, a COM API call allows the method to associate with the logical thread. The method now returns an HRESULT[2] that indicates to the caller that an error has occurred. It is important to note that the ErrorInfo object will then remain associated with the logical thread until some method higher up the chain explicitly removes it with another COM API call.

Of course, putting an ErrorInfo object on the logical thread doesn't do any good unless the client knows it is there. An object must have some way to alert a client that it is playing by COM's rules. It's probably not a surprise that COM has this covered as well. An object that supports COM error handling should implement the ISupportErrorInfo interface. This interface provides a method (InterfaceSupportsErrorInfo) that will tell the client whether or not an ErrorInfo object can be expected from this interface for this object. This concept of telling the client that you are playing by the rules illuminates another reason that you should follow the rules yourself. Suppose you are making use of a third-party object inside one of your methods. This third-party object is a good citizen, so when it has an error, it creates an ErrorInfo object and informs you that the ErrorInfo object is out there. You, on the other hand, did not bother implementing COM error handling, so when you handle the third-party object's error by returning an error HRESULT to your caller, you also tell the caller that you do not support the ErrorInfo object paradigm. Your caller, on hearing this, doesn't bother looking for an ErrorInfo object, even though one exists for the logical thread! By not playing by the rules, you not only make your errors harder to deal with, you also hide any errors that occur within servers you use from your clients.

Visual Studio to the rescue

Although the preceding example makes the concept of ErrorInfo objects seem like a lot of work, thanks to some wizards and functions in Visual Studio, they are actually quite easy to deal with. Here is a quick summary of each language's support for ErrorInfo objects.

Visual C++

When you write an ATL object, the Error method of the CComCoClass will take a large variety of arguments and create the ErrorInfo object automatically. There is also a check box on the Create Object Wizard that will add an implementation of the ISupportErrorInfo interface to your object.

Using the Visual C++ #import directive to import a COM library will create a set of smart pointers for that library's COM objects. In addition to providing simple access to the object's properties and methods, these smart pointers provide a wrapper function around every method. These wrapper functions check the HRESULT returned from the wrapped COM method and, in the event of an error, retrieve the ErrorInfo object and convert it to a C++ exception.

Visual Basic

When writing an object in Visual Basic, you can create an ErrorInfo object by using the Visual Basic Err object. The Raise method of the Err object takes all the information required to create the ErrorInfo object as arguments. Inside the Raise method, the object is created and associated with the logical thread. Any Visual Basic objects you write automatically implement the ISupportErrorInfo with no special action required on your part.

If you're a Visual Basic developer, all this talk of COM methods returning only HRESULTs has probably left you confused. From a Visual Basic perspective, COM methods return numbers, strings, and so on without an HRESULT in sight. This is because when acting as a client, Visual Basic always provides a layer of abstraction around COM calls that prevents the developer from having to worry about HRESULTs. When Visual Basic intercepts a bad HRESULT, it gets the ErrorInfo object and converts it to the Visual Basic Err object and throws a Visual Basic error that can be caught with an On Error Goto statement.

Visual J++

Visual J++ uses the ComFailException class to translate between Java exceptions and ErrorInfo objects. When a COM server encounters an error, it will create and throw a ComFailException object that contains all the information required to create an ErrorInfo object. The ComFailException is found in the com.ms.com package.

When Visual J++ acts as a COM client, it still uses ComFailException to handle COM errors. In this case, the ErrorInfo object is retrieved, converted to a ComFailException object, and thrown.

Rule #6: An Object Might Not Have the Privileges You Expect

Suppose you have written an object that, as a part of its responsibilities, reads some configuration data from the registry. As a careful developer, you've also written a test program in Visual Basic that thoroughly exercises all the methods and attributes of the object. You've run stress tests on the object to test for memory leaks. You've finally declared the object to be complete and robust and have loaded it on your Web server. Unfortunately, the first time you used the object from your ASP code, the exact same code that you used in Visual Basic, the object failed miserably. You have just learned your first lesson in Windows NT security.

When you run a Visual Basic program, the program and any objects it instantiates have the same privileges as the currently logged on user. Being a developer, chances are pretty good that you have Administrator privileges on your local machine, and your programs are the baddest dudes in the land, strutting around your machine unmolested by the security issues that may hinder lesser programs. ASP runs under the auspices of an NT service, however, so it doesn't even require a user to be logged onto the computer to execute. Instead, it operates under the auspices of a special username, IUSR_*machinename*. This username, usually called the anonymous user account, is given only guest privileges to the resources of the computer. It is possible to increase the privileges of the anonymous user account, but because many IIS machines are outside the company firewall, it is probably not a good idea. Limited to the usual guest privileges, your objects may not have the privileges to do some of the things that you expect. Like all guests, however, your objects will have the right to hog the remote, eat all your food, and stick around too long.

The bug in the first paragraph is based on a true story. It seems the object was attempting to open the registry in read/write mode when read only mode would have been sufficient. This was fine when the object had the user's Administrator rights but impossible for a guest account. Changing the open mode of the registry to read only solved the problem, and everything turned out fine. There are a lot more details to NT Security, but just knowing this rule should steer you clear of your first few potential problems.

Rule #7: Learn the Relationship Between Object Scope and Threads of Execution

Did you know that there are certain instances where it is completely inappropriate to use a Visual Basic object on your server? If you do not follow Rule #7, you may fall into this trap. This is probably the most complicated rule in this chapter, but ignoring the relationship between object scope and threads can have a huge impact on your site's performance. To understand this relationship, you first need to understand what each of these terms means.

Object scope

An object's scope defines where it can be accessed in a Web application. This availability is determined by where the object is created and how it is stored. In a Web application, there are three possible scopes for an object:

- **Application Scope.** Objects stored in the ASP Application variable have application scope. Unless they are explicitly removed from the Application variable, they will exist as long as IIS is running the Web application where they are housed. Any http request by any user can access them, and every one of the requests will use the exact same instance of the object.

```
<%
' This ASP code creates and stores an
' application scope object
Set Application("AppObj") = _
    Server.CreateObject("WebApp.MyObject")
%>
```

- **Session Scope.** Objects stored in the Session variable have session scope. Like objects with Application scope, unless they are explicitly removed from the Session variable, they will exist until the session (one user's interactions with the site) is completed. All the http requests from a user share the same session scope objects, but different users cannot share objects stored at the session level.

```
<%
' This ASP code creates and stores a
' session scope object
Set Session("SessionObj") = _
    Server.CreateObject("WebApp.MyObject")
%>
```

■ **Request scope.** Objects created, utilized, and freed during the course of one http call have request scope. These objects exist strictly for the duration of the call and cannot be shared between requests, regardless of which user is making the requests.

```
<%
' This ASP code creates and stores a
' request scope object
Set Obj = Server.CreateObject("WebApp.MyObject")
%>
```

As you will soon learn, the scope of an object determines a great deal about how the object is accessed and, therefore, how it must be written.

Threads

Let's go back to Computer Science 101 for just a moment. A computer program is merely a list of instructions executed in order. The process of executing these steps is known as a "thread of execution." As long as only one step is being executed at a time, the program is single threaded. If the process of executing the steps in a program is going on in several parts simultaneously—that is, if something is executing Step 2 at the same time something else is executing Step 4—then the program is multi-threaded. This is a very hard concept to visualize the first time. Let's use a real-world example to make it clearer.

Think of your last trip to the department of motor vehicles to get your driver's license. When you arrive, there is a sign with a list of steps you must take to get your license renewed. These steps might include:

1. Go to station 1 and pick up a form to fill out.

2. Take the completed form to station 2 to pay your fee.

3. Take your receipt and form to station 3 to get your picture taken.

4. Go to station 4 to await your completed license.

This set of steps is illustrated in Figure 10-10. The dotted line indicates your path around the stations.

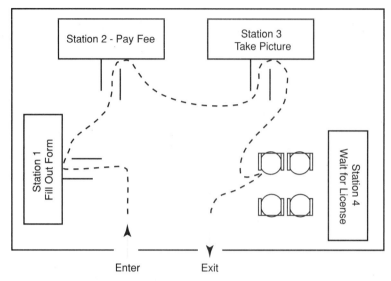

Figure 10-10. *Executing the steps of the "Get Your Driver's License" program.*

If you think of the steps of getting a driver's license as a computer program, your path through those steps is a thread of execution. If only one person were allowed in the department at a time, getting your license would be a single-threaded process. A computer program works the same way: If only one instruction can be executed at a time, the process is single threaded. In reality, the concept of only one person going through the process of obtaining a driver's license would be very wasteful, because three stations would be sitting idle for long periods of time. In fact, it would take even longer to get a driver's license than it does now!

It's much more efficient to have many people executing the steps to get their licenses simultaneously, with each one either performing the function of a station or waiting in line for their turn to use the resource found at a station. Getting your license is then a multi-threaded process, as illustrated in Figure 10-11. Each person can be thought of as a thread of execution, with each thread executing a different function simultaneously. A multi-threaded computer program works the same way, with many threads executing instructions in different parts of the code at the same time. When two threads of execution require the same resource—for example, the same block of memory, there are special programming constructs to make sure that one thread waits patiently for the other to finish using the resource before beginning. This is similar to how patrons of the DMV wait patiently for their turn to have their picture butchered by the camera at station 3!

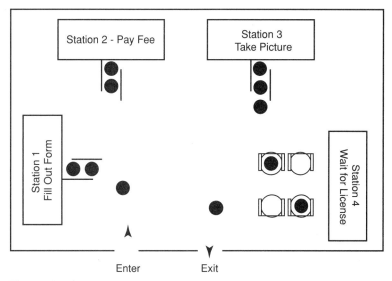

Figure 10-11. *"Getting Your Driver's License" as a multi-threaded program.*

Threads and COM

How does the concept of threads affect COM objects? Your program, be it single or multi-threaded, can use any COM object registered in the operating system. But if your multi-threaded object starts sending multiple threads through a COM object that doesn't protect its resources from multi-threaded access, trouble will surely result. Imagine if social mores broke down at the DMV and everyone tried to get their picture taken at the same time. Most likely, no one would ever get their picture taken successfully, and the whole process would grind to a halt. Similar things can happen inside a component in a situation like this.

What is needed, then, is a method for an object to inform the operating system and clients as to how it feels about threads. COM does this through the concept called *threading models*. There are four types of threading models, two of which will be discussed here.[3] Once instantiated on a thread, apartment-threaded objects may only be accessed by that same thread. This limitation to one thread is known as "thread affinity." Because they are limited to one thread, their resources need not be protected from multiple-thread access. Conversely, free-threaded objects may be accessed directly by any thread in the process. Because multiple threads may execute within the object simultaneously, all the resources in the object must be protected from multiple-thread access. Because of the lack of thread affinity, a free-threaded object is obviously much more flexible but, unfortunately, much more difficult to write. Visual Basic is unable to create free-threaded objects.

When an object is registered with the operating system, it tells the operating system what type of threading model it prefers. Depending on the threading model supported by the object, COM will load the object into something called an *apartment*. An apartment is kind of a "virtual area" that partitions how threads are allowed to access objects. An apartment model object is loaded into a Single-Threaded Apartment (STA). Only one thread is allowed to enter an STA and all the objects housed within it. Because any thread can instantiate an apartment-threaded object requiring an STA, a process can create as many STAs as it has threads. A free-threaded object is loaded into a Multi-Thread Apartment (MTA). MTAs and the objects within them can be accessed by any thread in the application. Because any thread can access an MTA, a process only needs to, in fact is only allowed to, create one MTA to service the whole process.

It is possible for threads to access other threads' STAs, but this access cannot be made directly. Instead, the requests made of objects in other apartments are marshalled across the apartment boundaries similar to the marshalling between processes discussed earlier. The same performance issues described in that section make cross apartment access a very unattractive situation for Web applications.

Threads, object scope, and IIS

If you've made it this far, congratulations! Now comes the payoff pitch: what all this means to your COM objects and IIS. Okay, read carefully and hang on; Internet Information Server maintains a pool of threads to service http requests. Each of these threads may access both its own STA and the IIS MTA directly. Nothing new so far; this is the same for all applications. IIS guarantees that a single thread will service an entire request. Because an object in Request scope can only be accessed by the thread servicing that request, that may reside either in the IIS MTA or in the thread's STA, meaning that the object may safely and efficiently be apartment threaded. An object in Session or Application scope can be accessed by any thread servicing a request for that Session or Application. Because IIS does not guarantee that all Session or Application requests will be serviced by the same thread, any object stored at Session or Application scope can be accessed by multiple threads. Further, because the only objects accessible by multiple threads directly are free-threaded objects in the MTA, all objects stored at Session or Application scope must be free threaded.

What does this mean from a practical standpoint? What kind of objects should you use for what functionality? Here's a quick set of rules to help you decide what type of functionality should be implemented where:

■ Write free-threaded objects to store in the Application variable to hold state variables that are shared by all clients of the application. This might include values like how many users are currently connected or have used the system in the past.

■ Write free-threaded objects to store in the Session variable. These objects hold state variables that pertain to the user's current session. This might include values like how many items a user has ordered to this point.

■ Write apartment-threaded objects to be instantiated in Request scope. Objects in Request scope are objects that are instantiated and released within the lifetime of one request. These objects might include functionality like data retrieval and mathematical calculations that have no need to keep a state longer than the duration of one request.

SUMMARY

In this chapter, you learned important rules to follow for implementing COM objects to run on your server. Here's a consolidated list of these rules. Keep these in mind as you read the rest of this book and develop your Web applications, and you will be a happier (or at least a better rested) developer.

1. Server-side COM objects may have no user interface.

2. Report user errors to the user and system errors to the system.

3. If at all possible, server-side objects should be in process.

4. Server-side objects must be as small as possible.

5. Handle errors according to COM conventions.

6. An object might not have the privileges you expect.

7. Learn the relationship between object scope and threads of execution.

---

[1] If your COM is a little rusty, check out Chapter 9, "COM Primer."

[2] According to the rules of COM, all methods return a type called an HRESULT. HRESULTs contain information on success or failure and the general nature of any errors that occurred. For more information on HRESULTs, see Chapter 9, "COM Primer."

[3] The other two threading models are single threaded and both threaded. Both-threaded objects support apartment threading and free threading and allow COM to choose the most appropriate model for the situation. Single-threaded objects are strictly limited to executing on the main thread of the application – such a loathsome context that we will speak of them no more!

Chapter 11

Scalability and Transactions with Microsoft Transaction Server

by Biff Gaut

The Internet has created an entirely new platform for providing electronic commercial services to users. Now software you write might be used by thousands, even millions of users. This gives you a great deal of potential for your business, but also introduces significant challenges you must consider when writing your applications. Microsoft Transaction Server (MTS) addresses several of these problems without requiring you to write a lot of code. Its powerful capabilities and solid foundation leave you free to get on with what's really important, like drawing the perfect animated GIF file.

COMMON WEB DESIGN PROBLEMS

If you are designing your first commercial site, several of the common problems faced by Internet developers might not yet be readily apparent to you. This section goes over several of these problems, explaining the origins and effects of each.

Scalability

What is *scalability*? In the early days of personal computing, a developer might write a small database program to satisfy some personal business need. Gradually, the program made its way from person to person until 20 people were accessing the same database using a program written for one user. Around this time, the overloaded system crashed regularly. The program written for one user did not *scale* to accommodate 20 people.

As demands on applications continued to grow, different architectures (for example, monolithic, two-tier, tree-tier) have been employed to service more and more users. Architecture alone cannot solve the problem, however. Now that applications use the Internet as their infrastructure, they have to be prepared to conceivably accommodate thousands of users simultaneously. What does that mean to your Web site? If your site uses a typical three-tier architecture, thousands of simultaneous users means:

- Thousands of COM objects taking up memory on your server machine

- Thousands of SQL Server connections constantly being acquired and released

- Dependence on client code to release resources promptly

Addressing these concerns efficiently involves filling your application with code that is geared more toward scalability than your business process. It also means trusting your client applications to release their resources effectively to keep server traffic down. While the first application written against your business layer is probably quite trustworthy (you probably wrote it yourself!), you have no way to monitor the client application written next year by the developer down the hall. A few ill-behaved clients can kill an otherwise efficient business layer. Wouldn't it be nice to have a system where the operating system frees unused server resources without requiring extensive code in the application?

Transactions

Internet commerce has gone way beyond selling books and software. The array of products on the Web ranges from booze to cars to houses to barbershop quartet music (you can even log on to the Net to buy a book on how to log on to the Net!). Chances are, if you are doing a large-scale Internet commerce site, you, too, are selling something.

Anyone writing software that deals with moving money and merchandise has to address the concept of transactions. A transaction is two or more activities that have to occur together or not at all. If you went to the local convenience store and gave the clerk your money without getting your frozen burrito and tub-o-soda, you would be understandably upset. The same principles apply on the Web. If your credit card gets billed and you don't get your product, you are unhappy.

Most databases already have the capability to manage transactions. Unfortunately, in an enterprise application such as a commerce Web site, transactions might involve many different databases and services from several corporate departments. Whether this situation occurs as the result of office politics or technical realities, as the creator of the site you have to have a way to make sure that transactions are always handled correctly, regardless of hardware, software, or user error.

Enter Microsoft Transaction Server

Microsoft Transaction Server was built to address these problems and more. Without requiring a significant amount of extra code, it will improve your site's scalability by automatically reclaiming objects that are not being used and pooling them for reuse by other clients. In addition, it will ensure the integrity of transactions across multiple databases and services. Finally, it eases the hassle of setting up security in a Web environment.

SCALABILITY

If you were going to specify an operating system service that improved your site's scalability, where would you start? What features would you have this new service provide to ensure that your site would remain responsive and robust as your user base climbed by orders of magnitude? This section explores the various design challenges you would face if you were to design an operating system service to increase scalability on your own.

Figure 11-1 shows the simplest architecture of objects being instantiated and used by a Web site using Microsoft's Internet Information Server (IIS). A thread in IIS creates an object, maintains a reference to it while it is being used, and releases it sometime after it is no longer being used. The advantage of this architecture is that it is easy to understand and makes it very straightforward to write objects and clients. The disadvantage becomes apparent when you envision thousands of users on the site creating objects, with each object soaking up memory and other resources. It is apparent that using COM objects in this manner cannot support a Web site with thousands of users or more. Any service designed to increase scalability must begin with the goal to reduce the number of objects instantiated on the server at any given instant.

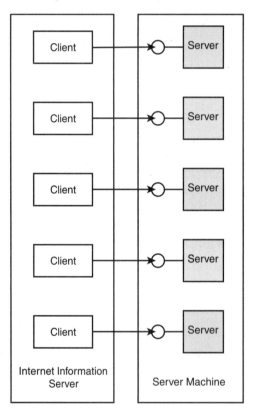

Figure 11-1. *Simple object use.*

Step 1. Don't Create Objects Until the Last Possible Instant

It is possible for an undisciplined client to instantiate an object long before it is actually necessary. In a situation like this, a scalability service should prevent any object from actually being created until the client has a need for the functionality. This should be a relatively simple thing to determine; the client needs the functionality of the object whenever it gets around to making its first method call on the object. The trick is to fool the client into thinking the operating system has provided a valid object while deferring the object's actual creation as long as possible.

What if the client were not given a reference to the object at all, but given instead something that only *looked* like the server object? This look-alike, provided by the operating system, would implement the same interface that was requested of the server object but would be very small and light. When the client actually makes a call to one of the methods of the look-alike interface, the look-alike immediately creates a real instance of the server object and passes all requests directly through to the new object. Not only does this system prevent bad clients from getting objects too early, it relieves good clients from having to worry about this issue in their design. In MTS, these look-alikes are called Context Wrappers (don't worry, the name will become more clear soon).

There will still have to be some sort of mechanism for the operating system to implement these Context Wrappers. MTS uses a DLL called the MTS Executive. For now, suffice it to say that the MTS Executive inserts itself between the client and object during the normal object creation operation.

The original COM architecture updated with Context Wrappers is shown in Figure 11-2. Assuming that MTS is able to create Context Wrappers that are much lighter than the actual server objects, it is apparent that some server machine memory has already been saved. All of the original clients still believe that they have valid object references and the server has only supplied objects to the clients that have actually made a functionality request. This first step is a good start, but there are still a lot of improvements to be made. What about objects that are kept around too long? Is there some way of allowing these objects to be deleted when they are not being used?

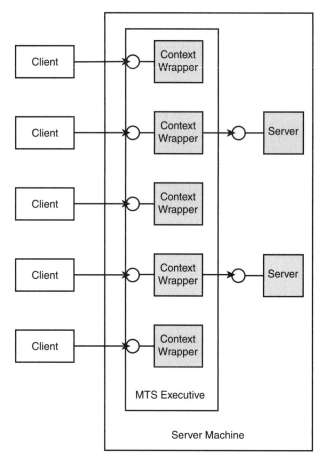

Figure 11-2. *An improved COM architecture.*

Step 2. Don't Maintain Unused Objects

The next step is to address objects that might have already been instantiated but are being kept around longer than their useful life or, perhaps, are just idle for a long period of time between calls. A truly efficient service would release these objects as soon as possible and re-create them only if they were actually needed by the client again. In this way, more resources could be freed.

A key aspect of this feature would be to assign the majority of this responsibility to the scalability service and the object itself. For instance, an object that allows a client to create a text message and send it via e-mail might decide that every time a message is sent, it has fulfilled its purpose. The object then instructs the service that it can be released. If the client needs the object again in the future, the Context Wrapper will create another instance of the server object at that time. In a situation like this, the client could obtain the object once and use it over and over again without ever monopolizing server resources, because the object and server would take responsibility for removing the object from memory when its not being used. This is exactly what MTS does.

For this to work, some method of communication must be set up between the object and MTS so that the object can declare when it can be released. MTS provides this communication path by creating its own object that it instantiates along with the Context Wrapper. This object, called the Object Context, is available inside the server object via an operating system call. When a server object knows that it has completed some logically associated group of steps, such as the e-mail example mentioned earlier, it uses the Object Context to notify MTS that it can be released. In MTS, a logically associated group of steps is called an *activity*.

Right about now some of you are probably saying "Wait just a cotton pickin' minute. This deletion and creation process is great for scalability, but what happens to any properties that might have been set when these objects were deleted?" Good question, as it would appear that any time an object declares itself to be done with an activity, any state that the object maintains will be lost.

And that's exactly what happens. MTS declares that as a rule, objects that want to take advantage of MTS's scalability features will forfeit state between activities. This isn't as bad as it sounds at first glance. If an object needs to maintain its state, it just won't instruct MTS that it is ready to be released until it is ready to lose that state. It is important to remember that this notification is the object's responsibility, not the client's. Although this design decision causes MTS-enabled objects to lose some OO purity, the benefits of the scalability features of MTS make it the pragmatic thing to do.

A diagram of the original COM architecture updated to include Object Contexts is shown in Figure 11-3. The features discussed so far have addressed two different locations in the original COM architecture where objects can be released:

■ Between the time an object is instantiated by the client and when it is actually used

■ When an object has completed a logically grouped series of steps

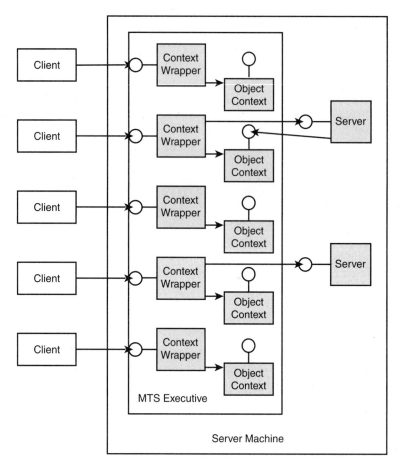

Figure 11-3. *Still more improvements.*

In addition, Object Contexts provide a great place for MTS to store information that it needs to manage the creation and deletion of multiple objects. Later sections of this chapter will give examples of the type of information MTS stores there.

The preceding features still don't appear to provide an optimal solution, however. The current method of deleting and creating objects that aren't being used does save memory, but it sure does lead to a lot of object creation and deletion that will definitely have a negative influence on performance. Limiting the number of creates and deletes would be a great way to squeeze a little more performance from the new service.

Step 3. Recycle Used Objects Among Various Clients

The last step in designing a scalable service is to define a way to reduce object creations and deletions. Because MTS has already declared that objects must be stateless, there doesn't seem to be any reason why client B can't use the object that just declared itself finished servicing Client A. That's a good idea; the service can create a pool of objects and allow instances to be shared among various clients. Think for a minute about what this means. Instead of hundreds of objects being constantly created and deleted for extremely short periods of existence, a much smaller number of objects will exist for a long period of time and be used as needed by hundreds of clients.

The only drawback to this idea is the fact that client B is going to get an object that client A has left in an undetermined state. Remember that while objects forfeit state between activities, they do have state that is created and maintained *during* an activity. Client B might be willing to accept a used object, but Client B should be confident that it is not receiving an object that still has the state set by Client A.

Objects are normally set to an initial state when they are created, by constructors in C++ and Java and the Initialize subroutine in Visual Basic. Because the object is not being deleted and re-created when it is sent to the object pool, the normal initialization code is not getting called, and the object's state is not being reset between clients. In this situation, another method must be used. MTS solves this dilemma by defining a new object state besides existing and not existing. An existing object can either be either *activated* (assigned to a Context Wrapper) or *deactivated–* (waiting in the MTS Executive object pool). MTS has defined an interface, IObjectControl, that it will look for on an object when it is changing the object's state. Any object that wants to be alerted when it is being changed from activated to deactivated (or vice versa) can implement IObjectControl, and MTS will call the COM methods Activate and Deactivate, and it is here that the object can initialize its properties or clear its used properties, respectively. If an object doesn't care about its current activation condition, it does not implement this interface. Adding Object Pooling to the COM architecture previously discussed yields the architecture shown in Figure 11-4.

> **NOTE** Microsoft Transaction Server 2.0 does not support object pooling. The IObjectControl interface has been defined so that objects can be written now to take advantage of object pooling in the future. Activate and Deactivate are currently called in the same manner they will be called when object pooling is implemented.

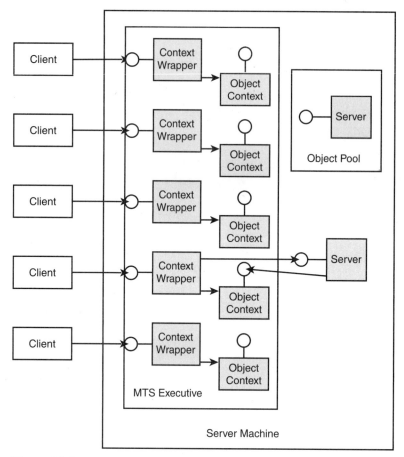

Figure 11-4. *MTS Architecture with Object Pooling.*

The only thing left to add at this point is a way to create these objects within the MTS framework. The creation process, along with a summary of everything explored so far, is shown in Figure 11-5 and described in detail here.

1.   A client calls CreateObject for a COM object registered in MTS.

2.   Registry settings instruct the operating system that this object is being handled by MTS and creation should be delegated to the MTS Executive.

3. The COM runtime loads the MTS Executive into the MTS surrogate process (A). The MTS surrogate process (MTX.EXE) is just a program that provides a process space to run MTS objects. Depending on configuration information, an MTS object can also be run in the client's process.

4. The MTS Executive loads the server's DLL and requests an instance of the Class Factory object (B). Remember from the COM Primer that the Class Factory is responsible for creating instances of COM objects for clients. MTS also creates a wrapper object for the class factory.

5. The MTS Executive then creates an Object Context and a Context Wrapper object. The Context Wrapper object implements the interface requested from the real server object (C).

6. The MTS Executive returns the Context Wrapper interface to the client. Note that at this point, the client thinks it has an object, but no object has been created.

7. When the client makes a call on the Context Wrapper interface, the MTS Executive obtains the Class Factory wrapper from the Object Context and creates a server object (D).

8. The MTS Executive calls Activate on the IObjectControl interface of the server object.

9. The client makes the method calls that constitute the activity.

10. When the object has completed this activity, it calls SetComplete on its Object Context.

11. The MTS Executive calls Deactivate on the IObjectControl interface on the object, removes the object from the Object Wrapper, and places it in the object pool (E).

12. If the client makes another call to the object in the future, the MTS Executive will obtain an object from the object pool, call Activate, and then make the call on the newly acquired server object.

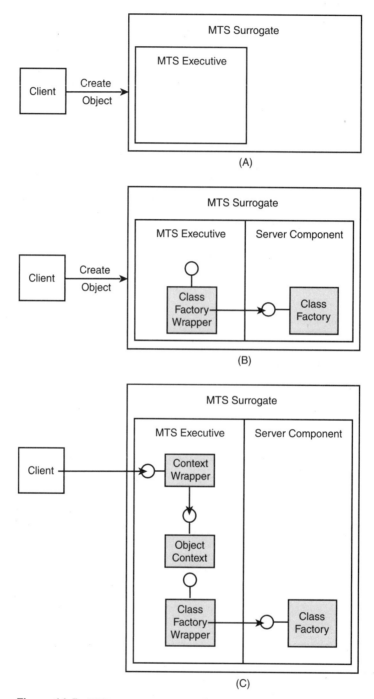

Figure 11-5. *MTS manages a COM object.*

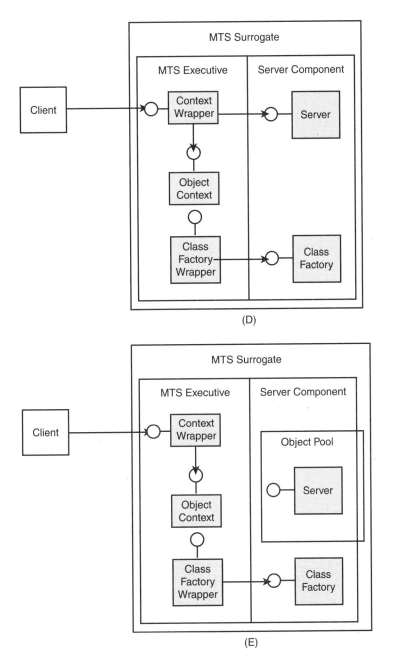

(D)

(E)

Figure 11-5. *(continued)*

Managing Microsoft Transaction Server Components

All this knowledge of MTS architecture is useless unless you can register your components with MTS and configure their handling. The Microsoft Management Console (MMC) makes this easy. This section discusses how to use MMC to manage your MTS components, introducing a couple of new MTS concepts along the way.

MMC is actually a generic program shell that does nothing but house in-process COM applications that manage various operating system services such as IIS and MTS. The COM applications that provide the actual functionality are called *snap-ins*. The Windows NT Option Pack comes with snap-ins for IIS and MTS, and Microsoft has published the specifications and interfaces so that you can create your own snap-ins to administer your own programs. To run the MMC with the MTS snap-in loaded, from the Start menu on a machine with NT Option Pack installed choose Programs/Windows NT 4.0 Option Pack/Microsoft Transaction Server/Transaction Server Explorer.

Figure 11-6 shows a running instance of MMC. You might have to expand the tree to see all the information shown here. A casual look at the MMC display reveals a concept that has not yet been covered: MTS packages. A *package* is a group of COM components that are grouped logically together. Typically, these can be all the components used in one application. To add a component to a package, highlight the components subfolder of the package in the tree view, right-click, and choose New\Component from the context menu. A dialog box will appear that leads you through adding one or more COM objects to the package.

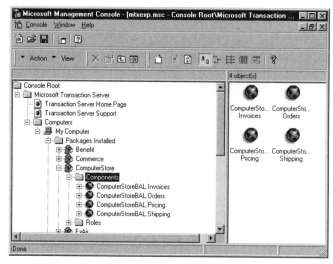

Figure 11-6. *Microsoft Management Console.*

One of the benefits of packages is that they allow configuration settings to be set on all objects in a package at once. If you right-click on a package, you can bring up the properties dialog box shown in Figure 11-7. The Activation tab of the properties window (shown in Figure 11-8) allows you to select how components in a package are loaded.

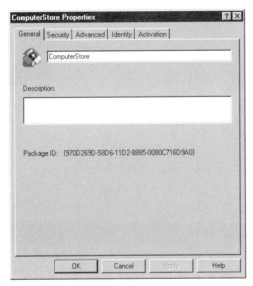

Figure 11-7. *MTS Package Properties*

- Library Package means that the component DLLs (along with the MTS Executive) will be loaded into the client's process space. Don't be confused by the word *client* as it is used here. For Web applications, the MTS client is IIS, not the browser. This will provide better performance because it eliminates cross-process calls but leaves the client vulnerable to rogue components that may misbehave and lock up the application.

- Server Package means that the components will be loaded in an instance of the MTS surrogate process, MTX.EXE. MTX.EXE exists simply to create a process space for MTS components to run in. Using Server Package protects your client but introduces a performance penalty because of cross-process calls. If you intend to run your objects on a separate machine than your client via DCOM, you should use Server Package.

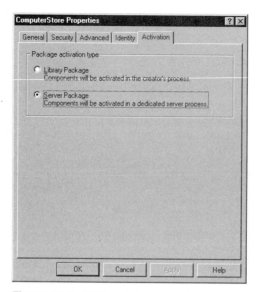

Figure 11-8. *MTS package properties—Activation tab.*

It is important to note that every DLL represented in a package is loaded into the process simultaneously. This means that when an object in a package is requested, in addition to the DLL implementing the requested object being loaded in the process space, every DLL with an object registered in the package is loaded as well. If any of these DLLs is corrupt or cannot be found, the package cannot be loaded, and the request to create the server object will fail *even if the server's DLL is present and valid.* For instance, if you have a package with two objects, A and B, implemented by A.DLL and B.DLL, a request to create an A object will entail loading both A.DLL *and* B.DLL into the process. If B.DLL cannot be loaded for any reason, the request to create object A will fail.

Sample Program

Okay, enough theory; it's time to talk about actually coding an object to take advantage of the scaling features of MTS. The goal of this demo is to demonstrate how MTS manipulates COM objects. The program does this by implementing an object that does nothing but log everything that happens to it to a file. When the program finishes, you can open the resulting text file and examine exactly when the object was instantiated, activated, deactivated, and deleted.

General Guidelines

When writing MTS objects, there are several rules you should follow. Some of these rules are just MTS requirements; others are suggestions that will ensure you get the best possible performance.

- All MTS objects must be In-Process (MTS requirement).

- All MTS objects must be Apartment threaded (MTS requirement).

- When writing an MTS client, always use CreateObject or CoCreateInstance to instantiate an object to ensure that the operating system is involved and has the chance to get the MTS Executive into the game. If you instantiate objects using the VC or VB "New" operator, you will bypass the operating system and lose the benefit of MTS.

- Call SetComplete as often as possible to allow MTS to work its magic.

- Use methods with many arguments instead of setting a lot of properties. This is for two reasons: your MTS objects shouldn't rely on state anyway, and it will reduce the number of cross-process trips if the object is loaded in the MTS surrogate, or worse, on another machine.

- If you are going to save a reference to the ObjectContext, always acquire it in the Activate method as opposed to the constructor. Because the same object can be passed from context to context through object pooling, an ObjectContext acquired in the constructor might be invalid when the object is reactivated.

Coding the Example

The sample program found on the enclosed CD shows how to write an MTS object in Visual Basic and illustrates the exact order of steps involved in managing an MTS object. The program is written in Visual Basic for the clearest possible presentation of the subject matter but could just as easily be written in Visual C++ or Visual J++.

The sample consists of two different programs: VbMtsLib, which implements the VbMtsObject object; and VbMtsDriver, a simple GUI application that instantiates and manipulates the VbMtsObject object.

> **NOTE** The VbMtsLib sample can be found on the CD under the directory Chapter 11\Samples\VbMts. The install.rtf file gives detailed instructions for installing the program on your machine.

VbMtsObject exposes one property, Count, and one method, SetComplete. Count is a simple property value stored in a private variable and accessed through Get/Set routines. One important concept to remember about Count is that it is set to 0 when the object is initialized. SetComplete is a one line method that calls SetComplete on the object's ObjectContext. This is the only place in the object where SetComplete is called, providing the client complete control over when the object relinquishes its state. Although this is not necessarily a wise choice in a normal MTS object, in this sample it allows you to clearly see the effect of calling SetComplete.

```
...
'    This method is called when MTS activates this object
'
Private Sub ObjectControl_Activate()
    On Error GoTo ReportError
    Output "Activating"
    '    Acquire and save a reference to the object context
    Set oContext = GetObjectContext()
    If oContext Is Nothing Then
        Output "No Context"
    End If
    Exit Sub

ReportError:
    Output "Error during Activate - " & Err.Description
    Exit Sub

End Sub


'
'    This method is called when MTS deactivates this object
'
Private Sub ObjectControl_Deactivate()
    On Error GoTo ReportError
    Output "Deactivating"
    '    This context means nothing now, so release it
    Set oContext = Nothing
    Exit Sub

ReportError:
    Output "Error during Deactivate - " & Err.Description
    Exit Sub

End Sub
```

The preceding listing shows the code for the ObjectControl Activate and Deactivate methods. In the Activate method, the object acquires a reference to the object context and records the fact that the object is being activated in the output file. In the Deactivate method, the object releases the object context and records the deactivation in the output file. The Initialize and Terminate methods have a similar implementation, although they do not manipulate ObjectContext. Everything MTS does with VbMtsObject will be written to the output file. The Count property will allow you to monitor when the object has lost its state as well.

The GUI program, VbMtsDriver, allows you to exert a high level of control over the manipulation of the VbMtsObject object. The dialog box implemented by VbMtsDriver appears in Figure 11-9.

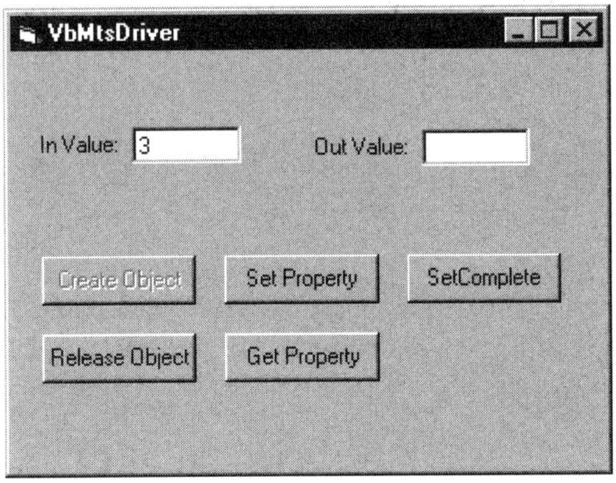

Figure 11-9. *The VbMtsDriver program.*

It is important to understand how the VB client is manipulating the VbMtsObject when each button is clicked to have a full understanding of the output file. The Create Object button instantiates an object and stores a reference to it in a global variable. It does not call any methods on the object. Once the object is successfully instantiated, the other buttons are enabled to allow manipulation of the object. SetProperty sets the Count property of the VbMtsLib object to the value in the In Value text box. GetProperty retrieves the value of the Count property and displays it in the Out Value text box. SetComplete calls the SetComplete method of the object, and ReleaseObject releases the client's reference to the VbMtsObject object.

Now that you understand what the object does and how the GUI works, it's time to run the program. Run VbMtsDriver and perform the following steps in order:

1. Click CreateObject.

2. The client has now created an object. Unbeknownst to the client, it has a reference to an MTS Context Wrapper, not a real object.

3. Type **3** in the In Value field.

4. Click "Set Property." MTS has now created a real object to hold the property.

5. Click "Get Property."

6. Click "SetComplete." The object has now told MTS that it can relinquish its state, so MTS has deactivated the object. In the current version of MTS, this means that the object has been destroyed. In future versions, the object will be placed in a pool.

7. Click "Get Property." MTS will now create a new object to satisfy this request. Note that the property is now 0, not 3.

8. Click "Release Object." The client releases the object, and it is deactivated and destroyed/pooled.

Now go to your C: drive and open the VbLog.txt file. Table 11-1 shows the contents of VbLog.txt in the left column and the client actions that created that output on the right.

Table 11-1

VBLOG.TXT CONTENTS AND THE CLIENT ACTIONS CREATING IT

VbLog.Txt Contents	Client Actions
	CreateObject called
	SetProperty called
Initialize	
Activating	
	SetComplete called
Deactivating	
CanBePooled called	
Terminate	
	GetProperty called
Initialize	
Activating	
	Object released
Deactivating	
CanBePooled called	
Terminate	

Take some time to play with the client program and examine the output of various combinations of steps.

TRANSACTIONS

At this point, you might be starting to realize, "Hey, I've read half a chapter on Microsoft *Transaction* Server, and I still haven't learned diddley about transactions!" MTS is actually about a lot more than transactions. A solid understanding of the architecture makes understanding transactions a breeze. This section goes over what transactions are and how they work in MTS.

What Is a Transaction?

What is a *transaction*? The short answer is *a series of steps that must occur on an all-or-nothing basis.* Remember in grade school when you and a classmate would be ready to trade something, and neither of you was willing to give up your precious item first? Neither one of you was convinced of the integrity of the transaction; you each thought the other would take your stuff and run off. Finally, you would work up some bizarre situation where both of you would be touching both items at the same time, each of you would tug on each of them for a moment, and then finish the trade. This was a transaction: neither of you could surrender your commodity without receiving the other's, so you made the steps happen simultaneously. Unfortunately, steps can't happen simultaneously in a computer program, so you need a way to treat them as if they do. That's where Microsoft Transaction Server steps in.

A set of properties that define a correctly behaving transaction can easily be remembered by the term *ACID*. The conditions of the ACID test are defined here:

- **Atomic.** The series of steps making up the transaction are encapsulated in one single action. In the playground example, this is the condition that required the simultaneous, two-handed swap. In a business example, this could be the ability to transfer money from one account to another by calling a single function.

- **Consistent.** The transaction must leave the databases and resources it touches in a valid state. In the case of the account transfer, this means that the money is both removed from the first account *and* added to the second (or to stretch the playground metaphor to the breaking point, suppose the item you were trading was a squirt gun or some other sort of illicit contraband, and a teacher saw the exchange and you ended up in the principal's office. In the operations of a child, this is definitely an error condition, and this transaction did not leave you in a consistent state).

■ **Isolation.** Each transaction in a system acts independently; the results of each are hidden until they are committed. For example, the money transfer between two accounts consists of two steps: removing some amount from the first account and depositing it into the second account. There will be a period of time, albeit very short, when the first account's balance has been reduced and the second account has yet to be credited. Until the second account has been credited and the transaction committed, other transactions operating on the first account see no effects of the debit action. (Because this condition would really destroy the playground metaphor, we won't even attempt it here.)

■ **Durable.** Once a transaction has been committed, its effects should be persisted in such a manner that they survive system shutdown or failure. This means that our account transfer is safely written to permanent storage in the database (and back to our playground, this means that no matter who you go to play with next, you have your newly acquired trinket safely in your pocket).

If all the steps of a transaction complete successfully, the transaction is committed. Once committed, the changes are stored permanently in the database (they are durable) and exposed to the rest of the world (they are no longer isolated). If any step of the transaction fails, the transaction is aborted. In this situation, all of the steps previously executed are rolled back (or undone) so that the database remains consistent, ensuring that the steps remain atomic.

MTS Transaction Support

So, a transaction is a group of operations that must occur together. Hey, that sounds a lot like the activities that an object performs before releasing its state in MTS. That is not an accident, the same methods that objects use to control state are the ones they use to manage transactions.

Processing transactions introduces two new concepts to the MTS architecture described so far:

■ **Resource Manager.** A resource manager is a software entity that controls a resource participating in a transaction. In practice, a resource manager usually represents a database, but the term is abstracted to reflect the idea that other items, such as message queues (see sidebar) may participate in transactions.

■ **Distributed Transaction Coordinator (DTC).** The DTC is a Windows NT service that manages transactions that occur over different resources. For instance, SQL Server and Oracle both have their own transaction support, allowing them to keep track of all the steps of a transaction that occur within themselves. Each time MTS starts a transaction in a resource, it registers that resource's individual transaction with the overall DTC transaction. When the resource-specific transaction is finished, MTS notifies the DTC whether to commit or abort the overall DTC transaction, which then leads to the same action being performed on all the resource-specific transactions registered within the overall DTC transaction.

MICROSOFT MESSAGE QUEUE

What Is It?

Microsoft Message Queue (MSMQ) is an operating system service providing a mechanism for transferring packets of data from one component to another. The great aspect of this mechanism is its flexibility, as the information may be text, binary or even a COM object like an Excel spreadsheet. The two components may be part of the same process, two process on the same machine or two processes on different machines.

The two machines need not even be connected when the message is sent; the message will be sent the next time the machines are connected. Although this is an intriguing feature technically, you may be wondering what application it has in real world situations. Essentially, it can be used anywhere asynchronous processing is required. A few examples are:

■ **Disconnected Computing.** MSMQ is ideal for situations where laptops are being used to record information while not connected to the main network. Applications may send the information to a message queue and be certain that the messages will be delivered the next time the laptop is connected.

■ **Poor Man's Load Balancing.** Load balancing is a huge issue in distributed applications. Extremely complex infrastructures can be created to ensure that processing is distributed evenly over multiple machines. In fact, Windows 2000 has built in features that address this very issue. A very rudimentary load balancing scheme (hence "poor man's load balancing") can be devised by sending all processing requests to a message queue

(continued)

> ### Microsoft Message Queue *(continued)*
>
> and having each processing machine poll the queue whenever it has available capacity. MSMQ ensures that only one processing machine retrieves each message. Fault tolerance is automatic, because if a processing machine goes down it automatically stops retrieving requests and MSMQ's transaction capabilities ensure that no request is lost in the process.
>
> - **Workflow Applications.** MSMQ is ideal for workflow applications, where documents are processed in several stages. For instance, someone in the Human Resources department may create an Excel spreadsheet for a new employee with basic information and place it in a message queue for the Facilities department. Facilities enters in information like office location and furniture requirements and puts the spreadsheet in a message queue for the Information Services department. IS then fills in hardware information and, well, you get the picture. After winding through the entire process, the spreadsheet ends up back in IS where the information is stored in the corporate database. This entire application can be created with Microsoft Office products and MSMQ.

How Does It Work

The entire architecture of MSMQ is dependent on operating system artifacts called queues, which are essentially areas of memory set up to hold messages. Queues are set up by the Administrator using the Microsoft Message Queue Explorer. Among the queue properties Administrators can specify are:

- **Queue size.** How much space is reserved for messages?

- **Security.** Who and what is allowed to access the queue?

- **Transactions.** Whether the queue access can be part of a transaction.

- **Name.** A text string allowing programs to specify the queue.

Once a queue is created, programs can write messages to it and retrieve messages from it. The steps involved in placing a message in a queue are:

1. Open the queue.

2. Create and populate a message.

3. Send the message to the queue.

4. Close the queue.

Conversely, the steps involved in retrieving a message from a queue are:

1. Open the queue.

2. Request a message from the queue, specifying a timeout to wait if no messages are currently in the queue.

3. Extract message information from the new message object.

4. Close the queue.

MSMQ provides two programming constructs to access a queue. The first, the raw C API, provides faster performance but is more difficult to use and requires the use of a language like C or C++. The second, a COM object wrapper, doesn't have quite the performance of the C API, but is much simpler to use and allows access from languages such a VB and ASP.

MSMQ allows two different types of messages, *Express* and *Recoverable*. Recoverable messages are persisted to disk while in the queue, ensuring that messages will not be lost in the event of a system crash. Express messages are not persisted to disk, leaving them vulnerable to system failure. Express messages achieve a better performance, but do so at the expense of the reliability provided by recoverable messages. Which message type to use depends on the performance and reliability requirements of the specific application you are designing.

Transactions

The key to MSMQ working in an MTS application is the transaction capabilities of MSMQ. MSMQ has an internal transaction mechanism that encapsulates calls inside transactions. This mechanism applies only to MSMQ operations, similar to the internal transaction capabilities of other resources like SQL server. The MSMQ internal transaction mechanism is controllable by DTC, making MSMQ transactions eligible to participate in MTS transactions.

You may not find the behavior of a messaging service inside a transaction intuitive—after all, all discussion of transactions up to this point concerned databases. Messages may be sent to a queue or retrieved from a queue within a transaction. When a message is sent to queue within a transaction, it does not actually appear in the queue until the transaction is committed—the message never gets to the queue if the transaction is aborted. Although the queue provides the durability after the transaction, the transaction does not guarantee that someone reads the message once it is in the queue. When a message is retrieved inside a transaction, it is immediately removed from the queue so that other applications can no longer retrieve it. If the receiving transaction is aborted, the message reappears in the queue.

Figure 11-10 and the following list document all the steps performed by MTS when processing a transaction:

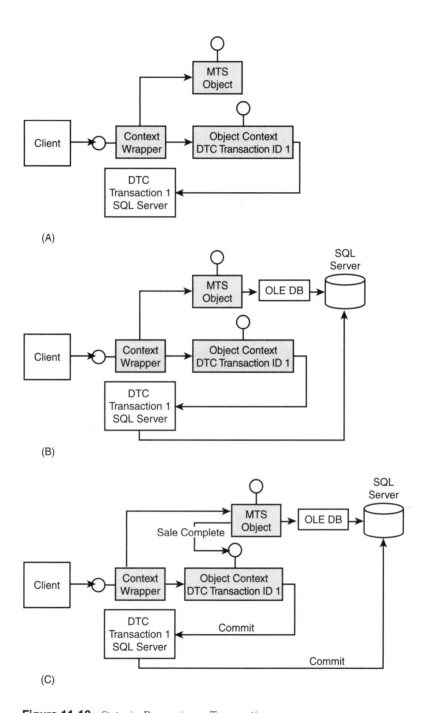

Figure 11-10. *Steps in Processing a Transaction.*

1. An MTS object configured to require a transaction becomes activated in response to an COM call.

2. The Object Context contacts the DTC to request a new transaction and records the transaction identifier for future reference (A).

3. The MTS object performs some sort of transacted function, in this case an OLEDB call on SQL Server.

4. A new transaction internal to SQL Server is created.

5. SQL Server is registered with the DTC as a participating database in the overall transaction (SQL Server is functioning as a Resource Manager) (B).

6. The previous three steps are repeated multiple times for as many resource managers as required.

7. When the transaction is complete, the MTS Object tells MTS whether the transaction was successful (commit) or unsuccessful (abort). Earlier you learned that objects communicate with MTS through the ObjectContext. In this case, you inform MTS of the status of the transaction by calling the SetComplete or SetAbort method of the ObjectContext.

8. The Object Context informs the DTC that the transaction is complete.

9. The DTC informs all the registered resource managers to commit their resource manager specific transactions.

Complex Transactions

The key to creating complex transactions in COM is to create many objects that each perform some small function and use them together to create a more complex transaction. It's pretty clear from the preceding explanation how DTC allows a transaction to span different resources, but how do you make a transaction span different MTS Objects?

The solution to this problem lies in the configuration of the MTS Objects themselves. Objects can be configured in one of four ways:

1. Requires a transaction. These objects operate within the context of the client's transaction, if there is one, or create a new transaction if there is not.

2. Requires a new transaction. These objects ignore the client's transaction and start a brand new transaction of their own.

3. Supports transactions. These objects operate within the client's transaction, if there is one, and operate independent of a transaction if there is not.

4. Does not support transactions. These objects ignore any client transaction and operate independently of any transaction.

What does it mean to operate within the context of the client's transaction? It means that status of the overall transaction is dependent on every object in the transaction. Consider a transaction that utilizes several MTS based objects to provide its service. Whether the transaction is committed is dependent upon input by all the objects participating in the transaction. Any object configured to operate in the transaction is allowed to vote by calling SetAbort or SetComplete. The trick is, the vote must be unanimous—one object calling SetAbort aborts the whole thing. The votes are tallied when the top level object (the object that started the transaction to begin with) casts its vote.

The other problem to solve is how an object gets access to the client object's transaction. Watch out for the word client as it's used here. In this situation, a client is anything that instantiates an object, including another object. An object functioning as a server to some client can simultaneously be a client of another object. If an object operating inside a transaction creates a server object by calling CoCreateInstance, the new object instantiated will be created within MTS, but will exist completely on its own, with no knowledge of the original object's transaction. In order to pass transaction information from client to server, MTS provides the CreateInstance method on the ObjectContext. When an object is created using the CreateInstance method, information from the client's ObjectContext is passed on to the ObjectContext of the server, including the transaction. Several examples of how the different configuration options interact in different scenarios is show in Figure 11-11.

It is important that you not confuse Object Contexts and transactions. Every object residing in MTS has it's own Object Context. An object's Object Context may have copied information from a parent object's Object Context when it was created, but even in that case both parent and child have their own distinct Object Context object. Conversely, MTS objects do not need to be associated with a transaction, and several MTS objects may share the same transaction.

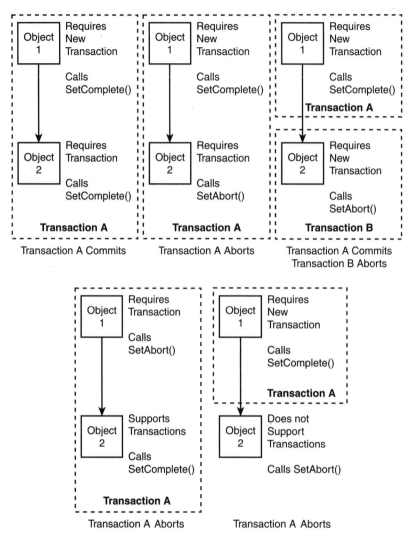

Figure 11-11. *Multiple Object Transaction scenarios.*

Use the MMC to set the transaction properties for an MTS object.. Right clicking an object and choosing properties displays the property dialog shown in Figure 11-12. This dialog gives you the ability to select any of the four configuration choices for each individual component.

ODBC CONNECTION POOLING

An additional NT feature supporting scalability is ODBC connection pooling. This feature maintains open ODBC connections in a pool to be assigned to clients as they are requested. Although this concept is often attributed to MTS, it is actually a feature of ODBC 3.0.

Opening a database connection is relatively slow procedure. After a client is finished with an ODBC 3.0 connection, closing the connection abandons the investment in resources already made to get it open in the first place. Instead of sacrificing this investment, ODBC tells the client it has closed the connection, but actually stores it in an internal pool. The next time a compatible connection is requested, ODBC provides the already open connection from the pool.

Receiving an already open connection in response to a request for a connection makes opening connections very quick. One result of this system is that the less time that objects retain connections, the more connections will be available in the pool at any given time. To this end, objects want to obtain connections as late as possible and release them immediately after use. This will leave connections in the pool as long as possible and not slow the application unnecessarily.

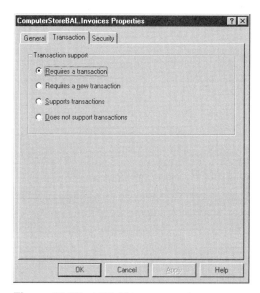

Figure 11-12. *MTS Object properties.*

Sample Program

The sample program described here and included on the CD demonstrates how to write applications that take advantage of MTS's transaction capabilities, both as a client and server. The sample consists of a very rudimentary commerce Web site.

> **NOTE**   The Computer Store sample can be found on the CD under the directory Chapter 11\Samples\ComputerStore. The install.rtf file gives detailed instructions for installing the program on your machine. Two versions of the UI are included, an ASP version to install on an IIS machine and a Visual Basic version to use if an IIS machine is unavailable.

Concept

The Computer Store is a fictitious enterprise that sells computer hardware. Customers may order machines over an 800 number or online through the company Web site. The sample program includes a business logic layer written for MTS along with two presentation layers, one written in Visual Basic for the telephone operators to use and one written in ASP to be used over the web. Only the ASP version will be discussed here.

The business requirements of the Computer Store Web site are:

- A customer must be allowed to specify his purchase by selecting from a variety of hardware options.

- A customer must be allowed to enter address information for shipping and billing.

- Due to the unpredictable nature of suppliers and pricing in the discount computer business, price calculations should be easy to change.

- Accounting and Shipping use completely different SQL Server databases (sure, this is ridiculous, but unfortunately, it is often true!).

- Shipping must be sent the customer's hardware configuration and customer address for each system sold. For simplicity, in this example the billing and shipping addresses are assumed to be the same.

- Accounting must be sent the price and customer address for each system sold.

These needs are similar to those faced by most commerce Web sites, although this sample has been greatly simplified for clarity. The design solutions it employs, however, can be applied to much more ornate and elaborate sites.

Implementation

In addition to the obvious UI requirements for entering information, these requirements break down to three basic business rules:

- Calculate a price

- Bill the user

- Ship the computer

  A fourth rule, a complex business rule incorporating the three simple rules, defines the order process.

Now that the business rules and their relationships have been identified, the next step is to specify MTS Objects and interfaces to implement the rules. The four objects required for the Computer Store sample, Shipping, Invoices, Pricing and Orders are shown in Figure 11-13.

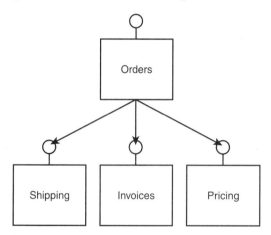

Figure 11-13. *The Business Layer for the Computer Store sample.*

Shipping

The Shipping object has one method, Add (shown later), that saves the hardware configuration and shipping address to a SQL Server database. If any error occurs during the saving of the information, the method calls SetAbort and generates an error. A successful SQL operation will lead to the object calling SetComplete, indicating that its portion of the transaction was successful. The Shipping object is configured to require a transaction.

```
Public Sub Add(LastName As String, _
                    FirstName As String, _
                    Address As String, _
                    City As String, _
                    State As String, _
                    Zip As String, _
                    Phone As String, _
                    HardDrive As Integer, _
                    Monitor As Integer, _
                    Memory As Integer, _
                    OperatingSystem As String, _
                    Modem As String, _
                    CurrentDate As Date)

    Dim AddCommand As ADODB.Command
    Dim nRows As Integer

    On Error GoTo ReportError

    Set AddCommand = New ADODB.Command

    AddCommand.ActiveConnection = ConnectionString
    AddCommand.CommandText = "Insert Shipping
(LastName,FirstName," & _
"Address,City,State,Zip,Phone,HardDrive," & _
"Monitor,Memory,OperatingSystem,Modem,Date)" & _
" values ('LastName & "', '" & _
                    FirstName & "', '" & _
                    Address & "', '" & _
                    City & "', '" & _
                    State & "', '" & _
                    Zip & "', '" & _
                    Phone & "', " & _
                    CStr(HardDrive) & ", " & _
                    CStr(Monitor) & ", " & _
                    CStr(Memory) & ", '" & _
                    OperatingSystem & "', '" & _
                    Modem & "', '" & _
                    CStr(CurrentDate) & "')"

    AddCommand.Execute nRows
    Set AddCommand = Nothing

    '   Let's see how we did
    If (nRows <> 1) Then
        '   Error, let's record it for the SysAdmin
```

```
        App.LogEvent "Could not add " & LastName & _
    " to Shipping", vbLogEventTypeError
        oContext.SetAbort
        Err.Raise ShippingError, "Shipping", Err.Description
    Else
        ' Success!
        oContext.SetComplete
    End If

    Exit Sub

ReportError:
    ' Error handling works a lot better in VB if you clean up
    ' objects before throwing the error
    Set AddCommand = Nothing

    ' Save it for the Administrator
    App.LogEvent "Error in Shipping - " & Err.Description, _
vbLogEventTypeError

    ' Raising the error will cause us to leave the routine, so
    ' let's explicitly abort the transaction here
    oContext.SetAbort

    ' OK, let's notify the client and get out
    Err.Raise ShippingError, "Shipping", "Error in Shipping - " & _
Err.Description

    ' This is here for clarity, it will never be called
    Exit Sub

End Sub
```

Invoices

The Invoices object has one method, Add, that saves the price and billing address to a SQL Server database. If any error occurs during the saving of the information, the method calls SetAbort and generates an error. A successful SQL operation will lead to the object calling SetComplete, indicating that its portion of the transaction was successful. It is configured to require a transaction.

Pricing

The Pricing object, in contrast to the Shipping and Invoices objects, has no interaction with the database. It has one method, Calculate, that takes the hardware configuration information as input and returns a price. The only way the

Pricing object will abort the transaction is if an invalid hardware configuration option is specified. The Pricing Object is configured to support transactions.

Orders

The Orders object has one method, Add, that uses the Shipping, Invoices and Pricing objects to carry out the logic involved in ordering a computer. If anything goes wrong, the transaction is aborted by calling SetAbort and an error is thrown. Note that MTS does not care how many or which of the steps in making an order are carried out. Conceivably, if the Pricing object fails but the Orders object ignores that fact and continues to save the Invoice information and calls SetComplete anyway, the SetAbort called earlier by the Pricing object would still cause the overall transaction to abort. It makes more sense, however, to monitor all the operations and discontinue processing if one fails, since completing steps you know are going to be rolled back is just a waste of server time and resources. Also, notice that Orders uses the CreateInstance method of ObjectContext to create the Invoices, Pricing and Orders objects so that all the objects share the same transaction. The Orders object is configured to require new transactions.

```
Public Function Add(LastName As String, _
            FirstName As String, _
            Address As String, _
            City As String, _
            State As String, _
            Zip As String, _
            Phone As String, _
            HardDrive As Integer, _
            Monitor As Integer, _
            Memory As Integer, _
            OperatingSystem As String, _
            Modem As String, _
            CurrentDate As Date) As Currency

    Dim oShipping As Shipping
    Dim oInvoices As Invoices
    Dim oPricing As Pricing
    Dim cPrice As Currency
    Dim strError As String

    On Error GoTo ReportError

    Set oShipping = _
oContext.CreateInstance("ComputerStoreBAL.Shipping")
    Set oInvoices = _
oContext.CreateInstance("ComputerStoreBAL.Invoices")
```

```
    Set oPricing = _
oContext.CreateInstance("ComputerStoreBAL.Pricing")

    ' Add to Shipping. This will throw an error if it has problems
    oShipping.Add LastName, _
                  FirstName, _
                  Address, _
                  City, _
                  State, _
                  Zip, _
                  Phone, _
                  HardDrive, _
                  Monitor, _
                  Memory, _
                  OperatingSystem, _
                  Modem, _
                  CurrentDate

    ' Calculate Price. This will throw an error if it has problems
    cPrice = oPricing.Calculate(HardDrive, Monitor, Memory, _
                                          OperatingSystem,
Modem)

    ' Add to Invoices. This will throw an error if it has problems
    oInvoices.Add LastName, FirstName, Address, City, State, Zip, _
    Phone, cPrice, CurrentDate

    Add = cPrice

    Set oShipping = Nothing
    Set oInvoices = Nothing
    Set oPricing = Nothing

    oContext.SetComplete
    Exit Function


ReportError:
    strError = Err.Description
    ' Error handling works a lot better in VB if you clean up
objects
    ' before throwing the error
    Set oShipping = Nothing
    Set oInvoices = Nothing
    Set oPricing = Nothing
```

(continued)

(continued)

```
        ' Save it for the Administrator
     App.LogEvent "Error in Orders - " & strError,
  vbLogEventTypeError

     ' Raising the error will cause us to leave the routine, so
     ' let's explicitly abort the transaction here
     oContext.SetAbort

     ' OK, let's notify the client and get out
     Err.Raise OrdersError, "Orders", "Error in Orders - " & _
  strError

     ' This is here for clarity, it will never be called
     Exit Function

  End Function
```

In addition to the methods discussed above , all of the objects implement the ObjectControl methods Activate, Deactivate and CanBePooled. All the objects also follow all the rules for server objects described in Chapter 10.

Granted, this is not a real life web site. Your business rules will probably be more complex than those implemented here. The code you have to write to take advantage of MTS scaling and transactions, however, will probably be just as simple and straightforward as the code in this example.

SECURITY

An overview of Microsoft Transaction Server would not be complete without discussing, at least briefly, its security administration features. Using a feature called Declarative Security, administration is greatly simplified. Declarative Security allows administrators to control access by functionality as opposed to by resource. It also reduces the amount of tedious work required of administrators by using a system similar to Windows NT groups.

Declarative Security starts with configuring access of the applications resources (databases, etc.) based on *MTS packages*, not users. Once this baseline has been created, the resources need not be reconfigured whenever the user base changes. Security is then established by controlling access to the packages. This is accomplished through a concept called roles. Administrators can define a list of roles for each package. A role is a list of users with similar access rights. Windows NT users are then assigned to one or more roles in the package. Finally, roles can be assigned access to functionality based on either entire components or individual interfaces. This gives the administrator a great deal of control over the exact functionality, as opposed to just which resources, a user may access.

Expanding the business requirements of the Computer Store example, assume that although three users, Alan, Beth and Chris can enter orders, only managers, in this case Chris, may cancel orders. To allow cancellation of orders, the Orders object has an additional interface, IAdmin that allows cancellation of orders. Under the MTS Declarative Security model, an administrator would define two roles, Sales and Manager. The Invoices, Shipping and Pricing components would have Role Memberships assigned that allowed access to users in the Sales role, in this case Alan, Beth and Chris. For the Orders object, the Sales role would only be assigned to the IOrders interface. The new Manager role (consisting of only Chris) would be assigned to the IAdmin interface. This configuration is displayed in Figure 11-14.

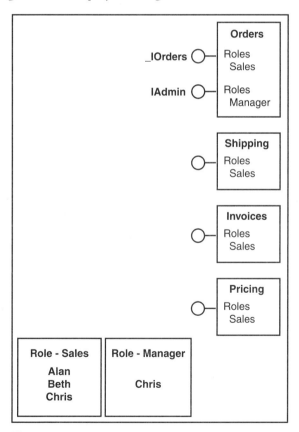

Figure 11-14. *Computer Store Security model.*

SUMMARY

Microsoft Transaction Server greatly simplifies programming large scale server applications, for the Web or the enterprise. It addresses scalability, transactions and security from within the operating system, allowing the developer to focus on the problem domain rather than the infrastructure. By utilizing MTS, you can make your Web site more responsive, safe and reliable while supporting larger number of users.

Chapter 12

The COM Language Decision

by John Intihar

For decades, the computing industry has seen hundreds of computer languages, yet none of them can claim the title as the best language for every situation. Some have a specific focus, such as ease of development, high execution speed, close adherence to object-oriented design, or fast GUI development. Others serve as decent all-around languages. You have many choices, as well as a responsibility to choose the right tool for the job.

To make this decision, you will undoubtedly need to make compromises. You might need to increase development time to gain in execution speed. You might need to settle for slower performance to gain an advantage in portability. You might even face the situation in which your team members might not know how to develop using the language best suited for the job. It takes a considerable amount of time to effectively learn a new language and all its personalities and pitfalls. When you set out to develop COM components, these decisions do not go away.

Due to COM's binary interface standard, you can use almost any language to develop COM components. Let's first look at how COM makes language choice possible.

COM's Binary Interface Standard

A COM component implements one or more interfaces that provide services. Each of these interfaces serves as a contract between the component and its clients. The client calls methods on the interface to access the services of the component. For a more in-depth explanation of COM interfaces, see Chapter 10. In this chapter, we will focus on how the structure of a COM interface supports you in building components with any language.

COM's interface standard defines the structure of the interface at the binary level. As shown in Figure 12-1, the interface simply consists of a virtual function table (vtbl) and a pointer (pVtbl), which points to the vtbl. The vtbl consists of one or more function pointers, which point to the object's implementation. A client of the object has an interface pointer, which points to the vtbl pointer. This double-indirection provides COM with numerous benefits including language independence.

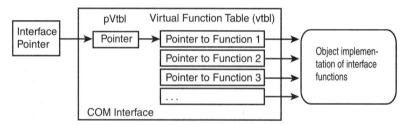

Figure 12-1. *The COM interface structure.*

If a compiler for a particular programming language can produce this interface structure, you can use the language to build COM components. This opens the COM door to most languages. Because you can express the COM interface structure in assembly language, any language that can reduce to assembly instructions can theoretically provide developers with the means to create COM components.

In this chapter, we will look at the pros and cons of developing COM components with C++, Java, and Visual Basic by examining performance, threading, portability, ease of development, and code libraries. Although there are many other languages that can be used to create COM components, these three are the most widely used and most appropriate to Web development on the Microsoft platform. You'll see that each of these languages has advantages over the others in the development of COM components.

PERFORMANCE

When designing a system, you will usually find that portions of it will need to perform their tasks very quickly. It, for example, might need to handle massive amounts of real-time data, such as the trading activity on a stock market or hundreds of simultaneous requests for messaging services. COM enables you to encapsulate these portions of the system into components that you can optimize to meet your performance requirements.

C++ for Superior Performance

When optimizing components for performance, you will obviously need to write efficient code. You will also want to choose the right language for the job. In looking at the three candidate languages, C++ will always provide the best opportunity for writing fast code. You can use Visual Basic and Java to write components, but you should have a good understanding of the drawbacks of implementing COM components with these languages where performance is an issue. Let's begin by looking at how to create a program from C++, Java, and Visual Basic code.

When you build a program using C++, you use a compiler to convert your code to an object file containing machine code instructions and data. Machine code consists of instructions understood by your computer's microprocessor. When you run a program that has been compiled into machine code, the operating system loads the program into memory and then manages the microprocessor's direct access to the program's instructions. This direct execution results in very fast performance.

Compilers of interpreted languages do not reduce code to machine code. Rather, these compilers translate code to p-code, bytecodes, or some other intermediate code not understood by the microprocessor. Running a program compiled to one of these intermediate forms requires a separate interpreter program. The interpreter reads each intermediate code instruction in sequence, analyzes it, and performs some action. Interpreted languages do allow developers to immediately debug their code without having to wait for the entire program to compile. Although this eliminates compile time from the development process, the interpreter overhead can seriously degrade performance in production, rendering the component slow and unable to scale effectively when execution speed is a limiting factor.

Visual Basic Slowed by Its Virtual Machine

Visual Basic first shipped as an interpreted language. In early versions of Visual Basic, the compiler would reduce the code to p-code. The Visual Basic interpreter would then handle the translation and execution of the resulting p-code program. Visual Basic 5.0 finally provided developers with the option to compile code to native machine code by using the same Win32 80x86 compiler back-end that Visual C++ uses. VB 5.0 programs, however, must dynamically link with the Visual Basic Virtual Machine to get access to the operating system. Therefore, while Visual Basic programs no longer require an interpreter, this intermediate step during execution makes them poor performers relative to their C++ counterparts.

Java and the JIT Compiler

Java also falls short of C++'s performance capability because it, too, requires execution assistance. The Java compiler translates code to an architecture-neutral object file containing bytecode instructions. This file can then execute on any platform with a Java Virtual Machine. The Java Virtual Machine interprets the bytecodes to machine code instructions and then executes them. Every time the program must execute a particular code segment, the Virtual Machine has to re-interpret it. All this interpreter overhead greatly reduces performance. You should experience great joy when you read on to discover that Java programs can run without interpretation.

Just-In-Time (JIT) compilation, available with some Java runtime environments including Microsoft's Win32 version, helps improve the performance of Java programs. When running a Java program without a JIT compiler, the Java Virtual Machine interprets a particular segment of code every time the segment must execute. To speed this up, a Virtual Machine can pass newly encountered bytecodes to a JIT compiler which will translate them to equivalent native machine code, as shown in Figure 12-2. The Virtual Machine need not interpret or recompile code once it has translated it using the JIT compiler. This one-time interpretation drastically improves the runtime performance of Java components.

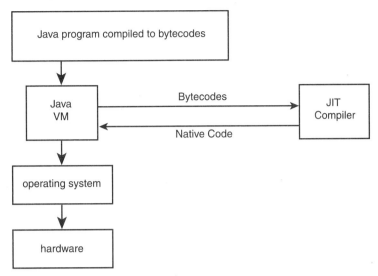

Figure 12-2. *Just-In-Time compilation of a Java program.*

Nevertheless, even with JIT compilation, Java performance still lags behind that of C++. You cannot avoid the overhead of runtime compilation. Java has other built-in features that hinder performance, such as background garbage collection and automatic bounds-checking when accessing arrays and manipulating strings. While these features make writing Java code easier than writing C++ code, they present an insurmountable performance drag on your components.

THREADING MODELS

Regardless of the language you choose, you can improve performance using additional threads. A client application, for example, can perform tasks in the background without freezing the GUI. Server components can receive and process multiple, simultaneous calls. Components can also leverage multiple processors to provide fast parallel processing. You'll have varying levels of success in trying to implement these designs based on the language you choose.

The COM Primer in Chapter 9 describes the single-threaded apartment (STA) and multi-threaded apartment (MTA) threading models supported by COM. The language choice comes into effect here because Visual Basic components currently do not support the MTA model. Therefore, if you use Visual Basic to develop a server component that provides services to clients running in multiple threads, COM will unfortunately synchronize all client calls to your component. In this case, you need to develop your component using the MTA model to prevent the need for clients to wait their turn for access to the component. You must use Java or C++ to build such a component, as these languages support both STA's and MTA's.

PORTABILITY

A cross-platform program runs on more than one platform. A portable program also runs on more than one platform, but you may need to perform some work, such as recompiling it, to enable it to run on all target platforms. You can think of cross-platform programs as perfectly portable programs. When you develop portable code, you end up with a single set of source code from which you can build your program to run on multiple platforms. For example, to break into the word processing market and create a program to sell to all your customers running Mac O/S, Solaris, Windows 3.1, Windows NT, or Windows 98, you would likely try to maximize shared code, write as little distinct code as possible, and compile a version of the program for each platform.

Historically, software developers created portable programs by writing code in a portable language, such as C or C++, and compiling the code once for each target platform. Using this approach, developers would have to concern themselves with all the platform differences in such areas as the sizes of data types, method calling conventions, and access to hardware devices. Code libraries released by many vendors improved this situation by taking care of most of these cross-platform issues and hiding them from the developer. Nevertheless, you will find it very difficult to build, test, maintain, and support an application that runs on multiple platforms.

The amount of work required to port programs to a particular platform will vary depending on the language used to develop them. When developing a program using C++, you will first need to recompile it before installing it on the new platform. You will then need to modify your test plan and fully test the program. For every platform to which you want to port your program, you will have to perform these steps. Java eliminates the majority of this work.

Java specifically addresses the portability issue by providing developers with a write-once, run-anywhere solution. Because you compile Java code to architecture-neutral bytecodes, you can run Java programs, without recompiling, on any platform for which someone has created a Java Virtual Machine. This makes Java a good candidate for developing cross-platform software.

To port programs developed with Java, you simply copy the file containing the components to the target machine. This works in theory. It works in reality when you develop the program using only Java code. Some implementations of the Java Virtual Machine contain architecture-specific extensions that allow you to forfeit portability for access to specific features of the operating system on which the Virtual Machine runs. If you write Java code that uses these extensions, your Java component will not run on a Virtual Machine that lacks the extensions. Microsoft has added one such extension to its Java Virtual Machine: COM.

The Java specification does not support COM. On Microsoft Windows platforms, however, Java programs can instantiate and use COM objects because the Microsoft Java Virtual Machine handles the communication with COM. Therefore, before you port your Java COM components to a non-Win32 platform, you must wait for that platform to have both a COM implementation and a COM-supporting Java Virtual Machine. Microsoft provides the only Java Virtual Machine that currently supports COM, and it runs only on Windows platforms. Some companies are currently developing Java-to-COM bridges to provide developers with the means to use COM objects from Java-only code. Using this approach, you won't need a COM-supporting Java Virtual Machine.

In the past, COM implementations existed only on Microsoft Windows platforms. Recently, however, vendors have released COM implementations on some UNIX platforms. Microsoft, for example, has released a COM implementation for Sun's Solaris operating system. This list of platforms with implementations of COM will most likely grow in the months and years to come.

You cannot currently port Visual Basic code to platforms other than Win32 operating systems. That may change some day, but for now, you cannot rely on Visual Basic as a portable tool set.

PRODUCTIVITY

Productivity refers to how quickly a developer can create measurable business functionality using a given tool. There is often a tradeoff between rapid creation of functionality and the flexibility to do low-level programming which may be necessary to tune for performance. The following section compares these productivity tradeoffs in detail.

C++ Delivers Flexibility at a Cost

C++ provides you with a very high degree of flexibility to write optimized, object-oriented, low-level code that takes full advantage of the target platform. This flexibility and speed, however, come at the price of reduced productivity. C++ does not come with features such as garbage collection, automatic array and string bounds checking, or automatic exception handling. Without these features, found in Java and Visual Basic, you must raise your level of caution when developing with C++. You must make sure that your code properly handles and disposes allocated memory. You must write your own exception-handling code to prevent your program from crashing. Compared with Java and Visual Basic, C++ requires you to spend more time testing, debugging, and reworking your code. C++ also requires that you compile your code before you can run it. In years past, it could literally take hours to compile some large programs. Today, with multi-processor, high-speed machines and nice development environment features such as incremental compilation, precompiled headers, and incremental linking, the build process takes much less time. Nevertheless, the larger the program, the longer you must wait for it to build. For example, a moderately sized component could take up to two minutes to build depending on its size, the speed of the development machine, and other factors. This time adds up.

Java: More Productive Than C++

The Java language resembles C++'s class-based, object-oriented structure. C++ developers seeing Java code for the first time have very little trouble understanding it. Java, however, has a different mission than C++. Java aims to provide developers with an environment, with a minimum number of implementation dependencies, in which they can write programs that will run anywhere. In its additional aim to help deliver robust programs, Java includes automatic bounds checking, default exception handling, and garbage collection. Java also supports Unicode-only strings, thereby preventing the development headaches and performance lags associated with string type conversions between components and across platforms. These and other features of the Java language let the developer spend more time implementing the logic of a program and less time debugging it.

VB: A Standard for Developer Productivity

The Visual Basic language has always provided developers with a highly productive environment. In the early 1990s, while Microsoft Windows rapidly grew in popularity, software developers were struggling to write Windows applications using C, C++, and the Windows API. Then Microsoft released Visual Basic, which gave developers a visual, interpreted, event-driven language and development environment that sent productivity levels soaring. Developers, who used to spend months writing user interface code, could now draw it in a matter of hours. Because of Visual Basic's interpreter, they could instantly debug code without compiling it, thereby freeing up literally hours of time per day previously allocated to the compiler. Using the Visual Basic development environment, developers could even change a line of code or the value of a variable while the program was running in the debugger. Visual Basic had set the standard for productivity in development tools.

Today, Visual Basic continues to provide developers with a highly productive tool set. With many of the same robust features of Java, including background garbage collection, Visual Basic enables developers to write robust programs more easily than with other languages. It's development environment also provides a seemingly endless amount of support for leveraging technology available on the Windows platforms, including COM. Visual Basic makes it very easy to create COM objects. Simply use the development environment to open a new COM DLL project, create a new class, and add public methods to it. Once you've implemented the methods, you can build the DLL with a single command.

Visual Basic makes using COM components just as easy. Using the development environment, just specify a reference to the type library of a COM library. Once you've done this, you can access the components packaged in the library directly from your code without any additional #include or #import statements. Although Visual Basic does not provide access to the complete set of COM technology, it does serve as a highly productive environment for general use and construction of COM components.

Java and C++ Catching Up

While Visual Basic provides you with a very highly productive development environment, some Java environments, such as Microsoft's Visual J++, do the same. Visual J++ includes many of the same development tools that Visual Basic does. You will have no more trouble creating and using COM components with Visual J++ than you will with Visual Basic. Visual J++ also ships with a code library called the Windows Foundation Classes (WFC), which will greatly increase your productivity.

The creators of C++ development environments and tools have made great strides in achieving higher productivity. Although the language itself requires you to spend more time developing, vendors continue to release tools and code libraries that increase productivity. For example, Microsoft's Visual C++ development environment and its ActiveX Template Library (ATL) combine to deliver a very easy way to create and use COM components.

PRACTITIONERS

If you manage a development team, you need to find people to create software and pay them to do it. You will have a difficult time doing this if you pick an unpopular language. When you finally find developers who know the language, they will probably charge you a high premium for their rare skill. Fortunately, you will not have too much trouble finding developers with experience in the languages discussed in this chapter. Software developers have used C++ for more than a decade and Visual Basic for just under a decade. Java has taken the software development community by storm. Just make sure that you choose a language you can continue to support.

CODE LIBRARIES

Once you choose the language, you might want to leverage a code library when writing components. Code libraries contain already written and tested source code upon which you can build components. For example, a C++ class library contains the definition and implementation of a set of base classes you can then extend to meet your system's specification. Although you don't need a code library to easily write COM components in Visual Basic or Java, you will definitely want to leverage one when using C++.

C++ Code Libraries

For C++ on the Win32 platform, you have two choices, both from Microsoft: the ActiveX Template Library (ATL) and the Microsoft Foundation Class Library (MFC). Both ship with Visual C++.

ATL

The ATL includes a set of template-based C++ classes you can extend to create small, efficient COM objects. ATL provides efficient, thread-safe implementations of most of the core COM features you will need in your components, including IUnknown, IDispatch, dual interfaces, connection points, and enumerator interfaces to name a few.

MFC

MFC provides you with a complete application framework with which you can create full-featured Windows applications. When Microsoft first released COM, it also added COM support to MFC. You can create COM components with this library by deriving a class from the CCmdTarget class. This class provides basic COM features. Although you can use MFC to create COM components, you should use the ATL unless you're building a component that takes advantage of MFC specific features not supported in ATL. ATL enables you to build smaller, faster components and spend less time doing it.

Java Code Libraries

Although you can easily build COM components using Java, you can now leverage a new code library for Java called the Windows Foundation Classes for Java (WFC). The WFC provides a large set of code you can use when developing components. With implementations for many standard COM features, user interface controls, data access, and much more, the WFC provides a very powerful set of code.

Sun Microsystems also ships a class library for Java called the Java Foundation Classes (JFC, a.k.a. Swing). The JFC extends Sun's original Java class library called the Abstract Window Toolkit (AWT). The JFC provides developers with a large number of classes from which they can build cross-platform programs that emulate the native look and feel of each target platform.

Visual Basic Code Libraries and Controls

There is a host of third-party code libraries and custom ActiveX controls available for Visual Basic. They range from simple widgets to handle data entry and validation to sophisticated data bound grids to multimedia controls to complete database reporting components. Code libraries for everything from sort algorithms to array manipulation are also available. Most of these third-party tools, however, are geared toward development of applications with user interfaces rather than UI-less business components. You will likely find that most COM components developed in VB will require that you write the majority of the functionality from scratch.

SUMMARY

Keep an open mind when choosing a language for your COM components. No matter what the situation, you will typically find that, to some degree, one language will outshine the others. The correct language choice can make a huge difference to the bottom line over the long run. While you will get the most COM support and the best performance from C++, you may want to forfeit these advantages for the increased productivity or other advantages offered by Visual Basic and Java. Perhaps you'll even choose a language not discussed in this chapter. In any case, consider how your language of choice stacks up to C++, Java, and Visual Basic for each of the categories in Table 12-1.

DECISION GUIDE: CHOOSING A COM LANGUAGE

Category	C++	Java	Visual Basic
General COM Support	Excellent	Good	Good
Performance	Excellent	Fair	Good
Developer Productivity	Fair	Good	Excellent
Portability	Good	Excellent	None (Windows only)
Threading Model support	Excellent	Good	Fair
Available Developers	Excellent	Good	Excellent
Available Code Libraries	Excellent	Good	Fair

Part V

Web User Interfaces

Chapter 13

HTML User Interfaces

by Steve Gilmore

Whether you're building your organization's retail commerce Web site or developing a business-to-business solution to exchange data with trading partners, chances are good you'll use HTML. Your Web-based user interfaces, whether intended for customers or partners, say a lot about your company. Your Web site is often the only image of your company your customers will see. Perceptions about whether you should be chosen over the competition are formed here. HTML is a valuable and common component of electronic commerce, so it's important to have a good understanding of what HTML is and what it can and cannot do.

HTML (HyperText Markup Language) is a tag-based language used to "mark up" specific parts of a Web page for display. By adding tags to the page, you give instructions to the Web browser about how you want the page displayed. Browsers read Web pages serially, and then interpret and display the various pieces of content based on the HTML tags surrounding that content. This process is called *parsing.* When parsing a Web page, the browser maps the HTML tags in the page to its own interpretation of how each tag should affect the enclosed content. For example, suppose you add the heading tags <H1></H1> around some text in your page. Web browsers will parse and display the enclosed text with a font that is bold and larger than normal text is displayed. However, each individual browser determines characteristics like font type and size. This inconsistent browser interpretation is important to understand, because it can cause varying results depending on the browser and the browser's platform.

The *HyperText* in HyperText Markup Language stands for its capability to link a text or graphic hotspot to other Web pages. This powerful feature, the hyperlink, is one of the main reasons HTML was adopted as the language for the Web.

HTML is maintained by a standards body called the World Wide Web Consortium (W3C). Though version 4.0 of HTML has been adopted by the W3C, it isn't widely supported. Browser makers offer varying support for the version 4.0 standard in addition to many of their own proprietary tags. For the best cross-platform results, use the core tag set of the currently supported HTML version 3.2. Using only the standard tags does not necessarily guarantee the expected results, however. As mentioned previously, the browser's interpretation of HTML varies by browser, platform, and browser version. You might notice in Figures 13-1 and 13-2 small differences in a Web page from the C|Net Web site, *www.cnet.com*, rendered on the same computer by Internet Explorer and Netscape Navigator.

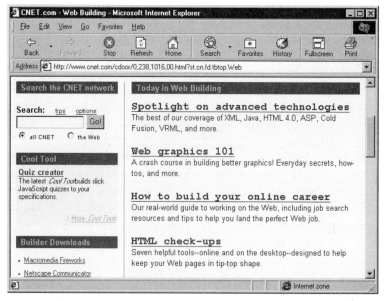

Figure 13-1. *Internet Explorer.*

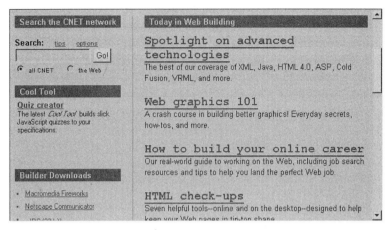

Figure 13-2. *Netscape Navigator.*

NOTE To find out more about the World Wide Web Consortium, the HTML standard, and where it is today, go to W3C's Web site at *http://www.w3c.org*.

TAG BASICS

The HTML language is a collection of tags that influence the display and formatting of a Web page's content. The HTML syntax is straightforward and easy for writers and non-programmers to learn. Tags give formatting and display instructions to the browser. All tags are enclosed in angle brackets, like <SomeHTMLTag>. Some tags, such as the line break tag <BR> used to add a line break to a page, require only a single tag. However, most tags are used in pairs consisting of a start tag and end tag. A start tag and its corresponding end tag are necessary to define the scope of the tag's effect. The difference in syntax is that the end tag is preceded by a backslash (/). For example, the heading tags and text <H1>My Title</H1> will display the text My Title in the largest HTML heading style. Text outside these start and end tags is not affected.

HTML tags are not case sensitive. To a browser, <BR> means the same as <Br> or <br>. Like any coding language, conventions are useful for readability and maintenance. Using all uppercase letters for tags is a common convention because it helps to distinguish the HTML from the content it affects.

Many tags have additional attributes that can be used for more granular control over the enclosed text. All attributes are placed inside the start tag's angle brackets. Attribute values can optionally be enclosed in quotes. For example, you can specify the size of text by using the font tag and its size attribute. The HTML would look like this:

```
<FONT SIZE=1>This text is very small</FONT>.
```

The size attribute of the font tag can have a value from 1 to 7, with 3 being the default. Many attributes can also be specified as relative values using the + or - characters. For example, the preceding HTML could also be written as:

```
<FONT SIZE=-2>This text is also very small</FONT>.
```

Page Structure

At a minimum, your HTML document should contain three basic sets of tags that identify it as a Web page and define a simple structure for that page.

The HTML tags <HTML></HTML> are the first and last tags in your page. Everything else on the page goes between these two tags. These tags tell the browser, or other program reading the page, that the file is a Web page.

Within these tags lie the header tags <HEAD></HEAD> and body tags <BODY></BODY>. The <HEAD></HEAD> tags must always be first and do not contain any of the page's actual content. The page title, which browsers use for their bookmarks and favorites list, should be included in the header tags, using the title tags <TITLE></TITLE>. Because browsers use title information for various reasons, a clear intuitive title is worth the extra few seconds it takes to create. The header tag <HEAD> can also contain script, which is discussed in the next chapter.

The body tag <BODY> contains the content of your page. Text, graphics, links, and other HTML elements go here. Three common attributes of the body tag are BGCOLOR, TEXT, and LINK. BGCOLOR specifies the background color of your page. TEXT specifies the color of the text of your page. LINK specifies the color of the hyperlinks on your page. To distinguish between text and hyperlinks on your page, choose different colors for the TEXT and LINK attributes. Color values are represented in either hexadecimal numbers (prefixed with a hash sign) or color names. Though you can specify any color by its hexadecimal value, you can specify only 16 colors by name. Table 13-1 shows the 16 HTML named colors and their equivalent hexadecimal values.

Table 13-1

HTML NAMED COLORS

Name	Hexadecimal
White	#FFFFFF
Yellow	#FFFF00
Fuchsia	#FF00FF
Red	#FF0000
Silver	#C0C0C0
Gray	#808080
Olive	#808000
Purple	#800080
Maroon	#800000
Aqua	#00FFFF
Lime	#00FF00
Teal	#008080
Green	#008000
Blue	#0000FF
Navy	#000080
Black	#000000

A Web page using hexadecimal values for a yellow background, olive text, and maroon hyperlinks has a body tag that looks like this:

<BODY BGCOLOR="#FFFF00" TEXT="808000" LINK="#800000">Though Web browsers can interpret body tags that contain both hexadecimal and named color values, your HTML coding conventions should define a consistent way to code color values.

The minimum Web page looks something like this:

```
<HTML>
<HEAD>
<TITLE>The basic Web page template </TITLE>
</HEAD>
<BODY BGCOLOR="#FFFFFF" TEXT="#0000FF" LINK="#FF0000">
 </BODY>
</HTML>
```

Creating a template file similar to this to use as the basis for each new page will reduce development time and typing errors.

Adding Comments

For maintenance reasons, you might want to document various sections of your page. HTML provides a special comments tag for this purpose. Though comments are contained in angle brackets like other HTML tags, its syntax looks a bit different:

```
<!-- Here's my comment -->
```

Everything within the start tag <!-- and the end tag --> is considered a comment by the browser and will not be displayed. The browser simply interprets the start comment tag and stops displaying everything after it until the browser finds the end comment tag. Although not displayed, what's between the comment tags isn't removed from the page. If you view the source of the page, you will see that the comments are still contained in the page. Good HTML code contains comments in every Web page, particularly complex pages.

> **NOTE** You can also use comments for indexing your pages. Many Internet search engines and index servers search through the entire document when indexing Web pages. By placing key words inside comment tags, your page can use reference words that don't actually appear in the displayed content of your page. For example, if your page contains a story about a hockey team, someone searching the Internet for the words *sports* and *story* won't find your page if those words are not in your page. By placing related words, like *sports* and *story*, inside a comment, you'll make sure your page is found even if the content of your page doesn't contain those words.

Working with Text

Now that you know how tags work and you have an understanding of the structure of a Web page, it's time to add some content. To add text to your page, simply insert it within the body tags <BODY></BODY> of the page. Once you do this and you view your page in a browser, you'll quickly realize that it's not very exciting. The first thing you'll want to do is improve the way it looks. You might also notice that any formatting you added to the text is gone. This is because the browser ignores every tab, carriage return, and extra space you placed in the text of the page. Only HTML tags can format a Web page.

Paragraphs and Line Breaks

One of the first formatting options you might want to use is to separate your text into paragraphs. The paragraph tags <P></P> take care of this for you. These tags add a blank line before and after the text they enclose. In older versions of HTML there was only a <P> tag. Many browsers allow the use of the <P>

tag without its corresponding </P> tag for backward compatibility. However, good HTML coding conventions require using these tags as a pair.

The line break tag <BR> places the text that follows on the left margin of the next line. As mentioned earlier, it has no associated end tag. Using two line break tags in succession looks similar to using one set of paragraph tags.

Emphasizing Text

HTML includes a number of tags that modify the style of words or characters so emphasis can be placed on them. Two of the most common such tags are the bold and italics tags. Use the bold tags <B></B> and the italics tags <I></I> like this:

```
The last word in this sentence will appear <B>bold</B>.
The last word in this sentence will appear in <I>italics</I>.
```

These tags can be placed inside other HTML tags as well, like this:

```
These words will appear<B><I>bold and italics</I></B>.
```

Notice that in the last example, the italics end tag </I> comes before the bold end tag </B>. This is necessary because HTML does not allow tags to overlap.

NOTE Avoid using the underline tag (<U></U>) because people viewing your page might confuse the underlined text as a hyperlink.

Headings and Horizontal Rules

Headings in HTML are used just like headings in books and newspapers. Headings divide various sections of text and improve the readability of the page. HTML defines six levels of headings for this use. Each of the levels is a different size, level one being the largest and six being the smallest. All heading tags contain an H and a number from 1 to 6 indicating the heading level. All headings are automatically bold. For example, the HTML code for a level two heading entitled *HTML Review* would look like this:

```
<H2>HTML Review</H2>
```

Heading tags, like all tags, are subject to the interpretations of different browsers. Test your pages on as many different types of browsers as you think might be used to access them to be sure they are being displayed as you intended.

A horizontal rule is another way of visually partitioning a page to improve readability and impact. If you add the horizontal rule tag <HR> to your page, the browser simply draws a line across the page. The horizontal rule tag has several attributes that make it useful. Thickness, alignment, width, and shading can all be set to give your page a unique look.

Lists

You can arrange your text in several types of lists. Most common are ordered (numbered) or unordered (bulleted) lists. Use the ordered lists tags <OL></OL> to create ordered lists and the unordered list tags <UL></UL> to create unordered lists. For each list item in the list within either of these sets of tags, use the *listitem* tag <LI>. For example, the HTML for an unordered list of product features could look like this:

```
<UL>
<LI>Available in sizes S-XXL
<LI>Comes in colors Black, Blue, Red, and White
<LI>Free delivery with purchase of two or more
</UL>
```

Notice that the listitem tag <LI> has no associated end tag. The lists are automatically indented when displayed. In addition, for unordered lists, the browser will use some character to represent a bullet. This character may vary from browser to browser and platform to platform. Lists can also be nested within other lists like this:

```
<UL>
<LI>unordered list 1 item 1
<LI>unordered list 1 item 2
<OL>
<LI>ordered list item 1
<LI>ordered list item 2
<LI>ordered list item 3
</OL>
<LI>unordered list 1 item 3
</UL>
```

Internet Explorer renders a Web page containing this ordered list nested in an unordered list as shown in Figure 13-3.

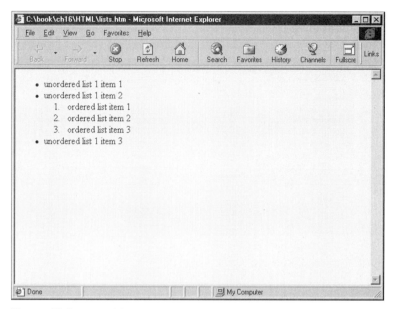

Figure 13-3. *Nested lists in Internet Explorer.*

One other list type worth mentioning is the definition list. A definition list can simulate the look of a glossary formatted as two parts: a term and a definition. You'll find this useful for your site's help pages when you explain site or business specific terminology. Use the definition list tags <DL></DL> to create a definition list. Within these tags, use the definition term tag <DT> for each list item term and use the definition data tag <DD> for each list item's data. Like other list items, both the <DT> and <DD> tags have no associated end tags. A section from a dictionary might look like this:

```
<DL><DT>mukluk
<DD>A soft Eskimo boot of sealskin ·or reindeer skin.
 <DT>mumbo jumbo
<DD>Complicated and confusing activity or language.
 </DL>
```

Internet Explorer renders a Web page containing this definition list as shown in Figure 13-4.

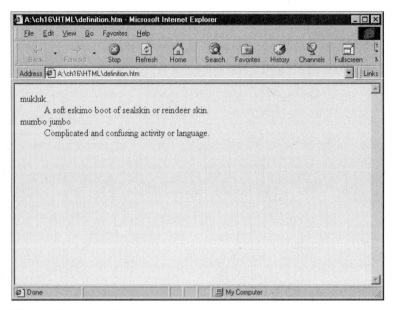

Figure 13-4. *Definition list in Internet Explorer.*

Font Size, Face, and Color

Adjusting the size, face, or color of a font for a phrase, word, or a single char-acter is common when authoring HTML. Earlier you got a quick look at the font tags <FONT></FONT> and one of the font attributes, SIZE. To reiterate, the size attribute can have a value from 1 to 7, with 3 being the default. The value can also be specified as a relative value using the + or - characters. For example, if you want the words *Shopping Basket* to appear in all capitals and you want the first letter of each word to be one size bigger than the other letters, your HTML will look something like:

```
<FONT SIZE=+1>S</FONT>HOPPING <FONT SIZE=+1>B</FONT>ASKET
```

To leave the first letter of each word the default size and make all other letters two sizes smaller, the HTML would look something like this:

```
S<FONT SIZE=-2>HOPPING</FONT> B<FONT SIZE=-2>ASKET</FONT>
```

Another useful font tag attribute is FACE. When creating your page, you'll want to use a variety of font types for some or all of the text on the page. To do this, enclose the value of the font tag's FACE attribute in quotes. You can specify one or more font names separated by commas, like this:

```
<FONT FACE="Verdana, Arial, Helvetica">What a face!</FONT>
```

The font tag can be combined with other HTML tags as well, like this:

```
<FONT FACE="Verdana, Arial, Helvetica"><H4>What a face!</H4></FONT>
```

When a browser parses the font tags, it tries to display the text within the tags using the first font specified in the list. If that font is on the browser's system, the text is displayed in that font. If the first font is not available, the browser tries again with the next font in the list. This continues until a match is found or the end of the list is reached. If no match is found, the browser uses its default font, which is user configurable.

It isn't safe to assume that all browsers viewing your page will have the same fonts available to them as you did when you created the page. Even if they do, the name of a font can vary from browser platform to platform, and a match still might not be found. When a page is dependent on specific fonts that the browser doesn't have, your intended look and feel may be displayed as poorly formatted pages. Here are a few simple techniques you can use to reduce this risk:

- Use a list of fonts instead of just one font to increase the browser's chance of finding a match as shown in the previous example.

- Use fonts common to your target browser's platform. For example, most computers have at least a Times or Courier font installed, while computers running Windows will also have the Arial font installed. If you can't be sure what fonts are available on the target browsers, avoid designing pages that depend on a specific font.

- Include a number of similar looking font types in the font list so the page will display similarly regardless of which font is used.

- Test your page with each font in the list and with the browser's default font. It's the only way to know for sure. Always test multiple browsers on multiple platforms.

The third font tag attribute is COLOR. It's used the same way the BGCOLOR attribute of the BODY tag is used. Specify the color by using a name or hexadecimal value. For example, making text red looks like this:

```
<FONT COLOR="#ff0000">You have a negative balance!</FONT>.
```

Use caution when working with colors. Many computers still display only 256 colors. The color you specify will have to be mapped to a color available on the browser's computer. Because this mapping is done by number and not by color, some unexpected color combinations can result. To test this, reduce the colors on your computer, and then view the page.

Alignment

If you're accustomed to sophisticated word processing applications like Microsoft Word, you'll be a bit frustrated with the limited alignment capabilities of HTML. However, you will find some tags and attributes very useful for arranging content on your page. By default, all text starts at the left margin. The ALIGN attribute can be used to override this and arrange text horizontally by using one of its three values: LEFT, CENTER, or RIGHT. The ALIGN attribute can be added to several tags, such as paragraph and heading tags. To align a heading on the right side of your page, your HTML would look like this:

```
<H1 ALIGN=RIGHT>This Heading is right-justified</H1>.
```

ALIGN can also be used with the division tags <DIV></DIV>. Using <DIV></DIV> allows you to align entire sections of content on your page. This allows you to specify alignment in one place to affect everything within these two tags. As a result, your pages are smaller in size and easier to maintain. If other HTML tags within the <DIV></DIV> tags use the ALIGN attribute, those individual tag's alignment are given precedence.

The center tags <CENTER></CENTER> are commonly used and are recognized by most browsers; however, they are not part of the HTML standard. Rather than using this tag, use the division tags with the ALIGN attribute, like this:

```
<DIV ALIGN="center">
   Text…
</DIV>.
```

Links

The most powerful feature of HTML is the user's ability to navigate via hyperlinks. Hyperlinks allow you to jump to other pages on the Web, to a particular place on a page, to other documents and programs on the user's computer, or onto Web servers anywhere in the world just by clicking a hotspot. You can add hyperlinks to your page by creating a hotspot using the anchor tags <A></A>. The content enclosed in the anchor tags is your hotspot. If you do not include any content between these tags, a hotspot is not created, and your hyperlink will not work. A hotspot is easy to identify because it is the color you specified with the LINK attribute of the BODY tag. It will normally be underlined, as well. Although underlined hyperlinks are the standard, browsers allow you to override this presentation through a configuration option.

Once you've created a hotspot, you have to tell the browser where to jump to when the hotspot is clicked. Specifying this target page or file is done by using the anchor tag's HREF attribute. The HREF attribute specifies the location, or URL, of the page to jump to when the hotspot is clicked. For example, the HTML for a hyperlink to the MMA home page looks like this:

```
<A HREF="http://www.micromodeling.com">Click here to go to MMA</A>.
```

Most often, you'll want to link to other pages that are part of your Web site. You can specify these "local" file locations one of two ways: with absolute or relative pathnames.

A relative pathname is relative to the location of the current page. If the target page is in the same directory as the current page, only the filename of the target page is needed. For example, if a target page named *catalog.btm* is located in the same directory as the current page, the anchor tag looks like this:

```
<A HREF="catalog.htm">Click here to see our catalog</A>.
```

If a target page is not located in the same directory as the current page, use a slash (/) to represent subdirectories and two dots and a slash (../) to represent parent directories. So, if a target page named saleitems.htm is located in a subdirectory /christmas/ of the current page, the anchor tag looks like this:

If the target page home.htm is located in the parent directory of the current page, the anchor tag looks like this:

```
<A HREF="../home/christmas/saleitems.htm">Click here to go to our home
page</A>.
```

You can also specify the location of a target page by using an absolute pathname. An absolute pathname is absolute to the file system of the current page. Absolute pathnames hard-code target locations into your pages and are necessary when referring to sites outside your own. Within your own site, though, this method increases the maintenance burden and reduces the flexibility of your pages. Generally, only relative pathnames are used when targeting files on the same Web site as the current file.

Another thing you can do with hyperlinks is jump to a specific place or "anchor" in a page. You can jump to an anchor in another page or to an anchor in the current page you're viewing—not just to the top of the page. This is particularly useful if your hyperlink's target page is long. To do this, create an anchor tag using the NAME attribute instead of the HREF attribute. If you created a page to sell CDs, you could make an anchor for each style of music on the page. For example, an anchor for the Jazz CDs section could look like this:

```
<A NAME="Jazz">Jazz CDs</A>.
```

Notice that this is not a hyperlink but a "bookmark," "anchor," or "target" for a hyperlink. Without the HREF attribute, the content between the anchor tags is not underlined. At the top of your page, you could create an index of hyperlinks: one hyperlink for each music type anchor. To reference each anchor, set the HREF attribute's value to the anchor's name prefixed with the pound sign (#). The hyperlink that jumps to the Jazz CDs anchor looks like this:

```
<A HREF="#Jazz">Go to our Jazz CD section</A>.
```

When this hyperlink is clicked, the browser jumps down to the Jazz CDs section located on the same page. To jump to an anchor on another page, just prefix the anchor name with its filename like this:

```
<A HREF="cds.htm#Jazz">Go to our Jazz CD section</A>.
```

Tables

Tables are the most sophisticated formatting element of HTML. If you view the source of some of the more advanced pages on the Web, you'll notice many of these pages use several tables to achieve their look. A table is just like any other grid in that it consists of cells arranged in columns and rows. Each cell can contain content or be used for spacing. Each cell can also span more than one row or column.

To specify a table, a few tags are needed. The table tags <TABLE></TABLE> define the scope of a table. <TABLE> has several attributes. The BORDER attribute is used to set the table's border width in pixels. Setting BORDER to 0 hides the border entirely. Use the WIDTH attribute to set the table's width in pixels or as a percentage of the browser's screen width. Specifying WIDTH as a percentage should be done with caution, because the screen width of the browser can't be determined at design time. Content in tables will wrap around or be pushed off the screen on lower resolution monitors. The BGCOLOR attribute is for setting the table's background color by using either hexadecimal numbers or color names.

Within the table tags, you need to define one or more table rows with the table row tags <TR></TR>. Within each of these rows, you can then define one or more cells using the table data tags <TD></TD>. The table heading tags <TH></TH> can be substituted for the table data tags. The difference is that the text enclosed in the table heading tags is bold. Like the table tag, the table data and table heading tags also have WIDTH and BGCOLOR attributes.

Within table cells, you can place any HTML element, including another table. If you want your table to have a title, enclose it in the <CAPTION></CAPTION> tags just after the <TABLE> tag. The HTML for a table with four cells—two rows and the two columns—looks like this. Figure 13-5 shows how this HTML is rendered in a browser.

```
<TABLE WIDTH=300 BORDER=0 BGCOLOR="#00008b">
     <CAPTION>
        <FONT COLOR="#00008b">Our Current Publications</FONT>
</CAPTION>
<TR>
   <TD WIDTH=200>
             <FONT COLOR="#ffffff">Fast Track HTML</FONT>
</TD>
<TD BGCOLOR="#ffffff">
             $29.95
</TD>
</TR>
<TR>
<TD WIDTH=200>
             <FONT COLOR="#ffffff">Web Development Overnight</
FONT>
</TD>
<TD BGCOLOR="#ffffff">
             $39.95
</TD>
</TR>
</TABLE>
```

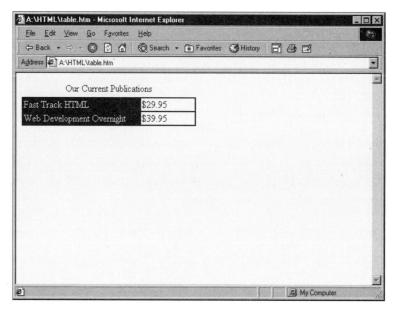

Figure 13-5. *A simple HTML table.*

Some new tags for organizing groups of columns and rows within tables have been added to the HTML standard with the approval of HTML version 4.0. The <THEAD>, <TFOOT>, and <TBODY> tags are available for grouping table rows into three distinct groups. The <COLGROUP></COLGROUP> and <COL> tags are used for grouping table elements into columns and groups of columns. Simplicity is the basic advantage of using these new tags. Previously, formatting a set of rows or columns required applying the same format attribute(s) to every individual table element involved. Now by identifying a set of columns or rows as a group, attributes set once in the group tag apply to all elements in that group. The result is a smaller page that is faster for browsers to parse and easier for authors to maintain.

TIP   While you are developing tables, a useful debugging technique is to set the table's BORDER attribute to 1 to make the table border visible. This shows you the size and shape of each cell. When you've got the positioning you want, set the BORDER attribute back to 0.

Frames

Frames are used to present an organized layout of multiple windows. Frames allow you to display several Web pages on a single screen, one page per frame.

To do this, you need to create a separate "frameset" file that defines this set or collection of frames. This file looks just like any other Web page except it replaces the <BODY> tags and everything between them with the frameset tags <FRAMESET></FRAMESET>.

> **NOTE** An HTML file can contain a BODY tag or a FRAMESET tag, but not both.

You control the number of frames and the size of each frame in the frameset by using either the ROWS or the COLS attribute. The ROWS attribute divides the screen horizontally into frames from top to bottom. The COLS attribute works the same as ROWS except it divides the screen vertically into frames from left to right. You separate each frame in the definition by a comma and define the size of each frame in absolute pixels, as a percentage of the entire screen, or by using an asterisk (*) to tell the browser to use whatever space is left on the screen. A frameset tag can contain any combination of these three sizing values.

> **NOTE** Using a percentage or an asterisk can produce unexpected results because the screen resolution of the browser displaying your frameset might be different than your screen resolution. Therefore, if a specific size of a frame is important to your design, define it in absolute pixels.

You can define as many frames in a frameset as you like, but you'll find using more than three frames is rarely useful. The HTML to specify a frameset with an 80 pixel frame at the top, a frame the size of 40 percent of the screen in the middle, and a frame the height of the remainder of the screen at the bottom looks like this:

```
<FRAMESET ROWS="80,40%,*"></FRAMESET>
```

A FRAMESET tag defining columns instead of rows looks like this:

```
<FRAMESET COLS="30,75%,*"></FRAMESET>
```

After you define the frameset, you need to tell the browser what Web page goes into each frame. To do this, use the frame tag <FRAME> and its SRC attribute to reference a Web page.

Putting all this together, the complete frameset file would look like this:

```
<HTML>
<HEAD>
<TITLE>
Frameset File
</TITLE>
</HEAD>
```

(continued)

(continued)

```
<FRAMESET COLS="30,75%,*">
      <FRAME SRC="left.htm">
      <FRAME SRC="center.htm">
<FRAME SRC="right.htm">
</FRAMESET>
</HTML>
```

Framesets can also be nested into other framesets. This gives you the ability to combine columns and rows of frames. To create a common frame design displaying a heading across the top of the screen, a table of contents on the left below the heading, and content filling the rest of the screen, the frameset file could look like this. Figure 13-6 shows how this is rendered in a browser.

```
<HTML>
<HEAD>
<TITLE>
Frameset File
</TITLE>
</HEAD>
<FRAMESET ROWS="75,*">
      <FRAME SRC="heading.htm">
<FRAMESET COLS="100,*">
            <FRAME SRC="index.htm">
      <FRAME SRC="content.htm"
</FRAMESET>
</FRAMESET>
</HTML>
```

A <FRAME> tag or another <FRAMESET> tag must exist for each frame defined in a frameset. By default, frames are sizable and display scroll bars if the page inside the frame is larger than the frame itself. The SCROLLING and NORESIZE attributes let you customize this behavior and are used like this:

```
<FRAME SRC="index.htm" SCROLLING="NO" NORESIZE>
```

Another important attribute of the <FRAME> tag is NAME. The NAME attribute lets you uniquely identify each frame. When used with the anchor tag's TARGET attribute, you can control which Web page is loaded into each frame in the frameset when a hyperlink is clicked. The frameset looks like this:

```
<FRAMESET COLS="100,*">
      <FRAME SRC="index.htm">
      <FRAME SRC="content.htm" NAME="main_content">
</FRAMESET>
```

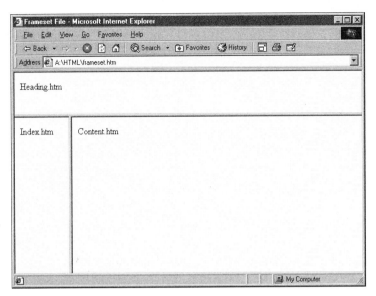

Figure 13-6. *A frameset example.*

An anchor tag in index.htm that updates the main_content frame with the content2.htm page looks like this:

```
<A HREF="content2.htm" TARGET="main_content">Page 2 </A>
```

To clear the current frameset and load the entire browser window with a different Web page, use the reserved HTML name "_top" like this: TARGET="_top".

Another type of frame, the inline frame, can be added directly to a page using the inline frame tags <IFRAME></IFRAME>. Inline frames are used to insert one Web page into a defined block of space in another page. The inline frame tag's attributes, SRC, HEIGHT, WIDTH, SCROLLING, and FRAMEBORDER, provide additional control over formatting and placement. Originally a proprietary tag of Microsoft's Internet Explorer, the inline frame is now part of the HTML 4.0 standard. However, as of its Navigator 4.3 browser, Netscape still does not support the <IFRAME> tag.

GRAPHICS

Graphics are an essential contributor to the success of the Web. While content is valuable, the Web's graphical interface interests people the most. From corporate logos to product photos and even images of text, many Web pages contain more graphics than anything else. While you won't learn how to become a graphic artist by reading this introduction, you will find out how to effectively work with images in your Web pages.

Sources of Images

From a quick search on the Web, you'll find many sites offering individual graphics files for sale or for free. You can also find catalogs of photography and clip art for sale on the Web or at your favorite software retailer. A large number of images come from scanned photos and, increasingly, digital cameras. If you're artistically inclined (you know who you are), you can use any of several popular image creation programs to create your own images. Making your own images by modifying selections from a purchased catalog is the best choice and will save you time and money. Personalizing these images will help ensure your graphics are relevant to your page's message and ensure that your page doesn't look like those created by everyone else who bought the same image catalog.

GIF or JPEG

The two dominant image file formats on the Web are the CompuServe Graphics Interchange Format (GIF) and the Joint Photographic Experts Group (JPEG) format. How do you decide when to use one file format over the other? Here's the general rule: for displaying high-quality photographs, images with many colors, or images with few blocks of repeating colors, use JPEG. Unlike GIF, JPEG isn't limited to 256 maximum colors. GIF's compressed format and limited color support are better for images with few colors or with repeated blocks of colors. Using the GIF format results in a smaller file for most images, which minimizes file transfer time over the Web.

One other feature of the GIF format is its support for transparent backgrounds. Transparent backgrounds let the background color of the Web page show through the image, allowing the image to visually integrate better with the page. If this is something your images need, you'll have to use the GIF format.

Colors vs. Size

There is a direct relationship between the amount of color information (number of colors) in an image and the size of the image file. There is also a relationship between the number of pixels in an image and the size of the image file. The goal is to produce the highest quality image and the smallest file size so your graphics will look good *and* download fast. You'll need to weigh the tradeoffs between whether those viewing your page should wait longer for a high-quality image to download or view lower quality images that download faster. Knowing your potential audience will influence your decision. Generally, users prefer speed over quality.

The Browser-Safe Color Palette

Though it's true that almost all new computers are capable of displaying millions of colors, the lowest common denominator for Web users is still a 256-color palette. Forty of these colors do not display consistently across different platforms. This leaves 216 browser-safe colors for you to create your graphics with if you want all browsers and platforms to properly display your images using the same colors you used to create them. The more colors over the 216 browser-safe colors you use to create your images, the more likely *dithering* will occur. Dithering happens when a color you used to create your image doesn't exist on the browser's platform. The browser tries to create the missing color by alternating pixels of available colors that are close to the missing one. The result of dithering is often less than desirable. Most good imaging programs have recognized this problem and will allow you to save your images using a 216 browser-safe color palette.

> NOTE   To find out more about the 216 browser-safe color palette, go to Lynda Weinman's Web site at *www.lynda.com/hex.html*.

Adding Images to Web Pages

To add the images you've created to your page, use the image tag <IMG> and its SRC attribute.

For example, to insert /images/product02.gif into your page, enter the following HTML code:

```
<IMG SRC="/images/product02.gif">
```

It's that simple. To make the image a hyperlink, the image tag can also be enclosed in other HTML tags such as the anchor tag, like this:

```
<A HREF="home.htm"><IMG SRC="home.gif"></A>
```

When the image is clicked, the browser will jump to the home.htm Web page.

Images can also be aligned with surrounding text using the <IMG> tag's ALIGN attribute. Three attributes you should use with your images are HEIGHT, WIDTH, and ALT. HEIGHT and WIDTH tell the browser how much space (in pixels) to allocate on the page for the image. When the browser parses the page, it reserves space for the image before downloading the actual image. Specifying HEIGHT and WIDTH saves the browser from having to repaint the page as each image is downloaded and its size is determined. By using these two attributes, your pages will load faster. The third attribute, ALT, is used for specifying the image's alternate text. This text will display instead of the image in one of two cases: before the image is fully downloaded or when the user configures his or her browser not to download images. This is a great way to make the page "perform" better because users can know what images are for and click on them before they appear.

Here's what an image tag using all three attributes looks like:

```
<IMG SRC="/images/newprd.gif" HEIGHT=75 WIDTH=150 ALT="Our latest
release">
```

Adding Background Images

To add an image to the background of your page, use the BACKGROUND attribute of the <BODY> tag. Again, just specify where the image is located using the same HTML syntax as an anchor tag's HREF attribute. For example:

```
<BODY BACKGROUND="/images/backdrop.gif">
```

The image is repeatedly tiled until it covers the entire page. An Internet Explorer-specific <BODY> tag attribute you can use is BGPROPERTIES. Setting BGPROPERTIES to "fixed" creates a *watermark*. A watermark is a background image that remains stationary even while the page's content is scrolling. The HTML looks like this:

```
<BODY BACKGROUND="/images/backdrop.gif" BGPROPERTIES="fixed">
```

However, when Netscape browsers see this attribute, they ignore it. It's a good idea to keep your background images small and let the browser do the work of tiling rather than make the network transfer an image file the size of a whole page. Keep your backgrounds simple and make sure your images don't distract from the page's content or message. Also, make sure that they don't leave the page illegible by blending in with the page's content.

IMAGE MAPS

Image maps are a technique of separating an image into specific areas or regions that then become individual hyperlinks. Each area, which is determined by a series of X and Y coordinates, can be one of several shapes like circles, squares, or polygons. Most commonly used for menus and indexes, image maps can be effective alternatives for text-based hyperlinks when used for Web site navigation. They are also an alternative to using multiple images each with their own hyperlink.

Creating Image Maps

The easiest way to figure out the coordinates for each area is with an image map editor. A good tool for this is a shareware program called Map This! (pictured in Figure 13-7), which you can find at *www.5star-shareware.com*. With Map This! you can create both client-side and server-side image maps by opening an image file (GIF or JPEG), outlining each area that will become a hyperlink, and then typing in the target URL the browser will go to when the area is clicked. Select the map type, client or server, when you save the map file. Map This! creates all the HTML needed. The Map This! help system provides instructions on adding the image maps you create to your pages.

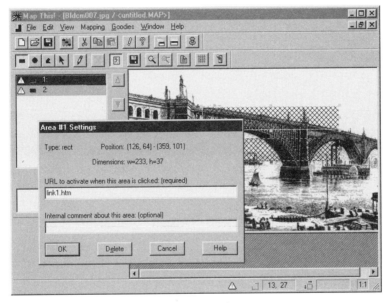

Figure 13-7. *The Map This! image map editor.*

Client-Side Image Maps

If you use Map This! and create a client-side map, the resulting HTML has an <AREA> tag for each area you marked on the image. Each <AREA> tag has SHAPE, COORDS, and HREF attributes already populated for you. All the <AREA> tags are surrounded by <MAP></MAP> tags. Notice that the <MAP> tag has a NAME attribute. The NAME attribute identifies the map so you can associate an image with it. This association is made by using the USEMAP attribute in the image tag. For example, suppose that the map tags generated by Map This! look like this:

```
<MAP NAME="clientmap1">
<AREA SHAPE=RECT COORDS="36,65,315,106" HREF="link1.htm">
<AREA SHAPE=RECT COORDS="36,122,315,164" HREF="link2.htm">
<AREA SHAPE=default HREF="home.htm">
</MAP>
```

You would then add an image tag just after the map that looked like this:

```
<IMG SRC="imagemap.gif" USEMAP="#clientmap1">
```

All of these image map tags go within the body of your page. Though working with image maps may seem complicated, using an image map editor makes it easy.

Server-Side Image Maps

Server-side maps require a separate .map file. This .map file resides on the Web server and holds all the image coordinate and hyperlink information. Place an anchor tag in your page to point to this .map file. Then, within that anchor tag, place an image tag specifying the image file that is mapped. The image tag also uses the ISMAP attribute. This attribute tells the browser to send the mouse coordinates to the server when hyperlinking to the .map file. The Web server uses these coordinates while checking the .map file to see if the X and Y coordinates are within any of the defined areas of the image. If they are, the server sends the URL associated with the image area back to the browser.

If you created a server-side map file, the anchor and image tags to reference it from your pages might look something like this:

```
<A HREF="serverimagemap.map"><IMG SRC="imagemap.gif" ISMAP></A>
```

Weighing the Options

Server-side image maps were the only option available before browsers supported client-side image maps. Image maps are predominantly client-side now, because they have a couple of notable advantages. First, client-side maps give users a visible indication, on the browser's status bar, that the area their mouse is over is a hyperlink. This makes for a more intuitive and less frustrating user experience. Server-side maps can't provide this, because hyperlinked areas of the image aren't known by the browser until it sends a request to the server.

The main difference between the two image map techniques lies in resource consumption of both the server and the network. Server-side maps consume considerably more resources because both a network round-trip and a server response are required every time the image in the browser is clicked. This is true whether a hyperlink is clicked or not. This resource consumption may be acceptable for a small number of users or for an intranet, but it will not scale well and will result in a less responsive Web site.

GIF ANIMATION

GIF animations, such as ad banners found on most commercial Web sites, have become standard Web page content. GIF animations are popular for several reasons: they effectively capture attention, are a major source of Internet revenue when used as banners, and don't require a lot of multimedia skill or technology to create. However, as with all user interface technologies, it's helpful to have an artistic background and design skills.

A *GIF animation* is a .gif file containing more than one image. It also contains some instructions about how the browser should display those images. The images are arranged in a progression just like the individual frames of a movie. If the objects in each image are repositioned slightly relative to those in the previous image, the illusion of motion is achieved when those images are displayed in succession.

To add animated GIF files to your pages, do exactly the same thing you did to add a single GIF image. Just use the <IMG> tag, and the browser will take care of the rest.

> NOTE If a browser doesn't support GIF animation, only the first image within the GIF file is displayed.

Creating Animations

Once you've created all the individual images you want to include in your animation, you'll need to package them into one file. One of the simplest tools to use to create animated GIFs is Microsoft's GIF Animator, shown in Figure 13-8. You'll find it included with Image Composer, which is part of Microsoft FrontPage. To create your animation, just add all the individual images you want to include in the order you want them displayed. You can then adjust settings such as how long each image is displayed and how many times you want the animation to loop or repeat. To test what you've done before saving your animation, click the Run button.

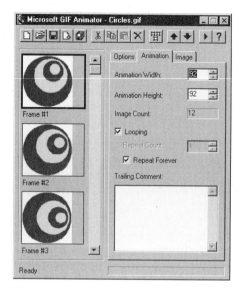

Figure 13-8. *Microsoft's GIF Animator.*

NOTE   Use caution when saving your animation because GIF Animator will, by default, use the filename of the last image you added to the series as the name for the resulting animation file, overwriting your last individual image file.

The GIF Animator is also a useful tool for learning from other animations. If you find an animation you like, open it with the GIF Animator to see how it was constructed.

GIF Animation Best Practices

- **Keep them small.** A typical standard for an animated image file is 50 K or less. Keep the image dimensions and number of colors to a minimum to ensure both a quick download and browser support for your image's color palette. The smaller you keep each individual image, the more images you'll be able to add to your animation, giving you greater creative flexibility and a smoother display.

- **Keep them simple.** Avoid annoying people. Some banners are guilty of trying to act like TV commercials, squeezing so much information and imagery into the animation that viewers tune out.

- **Take a break.** Animations that continuously loop, starting over as soon as they finish, get old fast. Try adding a few seconds to the end of your animation before starting it again.

- **Consider not using them at all.** While it's true that the best animated GIFs can be effective, the vast majority is not. If your animations are too big or poorly designed, they are likely to be ignored. If this is the case, it might be better to find other ways to get your message out.

ADDING MULTIMEDIA

Depending on your requirements, you might find that you need more than text and images on your Web pages. For example, adding sound samples to your CD music store may be a powerful sales tool. Or you might need to share product testing videos with partnering companies during R&D processes. This is easy enough to do, provided both the Web server and the browser know what to do when dealing with these types of files.

MIME and Content Types

MIME (Multipurpose Internet Mail Extensions) is a standard that indicates the content type and character sets encoded in each of many different types of files, including text, HTML, sound, and video. In the Web world, these MIME types are referred to using the term *content types* because they describe the content of files sent from the server to the browser.

When a browser tries to open a file on its local disk drive, it uses the file's extension to determine whether it can open and read the file or whether it needs help from another local application to work with that file. When browsers receive a file from a Web server, however, they don't always know the file extension. This is because the server often doesn't return a filename at all; it might instead return a stream of data. To make sure the browser knows what it's receiving, the Web server includes content type information as part of the data it returns to the browser. The browser uses this information to determine what type of data is being returned and then acts accordingly.

Content type information typically looks something like text/html or video/mpeg. Servers know what content types to send, and browsers know what content types they're receiving because each server maintains a content type map. These maps are basically lists of content types, their associated file extensions, an application that can handle that type of content when detected, and what action that application will take on the content. Both server and browser maps can be modified as new applications, and content types are created.

Embedding Multimedia Files

Use the object tags <OBJECT></OBJECT> to embed multimedia files directly into your pages. The object tag's DATA attribute specifies the URL of the multimedia file. The TYPE attribute determines the file's content type. The HEIGHT and WIDTH attributes are useful particularly for sizing video and images. Thus, HTML for an .avi file might look like this:

```
<OBJECT DATA="product01.avi" TYPE="video/msvideo" HEIGHT=100
WIDTH=100>
</OBJECT>
```

Linking to Multimedia Files

Linking to multimedia files is done by using the anchor tag discussed earlier. The value of the HREF attribute specifies the location, as a URL, of the multimedia file to retrieve when the hyperlink is clicked. For example, to play a .wav audio file stored in a sound subdirectory, the link would look like this:

```
<A HREF="/sound/newrelease1999.wav">Hear our latest release</A>.
```

DATA COLLECTION WITH HTML FORMS

Until now, this chapter has discussed only the one-way flow of information—from Web server to browser. But what if you want to send information from the browser to the server? While there are several ways of accomplishing this, such as developing and distributing a client application, HTML forms have several significant advantages. HTML forms can be written once and used on many different platforms. There is also no software distribution necessary, and all application maintenance is centralized at the Web server. On a typical retail Web site, you might want to collect order details, customer demographic survey data, or help desk problem information. HTML provides a form element and a number of input elements for collecting user responses. When the form is submitted by the user, all input element names and values within that form are collected and sent to a program or script on the server for appropriate processing.

Form Tags and Attributes

To set up a form, use the <FORM></FORM> tags. The form tag's ACTION and METHOD attributes complete a form declaration. The ACTION attribute is used to specify a program or script, in URL format, on the server that will process the data. For example:

```
<FORM ACTION="HTTP://www.yoursite.com/order.asp">
 </FORM>
```

Of course, you'll also need to specify what controls to show on the form via form element tags that appear between the FORM tags, but we'll explain that shortly. For now, we'll leave the space between the tags blank.

A Web page can contain multiple forms. However, a form cannot be nested within another form. HTML to declare multiple forms looks like this:

```
<FORM ACTION="HTTP://www.yoursite.com/order1.asp">
 </FORM>
<FORM ACTION="HTTP://www.yoursite.com/order2.asp">
 </FORM>
```

An example of form declaration that does *not* work looks like this:

```
<FORM ACTION="HTTP://www.yoursite.com/order1.asp">
<FORM ACTION="HTTP://www.yoursite.com/order2.asp">
</FORM>
</FORM>
```

The METHOD attribute is used to specify how the data is sent to the server. Its two possible values are GET and POST. GET appends the form's data to the URL specified in the ACTION attribute. POST, on the other hand, sends the input element information to the URL specified in the ACTION attribute as part of the HTTP request. Adding the METHOD attribute to the FORM tag would look like this:

```
<FORM ACTION="HTTP://www.yoursite.com/order.asp" METHOD="POST">
 </FORM>
```

Get vs. Post

The POST method is generally considered more robust for a couple of reasons. First, because POST doesn't append the form data to the URL, a hacker can't find out what data is being sent just by intercepting the URL. Second, Web servers don't have a limit on the amount of data they can receive with a POST as they do with a GET method. Though the actual limitation varies from Web server to Web server, if your forms have a lot of data to transmit, the GET method could lose some of that data.

Form Elements

Once the form is defined, you'll need to add some input elements to the form to allow your page to collect data from the user. The most commonly used tag for this is the <INPUT> tag. You can create several types of input elements by using the <INPUT>tag's TYPE attribute, including text boxes, buttons, passwords, and hidden fields. Each of these elements has additional attributes that are specific to it. For example, the HTML for a form containing input elements for a username, a password, a check box for first-time visitors, and a submit button could look like this. Figure 13-9 shows how this is rendered in a browser.

```
<H2>Please Login</H2>
<FORM ACTION="HTTP://www.yoursite.com/order.asp" METHOD="POST">
Username: <INPUT TYPE="TEXT" NAME="User" SIZE=40 MAXLENGTH=40>
<BR><BR>
Password: <INPUT TYPE="PASSWORD" NAME="Pwd" SIZE=8 MAXLENGTH=8>
<BR><BR>
Please check here if this is your first visit to our site:
<INPUT TYPE="CHECKBOX" NAME="FirstTime">
<BR><BR>
<INPUT TYPE="SUBMIT">
</FORM>
```

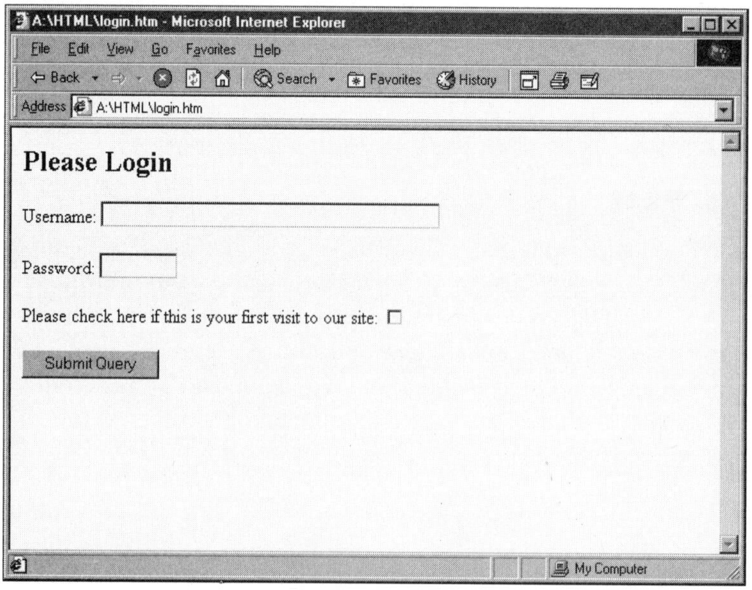

Figure 13-9. *An HTML Login form.*

Notice that the last input element in the form has its TYPE attribute set to "SUBMIT", which creates the Submit button seen in the browser. When clicked, this button does one thing: it sends the name and value of every input element between the form tags to the URL specified in the form tag's ACTION attribute. In this example, the data entered is sent to the order.asp script on the server.

NOTE If you place input elements on a page without form tags, Netscape browsers will ignore them and will not display them.

Other useful input elements include list boxes and text areas. List boxes are created with the <SELECT></SELECT> and <OPTION></OPTION> tags and their attributes. For example, a list box that makes four choices visible at once, allows multiple selection, and has the second choice set as the default selection looks like this. Figure 13-10 shows how this is rendered in a browser.

```
<SELECT NAME="CHOICELIST" SIZE=4 MULTIPLE>
  <OPTION>1st Choice</OPTION>
  <OPTION SELECTED>2nd Choice</OPTION>
  <OPTION>3rd Choice</OPTION>
  <OPTION>4th Choice</OPTION>
  <OPTION>5th Choice</OPTION>
  <OPTION>6th Choice</OPTION>
</SELECT>
```

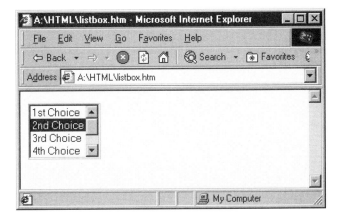

Figure 13-10. *A list box element.*

The text area element is used to collect multiple lines of information such as feedback or comments. By using the <TEXTAREA></TEXTAREA> tags with their NAME, COLS, and ROWS attributes, you can set up a text window for multi-lines data collection like this:

```
<TEXTAREA NAME="Feedback" ROWS=20 COLS=60>
  Enter your feedback here.
</TEXTAREA>
```

The FIELDSET and LEGEND elements aren't input elements, but they help organize input elements on your page. FIELDSET acts like a frame in the Windows environment by simply drawing a box around other input elements to visually group them. LEGEND adds a title to the FIELDSET. All input elements within the FIELDSET tags are placed inside the box. Unfortunately, the width of the FIELDSET covers the width of the screen. The HTML looks like this, and Figure 13-11 shows how it is rendered in a browser.

```
<FIELDSET>
  <LEGEND>Login Information</LEGEND>
Username: <INPUT TYPE="TEXT" NAME="User" SIZE=40 MAXLENGTH=40>
<BR>
Password: <INPUT TYPE="PASSWORD" NAME="Pwd" SIZE=8 MAXLENGTH=8>
</FIELDSET>
```

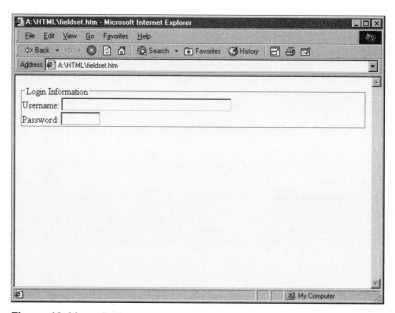

Figure 13-11. *A fieldset example.*

TOOLS FOR BUILDING WEB PAGES

Before HTML editors were available, it was common to use any text-based editor around, like Microsoft Notepad, and type in every tag. This approach was time consuming and prone to errors. Since then, many good editors have been developed for creating Web pages. Some claim to be WYSIWYG (What You See Is What You Get) and build pages entirely by drag-and-drop, insulating you from the HTML itself. If you use this approach, you'll inevitably need to do something to your page that the editor doesn't support or know how to do. Recognizing these two options, the best combination is an efficient editor and a thorough understanding of the underlying HTML it creates.

Some of the more popular editors include HotMetal (*www.softquad.com*), HomeSite (*www.allaire.com*), and PageMill (*www.adobe.com*). Microsoft FrontPage (pictured in Figure 13-12), another good choice, comes complete with graphics, wizards, templates, WYSIWYG support, and a Web server to get you started. A scaled-down version of FrontPage, called FrontPage Express, is included in the full installation of Internet Explorer. Chances are good that you already have an HTML editor on your computer. If you use Microsoft Office, you can use the Save As HTML option (Located on the File menu) of most Office applications to create Web pages from Office files.

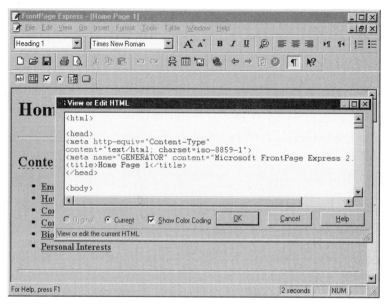

Figure 13-12. *Microsoft FrontPage.*

Microsoft's most sophisticated Web site development tool is Visual InterDev (pictured in Figure 13-13). Though Visual InterDev is designed for advanced Web site developers who create sites that contain much more than HTML, it's editor is well-suited for HTML development.

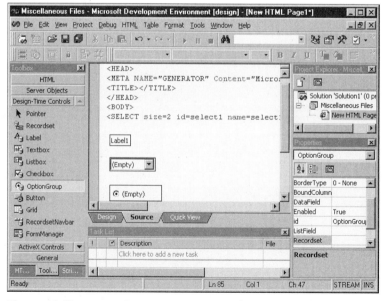

Figure 13-13. *Microsoft Visual InterDev.*

CHAPTER EXAMPLE: MEMBERSHIP REGISTRATION FORM

A popular page many Web sites include collects contact and demographic information from users. Requiring this information before granting users access to valuable content or before allowing a file to be downloaded is common practice and ensures that you get something of value in exchange for your content. The membership registration form applies many of the HTML features discussed throughout this chapter and can be found on the companion CD in the \Chapter 13\ directory. Table 13-2 provides a list of files, descriptions, and HTML features included in the membership registration form example, and Figure 13-14 shows the sample application in action.

> NOTE This example collects all the input element names and values within the HTML form and sends them to the program or script specified in the form tag's ACTION attribute. An actual script or program for handling the data on the Web server is beyond the scope of this example and is not included. For more information on server-side scripts, please refer to Chapter 7.

Table 13-2

CHAPTER EXAMPLE FILE LIST

File Name	Description	Features
Chapter13_example.htm	Frameset file defining a borderless frameset containing two frames. The first frame has scrolling and resizing turned off.	Tags: <FRAMESET>, <FRAME> Attributes: ROWS, BORDER, SRC, SCROLLING, NORESIZE
heading.htm	Web page that is placed in the top frame. It contains an animated GIF banner that's a hyperlink, and text. The page's colors are adjusted by both body tag and font tag attributes.	Tags: <BODY>, <DIV>, <A>, <IMG>, <FONT>, <H3>, <P> Attributes: BGCOLOR, TEXT, LINK, ALIGN, HREF, TARGET, ALT, HEIGHT, WIDTH, FACE, SIZE, COLOR
Registration.htm	Web page containing the HTML form and its input elements. The last element has a type of "submit". This creates a Submit button. When the Submit button is clicked, all input element names and values within the form are collected and sent to the program or script specified in the form tag's ACTION attribute.	Tags: <!— —>, <FORM>, <TABLE>, <CAPTION>, <TR>, <TD>, <B>, <HR>, <INPUT>, <SELECT>, <OPTION>, <TEXTAREA> Attributes: ACTION, METHOD, TYPE, NAME, LENGTH, SIZE, COLSPAN, VALUE, ROWS, COLS, VALIGN, CHECKED
Banner_ani.gif	Animated GIF advertising banner.	

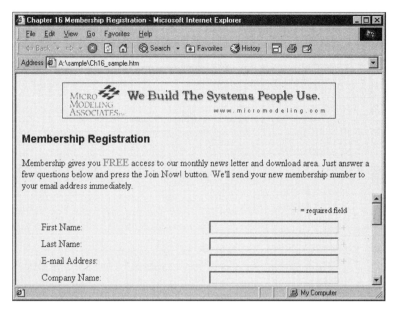

Figure 13-14. *Chapter example: Membership registration form.*

DESIGN CONSIDERATIONS

While it's helpful to have the technical ability to master the HTML syntax, a strategic plan and site design skills are critical. Most companies' first attempts at creating their Web sites are driven by the need to simply have a presence on the Web. These first-generation Web sites usually lack functionality, an understanding of who's using the site, how those users navigate the site, and what they might need or want once there. Identifying and analyzing a target market, and then designing Web-based services (features and functionality) that cater to those users will prove more effective.

Several issues are often overlooked and should be considered before you start building your site:

■ **Know your site.** What exactly is this site for? What value will it offer its users?

■ **Know your visitors.** Are they internal, external, people between 18 and 23, or first-time car buyers? Are they experienced with computers? Don't forget who they are and what they need or want.

■ **Keep it simple.** Use lots of space. Content should be easy on the eyes. Don't frustrate viewers with excessive clutter. Content should be straightforward and easily understood, not esoteric.

- **Visually partition your content.** Separate your page or frameset into distinct areas of logically related information.

- **Avoid using too many images.** Only use an image if it adds to or enhances your message.

- **Keep images small.** Users will usually trade speed for graphics.

- **Use colors and font types sparingly.** Many computers still don't support anything more than the bare minimum.

- **Follow standards.** Avoid using multiple terms that mean the same thing. Is it your home page or storefront? Today's balance or Current balance? Use the same graphics, toolbars, headings, colors, fonts, and navigation throughout your site.

- **Include a help page or pages.** Explaining site- or business-specific terms, supplying contact information, or providing a Frequently Asked Questions (FAQ) section improves site value and reduces your company's human effort and expense for these tasks.

- **Provide feedback and contact information.** For problems with the site, and for your potential clients to contact you! Interaction builds relationships!

BROWSER COMPATIBILITY

This chapter has noted some differences in the way browsers parse, interpret, and display Web pages. In addition, many browsers support proprietary tags that are not part of the HTML standard. Before deciding to take advantage of the latest proposed or proprietary features, you should ask some questions:

- **Who is my target audience?** If you're developing for a fixed audience like your company's intranet, you likely know what kind of browsers and platforms are viewing your pages. You can then take full advantage of features those browsers support. If you're creating a public site available to anyone with a browser, stick to the basic HTML standard. You'll reduce your support efforts and your user's frustration level.

- **Which browsers support the features I want to use?** It's common for the major browsers to support generally accepted tags that are not standard HTML. The <EMBED></EMBED> tags are good examples of this. Make sure your target browsers support the tags you're considering.

■ **Is it likely these features will become part of the HTML standard in the future?** Even before it's official, there's a good indication of what will be included in the next version of the HTML standard. You won't want to rewrite your entire site because tags you originally used were never adopted.

SUMMARY

Because HTML is still the fundamental language of the Web and because the HTML standard continues to evolve, you can expect it to be around for some time. You'll need to know what HTML can and cannot do, and when it's time to use another technology. While many of HTML's core features were discussed here, you'll need to look further for a complete understanding of the language.

WHERE TO GO NEXT

Though we've covered quite a bit, this is by no means a definitive HTML resource. Your next step is your favorite book store or search engine. A quick search on the Web will produce dozens of HTML references and tutorials. You'll also find the following Web sites useful:

■ **www.w3c.com.** The W3C is the authority for past, current, and proposed HTML standards. Their site also includes information on several other standards governed by the W3C, like cascading style sheets (CSS) and extensible markup language (XML).

■ **www.microsoft.com/sitebuilder.** This site is a complete resource for everything from the latest Web-related news and technical articles to free tutorials and software downloads. For access to some areas of the site, you'll need to complete the free registration.

■ **www.netscape.com.** This site is another good site for answers to HTML questions.

■ **www.download.com.** This site is part of the C|Net Web site. Check here for downloadable tools and utilities.

■ **www.zdnet.com.** This site, from computer magazine publisher Ziff Davis, contains industry news, product evaluations, technical articles, and downloads.

- **www.webreference.com.** This site covers it all, including HTML.

- **www.hotwired.com/webmonkey.** Just one more site full of informative HTML tutorials and examples.

- **www.lynda.com.** The site of author and Web design expert, Lynda Weinman, tells you all about color, graphics, and Web page design.

CHAPTER TAG SUMMARY

Tag	Use	Support by Internet Explorer and Netscape Navigator
<HTML></HTML>	Delimits an HTML document	All
<HEAD></HEAD>	Contains meta-data, script, and title information	All
<TITLE></TITLE>	Defines a document title	All
<BODY></BODY>	Defines Web page content	All
<!-- -->	Defines comments	All
<P></P>	Defines a paragraph	All
 	Defines a line break	All
<B></B>	Defines bold text	All
<I></I>	Defines italicized text	All
<H1></H1> through <H6></H6>	Defines headings 1 through 6	All
<HR>	Defines a horizontal rule	All
<UL></UL>	Defines an unordered (bulleted) list	All
<OL></OL>	Defines an ordered (numbered) list	All
<LI>	Defines a list item	All
<DL></DL>	Defines a definition list	All
<DT>	Defines a definition list term	All
<DD>	Defines a definition list description	All
<FONT></FONT>	Modifies font color, size, and typeface	NS 2+, IE 2+
<DIV></DIV>	Aligns sections of content	All
<A></A>	Defines a hyperlink	All

Tag	Use	Support by Internet Explorer and Netscape Navigator
<TABLE></TABLE>	Defines a table	NS 3+, IE 3+
<CAPTION></CAPTION>	Defines a caption for a table	NS 3+, IE 3+
<TR></TR>	Defines a table row	NS 2+, IE 2+
<TH></TH>	Defines a table header cell	NS 2+, IE 2+
<TD></TD>	Defines a table cell	NS 2+, IE 2+
<THEAD><TFOOT> <TBODY>	Defines table row grouping	NS 3+, IE 3+
<COLGROUP></ COLGROUP><COL>	Defines table column grouping	NS 3+, IE 3+
<FRAMESET> </FRAMESET>	Defines a group of frames	NS 2+, IE 3+
<FRAME>	Defines each frame	NS 2+, IE 3+
<IFRAME></IFRAME>	Defines an inline frame	IE 3+
<IMG>	Defines an image	All
<MAP></MAP>	Defines a client-side image map	All
<AREA>	Defines a hyperlink within a map	All
<OBJECT></OBJECT>	Defines an object	NS 3+, IE 2+
<FORM></FORM>	Defines a form containing input elements	All
<INPUT>	Defines input elements for collecting user entry	All
<SELECT></SELECT>	Defines a user input list box	All
<OPTION></OPTION>	Defines individual list box items	All
<TEXTAREA>	Defines a multi-lined text box </TEXTAREA>	NS 2+, IE 3+
<FIELDSET> </FIELDSET>	Defines a box around related elements	IE 3+
<LEGEND></LEGEND>	Defines a caption for a fieldset	IE 3+

Chapter 14

Cascading Style Sheets, Client-Side Scripting, and Dynamic HTML

by Steve Gilmore

Though the current HTML standard is a dramatic improvement over its early beginnings, HTML itself still lacks features for advanced formatting, logic, and user event handling. This chapter discusses three technologies designed to address each of these issues: Cascading Style Sheets (CSS), client-side scripting, and Dynamic HTML (DHTML).

CASCADING STYLE SHEETS

Cascading Style Sheets (CSS) are a standard way to format Web pages, extending HTML functionality. A standard maintained by the World Wide Web Consortium (W3C), CSS provides over 70 style properties for color, fonts, spacing, positioning, and margins that can be applied to HTML tags. The term *Cascading* refers to the fact that multiple styles can be applied to a single HTML page or a single HTML element within that page. When multiple styles are applied to the same HTML element, CSS-compliant browsers decide which style has precedence based on the cascading rules defined in the CSS standard. CSS is supported by Internet Explorer 3.x and later and Netscape Navigator 4.x and later. Browsers that don't support CSS interpret only the page's HTML, ignoring all CSS code entirely.

> **NOTE**   Cascading Style Sheets Level 1 (CSS1) is the current standard and, like the HTML standard, is maintained by the World Wide Web Consortium (W3C). Throughout this chapter, CSS1 will be referred to as CSS for simplicity. To find out more about the World Wide Web Consortium and the CSS standard, go to W3C's Web site at *http://www.w3c.org*.

Why use CSS? The level of formatting and layout control available with CSS is substantially greater than with HTML alone. Previously, HTML page developers often created images with graphics programs that contained formatted text and space to get a look and formatting that HTML didn't support. While somewhat effective, these image files increased the download time of such HTML pages, were more difficult than HTML to maintain and update, and added to the complexity of the Web site. By applying CSS to your HTML page's content, you can create many effects from shadows to absolute positioning without the need for image files. The result is smaller HTML pages that download faster. You'll also have fewer files to maintain, and you'll be less dependent on artists to create your graphics.

Another advantage of CSS is that it allows you to have a single style declaration apply to many HTML elements on a page. For example, let's say you had three sets of paragraph tags (<P></P>) on your page and wanted the text contained in each of them to be red. With HTML, you need to put font tags with the color attribute (<FONT COLOR="#ff0000"></FONT>) inside all three sets of paragraph tags. This approach is error prone and difficult to maintain. With CSS, you declare a style for the paragraph tag once, and then the browser automatically applies that style to all paragraph tags in your HTML page, reducing errors and easing maintenance.

Adding CSS to Your Web Pages

With CSS, styles are added to an HTML page by first declaring the styles and then adding those styles to the HTML elements you want them to affect. The three ways to include styles in your HTML pages are inline, embedded, and linked. Any combination of these three can be used in a single HTML page. If more than one style affects an HTML element, the style that takes precedence is determined by the cascading priority rules of CSS. Inline has top priority, then embedded, followed by linked. Let's take a closer look at each.

Inline styles

To add an inline style, you use the STYLE attribute with the HTML element you want the style to affect. Only the specific element that contains the STYLE attribute is affected. The value for the STYLE attribute is one or more CSS property:value pairs separated by semicolons. For example, specifying a paragraph that has a one-half inch left margin and text 14 points in size looks like this:

```
<P STYLE="margin-left:0.5in; font-size:14pt">
Only content within these paragraph tags is affected by this inline
style.
</P>
```

Inline styles can be useful when you need to modify a specific HTML element. However, inline styles are no easier to maintain than HTML because they are located throughout the page like individual HTML tags. They defeat one of the main purposes of CSS, which is to be able to create one style and consistently apply it to many HTML elements. To accomplish this, CSS offers embedded styles.

Embedded styles

Embedded styles are useful when you need to apply a style to many HTML elements in a page. Because they reside only at the top of an HTML page, embedded styles are easier to maintain than inline styles. To add an embedded style, use the style tags <STYLE></STYLE>. The style tags are placed between the <HEAD></HEAD> tags like this:

```
<HTML>
<HEAD>
<STYLE>
</STYLE>
</HEAD>
<BODY>
</BODY>
</HTML>
```

Within the style tags, define styles using property:value pairs for the various HTML elements you want to affect. The syntax for creating styles looks like this:

```
selector { property:value }
```

A selector is the HTML tag you want the style to affect. A property is placed between curly brackets and followed by a colon and its value. For example, changing the preceding inline example to an embedded style looks like this:

```
<HEAD>
<STYLE>
<!--
P {margin-left:0.5in; font-size:14pt}
-->
</STYLE>
</HEAD>
```

Notice that multiple property:value pairs are specified by separating them with a semicolon, just like the previous inline styles. You can also specify multiple selectors by adding them inside the same style tags, like this:

```
<HEAD>
<STYLE>
<!--
H1 {color:#ff0000}
H2 {color:#ff0000}
H3 {color:#ff0000}
-->
</STYLE>
</HEAD>
```

This code sets the color of the heading tags H1, H2, and H3 to red everywhere they're used throughout the HTML page.

> **NOTE** The previous embedded style examples contain HTML comment tags <!-- -->. Your embedded style declarations should always include comment tags, because older browsers that don't support CSS and the style tag will ignore the style tag and display all your style rules as text in the browser.

The embedded style technique can be effective if the style applies to a single HTML page or a few pages. However, for large Web sites with tens, hundreds, or even thousands of pages, cutting and pasting embedded styles from page to page can create maintenance problems of its own. To address this situation, CSS offers linked styles.

Linked styles

Linked styles allow you to keep your style definition in a separate file and link to that file from your HTML pages. The maintenance advantage of linked styles is that you can make changes to one linked CSS file, and all Web pages that reference it will be updated automatically.

Converting the preceding embedded style example into a linked style sheet involves two steps:

1. Cut the <STYLE></STYLE> tags and everything between them from your HTML page and paste them into another file. Save the new file with a .css extension.

2.. Add a <LINK> tag between the <HEAD></HEAD> tags that references the linked style .css file. The link tag and its three necessary attributes could look like this:

```
<LINK REL="stylesheet" TYPE="text/css" HREF="linkedstyle.css">
```

The REL attribute specifies the relation of the linked file. In the case of linked style sheet files, The REL attribute's value is always "stylesheet." The TYPE attribute specifies the MIME type of the linked file and is always "text/css." The HREF attribute references the linked style sheet file you created earlier. Under IIS, none of these values is case sensitive.

Grouping Styles

Grouping styles allows you to simplify your style rules. With CSS, you can group both style selectors and style properties. For example, let's take the embedded style definition that contained multiple headings and convert it to a grouped style by separating the selectors with commas. Before grouping, the style definition looks like this:

```
<HEAD>
<STYLE>
<!--
H1 {color:#ff0000}
H2 {color:#ff0000}
H3 {color:#ff0000}
-->
</STYLE>
</HEAD>
```

Grouping the three heading tags looks like this:

```
<HEAD>
<STYLE>
<!--
H1, H2, H3 {color:#ff0000}
-->
</STYLE>
</HEAD>
```

Grouping style properties is the same concept, but the syntax is a little different. In this case, multiple properties are separated by a blank space. Before grouping properties, the definition looks like this:

```
<HEAD>
<STYLE>
<!--
P {font-family: arial; font-size: 10pt}
-->
</STYLE>
</HEAD>
```

Grouping the style properties looks like this:

```
<HEAD>
<STYLE>
<!--
P {font: arial 10pt}
-->
</STYLE>
</HEAD>
```

While grouping selectors is intuitive shorthand for defining styles, grouping properties often makes a style definition more difficult to read. This becomes increasingly true with the more properties contained in the style. Consider this maintenance issue when you define your coding standard for style sheets.

Using Style Classes

Style classes let you create multiple styles for a single HTML tag. This is a useful alternative to inline styles when you have a single tag you want to display using various styles. To include a class in your style definitions, add a period and a class name to the end of a selector like this:

```
selector.classname { property:value}
```

You can use any names you like for classes—the more descriptive the better. For example, let's say you're using a level 2 heading tag <H2> in three places on your page, each with a different color of text. Instead of adding inline styles to each tag to specify their individual colors, you could define an embedded style definition with three classes like this:

```
<HEAD>
<STYLE>
<!--
H2.color_red {color: red}
H2.color_blue {color: blue}
H2.color_yellow {color: yellow}
-->
</STYLE>
</HEAD>
```

Then you can reference these classes using the CLASS attribute within the <H2> tags, like this:

```
<BODY>
<H2 CLASS="color_red">This heading is red.</H2>
<H2 CLASS="color_blue">This heading is blue.</H2>
<H2 CLASS="color_yellow">This heading is yellow.</H2>
</BODY>
```

If you use the <H2> tag but don't include the CLASS attribute, no style will be applied. This is because there is no style defined specifically for the <H2> tag without a class.

However, you might find it useful to define a style for a tag without a class. The style will then apply to all instances of that tag whether they have a class or not. For example, let's say you still want the three <H2> tags to be different colors, but you want them all to be 16 points in size. Rather than add the same font-size property to each of the three previous <H2> style rules, just add one style rule defining the size for all <H2> tags, like this:

```
<HEAD>
<STYLE>
<!--
H2 {font-size: 16pt}
H2.color_red {color: red}
H2.color_blue {color: blue}
H2.color_yellow {color: yellow}
-->
</STYLE>
</HEAD>
```

The result is that all <H2> tags, regardless of whether they contain the class attribute, will be 16 points in size.

Using Style IDs

Style IDs are useful alternatives to inline styles when you have many tags you want to display with the same style throughout your Web page or pages. Style IDs let you create a single rule for any number of different HTML tags. To include an ID in your style definitions, prefix an ID name with a pound sign (#) like this:

```
#IDname {property:value}
```

For example, you can define a style rule that creates a border using an ID like this:

```
<HEAD>
<STYLE>
<!--
#border1 {border-width:1; border-style:solid}
-->
</STYLE>
</HEAD>
```

Then you can use this style rule on several different HTML tags like this:

```
<BODY>
<H3 id="border1"> This H3 has a border.</H3>
<H3> This H3 does not.</H3>
<H4 id="border1"> This H4 also has a border.</H4>
</BODY>
```

Using the <DIV> and <SPAN> Tags

Styles can be applied to almost all HTML elements, but styles are most often applied to two elements: DIV and SPAN. These two elements define blocks or sections of content. They don't actually change the content's appearance. This unique behavior makes DIV and SPAN very useful for extending HTML with CSS. For example, by creating a style rule for a <DIV> tag, you can apply a style to all the different tags and content contained within the <DIV> tag, without each of those individual elements needing their own style rule.

Let's say your style definition looked like this:

```
<HEAD>
<STYLE>
DIV.center {text-align:center}
</STYLE>
</HEAD>
```

You can then apply this style rule to all the different HTML elements contained inside the DIV tags like this:

```
<BODY>
<DIV class="center">
  <H1>This heading is centered</H1>
    <P>All of this content within the DIV tags is also centered.</P>
</DIV>
</BODY>
```

Useful CSS Properties

Now that you know how to work with style sheets in your Web pages, you can use Table 14-1, containing several commonly used style properties, to build your style rules.

Table 14-1

CASCADING STYLE SHEET
PROPERTIES REFERENCE

Property	*Description*	*Values*	*Example*
text-align	Justifies an HTML element	left, center, right, or justify	{text-align: center}
text-indent	Sets space before first sentence	inches (in), or width of the letter *m* (em)	{text-indent: 0.5in}
line-height	Sets the distance between text baselines	points (pt), inches (in) percentage of the parent object's height (%), or pixels (px)	{line-height: 18pt}
word-spacing	Sets space between words	Default spacing between ("normal"), or width of the letter *m* (em)	{word-spacing: 3em}

(continued)

Table 14-1 *(continued)*

Property	Description	Values	Example
letter-spacing	Sets space between letters	Default spacing ("normal"), or width of the letter *m* (em)	{letter-spacing: 2em}
font-family	Sets the font's typeface	The name of a specific font family or typeface	{font-family: Arial}
font-style	Sets the font style	normal, italic, or oblique	{font-style: italic}
font-size	Sets text size	pixels (px), points (pt), or inches (in)	{font-size: 14px}
display	Displays or hides content	Inline, block, list-item, or none	{display: none} color
color	Sets text color	HTML named colors, hexadecimals, or or RGB values	{color: red} or {color: #FF0000} {color: rgb(255,0,0)}
background-color	Sets background color of body or :rgb(255,0,0)}	HTML named colors hexadecimals, or RGB values	{color: red} or {color: #FF0000} or {color: rgb (255,0,0)}
background-image	Sets the back-ground image	Valid URL of an image file	{background-url(image.gif)}
background-attachment	Used with background-image to deter-mine whether background image scrolls with text or remains fixed scrolls with text or remains fixed	scroll or fixed	{background-image: url (image.gif); background-attachment: fixed}
margin-left, margin-top, margin-right, or margin-bottom	Sets distance from left, top, right, or bottom edge of page	points (pt), inches (in), or centimeters (cm)	{margin-left: 0.5in}
border-color	Sets color of all four sides of a border	HTML named colors, hexadecimals, or RGB values	{border-color: red}

Table 14-1 *(continued)*

Property	Description	Values	Example
border-style	Sets style of all four sides of a border	none, dotted, dashed, solid, double, groove, ridge, inset, or outset	{border-style: dashed}
border-left, border-top, border-right, or border-bottom	Sets style and color of left, top, right, or bottom border around an element	styles: none, dotted, dashed, solid, double, groove, ridge, inset, or outset color: HTML named colors, hexadecimals, or RGB values	{border-left: dashed red}

Positioning Elements

Web page designers have traditionally spent much of their time trying to control the layout of their Web pages. With HTML, support for element layout is limited to images, tables, frames, and some element's ALIGN attribute. CSS addresses this need for more sophisticated layout control with four properties for positioning elements on Web pages: Position, Top, Left, and Z-Index.

The Position property

The Position property is used to specify how an element is positioned on a Web page. It can have one of two values: relative or absolute. Relative means that the element will be positioned relative to the end of the previous element on the Web page. Absolute means that the element will be positioned absolute to the top-left corner of the element's parent, like a frame or the Web browser window itself.

The Top and Left properties

The Top and Left properties are used for specifying the distance between an element and its parent or another element. These properties specify, in pixels, how far down and to the right the element will be positioned from either the top-left corner of the parent (absolute positioning) or from the end of the previous element (relative positioning).

The Z-Index property

Using the Top and Left properties might cause elements to layer or stack on top of each other. The Z-Index property is used to control the order in which those elements are stacked. The higher the number, the closer to the front or top the element is positioned. A value of –1 means the element will be place behind the default text on the page. This is a useful setting for background images and designs.

Let's look at these properties working together in a positioning example. If you want to create an HTML level 2 heading that is white with a shadow on a blue background, you could declare a style definition that looks like this:

```
<HEAD>
<STYLE>
#white {color:white; position:absolute; top:10px; left:15px;
z-index:2}
#black {color:black; background-color:blue; position:absolute;
top:12px; left:17px; z-index:1}
</STYLE>
</HEAD>
```

Notice that the #white style rule has a Z-Index that is higher than the #black style rule. This will cause the content referencing the #white style rule to be placed in front of the #black style rule. In the body of your page, add references to the preceding styles that look like this:

```
<BODY>
<DIV ID="white">
<H2>Drop Shadow Heading 2</H2>
</DIV>
<DIV ID="black">
<H2>Drop Shadow Heading 2</H2>
</DIV>
</BODY>
</HTML>
```

This example is located on the companion CD in the \Chapter 14\ directory and looks like Figure 14-1 in Internet Explorer.

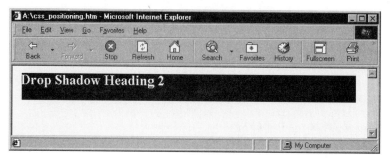

Figure 14-1. *CSS Positioning in Internet Explorer.*

CSS Example 2

This next Web page is also on the companion CD in the \Chapter 14\ directory and demonstrates how CSS can be used in place of graphics and images. The Web page has a graphical heading built with only text and style sheets. The style sheets make extensive use of absolute positioning and the Z-Index property. Figure 14-2 shows what this page looks like when rendered in a browser.

```
<HTML>
<HEAD>
<TITLE>CSS Example 2</TITLE>
<STYLE>
 P.arial {font-family:arial}
 #c1 {background-color:#777744; position:absolute;
      top:20px; left:30px; z-index:1}
 #c2 {background-color:#7777aa; position:absolute;
      top:35px; left:80px; z-index:2}
 #c3 {background-color:#7777ff; position:absolute;
      top:50px; left:180px; z-index:3}

 #css1 {color:#ffffff; font-size:96pt; position:absolute;
      top:20px; left:300px; z-index:6}
 #css2 {color:#000000; font-size:96pt; position:absolute;
      top:23px; left:303px; z-index:5}
 #css3 {color:#444444; font-size:96pt; position:absolute;
      top:26px; left:306px; z-index:4}
 #cs {color:#bb0000; font-size:24pt; letter-spacing:4;
position:absolute;
      top:84px; left:50px; z-index:7}
 #dh {color:#ff0000; font-size:16pt; letter-spacing:24;
position:absolute;
      top:110px; left:30px; z-index:8}
</STYLE>
</HEAD>

<BODY>
<DIV ID="css1">
<P class="arial">CSS</P>
</DIV>
<DIV ID="css2">
<P  class="arial">CSS</P>
</DIV>
<DIV ID="css3">
<P  class="arial">CSS</P>
</DIV>
<DIV ID="dh">
```

(continued)

(continued)

```
<P><I>Dynamic</I>HTML</P>
</DIV>
<DIV ID="cs">
<P>CLIENT-SIDE SCRIPTING</P>
</DIV>
<DIV ID="c1">
<H4> </H4>
</DIV>
<DIV ID="c2">
<H5> </H5>
</DIV>
<DIV ID="c3">
<H6> </H6>
</DIV>
</BODY>
</HTML>
```

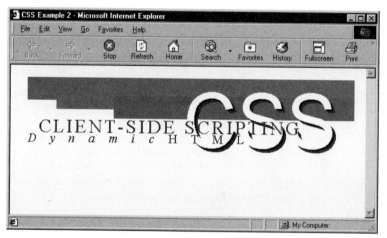

Figure 14-2. *Using CSS instead of image files.*

For More Information on CSS

This section on Cascading Style Sheets is enough to get you started, but it is not a complete resource. You'll find the following Web sites useful for deepening your knowledge of CSS:

■ *www.w3c.com.* The W3C is the governing body of the CSS standard. Here you can find out about both the current standard and future versions. This site also includes information on several other standards governed by the W3C like HyperText Markup Language (HTML) and eXtensible Markup Language (XML).

■ *msdn.microsoft.com.* In this site, you'll find CSS articles, products, and samples.

■ *www.hotwired.com/webmonkey.* This is a good site for HTML-related technologies, including CSS.

CLIENT-SIDE SCRIPTING

HTML and CSS are useful for formatting and displaying Web pages. However, neither HTML nor CSS supports the logic and data handling characteristics of a robust user interface. Client-side scripting technology addresses these shortcomings. Client-side scripting enables you to add logic and work with data within the HTML of your Web page.

Client-side scripting is often used for detecting browser features, responding to user actions, validating form data, and displaying dialog boxes. For these tasks, the alternative to client-side scripting is to have programs or scripts on the Web server perform them. While Web server programs for such tasks were common before client-side scripting was available, client-side scripting has several advantages over performing these tasks on the Web server. Because the script resides on the client, your page can perform validation and respond to user actions without communicating with the Web server over the network. This reduces network traffic and Web server load. Scripts residing on the client are also able to respond to user actions almost instantly, reducing response time and improving the user's experience.

Scripting Language Options and Comparison

Client-side scripts are interpreted, not compiled. This means that the client-side scripts added to your Web pages are read, interpreted, and run line by line as the scripts run. An advantage of this approach is that there are no code compilers and other tools required to convert the code into an executable form before it is run. You simply add script to your Web pages with the same editor you use to add content, HTML tags, and CSS. A disadvantage of having client-side scripts interpreted is that they execute slower than compiled code. Scripts are usually small, however, so this performance difference isn't significant. A more important disadvantage of client-side scripting is that the code in the non-compiled script can be seen when the Web page source is viewed in the browser. For this reason, you should avoid including sensitive or proprietary business logic in your client-side scripts.

The two dominant scripting languages available today are Visual Basic Scripting Edition (VBScript) and JavaScript. VBScript, developed by Microsoft, is a "safe for the Web" version of Visual Basic for Applications (VBA) and Visual Basic (VB). "Safe for the Web" means all functionality for accessing the client machine's operating system or files has been removed. Because it's a subset, VBScript is syntactically the same as VBA and VB. This means it's easy to learn for those new to VB, and the legions of current VB developers can leverage their existing skills. JavaScript, developed by Netscape, is also a "safe for the Web" language syntactically similar to C++ and Java.

> **NOTE:** You may encounter the term "ECMA-262" in the context of scripting languages. Here's what it is. The ECMA (European Computer Manufacturers Association), a European-based standards organization, recently approved the ECMA-262 scripting language. ECMA-262 is a standard scripting language that combines features from Microsoft's JScript language and Netscape's JavaScript language. JScript is Microsoft's implementation of ECMA-262, and JavaScript is Netscape's implementation. Because the term "ECMA-262" or any variation of it has not been successfully marketed yet, this chapter refers to the language as JavaScript to avoid confusion. To find out more about ECMA-262, visit the ECMA Web site at *http://www.ecma.ch*.

Interpreters for both VBScript and JavaScript come with Internet Explorer. You can even use both of these scripting languages in the same Web page, and Internet Explorer will interpret both. Netscape Navigator, however, supplies only an interpreter for JavaScript and does not support VBScript. VBScript will not run in Netscape browsers.

Your decision on which language to use will likely be driven by two factors: what languages your target browsers support and what skill set you or your developers already have.

- If you are developing an intranet site and Internet Explorer is your company's standard browser, VBScript is a good fit.

- If you are developing for unknown browsers on the Internet, JavaScript is a better bet.

- If you or your company has VB and VBA developers, VBScript is a logical choice to speed development and reduce maintenance expense.

- If you are C++ or Java focused, JavaScript makes sense.

Scripting Object Models

An object model is a hierarchy of objects representing various entities of a Web page and its environment. By manipulating an object's properties and calling its methods, you can provide a rich, interactive user interface in your Web pages. Object models also make user actions available to your scripts in the form of events. Actions like button clicks and mouse movement can be responded to by writing event handler functions or subroutines.

JavaScript has an object model built into its language. VBScript, however, does not. Instead, Microsoft has created an object model for Internet Explorer. This approach makes the object model language-independent and, therefore, more extensible as new languages are developed. Though they are very similar, these two object models are different and changing. As new versions of VBScript and JavaScript (as well as new versions of Web browsers) are released, the object models will be updated and enhanced. Be sure to check your target browser's object model documentation when developing client-side scripts.

Table 14-2 contains a partial list of objects that are common to both the JavaScript and IE object models with a description of their functionality.

Table 14-2
COMMON SCRIPTING OBJECTS

Object	Description
Window	Represents the top-level object for the current Web browser window
Document	Represents the current Web page itself
Frame	Represents a frame in a frameset
Link	Represents a hypertext link on a Web page
Form	Represents an HTML form on a Web page
History	Represents the Web browser's history list
Navigator	Represents the Web browser
Location	Represents the URL of the current Web page

Table 14-3 lists the 18 intrinsic HTML 4.0 events exposed by both object models, and describes each event's functionality.

Table 14-3

INTRINSIC HTML 4.0 EVENTS

Event	Usage	Applies to
onload	Occurs when the Web browser finishes loading a window or FRAMESET	Used with BODY and FRAMESET elements
onunload	Occurs when the Web browser unloads a document from a window or frame	Used with BODY and FRAMESET elements
onclick	Occurs when an element is clicked by the mouse	Used with most elements
ondblclick	Occurs when an element is double-clicked by the mouse	Used with most elements
onmousedown	Occurs when the mouse is pressed while over an element	Used with most elements
onmouseup	Occurs when the mouse is released while over an element	Used with most elements
onmouseover	Occurs when the mouse is moved over an element from somewhere else on the page	Used with most elements
onmousemove	Occurs when the mouse is moved while over an element	Used with most elements
onmouseout	Occurs when the mouse is moved off an element	Used with most elements
onfocus	Occurs when an element receives focus either by the mouse or by the keyboard	Used with LABEL, INPUT, SELECT, TEXTAREA, and BUTTON elements
onblur	Occurs when an element loses focus either by the mouse or by the keyboard	Used with LABEL, INPUT, SELECT, TEXTAREA, and BUTTON elements

Event	*Usage*	*Applies to*
onkeypress	Occurs when a key is pressed and released over an element	Used with most elements
onkeydown	Occurs when a key is pressed down over an element	Used with most elements
onkeyup	Occurs when a key is released over an element	Used with most elements
onsubmit	Occurs when a form is submitted	Used with the FORM element
onreset	Occurs when a form is reset	Used with the FORM element
onselect	Occurs when text is selected	Used with the INPUT and TEXTAREA elements
onchange	Occurs when an element loses focus and its value has changed	Used with the INPUT, SELECT, and TEXTAREA elements

NOTE   Though the W3C has defined these 18 standard events, they have not defined the order in which the events take place. This can be an issue if you are using multiple events for the same element, because you can't rely on the order in which the events will take place on different Web browsers. For example, the onclick, ondblclick, onmouseup, and onmousedown events may happen in a different order with different Web browsers. To avoid this problem, limit the number of events you are handling for any given element and be sure to check the target browser's event model documentation.

Adding Scripts to Web Pages

There are three ways to add scripts in your HTML pages:

- Add script using the <SCRIPT> tag.
- Add inline script inside the tags of individual HTML elements.
- Reference an external file that contains script.

Let's take a closer look at each.

Adding scripts using the <SCRIPT> tag

Add scripts to your Web pages by placing the script tags <SCRIPT> </SCRIPT> in the HEAD section or BODY section of your Web page. You can use these tags in multiple places throughout your Web page, but placing your code at the top of the page in the HEAD section is the best technique. It ensures that the browser reads the code and makes it available before events from the BODY section call it. It's also easier to maintain Web pages if all script is in a central location.

Prior to HTML 4.0, the SCRIPT tag's LANGUAGE attribute was used to specify whether the scripting language inside the tags was VBScript or JavaScript. With HTML 4.0, the W3C suggests using the TYPE attribute instead. The following table shows these attributes and their values by HTML version.

SCRIPTING LANGUAGE ATTRIBUTES

	HTML 4.0	*Prior Versions*
VBScript	TYPE="text/vbscript"	LANGUAGE="VBScript"
JavaScript	TYPE="text/javascript"	LANGUAGE="JavaScript"

You might be asking yourself, "How am I going to know which to use?" It's simple—use them both. Web browsers ignore tags and attributes they don't understand. When you include both attributes, a Web browser uses the attribute it understands and ignores the attribute it does not understand. You can also use both scripting languages in the same page.

NOTE   You can set the default scripting language for the entire page by placing the <META> tag between the <HEAD></HEAD> tags and before the <SCRIPT></SCRIPT> tags. Set the <META> tag's HTTP-EQUIV attribute to "Content-Script-Type" and set its CONTENT attribute to either "text/vbscript" or "text/javascript" like this:

```
<HEAD>
<META http-equiv="Content-Script-Type" content="text/
vbscript">
<SCRIPT>…</SCRIPT>
</HEAD>
```

A VBScript declaration looks like this:

```
<HEAD>
<SCRIPT LANGUAGE="VBScript" TYPE="text/vbscript">
<!--
  VBScript goes here.
-->
</SCRIPT>
</HEAD>
```

A JavaScript declaration looks like this:

```
<HEAD>
<SCRIPT LANGUAGE="JavaScript" TYPE="text/javascript">
<!--
JavaScript goes here.
//-->
</SCRIPT>
</HEAD>
```

Notice that both of these declarations include HTML comment tags just like the previous CSS embedded style declaration. Also notice that the end comment tag in the JavaScript declaration looks a little different: It's preceded by two slashes (//). These slashes are comments in the JavaScript language and are needed just before the end comment tag. Without them, the JavaScript interpreter will try to interpret the HTML end comment tag as JavaScript and produce an error message.

Within the script tags, place code inside or outside functions (VBScript also supports subroutines). If you write code outside functions, it will execute once when the Web page loads. This is useful for tasks like initializing input elements and checking browser characteristics. If you write code inside a function, it doesn't execute until that function is called.

To demonstrate, the following Web page counts how many times its Input button is clicked. Each time the Input button is clicked, its onclick event calls the add function event handler. The add function increments a counter variable and then displays the count in a message box. The Web page also displays the name of the Web browser used to view the Web page. Because the code for this is not contained in any function or subroutines, it is executed only once when the page loads.

The navigator object supplies information about the user's Web browser. The navigator object's appname property is used to retrieve the Web browser name, and the document object's write method is used to display that information on the Web page.

A JavaScript version of a Web page implementing this functionality can be found on the companion CD in the \Chapter 14\ directory and looks like this:

```
<HTML>
<HEAD>
<TITLE>Example 1 - JavaScript</TITLE>
<SCRIPT LANGUAGE="JavaScript" TYPE="text/javascript">
<!--
    //initialize counter
    var counter = 0;
    document.write("You're using " + navigator.appName);

    function add(){
        counter++;
         alert (counter);
    }
//-->
</SCRIPT>
</HEAD>
<BODY>
<FORM>
    <INPUT TYPE="Button" onClick="add();" VALUE="Add One">
</FORM>
</BODY>
</HTML>
```

The same Web page using VBScript for this functionality can be found on the companion CD in the \Chapter 14\ directory and looks like this:

```
<HTML>
<HEAD>
<TITLE>Example 1 - VBScript</TITLE>
<SCRIPT LANGUAGE="VBScript" TYPE="text/vbscript">
<!--
    'initialize counter
    Dim counter
    counter = 0
    document.write "You're using " & navigator.appName

    function add()
        counter = counter + 1
         MsgBox counter
    End function
-->
</SCRIPT>
</HEAD>
<BODY>
<FORM>
    <INPUT TYPE="Button" onClick="add()" VALUE="Add One">
```

```
</FORM>
</BODY>
</HTML>
```

Regardless of the scripting language used, both Web pages function the same and create the same output, which looks like Figure 14-3.

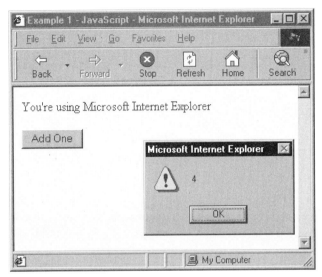

Figure 14-3. *Browser information and count function.*

While trying this example, you might notice that if you reload the Web page, the counter variable is reset to zero. This is because this variable is declared outside any functions. This global variable is created when the Web page loads and persists until the Web page unloads. In contrast, a local variable (declared inside a function) is created each time that function is called and is destroyed when the function finishes executing.

Adding inline scripts

You can also add inline scripting to your Web pages. Like inline CSS styles, inline scripting is placed within your HTML form's input element tags to respond to the input element's events. Add code, prefixed with the scripting language and a colon, for the event you want to handle. In the following example, found on the companion CD in the \Chapter 14\ directory, it's the onClick event of a button. Using JavaScript, a Web page that displays a message box with the date and time when a button is clicked looks like this. Figure 14-4 shows the page in action.

```
<HTML>
<HEAD>
<TITLE>Example 2 - JavaScript</TITLE>
</HEAD>
<BODY>
<FORM>
<INPUT TYPE="Button" onClick="Javascript:alert(Date());"
VALUE="Show Time">
</FORM>
</BODY>
</HTML>
```

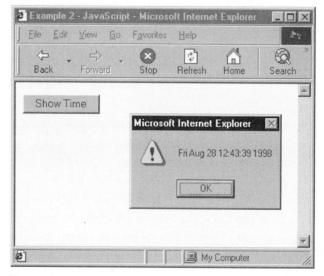

Figure 14-4. *Date and time via inline scripting.*

An Internet Explorer-only variation of inline scripting uses the FOR, EVENT, and LANGUAGE attributes of the script tag to specify the input element the script is specifically for, which event to handle, and what language to use. The following example can be found on the companion CD in the \Chapter 14\ directory. It's the same Web page described earlier, built using this technique and VBScript, and looks like this:

```
<HTML>
<HEAD>
<TITLE>Example 2 - VBScript</TITLE>
</HEAD>
<BODY>
<FORM>

    <INPUT TYPE="Button" NAME="TimeButton" VALUE="Show Time">
    <SCRIPT FOR="TimeButton" EVENT="onClick" LANGUAGE="VBScript">
<!--
        msgbox now
    //-->
    </SCRIPT>
</FORM>
</BODY>
</HTML>
```

Referencing an external script file

If you have script that you use in several Web pages, you might find it difficult to maintain the same redundant code in multiple places. To solve this problem, you can put the script in a single file and then reference that file from any Web page that needs it. To reference external script files, use the script tag's source attribute, SRC, to specify the URL of an external script file. Using the SRC attribute is an excellent way to reuse common scripts and reduce your maintenance effort. If you use this attribute, the Web browser uses only script in the external file and ignores any script that has been placed between the script tags.

Scripting Examples

Now that you have seen how to add script to your Web pages, let's look at a few more examples. These examples can all be found on the companion CD in the \Chapter 14\ directory and work using either Internet Explorer or Navigator.

Example: Displaying the current date

The first Web page (shown in Figure 14-5) uses an array of months and the JavaScript date object to determine the current month. It also uses the document object to build a new Web page on the fly that displays the current month (shown in Figure 14-6). Notice that when the document object's close method is executed, the Web browser automatically navigates to the new page just built.

```
<HTML>
<HEAD>
<TITLE>Example 3 - JavaScript</TITLE>
<SCRIPT LANGUAGE="JavaScript" TYPE="text/javascript">
<!--
function showMonth() {
        //create an array to hold the months
        var theMonths = new Array
                    ("January",
                     "February",
                     "March",
                     "April",
                     "May",
                     "June",
                     "July",
                     "August",
                     "September",

                     "October",
                     "November",
                     "December");
        //create a date variable
        var sysDate = new Date();

        //create an HTML page on the fly that shows this month
        document.open()
        document.write("<HTML><HEAD>")
        document.write("<TITLE>This page is built on demand
        </TITLE></HEAD>")
        document.write("<BODY TEXT='red'><H2>The current month
        is:</H2>")
        document.write("<H1>"+ theMonths[sysDate.getMonth()]+"
        </H1>")
        document.write("</BODY></HTML>")
        document.close
}
//-->
</SCRIPT>
</HEAD>
<BODY>
<FORM>
<INPUT TYPE="button" VALUE="Show current month"
onClick="showMonth()">
</FORM>
</BODY>
</HTML>
```

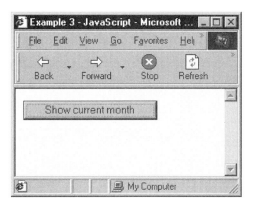

Figure 14-5. *Building a Web page on the fly.*

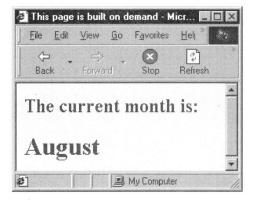

Figure 14-6. *Resulting output.*

Example: Implementing an adding machine

This next example is a simple adding machine. When you enter two two-digit numbers in the input boxes, the Web page adds them together and then displays the result in the form of three LCD-number images (as shown in Figure 14-7). There are a number of things going on behind the scenes. Here is what's happening:

- **Input validation.** When the Add button is clicked, the checkInput function is called once for each input element. It removes any non-numeric characters the user enters and inserts a zero if the user doesn't enter anything.

- **Data conversion.** In the displayresult function, the two input fields are converted to numbers using the JavaScript parseInt function, and then they are added together.

■ **For loops.** The result of the addition is converted back to a string and is then used in a reverse loop starting at the last character and working toward the first character. This loop is done backward so the result of the addition can be right-justified in the three images.

■ **String concatenation.** Each character in the result string is concatenated with other characters to form a complete filename that corresponds to an image file in the same directory as the Web page.

■ **Dynamic image swapping.** Each of the three image elements in the document.images collection is updated with the appropriate digit image file that reflects the correct result of the addition.

```
<HTML>
<HEAD>
<TITLE>Example 4 - JavaScript</TITLE>
<SCRIPT LANGUAGE="JavaScript" TYPE="text/javascript">
<!--
function displayresult(form) {

        //check for non-numerics
        checkInput(form,0);
        checkInput(form,1);

        //add numbers
        a = parseInt(form.num1.value) + parseInt(form.num2.value);

        //convert result to a string (the easy way) so the
        //length property can be used.
        a = a + ""

        //n is the counter used to start at the end of the result
         //string and work toward the beginning
        n = 1
        //this loop starts at the last image in the array
        //this way it's possible to right-justify the result
        for (var i = 2; i >= 0; i--){

          //this displays leading zeros if the result string
          //is shorter than three digits which is the total number
          //of images displayed
            if (a.length-n >= 0){
                document.images[i].src="dg" + a.charAt(a.length-n)
+ ".gif"
```

```
                    n++
        }else{
            document.images[i].src="dg0.gif"
        }
    }
}
// this function ensures only numeric values are
// in the input elements when the add button is clicked
function checkInput(form, index){
    var a = form.elements[index].value
    for (var i = 1; i <= a.length; i++){
        if ((a.charAt(i-1) != "0") &&
            (a.charAt(i-1) != "1") &&
            (a.charAt(i-1) != "2") &&
            (a.charAt(i-1) != "3") &&
            (a.charAt(i-1) != "4") &&
            (a.charAt(i-1) != "5") &&
            (a.charAt(i-1) != "6") &&
            (a.charAt(i-1) != "7") &&
            (a.charAt(i-1) != "8") &&
            (a.charAt(i-1) != "9")){
          a = a.substring(0,i-1)+a.substring(i,a.length)
            i = 0
        }
    }
    if (a.length == 0){
        form.elements[index].value = 0;
    }else{
        form.elements[index].value = a;
    }
}


//-->
</SCRIPT>
</HEAD>
<BODY BGCOLOR="#000000" TEXT="#FFFFFF">
<FORM>
Enter two numbers then click the add button:
<BR><BR>
<INPUT TYPE="text" SIZE=2 MAXLENGTH=2 NAME="num1">
<FONT SIZE=+2>+</FONT>
<INPUT TYPE="text" SIZE=2 MAXLENGTH=2  NAME="num2">
<FONT SIZE=+2>=</FONT>
```

(continued)

(continued)

(continued)

```
<IMG ALIGN=MIDDLE SRC="dg0.gif" WIDTH=20 HEIGHT=30>
<IMG ALIGN=MIDDLE SRC="dg0.gif" WIDTH=20 HEIGHT=30>
<IMG ALIGN=MIDDLE SRC="dg0.gif" WIDTH=20 HEIGHT=30>
<BR>
<INPUT TYPE="button" VALUE=" Add "
onClick="displayresult(this.form)">
</FORM>
</BODY>
</HTML>
```

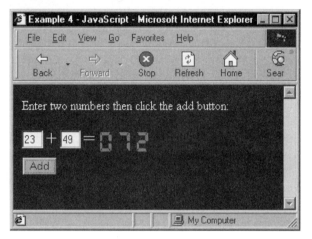

Figure 14-7. *Adding machine.*

The IE Script Debugger

After you start writing client-side scripts, you'll make two discoveries: The scripts have bugs, and you need a debugger. Microsoft addresses this need by including a free script debugger, shown in Figure 14-8, with the full installation of Internet Explorer. You can also download the script debugger from the Internet Explorer Web site at *http://www.microsoft.com/ie*. Once installed, the script debugger is visible on the View menu of Internet Explorer. If you are familiar with the debuggers from Microsoft's Visual Studio development suite tools like Visual Basic, Visual J++, or Visual InterDev, you'll be right at home. Like those debuggers, the script debugger allows you to step through code, set break points, check variable values, and view the call stack. If you haven't used a debugger like this before, the online documentation will get you up to speed quickly.

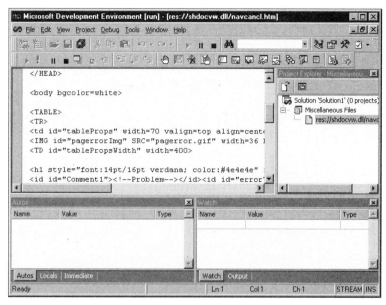

Figure 14-8 *The Microsoft script debugger.*

For More Information on Client-Side Scripting

This section on client-side scripting provides you with a working knowledge of what client-side scripting is, how scripting languages compare, and how to add script to your Web pages. You can further your understanding of client-side scripting by visiting the following scripting Web sites:

- *msdn.microsoft.com/scripting.* Microsoft's scripting site is a good source of articles, downloads, samples, tutorials, and references for both VBScript and JavaScript.

- *javascript.developer.com.* This site is dedicated to JavaScript.

- *www.netscape.com/developer.* This site offers lots of documentation, samples, and how-to articles on JavaScript.

- *www.hotwired.com/webmonkey.* This is a good site for HTML-related technologies, including client-side scripting.

DYNAMIC HTML

With HTML, CSS, and client-side scripting, you can create Web pages with static content and limited user interaction. Dynamic HTML (DHTML) takes these technologies a step further by enabling you to dynamically manipulate all the elements in your Web page—even after the page is loaded. With DHTML, you can dynamically hide and display content, modify styles, and animate and position elements. All of this can be accomplished by the browser without making requests to a Web server and without reloading the Web page. This makes for an improved user experience while reducing download time, network traffic, and Web server load. DHTML also allows you to present external information on your Web pages by binding elements to external data sources like files and databases.

So what exactly is DHTML? DHTML builds on existing technologies and can be broken down into three distinct areas:

- **HTML and CSS.** They are what are actually manipulated dynamically and include all HTML elements and CSS definitions.

- **The Document Object Model (DOM).** This enables HTML and CSS to be manipulated by exposing each Web page element as an object with properties, methods, and events.

- **Client-side scripting.** Client-side scripts work with the objects in the DOM to manipulate HTML and CSS on Web pages.

You have already learned about HTML, CSS, and client-side scripting. So let's look at what really makes DHTML possible: the Document Object Model (DOM).

The Document Object Model (DOM)

The DOM, another specification governed by the W3C, is what makes HTML and CSS dynamically changeable. The DOM isn't a new concept; Web page object models have been around since JavaScript was introduced, exposing HTML form elements, links, and Web browser information. The latest DOM specification proposed by the W3C is simply a language-independent superset of the JavaScript object model. Unlike the limited JavaScript object model, the DOM exposes all the HTML elements on a Web page to any scripting language. Therefore, all HTML elements and CSS definitions are accessible to scripting languages as objects with properties, methods, and events. Because the DOM specification continues to evolve, each Web browser's DOM support will vary. Figure 14-9 shows some of the structure of the Internet Explorer object model.

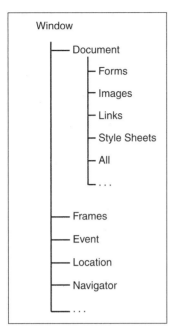

Figure 14-9   *Part of the Internet Explorer object model.*

Notice two of the objects under the document object: all and style-sheets. These two objects are actually collection objects—objects containing groups of other objects—that expose all the HTML elements and style sheets on the Web page.

> **NOTE**   The W3C DOM specification includes many requirements that currently only Internet Explorer supports. DOM features like exposing all HTML elements and CSS, language independence, and dynamic behavior after the Web page is loaded are not yet supported in Netscape's browsers. Therefore, the examples in this section of the chapter are designed for Internet Explorer browsers.

Accessing HTML and CSS through the DOM

Because the DOM includes objects that represent all elements on a Web page, an understanding of how parent and child elements relate to each other is necessary. The HTML element is at the top of every Web page structure. All other elements are subordinate to it. For example, consider the HTML code displayed here. Using the language of "parent" and "child," one can say that the HTML element is parent to HEAD and BODY. HEAD and BODY are children of HTML. HEAD is parent to TITLE, BODY is parent to H1 and DIV, and so on. In general terms, child elements are contained within parent elements, and parent elements contain child elements. Figure 14-10 depicts these relationships graphically.

```
<HTML>
<HEAD>
<TITLE>
</TITLE>
</HEAD>
<BODY>
<H1 ID=head1>Page heading</H1>
<DIV ID=divmain>
<P ID=ptag>This paragraph text is <I>italicized</I></P>
</DIV>
</BODY>
</HTML>
```

The Web page's I element is a child of the P element, which is a child of the DIV element. Both DIV and H1 are child elements of the BODY element, which is a child of the HTML element. The object model reflects all the Web page elements in the preceding Web page in an object hierarchy that looks like this:

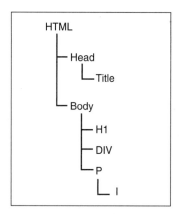

Figure 14-10. *Web page object hierarchy.*

This hierarchy can be referenced through script using the All object mentioned previously. The All object is a collection object including one element object for each HTML tag in the document. Therefore, the actual members of the All collection are different for every document. This is not a problem because the All collection provides access to every element object through its Item method and its Length and TagName properties. You use the Item method to access element objects by the HTML element's name or ID attribute, or by a zero-based index.

For example, accessing an element with its ID set to "menu1" looks like this:

```
document.all.item("menu1")
```

Alternatively, you can access elements sequentially by index like this:

```
document.all.item(2)
```

You can determine how many items are in the collection by using the Length property. Using the TagName property, you can determine an element's tag name (H1, DIV, and so on). For example, looping through the All collection and displaying each element's tag name looks like this in JScript:

```
for ( i = 0; i < document.all.length; i++ )
{
    alert(document.all(i).tagName);
}
```

The following example uses Item, Length, and TagName to determine the tag names of all elements with ID's set to menu:

```
var oColl = document.all.item("menu");
for ( i = 0; i < oColl.length; i++ ){
  alert(oColl(i).tagName);
}
```

Dynamic Content, Styles, and Positioning

If you're wondering what you can use DHTML for in your Web pages, the answer is you can use DHTML for almost anything. The following examples can be found on the companion CD in the \Chapter 14\ directory, and show the use of script and the DOM to manipulate Web page content, CSS, and the positions of HTML elements.

It's often necessary to customize Web page content based on user actions. For example, you could display one of several page headings based on the user's choice from a list box or menu without having to request a new page from the Web server. This first example works with the Web page's content and replaces the text in a paragraph tag each time a button is clicked. The code for the Web page looks like this:

```
<HTML>
<HEAD>
<TITLE>DHTML Example 1 - JavaScript</TITLE>
<SCRIPT>
<!--
   var toggleT = 0;
function changeText(){
      if (toggleT==0){
              document.all.ptag.innerText = "Replacement
paragraph text";
              toggleT = 1;
      }else{
              document.all.ptag.innerText = "Default paragraph
text";
              toggleT = 0;
      }
}
//-->
</SCRIPT>
</HEAD>
<BODY onLoad="changeText();">
<P ID=ptag></P>
<FORM>
   <INPUT TYPE="Button" onClick="changeText();" VALUE="Change
text">
</FORM>
</BODY>
</HTML>
```

Using color is an effective way of reducing user input errors and user frustration. For example, you could indicate if a form field contains invalid data by changing the color of its title to red. The user can immediately see the field is incorrect without having to respond to error messages or wait for the Web server to determine there's an error. This next Web page works with styles and toggles the color style of a heading tag between red and blue each time a button is clicked. The code for the Web page looks like this:

```
<HTML>
<HEAD>
<TITLE>DHTML Example 2 - JavaScript</TITLE>
<STYLE>
  H2.red {color:red}
</STYLE>
<SCRIPT LANGUAGE="JavaScript" TYPE="text/javascript">
<!--
```

```
function changeColor(){
    if (document.all.hd2.style.color !="red"){
        document.all.hd2.style.color ="red";
    }else{
        document.all.hd2.style.color ="blue";
    }
}
//-->
</SCRIPT>
</HEAD>
<BODY onLoad="changeColor();">
<H2 class="red" ID=hd2> Level 2 heading </H2>
<FORM>
<INPUT TYPE="Button" onClick="changeColor();" VALUE="Change
color">
</FORM>
</BODY>
</HTML>
```

From games to ad banners, it's common to see animation on the Internet. For example, most Web page ad banners are animated. Many of these animations can be easily created with DHTML. This next example, shown in Figure 14-11, uses CSS positioning and animates a heading tag by changing its position based on a random number and a timer. Notice the heading's z-index style attribute is set to -1 to make it display beneath the Web page's text. The code for the Web page looks like this:

```
<HTML>
<HEAD>
<TITLE>DHTML Example 3 - JavaScript</TITLE>
<STYLE>
 #head1 {color:yellow; position:absolute; top:25px; left:25px;
z-index:-1}
</STYLE>
<SCRIPT LANGUAGE="JavaScript" TYPE="text/javascript">
<!--
    function StartChangePosition(){
        window.setInterval("changePosition()",500);
    }

    function changePosition(){
        document.all.head1.style.top = Math.random() * 50;
        document.all.head1.style.left = Math.random() * 50;
    }
//-->
```

(continued)

```
</SCRIPT>
</HEAD>
<BODY onLoad="StartChangePosition();">
<DIV ID=head1>
<H1> Animated Level 1 heading </H1>
</DIV>
<B>
<BR>
Here's the content of the Web page.
<BR>
You can see that the animated heading is moving underneath this
text.
</B>
</BODY>
</HTML>
```

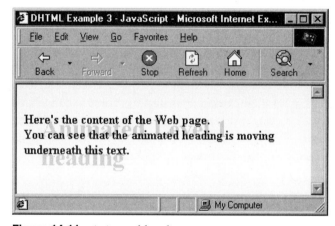

Figure 14-11. *Animated heading tag.*

Event Bubbling

One of the things that makes the DOM so powerful is its capability to expose events of Web page elements to scripting languages. Earlier in the chapter, you learned about events and how to respond to them in your scripts. To help simplify the error handling process, both Navigator and Internet Explorer introduced mechanisms to deliver events in an orderly fashion. These mechanisms are different. Netscape's mechanism, called *event capturing*, is a top-down design, allowing objects higher in the DOM to capture or intercept events before they reach the element that generated the event. Microsoft's mechanism, called *event bubbling*, does just the opposite. Its bottom-up approach delivers the event to the target element first and then moves up the DOM hierarchy, giving each parent the capability to handle the event. This bottom-up design is a common technique for processing user interface events in many operating systems. It allows you to centralize common event routines, reduce the amount of code and the Web page's size, and simplify maintenance.

The following Web page, found on the companion CD in the \Chapter 14\ directory and shown in Figure 14-12, shows how event bubbling works. It has two paragraph tags that are child elements of the DIV tag. The first paragraph tag has an event handler, but the second does not. The DIV tag also has an event handler. Both event handlers display a message box with the ID of the source element when you click the mouse.

When the mouse clicks over the first paragraph, the paragraph tag's event handler responds and then the event bubbles up to its parent, the DIV tag. Because the DIV tag has an event handler, it also responds to the event and displays two message boxes. When the mouse clicks over the second paragraph (which has no event handler), the event is bubbled up to the DIV tag's event handler that responds with a single message box. To stop events from bubbling up, cancel an event by setting the event object's cancelBubble property to "true."

```
<HTML>
<HEAD>
<TITLE>DHTML Example 4 - JavaScript</TITLE>
</HEAD>
<BODY>
<DIV ID=div1 onclick="alert(window.event.srcElement.id);">
<P ID=paragraph1 onclick="alert(window.event.srcElement.id);">
Paragraph with an event handler
</P>
<P ID=paragraph2>
Paragraph without an event handler
</P>
</DIV>
</BODY>
</HTML>
```

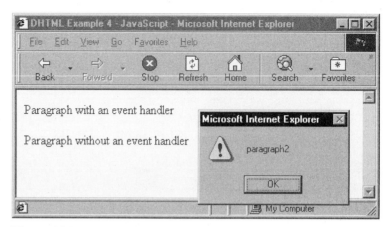

Figure 14-12. *Web page event bubbling.*

Data Binding

Data binding, a Microsoft technology introduced with Internet Explorer 4.0, allows you to "bind" elements on your Web page to data sources like text files and databases. Data binding lets you do things like dynamically generate tables containing information from your data source without making continuous requests to a Web server. You can also bind HTML form input elements to the data source and scroll through the data one record at a time. Data binding is implemented by adding a Data Source Object (DSO) to your Web page. DSOs are ActiveX controls or Java Applets provided by Microsoft and third parties. Internet Explorer comes with DSOs for accessing text files and ODBC data sources. To implement data binding, add a DSO to your Web page and configure it with information about your data source. Then bind HTML elements to the DSO using some additional HTML tag attributes.

For example, the following Web page (shown in Figure 14-13) references a text file with a DSO and then binds an HTML table to the DSO using the table tag's DATASRC attribute and the SPAN tag's DATAFLD attribute. It also includes a function that dynamically sorts the table when the column headings are clicked. It can be found on the companion CD in the \Chapter 14\ directory.

You'll notice that this Web page uses an ActiveX DSO that is added to the page using the object tags <OBJECT></OBJECT>. Working with ActiveX controls and the object tag is covered in detail in the next chapter. To find out more about data binding, check out the Internet Explorer Software Development Kit at *http://msdn.microsoft.com/developer/sdk/inetsdk/*.

```
<HTML>
<HEAD>
<TITLE>Data Binding Example</TITLE>
<SCRIPT LANGUAGE="JavaScript">
<!--
function reSort(sortcolumn) {
  orders.Sort = sortcolumn;
  orders.Reset();
}
//-->
</SCRIPT>

</HEAD>
<BODY>
<OBJECT ID="orders"
      CLASSID="clsid:333C7BC4-460F-11D0-BC04-0080C7055A83"
      BORDER=0 WIDTH=0 HEIGHT=0>
      <PARAM NAME="DataURL" VALUE="order.txt">
      <PARAM NAME="UseHeader" VALUE="True">
</OBJECT>
<DIV ALIGN=CENTER>
<P>
By Clicking on the Product ID, Description, Quantity,
or Total column headings, the table below can be sorted.
</P>
<H2>Unfilled Orders</H2>
<TABLE BORDER="1" ID="elemtbl" DATASRC="#orders">
<THEAD>
<TR>
<TH><FONT COLOR="#0000FF"><U>
    <DIV ID=prodid onclick="reSort(this.id);">Product ID</DIV>
    </U></FONT></TH>
<TH><FONT COLOR="#0000FF"><U>
    <DIV ID=desc onclick="reSort(this.id);">Description</DIV>
    </U></FONT></TH>
<TH><DIV ID=uprice>Unit Price</DIV></TH>
<TH><FONT COLOR="#0000FF"><U>
    <DIV ID=qty onclick="reSort(this.id);">Quantity</DIV>
    </U></FONT></TH>
<TH><FONT COLOR="#0000FF"><U>
    <DIV ID=tot onclick="reSort(this.id);">Total</DIV>
    </U></FONT></TH>
</TR>
</THEAD>
<TR>
<TD><SPAN DATAFLD="prodid"></SPAN></TD>
```

(continued)

555

(continued)

```
<TD><SPAN DATAFLD="desc"></SPAN></TD>
<TD><SPAN DATAFLD="uprice"></SPAN></TD>
<TD><SPAN DATAFLD="qty"></SPAN></TD>
<TD><SPAN DATAFLD="tot"></SPAN></TD>
</TR>
</TABLE>
</DIV>
</BODY>
</HTML>
```

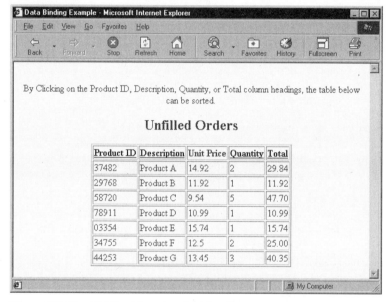

Figure 14-13. *HTML table using data binding.*

New DHTML Features in Internet Explorer

Internet Explorer 5.0 provides many significant new DHTML features from table enhancements to drag and drop support. The following list provides an overview of some of these new features.

■ **Data persistence.** Internet Explorer 5.0 provides the ability to store Web page information on the client. Data from HTML forms, scripts, or styles can be saved and used later.

■ **HTML table enhancements.** Internet Explorer 5.0 allows individual table rows and cells to be hidden. This lets you add functionality like dynamically collapsing tables.

- **Drag and drop.** Additions to the DOM provide support for the same drag and drop functionality that is characteristic of Windows applications.

- **Dynamic behaviors.** Dynamic behaviors are lightweight DHTML components that can be referenced from Web pages to provide encapsulated functionality. This encapsulation simplifies Web pages because the script is contained in the dynamic behavior component. These components also promote reuse of common DHTML functionality. You can create your own dynamic behaviors or use one of several that come with Internet Explorer 5.0.

- **Client capabilities.** One of the dynamic behaviors provided by Microsoft is called CLIENTCAPS. CLIENTCAPS makes client information like screen resolution and color depth available to the scripts in your Web pages.

- **Dynamic properties.** Dynamic properties allow you to declare property values as an expression or formula. Using dynamic properties, you could simulate the behavior of a spreadsheet by automatically updating the totals of a table when the values of the table's individual cells change.

DHTML Example

A common use for DHTML is to have it perform tasks that previously required Java applets or ActiveX controls. One such task is a collapsible menu. By clicking on menu items, their submenus are displayed and hidden dynamically. To make the menu more visually intuitive, the cursor icon turns into a hand when the mouse is over a menu item, and each submenu item turns red when the mouse is over it. This Web page, show in Figure 14-14 and found on the companion CD in the \Chapter 14\ directory, includes style sheets, scripting, and event handling. However, the core functionality of this Web page is the menuChange function that toggles an element's Display property on or off.

```
<HTML>
<HEAD>
<TITLE>DHTML Example 5 - JavaScript</TITLE>
</HEAD>
<STYLE>
    BODY {background:white; color:#0000ff; font-family:Arial;
font-size:10pt}
```

(continued)

(continued)

```
      A {color:#0000cc; font-family:Arial; font-size:8pt}
      A.red {color:#ff0000}
      DIV.indent {margin-left:.25in}
</STYLE>
<script language=JavaScript>
<!--
function menuChange() {
  var src;
  var subId;
  src = window.event.srcElement;
  if (src.className == "menu") {
     subId = "sub" + src.id;
     if (document.all(subId).style.display == "none") {
        document.all(subId).style.display = "";
     } else {
        document.all(subId).style.display = "none";
     }
  }
}


//-->
</script>
<BODY onClick="menuChange();">

<H3>Click on a menu group below to expand it and view its sub
menu.</H3>
<SPAN ID="menu1" CLASS="menu" STYLE="cursor:hand">+ MENU GROUP 1
</SPAN>
<DIV ID=submenu1 STYLE="display:None">
      <DIV CLASS="indent">
      <A onmouseover = "this.className = 'red'"
         onmouseout = "this.className = ';'">GROUP 1 SUB ITEM 1
</A><BR>
      <A onmouseover = "this.className = 'red'"
         onmouseout = "this.className = ';'">GROUP 1 SUB ITEM 2
</A><BR>
      <A onmouseover = "this.className = 'red'"
         onmouseout = "this.className = ';'">GROUP 1 SUB ITEM 3
</A><BR>
      <A onmouseover = "this.className = 'red'"
         onmouseout = "this.className = ';'">GROUP 1 SUB ITEM 4
<A><BR>
      <A onmouseover = "this.className = 'red'"
         onmouseout = "this.className = ';'">GROUP 1 SUB ITEM 5
</A>
      </DIV>
```

```
</DIV>
<BR>
<SPAN ID="menu2" CLASS="menu" STYLE="cursor:hand">+ MENU GROUP
2</SPAN>
<DIV ID=submenu2 STYLE="display:None">
        <DIV CLASS="indent">
        <A onmouseover = "this.className = 'red'"
          onmouseout = "this.className = ';'">GROUP 2 SUB ITEM 1
</A><BR>
        <A onmouseover = "this.className = 'red'"
          onmouseout = "this.className = ';'">GROUP 2 SUB ITEM 2
</A><BR>
        <A onmouseover = "this.className = 'red'"
onmouseout = "this.className = ';'">GROUP 2 SUB ITEM 3</A><BR>
        <A onmouseover = "this.className = 'red'"
          onmouseout = "this.className = ';'">GROUP 2 SUB ITEM 4
</A><BR>
        <A onmouseover = "this.className = 'red'"
          onmouseout = "this.className = ';'">GROUP 2 SUB ITEM 5
</A>
        </DIV>
</DIV>
<BR>
<SPAN ID="menu3" CLASS="menu" STYLE="cursor:hand">+ MENU GROUP
3</SPAN>
<DIV ID=submenu3 STYLE="display:None">
        <DIV CLASS="indent">
        <A onmouseover = "this.className = 'red'"
          onmouseout = "this.className = ';'">GROUP 3 SUB ITEM 1
</A><BR>
        <A onmouseover = "this.className = 'red'"
          onmouseout = "this.className = ';'">GROUP 3 SUB ITEM 2
</A><BR>
        <A onmouseover = "this.className = 'red'"
          onmouseout = "this.className = ';'">GROUP 3 SUB ITEM 3
</A><BR>
        <A onmouseover = "this.className = 'red'"
          onmouseout = "this.className = ';'">GROUP 3 SUB ITEM 4
</A><BR>
        <A onmouseover = "this.className = 'red'"
          onmouseout = "this.className = ';'">GROUP 3 SUB ITEM 5
</A>

        </DIV>
</DIV>
</BODY>
</HTML>
```

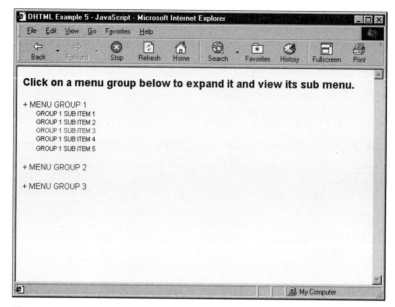

Figure 14-14. *Collapsible DHTML menu.*

For more information on DHTML

This section on DHTML is enough to give you a clear understanding of what DHTML is, what it can do, and how to add it to your Web pages today. However, like any new technology, DHTML's features, acceptance, and vendor support are constantly evolving. You'll find the following Web sites useful for keeping up with DHTML as it matures:

■ *www.w3c.com.* The W3C is the governing body of the DHTML specification. Here you can find their updated draft of the DHTML specification along with documents on the other related standards they also manage, including Cascading Style Sheets (CSS), ECMA-262 Scripting Language, and eXtensible Markup Language (XML).

■ *msdn.microsoft.com.* In this site, you'll find the latest on Microsoft's implementation of DHTML, including articles, products, and samples.

■ *www.netscape.com.* This site will keep you abreast of how Netscape is complying with and implementing the DHTML specification.

■ *www.hotwired.com/webmonkey.* This is a good site for DHTML 5 which features articles and sample code.

BRINGING IT ALL TOGETHER: AN EXAMPLE LOGIN PAGE

The following example brings all the technologies discussed in this chapter together to solve a real-world problem: membership login pages. While the vast majority of information on the Web is free, many Web sites have restricted or secure areas that require special membership access. These areas contain valuable content that can be accessed only by valid accounts on the Web server. The Web server needs to verify the identity of each user before users are granted access to restricted areas. User verification is typically done through a membership login page.

The example, shown in Figure 14-15, doesn't connect to a Web server but focuses instead on the user interface, applying the technologies discussed throughout the chapter. A combination of several of the chapter examples, the membership login page uses CSS instead of image files for all graphics effects and formatting. Client-side scripting is used to check that the e-mail address entered by the user has an "@" in it and that the membership number entered is at least six characters long. DHTML is used for the collapsible menu that includes dynamically expanding submenus, changing colors, and changing cursor icons. The code for the membership login page can be found on the companion CD in the \Chapter 14\ directory.

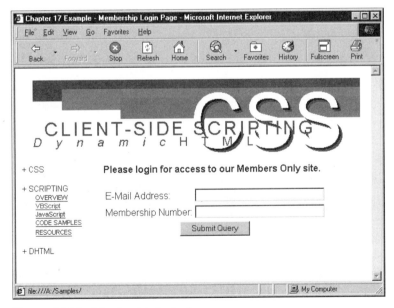

Figure 14-15. *Membership login form.*

DESIGN CONSIDERATION

While it's tempting to want to utilize the latest technologies in your Web pages right away, this is not always the best approach. A thorough understanding of the functionality required by your Web site and the technology options available for satisfying those requirements is a better place to start. While it's important to understand new Web technology developments, it's equally important to understand whether individual technologies and their companies will survive and prosper, given the competitive business environment of the industry. Identifying standards-based technologies from companies with intellectual and financial resources to evolve the product is critical to your success as a Web technology user.

Throughout the chapter, you learned some differences in the way browsers support CSS, client-side scripting, and DHTML. Because these three technologies are even younger than HTML, the differences in browser support are even greater. The biggest difference is Internet Explorer's extensive support of DHTML compared to Navigator's more limited functionality. Before deciding to take advantage of the latest proposed or proprietary features, you should ask this question: Is it likely these features will become part of a standard in the future? You can find out from the W3C Web site what new technologies vendors have submitted for standardization. You don't want to find out that a technology you built your Web site around won't become a standard with support from multiple vendors.

Here are some specific considerations to think about while choosing technologies:

- **Know your target Web browsers.** How advanced are the Web browsers that will be using your Web pages? What technologies do these Web browsers support? Is it possible to easily upgrade these Web browsers if necessary?

- **Follow the standards.** As most technologies mature, they become more standard and stable. The W3C is helping make sure this is true of CSS, client-side scripting, and DHTML. Because both Microsoft and Netscape contribute to the W3C standards, it's likely the W3C's recommendations will be supported by these vendors soon after the standards are finalized.

- **Let business reasons drive your technology decisions.** Ultimately, the technical direction you take and the Web sites you build should be based on business decisions, not the other way around.

SUMMARY

Though these technologies are young, Cascading Style Sheets (CSS), client-side scripting, and Dynamic HTML (DHTML) all appear to have solid, standards-based futures. All three add critical functionality to HTML that address formatting, logic, and user event and data handling needs. A thorough working knowledge of these three technologies and an understanding of their future direction will enable you to create rich, full-featured Web-based applications.

Chapter 15

Extending the HTML User Interface with Components

by Steve Gilmore

A component is a unit of compiled or scripted code that encapsulates a set of business functionality. Components such as ActiveX controls, Java applets, and DHTML scriptlets play an important role in extending the user interfaces of Web pages. For purposes of this chapter, a component is defined as having a user interface of some kind. This user interface could be very elaborate with many input fields, graphics, or animations, or it could simply display a message when an event takes place. A component's functionality, accessible through its interface, is simply the component's properties, methods, and events.

Components allow developers to provide the same sophisticated business logic and user interfaces in Web pages as in applications written in languages like Microsoft Visual Basic or Microsoft Visual C++. Because the code is encapsulated, components provide consistent, reusable functionality that users can't see when viewing the Web page's source code in the Web browser.

COMPONENT TECHNOLOGIES: ACTIVEX CONTROLS, JAVA APPLETS, AND DHTML SCRIPTLETS

This chapter focuses on three options for extending the functionality of Web pages: ActiveX controls, Java applets, and DHTML scriptlets.

- ActiveX controls are the most evolved of these component technologies and can be created using several languages. Developed by Microsoft, ActiveX technology was initially Windows based. However, ActiveX controls now also run on Macintosh and several UNIX platforms. ActiveX controls can be used by any COM-aware application and are not limited to Web browsers.

- Java applets, unlike ActiveX controls, must be created using the Java language. Java applets can run on any platform that has a Java Virtual Machine to interpret the code. Today, they are used most often in Web browsers on those platforms.

- DHTML scriptlets are Web pages containing DHTML functionality. Like ActiveX controls, DHTML scriptlets can be used by COM-aware applications in addition to Web browsers, and they are supported by Microsoft Internet Explorer on Windows, Macintosh, and UNIX platforms.

This chapter discusses how these technologies compare to client-side scripting and DHTML. You'll also learn how to add each of these components to your Web pages and how to communicate with them using script.

Benefits of Using Components

With so many Web technologies available today, such as client-side scripting and DHTML, why would you want to use components? Using components in your Web application offers several advantages over using DHTML alone. The following list highlights some of the benefits you can realize by deploying components as part of your Web solution:

■ **More robust functionality.** While technologies like Cascading Style Sheets (CSS), client-side scripting, and DHTML have substantially increased the capabilities of Web pages, these technologies can't compare with what's possible with languages like Visual Basic, C++, and Java. If you can write code in one of these languages, you can turn that code into a component and put it on your Web pages.

■ **No duplication of functionality.** For example, if several different Web pages need to validate the ZIP code entered by the user, those pages could simply use a ZIP code validation component instead of duplicating script to do the same thing. This greatly reduces the number of bugs introduced into the system, improving quality and, ultimately, saving money.

■ **Easy maintenance and reusability.**–Though many Web pages might use a component, the source code for that component is stored only in one. This centralized and modular approach improves maintenance. Encapsulating code for accomplishing a task or tasks in a single, well-defined unit makes it easy to reuse the component in other applications.

■ **No concern for implementation.** Implementation is defined here as how (and with what technologies) the component actually accomplishes its tasks. Developers using the component need to know only what it does, not how. Developers can therefore concentrate on the component's interface and functionality rather than worry about the internals of the underlying code.

■ **Consistent behavior.** Because there is only one set of source code for each component, it will behave the same wherever it is used.

■ **Increased security.**–ActiveX controls are compiled, and Java applets are partially compiled. Therefore, sensitive or proprietary business logic is safer inside these components than script placed directly in a Web page where users can view it.

■ **Readily available.**–Components are available for sale from hundreds of companies and are usually less expensive to buy than to build. In fact, your computer and your company's computers already have many components on them. You might even find that you already own the component you are looking for.

■ **Reduced development expense.**–The preceding benefits add up to cost savings throughout the software development lifecycle. This is true during the development and maintenance phases where encapsulated behavior, fewer bugs, more reuse, and less maintenance really begin to save time and money.

COMPARING COMPONENTS TO CLIENT-SIDE SCRIPTING

ActiveX controls, Java applets, and DHTML scriptlets offer varying benefits over client-side scripting and DHTML. Table 15-1 compares several specific aspects of client-side scripting and DHTML to these three component technologies.

Table 15-1
COMPONENT TECHNOLOGIES COMPARED TO CLIENT-SIDE SCRIPTING AND DHTML

	Client-Side Script / DHTML	ActiveX Controls	Java Applets	DHTML Script-lets
Browser Support.	Navigator and Internet Explorer.	Navigator (with plug-in) and Internet Explorer.	Navigator and Internet Explorer.	Internet Explorer only.
Perfor-mance.	Slowest option because scripts are interpreted.	Fastest because controls are compiled into native code.	Slower than controls but faster than other options.	Same as client-side script.
Function-ality.	Limited to scripting language features.	Almost unlimited.	Limited to Java language features.	Limited to scripting language features.
Security for the User.	Scripting languages have no function capable of doing damage to user's computers.	Managed by code signing and digital-based security certificates.	Managed by trust-based security model.	Scripting langua-ges have no func-tion capable of doing damage to user's computer. DHTML.

	Client-Side Script / DHTML	*ActiveX Controls*	*Java Applets*	*DHTML Script-lets*
Security for Business logic.	None. Source code can be seen in the Web browser.	Source code is compiled and is not accessible.	Source code is compiled and is not accessible.	Same as client-side script-ing DHTML.
Download speed.	Fastest.	Slow during the first download. ActiveX controls then remain on the client, so subsequent downloads aren't required.	Slowest because class files have to be downloaded every time the Web page containing the applet is requested.	Slower than client-side script-ing alone because DHTML scriptlet must be located in a separate file before being down-loaded
Required Skillset.	HTML, CSS, JavaScript, VBScript, DHTML.	C, C++, VB, Java, or third-party tool that can create Active X controls.	Java.	HTML, CSS, JavaScript, VBScript, DHTML.
Reuse and Mainten-ance.	Most difficult.	Easily reused. Maintenance requires a develop-ment tool for the language used to create the control.	Easily reused. Requires Java skills and Java develop-ment to maintain.	Easily reused. Can be maintained with any text editor.

Now that you have a general understanding of what your options are for extending the HTML user interfaces of your Web pages, let's take a closer look at each technology.

ACTIVEX CONTROLS

ActiveX is a mature technology that has been around since the early 1990s when it was called Object Linking and Embedding (OLE). Based on Microsoft's Component Object Model (COM), which defines how objects interact with each other. ActiveX controls are components that can be added to Web pages and used within Internet Explorer or other ActiveX containers like Visual Basic forms.

> **NOTE**   ActiveX containers have the capability to host embedded ActiveX control objects. Containers display and synchronize messages with those objects. Netscape Navigator is not natively an ActiveX container; therefore, Web pages containing ActiveX controls will not function properly in Netscape browsers.

From text boxes, list boxes, and menus to calendars, media players, and the Microsoft Wallet, ActiveX controls are an integral part of all 32-bit Windows operating systems. When you use Windows, you are likely using ActiveX controls.

An ActiveX control is a compiled unit of code that has an .ocx file extension. ActiveX controls are language independent. This means you can leverage your existing skills and write controls using your favorite language, such as C++, Visual Basic, or even Java.

> **NOTE**   When Java was first introduced, many industry experts labeled it a competitor of ActiveX technology and suggested that IT professionals must choose between Java and ActiveX. In fact, ActiveX is language independent object architecture, whereas Java is a programming language. Because of their language-independent nature, ActiveX controls can be developed in many languages, including Java.

Adding Controls to Web Pages

Once you have a control you want to add to your Web page, use the HTML object tag <OBJECT></OBJECT> and its attributes to add it to your page. Although the <OBJECT> tag has several attributes, six of these attributes are of particular importance: CLASSID, CODEBASE, ID, WIDTH, HEIGHT, and BORDER.

<OBJECT> Tag Attributes: CLASSID, ID, and CODEBASE

CLASSID is the only required attribute of the <OBJECT> tag and contains the control's class ID, a unique identification tag generated when the control is compiled so that the control can be uniquely recognized and referenced. When an ActiveX control is installed on a user's computer, it is registered in the system registry with this unique class ID. The following example shows the <OBJECT> tag and its CLASSID attribute for the Microsoft Chart ActiveX control:

```
<OBJECT
  CLASSID="CLSID:31291E80-728C-11CF-93D5-0020AF99504A">
</OBJECT>
```

Microsoft tools like FrontPage, Visual InterDev, and the ActiveX Control Pad will automatically generate the correct HTML <OBJECT> tag code (including the CLASSID information) when you use one of them to add an ActiveX control to your Web page. You can also manually find the class ID of a control by searching for the control in the system registry using the registry editor, REGEDIT.EXE.

NOTE Use caution when running REGEDIT.EXE. Inadvertently changing entries in the registry can leave software, or even the system itself, inoperable.

For users to access an ActiveX control on your Web page, the control must be installed and registered on the user's computer. So how do you ensure the user has your control installed before accessing your Web page? The <OBJECT> tag's CODEBASE attribute takes care of this for you. The CODEBASE attribute is used to specify a relative or absolute URL from where the control should be downloaded. Here's how it works: When Internet Explorer sees an <OBJECT> tag in your Web page, it checks to see if the control is installed on the user's computer by searching the user's system registry. If the control is installed, Internet Explorer uses this "local copy" of the control on the Web page. If the control is not installed on the user's computer, Internet Explorer downloads the control from the URL specified in the CODEBASE attribute, installs it, and then uses the control on the Web page. The control then resides on the user's computer, serving future requests and eliminating the need for subsequent downloads of the same control. An <OBJECT> tag with a CODEBASE attribute looks like this:

```
<OBJECT
  CLASSID="CLSID:31291E80-728C-11CF-93D5-0020AF99504A"
  CODEBASE="/control_directory/control.ocx"
>
</OBJECT>
```

Because ActiveX controls are often updated and enhanced, it's common for multiple versions of the same control to exist on a single computer. Though properly designed components should be backward compatible, you might want to reference a specific version of a control in your Web pages. To do so, you can add the version number to the end of the control name in the CODEBASE attribute. The syntax for the CODEBASE attribute with a version number looks like this:

```
CODEBASE="filename.ocx#Version=N,N,N,N"
```

To find the version number of a control, right-click the control's .ocx file in Microsoft Windows Explorer, click Properties, and then click the Version tab.

If you do not specify a version, the control that is installed on the user's computer will be used—regardless of the version. If you want the control to download every time, even if it's already installed on the user's computer, set the version number to -1,-1,-1,-1.

The following example shows the object tag for a specific version of the Microsoft Calendar control:

```
<OBJECT
  CLASSID="CLSID:8E27C92B-1264-101C-8A2F-040224009C02"
  CODEBASE="mscal.ocx#Version=8,0,0,3432">
</OBJECT>
```

The ID attribute works with the <OBJECT> tag just as it does with other HTML element tags, allowing you to reference the element from scripting languages. Adding the ID attribute to the preceding example looks like this:

```
<OBJECT ID="Calendar1"
   CLASSID="CLSID:8E27C92B-1264-101C-8A2F-040224009C02"
   CODEBASE="mscal.ocx#Version=8,0,0,3432"
   ID="MyCalendar">
</OBJECT>
```

<OBJECT> Tag Attributes: WIDTH, HEIGHT, and BORDER

The WIDTH, HEIGHT, and BORDER attributes affect a control's size and border and work the same with the <OBJECT> tag as they do with many other HTML elements, such as the image tag <IMG>. By default, WIDTH and HEIGHT both have a value of zero. This means the control will not be visible on your Web page unless you set both of these attributes to values greater than zero. Adding these three attributes to the preceding example looks like this:

```
<OBJECT
  CLASSID="CLSID:31291E80-728C-11CF-93D5-0020AF99504A"
  CODEBASE="/control_directory/control.ocx"
  ID="MyChart"
  WIDTH=100
  HEIGHT=150
  BORDER=1>
</OBJECT>
```

The <PARAM> Tag

The <PARAM> tag and its NAME and VALUE attributes are placed between the <OBJECT> and </OBJECT> tags to assign initial values to a control's properties. Use a separate <PARAM> tag for each control property to which you want to assign a value.

The following code was generated by inserting the Microsoft File Upload Control into a Web page using the ActiveX Control Pad. You can see the control's _ExtentX and _ExtentY properties are being initialized with two <PARAM> tags.

```
<OBJECT ID="FlUpll" WIDTH=100 HEIGHT=51
  CLASSID="CLSID:886E7BF0-C867-11CF-B1AE-00AA00A3F2C3">
    <PARAM NAME="_ExtentX" VALUE="2646">
    <PARAM NAME="_ExtentY" VALUE="1349">
</OBJECT>
```

You can find out the properties, methods, and events an object has by using the Object Browser included with Microsoft Visual Studio tools like Visual Basic. The Object Browser looks like Figure 15-1.

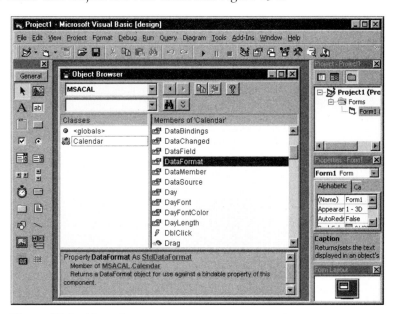

Figure 15-1. *Object Browser.*

Cabinet Files

You have learned how to use the <OBJECT> tag to download a single, uncompressed ActiveX control. However, some ActiveX controls require additional support files like a dynamic link library (DLL). All supporting DLLs must also be installed and registered on the user's computer before the control will function properly.

To download a control and its required support files, use a cabinet file. A cabinet is a single file (usually suffixed with a .cab file type) that stores several compressed files in a file library. Cabinet files are used to organize all the files that need to be copied to the user's system.

The .cab file contains one or more files, all of which are downloaded together in a single compressed cabinet file. Installing an ActiveX control by referencing its .cab file looks like this:

```
<OBJECT
  CLASSID="CLSID:31291E80-728C-11CF-93D5-0020AF99504A"
  CODEBASE="/cab_dir/control.cab">
</OBJECT>
```

Located within the .cab file is the .inf file, which provides further installation information. The .inf file specifies the support files that need to be downloaded and set up before an .ocx can run. The syntax of the .inf file supports URLs. This provides you with very flexible configuration options that can span multiple .cab files and multiple Web or FTP servers.

NOTE   For more information on cabinet technology and the cabinet SDK, see the Web Content Management area of the Microsoft Sitebuilder Web site at *www.microsoft.com/workshop/management.*

Licensed Controls

Many controls are licensed by their authors to protect the controls from being pirated or used without permission. There are two types of licenses: design-time and runtime. Design-time licenses allow controls to be used in development environments such as Visual Basic or Visual InterDev when designing applications. Runtime licenses allow controls to be executed or run, but not used in development environments. The required licenses need to reside on the computer where the control is being used. Most authors require design-time licenses for their controls, yet they usually allow the control to be freely distributed and executed. Some authors required both design-time and runtime licenses for the control to be used. This means that to use these controls on your Web pages, their runtime licenses must reside on the user's computer. To provide licenses for the controls, you need to reference the License Control Manager on your Web page using the <OBJECT> tag.

The License Manager

The License Manager, which is included with Internet Explorer, ensures that runtime licenses (for controls on a Web page requiring them) are included in a license package file. A license package file (.lpk) is required for every Web page that uses licensed controls. While it's possible to include several license package files on a Web page, the License Manager looks only in the first .lpk file. This means the first .lpk file must contain the required runtime licenses for all the licensed controls on the Web page.

To create the license file, use the License Package Authoring Tool, lpk_tool.exe. When you run lpk_tool.exe, you'll see a list of all the controls registered on your computer. Simply select the controls you want to include in the .lpk file, and then click Save And Exit. The License Package Authoring Tool looks like Figure 15-2.

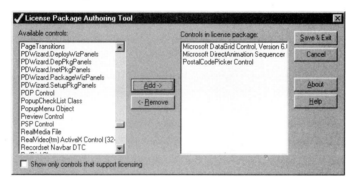

Figure 15-2. *License Package Authoring Tool.*

NOTE You can find the License Package Authoring Tool included with the Microsoft ActiveX SDK and with Microsoft Visual Studio.

Once you have a created a license package file, you'll need to add it and the License Manager to your Web page. As in the previous examples, the License Manager is added to a Web page by specifying its CLASSID using the <OBJECT></OBJECT> tag. To have the License Manager reference the .lpk file you created, add a <PARAM> tag with its NAME attribute to "LPKPath" and its VALUE attribute to the .lpk file you created.

Adding the License Manager and an .lpk file to a Web page looks like this:

```
<OBJECT CLASSID="clsid:5220CB21-C88D-11CF-B347-00AA00A28331">
  <PARAM NAME="LPKPath" VALUE="mylicenses.lpk">
</OBJECT>
```

When Internet Explorer loads the Web page, it invokes the License Manager, which then reads the .lpk file and verifies the runtime licenses of the controls on the Web page. If a control on a Web page requires a runtime license and its license information is not in the .lpk file, the control will not be loaded, and its associated functionality will not be available.

Digital Signatures

Digital signature technology was developed as a way of ensuring that the people claiming to have authored a piece of software available on the Internet actually created it and that the software has not been tampered with. Digital signatures are created using sophisticated public- and private-key algorithms. The private-key is known only by the owner, but the public-key is available to everyone. The private-key generates and encrypts the signature, and the corresponding public-key decrypts and validates that signature. With this identity validation, digital signatures remove the anonymity of the Internet and ensure accountability. When a digital signature is applied to an ActiveX control, the control is considered digitally signed.

However, a digitally signed control is not necessarily a safe control. The digital signature verifies only the author and that the code hasn't been tampered with. Controls, whether digitally signed or not, are like any other piece of software in that they can damage a user's computer if they inappropriately access the operating and file systems.

To sign code such as an ActiveX control or a cabinet file, you need to first get a digital certificate by applying to a Certificate Authority (CA) such as VeriSign at *www.verisign.com*. A CA verifies your credentials (and Dun & Bradstreet rating if you're a corporation) before giving you a unique digital certificate. The certificate identifies you as a legitimate entity that has pledged not to knowingly create, sign, and distribute software that will damage a user's computer. Certificates typically expire after a specific period—usually one year.

After you receive your digital certificate, you can use signcode.exe to apply your digital certificate to your code. Signcode.exe is included with the ActiveX SDK and can be used to digitally sign .exe, .dll, .ocx, .ctl, and .cab files. Although you can sign all these types of files, it's easiest just to sign the .cab files that contain all these other types of files, because the signature on the .cab file applies to all the compressed files contained within it.

For more information about digital certificates and code signing, go to the Security and Cryptography area of the Microsoft SiteBuilder Workshop at *www.microsoft.com/workshop*.

Security Levels

Whether the controls on your Web page are signed or not, users have the ultimate say over the downloading of ActiveX controls to their computer. Users determine whether to download signed and unsigned controls by selecting one of four security levels in Internet Explorer: High, Medium, Low, or Custom. Each of these settings varies with regard to whether downloads are enabled, disabled, or the user is prompted for both signed and unsigned controls.

The following table shows how these security levels affect the downloading of a control:

Security Controls	*Download Unsigned Controls*	*Download Level Signed*
High	Dialog box is displayed warning of unsafe content, and the control is not downloaded.	Dialog box is displayed warning of unsafe content, the control is not downloaded.
Medium	User is prompted to download the control or not.	Dialog box is displayed warning of unsafe content, and the control is not downloaded.
Low	User is not prompted, and the control is downloaded.	User is prompted to download the control or not.
Custom	User can set to Enable, Prompt, or Disable.	User can set to Enable, Prompt, or Disable.

To further customize Internet Explorer security, users can apply any of these four security levels to Internet Explorer security zones. Security zones can be thought of as areas on the Web that various Web sites reside in. To change security settings in Internet Explorer, select Internet Options from the View menu and click the Security Tab.

The following table describes the four security zones in more detail:

Security Zone	*Web Sites Security Level*	*Default*
Local intranet	Any Web site that doesn't require a proxy server. Typically internal sites only.	Medium
Trusted Sites	Any Web site believed to contain content safe to download.	Low

(continued)

Security Zone	Web Sites Security Level	Default
Restricted Sites	Any Web site believed to contain content that cannot be trusted to download.	High
Internet	By default, this zone contains all sites that are not assigned to one of the other three security zones.	Medium

In a sense, there is a fifth security zone: the user's computer. Internet Explorer assumes all files already on the user's computer are safe, so it does not apply security settings or zones to them.

NOTE Even if your controls are signed, your Web page might not function properly for users. Users can choose whether the controls on your pages are downloaded onto their computers. If a user chooses not to download an ActiveX control on your Web page, Internet Explorer displays a small icon as a placeholder instead of the control.

Code Marking

In addition to being digitally signed, controls can also be marked as safe for scripting and safe for initialization.

Safe for scripting

When an author marks a control safe for scripting, that author is guaranteeing that script cannot manipulate the control so that it damages the user's computer. Safe for scripting means the control should not be able to obtain unauthorized user information or corrupt their system in any way.

Two general guidelines for what a control marked as safe for scripting should *not* do are:

■ **Access the registry or any .ini file information.**—Registry and .ini files specific to a control are an exception to this.

■ **Accept a filename as a parameter.** Reading and writing files whose names were passed in from scripts could potentially damage a user's system.

Safe for initialization

When an author marks a control safe for initialization, that author is guaranteeing that the control cannot be initialized so that it damages the user's computer. *Safe for initialization* means the control should not obtain unauthorized user information or damage the user's system. As discussed earlier, controls are initialized by setting initial values to properties using the <PARAM> tags. Internet Explorer will read the <PARAM> tags only if the control is marked as safe for initialization.

Code marking and security levels

Internet Explorer looks at each control to determine if the control is safe for scripting and safe for initialization. The following table shows how the security levels affect whether a control can be initialized and scripted or not:

Security Level	Script Safe Controls	Initialize and Script Unsafe Controls
High	User is not prompted, and the control is scripted.	Dialog box is displayed warning of unsafe content, and the control is not downloaded.
Medium	User is not prompted, and the control is scripted.	User is prompted whether to allow the control to be initialized or scripted.
Low	User is not prompted, and the control is scripted.	User is prompted whether to allow the control to be initialized or scripted.
Custom	User can set to Enable, Prompt, or Disable.	User can set to Enable, Prompt, or Disable.

NOTE You can mark controls as safe for scripting and initialization by using the Package and Deployment Wizard included with Visual Studio.

Accessing Controls with Script

Once you have added an ActiveX control to your Web page, you will want to write script to interact with that control via its properties, methods, and events. In the previous chapter, you learned how to create event handler functions with script to capture an object's events like an input element's onClick event. You learned how to use methods like the document object's write method, and how to use object properties like the Navigator object's appName property.

Script that interacts with ActiveX controls is almost identical to script that interacts with intrinsic HTML form elements and Document Object Model (DOM) objects. Let's quickly review how to reference an object's properties, methods, and events.

Setting and getting properties

To set the values of an object's properties in VBScript and JavaScript, place the object and its property to the left of the equal sign and the new value of the property on the right, like this:

```
Object.Property = Value
```

To get values contained in an object's properties in VBScript and JavaScript, do the opposite, like this:

```
Value = Object.Property
```

Value can be a constant, variable, the results of a function or method call, or the property of another object. This line of code moves the value of a property of one object to the property of another object:

```
Object1.Property = Object2.Property
```

Calling methods

Calling methods in VBScript is slightly different than in JavaScript. Object method calls in VBScript can be written two ways:

```
Object.Method [Param1, Param ...]
```

Or

```
Call Object.Method([Param1, Param ...])
```

Parameters are optional. However, if the Call keyword is used, the parameters must be included in parentheses. If the call keyword is used and the method has no parameters, empty parentheses are required. The syntax for calling Object methods in JavaScript is the same as the second VBScript option without the call keyword, and looks like this:

```
Object.Method([Param1, Param ...])
```

Method return values can be captured in variables using syntax similar to that of setting properties earlier, like this:

```
MethodResults = Object.Method([Param1, Param ...])
```

Handling events

You need to write event handlers for ActiveX controls just as you do for intrinsic HTML elements. The following is the event handler in VBScript for the TimerStarted event of a control named Animator:

```
<SCRIPT LANGUAGE="VBScript">
<!--
Sub Animator_TimerStarted()
  'script to handle the event goes here
end sub
-->
</SCRIPT>
```

This looks a little different in JavaScript because the FOR and EVENT attributes of the <SCRIPT> tag are required to specify the object and the event associated with the event handler. The JavaScript equivalent looks like this:

```
<SCRIPT LANGUAGE="JavaScript" FOR="Animator" EVENT="TimerStarted()">
<!--
  //script to handle the event goes here
-->
</SCRIPT>
```

ActiveX Control Example

ActiveX controls are often used to reduce user-input errors by limiting the number of options and the amount of free-form text a user can enter. It's common to have several ActiveX controls interact with each other on a Web page. This is particularly effective because it's easy to make controls communicate with each other and because so many sophisticated controls are readily available. The sample Web page, found on the companion CD in the \Chapter 15\ directory, contains two ActiveX controls (a calendar control and a listbox control) and an HTML button element that all interact with each other. The calendar and list box ActiveX controls included in the sample ship with Visual Studio.

Here's how the Web page works: When a date on the calendar control is clicked, that date is added to the list box control. This is done by passing the calendar's value property as a parameter to the list box's additem method. This takes place inside an event handler for the calendar's Click event. Here's how the VBScript looks:

```
Sub Calendar1_Click()
  Listbox1.additem Calendar1.value
end sub
```

The list box entries can be deleted by clicking an HTML button element. The onClick event of the button calls the ClearList subroutine, which looks like this:

```
Sub ClearList()
```

```
   ListBox1.clear
end sub
```

Finally, a list box item and its value are displayed in a message box when that item is clicked. The VBScript looks like this:

```
Sub Listbox1_Click()
  msgbox "Item " & Listbox1.Listindex + 1 & " in the listbox has a
value of " & Listbox1.Value
end sub
```

Each of these subroutines contains only one line of code. As shown in Figure 15-3, you can see how easy it is to interact with ActiveX controls on a Web page.

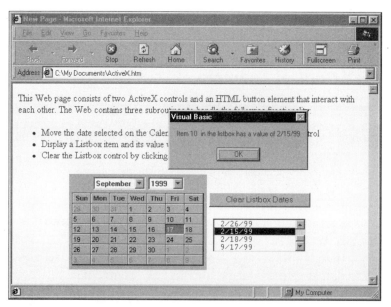

Figure 15-3. *Web page with multiple ActiveX controls.*

JAVA APPLETS

Java applets are similar to ActiveX controls in several ways. Like ActiveX controls, applets are components designed to do a specific task that can be added to Web pages and used within Internet Explorer and Navigator.

Unlike ActiveX controls, applets are not language independent and must be written using Java. An applet is both compiled and interpreted. When compiled, the source code for an applet is turned into byte code and placed in a file with a .class extension. This byte code in this .class file is then interpreted by the browser at runtime using a Java Virtual Machine. Applets can run on any platform that has a Java Virtual Machine installed on it. Platform-specific Virtual Machines are included with browsers and are installed automatically with the browser.

Adding Applets to Web Pages

Adding an applet to a Web page is similar to adding an ActiveX control. Once you have an applet you want to add to your Web page, use the HTML applet tag <APPLET></APPLET> and its attributes to add applets to your Web pages. Although the <APPLET> tag has several attributes, five of these attributes are of particular importance: CODE, CODEBASE, WIDTH, HEIGHT, and NAME.

<APPLET> Tag Attributes: CODE and CODEBASE

The CODE attribute is required and points to the .class file containing the applet to be downloaded. The value of the code attribute is case sensitive and cannot be an absolute URL; it must be relative to the URL of the Web page. If you want to put the .class files for an applet in a different location than where the Web page is, you use the CODEBASE attribute. The CODEBASE attribute can be an absolute or relative URL.

Using these two attributes with the <APPLET> tag looks like this:

```
<APPLET
  CODE="myApplet.class"
  CODEBASE="applets">
</APPLET>
```

<APPLET> Tag Attributes: WIDTH, HEIGHT, and NAME

The WIDTH and HEIGHT attributes are required. They affect a control's size and work the same with the <APPLET> tag as they do with the <OBJECT> tag. By default, WIDTH and HEIGHT both have a value of zero. This means the applet will not be visible on your Web page unless you set both of these attributes to values greater than zero. The NAME attribute works with the <APPLET> tag just like the ID attribute does with the <OBJECT> tag, allowing you to reference the element with scripting languages.

Adding these three attributes to the preceding example looks like this:

```
<APPLET
  CODE="myApplet.class"
  CODEBASE="/applets"
  HEIGHT=200
  WIDTH=200
  NAME="Animator">
</APPLET>
```

The <PARAM> Tag

As with ActiveX controls, the <PARAM> tag and its NAME and VALUE attributes are used to assign initial values to an applet's properties. You use a separate <PARAM> tag for each applet property you want to assign a value. These initial property values define how an applet appears when the Web page is first loaded by the browser.

Setting initial values using the <PARAM> tag looks like this:

```
<APPLET
  CODE="myApplet.class"
  CODEBASE="/applets"
  NAME="Animator"
  HEIGHT=200
  WIDTH=200>
  <PARAM NAME="interval" VALUE=.5>
  <PARAM NAME="repeat" VALUE="True">
</APPLET>
```

JAR Files

JAR files are the Java equivalent of Cabinet files. *JAR* stands for *Java ARchive*, which was added to the Java Development Kit in version 1.1. JAR files are based on the popular PKZIP file format. Like cabinet files, JAR files can contain several compressed, digitally signed files in a single library file.

JAR files can be used to package all the files an applet needs to run. JAR files will typically contain image, sound, and additional class files. To specify a JAR file containing the applet in the CODE attribute, use the <APPLET> tag's ARCHIVE attribute. An <APPLET> tag using a JAR file looks like this:

```
<APPLET
  CODE="myApplet.class"
  CODEBASE="/applets"
   ARCHIVE="myApplet.jar"
  NAME="Animator"
   HEIGHT=200
  WIDTH=200>
  <PARAM NAME="interval" VALUE=.5>
  <PARAM NAME="repeat" VALUE="True">
</APPLET>
```

Alternatively, you can create a ZIP file instead of a JAR file. If you specify a .zip file instead of a .jar file in the archive attribute, the Java Virtual Machine will read the ZIP file and extract the .class and other support files from it.

In addition, you can specify more than one JAR and ZIP file by separating each with a comma. For example, the <APPLET> tag could look like this:

```
<APPLET
  CODE="myApplet.class"
  CODEBASE="/applets"

   ARCHIVE="myApplet.jar,myApplet.zip"
  NAME="Animator"
   HEIGHT=200
  WIDTH=200>
  <PARAM NAME="interval" VALUE=.5>
  <PARAM NAME="repeat" VALUE="True">
</APPLET>
```

Packaging Applets in Cabinet Files

If your target browser is Internet Explorer, you can use cabinet files to package and download your applets. To specify a cabinet file containing the applet, add a <PARAM> tag to the applet definition. Set the <PARAM> tag's NAME attribute to "cabbase" and its VALUE attribute to the name and location of the cabinet file. Like .class files, a .cab file must be in the same location as the Web page or in the location specified with the CODEBASE attribute. An <APPLET> tag referencing a cabinet file looks like this:

```
<APPLET
  CODE="myApplet.class"
  NAME="Animator"
   HEIGHT=200
  WIDTH=200>
  <PARAM NAME="cabbase" VALUE="myApplet.cab">
</APPLET>
```

Like JAR and ZIP files, you can specify more than one cabinet file by adding a <PARAM> tag and setting its NAME attribute to "Cabinets." The VALUE attribute then contains a list of cabinet files separated by commas. For example, the <APPLET> tag could look like this:

```
<APPLET
  CODE="myApplet.class"
  NAME="Animator"
  HEIGHT=200
  WIDTH=200>
  <PARAM NAME="cabinets" VALUE="myApplet1.cab,myApplet2.cab">
</APPLET>
```

> **NOTE** If you include JAR or ZIP files and cabinet files in the same <APPLET> tag, Internet Explorer will search only the cabinet files. Any JAR or ZIP files will be ignored. Non-Internet Explorer browsers will ignore the cabinet files and use the JAR or ZIP files.

An <APPLET> tag referencing both a ZIP file and a cabinet file looks like this:

```
<APPLET
  CODE="myApplet.class"
  NAME="Animator"
  ARCHIVE="myApplet.zip"
  HEIGHT=200
  WIDTH=200>
  <PARAM NAME="cabbase" VALUE="myApplet.cab">
</APPLET>
```

The Future of the <APPLET> Tag

The W3C is proposing that the <OBJECT> tag be used to insert any type of object into a Web page. When this proposal is standardized, several existing HTML tags—including the <APPLET> tag—will become obsolete. Though both Microsoft and Netscape support the <APPLET> tag, only Microsoft browsers currently support the <OBJECT> tag.

Security

Microsoft's security implementation for Java is a trust-based model that supports granting a very granular level of permissions to applets and class libraries. This security model includes the following areas where access rights and permissions can be fine-tuned:

- The permission model provides control over what Java classes can do by allowing permissions to be associated with a class.

- Permission signing allows both digital signatures and permissions to be added to cabinet files.

- Permission scoping allows developers to control which specific parts of their trusted code are granted particular permissions.

- A Package Manager allows the installation of local class libraries that are not fully trusted by using permission signing.

NOTE: For complete details and in-depth information on Java security, see the Microsoft Java Software Development Kit at *msdn.microsoft.com/ java/techinfo.htm*.

Accessing Applets with Script

After you have added an applet to your Web page, you will want to write script to interact with that applet via its properties, methods, and events. Previously in this chapter, you learned how to script event handler routines to capture the events of controls as well as how to use a control's methods and properties. To script applets, you use the same techniques, because script that interacts with applets is identical to script that interacts with ActiveX controls.

DHTML SCRIPTLETS

DHTML scriptlets provide script authors with the ability to create robust and reusable controls without needing to know sophisticated development languages like C++ or Java. DHTML scriptlets can often duplicate the functionality and user interface of an ActiveX control or applet with much less code and effort. DHTML scriptlets can be built by using your favorite Web page creation tool or text editor so they're easy to develop and maintain. Their functionality can be written in any scripting language including VBScript and JavaScript. Because DHTML scriptlets are typically small and don't require additional support files, they also download faster than ActiveX controls and applets. DHTML scriptlets are supported by Internet Explorer on all platforms: Windows, Macintosh, and UNIX.

A DHTML scriptlet is a self-contained Web page containing Dynamic HTML (DHTML). DHTML scriptlets, like ActiveX controls, act as visual components that can be added to other Web pages and used within Internet Explorer or other ActiveX containers like Visual Basic forms.

DHTML Scriptlet Architecture

A DHTML scriptlet consists of a user interface created with DHTML and a control interface (publicly exposed properties, methods, and events) created with script. For example, a DHTML scriptlet could be a calendar control. The calendar's buttons and display fields could be created with DHTML and its control interface created with script. Web pages can then use the control interface to communicate with the DHTML scriptlet.

> NOTE   For more information on creating DHTML scriplets, see the Visual InterDev documentation or the Component Development area of the Microsoft Sitebuilder Web site at *www.microsoft.com/workshop/components/*.

A Web page or container application doesn't host a DHTML scriptlet directly. As shown in Figure 15-4, it hosts a scriptlet container object, which in turn hosts, or contains, the DHTML scriptlet. The scriptlet container object is responsible for displaying the DHTML scriptlet and providing an interface so the container application can access the DHTML scriptlet's properties, methods, and events. The scriptlet container object acts as a broker, passing property requests, method calls, and events back and forth between the Web page and the DHTML scriptlet.

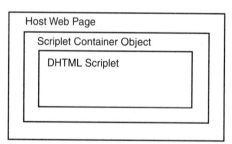

Figure 15-4. *Hosting a DHTML scriptlet via the Scriptlet Container object.*

Adding DHTML Scriptlets to Web Pages

As with Active X controls, you use the HTML object tag <OBJECT></OBJECT> and its attributes to add DHTML scriptlets to your Web pages. Five of these attributes are of particular importance for DHTML scriptlets: TYPE, DATA, ID, WIDTH, and HEIGHT.

<OBJECT> tag attributes: TYPE and DATA

The TYPE and DATA attributes of the <OBJECT> tag are required for DHTML scriptlets. The TYPE attribute is set to "text/x-scriptlet." This tells Internet Explorer that the object being inserted should be treated as a DHTML scriptlet. The DATA attribute is set to the DHTML scriptlet's filename using standard URL syntax. For example, adding a calendar DHTML scriptlet named myCalendar.htm to a Web page looks like this:

```
<OBJECT
  TYPE="text/x-scriptlet"
  DATA="myCalendar.htm">
</OBJECT>
```

<OBJECT> tag attributes: ID, WIDTH, and HEIGHT

The ID attribute works with the <OBJECT> tag just as it does with other HTML element tags, allowing you to reference the DHTML scriptlet from script in your Web page. Like ActiveX controls and applets, the DHTML scriptlet will not be visible unless you add WIDTH and HEIGHT attributes and set them both to values greater than zero. Adding these three attributes to the preceding example looks like this:

```
<OBJECT
  ID="myCalendar"
  WIDTH=200
  HEIGHT=150
  TYPE="text/x-scriptlet"
  DATA="myCalendar.htm">
</OBJECT>
```

Accessing DHTML Scriptlets

Properties and methods of DHTML scriptlets are manipulated the same way that properties and methods of ActiveX controls are, as shown earlier in this chapter. However, scripting event handlers for DHTML scriptlets are more complicated than for other components. Two types of events can occur:

■ **Standard events.** The Scriptlet Container object provides these events for all DHTML scriptlets automatically, like the events of intrinsic HTML elements. This means the developer doesn't have to explicitly write code to raise these events from within the DHTML scriptlet. The following standard events are automatically exposed by the Scriptlet Container object: onclick, ondblclick, onkeydown, onkeyup, onkeypress, onmousedown, onmouseup, and onmousemove. Event handlers are created in Web pages for standard events of DHTML scriptlets the same way event handlers are created for ActiveX controls, as discussed earlier.

■ **Custom events.** These are events, other than the standard events discussed earlier, that the DHTML scriptlet developer must write code to raise. For example, a DHTML scriptlet can contain a custom event that is raised when a timer is started.

Handling custom events

A DHTML scriptlet exposes events by bubbling them up to its parent, the Scriptlet Container object. The Scriptlet Container object passes all DHTML scriptlet events to the Web page through its Onscriptletevent event. Therefore, to handle any and all custom events bubbled up from a DHTML scriptlet, you must write script to handle the Scriptlet Container object's OnScriptletEvent event. The OnScriptletEvent event has two input parameters: eventName and eventObject. These two parameters can be evaluated to determine what event is being raised and which object in the DHTML scriptlet raised it. You can then handle multiple events from within this single routine.

The following two examples show the basic structure of a DHTML scriptlet custom event handler in VBScript and JavaScript:

```
<SCRIPT LANGUAGE="VBScript">
<!--
Sub ScriptletContainerID_ OnScriptletEvent
(MyEventName,MyEventObject)
        'script to evaluate and handle
     'multiple events go here
end sub
-->
</SCRIPT>
<SCRIPT LANGUAGE="JavaScript"
     FOR="ScriptContainerID"
     EVENT=" OnScriptletEvent (MyEventName, MyObjectName)">
        //script to evaluate and handle
     //multiple events go here
</SCRIPT>
```

DHTML Scriptlet Examples

It is common for DHTML scriptlets to perform tasks that previously required Java applets or ActiveX controls. Such tasks include menus, tab buttons, and even calculators. In the \Chapter 15\ directory on the companion CD, there are three ZIP files containing DHTML scriptlet examples of each of these tasks. These examples (shown in Figures 15-5, 15-6, and 15-7) were taken from the DHTML scriptlet samples gallery, which is part of the Microsoft Scripting Web site located at *http://msdn.microsoft.com/scripting/*. These and the other samples on the Web site show how to create DHTML scriptlets and use them in other Web pages. These examples demonstrate just how powerful a technology DHTML scriptlets is.

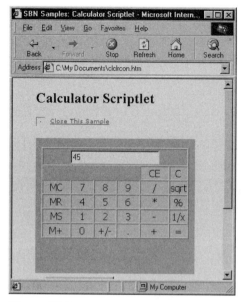

Figure 15-5. *Calculator DHTML scriptlet.*

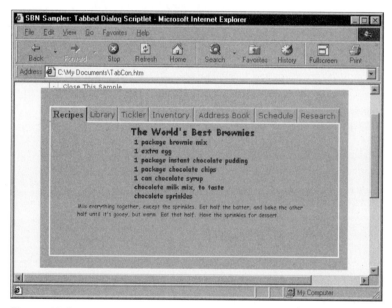

Figure 15-6. *Tabs DHTML scriptlet.*

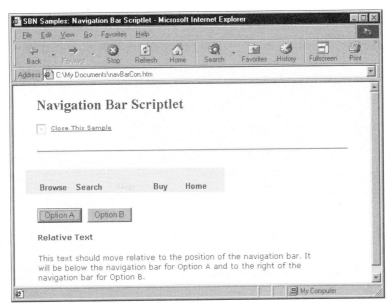

Figure 15-7. *Navigation Bar DHTML scriptlet.*

Security

Internet Explorer security will be applied to scriptlets and any controls contained within them. For users to access your DHTML scriptlet, both "Script ActiveX Controls Marked Safe for Scripting and Initialize" and "Script ActiveX Controls Not Marked As Safe" must be set to either Prompt or Enable. This can be done by setting security for the zone containing the DHTML scriptlet's Web site to Medium, Low, or Custom. DHTML scriptlets will not be downloaded if Internet Explorer's security is set to High for that zone.

Design Considerations and Browser Compatibility

While it's tempting to want to utilize new or proprietary technologies in your Web pages, use caution in your approach. A dominant factor in Web technology decisions remains the target Web browser. How advanced are the Web browsers that will be used to view your Web pages? Do these browsers support the technologies you have chosen to implement?

In this chapter, you learned about ActiveX controls, applets, and DHTML scriptlets. While all three are useful and effective technologies, only Internet Explorer supports them all. Netscape's browsers do not support DHTML scriptlets, and they support only ActiveX controls via a third-party plug-in called ScriptActive from NCompass Labs (*www.ncompasslabs.com*). Spending the time to analyze which of these technologies your environment and target browsers support is an important next step.

More Information on ActiveX Controls, Applets, and DHTML Scriptlets

This chapter got you started working with and reusing components in your Web pages, but it is not a complete developers guide. You'll find the following documentation and Web site references useful for deepening your knowledge of these technologies:

- ■ *microsoft.com/workshop.* The Microsoft Site Builder Network. This includes in-depth samples, documentation, and so on, on everything related to Internet client development, including ActiveX controls and DHTML scriptlets.

- ■ *msdn.microsoft.com/developer/sdk/java.htm.* The Microsoft Java Software Development Kit. This is an excellent resource for applet developers.

- ■ *www.microsoft.com/workshop/components/.* The   Component Development area of the Microsoft Sitebuilder Web site.

- ■ *msdn.microsoft.com/scripting/.* The Microsoft Scripting Technologies Web site. The information here includes excellent examples and downloads of DHTML scriptlets.

- ■ *The Visual InterDev documentation set.* Now part of the MSDN Library for Visual Studio, this online documentation provides thorough coverage of component technologies as they apply to Web development.

SUMMARY

ActiveX controls, Java applets, and DHTML scriptlets play an important role in extending the user interfaces of Web pages by providing sophisticated technologies to build business logic and user interfaces encapsulated in consistent, reusable components.

All three technologies add critical functionality to Web pages that can address presentation, logic, user event, and data handling needs. Leveraging component technologies in your development efforts will enable you to create sophisticated and robust Web-based applications not possible with HTML alone.

Chapter 16

Information Exchange with XML

by Steve Gilmore

It is difficult to have a conversation about electronic commerce, extranets, or any multi-tiered system today without including XML. Like HyperText Markup Language (HTML), the Extensible Markup Language (XML) is a standard tag-based language maintained by the World Wide Web Consortium (W3C). However, unlike HTML, which is used to display and present content, XML is used to describe structured data.

XML is really a meta-language that makes it possible to create other languages that describe data structures: hierarchies of data elements described by their surrounding tags and attributes. Because XML data has this "self-describing" nature, it is easier to understand and, therefore, easier to develop, maintain, and share than traditional data formatted as columns and rows.

XML also provides a way of transferring structured data between applications and systems. XML, a subset of Standard Generalized Markup Language (SGML), is optimized for the Web to ensure that structured data that is vendor- and application-independent can be efficiently exchanged over the Web. This open interoperability is one characteristic that makes XML extremely useful for electronic commerce applications. Diverse systems can now share and exchange structured data using XML over HyperText Transport Protocol (HTTP) as easily as HTML pages are transmitted over HTTP from Web server to browser.

Data such as customer information, credit card transactions, purchase orders, and fulfillment requests can be converted to XML and shared across applications without changing legacy systems. XML can be used to exchange data between Web server and browser or between trading partners without the existing systems needing any prior description of the data's structure.

NOTE   Because many of the W3C's XML recommendations are still in the definition stages, this chapter is presented as a survey to show several of the more evolved features of the language and to point you to the latest information. Microsoft currently supports XML in Internet Explorer 4.0 and 5.0, and you can learn more about most of the topics discussed in this chapter at *http://www.microsoft.com/xml.*

XML Benefits

For developing Web-based applications, XML offers several benefits to both the users and developers. Here are just a few of the things that can be gained:

- **Separation of Data from Presentation.** XML data structures are separate from the HTML used to display them. Multiple views and customizable presentations of the same data set can be used without making additional requests to the Web server.

- **Improved User Interface.** XML data can reside on the client and provide local data to the browser without requiring repeated requests to the Web server over the network. XML data on the client can be manipulated and displayed almost instantly, reducing response time and improving the user's experience.

- **Data Integration.** XML enables you to create structured data from almost any application and data source. Disparate legacy data can be converted into XML data structures on the fly and transmitted over the Web.

- **Scalable.** XML data can be granularly updated, eliminating the need to retransmit an entire data structure each time data is changed or added. This reduces the Web server's workload.

- **Compression.** XML compresses extremely well due to the repetitive nature of the tags used to describe data structure. Compression can improve the transfer speed of large data structures.

- **Open Standards.** XML is based on proven standards-based technology optimized for the Web (such as SGML and HTTP), ensuring interoperability and support for multiple systems and browsers.

XML FEATURES IN INTERNET EXPLORER

Internet Explorer 4.0, the first IE version to provide XML support, offered three core features:

- **XML Parsing Engines.** Each XML parsing engine reads in and exposes XML via the W3C Document Object Model (DOM) standard. Microsoft included two parsers: a C++ parser (that ships with Internet Explorer 4) and a downloadable Java parser.

- **XML Object Model.** A subset of the DOM used to allow programmatic access to structured XML data.

- **XML Data Source Object.** Allows Dynamic HTML data binding to structured XML data.

XML support in Internet Explorer 5 is taken to the next level, adding the following features:

- **Improved Parsing Engines.** Improved performance with full support for the W3C XML recommendation.

- **Enhanced XML Document Object Model (DOM).** Includes full support for the W3C XML DOM recommendation. The XML DOM is accessible from script and COM-compliant programming languages.

- **Improved XML Data Source Object.** Increased performance and improved ability to bind to XML data to Dynamic HTML.

- **XML Schemas Preview.** Schemas are an unfinished W3C recommendation offered as an improved replacement for Document Type Definitions (DTD), which define the rules and characteristics of an XML document.

- **Extensible Stylesheet Language (XSL) Support.** Based on the W3C XSL recommendation, XSL provides a presentation language for displaying structured XML data.

- **XML Viewing.** Displays XML in the Internet Explorer 5 browser just as an HTML document would be displayed.

THE XML LANGUAGE

XML is a tag-based language designed for storing and transmitting data. An XML data structure is a collection of one or more data elements, where each data element consists of start and end tags surrounding element data. Unlike HTML's predefined tags, XML allows unlimited user-defined tags—each describing data elements without providing display instructions. You decide what kind of data to use and what tag names will best describe the data. Any application that receives your data can then understand and decode the data based on the element tag names.

For example, a traditional comma-delimited bank transaction record might looks like this:

```
87334258,57489024,13672.74,230.45,19990812
```

You can see that the record, by itself, does not contain enough information to be useful. Converting this record into XML looks like this:

```
<transaction>
<account_from>87334258</account_from>
<account_to>57489024</account_to>
<previous_bal>13672.74</previous_bal>
<transaction_amt>230.45</transaction_amt>
<transaction_date>19990812</transaction_date>
</transaction>
```

Anyone looking at this data can now immediately understand and use the data. Notice that the tag names are determined by the author of the data and should be as descriptive as possible. XML element data can also contain additional element tags. For example, further defining the date in the preceding data structure looks like this:

```
<transaction>
    <account_from>87334258</account_from>
    <account_to>57489024</account_to>
    <previous_bal>13672.74</previous_bal>
    <transaction_amt>230.45</transaction_amt>
    <transaction_date>
        <year>1999</year>
        <month>08</month>
        <day>12</day>
    </transaction_date>
</transaction>
```

Elements can also have attributes to further define the data. Like HTML, attributes are added within the start tag in XML. However, unlike HTML, an XML attribute's value must be enclosed in quotes. For example, a currency attribute could be added to the transaction_amt element like this:

```
<transaction_amt currency="USD">230.45</transaction_amt>
```

XML requires that each data element be terminated with an end tag. A data element that contained no data would therefore look like this:

```
<savings_account></savings_account>
```

Empty data elements can also be represented as follows:

```
<savings_account/>
```

Using this second option will reduce the physical size of your XML data structure because there are fewer characters, but it is less intuitive and requires additional parsing of the data.

XML is a case-sensitive language. Consequently, the following three empty elements are not the same:

```
<savings_account/>
<Savings_Account/>
<SAVING_ACCOUNT/>
```

Like HTML, XML allows nested elements, but they cannot overlap. This means that the first group of elements in the following listing uses incorrect syntax, while the second is correct:

```
<account_1>
<account_1a>
</account_1>
</account_1a>
<account_1>
  <account_1a>
  </account_1a>
</account_1>
```

In addition, XML comments are identical to HTML comments:

```
<!-- This comment syntax is the same in HTML and XML -->
```

Unlike HTML, XML does not ignore white space (including line feeds and carriage returns). This means that the following two elements' data are different:

```
<model>4 door sedan</model>

<model>4 door
sedan</model>
```

This is particularly important to understand when performing data element comparisons because the data in the two previous elements are not equal.

Like any development language, XML contains reserved words and characters. At some point, you will inevitably create an element that contains a character or phrase that is a reserved word or character in XML. For example, suppose an XML element contained angle brackets. When this happens, the XML parser won't be able to tell what is XML syntax and what is data. To tell the XML parser that a section of data is not XML, the CDATA construct is used. The CDATA syntax looks like this:

```
<![CDATA[this data will be ignored]]>
```

If your element data consisted of a<b, the XML parser would see the angle brackets and try to interpret this as XML tags unless you placed it inside a CDATA section like this:

```
<![CDATA[a<b]]>
```

Here is a summary of the main XML syntax rules discussed:

XML SYNTAX SUMMARY

XML is case-sensitive.

XML does not ignore white space.

XML elements must have a start and end tag unless empty. If empty, they must have a single tag with the slash after the element name.

XML attributes must be enclosed in quotes.

XML elements cannot overlap.

XML comments use the same syntax as HTML comments.

XML's CDATA construct is available for insulating content from the parser.

Document Structure

An XML document must consist of at least one XML element (the root element). This root element may or may not include additional nested XML elements. In addition, all XML documents should begin with the XML declaration literal:

```
<?xml version="1.0">
```

This is a processing instruction used to identify the contents of the document as XML. The complete structure of an XML document therefore looks like this:

```
<?xml version="1.0">
<order>
  <product_id>346553</product_id>
  <unit_price>12.95</unit_price>
  <quantity>3<quantity>
</order>
```

ADDING XML TO HTML PAGES: XML DATA ISLANDS

HTML has always lacked a way of embedding data inside HTML pages. Internet Explorer 5 addresses this with *data islands*, XML data structures that are embedded within an HTML page. Once the XML is integrated into an HTML page, you can access the XML without having to use a control or Java Applet. Anything that can be placed in a well-formed XML document can be placed inside a data island on an HTML page.

The XML Tag

There are two ways to embed a data island into an HTML document. The first is inline, where the XML data structure is surrounded by the <XML></XML> tags. Notice the <XML> tag's ID attribute. This is used to reference the data structure from a scripting language.

```
<XML ID="xmlid">
<transaction>
  <account_from>87334258</account_from>
  <account_to>57489024</account_to>
  <previous_bal>13672.74</previous_bal>
  <transaction_amt>230.45</transaction_amt>
  <transaction_date>19990812</transaction_date>
</transaction>
</XML>
```

The second way to embed a data island is to specify an external XML file using the <XML> tag's SRC attribute. That syntax looks like this:

```
<XML ID="xmlid" SRC="transaction.xml"></XML>
```

A complete HTML page with an embedded XML data island looks like this:

```
<HTML>
<HEAD>
<TITLE>HTML with XML</TITLE>
</HEAD>
<BODY>
<XML ID="xmlid">
    <transaction>
        <account_from>87334258</account_from>
        <account_to>57489024</account_to>
        <previous_bal>13672.74</previous_bal>
        <transaction_amt>230.45</transaction_amt>
        <transaction_date>19990812</transaction_date>
    </transaction>
</XML>
</BODY>
</HTML>
```

THE DOCUMENT OBJECT MODEL (DOM)

In Chapter 14, you saw how the DOM exposes the various elements of an HTML page, allowing them to be manipulated. The DOM also exposes an XML document and its various data elements, allowing them to be manipulated.

When the XML document is parsed and loaded, an object in the DOM representing your XML document is created that can be referenced by the document's ID value. The object that is created is really an XML Object Model consisting of a hierarchical tree of nodes (elements, attributes, and so on), representing the complete XML document. The XML document's data can then be manipulated using the properties and methods of the XML Object Model.

Using the XML document with the ID of xmlid referenced in the previous code sample, you would access the account_from element's data using the following syntax:

```
xmlid.documentElement.childNodes.item("account_from").text
```

For more information on the DOM, see the W3C's Web site at *www.w3.org/ DOM/.* -

THE DATA SOURCE OBJECT (DSO)

You'll recall from Chapter 14 that an ActiveX Data Source Object (DSO) was embedded in an HTML page to provide DHTML data binding. Internet Explorer 5 ships with an updated DSO written in C++ that offers better performance than the previous version. This DSO can also be used to bind DHTML to XML (including binding directly to an XML data island). In addition, the DSO provides the capability to create XML-driven Web applications without needing to declare an APPLET or OBJECT. This simplifies development and eliminates the need to download additional files from the Web server.

Binding DHTML Elements to XML Data Sources

Let's assume you have product information in the following XML file, products.xml, that you want to display:

```
<products>
    <product>
        <product_id>37482</product_id>
        <description>Product A</description>
        <unit_price>14.92</unit_price>
    </product>
    <product>
        <product_id>29768</product_id>
        <description>Product B</description>
        <unit_price>11.92</unit_price>
    </product>
    <product>
        <product_id>58720</product_id>
        <description>Product C</description>
        <unit_price>9.54</unit_price>
    </product>
    <product>
        <product_id>78911</product_id>
        <description>Product D</description>
        <unit_price>10.99</unit_price>
    </product>
    <product>
        <product_id>03354</product_id>
        <description>Product E</description>
        <unit_price>15.74</unit_price>
    </product>
</products>
```

The following HTML page binds DHTML to the XML products.xml document.. You'll notice that this HTML page is almost identical to that in the DHTML data binding example in Chapter 14. Besides cosmetics, the main difference is that the <object></object> tags were replaced by the <XML></XML> tags so that an XML document could be referenced instead of a text file.

```
<HTML>
<HEAD>
<TITLE>XML Data Binding Example</TITLE>
</HEAD>
<BODY>
<DIV ALIGN=CENTER>
<P>The following table is bound to the products.xml document.</P>
<H2>Product Inventory</H2>

<XML ID="XMLproducts" SRC="products.xml"></XML>

<TABLE BORDER="1" DATASRC="#XMLproducts">
<THEAD>
<TR>
<TH>Product ID</TH>
<TH>Description</TH>
<TH>Unit Price</TH>
</TR>
</THEAD>
<TR>
<TD><SPAN DATAFLD="product_id"></SPAN></TD>
<TD><SPAN DATAFLD="description"></SPAN></TD>
<TD><SPAN DATAFLD="unit_price"></SPAN></TD>
</TR>
</TABLE>
</DIV>
</BODY>
</HTML>
```

This example can be found on the companion CD in the \Chapter 16\ directory and looks like Figure 16-1 in Internet Explorer.

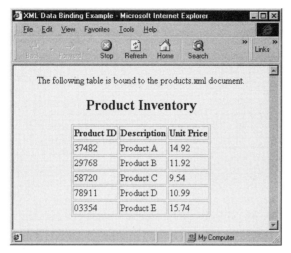

Figure 16-1. *Binding DHTML elements to XML data sources.*

TURNING RELATIONAL DATA INTO XML DATA

While it is true that XML documents offer many benefits, it is also true that most of your legacy data resides in relational databases, not in XML documents. By combining a couple of technologies discussed in this book, this problem is easily solved. Using ASP and ADO, you can create XML documents from relational data on the fly.

The following ASP page creates a file identical to the preceding products.xml file on the fly. It uses the File System Object and ADO to open a Microsoft Access database, execute a query, and write the results into a formatted XML document. It then returns a page to the browser displaying the name of the XML document that was created.

```
<%@ Language=VBScript %>
<?xml version="1.0">
<%
'set file path and name using the Server and Session objects
DefaultDir = Server.MapPath("\")
sFileName = session.SessionID & ".xml"

'open file
Set fs = CreateObject("Scripting.FileSystemObject")
Set sFile = fs.CreateTextFile(DefaultDir & "\" & sFileName)

'create ADO connection and recordset
```

(continued)

(continued)

```
Set cnProducts = Server.CreateObject("ADODB.Connection")
cnProducts.Open "productsDB"
Set rsProducts = cnProducts.Execute("select * from products")

'write the root element
sFile.WriteLine ("<products>")

'write all DB records
Do While Not rsProducts.EOF
sFile.WriteLine ("    <product>")
sFile.WriteLine ("        <product_id>" &rsProducts("prodid")& "</
      product_id>")
sFile.WriteLine ("        <description>" &rsProducts("desc")& "</
      description>")
sFile.WriteLine ("        <unit_price>" &rsProducts("uprice")& "</
      unit_price>")
sFile.WriteLine ("    </product>")
      rsProducts.MoveNext
Loop

'close the root element
sFile.WriteLine ("</products>")

'close file
sFile.Close

'close and release DB objects
rsProducts.close
cnProducts.close
%>
<HTML>
<HEAD>
<TITLE>Chapter 16 Example</TITLE>
</HEAD>
<BODY>
<H3>Results</H3>
The product file <%=DefaultDir & "\" & sFileName%> was just
created.
</BODY>
</HTML>
```

The resulting XML document looks like this:

```
<products>
      <product>
      <product_id>37482</product_id>
      <description>Product A</description>
      <unit_price>14.92</unit_price>
      </product>
       <product>
      <product_id>29768</product_id>
      <description>Product B</description>
      <unit_price>11.92</unit_price>
   </product>
   <product>
      <product_id>58720</product_id>
      <description>Product C</description>
      <unit_price>9.54</unit_price>
   </product>
   <product>
      <product_id>78911</product_id>
      <description>Product D</description>
      <unit_price>10.99</unit_price>
   </product>
   <product>
      <product_id>03354</product_id>
      <description>Product E</description>
      <unit_price>15.74</unit_price>
   </product>
</products>
```

This example can be found on the companion CD in the \Chapter 16\ directory, and looks like Figure 16-2 in Internet Explorer.

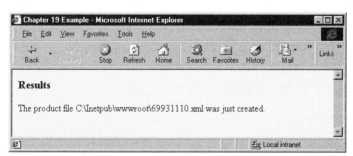

Figure 16-2. *Creating an XML document from a database.*

NOTE An ODBC data source named productsDB pointing to the products.MDB file is needed to run this example. To create this data source, follow these instructions:

1. Go to the Windows control panel and double-click the ODBC icon.

2. Select the System DSN tab, and then click the Add button.

3. Select the Microsoft Access driver and click Finish.

4. Type **productDB** in the Data Source Name text box.

5. Click the Select button and browse to the products.MDB file on the companion CD.

6. Click OK.

With a little modification, this same example could embed an XML data island directly into an HTML page. Creating XML documents from flat files or transferring data from an XML document to a relational database is also easily done.

NAMESPACES

It's common for commerce applications to access data from multiple sources. If XML documents are used to supply data for an e-commerce application, it is likely that an element in one XML document could have the same name as an element in another, causing a conflict. For example, two XML documents could have an element named <account>.

To solve this problem, namespaces were added to XML to avoid duplicate and thus conflicting names defined in different XML documents. Namespaces let you eliminate duplicates by attaching a namespace prefix to uniquely qualify element names. XML namespaces are supported by Internet Explorer 5 and higher.

For more information on XML Namespaces, see *http://www.w3.org/TR/WD-xml-names*.

FORMATTING XML WITH XSL

The Extensible Stylesheet Language (XSL) defines rules for mapping structured XML data to HTML for display. XSL allows XML elements to be formatted and displayed anywhere on a page and in any order. The resulting presentation can be completely different from the underlying XML data structure.

XSL can be thought of as the next generation of Cascading Style Sheets (CSS). Chapter 14 showed how to use CSS to format an HTML page. XSL takes formatting to the next level by allowing you to manipulate, sort, and filter XML data before displaying it. With XSL, you define templates (or style sheets) consisting of construction rules that describe how an element is transformed into

HTML. When the template is processed, the XSL style sheet and XML data are merged to produce HTML output. Because XML can represent data from any relational database, XSL allows you to manipulate, sort, and filter relational database information and display it for HTML-only browsers.

XML VOCABULARIES

XML vocabularies, also known as data formats, are standard collections of elements used in particular applications or industries. Vocabularies provide a common language that makes interoperability between applications and business partners possible. It will soon be common to have standard XML vocabularies defined for applications and industries such as messaging, decision support, telecommunications, and electronic commerce. For example, a dental trade group could define a specialized vocabulary containing elements such as <denture>, <filling>, and <last_cleaning> that could be exchanged with insurance companies to streamline the claims process. You can also build your own vocabularies to use within your organization or to exchange with business partners.

Although many XML vocabularies are on the way, several are already in use today. The following list describes some of the most common:

- **Open Finance Exchange (OFX).** OFX is used to allow financial institutions and personal finance applications to communicate and exchange data over the Web. Popular applications such as Microsoft Money and Intuit Quicken use OFX today.

- **Open Software Description (OSD).** OSD is used to automate software distribution. It describes software packages and their dependencies for heterogeneous clients.

- **Channel Definition Format (CDF).** CDF is used in Internet Explorer for describing Active Channel content. CDF contains elements, such as <Schedule>, <Channel>, and <Item>, that make up the vocabulary for describing collections of HTML pages, when and how often these pages should be downloaded, and so on.

TOOLS AND UTILITIES

One of the benefits of XML is that it's text-based. This means that you can create and modify XML with your favorite text or HTML editor. If you would like a tool designed specifically for XML, there are dozens available from third-party vendors. The following tools and utilities are free from Microsoft and can be found on the companion CD in the \Chapter 16\ directory.

■ The XML Notepad, shown in Figure 16-3, allows you to create XML documents and data structures quickly and easily.

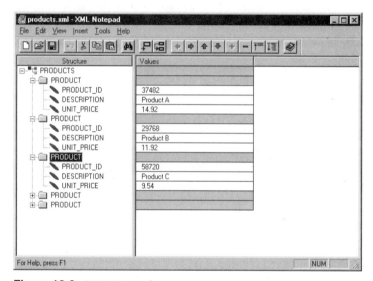

Figure 16-3. *XML Notepad.*

■ XMLINT validates XML document files (or directories of files). With this command line utility, you can verify that your XML documents are valid or well formed.

■ The CDF Generator (see Figure 16-4) provides an excellent wizard and editing environment for creating and modifying CDF files.

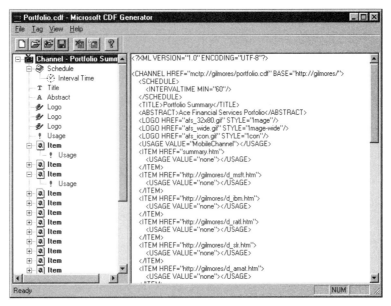

Figure 16-4. *CDF Generator.*

■ CDFTest is a program that will verify the structure and syntax of a CDF or OSD file. It will find mistakes such as missing end tags as well as incorrect or misspelled tags, saving you lots of time.

SUMMARY

Although XML is young, it appears positioned to be the primary data storage and transfer mechanism for Web-based commerce applications. A thorough working knowledge of XML technologies and an understanding of their future direction will enable you to create robust Web-based commerce applications.

Although XML is young, it is the fastest evolving technology on the Web. While you've learned about many of the standards and recommendations that fall under the XML umbrella today, this is by no means a definitive XML resource. Here are two Web sites to help you stay on top of XML as it matures:

■ **www.w3c.org/XML.** The W3C is the authority for the current XML standard and the proposed recommendations. Their site also includes information on several other related standards such as XSL and XML Schemas.

- **www.microsoft.com/xml.** This site is an excellent resource for everything Microsoft is doing with and has planned for XML. You'll find the latest news, technical articles, tutorials, and software downloads. For access to some areas of the site, you might need to complete the free registration.

Chapter 17

Microsoft Office 2000 and the Web

by Charles Maxson

It may or may not be strikingly obvious, but one of the key ingredients to your success in creating Web-based commerce solutions is probably one of your favorites: old tools. Microsoft Office, more specifically Microsoft Office 2000, is a supercharged application for the Web. It will allow you to extend your business further, while starting from a point where you and your business partners already spend a lot of time working. And that's with desktop tools.

But after reading the other chapters of this book, you may be wondering how does a desktop productivity suite fit in with building great E-commerce sites? Your first reaction might be that Microsoft Office is just an end user tool. Hasn't it been around long before the Web became prominent? How can it add value to the Web?

Well let's start with the basics. You're probably already an Office user. Your colleagues probably use it almost every day. Chances are that it's installed throughout your entire organization. In fact, the revolution called Microsoft Office has reached epic proportions across desktops around the world. And frankly, it's where an awful lot of real business is being conducted.

Knowing this, what if you were building an extranet to bolster your relationship with your trading partners? Wouldn't they be more impressed if you delivered a solution for them in the tools *they* use and understand? Instead of creating a report in HTML they could merely look at in a browser, what if you delivered a *working* spreadsheet model they could use to perform analyses, draw conclusions, make decisions, *buy your product, see you as a preferred partner...*? Well, you get the picture!

In this chapter, we will examine how Microsoft Office 2000 allows you to take advantage of common functionality you expect from desktop applications as well as some of the newer features that truly Web-enable Microsoft Office.

USING MICROSOFT OFFICE DOCUMENTS WITH THE WEB

For years, users have been creating and sharing Microsoft Office documents to conduct business. Originally, the "sneaker-net" (the passing of a floppy diskette from user to user) was a protocol for "working together." Then as LANs, WANs, and e-mail became the norm, information flowed much more freely as documents routed their way to other users. This was great for internal operations, but did little to help clients, outside partners, or anyone else not privileged to the network. So you printed, you faxed, you mailed, you waited for a response. But then you realized someone in accounting made a mistake. So you went through the same motions and re-sent the whole project over again, with your apologies attached.

But then, of course, came the Internet. And the rest, you can say is, well, history. With the release of Office '97, Microsoft saw this changing tide in the way people shared information, and introduced features that allowed users to push Office-created content to the Web. Files could be saved as HTML, Web page templates were included for all of the products, and features like hyperlinks in Office documents were included. While this version of Office was a significant breakthrough, certain limitations made it less than robust as a Web tool. However, it did lay the underlying foundation for the follow-up version, Office 2000.

In this latest release of Microsoft Office, much of the wish list that remained from Office '97 has been fulfilled. HTML document creation is both realistic and reliable. In Office 2000, Microsoft has added HTML as a companion file format to its own proprietary binary file format. So saving a document as HTML is as seamless as saving it natively.

Office 2000 Document HTML File Format

Traditionally, an Office document was stored as a single binary file: .DOC (Word), .XLS (Excel), .PPT (PowerPoint), or MDB (Access). With Office 2000, you have a choice. You may select to use an application's inherent format to create files or the new HTML file format. But what's even more impressive is that you can go back and forth with the same document, "round-trip," between binary and HTML formats without losing any content or functionality. The ramifications here are huge. You can leverage your knowledge of Office to create very serious Web pages without having to learn HTML or use other Web publishing software. And just think of all of the Office documents that already exist in your organization that can now be utilized as Web content and still function in their respective Office applications as you would expect.

From the desktop to the Web

Let's take a look at how this high-fidelity HTML support is obtained by first seeing how easy it is to achieve. Let's use Microsoft Word, which is the default HTML editor for Office, as the application for this scenario. Note that although the Office applications operate similarly, the obvious differences between products cause them to have some of their own unique characteristics in how they react when creating HMTL. Word happens to be the truest of the Office suite in HTML content creation and retention, and probably the product that will be most often called upon to create HTML.

Suppose you have created a document in Microsoft Word that you want to publish as content for your intranet. When you are done working with it, instead of saving it to your hard drive or network as a ".DOC" binary file, you can publish it directly to any Web server. To do so, choose "Save as Web Page" from the "File" command bar, as shown in Figure 17-1.

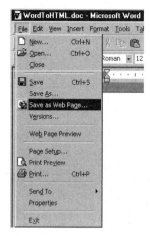

Figure 17-1. *Word's File Command bar.*

NOTE This scenario requires Office Server Extensions (OSE), which is a set of server extensions installed to an IIS server that enables Office to work directly with the Web server. OSE will be covered in more detail later in the chapter.

Also note that on the "File" command bar just below the "Save as Web Page" function, is the "Web Page Preview" option. Web Page Preview, similar to Print Preview, will allow you to see how your document will appear in your *default* browser without having to save the document as HTML and without leaving the application.

Next, you are presented with the Office 2000 common "Save As" dialog (seen in Figure 17-2) that has been extended to support Web integration. For this figure, the "Web Folders" icon at the bottom left of the dialog has been clicked, which reveals all of the Web servers available at this time. Next, you just save the document to the folder in the site you want and you are published!

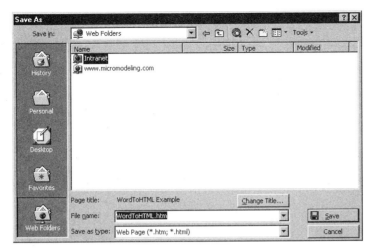

Figure 17-2. *Office 2000's common "Save As" dialog—shown in Word.*

Since this makes publishing to the Web as easy as saving a file or printing, it opens up possibilities of relieving the Webmaster's burden by allowing others to contribute content to a Web site with little effort or technical assistance. (This may be a good or bad thing depending on your view of securing a Web site.) Wouldn't it be nice if the guys in your Procurement Department could speed up the RFP process by posting them to an extranet dedicated to all your suppliers and vendors?

Behind the Office HTML file format

So what physically happens to an Office document when you save it as HTML? Let's examine that closer. On the companion CD in the \Chapter 17\ directory is a sample Word document named "WordToHTML.doc" that was saved as an HTML document named "WordToHTML.htm." You can use this document as reference in this discussion of the HTML file format.

The first noticeable difference between creating an Office binary file and a new Office HTML file is the quantity of files created. A file saved in its native binary creates only one physical file. But depending on the complexity and the content of the Office document going into HTML, the number of actual files created for an HTML "file" can vary drastically. Why this occurs will be explained in greater detail in the upcoming sections in this chapter.

The Office HTML file format is built upon standard HTML (HyperText Markup Language), CSS (Cascading Style Sheets), and XML (eXtensible Markup Language).

> **NOTE** For a much more detailed look at these languages, refer to Chapter 13 for HTML, Chapter 14 for CSS, and Chapter 16 for XML.

HTML

Office begins with HTML to define the structure of a document. Items like content, document layout, paragraphs, basic formatting are represented in HTML. Office 2000 preserves all unknown HTML that it encounters, so that it won't damage HTML documents containing unknown tags when opened in Office.

CSS

CSS is used to represent the more sophisticated formatting and positioning that HTML is not capable of supporting. You can think of CSS as "Styles" that you would use in Word. Office uses CSS to manage headers/footers, margins, page setup, character and paragraph formatting such as fonts and borders.

CSS allows Office 2000 documents to avoid being compromised by preserving information in the file that isn't rendered by the browser. An example of this is how Office handles border styles with CSS. Complex border formats that cannot be duplicated by the browser are "replaced" by the best alternate the browser can provide. The CSS property set by Office to represent the border is still a part of the HTML file, but ignored by the browser. But when the document is loaded back into Word for editing, the rich border styles remain as Office intended.

XML

Similar to CSS, Office uses XML to capture data that is resident in a document that isn't represented in HTML. It acts like a storage mechanism for Office files when they are being used in a browser, but when they are re-edited in an Office application, the data is reloaded to complete the round-trip. Office-specific features like file properties, document settings, OLE document properties, Office Art, formats for Excel charts and PivotTables are stored in XML.

The following Office-generated XML is an excerpt from our sample file's HTML source code. Basically, it stores the document's View property as "Print" so when it is edited in Word that setting is applied.

```
<!--[if gte mso 9]><xml>
<w:WordDocument>
<w:View>Print</w:View>
</w:WordDocument>
</xml><![endif]-->
```

For an in-depth look at the HTML, CSS, and XML code that Office generates, open the sample file WordToHTML.htm in Internet Explorer and select "View, Source." Since this is a rather simple example, create some of your some own documents and see what Office 2000 uses to produce them as HTML. You may be amazed at how little it takes to make all this happen.

Supporting binary files

One last thing to mention about Office HTML File Format is what happens to
those things that HTML, CSS, and XML do not handle. To ensure that *none* of
the Office functionality gets left behind en route to HTML and back, Office
employs a "catch-all" binary to hold those items. Items not represented by HTML,
CSS, or XML include:

- Visual Basic for Applications (VBA) projects
- Customized command bar information
- Embedded fonts
- OLE object edit data

The one(s) that got away

Microsoft has gone to great lengths to make the binary and HTML file formats
as identical as possible. In fact, they claim that Microsoft Word is $99^{44/100}$ percent pure at handling full round trips. Judging by how close the sample file
"WordToHTML.*" looks and acts in both Word and IE, this claim appears to true.
Well, almost. On creating the HTML version of "WordToHTML.doc," the message shown in Figure 17-3 was generated.

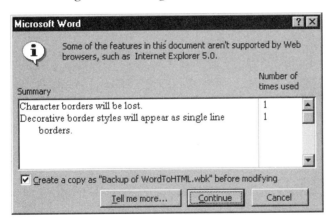

Figure 17-3. *Warning about unsupported features when saving as HTML.*

And if you round trip the HTML file back to a Word binary file (save as

.DOC), the fancy borders are not maintained. But overall, the results are very impressive.

File management for Office HTML

As you may have gathered from reading the last few sections, creating an Office document as HTML doesn't come without cost. One such cost is the usage of multiple physical files. When an HTML document is created, an HTML file (.HTM) is saved at the location specified by the user, whether on a file server or a Web server. Additional supporting files that may be required are then automatically placed in a folder created by Office. The new folder bears the same name as the .HTM file with the word "files" appended to it. Figure 17-4 shows the outcome of saving the sample WordToHTML.doc as HTML.

Figure 17-4. *File structure for the sample WordToHTML.doc saved as HTML*

Depending on the complexity and content of the Office document being saved, the HTML file format can require supporting files that include:

- **.mso.** A binary file that maintains Office-specific features such as a VBA project

- **.css.** Additional information relevant to Cascading Style Sheets (CSS)

- **.xml.** XML-supported information including one file specifically used to manage the list of all of these supporting files

- **.gif.** A picture file for each drawn object found in the document

- **.htm.** Additional HTML support that cannot be included in the main file such as a file for each worksheet in an multisheet Excel workbook, or each slide in a PowerPoint presentation.

- **.wmz.** Binary file support for Office-specific components

- **.js.** Java script files that allow Office to support buttons for navigation between sheets in Excel, or slides in PowerPoint.

One of the challenges with this *one document to many files* format is that if you move, copy, or delete any part of the HTML file structure, *you*, not the operating system, must account for all of the files and directories that make up the document. So if you use a Windows Explorer to copy an HTML document, you have to make sure you copy all of the supporting files to the new location yourself. The risk here is obvious; without careful management, users may encounter lost file components, cross-version document issues or hanging fragments. If you intend to move files around a lot or share them with others via e-mail, think about using the traditional binary file format for simplicity of management. Note that Windows NT 5 will introduce a new technology, IntelliMirror, which will help alleviate this issue by treating the files as one when performing OS functions.

The ultimate Office viewer

Web browsers are the "universal viewers" for Office 2000 documents. The support of the HTML file format serves as a standard format for sharing with non-Office users, or those using older versions. This enables Office 2000 users to freely share their work without regard to the platform their audience uses, as long as they have access to a browser.

USING THE "RIGHT" BROWSER WITH OFFICE 2000 DOCUMENTS

Office 2000 documents will work with good results with most commonly used browsers, specifically Netscape Navigator 4 or Internet Explorer 4. They even work reasonably well with earlier ones. But with older browsers, you must be very careful in selecting some of the Office features you use, since they may support different levels of HTML/CSS. For example, Access Data Pages (discussed later in the chapter) only work with IE 4 or higher. The best way to really optimize the experience of Web-based Office 2000 documents is by using Microsoft Internet Explorer 5.

If you have no control over the browser choice of your audience, you can instruct Office 2000 to ignore some of its advanced features or "aim" your content at a specific browser. To do this from any of the Office applications, select "Tools, Options" from the command bar, then select the "General" tab and click the "Web Options" button. Each Office application has its own set of features that can be altered or removed from this Web Options dialog to suit different browsers.

Above all, review any content created with Office 2000 in the specific version of browser that your audience will use to ensure it performs as you intended.

Intelligent Editing

Since all Office 2000 documents saved in HTML file format have an .HTM extension, Office creates tags within the HTML code that identify which application is actually the owner. The following code was taken from our sample document created in Microsoft Word:

```
<meta name="ProgId" content="Word.Document">
<meta name="Generator" content="Microsoft Word 9">
<meta name="Originator" content="Microsoft Word 9">
```

This allows HTML files to be recognized properly by Office and allows editing to be done in the right Office application. A nice feature in Microsoft Internet Explorer 5 is that it uses these tags to launch the Office 2000 application that created the HTML file, making editing within Web browsers much easier. Figure 17-5 shows the IE 5 tool bar with the cursor over the edit Office component.

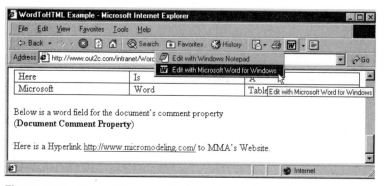

Figure 17-5. *Microsoft Internet Explorer 5 with the Intelligent Editing feature.*

HTML Script authoring

Adding to the capabilities of the HTML support in Office 2000 is the ability to create HTML scripts and HTML-based client solutions. HTML scripts can be authored in Office with the Microsoft Script Editor, shown in Figure 17-6, which is very similar to the script editing environment found in Microsoft's Visual Studio. There is full browser support for debugging. Script anchors are available in Office documents, allowing programmatic control of a document using the Scripting Object Model. The integrated Script Editor will enable developers to build Office-based solutions without having to rely on other development tools.

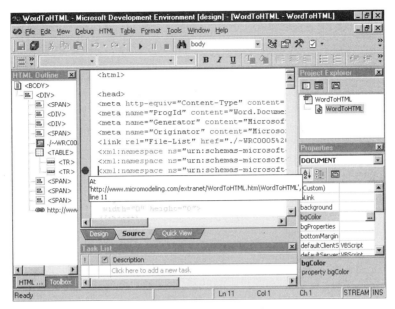

Figure 17-6. *The Microsoft Office 2000 Script Editor.*

NOTE See Chapter 14 for a deeper look at Web Page Scripting.

FYI about Office Web documents

When all is said and done, Microsoft Office 2000 may not always be the right tool for all of your HTML creation needs. While it does provide a lot of very nice features, it is not as sophisticated as FrontPage or DHTML. But for many situations, like working with corporate intranets or with users who demand more from Web content than just flash and pizzazz, Microsoft Office 2000 can lend more to the way you work than just traditional content creation. Here are some of the things you may want to consider when deciding whether Office makes your next Web page.

Limitations of creating HTML with Office 2000:

- **WYSIWEB:** "What you see is what everyone browses."

  ❏ Not always true, especially when supporting earlier versions of browsers.

  ❏ Microsoft Word does the best job of this out of all the Office suite of applications.

- **HTML** is not a universal file format among Office 2000 applications.

  - ❏ Each Office application actually writes out HTML its own way.

  - ❏ Common Office elements, such as document properties, shapes, and OLE objects, are written out the same.

- **Security**: Remember HTML is very open to file tampering. Does anyone have Notepad? Cannot rely on document-level security with HMTL. File password protection is not valid outside of binary.

- **File Management**

  - ❏ Increase in the quantity of files.

  - ❏ Potentially confusing for users when copying, moving, or deleting (unless using Windows NT 5).

  - ❏ Slower loading speed versus binary.

  - ❏ May (not always) dramatically increase footprint created versus binary.

- **Saving HTML** as Office Binary may sometimes reorder HTML tags or change representation of white space found in the document.

COLLABORATION WITH MICROSOFT OFFICE

So you and your team are working on the functional specification for the largest project any of you has ever been involved with. The deadline is tight. In fact, it's tomorrow. Of course, the client would've liked it yesterday. You've had two months and the team has made some pretty impressive progress. The team is scheduled to meet early tomorrow morning for a final review of the document before presenting it at noon. One of the senior project managers who has been working on the client's site this past week, dials in to your network and e-mails you his version of the document. He'd like you to incorporate his changes with everyone else's for tomorrow's conference call. Okay, will do. But after you've started looking through his copy, you think to yourself, "Are we on the same project?" You read on, seeing he's made some really good points, but he's also made some that may take a bit of time to digest. Do you make the changes without consulting the others first? Or do you risk having to explain to him that you've taken some liberties in the interpretation of his ideas? You think to yourself, "There's gotta be a better way to work together, isn't there?"

Office 2000 not only makes it easy for anyone to publish information on the Web, it can be extended to become a central workspace for collaboration and communication. The vision is to have teams post documents to Web sites — either the corporate intranet or an extranet. Then team members can refer to this central repository to view, comment, discuss, and even have online meetings around documents. No more waiting for documents to be routed through e-mail, stalling in someone's in-box, only to be returned to you full of so many edits, you're not sure if this was the original document you sent out.

These collaborative services are provided by the implementation of Office Server Extensions.

Office Server Extensions

Office Server Extensions (OSE) are a set of server extensions that augment the functionality of a Web server by providing additional publishing, collaboration, and document management capabilities. When OSE is present on a server, it enhances the functionality of Office 2000, Windows Explorer, and the Web browser. OSE can be installed on any Web server capable of supporting FrontPage extensions. This includes any server that supports HTTP 1.1 such as Internet Information Server (IIS).

Web publishing

As mentioned earlier in the chapter, OSE simplifies Web publishing. Users can now save to a Web site as easily as saving to their hard drive. OSE creates a Namespace extension for Web locations so that they are presented just like another mapped network drive. As shown in Figure 17-7, Web folders are displayed as top-level folders within the Windows Explorer. Users can create folders, view properties, and perform file drag-and-drop operations on Web servers just as they would on normal file servers. In Internet Explorer, OSE enables on-the-fly display of Web directory listings, files, and HTML views of Web folders. In Office 2000, the common "Open" and "Save As" dialogs display Web sites as simply another option for storing files.

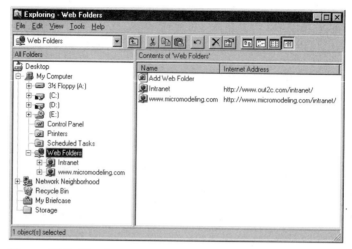

Figure 17-7. *Windows NT4 Explorer with OSE and the Namespace extension for Web Publishing.*

For all practical purposes, users can forgo using the standard file server approach and save all of their work directly to a Web server. No longer would you have to explain to that financial analyst looking for your Excel monthly budget file the finer points of network administration to connect to the "X" drive on your server on the WAN. Just point him to your spot on the company intranet. Operating a browser doesn't require you to read "NT Networking Essentials," right?

Working Web documents offline

As more and more people conduct business from the road, at home, or at the client's site, not only is the need to stay in touch paramount, but also the need to be able to keep working has become a requirement. If the Web is to become a central repository for document management, then there is one binding challenge—staying connected. Office Server Extensions will help with that by automatically taking Web-based documents offline and online with a Replication and Synchronization feature (see Figure 17-8).

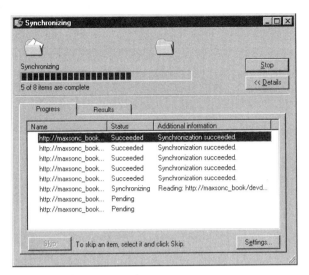

Figure 17-8. *Web Synchronization in progress.*

Basically a transparent process, users can continue to work on documents even when they log off the network. Office maintains a list of recently used documents by taking the most recently used (MRU) lists from all of the Office applications and caching them on the local machine. This caching is performed while the user is working online without user awareness. If the user goes offline, he can still access those files, just like he would if he were online. When the user logs back on to the network, all of his or her local changes are automatically replicated to the server and any changes that occurred on the server are replicated back to the local machine.

Users can tag specific files or folders to be available offline in addition to the MRU files automatically cached (see Figure 17-9). This can be done from the Windows Explorer by selecting the files/folders, then right-clicking and selecting "Make Available Offline." Users can also force files to synchronize now by selecting "Synchronize" from the same menu.

NOTE The offline features only work with Microsoft Internet Explorer 5.0, making it suited best for intranet use or situations where the user's browser is well known.

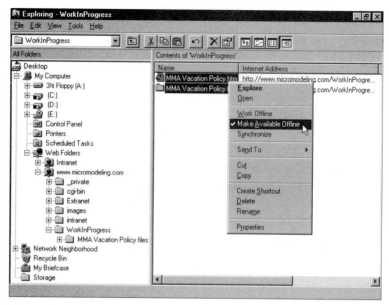

Figure 17-9. *Tagging documents to be available offline from Windows NT Explorer.*

Users can also control advanced synchronization functionality such as different connection settings and scheduling (Figure 17-10).

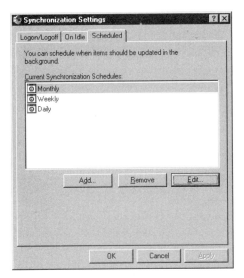

Figure 17-10. *Advanced synchronization settings dialog.*

But what happens when a user *offline* changes a document and someone else changes the same document *online*? (I anticipated this question.) There is a conflict-resolution mechanism that prompts the *offline* user when they reconnect as to which document should take precedence. The bad news here is that this is resolved at the document level, so if both sets of changes are valid, the conflicting changes will have to be merged manually.

Security with Office Server Extensions

Office Server Extensions does not employ its own security model, but instead it uses the security already being used on the Web server. OSE running with IIS on an NT server would adopt the NT's inherent security. In that case, access can be set to files and folders on the Web site just as they would with NT file servers.

Web Discussions

With the Office Server Extensions installed on a Web server, users can have threaded discussions in Word, Excel, and PowerPoint documents, as well as any HTML or RTF file (rich text format). Discussions can be through the originating Office application or simply through the browser (support for Internet Explorer 3.0 and Netscape Navigator version 3.0 or later).

Users can work in teams via the Web, either locally or remotely, ad hoc or real time, have staged document reviews or ongoing threaded discussions. Users can make inline comments that are displayed at the relevant position in the document (Figure 17-11). Inline comments are intelligently anchored and will move with the content as it changes.

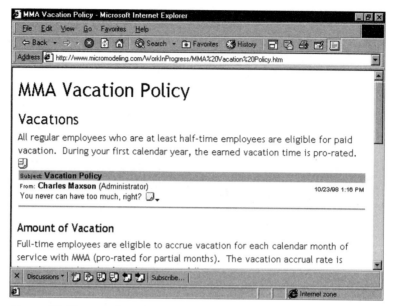

Figure 17-11. *An inline discussion on an HTML document in Internet Explorer 5.*

General discussion comments pertain to the document as a whole and can be viewed in the discussion pane at the bottom of the application window (see Figure 17-12). There is a Discussions toolbar that allows users to insert new comments, navigate through, edit, and reply to existing comments as well as subscribe to a particular document ("Web Subscription" is described further in this section).

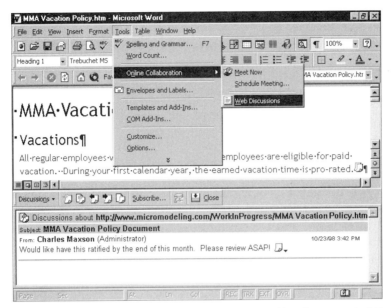

Figure 17-12. *A document-level discussion on an HTML document in Microsoft Word 2000.*

As you would expect, discussions can only be edited or removed by the original creator (or administrator), which is determined by the permission of the account used by the creator when he or she logged on the server. With anonymous authentication, any comment made by users logged on anonymously can be edited or deleted by any other users.

Another useful feature is the ability to filter Web Discussions by creator and timeframe. This helps you narrow down comments to specific people or weed out older comments that you may have read already or might no longer be relevant (see Figure 17-13).

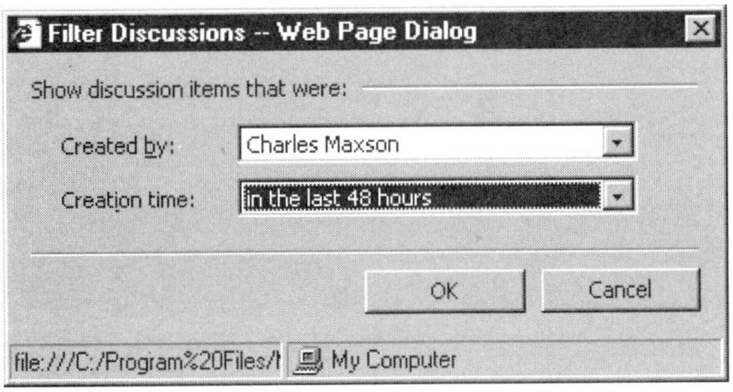

Figure 17-13. *Discussion Filter based on Creator and Time.*

Independent discussions can be added to the same document with the use of multiple OSE-enabled Web servers. This may be useful practice for teams that work anomously and require privacy. This is easy to administer and may be setup in a user's Office 2000 installation at deployment time.

Web Discussion architecture

Discussion threads are not physically stored within the document file. They are stored in a SQL server database. Therefore, documents can be modified without affecting the collaborative discussion. This enables read-only documents to have Discussion items added to them, as well as the simultaneous creation and editing of comments by multiple users.

You have some options when selecting which SQL database to use to store Discussion information. You can elect to store them within any existing SQL server database (6.5 or later) you have, provided that it does not reside on the Web server, or you can opt to use the version of embedded SQL server database that is installed with Office Server Extensions. The embedded version does reside on the Web server. Figure 17-14 depicts the schema of an implementation of both database solutions. Note that the two databases cannot coexist on the same machine.

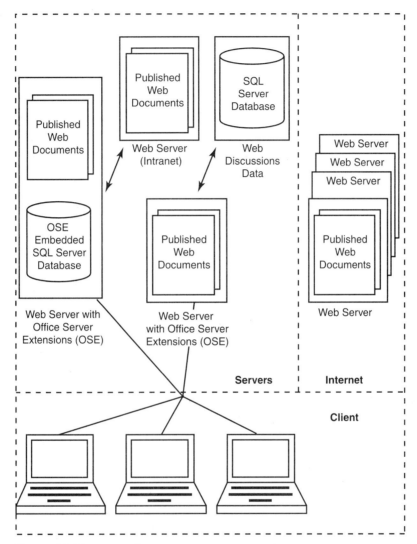

Figure 17-14. *OSE Architecture.*

How Web Discussions work for each Office application

Each Office 2000 application performs differently in terms of discussions. Word, HTML, and RTF documents are the most flexible, allowing both inline and general document-level discussions. Excel and PowerPoint only support document-level discussions. Access does not support any form of discussions directly, but Data Access Pages (discussed later in the chapter) are created in Access and saved as HTML files, which fully support Web discussions.

For programmatic manipulation of discussions, there is a simple Discussions Object Model available with functions like adding or deleting discussions to a document. And since the data for Discussions is stored in SQL server databases, the possibilities for creating custom tools and reports for Web Discussions is unlimited.

Browser support for Discussions begins with Microsoft Internet Explorer 3 and Netscape Navigator, which both allow users to view and contribute to Discussions, but all Discussion items, including inline items, are displayed in a frame separate from the document. Only Internet Explorer 4 and above can display inline Discussions directly in a document.

Web Subscription and Notification

Web Subscription and Notification are other features provided by Office 2000 and Office Server Extensions that enrich the usage of the Web. Users can "subscribe" to documents or folders on any Web server running OSE using the dialog shown in Figure 17-15. Then if the status of a subscribed document changes, they are automatically "notified" by e-mail. A change in status includes "edited," "added," "renamed," "moved," or "deleted."

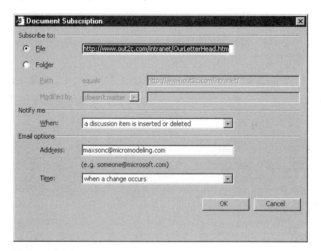

Figure 17-15. *Web Subscription dialog.*

A subscription can be tied to a particular document, an entire folder, or documents by a specific author. This is a great feature if you are tracking a document through the editing process or you want to know when additions to a folder are made. You can subscribe to receive e-mail for each change and you won't have to worry about monitoring a Web site to stay up to date.

Subscriptions can also be created in reference to Discussions items. If a Discussion is added, edited, or receives a reply, a user can be notified. Note that Subscriptions tied to Discussions can refer to documents anywhere on the Web, but Subscriptions tied to documents or folders must be on an accessible Office-extended Web server.

Web Notifications are sent when documents change. Notifications also have several options. So you aren't bombarded by email, Notifications can be managed over different intervals of time, from immediately, to daily, to weekly. Anything you tag "immediate" will be sent to you as soon as the event occurs. The OSE server stores any other messages according to the longer time periods you have designated, and then sends a single e-mail message to you when the time period is met with all of the events that transpired. The notification e-mail message contains a link to the document(s) that is affected, but not the document itself. The e-mail also contains a link that will enable a user to cancel or "unsubscribe" to a document, allowing easy one-time usage. When creating a Subscription, you can even have the Notification routed to someone else. For users with Internet Explorer, Notifications can also be received through a channel in IE in addition to e-mails.

NOTE Web Notifications can be implemented with any server using SMTP to send e-mail.

Online Meetings with Office Documents

For an even more interactive, real-time collaboration process, teams can collaborate around Office documents with Online Meetings. Office 2000 provides an interface to Microsoft NetMeeting. NetMeeting provides network conferencing and enables documents to be shared and reviewed with a team of people. It provides tools like Chat and Whiteboard (see Figure 17-16).

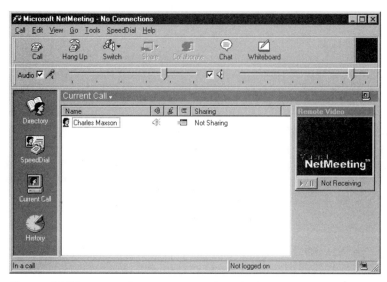

Figure 17-16. *Microsoft NetMeeting and Outlook.*

From Office 2000, via Microsoft Outlook, users can set up and schedule Online Meetings that use NetMeeting (see Figure 17-17).

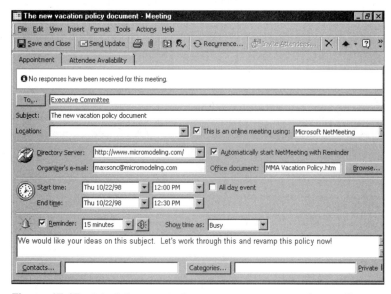

Figure 17-17. *Scheduling an Online Meeting NetMeeting from Office 2000 and Outlook.*

In addition to NetMeeting integration around documents, PowerPoint can broadcast a slide presentation with live narration over the Web (see Figure 17-18). With HTML file format support for PowerPoint presentations files, audiences require only a browser to be a part of an online presentation.

Figure 17-18. *Creating a PowerPoint Presentation Broadcast.*

An HTML "Events" or "Lobby" page created when a broadcast is set up, can be used to advertise a presentation or to allow users to tune in to a presentation already in progress. Microsoft Outlook 2000 can be used to schedule presentation broadcasts. Also, since the PowerPoint broadcasts are HTML based, they can also be stored on a Web server to facilitate viewing presentations on demand.

REPORTING ON THE WEB WITH MICROSOFT OFFICE

At the end of your status meeting with your boss, the CEO, he is concerned that like last year, the business unit leaders won't be prepared for the annual budget meeting. You tell him that your IT staff securely published each sector's financials on the intranet to help them get ready. He says "Yeah, I browsed those, but you can't really do anything with them. I want to play with the numbers, think about different scenarios, and really understand what drives our business. I realize you're trying to justify the cost of building that Web site, but maybe you should've just e-mailed them a spreadsheet." You really wished your performance review wasn't directly following this meeting.

Reporting has always been one of the key strengths of Microsoft Office. But creating static reports for the Web strips away one of the most useful functions of Excel, user interaction. When people work with spreadsheets and databases, they are used to entering their own formulas and parameters to create output that is more meaningful to them. Seeing a table of numbers or a list of data items stuffed into HTML forces a viewer to judge the message conveyed in the context of how it was published, but does not allow them to add their own interpretations to it. Many users end up copying data from a browser and pasting it in a spreadsheet anyway.

Likewise, another major feature of Microsoft Office is the ability to use data from various sources in the creation of reports. This has often been compromised when these documents are exported to static HTML for the Web. Let's discuss how we can extend the Office functionality we expect on the desktop to the Web.

An Interactive Web with Office Web Components

Since COM became a standard protocol for software development, developers look at Microsoft Office as a library of very robust features they can use inside their own applications, especially for reporting. Earlier versions of Office provided developers with rich, proven functionality, that users are very familiar with, and readily available to the developer through the fully exposed Application object models. The catch was, however, if you wanted to use a specific portion or subset of an Office application's functionality, you had to reference the entire application and be willing to load the whole thing. If you wanted to build a Web-based solution using an Office application, well that was even a less realistic option.

With that in mind, Microsoft developed the Office Web Components for Microsoft Office 2000. Office Web Components, comprising of a spreadsheet component, a chart component, and a PivotTable component, are COM controls that can be put into any container application that supports COM objects like Microsoft Visual Basic or Internet Explorer. They are "lighter weight" versions in both size (just under 3 MB in size at the time of writing) and functionality, but offer some of the best interactive analytic and publishing features found in Office and more specifically, Microsoft Excel.

When a Web page containing one of the components is run in a browser (IE 4.01 or higher, see "Browser Notes" in an upcoming section), users can interact with the data right on the page, performing tasks like changing values or formulas, sorting, filtering, formatting, pivoting, and so on. And for developers, the Office Web Components are fully programmable, just like the full-featured Office, enabling developers to enlist them in creating solutions.

NOTE Demonstrations of the Office Web Components in use can be found in the sample application on the companion CD in the \Chapter 17\ directory. A review of that application is discussed towards the end of the chapter.

Spreadsheet Component

The Spreadsheet Component (see Figure 17-19) takes the most commonly used functionality from Excel spreadsheets and makes it available in the browser. Any experienced Excel user will immediately feel comfortable working with this browser version. You can do things such as enter text and numbers, create formulas, sort data, use auto filter, change formatting, adjust the spreadsheet's appearance, manage calculations, and even undo operations. It supports frozen panes for keeping header rows and columns visible while scrolling larger spreadsheets and has in-cell editing capabilities and resizable rows and columns.

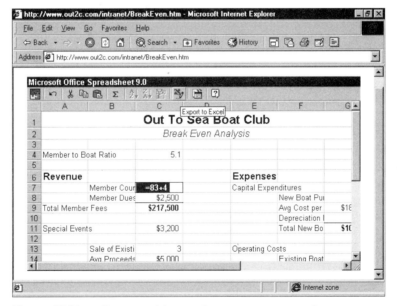

Figure 17-19. *Office Spreadsheet Web Component in a Web page in Internet Explorer.*

Besides the built-in control toolbar, a property toolbox (shown in Figure 17-20) is available with a right mouse click that provides an interface for users to perform additional functions. A few other operations still can be preformed with Excel shortcut keys such as Edit {F2} and Calculate {F9}.

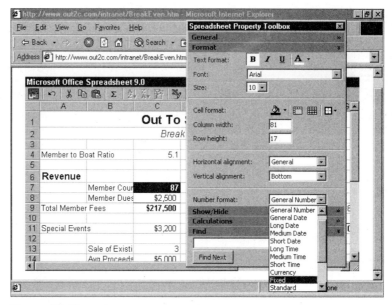

Figure 17-20. *Web Component Toolbox - shown with the Spreadsheet Web Component in runtime.*

PivotTable Component

Like the spreadsheet, another powerful feature of Excel comes to the Web with the PivotTable Web Component, shown in Figure 17-21. Users can analyze information by grouping rows and columns, dynamically sorting and filtering data, outlining items, pivoting fields, and adding totals. Data can be compiled from a spreadsheet range, from database tools such as Access and SQL server, as well as any other data source that supports multidimensional OLEDB. Data can be stored with the PivotTable as a static source or it can be dynamically tied to the data source to reflect changes as the underlying data changes.

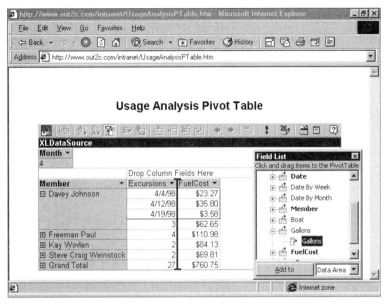

Figure 17-21. *Office PivotTable Web Component.*

EXCEL'S PIVOTTABLE

If you are not familiar with the PivotTable in Microsoft Excel, you may want to take a closer look at it. It is an interactive table that allows you to summarize and analyze data in Excel (and now in a Web browser). Data can be compiled from an Excel list, a consolidation of lists, or from any external ODBC data sources.

Now with Office 2000, you can link a PivotTable to operate interactively with the new PivotChart for a greater visual demonstration of your data. A comprehensive wizard built into Excel walks you through the creation of PivotTables and PivotCharts. From Excel, select "PivotTable and PivotChart Report" from the "Data" command bar.

Chart Component

The chart component, shown in Figure 17-22, provides a graphical representation of data on a Web page. With the majority of the Charting features found in the full Excel version, the Chart Component is bound directly to other controls on a Web page such as a Spreadsheet Component, a PivotTable Component, a Data Source Component, or any ADO recordset. This allows the chart to be dynamically updated to reflect the current view of the data on the page update without having to be refreshed from the server. When a user makes changes to the bound control or if the data on the back-end server changes, the Chart Component automatically updates, scales, and sizes appropriately.

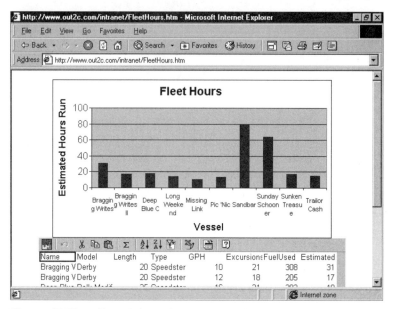

Figure 17-22. *Office Chart Web Component (with accompanying Spreadsheet Web Component below).*

Implementing Web Components

You can create Web Components by either saving Excel workbooks as Web pages, or by creating them from scratch using the Data Access Pages Designer in Access. From Excel, you can create a Web page by selecting "Save as Web Page" from the "File" command bar and checking "Add interactivity" as shown in Figure 17-23. Excel offers you several options to publish your page such as what portion of the workbook to include, what type of component you would like it published as, and the page's title.

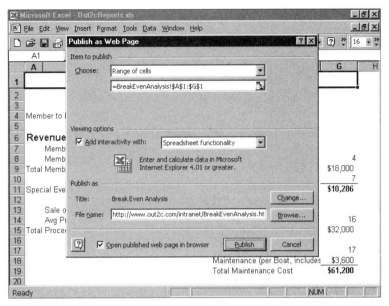

Figure 17-23. *Web Publishing Options from Excel.*

Creating a Web page from Access is very much like creating an Access Report or Form. In Data Access Page Design mode, any of the Web Components can be applied to the page from the Design toolbox (shown in Figure 17-24) just like traditional controls are. (Data Access Pages are discussed in greater detail in an upcoming section in this chapter.)

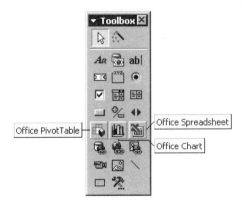

Figure 17-24. *Access Data Access Page Design toolbox.*

In addition to the Data Access Pages Designer, any HTML editor that supports COM controls, such as Microsoft FrontPage, Visual InterDev, the Office Visual Script editor, and Microsoft Word 2000, can edit pages with the Web Components.

When a control is added to a Web page, Office generates HTML that contains an OBJECT tag that refers to the Web Component. The component's properties that were established by the creator of the page are also stored as HTML. Once a page is built and published, users can interact with it and change those properties (such as formatting, values, display settings, and so on), but their interaction only affects the version running in their browser. If the page is refreshed from the server, the original property settings are restored to what the author of the page designated at design time.

If a user wants to save the changes they have made while interacting with a page, they can export the component into Excel 2000 and use it in a regular Excel workbook. By clicking the "Export to Excel" command button on the Component toolbar, the component will be opened in Excel as it appears in the browser. A user can then perform additional analysis using all of the features of Excel, take advantage of Excel's printing features, or even republish their own version of the information.

Advanced Web Component usage

Web Components are fairly simple to use for anyone who is familiar with Microsoft Office. But with just a little more effort, their "out of the box" functionality can be built upon to create even more sophisticated solutions. Let's start by looking at data binding.

Web Component supports the OLE Simple Provider data-binding interface (OLEDB). This enable controls on a Web page to work together using Microsoft Internet Explorer data binding. For example, in Figure 17-25, the Spreadsheet Component on the bottom is referencing the value for its Cell "C2" from the top Spreadsheet Component's Cell "C2" through the document object model with the following formula:

```
=Document.WebCalc0.Range("C2").Value
```

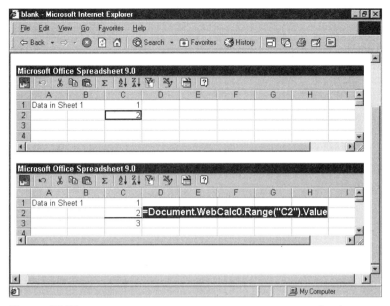

Figure 17-25. *Component-to-component communication—the document object model.*

With this ability to share data among controls, the possibilities for creating robust pages can be extended to multiple controls and it isn't limited to just the Office Web Components. A text box control, for instance, can be bound to a cell in a spreadsheet on a page.

Another example of extending the Web Components is to use the Spreadsheet Component as a calculation engine for a Web page. By placing a Spreadsheet Component on a page and setting its "Visible" property to FALSE, you can then bind it to other controls on the page that you would like users to see. This is a nice way to present the results of complex or extraneous calculations to your users without relying on functionality from outside of the Web page. This "Recalc Behind HTML" feature can be instituted without any programming or HTML editing. After all, you're simply using Excel to create the underlying formulas.

Developers can also take advantage of using the Web Components as Web page-building blocks. After creating a page with a Web Component(s), a developer can open the page in the Data Access Pages Designer, the Visual Script Editor, or Microsoft Visual InterDev, to add additional scripting or logic. The components can also be used in server-side implementations with ASP and Microsoft Internet Information Server (IIS). Calculations can be made with an instance of a Web Component running on a server and the results shipped back to the browser. Developers can remove the processing away from the user's machine while taking advantage of the power of the server. This also enables solutions employing the Office Web Components to be browser independent.

Getting Office Web Components to the client

Before a user can interact with the Office Web Components in IE, the components must be installed on the client machine. The Office 2000 setup program by default will automatically install them. Alternatively, they can be downloaded via the Internet Explorer built-in component installer when a user browses a component-based Web page for the first time. To make this possible, you must check the "Enable Auto-download" option of the Office Web Components page of the Custom Setup wizard and make sure that the Web Components automatic installation files (msowcin.cab and msowc.cab) are available on your Office installation server.

FYI about Office Web Components

Don't get too excited about using Office Web Components on your firm's Internet site. They are targeted specifically for *intranet* usage for a fairly obvious reason: licensing. In order to use these controls interactively, the client machine must be licensed for the use of Microsoft Office 2000. (Which version of Microsoft Office 2000 that is required wasn't announced at the time of this writing.) This is understandable. Microsoft has spent the last decade developing and refining Office. It's unlikely that they would want to give it away to anyone who browses the Web.

Browser notes

Any browser that doesn't support COM controls (for example, Netscape Navigator) is reduced to seeing a static HTML representation of any Office Web Components in a Web page. This allows sharing across browser platforms, but not with the features the components were designed to achieve. For Internet Explorer users, Version 4.01 or higher is required to browse with all of the intended functionality.

> **NOTE**   Machines that do not have a license for Office 2000 will also see a static HTML representation of any Office Web Components in a Web page, just like non IE 4.01+ users.

The good news is if you are working in a mixed browser and/or desktop suite environment, you still only need to create one version of each page and you can use the Office Web Components throughout.

Static Reporting, If You Must

A lot of companies have made large investments in creating reporting applications with Microsoft Access. There is a way that they can leverage that investment while reaching a broader audience via the Web. Microsoft has made available a product called the Snapshot Viewer, which allows you to distribute Access reports to users inside and outside your organization without requiring them to have Microsoft Access.

A Snapshot file (.snp) is basically a saved version of a Microsoft Access report that maintains the data and formatting of the entire report. Once you have created a snapshot from Access, anyone can use the Snapshot Viewer (Snapview.exe) to scroll through the report, print any combination of pages, or even send it via e-mail.

In addition to the stand-alone executable version, there is an ActiveX Snapshot Viewer control (Snapview.ocx) that enables snapshot reports to be viewed from a browser or from any application that supports ActiveX controls (see Figure 17-26). So you can eliminate printing and sending reports to people by simply sending them a URL that points to your Web page and let them view and print reports straight from the Web.

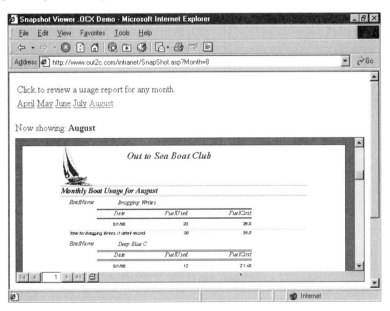

Figure 17-26. *Snapshot View in a Web page.*

Now although snapshot reports are static and the Snapshot Viewer control can only represent one report at a time, with a little server-side creativity, you can easily present static reports "dynamically" to your users. In the samples for this chapter on the companion CD, there is an example of a Snapshot Viewer control on an Active Server Page (ASP) that has its "SnapshotPath" property changed to reference a different snapshot file depending on a user's selection. These snapshot files were already made, but this could be enhanced further by allowing the page to accept more arguments, and then using them as parameters to create new snapshot reports on the fly by automating Access, making static reporting become real time.

By default, the Snapshot Viewer Components are automatically installed by Access 2000 the first time you create a report snapshot. For users without Microsoft Access, the viewer can be installed separately via its own setup program. It can be downloaded from the Microsoft Access Developer's Web site at *http://officeupdate.microsoft.com/welcome/access.htm*.

The Web as a Data Source

Microsoft Office is not only able to turn content into Web pages, but it can also turn Web pages into content. Starting with the simple process of opening a Web page from the File Open dialog in Word, this capability extends to actually being able to retrieve specific parameterized data in Excel with Web Queries.

From any of the Office applications you can open a Web page just as you would a traditional file. Instead of a file name relating to a disk location, you can use the URL of a Web page on the Internet or an intranet. This allows you to bring Web content into a document without having to cut and paste from the browser. Microsoft Word is the best "interpreter" of HTML, while Excel does a very good job at handling figures and tables. Access works surprisingly well, but PowerPoint doesn't quite make sense. But if you decide to simply copy from a browser, Office 2000 treats HTML as a premium Clipboard format, which makes content copied from the Web appear very much like it did in the browser when pasted into an Office document.

Web Queries

The Web Query is a feature of Microsoft Excel that allows you to bring data from the Web into a spreadsheet so that you can analyze the information with the tools of Excel. Web Queries were first introduced in Excel '97 but they lacked an interface for building ad hoc queries. Excel 2000 has added that interface so you can create your own, as well as use the canned ones that ship with the product.

Excel's canned Web Queries link to popular Web sites that provide real-time information such as stock quotes and currency exchange rates. They accept parameters like stock tickers and return the up-to-moment data that you ask for, directly into a worksheet. You can use them for building tools like a stock portfolio model or a net worth calculator in Excel. Best of all, you can retrieve the data into your projects free of charge and use features like automatic data refreshing and the ability to reference cell values or formulas for criteria. Microsoft includes a query named "Get More Web Queries.iqy" with Excel that returns a list of many more useful query templates.

If you would like to create your own Web Queries, you can select the "New Web Query" command from "Get External Data" option on Excel's "Data" menu and Excel will guide you through the process. It is basically as easy as pointing to the Web page you want to query and clicking OK (see Figure 17-27). You can retrieve data from a specific table on the page, from multiple tables, or retrieve the entire page. You can also elect to bring in the formatting of the Web page or retain the formatting of the worksheet.

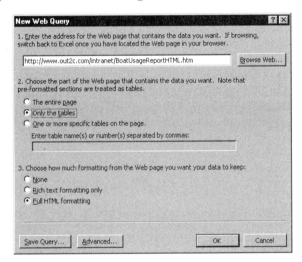

Figure 17-27. *Excel's Create New Web Query dialog.*

You can save a Web Query for future use as an .IQY file or save the query definition embedded in a worksheet. You can run a saved query from the "Run Saved Query" menu option under "Get External Data" or let a Web Query be automatically refreshed when a workbook is opened or on a regular time interval.

USING MICROSOFT OFFICE AS A DECISION SUPPORT TOOL

You just get off the phone after closing a sale with a key account, when your sales assistant asks you how it went. You reply, "Great, I got the deal done by cutting the price by 2 percent and they bought a lot more! I figured an 8 percent margin was better then no sale at all." He looks at you kind of puzzled and says "Eight percent margin? Didn't you get the new numbers from manufacturing? They're estimating that our cost of production is going to go up almost 4 percent this quarter. That pricing report you've got on your desk is over two months old! We'll barely cover costs on that deal!" Then he asks you in horror, "They won't try to make this up with our commissions, will they?"

With business changing as fast as it does today, decision making is dependent on timely, accurate data and the ability to realize conclusions with powerful, yet easy-to-use tools. It's no surprise that the intranet has become an integral mechanism for disseminating timely information throughout organizations. Intranets offer the centralization of information mixed with the relative ease of use. And more and more, users expect to formulate answers by what they find on their corporate intranet.

Since organizations store their essential data in corporate databases, getting this information onto the intranet can greatly enhance the decision-making process. Office 2000 offers such a feature in the form of Access Data Pages.

Access Data Pages—Bringing Data to the Web

You can start off by thinking of Access Data Pages as Access forms or reports for the Web. But Data Access Pages are actually dynamic HTML pages that use the client-side data binding capabilities of Internet Explorer allowing you to view and edit data from a browser that is linked back to a database. They are as easy to create as Access forms and reports with the same design-time tools available plus some additional Web-enabled features. The pages can be run from either Access databases or from Microsoft Internet Explorer 5.0.

Unlike the standard forms and reports, Data Access Pages are stored as HTML files outside of Microsoft Access databases (.MDB) file or Access database projects (.ADP — See the sidebar "Connecting to Enterprise Data with Microsoft Access 2000" for a greater explanation of the database project). Only a reference to the Data Access Page file is added to an Access database. Since this is the case, you can load a Data Access Page as a stand-alone file into Microsoft Access without having a database open. You can also send Data Access Pages through e-mail or post them on the Web as static HTML pages. Like other

Office 2000 HTML files, Data Access Pages consist of several files as described earlier in the chapter.

CONNECTING TO ENTERPRISE DATA WITH MICROSOFT ACCESS 2000

Microsoft Access 2000 supports the OLE DB component architecture for data access. This enables Access to connect directly to Microsoft SQL server databases instead of going through the JET engine, the default database engine of Access. A new file type has been created called a Microsoft Access Project (.ADP) to work with SQL server databases. When you create a new database in Access 2000, you can choose JET or SQL as the data storage medium.

The Microsoft Access Project functions much like you would expect from working with SQL server. It doesn't contain tables or queries, but instead it is connected directly to the SQL server database that contains tables, stored procedures, views, and database diagrams. Changes you make to any of the database objects and data are actually made directly to the SQL database itself.

With this new integration technology, you can create solutions that combine the ease of use of the Microsoft Access interface with the scalability and reliability that you'd expect from SQL server.

Access 2000 also allows you to open any HTML file directly into the Data Access Page Designer shown in Figure 17-28 (unless it contains frames). This is a nice feature because it lets you use other HTML editors like FrontPage or the other Office applications to start creating a page, as well as using any existing content you already have. Once you have an HTML page open in Access, you can then add data bound controls to it. You can also take advantage of the design tools like the property sheet, a field list, toolbox, and miscellaneous wizards just like you would use to build forms and reports, only with a Web page slant.

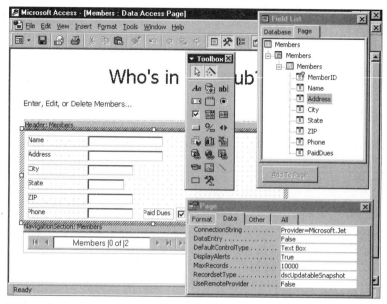

Figure 17-28. *Microsoft Access Data Access Page Design surface.*

The different faces of Data Access Pages

Data Access Pages are flexible enough to allow you to use them in a variety of different capacities. You can create a simple page that enables Web-based data entry. Extend that page by representing a one-to-many relationship as a hierarchical view of the data for an interactive report. Or you can add an Office Web Component to the page and make it a data analysis tool.

Data entry

Much like a regular form in Access, a Data Access Page can be built to allow users to enter, edit, and delete data in a database, *but* via the Web. When the page is posted on the Web, users won't need to know where your database is or how to operate it. With features like the navigation bar control, shown in Figure 17-29, Data Access Pages are fairly intuitive to use. They can make gathering information from all around your organization easier and without the issues involved in distributing traditional database applications.

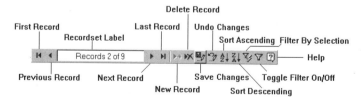

Figure 17-29. *Record navigation bar.*

You can even restrict access to the page's data. By setting the page's "DataEntry" property to TRUE, new records may be added but existing records won't be displayed. Now your page will be truly a data entry form (see Figure 17-30).

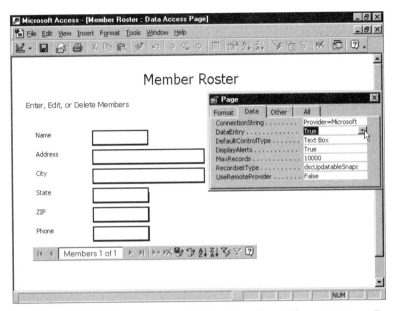

Figure 17-30. *Data Access Page built for Data Entry (shown in Access Page View).*

Interactive reporting

Data Access Pages provides a new way to interact with data. Instead of just seeing the data in a report, you can explore it. A "Grouped" Data Access Page (sometimes referred to as a "Banded" page) gives you the ability to navigate through data on a page, and allows you to drill into a hierarchical view of data in an interactive manner. By expanding and collapsing groups of records, you can work with larger volumes of data easier, while focusing just on what's important to you.

Figure 17-31 shows an example of a Grouped Data Access Page. The page (taken from the sample application found on the CD) allows users to scroll through a list of boats. You could drill down into the data to reveal a secondary list of data (the boat's log) that is related to the currently selected boat by clicking the Expand/Collapse button just under the boat name. Note that both the boat and voyage data sets have their own record navigation control tied to them.

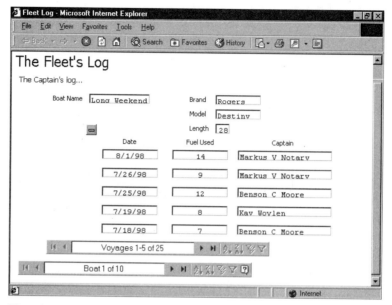

Figure 17-31. *Grouped Data Access Page in IE 5.*

Data analysis

Data Access Pages bring better data analysis capabilities to the Web than ever before, specifically because not only do you see data, you can experience it. You can slice and dice data, apply filters, drill down a level for more clarification, add your own formulas, and have your changes automatically reflected graphically. Data pages integrate the best of the tools that people use for analytics, things like spreadsheets, PivotTables, and graphs and interactively links them to the data that helps them make decisions.

A Pivot List, which is a slight variation of the PivotTable, is another useful way to view data. A Pivot List is somewhat of an alternative to the Grouped Data Access Page. It is actually just a PivotTable Component that a Data Access Page creates with a look that is similar to an Access table in datasheet view. Since it is still a PivotTable, you can manipulate the data just like you would expect. Figure 17-32 displays a Pivot List which actually represents the same data as the Grouped page does in Figure 17-31.

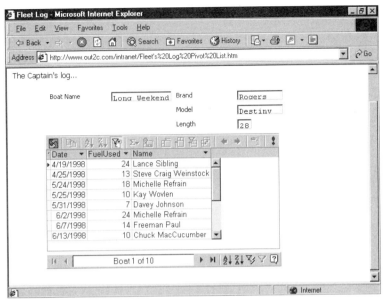

Figure 17-32. *Pivot List in a Data Access Page.*

DAP data options

Data Access Pages can get data from a Microsoft Access database or a Microsoft SQL server database version 6.5 or higher. When you create a new page, it is automatically connected to the current database you are working with, storing a reference to the database in the ConnectionString property of the Data Access Page.

Where the database is located is very important. If you create a Data Access Page within a local database on your hard drive, and then publish the page to a Web site, other users will not see the underlying data when they browse to the page. (The ConnectionString will be pointing to *your* hard drive.) If you work with the database from a network share and open the database using the UNC address of the database (Universal Naming Convention e.g. \\ServerName\SharedDrive\MyDataBase.MDB), any Data Access Page you create will have the UNC as its ConnectionString property, allowing anyone with access to that network location to properly use the page. Restricting usage of your Data Access Page can be implemented through either NT networking security or adding security to the database itself.

Microsoft Office Web Components on a Data Access Page can get their data from other sources besides the current database. For example, a PivotTable on a DAP may be created with data from an Excel worksheet or a database other than Access or SQL server. Depending on the data source and how the component was created, the component can be linked live back to the data source with its own separate connection, or the data can be embedded statically with the control.

Other FYI about Data Access Pages

Like a lot of the new Web-based technologies available in Office 2000, Data Access Pages are dependent on Microsoft Internet Explorer 5. If you would like to build pages with Office Web Components, users of your pages will require a license for Office. Here are some other notable comments about Data Access Pages.

Linking Access Data Pages

Building a single Access Data Page doesn't necessarily mean that you have met all of the requirements for completing an "application," typically you need a bit more. It may be necessary to build a multiple-page application and pass data between them. The easiest, code-free way to do this is with hyperlinks. By setting the filter criteria when creating a hyperlink (shown in Figure 17-33), you are attaching a server filter. When the hyperlink navigates to the destination page, the server filter is applied against the page's recordset, displaying it with only the desired data.

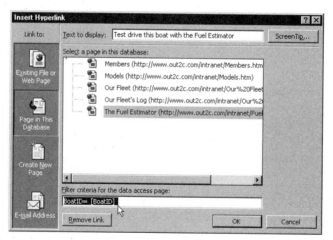

Figure 17-33. *Insert Hyperlink dialog.*

Field List

Using the Field List is the simplest way to build a Data Access Page (see Figure

17-34). It is much more than a graphical, drag-and-drop component. It allows you to build complex, hierarchical pages *without* having to build queries beforehand. You may come across some complex tasks that still require queries, which are also available through the Field List, but the use of queries for simple joins is not required for creating Data Access Pages.

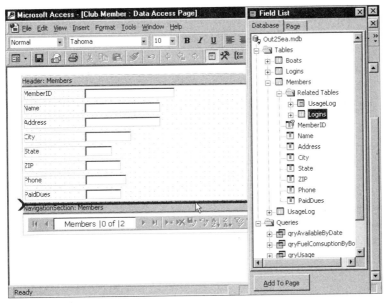

Figure 17-34. *Using the Field List to drag a table into a Data Access Page.*

TYING IT ALL TOGETHER—A SAMPLE APPLICATION

If you have read all the way through this chapter, you are probably thinking, "this stuff sounds great, but what does it look like?" On the companion CD for the book, there is a sample application that will demonstrate most of the things we covered throughout the chapter, with the exception of some of the collaboration features.

To get started with the sample, you will need to have a few things:

- **Office 2000.** Kind of obvious, but I thought I'd mention it.

- **Office Web Components.** If you've got Office 2000 installed, you probably have these installed, too.

- **Office Server Extensions.** Need to put these on your Web Server (Yep, I'm leading up to that). They're not 100 percent critical for demo, but they make things a lot easier. And if you want to play with the any of the collaboration functionality, you will need them anyway.

- **Web server.** IIS or something capable of supporting HTTP 1.1 and Active Server Pages.

- **A Web site.** If you want the full flavor, name it *www.out2sea.com* after my fictitious site and set your home page to *http://www.out2c.com/intranet/OurLetterHead.htm*. The name is really not important though, as long as the files remain in the same directory like they do on the CD.

- **Microsoft Internet Explorer 5.0.** Can run without this, but the sample application would just be a lot of static data.

   And then you'll have to do a couple of things:

- Copy the Out2Sea.mdb to the root of the C Drive (C:\) on the Web Server. Somewhere out there I hear a network administrator grumbling—this is to enable data access over the sample Web. You can put it somewhere else, but you will have to change the connection strings for all of the Data Access Pages.

- Create an "intranet" directory off of the www.out2sea.com Web site and copy all of the files and folders from the Chapter 17\ Out2Cintranet directory on the CD into it.

If you were able to do all that, you're probably qualified to be a Microsoft Certified Systems Engineer, if not that's okay, you can still get some of the feel of what Office can do through the samples without being "online."

Either way, the first file you should check out is "SampleGuide.htm." It contains an explanation and hyperlinks to all of the files for this chapter.

The Out-to-Sea Boat Club

The goal in creating the sample application was not to show you my brilliant creativity and design skills (good thing!), but more importantly, what Office can do for you when building Web-based solutions. So pardon the "creativeness" or lack thereof, of the sample, but keep one thing in mind; this was 100 percent developed with Microsoft Office 2000 (well, okay there was a tiny bit of Notepad to tweak the beta code I was working with).

The backdrop for the site is kind of simple. It's for a boat club, which is a cooperative of boating enthusiasts. The members don't own the boats personally, but they pay dues to the club, and the club owns and maintains the boats. Therefore, the members like to stay in touch with the club's finances and watch who's using which boats. (You need to use your imagination a little.)

The members of the club realized that a Web site would be the best way to stay in touch with the club's activity, financials, membership list, and so on, as well as a way to market themselves. So, with little time, technology, or money to spare, the club leveraged their ownership in Microsoft Office 2000.

Starting with only the materials that the club had from using Office, Out to Sea Web site was built:

- The club's letterhead (Word document)

- A database (Access)

- A financial model in a spreadsheet (Excel workbook)

- A marketing slide show (PowerPoint presentation)

Tour the site

The site consists of four major sections: a home page, marketing presentation pages, a login page, and private member pages. The following walks you through each section.

The home page

Start off by pointing your browser to *http://www.out2c.com/intranet/ OurLetterHead.htm* (shown in Figure 17-35). This home page was originally the club's letterhead, a Word document named "OurLetterHead.doc." The document's layout still has that "letterhead look," because all I did to create the page was apply a theme to give the page some color and character, add hyperlinks to the login page and to the club's marketing page, and saved the document as HTML. That's it!

Figure 17-35.   *he Out to Sea Boat Club's "Letterhead" homepage.*

The Marketing Presentation Pages

Click on the "Thinking about joining, click here..." hyperlink to see the club's marketing page. Creating this was even easier than the home page, by simply saving the "Out2cMarketing.ppt" PowerPoint presentation as HTML. It creates an awful lot of files, forty-one to be exact, but it also adds a lot of features that can be used when running in the browser. Things like a framed, expandable outline bar, slide navigation controls and the ability to run a normal or full screen presentation with graphics, animations, sounds, videos, voice narration. Not bad for no effort.

The Login Page

From the home page, click the "Member Login" hyperlink to go to the Member's Login Page. The only reason I included this "security" feature was to demonstrate the extensibility of using Office 2000 to create more sophisticated content. You may have noticed that the URL ends with "OurLetterHeadLogin.asp?LoggedIn=False"? That's because I started with the original home page I created in Microsoft Word, through in a few lines of code using Office's Script Editor (Word Menus : "Tools," "Macros," "Micro Script Editor") and saved the file as with an .ASP extension and created an Active Server Page. Yes, with Microsoft Word.

To run the page, click on the submit button (both password and ID or optional), and you are "logged in" via client side VB Script, then the table site's table of contents is built when the on the server when it receives the "LoggedIn" parameter as TRUE. Look at the HTML source for this file ("OurLetterHeadLogin.asp") and see for yourself how simple this was to do.

The Member Pages

The table of contents reveals all of the remaining pages for the site. They demonstrate many of the features of Office 2000 covered in this chapter. Explore and interact with each one of them to see Office 2000 can perform in the browser. Here is a summary of what each page will do:

- **Break Even Analysis Spreadsheet.** Demonstrates the Office Web Component (OWC) spreadsheet control with a break-even model that allows club members to play with the club's financials. All of the spreadsheet's characteristics were turned off to make it blend into the page. You can right-click with the mouse to change any of the component's properties as well as change values and formulas.

- **Fleet Usage Chart.** Uses a Web Chart Component to depict how many hours each boat has been used. It was originally created from an Excel chart and the data is saved with this page (static). Data with an OWC Chart can also be tied to a backend data source.

- **Member Usage PivotTable.** This PivotTable component lets the members analyze boat usage in the club. You may move fields, filter by different criteria, and so on, to understand the way that means the most to you. Like the chart page before, the data is saved with this page but it can be dynamically tied to other data sources as well. (Play with this; it is very cool!)

- **Historical report snapshots.** This is an ASP page that demonstrates the Access Snapshot Viewer ActiveX control. It takes "Month" as a parameter back to the server, which changes the "SnapshotPath" property of the control to point to the appropriate Snapshot file.

- **Members.** This is a simple Data Access Page designed for data entry. Members can browse the list of club members, edit, delete or add new records, which are stored in an Access database. This one took literally seconds to create with Data Access Page Wizard.

- **Brands and models.** A Data Access Page that uses a Group Filter Control to simplify browsing through the brands of boats the club owns.

- **Grouped Report.** A common layout of a Grouped Data Access Page allowing club members to display the log for any boat in the club.

- **Pivot List.** Basically the same information that is in the Grouped Report, but displayed using a Pivot List.

- **Fuel estimator.** This page includes every Web feature but the kitchen sink. It uses the HTML Document function to tie a Grouped Data Access Page to a Web Spreadsheet and Chart Component (via gallons per hour). It helps members project fuel costs while in a very slick page.

SUMMARY

Microsoft Office 2000 makes working with the Web easy and powerful. It enables you to leverage existing Office skills and content to create robust Web pages. While it may not be the editor of choice in creating *all* Web content, it does bring a lot of features and functionality to the Web that have not been available before. Combining those Web features with the traditional productivity of Office, its large, knowledgeable user base and prevalent position as a critical business tool throughout organizations everywhere, you will want to consider how you can leverage it in creating Web solutions for your business. It can help you establish credibility with clients, communicate better with your peers, get information to decision makers, and let people be interactive with information. Why would you consider using Microsoft Office 2000 as a tool for building Web-based Commerce solutions? Simply because it's where people work.

Chapter 18

Integrating Workflow

by Raffaele Piemonte and Scott Jamison

Today, major corporations conduct an enormous amount of business over the Internet. Timeliness, or the ability to react to a customer quickly, becomes more and more critical, because customers who suffer delays have time to look elsewhere to fulfill their business needs.

This chapter discusses how to create applications on the back end of a Web commerce site that facilitate the customer service function. We'll use a case study of Awesome Computers, a fictitious computer distributor, to illustrate the key points and build a working example around accepting customer support requests from the company's Web site, and then routing them to appropriate individuals within the company for follow-up. The technologies discussed include Microsoft Exchange as the message store and routing engine, Microsoft Outlook as the forms manager and user interface, two distinct but related programming interfaces, Collaboration Data Objects (CDO) and the Outlook object model, and Routing Objects as a means to automate workflow. This chapter will also show how and why to integrate Web and non-Web technologies. Although the customers of this company can use a Web site to request support, the internal support staff will not use a Web application to manage the support process. Rather, they will work within Outlook, which is much better suited to this task than a browser interface. This chapter is organized as follows:

- Review and comparison of the Outlook and CDO object models
- Description of the business problem in detail
- Creation of custom Outlook forms
- Retrieval of data from a corporate database via ODBC
- Microsoft Exchange Routing Objects
- How Exchange agents are used
- How to render information in Outlook/Exchange on the Web

Development components utilized for this chapter include:

- Microsoft Exchange 5.5 Service Pack 1
- Microsoft Outlook 2000
- Microsoft Routing Wizard
- Visual InterDev 6.0

MICROSOFT OUTLOOK AND COLLABORATION DATA OBJECTS

When incorporating messaging functionality into an application, there are two techniques you can use. The first technique involves automating the Outlook application via its programmable object model and creating custom Outlook forms. The second uses *Collaboration Data Objects (CDO)*, a server-side programmable object model.

Automating Outlook via its object model is typically used to extend or customize the Outlook interface on client machines. Most of the things you can do with Outlook can be implemented programmatically. Custom Outlook forms provide a way to create specific forms to automate specific tasks or workflows.

CDO is an in-process, self-registering COM server that provides messaging services via a programmable object model. CDO is typically used on an application or Web server as it talks directly to the messaging server (for example, Microsoft Exchange) bypassing the need to go through the Outlook client application layer. For example, CDO can be called by ASP scripts on a Web server to integrate a Web application with back-end messaging functionality. As you'll see in the examples to come, both CDO and the Outlook object model have a place in the customer support solution discussed in this chapter. But first, let's start with a quick overview of how each of these technologies works.

Microsoft Outlook

Microsoft Outlook, a core part of the Office 2000 family, is the client application for correspondence and collaboration. As shown in Figure 18-1, it provides personal information management capabilities, such as e-mail, scheduling, and contact management. It also includes many other information management features such as journal entries, task/to do list tracking, and even sticky notes.

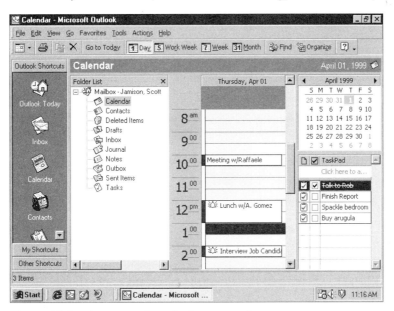

Figure 18-1. *The Microsoft Outlook user interface.*

Outlook's built-in features and extensive customization capabilities make it a good choice for custom business solutions requiring messaging, routing, and collaboration:

- Sales Force Automation (SFA)

- Order Fulfillment

- Document Routing

- Job Applicant Tracking

- Customer Service

Outlook provides a powerful but lightweight scripting interface that allows programmers to add business logic. Using Microsoft Exchange, you can then add workflow features with ease. In the next section, we will look at a simple example of how to automate Outlook to send an e-mail message.

Programming with Outlook

Outlook can be programmed using VBA or through embedding VBScript in its forms. This chapter will review both of these options.

The following example shows how to use the Microsoft Outlook Object Model to send an e-mail message including an attachment. First, declare all variables that will be used in the function:

```
Function OutlookSendMailExample()
    Dim objOutlook As Outlook.Application
    Dim objNamespace As Outlook.NameSpace
    Dim objMessage As Outlook.MailItem
    Dim objAttach As Outlook.Attachment
    Dim objToRecipient As Outlook.Recipient
```

Next, create a reference to the Outlook application object using the CreateObject statement:

```
    Set objOutlook = CreateObject("Outlook.Application")
```

From here, use the GetNamespace method to return the only data source presently supported in Outlook, "MAPI," and logon to the mail server using the default profile:

```
    Set objNamespace = objOutlook.GetNamespace("MAPI")
    objNamespace.Logon
```

Now that a connection to the server has been made, use the CreateItem method to return a mail message item using the "MailItem" type, and then set its relevant properties:

```
    Set objMessage = objOutlook.CreateItem(olMailItem)
    With objMessage
        .Subject = "New processor announced"
        .Body = "Please read the attached press release."
        Set objAttach = .Attachments.Add("C:\My
Documents\Release.doc", olByValue, 1, "Release.doc")
    End With
```

Then add your favorite recipient using the Add method of the Recipients collection:

```
Set objToRecipient = objMessage.Recipients.Add("Jamison, Scott")
```

To send the message on its way, use the Send method of the Message object:

```
    objMessage.Send
```

And don't forget to log off and free up your objects:

```
    objNamespace.Logoff

    Set objOutlook = Nothing
    Set objNamespace = Nothing
    Set objMessage = Nothing
    Set objAttach = Nothing
    Set objToRecipient = Nothing
End Function
```

Figure 18-2 shows a high-level view of the Outlook Object model and the different types of objects supported by Outlook. The model has objects for accessing data as well as user interface features.

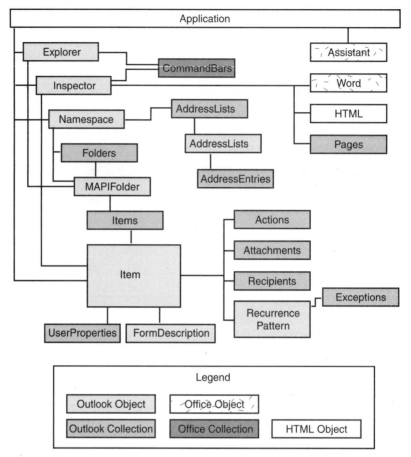

Figure 18-2. *The Outlook 2000 Object model.*

The Namespace Object is the topmost layer in the Outlook Object model relating to data. It deals with the underlying data but not with any user interface aspects of Outlook, and it's the object used in the preceding example. The Explorer, Inspector, Assistant, Outlook Bar, and Command Bar objects let you programmatically control the visual aspects of the Outlook interface.

The Explorer Object represents the Outlook interface as a whole, while the Inspector Object represents a view of a single Outlook item. Use the Namespace, Explorer, and Inspector Objects together as appropriate to create an application that best fits your company's specific needs.

Collaboration Data Objects

CDO, a small, lightweight DLL, is essentially a programmable object model wrapped around the MAPI function library. (Note: MAPI is the layer that communicates with mail servers such as Microsoft Exchange) CDO has no display capabilities because it is used only when an application needs to access MAPI data without any client-side display-related functionality. CDO eschews the user interface and functions behind the scenes and is a quick and efficient way to add messaging functionality to existing applications such as a Web page, or to create a desktop collaboration application from the ground up. In fact, CDO is absolutely crucial when doing server-side scripting, where there is no user interface. Server-side scripting is discussed in further detail later in the chapter in the routing example.

> **NOTE** Microsoft realized that developers needed a heavy-duty object library, so it replaced Active Messaging with Collaboration Data Objects. CDO supports roughly 1,000 concurrent users per server and is thread safe, allowing for the creation of large-scale enterprise applications. CDO also supports caching, making it two to three times faster than Active Messaging.

CDO has an easy-to-use object model. The code needed to send an e-mail looks very similar to the Outlook code provided earlier:

```
Function CDOSendMailExample()
    Dim objMAPISession As MAPI.Session
    Dim objMessage As MAPI.Message
    Dim objAttach As MAPI.Attachment
    Dim objToRecipient As MAPI.Recipient

    Set objMAPISession = CreateObject("MAPI.Session")

    objMAPISession.Logon

    Set objMessage = objMAPISession.Outbox.Messages.Add
    With objMessage
        .Subject = "New processor announced"
        .Text = "Please read the attached press release."

        Set objAttach = .Attachments.Add
        With objAttach
            .Type = CdoFileData
            .ReadFromFile "c:\My Documents\Release.doc"
            .Name = "Release.doc"
        End With
        .Update
    End With

    ' Add our recipient
    Set objToRecipient = objMessage.Recipients.Add
```

(continued)

(continued)

```
    With objToRecipient
        .Name = "Erica Jamison"
        .Type = CdoTo
        .Resolve
    End With

    objMessage.Send
    objMAPISession.Logoff

    Set objMAPISession = Nothing
    Set objMessage = Nothing
    Set objAttach = Nothing
    Set objToRecipient = Nothing
End Function
```

Because both Outlook and CDO are scripting layers into MAPI, both of these examples look very similar. With CDO, however, you do not get the specific interface features of Outlook such as the Outlook Bar. Looking at the CDO Object model, shown in Figure 18-3, you can see that it provides access to MAPI data, but it does not provide Outlook interface features.

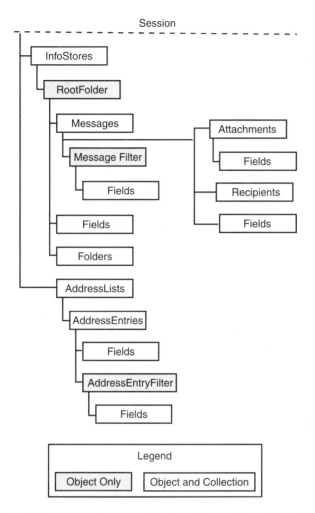

Figure 18-3. *The Collaboration Data Objects hierarchy.*

Which Object Model Do I Use?

Knowing when to use each model, Outlook or CDO, is pivotal to implementing a proper solution.

■ The Outlook Object model is often the best choice to use on a client computer. It is typically used to present custom forms and has the added advantage of integrating with the user's familiar tools. In addition, Outlook is probably already present on the user's computer because it is included with Office 2000.

■ CDO is typically used as a server component when no user interface is needed. CDO is designed to be used as a scripting layer between an Active Server Page application and the Microsoft Exchange Server. Figure 18-4 shows where the Outlook executable and the CDO library normally reside in the environment.

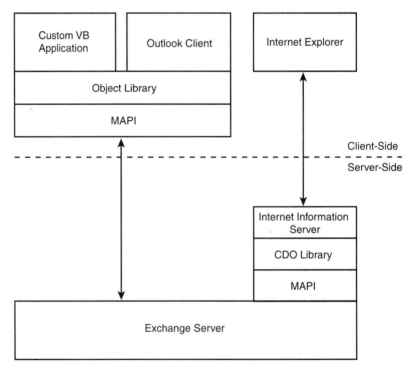

Figure 18-4. *Collaboration Data Objects normally reside between Internet Information Server and Microsoft Exchange Server. Outlook sits on the desktop.*

THE CUSTOMER SUPPORT SAMPLE APPLICATION

With this background now in place, let's jump into a case study that will illustrate this technology in more detail, using the fictitious Awesome Computers Company. Awesome Computers is a PC distributor that wants to deploy an application that quickly routes relevant information through support channels to obtain a speedy response from the company's service department. Customer service requests should be treated identically whether the request arrives via the Web site or through Awesome Computer's call center. The only difference between the processes is the origin of the ticket. If a phone call comes in to a representative, the representative manually enters data into a custom Outlook form. If the customer enters the support request via the Web, he or she enters information into a Web-based form, and an Active Server Page will then initiate the routing process. To move ahead of their competition, Awesome Computers has imposed a 24-hour time response time frame, no matter the origin of the request. This process is depicted in Figure 18-5.

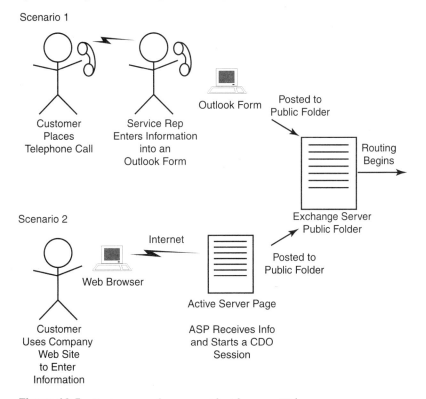

Figure 18-5. *Customer makes request by phone or Web.*

At the top, the customer places a phone call to the service representative. The representative uses an Outlook form to enter the customer's information. Below, the customer uses a browser instead to fill out a service request. The result is the same: prompt service.

Once a support ticket is generated by the customer or the service representative, the information must be routed to the appropriate response support employee and reviewed at particular time intervals to ensure that the client receives adequate service and response times. Customer requests can be routed to one of three departments:

- **Hardware**: Customers with hardware issues
- **Software**: Customers having trouble with software
- **Customer Service:** All other issues will be handled in customer service

Customers are required to submit the serial number that is located on the front of each Awesome Computer with their request for service. Service request will be escalated if the request falls behind schedule, and each request is evaluated every four hours. This means that the request will be escalated if it has not been acted upon within four hours. If an issue is not addressed within eight hours, the application will e-mail the support pager to ensure that the customer receives immediate attention.

Once the request is generated, the application searches the company's relational database to cross-reference any information it has on the customer and previous requests for service. This process is implemented using Visual Basic Scripting (VBS), either embedded in the Outlook form or Active Server Page. After retrieving the information from the database, the application applies business rules to determine which representative will be assigned the request and uses a dynamic Process Definition Map bound to a public Exchange Server folder to allow custom routing through resolution. There is always a default map stored in the public folder as well, but you can embed a map in an Outlook form that overrides the default map to create dynamic routes for an item to follow. This is demonstrated later in the chapter.

Once the appropriate member of the support team receives the request (in the form of an Outlook item), she now has all of the information she needs. Finally, managers are provided with an intranet-based report that lets them review all unresolved requests and provides detailed information on the number of support calls currently open, and the order they arrived in the queue.

Outlook Forms: The User Interface

Let's first discuss the customer who uses the telephone to call Awesome Computers to place a support request. The customer is having a problem with her computer, so she places a call to the Awesome Computers Hotline number. The answering service representative collects the Awesome Computer serial number from the customer and enters it into an Outlook form (shown in Figure 18-6). The form searches the company database and retrieves information related to the original sale of the computer. The representative also enters the type of problem (Hardware, Software, or Other), and with the click of a button, the form is posted to a public folder on the company's Exchange Server.

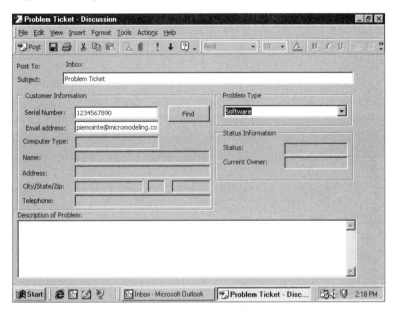

Figure 18-6. *A custom Outlook form, with all the relevant fields.*

Working in the Outlook environment

An Outlook form presents a set of information to the user. Developers can determine whether a *Compose* or a *Read* form is presented, depending on what action the user is taking. The Compose form is used when the message is initially created, and the Read form is used when the message is read. For this example, while designing an Outlook form, choose Form from the menu and check off Separate Read layout to keep one form. In addition to the Read and Compose options, Outlook has some very useful features for creating professional-looking forms, including auto-layout and control alignment tools.

On an Outlook form, each of the tabs across the tab control is called a *page*. If the page has parenthesis around it, this indicates that it is not visible.

You can make the second page visible by first clicking on the tab labeled (P.2), and then choosing Display This Page from the Form menu.

Different item types in Outlook are based on specific forms, which means that e-mail items are based on one form, while appointment items utilize another. Therefore, developers must create a separate form for each item type. Outlook allows the developer to prevent the user from manipulating a form. This security measure, along with built-in version control and very light forms (usually around 10 K after the form is installed on a client machine), make Outlook a very suitable development environment.

Building the form

To allow the service representative to capture all the necessary information and initiate a service ticket for the customer, you need to create a custom form. From the Outlook client, select Tools, Forms, Design a Form, and select Post from the Design Form dialog box. Once in Design mode, you can begin to add custom fields using the Field Chooser (see Figure 18-7). Click the New button to add a custom field and drag the field onto the form to create a suitable place to enter the information. Repeat this set of steps for each field on the form until it looks like Figure 18-7.

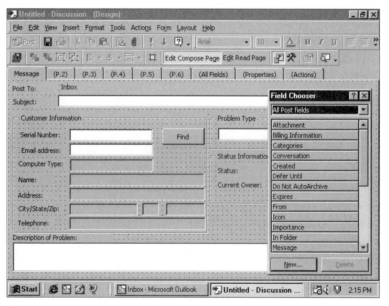

Figure 18-7. *The Outlook Forms development environment.*

Now that the form's been built, you need to put code behind the form for three particular tasks:

1. Look up the customer information in the database when a serial number is entered.

2. Obtain the list of technicians for routing the completed request.

3. Build the routing table and save it with the form.

The next section will focus on the VBScript to be included with the form.

Adding the code

Programming in Outlook forms is done using Visual Basic Scripting Edition, which is a subset of Visual Basic for Applications (VBA) used in Microsoft Office. Outlook 2000 is the first version of Outlook to support VBA.

VBA VS. VBSCRIPT

Some of the differences between VBA and VBScript include:

■ Only variants are used in VBScript.

■ VBScript does not include file I/O.

■ VBScript has only late binding of objects; VBA has both late and early binding.

■ No API support.

To add code in the Outlook environment, simply open a form for design and choose Form, View Code. Although Outlook's VBScript coding environment is not as rich as some others, an Object browser has been added to Outlook 2000, making it much easier to use. This section will concentrate on the code behind the Find button, pressed once a serial number is entered, to look up the customer's information in the corporate database. In the button's click event, code is added to query the database and return the customer's record.

The first three lines declare a constant (because VBScript does not provide constants in the way that Visual Basic does), set a reference to the current item's form, and set a reference to a control (txtSerialNumber) on the form:

```
Sub cmdFind_Click()
Const db_READ_ONLY = 4
        Set objPage = GetInspector.ModifiedFormPages
        Set objTXTSerialNumber =
        objPage("Message").Controls("txtSerialNumber")
```

The next three lines create a reference to the DAO 3.5 library and to the Awesome Computer data source:

```
Set daengMyEngine = CreateObject("DAO.dbengine.35")
Set wsMyWorkspace =
daengMyEngine.Createworkspace("ODBCWorkspace", admin, "", 1)
Set dbMydb = wsMyWorkspace.openconnection("Awesome")
```

Then, SQL is used to query the data source and find our record:

```
        'Query against SQL Server to return customer person
        sSQL = "select * from customer where Customer.SerialNumber
= '" & objTXTSerialNumber.Value & "'"
        Set rsReturnSearch = dbMydb.OpenRecordset(sSQL,
db_READ_ONLY)
        If rsReturnSearch.recordcount Then
            ' fill in customer information
            item.userproperties("Computer Type").value =
  rsReturnSearch.Fields("ComputerType")
            item.userproperties("Name").value =
rsReturnSearch.Fields("CustomerName")
            item.userproperties("Address").value =
rsReturnSearch.Fields("CustomerAddress")
            item.userproperties("sCity").value =
rsReturnSearch.Fields("CustomerCity")
            item.userproperties("sState").value =
rsReturnSearch.Fields("CustomerState")
            item.userproperties("sZip").value =
rsReturnSearch.Fields("CustomerZip")
            item.userproperties("sPhone").value =
rsReturnSearch.Fields("CustomerPhone")
        Else
            MsgBox "Serial number not found in database."
        End If

        Set objPage = Nothing
        Set objCBOProblemType = Nothing
        Set objTXTSerialNumber = Nothing
        Set daengMyEngine = Nothing
        Set wsMyWorkspace = Nothing
        Set dbMydb = Nothing
End Sub
```

Now that the application has the customer and computer information it needs, it must determine who should take care of the request. By classifying the type of problem into three different categories, the application can select the problem "hierarchy" by looking in its database. Different roles have been assigned to each of the customer service employees, and the assignment of each request gets determined in the following manner:

```
Function Item_send()
Const db_READ_ONLY = 4
        Set objPage = GetInspector.ModifiedFormPages
        Set objCBOProblemType =
objPage("Message").Controls("cboProblemType")

        Set daengMyEngine = CreateObject("DAO.dbengine.35")
        Set wsMyWorkspace =
daengMyEngine.Createworkspace("ODBCWorkspace", admin, "", 1)
        Set dbMydb = wsMyWorkspace.openconnection("Awesome")

        'Query against SQL Server to return customer person
        sSQL = "select * from customer where Service.SupportType =
'" & objCBOProblemType.Value & "'"
        Set rsReturnSearch = dbMydb.OpenRecordset(sSQL,
db_READ_ONLY)

        If rsReturnSearch.recordcount Then
            ' fill in customer information
            Tier1 = rsReturnSearch.Fields("Tier1Name")
            Tier2 = rsReturnSearch.Fields("Tier2Name")
            Tier3 = rsReturnSearch.Fields("Tier3Name")
        End If

        Set objPage = Nothing
        Set objCBOProblemType = Nothing
        Set objTXTSerialNumber = Nothing
        Set daengMyEngine = Nothing
        Set wsMyWorkspace = Nothing
        Set dbMydb = Nothing
End Function
```

The last thing the application needs to do before sending this off to the public folder is to create the Process Definition the Exchange Routing Objects need to properly route the request. We will come back to the Outlook item coding after we fully describe Routing Objects later in this chapter.

CDO Enters the Scene

A second scenario envisions the customer requesting support via the Web instead of the telephone. This self-service technique has been gaining prevalence as more and more companies do business over the Web. To incorporate this type of customer service into this sample workflow environment, you will need to use CDO. When the customer enters information into a Web-based form, an Active Server Page feeds the information into the same Outlook form that the representative used in our telephone scenario. Scripting code on Internet Information Server automatically opens the custom form and routes it to the proper public folder.

To accomplish this, first build a Web page for the customer to enter data (see Figure 18-8), making sure that the form submits code to an Active Server Page (in our case, it is called "ctr.asp"). The code for the HTML support request entry page follows this format:

```
<html>
<head>
<title>Awesome Computers Company</title>
</head>

<body>

<h1 align="center"><img src="AG00062_.gif" width="120" height="83"
alt="AG00062_.gif (7566 bytes)"></h1>

<h1 align="center"><big>Awesome Computers Company</big></h1>

<h2 align="center"><big>Service Request Form</big></h2>

<h4 align="center"><big>Please enter your information below and
press the submit button.</big></h4>

<form action="ctr.asp" method="post">
  <table border="1" width="100%" height="75">
    <tr>
       <td width="15%" height="23">Serial Number:</td>
       <td width="60%" height="23"><input type="text"
name="txtSerialNumber" size="20"></td>
    </tr>
    <tr>
       <td width="15%" height="1">Email Address:</td>
       <td width="60%" height="1"><input type="text"
name="txtEmail" size="20"></td>
    </tr>
```

```
     <tr>
       <td width="15%" height="1">Service Type:</td>
       <td width="60%" height="1"><select name="cboServiceType"
size="1">
          <option selected value="Hardware Problem">Hardware
Problem</option>
          <option value="Software Problem">Software Problem</option>
          <option value="Other">Other</option>
       </select></td>
     </tr>
     <tr>
       <td width="15%" height="30">Description of Problem:</td>
       <td width="60%" height="30"><input type="text"
name="txtDescription" size="89"></td>
     </tr>
     <tr>
       <td width="15%" height="25"></td>
       <td width="60%" height="25"><input type="submit"
value="Submit" name="cmdSubmit"></td>
     </tr>
   </table>
</form>
</body>
</html>
```

Figure 18-8. *A Web-based form.*

After the user submits the proper information, the application passes it to the following ASP page and starts a CDO session to post the form to a public folder. As the following code example demonstrates, the application logs on to a MAPI Session (Awesome), gets a reference to the Outbox, creates a message using information from the HTML form, and posts the form to the specified public folder. This process is depicted in Figure 18-9.

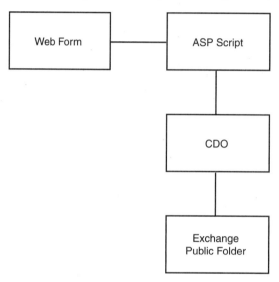

Figure 18-9. *Posting data from an HTML form to Exchange via ASP and CDO.*

```
<%
' create a CDO session and log on -- username and password in
      profile
Set objSession = CreateObject("MAPI.Session")
objSession.Logon "Awesome"
Set objMessage =
objSession.Outbox.Messages.Add(,,"IPM.Note.Issue")
objMessage.Subject = "Service Request for serial number " &
Request.Form("txtSerialNumber")
objMessage.Text = Request.Form("cboServiceType") &
Request.Form("txtDescription")
Set objOneRecip = objMessage.Recipients.Add
objOneRecip.Name = "Service Requests" ' Public Folder
objOneRecip.Resolve ' get MAPI to determine complete e-mail
      address
```

```
' send the message and log off
objMessage.Send
objSession.Logoff
Response.write "Your request has been processed."
%>
```

The customer entering via the Web unknowingly utilizes Active Server technology to e-mail the Outlook form and initiate routing. Active Data Objects (ADO) are used to retrieve data from the corporate database. (For additional information on ways to retrieve information from corporate data sources, see Chapter 9).

Once the message is posted to the public folder (from either source), it must get to the proper support representative so that the service request can be resolved. Microsoft Exchange Routing Objects are used to map a routing plan for the Outlook item. Routing Objects utilize a hub-and-spoke architecture; the public folder acts as the hub, and the recipients act as spokes (see Figure 18-10).

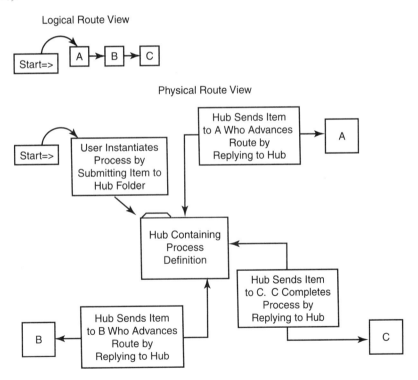

Figure 18-10. *The hub and spoke architecture of Routing Objects.*

To allow managers in the company to view the current service backlog, let's create a view for posting to the company's intranet. Use CDO rendering objects and ASP from Microsoft Exchange and Microsoft Outlook to accomplish this task. Now let's discuss how to show all requests in the system and how they have progressed through the workflow process.

Routing Objects

Routing Objects, added to Microsoft Exchange as part of Service Pack 1, were created to facilitate workflow applications. Anyone who has ever developed workflow applications knows how much effort it takes to program from scratch what Routing Objects are specifically geared to create. Examples of applications that would benefit from Routing Objects include order entry and processing, accounting, bug tracking, document management, expense reports, and, of course, customer call tracking as discussed here.

Routing Object components

Routing Objects consist of the following four components (see Figure 18-11):

- **Routing Engine.** A COM component that sits on top of the Event Service in Exchange Server whose main purpose is to track and execute multiple process instances within an Exchange folder. The engine supports all flow control activities and utilizes VBS for any additional activities.

- **A set of COM objects.** Used for programming the Routing Engine and that allow for the creation and manipulation of process maps. Process maps define the actions an item will follow when dropped into the public folder. The Routing Engine uses these maps to determine which steps will be taken. Routing Objects support two different types of routing: sequential and parallel. Sequential routing is dependent on time or an event in order to move to the next step in the workflow, as items are moved step by step through the workflow process. With parallel routing, the request is broadcast to more than one recipient at a time, so approvals can take place concurrently.

- **Routing Map.** Process maps define the actions that an item will follow when dropped into the public folder when Routing Objects are installed.

- **VBScript Actions.** Default set of VBScript (VBS) functions included with Routing Objects. This file, routing.vbs (included free on Exchange 5.5 SP 1), includes activities such as Send, Receive, and

Consolidate as well as IsTimeout or isNDR to evaluate scenarios and deal with them appropriately. Developers can also adapt VBS code to their development needs. Developers must use VBS to code within Routing Objects because VBS is the only supported scripting language.

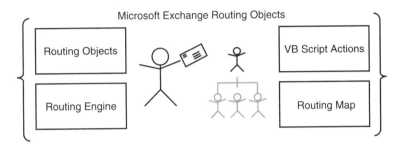

Figure 18-11. *Four components that make up Routing Objects.*

Together, these four components combine to include an effective solution for routing information. Prior to Routing Objects, corporate developers would have to create enterprise applications from scratch in order to custom design a specific workflow application need. With Routing Objects, the problem is simplified, and an integrated solution can be easily developed, leveraging an existing Exchange architecture.

Starting the Routing Process

Once an item is dropped into the public folder, the Routing Object technology is triggered. This event will be the launch pad for the workflow application; the public folder will act like mission control, maintaining status on the item throughout the routing process.

Routing Wizard

Included with Routing Objects is a simple-to-use Routing Wizard. The Routing Wizard is an application written in Visual Basic, and Microsoft has released the source code on the Microsoft web site (*http://www.microsoft.com/technet/download/exchange/*).

Once an item is dropped on the folder, the routing process and tracking begins. Let's review the steps required to create a simple routing application using the wizard. Remember, even if you start with the wizard, you can always customize the VB scripts and Route Map tables generated by the wizard later in the process using the Agents editor application (see Note later in chapter).

To use the Routing Wizard, all you need to know is the type of routing you want to use (parallel or sequential), the recipients or roles to which you want the item to be routed, and a public folder to which to bind the wizard code.

Routing Objects can route information to people based on roles. Roles are a way to define a position in a company, rather than hard-coding a person's name. For example, if a software technician in the company needs to receive a routed message, you should put the person's role in the event script, not the user's exchange login name. This way, if a new employee takes over the position, you do not have to change the scripting code. Another way to select recipients is to add their names dynamically in the script at the time the message is created. This process involves looking up a job function in a database and extracting the current employee. For this example, we will route requests to specific recipients obtained from our corporate directory.

Figures 18-12 through 18-15 depict some of the wizard screens. Again, the wizard is only for the simplest of applications and simply whets the developer's appetite to use Routing Objects to create more sophisticated applications. For more complex routing applications like this one, you will need to write custom VBScript code and customize the Routing Table.

Figure 18-12. *The first screen for Routing Objects shows all the steps.*

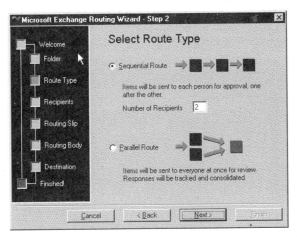

Figure 18-13. *Simply choose the type of routing required.*

Figure 18-14. *Choose to route using Roles or Recipients.*

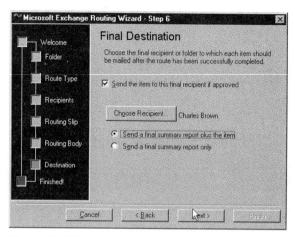

Figure 18-15. *Status report that is created when using Routing Objects.*

The Solution

To create this application, first install Routing Objects from Exchange 5.5 Service Pack 1 and set the proper permissions for scripting as described in the next section. The computer also needs Microsoft Windows NT Server 4.0 SP3 or higher, Exchange 5.5 SP1, and Internet Information Server 4.0 installed to run the application. You must have Exchange administrator privileges to set up the folder, but after it is set up, any person who has Owner permissions can modify the routes. Only users with "Owner" level security can set up folders, write the scripts, and establish event-server bindings. The following section describes setting up the event service in more detail.

Configuring the Exchange Event Service for Scripting

To use Exchange Server Routing Objects, the Event Service must be installed on the Exchange server. Any servers with the Event Service installed will appear under Events Root in Exchange Server Administrator. Permissions of Author or above must be granted on EventConfig_<server name> for the event service to work. You can test if you can edit scripts by right-clicking on the folder in the Outlook client and choosing Properties. In Properties, use the Agents tab to view/edit scripts in the folder. Only the owner of the folder can access its Agent properties (see Figures 18-16 and 18-17). If you don't see the Agents tab, check and make sure the Server Scripting Add-In is installed. Select Tools, Options, Other Tab, Advanced Options, Add-In Manager, and make sure Server Scripting is checked and you are using Outlook version 8.03 or later. If you still don't see the tab, you probably don't have the right permissions.

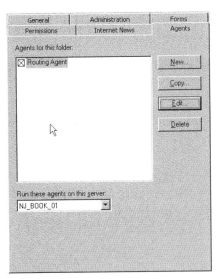

Figure 18-16. *The Agents tab appears only when the appropriate permissions are assigned by the administrator.*

Figure 18-17. *When Routing Objects is properly installed, it is an option on the Agents tab.*

Now let's create a logical map depicting the logical sequence of steps that take place. This map will ultimately evolve into a physical map as the steps are actually implemented. Some of the terms you need to be familiar with to work with Routing Objects are:

- **Activity ID.** The line number that identifies the code
- **Action.** The method to use
- **Argument.** Whatever parameter(s) are needed

Table 18-1 shows the logical map for the Awesome Computers routing process. Creating a logical map assures that both you and your users mutually understand the problem and suggested steps when creating workflow solutions.

Table 18-1
LOGICAL MAP FOR THE AWESOME COMPUTERS ROUTING PROCESS

Activity ID	Action	Argument
10	Send	Service-Level Recipient 1
20	Wait	240 minutes
30	OrSplit	IsTimeout
40	Goto	100
50	Goto	1000
100	Send	Service-Level Recipient 2
110	Wait	240 minutes
120	OrSplit	IsTimeout
130	Goto	200
140	Goto	1000
200	Send	Support Pager
1000	FinalizeReport	
1020	Send	Manager on Duty
10000	Terminate	

Every routing folder contains a default map that it will use if the item doesn't have its own map. In this example, you will generate the map using the Outlook form's script, so you can customize the route for different scenarios. This provides the flexibility of dynamically creating maps and routing the requests to different departments, depending on the specific customer service issues. MakeMap is used by the Outlook script to read information from the item and create the process map (see Figure 18-18).

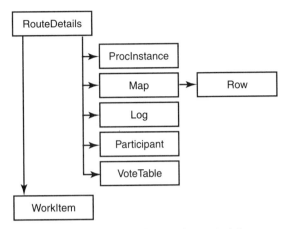

Figure 18-18. *Routing Objects Object Model.*

In the Outlook VB Scripting window of the form, add the following code to build the map to complete the routing. This code is based on the logical map created earlier.

To create the map, the following function comes in handy when adding a row to the table. This code creates a new Exchange Routing Row Object, sets the ID, Action, and Flags properties, and returns the newly created row. The function is included on the Exchange SP1 CD in the routing.vbs file:

```
Function MakeRow(ID, Action, Flags, Argv, Argc)
    Dim RTRow
    Set RTRow = CreateObject("ExRt.Row")

    RTRow.ActivityID = ID
    RTRow.Action = Action
    RTRow.Flags = Flags
    If Argc > 0 Then RTRow.SetArgs Argc, Argv

    Set MakeRow = RTRow
End Function
```

The next step in creating the map involves using the MakeRow method to insert the rows for the map. The first lines of code handle preprocessing such as non-delivery of messages (NDR) or resolving the recipient prior to beginning the routing process. Notice that because Outlook uses VBScript as its scripting language, you must use late binding.

LATE BINDING VS. EARLY BINDING

VB Script allows only late binding of object instancing. With early binding (Visual Basic/VBA gives you this option), you actually declare the type of object so that certain items are already loaded when you start the application, such as the type of object. What early binding means is quicker instancing of objects. In late binding, the application has no idea what kind of object you will instantiate until it is called in the line of code. Overhead is incurred in the process of running through the application and having to instantiate a new object.

```
Dim rtobMap
rtobMap.InsertActivity -1, MakeRow(1, "ORSplit", 0, Array("IsNDR"), 1)
rtobMap.InsertActivity -1, MakeRow(2, "Goto", 0, Array(1020), 1)
rtobMap.InsertActivity -1, MakeRow(3, "OrSplit", 0,
Array("IsReceipt"), 1)
rtobMap.InsertActivity -1, MakeRow(4, "Goto", 0, Array(1020), 1)
rtobMap.InsertActivity -1, MakeRow(9, "PreProcessing", 2,
Array(False), 1)
```

Next, the program will send the customer service request item to the first-level support representative. It will then wait four hours for a response. OrSplit is the equivalent of an IF statement; the flow of the programming logic skips to the next line if the evaluation is true and two lines if it is false.

```
rtobMap.InsertActivity -1, MakeRow(10, "Send", 2,
    Array(SupportRecip1, _
    False, "Trouble Ticket, please review (1st level)",
"<ATTACH>", False, False), 6)
rtobMap.InsertActivity -1, MakeRow(20, "Wait", 0, Array(240), 1)
rtobMap.InsertActivity -1, MakeRow(30, "ORSplit", 0,
Array("IsTimeout"), 1)
rtobMap.InsertActivity -1, MakeRow(40, "Goto", 0, Array("100"), 1)
rtobMap.InsertActivity -1, MakeRow(50, "Goto", 0, Array("10000"),
1)
rtobMap.InsertActivity -1, MakeRow(100, "Send", 2, Array
SupportRecip2, _
    False, "Trouble Ticket, please review(2nd level)", "<ATTACH>",
False, False), 6)
rtobMap.InsertActivity -1, MakeRow(110, "Wait", 0, Array(240), 1)
rtobMap.InsertActivity -1, MakeRow(120, "ORSplit", 0,
Array("IsTimeout"), 1)
rtobMap.InsertActivity -1, MakeRow(130, "Goto", 0, Array("200"),
1)
```

```
rtobMap.InsertActivity -1, MakeRow(140, "Goto", 0, Array("10000"),
1)
rtobMap.InsertActivity -1, MakeRow(200, "Send", 2,
Array("SupportPager", _
    False, "Trouble Ticket, Alert(3rd level)", "<ATTACH>", False,
False), 6)
```

For example, the code translates to:

- Send item to the tier-1 support person.

- Wait 240 minutes (four hours).

- Check if there is a timeout.

- If timeout is true, then go to line 100.

- If timeout if false (it was opened), go to line 1000.

The coding in Routing Objects is very rudimentary and may take you back a few years before Visual Basic existed. It is somewhat frustrating at first to code in the Outlook IDE after having worked in Visual Basic (see sidebar "VBScript vs. VBA" earlier in this chapter). Even so, the results are worth it, and we hope that Microsoft will improve on this capability in future versions.

The final part of code uses the FinalizeReport action, which generates a summary report. When the summary report is generated, the report is sent to the manager for review. Finally, the map logic is terminated.

```
rtobMap.InsertActivity -1, MakeRow(1000, "FinalizeReport", 2,
Array(False, False), 2)
rtobMap.InsertActivity -1, MakeRow(1010, "Send", 2, Array(Manager, "",
False, "<FINALIZED>", _
    "<ATTACH>", False, False), 7)
rtobMap.InsertActivity -1, MakeRow(10000, "Terminate", 0, Null, 0)
```

The result of the scripting code is a physical map, attached to the Outlook item in the public folder, which is used by the Routing Engine to override the default map. The scripting process has begun and will redirect the problem whenever it looks like it is not being resolved in a timely manner.

NOTE Microsoft has released an Agents Editor application that allows developers to modify, create, or delete process maps. It is included free on the MS Web site (http://www.microsoft.com/technet/download/exchange/) or on the Exchange EDK that was released at the PDC in 1998. This application is a Visual Basic 5 application, and all the source code is included.

When Outlook form development is complete, publish the form to a public folder called New Issues by choosing File, Publish Form As. Type in the name **Issue** (Name of the form) and choose Publish in the New Issues Folder.

When a representative takes a call, she simply clicks on the New Issues public folder and chooses Compose from the menu. She will see the New Issue form and choose it to create a new instance of the form.

Reporting

After the routing code is in place and customers begin to use the system, management will want to see how the system is working. To enable management to look at reports over the intranet, you can make use of the Outlook Web Access (OWA) feature of Exchange. OWA lets you configure an Active Server Page that automatically renders Exchange folder information in a browser-ready format. Because a simple view is easy to set up, there is no code required.

CONFIGURING OUTLOOK WEB ACCESS

To enable the Exchange server to automatically render information over the Web, you must first install the Active Server component of Exchange. To do so, run the Exchange Server setup program and select Add, Remove components. Select the Active Server component and enter the name of your IIS machine. To do a quick test to see if the install worked, open Internet Explorer and enter http://<servername>/exchange, which will open the Outlook Web Access screen. From here, you can enter your user ID and gain access to your Exchange mailbox or public folders.

You might not see any public folders yet, however, because they haven't been added to the list of rendered folders. To add public folders in Exchange Administrator, Open the HTTP (Web) Site Settings Object from the site-level Protocols container. Select the Folder Shortcuts tab. Using the New button, individually add the folders you want to publish. From the Properties dialog box of each published folder, select the General tab. Then select the Client Permissions button and make sure that the folder has at least the Folder Visible permission enabled for the anonymous account. To view the contents of the public folder, the anonymous account must have at least a role of Reviewer.

Now that you have a view into the folder, select just the fields you want, or even filter out whole items you don't need to see. Using a regular Outlook client, select the public folder you've created. Select View, Current View, Define Views... to open a dialog box for customizing a new view. Click the New button and enter **Open Service Requests** into the Name field. Click OK, and then use the Fields button to select only those fields you want to see. Use the Advanced tab of the Filter button to enter **Field: Status equals 'open'**. After saving the view, managers can use either Outlook or the Web to see the custom report.

Things to Consider

Some of the limitations and considerations of routing objects as of the time of this writing include:

- Signed and encrypted messages are not supported.

- It's possible to create a never-ending circular route, and the engine will simply follow your orders and keep routing data.

- Message flags are not copied to messages.

- One routing agent per public folder limit. This makes sense as two agents will only confuse the engine.

- Routing Objects work on a timer; therefore, some items might get routed slightly later than the elapsed time specified when creating the routing map.

- You must have Exchange administration privileges to use Routing agents or Exchange agents.

Exchange Agents

Although we do not detail the use of Agents, it is important to know they exist because the Routing Objects libraries are based on them. They can also be used to develop more complex Exchange applications and allow custom server-side scripting in Exchange. Scripts run as the result of events in a particular public or private folder. These events include timer events, such as how long an item is in a folder, as well as actions, such as posting, editing, or deleting a message. The same permissions and security discussed earlier for Routing Objects also applies to Event Agents.

In Routing Objects, you can code using only VBScript, whereas with Exchange Agents you can code using VBScript, Jscript, or any other supported language. You can even use Visual Studio as your script editor. You may also add custom COM objects to events. Agents can be customized to perform very specified processes when triggered by events in Exchange.

SUMMARY

Exchange, Outlook, and CDO make a great team for creating custom applications and providing support services for other applications, such as an e-commerce site. This chapter provided only one example, but the possibilities are endless when it comes to messaging, workflow, and collaboration. The next step is to install Routing Objects and begin experimenting and creating your own custom workflow applications.

Chapter 19

Streaming Multimedia

by John Intihar

In the past, to deliver multimedia over the Internet, you would provide your audience with links to .wav, .jpg, or .avi files. Users would click on one of these links, causing the browser to download the entire file before launching a default player to play it. This method limits the size of the content you can deliver, as no one wants to wait a long time for a file to download. You can now get past this limitation by sending a continuous stream of multimedia content to a client application that can play it to the user as the content arrives. You can also avoid serving multimedia as files altogether by broadcasting live content over the Internet.

Using these new capabilities, you can provide audio and video product presentations in your online store. You can also provide a multimedia annual report on your company's Web site. You can provide your employees with on-demand training videos, which they can view whenever they wish. You can even broadcast a live presentation, complete with video and slides, directly to the desktops of all your employees in all your offices worldwide. You can accomplish these and other production tasks using streaming multimedia products from Microsoft and RealNetworks.

When considering streaming technology, consider that businesses make money not only by increasing sales, but by lowering costs of operations and being more capable in what they do. Utilizing the best communications technology within an organization—for training, employee communication, group empowerment, and so on—can be a sufficient reason for using network multimedia, even if you never put it on the public Web page.

> NOTE   This chapter will explain streaming multimedia technology and the Microsoft NetShow products that implement it. Although the streaming multimedia line of products from RealNetworks gives you a comparable, high-quality solution, this chapter does not serve as a comparison of product lines from the two companies. If you plan to implement streaming multimedia in your organization or over the Internet, you should thoroughly evaluate all available products to find the best solution for your multimedia needs.

THE BASIC CONCEPTS

At the heart of this new technology lies the concept of *streaming* multimedia—a continuous data feed from a media server to a media player on a user's machine. The media player does not have to wait for an entire media file to download before it can start playing it, rather, it will play the media stream continuously as it receives it until the stream terminates. The player does not store the downloaded data in a file. This method not only frees the user from waiting a long time, but also, more importantly, allows you to provide content without worrying about its length. You can stream hours, days, or years of content because there are no file-size restrictions.

One of the immediately apparent problems with streaming has to do with unstable transmissions. You've probably noticed, on occasion, that data flowing to your computer from the Internet sometimes pauses briefly (and sometimes not so briefly). This results from unavoidable high network traffic, transmission errors, and other communication problems. If media players did not handle this common situation, the audio or video produced by a player would pause each time the stream experienced a delay. To avoid this problem, a media player stores the data received in a buffer. After a short delay, the player begins to resolve the stream to audio and video output as it reads the data from the buffer. Although it produces a slight delay at the beginning of the transmission, this method enables the player to hide transmission delays from the viewer. The buffering process is shown in Figure 19-1.

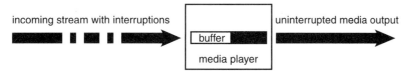

Figure 19-1. *The stream buffering process*

When the stream coming into the buffer experiences an interruption, the buffer shortens, but the player can still provide the user with continuous output from the buffer. When the stream coming into the buffer exceeds the rate at which the player outputs the media, the buffer grows. The user will experience a pause in the show only if the buffer empties. If this happens often, the user can increase the buffer length setting on his or her media player resulting in longer up-front wait time but fewer interruptions.

Streaming multimedia and stream buffers give you great advantages but do not represent the full solution to the problem of sharing multimedia across data networks. The network broadcast process requires optimization to make the transmission of media streams as efficient as possible.

CODECS

Every connection used to transmit media streams will have a particular *bandwidth*. Bandwidth refers to the amount of data that can pass through the connection over a fixed period of time and is expressed in terms of *bits per second*, or *bps*. With increased bandwidth, a media server can send more data in the same amount of time and the same amount of data in less time. Modems that most people use to connect to the Internet these days can provide a maximum bandwidth of either 28,800 bps or 56,600 bps. These connections provide enough bandwidth to send low- to medium-quality audio and video. Connections contained within a local area network typically support bandwidths of 10,000,000 to 100,000,000 bps. With this much bandwidth, you can send full-screen, high-quality video. No matter what level of bandwidth you have, you will want your transmissions to use as little bandwidth as possible so that you do not tie up the network with exorbitant amounts of traffic. You will want to minimize the amount of data you send without losing quality.

The media server and media player use *compression/decompression* algorithms, or *codecs*, to reduce the size of the data within the media stream. Codecs can either compress or decompress audio, video, and still images without significant loss in quality. Before streaming media to the player, the media server passes the data in the stream through a codec to shrink it, thereby decreasing the time it will take to reach the media player. When the media player receives the stream, it first passes the data in the stream through a codec to restore it to its original state. It then renders the stream into the audio, video, or still images it contains.

Because you can provide many different types of content over connections with a wide range of bandwidth, vendors give you many codec choices. Some codecs work best with high-quality video over high-bandwidth connections, some specialize in working with music, and others provide the best choice for speech over low-bandwidth connections. Table 19-1 shows some of the codecs that ship with NetShow Multimedia Services. These codecs also ship with the Windows Media Player.

Table 19-1

COMMON CODECS SHIPPED WITH NETSHOW MULTIMEDIA SERVICES

Codec Name	Description
FhG MPEG Layer-3	Good for CD-quality audio over the Internet and comes with different formats for different network bandwidths
Voxware MetaVoice	Used only for speech over very low bandwidth connections
Microsoft MPEG-4 Video	A video codec optimized for scalability and flexibility at most bandwidths
Microsoft H.263	Good for low- to medium- quality video; optimized for presentations and other low-motion video content
Duck TrueMotion RT	A high-quality video codec for high bandwidth connections (>1,000,000 bps)

NETSHOW STREAMING METHODS

When using streaming multimedia, you can deliver content from your server in a number of different ways. You can use *on-demand* streaming to provide stored content in files that users can request at will. You can also use a *broadcast* to stream content on a schedule that you announce to users ahead of time.

On-Demand Streaming

On-demand streaming occurs over a bi-directional connection between the media player and the media server. You initiate the connection by supplying the media player with the URL of the stored media file. The media player opens a connection with the server, and the server begins to stream the media. You not only have the ability to receive the media any time you want, you can also pause, fast-forward, and rewind the stream using your media player. You can even jump to a specific point in the stream.

Broadcast Streaming

While on-demand streaming provides the receiver of the media stream with many benefits, you will find you will not always want to deliver your media in such a manner. For example, you might want to provide prerecorded media on a pay-per-view basis and will therefore want to prevent the user from controlling the media stream. You also might want to broadcast a live event. For example, as I write this, I am using the Windows Media Player to view NASA's live broadcast of John Glenn's return to space aboard the space shuttle *Discovery*. We call these methods of media delivery *broadcast* streaming.

You can use two broadcast methods: *unicast* broadcast and *multicast* broadcast. With both methods, you control the media stream from the media server. Users connect to the server and request access to a media stream. As shown in Figure 19-2, with unicast broadcast, the media server delivers a separate stream to each connected user. When you use multicast broadcast, the server sends a single stream to all connected users.

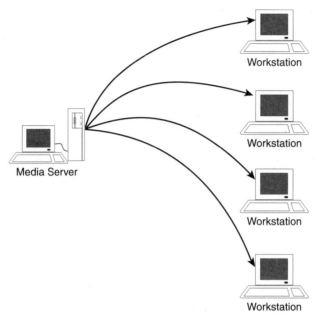

Figure 19-2. *A unicast broadcast requires the media server to send a copy of the media stream to each client workstation.*

A generic network broadcast involves a server sending data to every computer on a particular network segment. This restricts you from broadcasting information to other network segments in your local area network and to the computers on your wide area network located in other cities. These broadcasts also require that every computer receiving the broadcast decide whether it is interested in the message.

Using a multicast broadcast as shown in Figure 19-3, which requires multicast-enabled routers connecting your network segments, you can broadcast information to any computer on any segment of your network. The multicast broadcast gives you a great advantage over other broadcast methods. Using this method, you broadcast information only to recipients who have expressed interest in receiving it. Moreover, the server sends only a single copy of the information. If the recipients reside on more than one network segment, the multicast-enabled router will handle any data cloning necessary to reach all destinations. In contrast, a server sending information with a unicast broadcast must send one copy of the data to each recipient. Therefore, the multicast method gives you a lower bandwidth requirement and does not require non-recipients to waste time dealing with unwanted data.

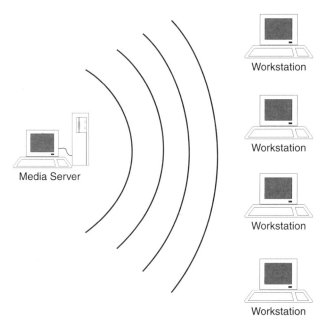

Figure 19-3. *A multicast broadcast requires the media server to send only a single media stream, which each interested client workstation monitors.*

Keep in mind that you can only multicast on the local network segment unless your network routers support multicasting. You will need to plan for this capability when designing the network hardware and selecting the hardware for it.

NETSHOW MULTIMEDIA SERVICES

As shown in Figure 19-4, Microsoft's NetShow Multimedia Services provide you with a full suite of software for organizing, publishing, and serving multimedia content. This suite of software includes NetShow's server components, which run on NT Server, a collection of codecs, a set of NetShow tools used to create and edit content, and the Windows Media Player. All of these components work with multimedia streams in the same format: the Advanced Streaming Format (ASF).

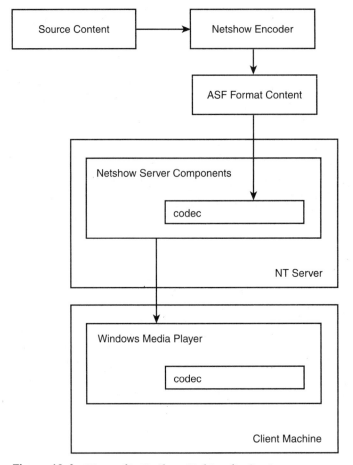

Figure 19-4. *Microsoft's NetShow Multimedia Services.*

Microsoft NetShow Server Components and Windows Media Player Advanced Streaming Format

NetShow's Advanced Streaming Format provides a single format with which you can deliver audio, video, still images, and script commands to the media player over both high- and low-bandwidth connections. Using NetShow tools, you can convert almost any form of media to this format, including compact disk recordings, live video feeds, video tapes, saved still images, Microsoft PowerPoint presentations, live audio, and audio stored in files. Once you have converted your media to ASF, you can immediately stream it to recipients or store it in a file. You store ASF streams in .asf files. The Advanced Streaming Format enables you to work with all media the same way. For more information on ASF, refer to *http://www.microsoft.com/ASF.*

ASF also enables you to implement scalable video streams. Scalable video streams contain multiple video streams. Each stream delivers the same content and uses slightly greater or slightly lesser amounts of the target bandwidth. This way, the media player can switch to a lower-bandwidth portion of the ASF stream during times of decreasing network throughput to continue to provide the user with continuous video. Likewise, the player can switch to a higher-bandwidth portion of the ASF stream when network throughput increases. While the user might see changes in video quality, the media player delivers continuous output. This technique always provides the user with the highest quality video.

Note that ASF scalable video, however, does not enable the media player to render a 56.6 kbps scalable stream adequately to a user with a 28.8 kbps connection. It strives only to provide the best-quality video to each type of network connection.

ASF also support *script commands*. You can include script commands in an ASF stream to instruct the media player to perform an action during the stream. Typical scripts tell the media player to display a caption or to display a Web page at various moments during the stream delivery. For example, you might want to add a video presentation to your Web site that instructs the visitor how to use various sections of the site. Using an ASF stream with script commands, you can walk the visitor through the steps of purchasing a product from your site. The user watches a video or listens to a recording of an instructor. As the instructor explains the purchasing steps, the media player executes synchronized script commands and tells the browser to display specific Web pages.

You can also send custom script commands to provide more information and to perform other application-specific actions. See the section titled, "Windows Media Player Control," for more information on custom script commands.

Windows Media Player

The Microsoft Windows Media Player runs on the client machine and plays the content delivered by the media server. This seemingly insignificant little gizmo actually packs a large number of features. The Windows Media Player can process ASF streams and files, freeing the user from worrying about media types.

It can handle just about anything you throw at it, including multiple audio and video file formats (.wav, .snd, .au, .aif, .aifc, .aiff, .avi), MIDI files (.mid, .rmi), MP3 files (.mp3, .m3u), MPEG files (.m1v, .mp2, .mpa, .mpe, .mpeg, .mpg), QuickTime files (.mov, .qt), RealMedia files and streams (.ra, .rm, .ram, .rmm), and Windows Media files and streams (.asf, .asx). As mentioned earlier in this chapter, the Windows Media Player can also switch between various streams in an ASF stream that contains scalable video. It can process ASF script commands. It enables you to control on-demand streams and stores lists of your favorite media-streaming Web sites.

"Gee whiz," you say, "I wish I could build applications that did all that." Are you ready for the good news? You can.

Windows Media Player Control

As shown in Figure 19-5, the Windows Media Player application wraps a COM component that provides the player with most of its apparent features. This COM component, called the Windows Media Player Control, has the following progid: MediaPlayer.MediaPlayer. You can plug the Windows Media Player Control into your applications as an ActiveX control. That means that you can build your applications, using VBScript, Javascript, Visual Basic, Delphi, Java, C++, or any other language or development environment that supports COM. You can even embed the Windows Media Player Control in your Web page, as shown in Figure 19-6.

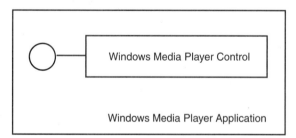

Figure 19-5. *The Windows Media Player derives most of its features from the Windows Media Player Control.*

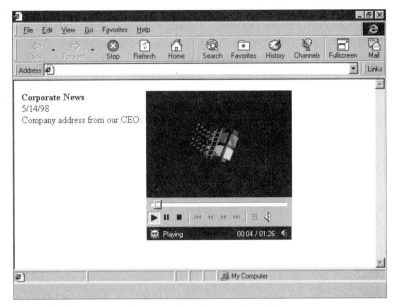

Figure 19-6. *The Windows Media Player embedded in a Web page.*

You can also use the Windows Media Player Control in your application to respond to script commands in an ASF stream. The ASF stream stores script commands in a header. When the control plays the stream, it fires each event at its specified time. Your application can handle the events that the control fires via a connection point by implementing the Windows Media Player Control ScriptCommand method on its _MediaPlayerEvents interface. If you use the control in an application developed with Visual Basic, the development environment will present the ScriptCommand method to you as an event subroutine.

Table 19-2 shows just some of the properties, methods, and events of the Media Player Control:

Table 19-2

SOME OF MICROSOFT MEDIA PLAYER'S METHODS, PROPERTIES, AND EVENTS

Property/Method/Event	Description
AnimationAtStart	Returns or sets whether or not the control shows its animation during initial file buffering
AudioStream	Returns or sets the current audio stream
AutoRewind	Returns or sets whether or not a file is rewound at the end of playback
Bandwidth	Returns the bandwidth of the file in bits per second
Buffering	Sent when the control begins or ends buffering
BufferingProgress	Returns the percent of buffering completed
Cancel	Cancels the current operation
ChannelDescription	Returns a description of the station
Click	Sent when a mouse button is clicked
ClickToPlay	Returns or sets whether or not clicking on the control starts the playback
ConnectionSpeed	Returns the network connection speed of the player
CurrentPosition	Returns the current position in the file
Disconnect	Sent when the control is disconnected from the server
Duration	Returns the play duration of the file
EndOfStream	Sent when the end of the file is reached
Error	Sent when the control has an error condition
FastForward	Fast forwards the playback
GetCodecURL	Returns the URL for a codec
GetStreamName	Returns the name of a media stream
IsBroadcast	Returns whether or not the source is a broadcast
Mute	Returns or sets the current mute state of the stream
Open	Opens the given filename asynchronously
Pause	Pauses the playback at the current position
Play	Begins playing from the current position or marker
SAMILang	Returns or sets the closed-captioning language
ShowControls	Shows or hides the control panel
WindowlessVideo	Returns or sets whether the player will render video without a window

Armed with the power to embed the Windows Media Player Control in your applications, you can produce some awesome applications. Here are a few ideas:

- Add audio and video presentations to your online store. During the presentation, update a list of product features as bullet points in a separate frame.

- Add customer service support videos to your online store, including a guided tour that helps your customer reach the checkout page without confusion.

- Create a "Message from the Top" application to let your company's CEO deliver late-breaking news to employees using live video streams.

- If you ship software, provide a product demonstration presentation on your Web site that actually controls a demo copy of your software on the client's machine while your client watches a presentation video.

Publishing Streams with NetShow Administration Applications

NetShow ships with administration applications for accessing and controlling the NetShow Server Components. Using the NetShow Administrator application, publish your content and control how clients access it. Configure your NetShow server differently depending on the format you will use to deliver your media streams.

On-demand unicasts

To provide a stream via an on-demand unicast, you must first create an on-demand unicast *publishing point*. Publishing points not only provide you with a virtual directory from which clients will access the stream, they also let you control the number of clients that can access the stream simultaneously and throttle the amount of bandwidth they use. Once you have created the publishing point using the NetShow Administrator application, you should store the .asf file that contains the stream you want to publish in the directory path of the publishing point. For example, create a publishing point with an alias of Products on a NetShow server named Acme_02, and then store a file named Demo_123.asf, which contains a product demonstration video, in the directory path of the publishing point. You need to do nothing more. Users can now access the demonstration video by specifying the following string in the Open dialog box in the Windows Media Player application:

```
mms://Acme_02/Products/Demo_123.asf
```

Remember that on-demand unicast streams can serve only one client at a time. If two or more users request the stream at the same time, the NetShow server will send one stream for each user. Nevertheless, the users can fully control their individual on-demand unicast streams.

Broadcast unicasts

To configure the NetShow server to provide users with live unicast streams, you must first create a broadcast unicast publishing point. Rather than specify a directory path, as required when creating an on-demand unicast publishing point, specify a remote stream source. The stream source can originate from a remote broadcast stream, either unicast or multicast, or from a live feed via the NetShow Encoder. The NetShow Encoder, described more fully later in this chapter, converts audio and video signals to an ASF stream. Once you have set up the publishing point, the NetShow server copies the incoming source stream into a separate stream for each connected client.

Multicasting using stations and programs

To publish streams with NetShow via a multicast broadcast, you need to create a *station*. Stations, like unicast publishing points, provide clients with a location from which they can access the media stream. Using the NetShow Administrator application, you create a station and configure its attributes such as its name and description. You must also set the distribution mode of the station. You can set this attribute to Multicast and Distribution, Multicast Only, or Distribution Only. You must enable multicast to deliver streams to clients and distribution if you plan to deliver streams to another NetShow server. See the "Distributing ASF Streams" section later in this chapter for more information on distribution.

You will also need to specify the station's *multicast IP address* and *port*. Similar to the scenario in which many people tune in to the same radio frequency to receive a radio broadcast, all clients that want to access the multicast stream will monitor the station's multicast IP address and port. The station also has a *time-to-live (TTL)* property that indicates the number of routers your multicast will pass through. You can also refer to TTL as *scope*. This attribute allows you to limit the reach of your multicast from a local network segment to the entire Internet.

On your multicast stations, you will publish *programs,* which contain one or more streams. NetShow plays each stream in a program sequentially, one at a time. You use programs to work with and control the streams they contain. For example, you can specify whether you want the streams to play just once or loop continuously.

When you create a station, you save all the information a client needs to connect to it and receive the stream in a station file with an .nsc extension. This file remains on your NetShow server. To announce your program, you provide the client with an *ASF stream redirector file,* which has an .asx extension. Clients will typically access this file via e-mail or a Web hyperlink. The .asx file will contain the program name and a link to the .nsc file of your station. When the Windows Media Player opens the .asx file, it will discover the location of the .nsc file and open it. Once it has read the .nsc file, it will know how to connect to your multicast station.

ASF Stream Redirector Files

ASF Stream Redirector Files have an .asx extension and describe the media content specified by a Uniform Resource Locator (URL). They use the Extensible Markup Language (XML) format to deliver information to the Windows Media Player efficiently. Typically, .asx files serve as hyperlinks to one or more media streams. Because most Web browsers do not know about the protocols used to deliver media streams, use an .asx file to transfer control from the browser to the media player. The media player then connects to the NetShow server to receive the media stream.

ASX files can provide the Windows Media Player with redirection to your published streams no matter which method you use to publish them on your NetShow server. The following code shows the contents of an .asx file used to redirect the Windows Media Player to a program called 6PM News on a station called News served on a NetShow server named news_01. Note that .asx file provides a hyperlink to the station file, News.nsc, on the NetShow server. The Windows Media Player will read the News.nsc file to learn how to access the media streams in the 6PM News program.

```
<asx version = "1.0">
<title>6PM News</title>
<entry>
<ref href = "http://news_01/News.nsc"/>
<title>6PM News</title>
</entry>
</asx>
```

We've only scratched the surface of what you can do with ASX files. Microsoft provides help on the structure and use of the ASX files on their Web site at *http://www.microsoft.com/directx/dxm/help/mmp_sdk/asx_intro.htm*. In addition, *http://www.Microsoft.com/NetShow* will get you to the Windows multimedia page that references NetShow Server components.

The ASX specification details a number of elements you can use in an ASX file to control streams. Table 19-3 shows some of the ASX elements you can use.

Table 19-3
COMMON ASX ELEMENTS

Element	Description
Author	A text string representing the name of the author of the ASX file. The text displays in the Display panel and Properties dialog box of the media player.
Banner	A URL to a graphic file that displays in the media player's display area. You can use banners for advertisements.
Copyright	A text string that specifies copyright information. The text displays in the Display panel and Properties dialog box of the media player.
Logo	A URL to a graphic file that displays next to the stream title in the media player.
Repeat	Defines the number of times the media player repeats a media clip.

Streaming protocols

You can connect NetShow components using a number of protocols as listed in Table 19-4.

Table 19-4

NETSHOW STREAMING PROTOCOLS

Protocol	*Comments*
HyperText Transfer Protocol HTTP	Although you can use this protocol to connect all NetShow components, it is not an efficient method. Use this protocol only when sending media streams across a firewall from one NetShow Server to another.
Microsoft Media Server Protocol (MMS)	This protocol is used to transfer unicast media content from a NetShow publishing point.
MMSU	The MMS protocol that works with the User Datagram Protocol (UDP) to provide the most efficient unicast streaming from a NetShow Server to a media player.
MMST	The MMS protocol that works with the Transfer Control Protocol (TCP) to provide unicast streaming from a NetShow Server to a media player. NetShow tries to connect using the MMSU protocol before trying to connect using the MMST protocol.
Media Stream Broadcast Distribution Protocol (MSBD)	This protocol is used to transfer media streams between NetShow Server components and the NetShow Encoder. It is also used to transfer media streams from one NetShow Server to another.

Distributing ASF Streams

NetShow Services allow you to stream media content not only to clients running media players, but also to other NetShow Servers. This often comes in handy when you need to send your stream across a firewall to reach your clients, and the firewall might not allow a particular transfer protocol. In this case, you can use distribution to send the stream across the firewall from one NetShow Server to another using HTTP, a protocol inefficient for media streaming but tolerated by many firewall configurations. Once the stream has crossed the firewall, you can broadcast it to clients using a more efficient protocol. You might also want to use distribution when you have to deliver your streams using unicast but you have too many clients to serve from a single NetShow Server. You can use distribution in this case to multicast the stream to multiple NetShow Servers, which can each then broadcast a subset of your required unicast streams. NetShow distribution provides you with a level of flexibility that will help you work around many broadcast problems.

NetShow Tools

NetShow ships with a number of useful tools to assist you in encoding, indexing, and editing content. These tool are described as follows.

NetShow Encoder

The NetShow Encoder encodes both stored and live audio and video to an ASF stream. With the NetShow Encoder, you can specify the media source and set the target bandwidth by selecting the proper codec. You can then specify that you want to either save the stream to an .asf file or send it to a NetShow Server for immediate broadcast. No matter what the input source—live video or audio feed, an .asf file, an .avi file, or a .wav file—the NetShow Encoder will encode the media to an ASF stream on the fly. This frees you from performing all sorts of preproduction work.

NetShow ASF Indexer

The NetShow ASF Indexer lets you add properties, markers, and script commands to your ASF files. Each .asf has properties such as Title, Author, and Copyright that you can edit to provide the audience with helpful information about your media stream. The ASF Indexer application displays your ASF file in a window, presents you with timeline controls, and lets you insert objects at any point in the stream. You can insert markers into the ASF file so that your audience can use them to jump to different locations in the stream. You can also use the ASF Indexer to insert script commands into the stream and edit them.

NetShow T.A.G. Author

Using the NetShow T.A.G. Author, you can orchestrate a series of images, audio files, and script commands into a single ASF stream. The tool presents a visual timeline with which you can graphically edit your stream. The T.A.G. Author handles compression of audio and image files using codecs you select. You will typically use the T.A.G. Author to create illustrated audio files such as a slideshow presentation. For example, you can take a presentation you have created using Microsoft PowerPoint and export it to a series of .jpg files. You can then import these files to a NetShow T.A.G. Author project, which will automatically space out the images along the timeline. You can then add audio tracks and script commands to the stream to create a completely automated presentation.

Windows Media On-Demand Producer

This new utility helps both novice and expert media authors create content. The On-Demand Producer lets you easily convert WAV and AVI files to ASF files using encoding templates that provide you with the best encoding settings for each particular bandwidth. This feature takes a lot of the guesswork out of creating streams. Once you have created your media stream, you can use the On-Demand Producer's Publishing Wizard to publish the stream on a NetShow server.

The On-Demand Producer also lets you tweak your content prior to encoding it to a stream. You can:

■ Fade audio in or out

■ Fade video in or out

■ Adjust the starting and end points of a media file

■ Adjust the brightness of a video file

■ Adjust the volume of an audio track

■ Limit any volume disparity in an audio track

The On-Demand Producer provides you with a very easy way to create and publish media streams. Command-line utilities include:

■ **VidToAsf.** Use this command-line utility to convert existing .avi or .mov video files to ASF stream files. Make sure you completely edit your video files using a video editor before converting them to ASF streams.

■ **WavToAsf.** Use this command-line utility to convert existing .wav or .mp3 audio files to ASF stream files. You can compress the file as you convert it using the codec of your choice.

- **ASX3Test.** Use the ASX3Test utility to check the validity of the syntax in your ASX files.

- **ASFCheck.** Use this utility to check your ASF files and repair them if it finds any errors. By using this utility, you can avoid having to play, in its entirety, each ASF file you plan to publish.

- **ASFChop.** Use the ASFChop command-line utility to delete sections of an ASF file. You can also use it to add and edit properties, markers, and script commands.

SUMMARY

This chapter has delivered an overview of streaming multimedia and NetShow Services. It has given you an understanding of this new technology and how you can use it to provide content in a very captivating way.

The NetShow Services from Microsoft provide you with a very good implementation of streaming multimedia technology. NetShow's tools and applications provide all the basics for creating, distributing, and publishing content. You can also fully access the NetShow Services and client components programmatically via their COM interfaces, opening the door to you and your development team to leverage fully these components and services in your custom systems and software.

For more complete information on programming with NetShow Services and the Windows Media Player Control, see the NetShow SDK and the Windows Media Player SDK. You can download these software development kits and a nice collection of sample programs and sample media content from the Microsoft NT Server Media Services site at *www.microsoft.com/ntserver/mediaserv/*.

Index

Index

About The Authors

Micro Modeling Associates, Inc. (MMA), founded in 1989, is a business technology consulting firm and Microsoft Certified Solution Provider Partner with 11 U.S. offices. We build innovative enterprise, desktop, Internet and e-commerce solutions using the latest Microsoft technologies to help companies make better business decisions, reduce costs and increase revenues. We combine deep business knowledge, focused technical expertise and a pragmatic, delivery-oriented approach. We are an *Inc. 500* company and the author of several Microsoft Press books, including *Official Microsoft Intranet Solutions, The Excel 97 Developers Handbook,* and *Inside Microsoft Windows NT Internet Development.* MMA can be found on the Internet at *www.micromodeling.com.*

Frank J. Campise is a senior developer in the Enterprise Solutions Group in MMA's Chicago office. His key discipline areas include object-oriented analysis and design, UML, distributed component architectures and web technology. He has spent the majority of his career working with Microsoft technologies. Prior to joining MMA in 1998, Frank was an architect at Andersen Consulting and earned his BS in Computer Science from the University of Illinois at Champaign/Urbana. He would like to thank his wife, Susan, for putting up with him while writing the chapter. Frank can be reached at *CampiseF@micromodeling.com.*

Paul Drumgoole joined MMA in 1996 and has since made the transition from client/server programmer to Web developer. Paul programs in Visual Basic and codes Web front-ends using JavaScript and Dynamic HTML. He has fled city life and currently lives in the woods of Orange County, NY with his beautiful wife Sharon and baby boy Liam. Paul has a BS in Computer Science from The Catholic University of America in Washington, DC. Paul can be reached at *DrumgooleP@micromodeling.com.*

Biff Gaut started programming personal computers professionally on an Osborne 1, a year before the introduction of the IBM PC. After bouncing around through a couple of operating systems, languages and jobs, he has found a home at MMA as a technical manager in the DC office, leading teams of C++ developers implementing high end enterprise applications. Along the way he acquired a beautiful wife, Holly, and two wonderful children, Amanda and Chris, all of whom he thanks for tolerating his prolonged absences while working on this book. No, Amanda, Daddy won't have to work on Sundays for a while. Biff can be reached at GautW@micromodeling.com.

Steve Gilmore is a manager in MMA's San Francisco Enterprise Solutions practice. When not on Safari or attending traffic school, he can be found developing Web and commerce initiatives on the Microsoft platform for a variety of MMA clients. Prior to joining MMA, he spent over ten years developing and managing enterprise and Internet projects in government and the private sector. Steve can be reached at GilmoreS@micromodeling.com.

John Intihar is a senior developer in MMA's DC Enterprise Solutions group. He and his beloved wife Janel live just outside of Charlottesville, VA with their friends Checkers, Tiger Lily, and Sam. His mom always tells him he can do whatever he wants to do if he puts his mind to it. His dad is his hero. John can be reached at IntiharJ@micromodeling.com.

Steve Harshbarger works out of MMA's San Francisco office. As a Director in MMA's Strategic Technology Practice, he focuses on emerging technology R&D, application design and architecture on key client engagements, and evangelism of new technologies to MMA clients and staff. Steve is a frequent writer in technical journals, and he recently co-authored Official Microsoft Intranet Solutions and Microsoft Excel 97 Developer's Handbook, both published by Microsoft Press. He is a regular speaker at industry events such as VBITS and TechEd. Steve lives in San Francisco with his wife Kathy, and in his spare time enjoys skiing, bicycling, martial arts, and picking the next great Internet stock. Steve can be reached at HarshbargerS@micromodeling.com.

Andy Hoskinson is a senior developer in MMA's Knowledge Management Group and develops n-tier Internet, intranet, and extranet applications using Microsoft BackOffice products and development tools. Prior to joining MMA, he was a senior software engineer for Systems Planning and Analysis, Inc., a defense contracting firm in Alexandria, VA. He was also a part-time Java instructor for the George Washington University Center for Career Education Information Technology program. Andy has a BA from the University of Virginia, a MS from Mississippi State University, and lives in Arlington, Virginia with his wife Angie. Andy can be reached at HoskinsonA@micromodeling.com.

Scott Jamison is a senior developer in MMA's Boston office. He's a frequent speaker at industry events such as Microsoft Explorer, and a contributor to both the Visual Basic Programmer's Journal and Access-Office-VB Advisor. Scott recently co-authored a book with MMA's Raffaele Piemonte on Outlook 2000 and Exchange for Addison-Wesley. When he's not feeding his cat or out on the town with his wife Erica, Scott can be found developing applications with the entire suite of Microsoft development tools. Scott can be reached at JamisonS@micromodeling.com.

Andy Maretz is the Chief Technology Officer of MeasuRisk, an MMA-funded venture which provides portfolio risk analysis services over the Internet to institutional investors. Prior to joining MeasuRisk, he was the manager of MMA's Enterprise Solutions practice in Chicago. Andy has a BA in the history of science from Harvard University and an MBA in finance and international business from Northwestern University (Kellogg). He can be reached at MaretzA@MeasuRisk.com.

Charles Maxson heads up the desktop development practice in MMA's Minneapolis office, where he and his team of developers incorporate Microsoft Office into innovative business solutions. Recently, he has been speaking at events such as Microsoft Developer Days and TechNet sessions to excite users and developers about the new release of Office 2000. His contribution to this book was "conveniently" scheduled so he could spend time at home with his wife Jane, and their newborn son Matthew. Charles can be reached at MaxsonC@micromodeling.com.

Lenore Michaels is MMA's Director of Marketing Communications and the internal editor and project manager for this book, reprising her role from MMA's first group book effort, *Official Microsoft Intranet Solutions (1997, Microsoft Press)*. While seeing this book to completion, she gave birth to her second son Stephen, whose day/night confusion gave her plenty of time to work on the project! At MMA, Lenore is responsible for all paper and Web-based collateral, internal communications, and oversees aspects of MMA's relationship with Microsoft. Prior to joining MMA back in 1993, she was an Assistant Vice President at CS First Boston Corporation in New York. Lenore can be reached at MichaelsL@micromodeling.com

Raffaele Piemonte is Micro Modeling's Visual Basic Champion and has worked with Microsoft Outlook since alpha code. As a manager in MMA's New Jersey Enterprise Solutions practice, he manages technical resources, and does analysis, system design, and development for enterprise business applications. He contributes frequently to Advisor Publications and co-authored a book with MMA's Scott Jamison on Outlook 2000 and Exchange for Addison-Wesley. He was featured on the cover of VB Tech Journal, who did an extensive article on his philosophy on application development. He lives in northern New Jersey with his wife, Jackie, and his two daughters, Lauryn and Marissa. Prior to working at MMA, he worked for ABC TV, United Parcel Service, and NYNEX. Raffaele can be reached at PiemonteR@micromodeling.com

Steve Waldon currently manages the Internet and E-commerce practice in MMA's Chicago Office. His key technical strengths are in the areas of software development process, web technology, distributed objects, and security. Steve has also been on the forefront of applying these technologies to the healthcare domain. Prior to joining MMA, Steve was a Senior Systems Architect in the advanced technology group of GE Medical Systems. Steve posses an MS degree in Computer Science from the University of Wisconsin - Madison and an MS degree in Electrical Engineering from Drexel University. He would like to thank his wife Mary, and two sons, Brandon and Harrison for putting up with him while he worked on this book. . Steve can be reached at WaldonS@micromodeling.com

MICROSOFT LICENSE AGREEMENT

Book Companion CD

IMPORTANT—READ CAREFULLY: This Microsoft End-User License Agreement ("EULA") is a legal agreement between you (either an individual or an entity) and Microsoft Corporation for the Microsoft product identified above, which includes computer software and may include associated media, printed materials, and "on-line" or electronic documentation ("SOFTWARE PRODUCT"). Any component included within the SOFTWARE PRODUCT that is accompanied by a separate End-User License Agreement shall be governed by such agreement and not the terms set forth below. By installing, copying, or otherwise using the SOFTWARE PRODUCT, you agree to be bound by the terms of this EULA. If you do not agree to the terms of this EULA, you are not authorized to install, copy, or otherwise use the SOFTWARE PRODUCT; you may, however, return the SOFTWARE PRODUCT, along with all printed materials and other items that form a part of the Microsoft product that includes the SOFTWARE PRODUCT, to the place you obtained them for a full refund.

SOFTWARE PRODUCT LICENSE

The SOFTWARE PRODUCT is protected by United States copyright laws and international copyright treaties, as well as other intellectual property laws and treaties. The SOFTWARE PRODUCT is licensed, not sold.

1. GRANT OF LICENSE. This EULA grants you the following rights:

  a. Software Product. You may install and use one copy of the SOFTWARE PRODUCT on a single computer. The primary user of the computer on which the SOFTWARE PRODUCT is installed may make a second copy for his or her exclusive use on a portable computer.

  b. Storage/Network Use. You may also store or install a copy of the SOFTWARE PRODUCT on a storage device, such as a network server, used only to install or run the SOFTWARE PRODUCT on your other computers over an internal network; however, you must acquire and dedicate a license for each separate computer on which the SOFTWARE PRODUCT is installed or run from the storage device. A license for the SOFTWARE PRODUCT may not be shared or used concurrently on different computers.

  c. License Pak. If you have acquired this EULA in a Microsoft License Pak, you may make the number of additional copies of the computer software portion of the SOFTWARE PRODUCT authorized on the printed copy of this EULA, and you may use each copy in the manner specified above. You are also entitled to make a corresponding number of secondary copies for portable computer use as specified above.

  d. Sample Code. Solely with respect to portions, if any, of the SOFTWARE PRODUCT that are identified within the SOFTWARE PRODUCT as sample code (the "SAMPLE CODE"):

    i. Use and Modification. Microsoft grants you the right to use and modify the source code version of the SAMPLE CODE, *provided* you comply with subsection (d)(iii) below. You may not distribute the SAMPLE CODE, or any modified version of the SAMPLE CODE, in source code form.

    ii. Redistributable Files. Provided you comply with subsection (d)(iii) below, Microsoft grants you a nonexclusive, royalty-free right to reproduce and distribute the object code version of the SAMPLE CODE and of any modified SAMPLE CODE, other than SAMPLE CODE (or any modified version thereof) designated as not redistributable in the Readme file that forms a part of the SOFTWARE PRODUCT (the "Non-Redistributable Sample Code"). All SAMPLE CODE other than the Non-Redistributable Sample Code is collectively referred to as the "REDISTRIBUTABLES."

    iii. Redistribution Requirements. If you redistribute the REDISTRIBUTABLES, you agree to: (i) distribute the REDISTRIBUTABLES in object code form only in conjunction with and as a part of your software application product; (ii) not use Microsoft's name, logo, or trademarks to market your software application product; (iii) include a valid copyright notice on your software application product; (iv) indemnify, hold harmless, and defend Microsoft from and against any claims or lawsuits, including attorney's fees, that arise or result from the use or distribution of your software application product; and (v) not permit further distribution of the REDISTRIBUTABLES by your end user. Contact Microsoft for the applicable royalties due and other licensing terms for all other uses and/or distribution of the REDISTRIBUTABLES.

2. DESCRIPTION OF OTHER RIGHTS AND LIMITATIONS.

  • **Limitations on Reverse Engineering, Decompilation, and Disassembly.** You may not reverse engineer, decompile, or disassemble the SOFTWARE PRODUCT, except and only to the extent that such activity is expressly permitted by applicable law notwithstanding this limitation.

  • **Separation of Components.** The SOFTWARE PRODUCT is licensed as a single product. Its component parts may not be separated for use on more than one computer.

  • **Rental.** You may not rent, lease, or lend the SOFTWARE PRODUCT.

  • **Support Services.** Microsoft may, but is not obligated to, provide you with support services related to the SOFTWARE PRODUCT ("Support Services"). Use of Support Services is governed by the Microsoft policies and programs described in the user manual, in "on-line" documentation, and/or in other Microsoft-provided materials. Any supplemental software code provided to you as part of the Support Services shall be considered part of the SOFTWARE PRODUCT and subject to the terms and conditions of this EULA. With respect to technical information you provide to Microsoft as part of the Support Services, Microsoft may use such information for its business purposes, including for product support and development. Microsoft will not utilize such technical information in a form that personally identifies you.

- **Software Transfer.** You may permanently transfer all of your rights under this EULA, provided you retain no copies, you transfer all of the SOFTWARE PRODUCT (including all component parts, the media and printed materials, any upgrades, this EULA, and, if applicable, the Certificate of Authenticity), **and** the recipient agrees to the terms of this EULA.

- **Termination.** Without prejudice to any other rights, Microsoft may terminate this EULA if you fail to comply with the terms and conditions of this EULA. In such event, you must destroy all copies of the SOFTWARE PRODUCT and all of its component parts.

3. **COPYRIGHT.** All title and copyrights in and to the SOFTWARE PRODUCT (including but not limited to any images, photographs, animations, video, audio, music, text, SAMPLE CODE, REDISTRIBUTABLES, and "applets" incorporated into the SOFTWARE PRODUCT) and any copies of the SOFTWARE PRODUCT are owned by Microsoft or its suppliers. The SOFTWARE PRODUCT is protected by copyright laws and international treaty provisions. Therefore, you must treat the SOFTWARE PRODUCT like any other copyrighted material **except** that you may install the SOFTWARE PRODUCT on a single computer provided you keep the original solely for backup or archival purposes. You may not copy the printed materials accompanying the SOFTWARE PRODUCT.

4. **U.S. GOVERNMENT RESTRICTED RIGHTS.** The SOFTWARE PRODUCT and documentation are provided with RESTRICTED RIGHTS. Use, duplication, or disclosure by the Government is subject to restrictions as set forth in subparagraph (c)(1)(ii) of the Rights in Technical Data and Computer Software clause at DFARS 252.227-7013 or subparagraphs (c)(1) and (2) of the Commercial Computer Software—Restricted Rights at 48 CFR 52.227-19, as applicable. Manufacturer is Microsoft Corporation/One Microsoft Way/Redmond, WA 98052-6399.

5. **EXPORT RESTRICTIONS.** You agree that you will not export or re-export the SOFTWARE PRODUCT, any part thereof, or any process or service that is the direct product of the SOFTWARE PRODUCT (the foregoing collectively referred to as the "Restricted Components"), to any country, person, entity, or end user subject to U.S. export restrictions. You specifically agree not to export or re-export any of the Restricted Components (i) to any country to which the U.S. has embargoed or restricted the export of goods or services, which currently include, but are not necessarily limited to, Cuba, Iran, Iraq, Libya, North Korea, Sudan, and Syria, or to any national of any such country, wherever located, who intends to transmit or transport the Restricted Components back to such country; (ii) to any end user who you know or have reason to know will utilize the Restricted Components in the design, development, or production of nuclear, chemical, or biological weapons; or (iii) to any end user who has been prohibited from participating in U.S. export transactions by any federal agency of the U.S. government. You warrant and represent that neither the BXA nor any other U.S. federal agency has suspended, revoked, or denied your export privileges.

6. **NOTE ON JAVA SUPPORT.** THE SOFTWARE PRODUCT MAY CONTAIN SUPPORT FOR PROGRAMS WRITTEN IN JAVA. JAVA TECHNOLOGY IS NOT FAULT TOLERANT AND IS NOT DESIGNED, MANUFACTURED, OR INTENDED FOR USE OR RESALE AS ON-LINE CONTROL EQUIPMENT IN HAZARDOUS ENVIRONMENTS REQUIRING FAIL-SAFE PERFORMANCE, SUCH AS IN THE OPERATION OF NUCLEAR FACILITIES, AIRCRAFT NAVIGATION OR COMMUNICATION SYSTEMS, AIR TRAFFIC CONTROL, DIRECT LIFE SUPPORT MACHINES, OR WEAPONS SYSTEMS, IN WHICH THE FAILURE OF JAVA TECHNOLOGY COULD LEAD DIRECTLY TO DEATH, PERSONAL INJURY, OR SEVERE PHYSICAL OR ENVIRONMENTAL DAMAGE. SUN MICROSYSTEMS, INC. HAS CONTRACTUALLY OBLIGATED MICROSOFT TO MAKE THIS DISCLAIMER.

DISCLAIMER OF WARRANTY

NO WARRANTIES OR CONDITIONS. MICROSOFT EXPRESSLY DISCLAIMS ANY WARRANTY OR CONDITION FOR THE SOFTWARE PRODUCT. THE SOFTWARE PRODUCT AND ANY RELATED DOCUMENTATION IS PROVIDED "AS IS" WITHOUT WARRANTY OR CONDITION OF ANY KIND, EITHER EXPRESS OR IMPLIED, INCLUDING, WITHOUT LIMITATION, THE IMPLIED WARRANTIES OF MERCHANTABILITY, FITNESS FOR A PARTICULAR PURPOSE, OR NONINFRINGEMENT. THE ENTIRE RISK ARISING OUT OF USE OR PERFORMANCE OF THE SOFTWARE PRODUCT REMAINS WITH YOU.

LIMITATION OF LIABILITY. TO THE MAXIMUM EXTENT PERMITTED BY APPLICABLE LAW, IN NO EVENT SHALL MICROSOFT OR ITS SUPPLIERS BE LIABLE FOR ANY SPECIAL, INCIDENTAL, INDIRECT, OR CONSEQUENTIAL DAMAGES WHATSOEVER (INCLUDING, WITHOUT LIMITATION, DAMAGES FOR LOSS OF BUSINESS PROFITS, BUSINESS INTERRUPTION, LOSS OF BUSINESS INFORMATION, OR ANY OTHER PECUNIARY LOSS) ARISING OUT OF THE USE OF OR INABILITY TO USE THE SOFTWARE PRODUCT OR THE PROVISION OF OR FAILURE TO PROVIDE SUPPORT SERVICES, EVEN IF MICROSOFT HAS BEEN ADVISED OF THE POSSIBILITY OF SUCH DAMAGES. IN ANY CASE, MICROSOFT'S ENTIRE LIABILITY UNDER ANY PROVISION OF THIS EULA SHALL BE LIMITED TO THE GREATER OF THE AMOUNT ACTUALLY PAID BY YOU FOR THE SOFTWARE PRODUCT OR US$5.00; PROVIDED, HOWEVER, IF YOU HAVE ENTERED INTO A MICROSOFT SUPPORT SERVICES AGREEMENT, MICROSOFT'S ENTIRE LIABILITY REGARDING SUPPORT SERVICES SHALL BE GOVERNED BY THE TERMS OF THAT AGREEMENT. BECAUSE SOME STATES AND JURISDICTIONS DO NOT ALLOW THE EXCLUSION OR LIMITATION OF LIABILITY, THE ABOVE LIMITATION MAY NOT APPLY TO YOU.

MISCELLANEOUS

This EULA is governed by the laws of the State of Washington USA, except and only to the extent that applicable law mandates governing law of a different jurisdiction.

Should you have any questions concerning this EULA, or if you desire to contact Microsoft for any reason, please contact the Microsoft subsidiary serving your country, or write: Microsoft Sales Information Center/One Microsoft Way/Redmond, WA 98052-6399.